Kurt Adler

THE ART OF
ACCOMPANYING AND COACHING

The University of Minnesota Press, Minneapolis

Lithographed in the United States of America at the
North Central Publishing Company, St. Paul

 3

Library of Congress Catalog Card Number: 64-25906

PUBLISHED IN GREAT BRITAIN, INDIA, AND PAKISTAN BY
THE OXFORD UNIVERSITY PRESS, LONDON, BOMBAY, AND KARACHI,
AND IN CANADA BY THE COPP CLARK PUBLISHING CO. LIMITED, TORONTO

I dedicate this book to the memory of the teachers who molded my
musical culture during my formative years

CANTOR JACOB FUERNBERG · PROFESSOR RICHARD ROBERT
MRS. FANNY BOEHM-KRAMER · PROFESSOR ALEXANDER MANHART
PROFESSOR DR. KARL WEIGL · PROFESSOR GUIDO ADLER
PROFESSOR WILHELM FISCHER · PROFESSOR FERDINAND FOLL
HERMANN WEIGERT · ERICH KLEIBER

Acknowledgments

MY SINCERE THANKS go first and foremost to Malcolm M. Willey, educational consultant to the vice chancellor of the University of Calcutta and former vice president of the University of Minnesota, and to the director of the latter institution's Department of Concerts and Lectures, Mr. James S. Lombard. Without their encouragement and active help I could not have undertaken to write this book.

I was furthermore very fortunate in getting expert advice and fruitful suggestions about many aspects of the book from many different sources. It is impossible here to mention all of them, but I should like to tender my sincere thanks to Dr. Frederick Brodnitz of Mount Sinai Hospital, New York City, for his patient explanations of the anatomy and physiology of the vocal apparatus; to Mr. William Vennard of the University of Southern California, Los Angeles, for permission to quote some passages from his excellent book, *Singing: The Mechanism and the Technic*; to Mr. Ralph Garcia of the Bell Telephone Laboratories, New York City, for permission to use some of the laboratories' splendid high-speed photographs of the human vocal cords in action; to Mr. Joseph S. Whitehead, president of the Aeolian-Skinner Company, Boston, for his invaluable corrections and additions to the difficult chapter about organ-building; to Yale University Press for permission to use the illustration on page 144, which is taken from their edition of Bach's *Clavier-Büchlein vor Wilhelm Friedemann Bach*, edited by Ralph Kirkpatrick, copyright 1959; to Mr. Felix Eyle, noted violinist and orchestra manager of the Metropolitan Opera, and to Mr. Frederick Steinway of Steinway & Sons, New York City, for their information about the construction of stringed instruments and pianos.

Miss Lieselotte Singer of New York City contributed her talents in drawing some complicated anatomical illustrations. The late Miss May Savage and Maestro Jean Morel of the Juilliard School of Music helped to unravel the intricacies of French musical diction; Miss Mattlyn Gavers and Mr. Vincenzo Celli, both of New York City, did likewise in the field of music for basic ballet steps. Mr. A. Gimson, London, secretary of the International Phonetic Association, furnished me with a copy of the latest I.P.A. chart. To all of them go my profound thanks.

I am also extremely grateful to my editor, Miss Marcia Strout, of the University of Minnesota Press, for improving the readability of my English and for sifting and organizing the bulky manuscript, and to the members of all departments of the University of Minnesota Press.

And — last but by no means least — my colleagues of the Metropolitan Opera musical staff have earned my lasting gratitude for their constructive criticism and their suggestions based on rich experience, tendered to me during long train rides on tour and in free moments at rehearsals and performances.

Table of Contents

INTRODUCTION   3

THE HISTORICAL BACKGROUND OF ACCOMPANYING   7

THE HISTORICAL BACKGROUND OF COACHING   18

THE MECHANICS OF MUSICAL INSTRUMENTS   21

PHONETICS AND DICTION IN SINGING   43

ITALIAN PHONETICS AND DICTION   48

FRENCH PHONETICS AND DICTION   65

SPANISH PHONETICS AND DICTION   89

GERMAN PHONETICS AND DICTION   92

ELEMENTS OF MUSICAL STYLE   111

PROGRAM-BUILDING   171

THE ART OF ACCOMPANYING AND COACHING   182

BIBLIOGRAPHY   243

INDEX   246

THE ART OF ACCOMPANYING AND COACHING

Introduction

IN WRITING a book for which there is no precedent (the last textbooks about accompanying were written during the age of thorough bass or shortly thereafter — the eighteenth and early nineteenth centuries — and dealt exclusively with the problems timely then) one must make one's own rules and set one's own standards. This freedom makes the task somewhat easier, if, on the one hand, one looks to the past: there is no generally approved model to be followed and to be compared with one's work; but, on the other hand, the task is hard because one's responsibility to present and future generations of accompanists and coaches is great. In short, to break a new trail and to set a standard for the future is a most gratifying but also a most difficult undertaking.

In our world of rapidly changing values — welcome changes when they are the results of technical and scientific progress — spiritual, ethical, and artistic values tend likewise to change, but much more slowly, and not always for the better. It is sad but true that ours is not an age of real cultural and creative artistic growth. And, in fact, a fast-growing culture, even in the era of nuclear energy and interplanetary travel, is unthinkable. Culture and art are the apparent *emanations* of an age, but not its *inceptors* — this notwithstanding the fact that occasionally some lone artistic genius may suddenly spring up to rebel against the existing order, break the chains of conformity, and create a new artistic age. Such lone geniuses — to mention but a few — were Michelangelo, Beethoven, Mussorgsky. Although their early development is anchored in the era in which they were born, they later traveled along hitherto uncharted roads. Beloved and admired by their progressive contemporaries, these geniuses did not become the idols of mankind until a later age caught up with their ar-

tistic achievements. But, alas, there has not been such a genius in the realm of music during the twentieth century. The creative musical genius of our space age has yet to be discovered, if he has been born.

Our time has perfected technique to such a degree that it could not help but create perfect technician-artists. Our leading creative artists master technique to the point of being able to shift from one style to another without difficulty. Take Stravinsky and Picasso, for instance: they have gone back and forth through as many periods of style as they wished. Only with a stupendous technique fortified by a certain lack of conviction as to what one's own style ought to be could these Proteans have attained their place in our artistic world. Compare the uncompromising spiritual loneliness of Beethoven's last quartets, not fully understood even today, with the modern commercialism of Picasso's cross-eyed beauties.

What the future will bring, no one can say. I should like to venture the opinion that the vistas opening for us will render us more humble, more concerned with inner or spiritual values. Our technological advances should give us more time; we shall need culture and be able to afford it. Two writers, both Nobel Prize winners, have recently raised the question of the future of music. Thomas Mann and Hermann Hesse, neither knowing of the other's efforts, came to very similar conclusions. They envisage music as rising to a much higher spiritual level than heretofore — as not just entertaining, but uplifting and cleansing.

Mann in *Doctor Faustus* models the life and death of a young German composer on the actual lives of a number of artists — Robert Schumann, Nietzsche, Hugo Wolf, Hindemith, Schoenberg. His hero's life's work is climaxed with a vocal-orchestral composition — a combination of medieval philosophy and modern twelve-tone music. It seems to me, however, that this road of atonality traveled by Schoenberg and Webern, and followed to some degree by Alban Berg and Křenek, is a one-way street which has already come to a dead end. To us, the importance of Mann's *Doctor Faustus* lies not in his hero's choice of musical language nor in his clinical end, but in the idea that the music of the future will revert to spiritual values.

Exactly the same idea is expressed in the Swiss writer Hermann Hesse's Nobel Prize–winning novel *Magister Ludi (Das Glasperlenspiel)*. Hesse goes so far as to imagine the music of the future as imbued with Pythagorean and scholastic ideas, founded on strict mathematical rules, taught and played by members of a monk-like brotherhood. After they have heard the music played on a musical instrument consisting of ethereal-sounding glass beads, the musicians of the future (the action takes place in the twenty-sixth century) derive sensual and spiritual enjoyment from just seeing the musical-numerological writings, without actually hearing the music except with the inner ear. Whether or not this kind of musical enjoyment may prove to be too ascetic for the real future, the fact remains that Hesse, like Mann, sees the future of music in the enrichment of spiritual and ethical values. This outlook is also represented by the conductor Bruno Walter, who in his old age restricted himself to conducting works of high spirit-

ual and ethical value, underlining these traits in his conducting, implanting them in his audiences, and drawing from them the life-prolonging waters. This almost religious, though non-sectarian, service reminds one of the ritual of the Grail's life-preserving power in Wagner's *Parsifal*.

What has all this to do with a book about accompanying and coaching? Nothing, and yet at the same time very much. I believe the reader has a right to know the author's artistic credo. I want to make mine clear to my reader in the very beginning, particularly since my point of view will be found wherever this book offers a choice of solutions to particular artistic problems.

This book is meant to be an aid to pianists who want to become or already are professional accompanists or coaches. The "or" between the two professions is only relative. One may be an accompanist *and* a coach. Though the two professions, accompanying and coaching, are really two different specialties, they will overlap most of the time. I am therefore justified in writing one book about their art instead of devoting a separate book to each of them. Only on the highest professional level does specialization usually take place with the result that a career is made as either accompanist or coach.

These two professions, then, are offshoots of the large family of pianists. They are not the only offshoots. Figure 1 shows how many branches the pedigree of the piano player consists of. Each of these groups of musicians may be divided into classical and popular pianists, but this

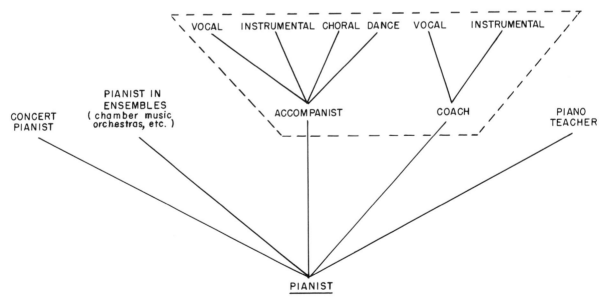

Figure 1. Diagram of the family tree of the pianist

book will be concerned only with the classical part, including the accompanist or coach for the semiclassical repertoire (light opera and operetta). Of the categories represented in Figure 1, this book will deal with the specialized fields as delineated by the trapezoid.

An accompanist, according to Grove's *Dictionary of Music and Musicians* (5th edition) is "the performer playing as a rule with a single singer or instrumentalist usually on the pianoforte, whose part is nominally subsidiary, but who, in all music that matters and especially in music dating later than the 17th- [and] mid-18th-century accompaniment from a thorough-bass, should be regarded as an equal partner in the interpretation of a type of music which in a broad sense appertains to the category of chamber music."

In a broad sense, yes; but nobody will speak of chamber music when vocalist and accompanist alone are performing, nor will anyone call a violin or violoncello recital with piano accompaniment chamber music unless it consists of an evening of sonata-playing. And neither, of course, are choral concerts and dance recitals chamber music. We may, therefore, exclude chamber music as specifically connected with accompanying, but keep it always in mind as representative of what Grove's *Dictionary* calls the "equal partnership."

In the next chapter I shall trace the art of accompanying back to its beginnings. The modern accompanist's instrument is the pianoforte. In religious concerts he may have to play the organ or the harmonium, which will create the same difficulties for a pianist as accompanying on a piano would create for a professional organist. The basic technique of the two instruments is different. But a pianist trained to play Bach's music may quickly adjust himself to using the Bach legato technique in playing the organ and the harmonium. This book will give useful hints for occasions when the pianist has to accompany on keyboard wind instruments. Another possible duty of an accompanist is to play for a rehearsal, usually under the direction of a leader — chorus master, ballet master, or one of the many teachers in the vocal, instrumental, and dance fields.

Our second concern, the coach, is more difficult to define. Both Grove's and Willi Apel's *Harvard Dictionary of Music* evade a definition. I would define a musical coach as a pianist with thorough musical background who teaches, guides, and advises vocalists, instrumentalists, or choral groups so that they will be ready to perform in public certain musical pieces such as songs, choral or instrumental compositions, roles in operas or operettas, or parts in oratorios. The main difference between an accompanist and a coach is the latter's teaching function.

"Coach" is used only in English. Since the profession is of comparatively recent origin, names have had to be created to describe the work. In German the coach is called *Korrepetitor*, a pianist who "repeats" music with somebody else. The French express the same idea in their *répétiteur*. The Italians elevate the position to *maestro sostituto* (substitute maestro). The Russians have no equivalent word but call him concert master (a term reserved in other countries for the leader of the first-violin section of an orchestra).

It is almost impossible for an amateur to coach well. This is not to say that not many amateurs are trying to coach. This book may help them to become professionals, though reading a book, of course, will not suffice in itself. Absorbing the many aspects of coaching, plus sufficient practice, will do the trick — if the amateur is sufficiently talented.

A musical coach of the long-hair category is needed mainly in an opera house, where American custom makes him assistant conductor or member of the musical staff. In an opera house there is need for vocal coaches and choral coaches; the ballet department can get along with good accompanists, but a real pianist who can coach will always be preferable, for he knows how to imitate orchestrations on the piano. Assistant conductors in opera houses must in the line of duty play the organ, harmonium, and celesta; they must know how to beat bells, drums, and anvils. They must learn to follow the hand of any conductor, be it clear, or — as happens in many cases — hardly understandable. They must efface themselves during stage rehearsals but show their authority as teacher in solo or group rehearsals.

But the United States' depressingly few opera houses cannot support more than a handful of coaches. So the main function of a coach here is teaching. Coaches teach singers and, less often, instrumentalists and dancers, preparing them for recitals and other performances. They guide singers until their roles are memorized and they are responsible for the development of every shade of dynamics, every nuance of interpretation. They are directly responsible if the singer's diction, his languages, or even his stage presence is at fault.

Coaches and accompanists must also at least help in building a program. In this preparatory work the functions of coaches, on the one hand, and voice or instrumental teachers, on the other, touch. Some space will later be devoted to defining the different spheres of interest of teacher and coach — spheres where their work should not overlap. Teachers and coaches must find a way to cooperate, so that the poor artist is not torn between them. With real cooperation, the results will be much more gratifying and more quickly achieved.

The cultural and musical background of accompanist and coach ought to be the same. For a long time their training, their duties, and their accomplishments travel the same road. At the public-performance level, however, specialization sets in. There, accompanists will be concerned with such things as the finesse of their profession, with the pianistic qualities, the shadings of touch, and the give and take between artist and accompanist. Coaches, on the other hand, will concentrate on the psychological, pedagogical, and interpretative aspects of their work until their charges are ready to be turned over to conductors or concert accompanists. Rarely, soloists are accompanied and coached by the same person. But only a few coaches have the pianistic ability to accompany in recitals, and few accompanists know all the coach's tricks to draw the best out of their pupils.

As in every other profession, one finds both artisans and artists among accompanists and coaches. This book will undertake first to describe fully the crafts of accompanying and coaching, by dividing the musical material they will have to cope with into historical, technical, and aesthetic elements. This is something that can be taught and learned. Anchored on the crafts, however, there towers the hardly definable something that we call Art.

Artistry cannot be analyzed satisfactorily in logical terms. It originates in human talent and personality. But it can be taught if the spark is in the pupil. More than by pure description, artistry can be developed in musicians by deepening and broadening their cultural background, by using the right psychology and pedagogy in bringing out their artistic endowment, and by implanting in them the spiritual and ethical values referred to at the beginning of this chapter.

Instrumentalists and singers are not the only real artists. Accompanists and coaches may also reach heights of interpretative artistry. To help them attain these heights, to lead them across the plains and over the hills of craftsmanship to the mountaintops of artistry — that is the real purpose of this book.

The Historical Background of Accompanying

ACCOMPANYING is almost as old as mankind. We may assume that the cave man, when he discovered his voice, used it to terrorize his enemies by yelling, and employed softer vocal colors to woo his spouse. Soon, however, he learned that he could be more terrifying to his foes if he underlined his stentorian outbursts by beating out rhythms on some such percussive object as a hollowed-out tree trunk. In more tender moments, his cave woman may have tried to follow his singing by blowing into a dried animal bone, or may even have collected bones of deceased and devoured enemies for this purpose. Thus was the art of accompanying born, dividing itself immediately into self-accompanying and accompanying others. We may deduce this development by observing aborigines in the wilds of Africa and Australia, and by watching babies happily and unendingly crow and babble, at the same time swinging their rattles wildly and triumphantly.

BIBLICAL AND ANTIQUE TIMES

In II Samuel: 6, the Bible says: "And David and all the house of Israel played before the Lord on all manner of instruments made of fir wood, even on harps, and on psalteries, and on timbrels, and on cornets, and on cymbals." In Psalm 92, which has as its theme the praise of the Lord in song, one accompanying instrument — probably a harp — is mentioned in even greater detail: "Upon an instrument of ten strings, and upon the psaltery; upon the harp with a solemn sound." Genesis calls Jubal the "father of all such as handle the harp and organ" — an organ not to be confused with even a primitive predecessor of ours. We do not know of any organ-like musical instrument that the Jews of biblical times may have used; probably it was a primitive system of pipes. The first organ deserving of the name was built on a hydraulic basis by the Greek Ktesibios in the second century B.C. Earlier, however, the Chinese had a wind instrument, the cheng (first described around 1100 B.C.), which was composed of a comparatively large number of pipes tied together with a string.

The ten-stringed instruments mentioned in Psalm 92 — and the instrument mentioned in Psalm 81, "the pleasant harp" — were most probably zithers. The "harp with a solemn sound" must have been a bigger harp which the Jews brought back from Egypt. The psaltery was a widely used ten-stringed instrument in a square frame. The Jews also used wind instruments like flutes, trumpets, cornets, and horns for accompaniments (the shofar, a ram's horn, was used only in religious services). Their percussion instruments were the cymbals and timbrels.

One must not imagine that these accompaniments were elaborate. Until polyphony came into being in the Middle Ages, players did nothing but repeat the melody at the same pitch or an octave higher or lower, whichever was most convenient for a particular instrument. Sometimes small embellishments were added, the accompaniment would momentarily deviate slightly from the tune, or vocal pauses would be filled with a few notes of accompaniment. The percussion instruments gave mainly rhythmical support to the voice or the instrument carrying the melody. These rhythms, judging by today's primitive African and Asian rhythms, were fairly complex. The accompaniments of the biblical Jews have inspired many composers (most of them to hideous anachronisms) and writers. One of the most touching poetic licenses was taken by Thomas Mann in his great novel *Joseph and His Brothers*. Mann, wondering how the message that his son Joseph was still alive could be brought to Jacob without the old patriarch's dying of joy, decided to have it said with music. He made one of Jacob's granddaughters a twelve-year-old singer who accompanied herself on the zither. Singing and playing, she brings the joyous message to Jacob, obscuring the dividing line between truth and poetry, and thus easing the shock.

Here is a partial account of this episode:

"On a little rock, against which a foam of blossoms beat like surf on a cliff, sat a figure almost, as seen from afar, like a flower itself. Soon they could tell it was a little maid, alone under the wide sky, in red smock with daisies in her hair. On her arm she held a zither and her slender brown fingers travelled up and down the strings. It was Serah, Asher's child; her father was the first to recognize her and with fatherly pride he said:

"'That is my little Serah, sitting there on a stone, playing herself a little tune on her zither. The little wench is like that, she loves to sit alone and practise herself in psalmody. She belongs to the tribe of whistlers and fiddlers, God knows where she gets it, but she has had it ever since she was born, she has to make psalter and psalm; she can play on the strings till they ring and mingle her voice in songs of praise, clearer and stronger than you could believe, seeing her wisp of a body. Some day she will be famous in Israel, the little monkey.' . . .

"'Gladly will I,' answered Serah in her ringing tones. 'Never before have I had such words to string on my strings, perhaps now I can show what they can do. Many sing, in tribe and town, but now I have better matter than they and will sing them out of the field.'

"So saying she took her instrument from the stone where she had sat and held it on one arm and spread her tapering brown fingers across the strings, the thumb here, the four fingers there. She began to move steadily through the flowers, now fast, now slow according to the measure of her song:

'Oh let my soul sing a new joy as it goeth,
For a fine chant on eight strings my heart knoweth.
Of what it is full let it run over in rhyme
More precious than gold and fine gold from the mine,
Sweeter than purest honey in the comb,
For the Spring's message I bring home.'"

The Greeks had an already highly developed art of accompanying. Their melodies, called *nomoi*, were created to fit the poets' words, and vocal music, therefore, is the main branch of Greek music. They used many different instruments to accompany their soloists and choruses. Even non-singing actors declaimed their verses with musical accompaniments. The roots of Greek music lie deeply embedded in mythology. Orpheus, Amphion, and Arion are among the first Greek composers, singers, and self-accompanists combined in one. Olympos, whose specialty was playing the aulos, a reed wind instrument, consisting of a pair tied together, composed famous nomoi around 700 B.C. The melody was played on one aulos, the other filling in the pauses with additional notes. If Olympos is important for the development of Greek wind playing, equal importance is due his contemporary, Terpander of Lesbos, a virtuoso on the kithara, in the realm of stringed instruments. Another Greek musician of the same period was Archilochos, who initiated faster tempi and embellishments in instrumental accompaniments. Among the younger generation (about 625–575 B.C.) of Greek lyric composers we ought to remember the famous school of Lesbos with Alcaeus, the great poetess Sappho, and the serene, life-loving Anacreon. Among their accompanied songs was the skolion, a tune sung in turn at table by the guests, each accompanying himself on the kithara.

Homer tells us how many were the occasions for accompanied music in Greece. There were songs of mourning and of jubilation, dancing songs and lullabies, songs of shepherds, reapers, vintners, warriors. Greece may also be called the mother of modern choral and dance accompaniments, for which a strong incentive was provided by the Olympic games; these included contests for choral and dance groups as well as for individual aulos and kithara players.

The principal exponent of Greek choral music is Pindar (522(?)–443 B.C.) whose odes are thought to have been its culmination. Choral singing was always combined with dancing, the dancers usually also playing the accompaniments.

In accordance with the Greek belief in the synthesis of all arts, tragedies and comedies were liberally supported by musical accompaniments. This accompaniment was the job of a single aulos player; the small, delicate tone of the kithara would not have carried in the big amphitheaters.

With time, Greek music degenerated. When the Romans inherited it, there was nothing worthwhile left. The Romans were not very musical, and left no examples of original music. What survived of the Greek tradition migrated to Alexandria, lingering there until the end of ancient civilization.

Though illustrations of Jewish musical instruments are scarce, we are fairly well informed about Greek instruments, not only from authors' descriptions but also from the many paintings and sculptures on graves, vases, and statues. Greek wind instruments in addition to the aulos were the syrinx or Panpipe of five pipes which is known to us as Papageno's calling card in *The Magic Flute*. Today's brass instruments were represented by the trumpet (salpinx) and the curved trumpet or horn (keras). Besides the kithara (the word zither is derived from it) the Greeks used the lyra widely. Both instruments had first four, then seven, and later eleven strings. The kithara had a flat but elaborate soundboard and was used mostly for concerts. The lyra's soundboard was curved, not so well designed as the kithara's, and it was used mostly as a musical instrument for lay people and for domestic use. Both were plucked with the help of a plectron, an arrow-shaped stylus. The trigonon is another stringed instrument, taking its name from its triangular form. The most common percussion instruments in Greece were the cymbals and the tympanum (a large drum). The hydraulic organ of Ktesibios has already been mentioned. To conclude the history of Greek music as it applies to accompanying, let me again quote a poet's vision of that age. Goethe, in his verse fragment "Pandora," has a shepherd urge a blacksmith to make him a trumpet whose sound could be heard further than the feeble aulos and syrinx.

The Shepherds

Who wants to guard the flocks
Never finds time brief.
Counting the shining stars
May he play on a leaf.
Trees give us tender leaves
Moors give us reeds so ripe;
Smith, clever artisan,
Hand us an iron pipe,
Slender, with pointed mouth,
Tenderly cut a slit;
Louder than human voice
Far will it sound;
Maidens in fields around
Hear and rejoice.

THE AGE OF THE TROUBADOURS

The history of accompaniment now makes a big jump of approximately a thousand years. The early Christian era and the very beginnings of the Middle Ages were not receptive to secular music — popular music, we would call it today. And it is exactly this popular music that used accompaniments. The sacred music of the early Christian period was sung unaccompanied, by and by developing into Gregorian chant, which is still used today. Undoubtedly there were some popular songs in Roman and post-Roman times, but we do not know them or how they were performed. We do, however, know by whom. The former Roman actors, the mimes, could no longer support themselves as Roman culture declined. They had to look out for other occupations, among them acrobatics, juggling, card tricks — if nothing more doubtful — and playing various instruments. The mimes did all these things; they were thoroughly disreputable, driven out of their towns by various edicts, and forced to become wayfarers. But as is true of much flotsam, they survived; and with time they were again tolerated, if not respected. They are our next group of accompanists: the jugglers, jongleurs, gauklers, gleemen, or minstrels. They hired themselves out and were widely employed by the troubadours and *trouvères* of the eleventh and twelfth centuries, aristocratic composers of secular music who also sometimes accompanied themselves. The troubadours' chivalrous song started in the south of France, in Provence. It was taken over and developed by the trouvères in the North.

The trouvères devised definite forms for their songs: chansons, rondeaus, virelais, and ballads. Although the songs of the troubadours and trouvères were annotated, they were open to wide improvisation. Undoubtedly, the jugglers added to their accompaniments some popular melodies that they had known before. Of course, the accompaniment was nothing more than an instrumental repetition of the melody with slight, improvised deviations. The jugglers' instruments were manifold — whatever was available. According to a twelfth-century German source, they were trained "to play the drum, the cymbals, and the hurdy-gurdy; to throw small apples and to catch knives; to perform card-tricks and to jump through four hoops; to play the citole and mandora, the manichord, the guitar, and many other instruments." We may add to this list fiddles, bells, and harps.

The German equivalents of the troubadours and trouvères were the *Minnesänger*. They also were dedicated to the service of chivalry but owing to the heavier German temperament their songs were more spiritual and chaste. These songs took two forms, the *Barform* and the *Leich* (from the French *lai*). The minnesingers are familiar to us through Wagner's *Tannhäuser* as the troubadours are through Verdi's *Il Trovatore*. Walther von der Vogelweide is the best known minnesinger, but Neidhard von Reuenthal (early thirteenth century) is more important for music because of the quality of his songs. Wagner, in his musical treatment of the "Sängerkrieg auf der Wartburg" takes advantage of poetic license. Historically this contest had nothing to do with music, but was simply a battle of poets and orators.

While the rest of Europe progressed far into polyphony, the homophonic movement of the minnesingers continued into the sixteenth century by the *Meistersinger*, a guild of craftsmen whose serious hobby it was to make music. Their rules were very strict and antiquated and their art was not very inspired. They used the barform of the minnesingers, but implanted in their songs all kinds of cadenzas and coloraturas. Hans Sachs, the most famous among them, is very near to our hearts because of Wagner's very human description of him in *Die Meistersinger von Nürnberg*.

The minnesingers usually accompanied themselves. Many of these wayfaring musicians traveled with the noblemen they served. Their instruments were mostly the predecessors of our violin—fiddles, rotas, rebabs, rubebes, vielles, and crwths. The prototypes of lutes and guitars appear, destined to dominate the field for centuries. Simple bagpipes were also used and some small harps and square and round psalteries. The hurdy-gurdy mentioned earlier was actually an organistrum with three strings set in vibration by turning a crank. Eight bridges shortened or lengthened the strings and thus some kind of music could be produced. This is the instrument referred to by Schubert in "Der Leiermann."

Another very important function of the wayfaring musicians was to accompany dances in towns and villages. Here, they could use any string, wind, and percussion instrument at their command. The tradition of having wayfaring musicians at peasant weddings, county fairs, and carnivals still lives in Europe, especially in Scandinavia.

The English gleemen were just as popular as their French or German cousins. They also had a reputation of being mountebanks and altogether disreputable. In time the word minstrel, which originated in France as

ménestrier, became popular in England. Minstrels were the accompanists of the trouvères. Later on, the word minstrel came to be applied to any musician, especially a fiddler or viol player. Richard the Lionhearted, a noted troubadour, invited many minstrels from France to serve at his court, among them Blondel de Nesle, hero of many stories. Most English minstrels sang and played in the style of the French troubadour.

Italy and Spain of the twelfth and thirteenth centuries were rather backward in developing accompanied secular music. Gregorian chant dominated church services, and most of the secular music known from this time, songs of flagellants and penitents, has a strong spiritual tinge. Italy's position in accompanied music had yet to be established. It took another hundred years for the ars nova to find its way across the Alps.

THE ARS NOVA

While the jugglers and minstrels were merrily accompanying their masters, sacred music had already made its first steps toward polyphony. Very primitive at first, polyphony grew as fast as the human ear's faculty to perceive more than one musical line at a time would allow. This newly discovered art was largely limited to church services and to choral singing or playing by several instruments. The rules were very strict; no room was left for improvisation. Thus we cannot speak of accompaniments during this period.

But with the beginning of the fourteenth century a change took place, emanating again from France, where a feeling had grown that the times needed a breath of fresh air. This break with formalism was effected in secular music—in the popular melodies of the times, tunes accompanied by subordinate voices, usually instrumental and usually by improvisation. These accompanying voices could go in any direction, as long as they did not overpower the leading voice that sang the melody. The principal exponent of the ars nova (new art) was Guillaume de Machaut, composer of a number of virelais and chansons, still mostly homophonic, as well as ballades and rondeaus, already polyphonic. With the beginning of the quattrocento the first stirrings of the Renaissance could be felt in Italy, where the ars nova was accepted with open arms, and Florence, leading the way in this as in all other arts, became its center. The blind organist Francesco Landino was the Florentines' favorite composer. The Italian ars nova concentrated more on instrumental than on vocal music, favoring dance music, madrigals, and ballads. Another Italian specialty of the time is the *caccia*, a two-part vocal composition in the form of a canon, with instrumental accompaniment. (One voice hunts the other; hence the name.)

The favorite Italian instrument for accompanying vocal music was the lute. Its larger number of strings — from six to eleven — enabled the lute to meet the growing requirements of polyphonic music. From 1500 on, the lute appears in the form in which we still use it today except that the neck with the pegs was bent back at a ninety-degree angle. The strings were no longer plucked with a plectron but with the fingers. In time the lute became the universal accompanying musical instrument everywhere in Europe except Spain. There the guitar (with shallow sounding board) was played with a virtuosity still to be admired as we listen to leading Spanish guitarists, such as Andrés Segovia and even some unknown improvising flamenco guitarists.

Other newer accompanying instruments that came into wider use during the early Renaissance were the portative organs (small hand organs), the whole array of recorders that is being revived today, the shawms (predecessors of our oboes and bassoons), the cromorne or Krummhorn (a curved wind instrument with concealed reeds), the straight or curved cornets or zinks, and the old trumpet and trombone or busine as it was called then. Another strange-looking musical instrument was used for bass accompaniments: the trumscheit, a long wooden instrument with one or two strings which when plucked or sounded by bowing gave forth a curious drumming sound.

The sixteenth century saw a tremendous growth of polyphony in the Low Countries. Perfection of the counterpoint technique and the development of mensural notation increased the importance of all voices of a composition. Its execution could no longer be called melody plus accompaniment. True, accompanied songs, ballads, and madrigals lingered on; but they were not very important. Even Renaissance Italy began importing the Flemish masters of polyphony. For instance H. Isaac, the leading master of polyphony in the Low Countries, was for some time employed by Lorenzo il Magnifico, the Medici prince who did most for the growth of art in Italy.

The transition from the ars nova to Flemish music was effected by the Burgundian school. Its outstanding composer, Guillaume Dufay, wrote many chansons, simpler in style than the overly ornamental pieces of the ars nova. These chansons could be accompanied by any or all possible instruments — viols, lutes, human voices, even keyboard instruments.

Some popular four-part songs, however, called frottole, had already been arranged by the Italian Ottavigno dei Petrucci (between 1509 and 1515) for solo voice with lute accompaniment, the ad libitum changed for the first time to a written obbligato accompaniment. France followed suit with similar four-part arrangements (Attaignant in 1529), and Spain too with the music of Narváez, Valderrabano, and others. Many of the polyphonic compositions of that age were also transcribed as dance music. In passing it may be remarked that these transcriptions are the first examples of a vocal score, or of a score in general.

The first scores were printed in 1577 (for madrigals) and the first orchestral score — for a ballet — was printed in Paris in 1582. In Germany, some lute songs by Schlick (1512) have survived. But all in all, the sixteenth was the century of the rich Flemish polyphony, of nascent orchestral music, of chamber music, and of perfection of organ construction and technique.

THE BAROQUE ERA

The baroque era (1600–1750) — musically, modern times — rested on several important developments.

First of all was the progress in the construction of keyboard instruments. By 1600, the clavichords, spinets, harpsichords, and virginals were able to execute all kinds of complicated accompaniments. The stringed instruments, too, were well on their way to their modern form. Unreliable and awkward looking reed instruments gradually vanished while others took on more importance. Technical improvements led to greater virtuosity.

The old church modes were gradually driven back by the major and minor tonalities. Overfed with polyphony, people began faintly to recognize harmony. Their ears adjusted themselves to hearing melodies and latent harmonies.

Now the Flamands were overwhelmed by their political problems — the Spanish occupation of the Low Countries and the beginning of the Thirty Years War. But the English, heretofore busy with wars, could breathe a little easier, and they took over the new movement of latent and patent harmonies with eagerness.

Whereas in polyphony all voices had been equally important, now the melody again assumed leadership and the bass became the skeleton — the bone structure of the music. This led to the development of the thorough bass (supposedly invented by Lodovico Viadana) which dominated the whole baroque period. It was a system of numbers written under the bass notes to indicate the intervals and chords to be played in accompaniment of the melody. The study of thorough bass led to a virtuoso technique of improvising middle voices imitating the melody, thus coloring a composition but always keeping every inside voice subordinate to the melody. A viola or violoncello usually played the bass; an archlute, an organ, or one of the other keyboard instruments filled in the middle voices.

With the invention of the thorough bass the need arose for keyboard musicians or lutenists who could improvise well. The professional accompanist in our sense had finally arrived. First called *maestro al cembalo*, his musical background had to be sound: not only must he know all the intricacies of linear and vertical counterpoint, he also had to keep all the other players in the ensemble together. He was thus the predecessor of our modern conductor. Even Mozart's operas were still led from and accompanied by the harpsichord.

The age of monody was reborn, but on a higher rung of the musical ladder than before. Monody found new expression in the form of opera, derived from the revival of the classical Greek conception of tragedy. Opera combines music, poetry, stage design, acting, dancing, and other allied arts. The first operas — *Dafne* and *Euridice* by Peri, and *Euridice* by Caccini — originated in Florence between 1597 and 1600. They had immediate appeal, and from then on, accompanists — and, in rudimentary form, even coaches — could be sure of making a living, however frugal.

The operatic accompaniment of that time consisted in executing the thorough bass of rather dry recitatives. Ensembles, choruses, and dances were usually written to end a scene or an act. It took a genius like Monteverdi to enrich the musical and spiritual values of early opera and to add expression to the recitative.

We now enter the era of the Arie Antiche, operatic solos with predominant melody, still to be found on the programs of our concert halls today. Caccini called his publication of arias and madrigals in monodic accompanied style (1602) *Nuove Musiche*, a term now used for the whole first period of baroque music.

Instrumental monody profited tremendously from the introduction of the thorough bass and the development

of our present string family. The sonatas and concertos written by Corelli, Veracini, Geminiani, Locatelli, and Vivaldi among others clearly show the influence that the Cremona school of violin-building had in establishing the violin as the instrument best suited to execute difficult and brilliant technical figurations. These works were not chamber music, but simply solo string compositions with harpsichord accompaniment.

In England, musicians caught up with the new style, but somewhat more slowly. Monody conquered the island through John Dowland's compositions (1597). His collection of songs required lute accompaniment, and the lute became one of the two leading accompanying instruments for the ensuing century and a half or so. Elizabethan composers wrote many songs still standard in our concert repertoire. The other dominant instrument was the virginal, which was favored by generations of English composers — Byrd, Morley, John Bull, Jones, and others. Besides songs (many of them composed to Shakespeare's lyrics), accompanists played dance music and transcriptions of madrigals. This Elizabethan period is one of the most fruitful eras of English music, characterized by deep feeling and artful settings. It reaches its climax in the beautiful music of Henry Purcell (1658–1695).

Germany's contribution to the history of sixteenth-century accompanied music is only indirect. During this time some of the most beautiful old German songs were collected and new ones composed: drinking songs, love songs, songs of the mercenaries (Landsknechte), political songs, rustic songs, and many more. But these songs, still under the influence of Flemish polyphony, were usually performed in four-part counterpoint. Occasionally there may have been lute accompaniments; we do not know much about the musical execution of these songs.

The gauklers and wayfaring musicians of the old days had become more respectable and consolidated their social position by forming guilds. These guilds were the beginning of later military bands and even orchestras. They did much to improve the quality of individual musicianship, but for accompanists a guild was not the right place.

With the advent of Protestantism in Germany in the sixteenth century, the way opened for even more secular music than before, but the Flemish influence did not favor the development of accompanied music. A famous musician's words fit this time very well: "The devil must have put the counterpoint into the cradle of the German."

The baroque era brought a decisive change. Influenced greatly by Italy's nuove musiche, monody became very popular in German secular and even sacred music. Thorough bass and keyboard instruments made elaborate accompaniments of melodies possible and desirable. Sacred motets, heretofore sung a cappella, were accompanied by thorough bass. One of the first composers in the new style was Michael Praetorius (1571–1621), to whom we are also indebted for an excellent book about the music and musical instruments of his time. The greatest composer of this pre-Bach era was Heinrich Schütz (1585–1672), who raised the elements of the nuove musiche to the highest level, imbued them with deeply spiritual and ethical values, and thus created a soil from which Bach could reap the noblest harvest of the baroque age. Schütz introduced passion music to the world and laid the groundwork for the oratorio. He also published arrangements of chorales for several voices accompanied by organ.

By 1600 the organ was already perfected to such a point that only new technical inventions could advance its construction. As far as versatility of the organ is concerned, nothing really new has been added since. Harpsichords and clavichords likewise were complete enough to fulfill any composer's wishes. The woodwinds and brass instruments attained more or less the form and the importance which they hold in today's orchestra, only the clarinets arriving later.

During this period, the French horn made its entrance on the musical scene. Wind playing was much more perfect than it is today, at least from the point of view of lip technique. One reason for the technical proficiency of the wind players is to be found in the strict schooling of the guilds. The invention of valves came much later.

The lute as the accompanying instrument of art music was on its way out. Keyboard instruments gave better service, being richer in sound and technical possibilities. All in all, the stage was set for the golden age of music. But before this age, with the classic and romantic school, appeared, the baroque era — yes, the whole of medieval music — was brought to its apotheosis by Bach and Handel.

Johann Sebastian Bach (1685–1750) appears to us as the greatest musical genius of all time. His contemporaries did not think so, at least not in the way in which we look upon him today: he was loved and revered as

organist, as improviser, as a technical wizard. But even at the end of his life the musical world was far removed from his universal world of ideas. His sons, composing in the new style, were better known than he. This did not faze the old man. Whether he composed his own works or whether he took somebody else's (Vivaldi's) and transcribed them, he soared higher and higher, ignoring fashion.

George Frederick Handel (1685–1759), belongs to Germany as well as to England where he lived for a long time. His works may not be so deep as Bach's, but for that very reason they are more in conformity with his times. He accepted the Italian operatic style and wrote numerous operas on biblical and classical subjects. These are rather static from a theatrical point of view and usually performed today in concert. Handel's arias, sonatas, and concerti are widely represented in our concert repertoire. People were not overawed by Handel's music as they were sometimes by Bach's. Even Beethoven, who loved Handel as the greatest composer he knew, and said of him, "I bend my knees before him," said of Bach: "Not a brook (Bach in German) but an ocean." This shows a deep but somewhat distant respect. It should be added, however, that only a relatively small number of Bach's compositions were known in Beethoven's time.

The accompanist — pianist or organist — will find dozens of Bach's and Handel's compositions along his professional path. I shall discuss their styles later (pp. 116–117, 127–128, 131–132, 144–145, 154–157).

Seventeenth-century France dramatically and suddenly switched to the operatic and balletic world of the Italian monody. The chief reformer was Jean Baptiste Lully (1633–1687). Italian by birth, he came to Paris as a boy. He may not have reached the height of the Italian school in richness of expression and invention, but in his operas he wed music with words and gave the chorus a much more important dramatic function. With his ballets he popularized an art form that has never left the French stage.

The other French innovator of the baroque period was Jean Philippe Rameau (1683–1764). He was not only a musician, composer, and virtuoso, but also a universal genius, theoretician, and scientist. His book, Traité de l'harmonie, established for the first time the scientific basis for our tonal system. He emphasized that our ears are accustomed to hearing latent harmonies in a melody. The human ear during the century before

Rameau had turned to vertical or harmonic, instead of horizontal or linear, hearing. Rameau also wrote books about new methods of accompanying — modifications of thorough-bass playing. Besides operas, he composed many concert pieces for clavecin (harpsichord) and violin.

The songs composed in France during that time were partly folk songs, shepherds' songs (bergerettes), and a kind of narrative song about all kinds of happenings among the people, such as hunting and marriage. French instrumental music, which is played to this day, includes violin sonatas by Leclair and pieces for flute by Monteclair.

The group of French composers called the clavecinistes wrote very pleasant music for the harpsichord; but with the exception of François Couperin (1668–1733), who towered above the rest, their importance lies in the fact that they successfully adapted the old style of composing for the lute to the harpsichord and thus greatly developed harpsichord technique by adding all kinds of embellishments to the melody.

THE PRECLASSICAL AND CLASSICAL PERIOD

In a general history of music these two movements, though almost simultaneous, would be treated separately. With respect to accompaniment they have much in common. The great innovator in vocal accompaniment was Schubert, with whom we may say that our modern age of accompaniment starts. The eighteenth century is characterized, for our purposes, by the following developments: (1) The impoverishment of musical accompaniment to the point of simple chords or arpeggios; the Italian musical center of gravity moves to Naples; the Neapolitan school and the opera buffa are born. (2) Opera (seria and buffa) finds its way into Germany, climaxed by Gluck's and Mozart's operas; the development of pianoforte changes the whole way of composing.

Every musical age has its zenith and its nadir, but they do not follow each other with regularity. Usually, when a high point is reached and degeneration sets in, another movement is starting from its low point and growing constantly. At one point, these two extreme curves cross. While Handel's and Bach's music formed the highest thinkable climax for the whole baroque age, the rococo period had already started and was shortly to become popular. In Italy, the line led upward from Monteverdi to Corelli to Vivaldi. The decline started with the trans-

fer of musical life to Naples. True, there were geniuses among Neapolitan composers, such as Alessandro Scarlatti (1659–1725), and the Neapolitan school created one masterful kind of music: the opera buffa, which sneaked into public success by being interpolated into opera seria as intermezzos between acts. Giovanni Battista Pergolesi (1710–1736) created the first opera buffa of lasting importance. Domenico Cimarosa (1749–1801) continued this trend with his buffa operas, especially *Il matrimonio segreto*. The latest representative of Neapolitan opera (seria and buffa) was Nicola Piccini (1728–1800), who became so popular that the public long preferred his operas to Gluck's. The composers of buffa operas added a new form of recitative to the accompanied recitative. It is the secco recitative, which consists of thorough-bass notation of chords under half-sung, half-spoken text which drove the action along.

But all in all, the eighteenth century brought a decline in accompanied music. The names Durante, Marcello, Paesiello, and Giordani can still be found on our concert programs. Their accompaniments degenerated into simple chords or arpeggios, leading to a stereotyped form of arpeggio called murky or Alberti bass figures (Fig. 2). This primitive harmonization and bass figuration can occasionally be found even in Haydn and Mozart.

Figure 2. Murky or Alberti bass figures

Thorough-bass notation became rarer and rarer. Toward the end of the eighteenth century, composers wrote out the bass and the harmony, except in recitatives.

In instrumental music, the Italians were very active. The newly perfected stringed instruments gave such composers as Tartini, Pugnani, Viotti, and Boccherini ample occasion to write acrobatically difficult pieces. The violoncello became a solo concert instrument around 1700.

In the eighteenth century, Italian opera conquered Europe and there was a lively exchange of musicians between Italy and other countries. One of the most important German composers of this time, Johann Adolf Hasse (1699–1782) studied in Naples with Scarlatti and Porpora. Italian composers accepted positions as court musicians in Germany and Austria — Antonio Salieri (1750–1825), for instance, who for years was to stand in Mozart's way in Vienna. One successful German composer was Georg Philipp Telemann (1681–1767), who wrote about forty operas. But on the whole, German operas were pompous, lacking in real drama and humor. The Germans up to the time of Mozart did not create a really good opera buffa. Even the comic episodes of Mozart's *Nozze di Figaro* and *Don Giovanni* are traceable to the Italian school. The Germans, however, introduced a new genre, the *Deutsche Singspiel* (inaugurated by J. A. Hiller) which does not use secco recitatives, but employs spoken dialogue between musical numbers. Mozart created the finest of these singspiels with *Die Entführung aus dem Serail*.

The German situation is quite different in the field of opera seria. Here, Christoph Willibald Gluck (1714–1787) may rightly be called the reformer of opera. He consciously counteracted the shallow dramatization and lack of ethical and spiritual values of the Italians and the French and lifted opera upon the shield of greatness. His stays in England and France made him more cosmopolitan than the other German composers of his time. Without him, neither Mozart nor Weber nor Richard Wagner would have been possible. Gluck used only the accompagnato recitative, but he imbued it with highly dramatic emotion.

Up to Mozart's time, German lied composition is not outstanding, and most of it is forgotten today. Karl Friedrich Zelter and Johann Rudolf Zumsteeg composed music for many poems by their friends Goethe and Schiller. Although the poets liked these lieder because the music merely accompanied and underlined the words, the songs themselves were formalistic and bare of invention. Another lied composer, Johann Friedrich Reichardt (1752–1806), who set many of Goethe's poems to music, is more important historically because he influenced Schubert's first period. Reichardt showed Gluck's influence. The piano accompaniment became richer, and pianistic interludes enlivened his songs.

We now approach the golden age of music, the classical period whose seat was in Vienna. In vocal accompaniment this period is not outstanding, so I shall confine myself to the most pertinent points from the point of view of an accompanist.

Joseph Haydn wrote songs and some rather humorous and some very insignificant operas. His genius proved itself in other fields of music.

Wolfgang Amadeus Mozart reached unsurpassed heights in his treatment of recitatives and concerted numbers, and originated the legato piano-playing which

is still our predominant style. There is no need to write more about Mozart's unique musical genius and his endearing personality; but we must look at his accompanied vocal compositions: one thin volume of songs, most of them in a rather conservative strophic style. The usual style of the lied of the period was simple musical accompaniment to several stanzas of lyrics, lyrics never overpowered by the music. The music was to fit the words in general, but not follow their emotional changes. Mozart's songs, although of much higher quality of invention and pianistic treatment, are not an exception. Some of his songs, however, point in their originality to the future. His simple "Das Veilchen," for example, breaks with the strophic system, and treats each stanza differently; he even introduces a short recitative into this song before he leads it back to the mood of the beginning. Another interesting song which employs for the first time a longer prelude and postlude is "Gesellenreise," emanating from his belief in Freemasonry. Another song, "Abendempfindung," surprisingly anticipates Schubert's moods and technique.

Ludwig van Beethoven's contribution to the accompanist's vocal literature is also not quite in keeping with his mastery of other musical forms. This giant could not make himself subservient to words; he had to use them for his creative purpose — which he did to perfection in the Ninth Symphony's last movement. He did, however, compose the first important German song cycles, the *Geistliche Lieder* and *An die ferne Geliebte*. The first is set to music in simple noble accompaniment and stresses the dignity of the words. In the second he found new ways of leading one song into the next, something Schumann later perfected. Beethoven's accompaniment in this second cycle is very original; at times he lets the piano take the melody while the voice subordinates itself. He also transcribed many Scottish and Irish folk songs for voice with piano and ad libitum violin or violoncello accompaniment.

In instrumental music, two of Bach's sons, Philipp Emanuel (1714–1788) and Johann Christian (1735–1782), brought the rococo style — the so-called gallant age — to Germany. Other composers of this time were Georg Benda (who also wrote the first German melodramas, where music accompanies and illustrates recitation), Johann Christoph Wagenseil, Georg Mathias Monn (whose concerto for violoncello is still in the repertoire), and Johann Stamitz (a Bohemian composer).

A very important connecting link between the preclassical and classical periods is Johann Schobert (died 1767). He broke with thorough-bass tradition to such an extent that he composed works for piano obbligato with accompanying violin. Mozart knew and was greatly influenced by Schobert's compositions.

In their sonatas, Haydn, Mozart, and Beethoven created pure chamber music. The pianist is no longer an accompanist, but a full-fledged partner of the instrumentalist. Haydn wrote no small pieces for violin or 'cello, but he did write concerti for these instruments, some of them still played in solo recitals and thus requiring accompaniment. He also wrote pieces for old instruments like the lyra and the barytone (both some kind of viola da gamba). Mozart's accompanied instrumental solo pieces are practically nil. Beethoven wrote a number of variations for violin and piano, and for violoncello and piano. The latter works are standard requirements for accompanists in the scarce literature for violoncello.

All our classic masters wrote great quantities of dance music. They had to eat, and minuets, German dances, and country dances were easier to sell than serious music. And accompanists were busy executing such dance music.

The French were too much concerned with opera to write any appreciable number of songs. They still used thorough bass and the few romances of the time are not of particular interest to the accompanist. Berlioz was still to come. More interesting is France's contribution to instrumental accompanied music. Here, the school of Giovanni Viotti had created some excellent virtuosos who not only enriched the pedagogical material but wrote some excellent concerti and smaller pieces. Among them are Charles Bériot, Jacques Rode, Rodolphe Kreutzer, Jacques Mazas, and Jean Charles Dancla.

The situation in England during the eighteenth century was not much better, if one excludes the much-played music of Handel. The principal composer of the time was Thomas Arne, who successfully incorporated into his songs some elements of folklore, mostly Scottish. The London Bach (Johann Christian) wrote most of his songs for English audiences. But most vocal music was imported from Italy, Germany, and Austria. In addition to being an eminent composer of songs, Arne was also one of the very few English instrumental composers. But with Purcell, a climax had been reached which could not easily be attained again.

SCHUBERT AND THE ROMANTIC PERIOD

For the accompanist and coach, Franz Schubert's work is not only the starting point for a tremendous growth of important accompanied vocal music, but it may be said that Schubert actually gave the accompanist the means to earn his bread — something Schubert was hardly able to do for himself. Just as an operatic coach could die of starvation if Mozart, Verdi, and Wagner never had lived, so Schubert, Schumann, and Brahms have supported generations of accompanists and coaches. If for no other reason, our gratitude must go to Schubert for this material fact.

Schubert may be called a classicist master in the same way that Beethoven may be called a romantic composer. They transcend categories into which they have been pushed by our musicologists and critics. With Schubert, the history of accompanying might as well end. All that follows — right up to the present — is only a logical continuation of his work. He elevated the piano accompaniment from a subordinate position and designated it as the carrier of psychological motivation for his songs' lyrics.

There is no human emotion for which Schubert did not find musical expression. Even when he used the strophic song, he enriched it by giving the piano part special significance. In some instances, one could even call this inner program music. The lover's impatience ("Ungeduld"), the pounding of the heart like the rhythm of the mailcoach ("Die Post"), the never-ceasing movement of the spinningwheel, leading to inevitable tragedy ("Gretchen am Spinnrad"), the hopelessness of lost love ("Der Doppelgänger"), the simple nobility of sound ("An die Musik"), the galloping hoofs of tragedy ("Der Erlkönig") — one could name hundreds of different emotions without scraping the bottom of the barrel of invention.

Pianistically, Schubert set very high standards. Songs like "Der Erlkönig" or "Frühlingstraum" are difficult technically and in interpretation. He also created a few works for violin and pianoforte and a sonata for arpeggione, an extinct instrument which is today replaced by a violoncello.

Schubert's work leads directly to a wide range of accompanied vocal music, characterized by such names as Loewe who developed the art form of the ballad, Schumann who challenged the pianist by composing preludes and postludes of considerable difficulty, and Mendelssohn, Cornelius, Robert Franz, Franz Liszt,

Brahms, Wolf, Mahler, Richard Strauss, and Alban Berg. I shall have something to say about these masters elsewhere in this book. Most of them have also contributed a great deal to instrumental accompanied literature.

German opera proceeds from Gluck via Mozart, Beethoven, Weber, and Marschner to Richard Wagner's music drama and Pfitzner's and Richard Strauss's operas. A temporary halt has been reached with Alban Berg's *Wozzeck*. Only the future will show whether Orff's and Egk's operas will endure. The deutsche Singspiel was continued by Lortzing, Nicolai, Cornelius.

Italy transferred all its efforts to composing opera. The line goes from Bellini, Donizetti, and Rossini through Verdi, Ponchielli, Mascagni, Cilea, and Puccini to Giordano and Respighi. A high spiritual plane has been attained by Pizzetti and Busoni who, in his *Doktor Faust*, presents a synthesis of Italian sensual sound and German philosophical depth.

The nineteenth century was the age of great virtuosos who also enriched the literature with many virtuoso pieces. The greatest was Paganini, and after him came Wieniawski, Ysaye, Joachim, Sarasate, Hubay, Kreisler, and many others.

During the nineteenth century, national compositions bloomed, and outstanding among them was the French art song. Based on the compositions of Berlioz, Cherubini, Halévy, Méhul, Meyerbeer, Gounod, Bizet, César Franck, Delibes, and Massenet, and on the impressionist paintings, French art songs reached their climax with works by Debussy, Fauré, Duparc, Ravel, Hahn, Honegger, Milhaud, and Poulenc. Other national schools sprang up in Scandinavia, Russia, Czechoslovakia, Poland, Hungary, Finland, Spain, and England. It may be enough to mention a few names: Grieg, Glinka, Tchaikovsky, Mussorgsky, Borodin, Rachmaninoff, Glazunov, Rimsky-Korsakoff, Stravinsky, Prokofiev, Shostakovich, Smetana, Dvořák, Sůk, Janaček, Szymanovsky, Bartók, Kodaly, Sibelius, Palmgren, Kilpinen, Granados, Turina, de Falla, Cyril Scott, Quilter, Delius, Vaughan Williams, Benjamin Britten.

The United States has made great progress in creating and developing American music. Griffes, Hageman, Carpenter, Ives, Taylor, Copland, Barber, Roy Harris, Dougherty, Bernstein, Menotti, and, above all, George Gershwin are some of the American composers of "long hair" music. Gershwin is also the connecting link to the true American kind of music, the popular jazz and swing music and the folk music of the spirituals and the regional American songs.

Obviously the accompanist and coach will have to store up and sublimate much knowledge and many different cultures if he really wants to reach the top in his profession.

The Historical Background of Coaching

COACHING is very recent in the history of music. Its beginnings can be traced back only to the introduction of vocal monody and the appearance of the first operas, roughly around 1600. Then, for the first time in history, large casts and choral masses, orchestras, dancers, and all kinds of complicated if very naive technical effects had to be coordinated and rehearsed. The maestro al cembalo had his hands full and needed assistance. How did he recruit his assistants? Where did he find them? Well, in the beginning of opera a musician had to be everything at once: composer, arranger, voice teacher, music teacher, conductor, coach. He was most often in the service of one of the Italian dukes or the wealthy rulers of an Italian state or city government. The Medici assembled the best musical talent at their courts and other rulers followed suit. These rulers took pleasure in sponsoring talented singers — usually young girls, sending them to their court musicians for tuition. The prime reason for this musical education was often amorous, but it must also be said that discovering and sponsoring talent in all fields was one of the most satisfying ways of advertising one's court and of immortalizing one's name. Tremendous amounts of money were paid by these Renaissance Maecenases to import famous composers, musicians, castrati and other singers, technical directors, stage designers, ballet dancers, choreographers. It is very interesting to read in the old sources how these princes and dukes, who more often than not were talented amateur composers and musicians themselves, tried to secure the highest artistic achievements for their court, their city, and their state.

One of the finest musical assemblages of the Renaissance could be found at the court of a member of the Gonzaga family, Vincent, Duke of Mantua — not the one in *Rigoletto*. Jacopo Corsi, a cultured composer and musician in the court, composed some arias for a performance of Peri's opera *Dafne* in 1608, having been harpsichord player at its very first performance in 1594. A near relative of the Duke of Mantua was a cardinal who in his leisure composed some not at all religious songs. He sent them to the court composer, Marco da Gagliano, another Florentine, for corrections, and received the following reply, dated August 5, 1608: "I am returning to your most illustrious Grace your sonnet which I have reduced to a better meter according to my judgement. As you will see I have also added a note in the bass which, it seems to me, adds gracefulness to it."

In another letter to the cardinal, Marco da Gagliano said: "The most illustrious Cardinal Montalto's lady is a most precious thing and if Signora Vittoria were not superior to her in vocal beauty I would say absolutely that she was more singularly endowed." Let us assume that this singular endowment lay in the musical sphere and that the situation is comparable with the recent Tebaldi-Callas rivalry.

One of the most famous operatic composers of the time, the above-mentioned Jacopo Peri, wrote to the Duchess of Mantua that he had chosen one of the girls she had sent him as prospective pupils and had started her musical development: "I have visited her often taking diligent care of her and I hope that she will have a very good success. She has a more than reasonably good voice, she likes to study and has excellent ears which is very important. She is very secure in reading in all the different keys and starts to sing very well from sight which in my opinion is necessary to lay a good foundation. She also sings some little arias with the accompaniment of a keyboard instrument and is learning to accompany herself which, in the short time of her studies, may be called a miraculous achievement." These are the words of a proud and successful coach, probably the first such report on record.

Other composer-arranger-teacher-coaches during the early seventeenth century were Giovanni del Turco, Gian Battista Strozzi, and, in fact, almost every musician of fame. The monodic age started in the house of Count Bardi in Florence, spread to Mantua, and moved on to Bologna, Rome, and Venice. The greatest operatic composer and innovator of the monodic age, Claudio Monteverdi, after having served in Mantua as singer and violinist, became court conductor there and stayed on in this capacity from 1601 until 1613, when he was called to Venice as conductor of the Cathedral of St. Mark. His influence on Venice's operatic life cannot be overestimated.

Venice was the first city to open an opera theater for the public in general. Up to then, operatic performances had taken place in private theaters of the courts or of wealthy noblemen. Venice's opera houses — there were already quite a number of them by 1650 — were highly competitive and must have been the first theaters where the managers employed coaches or assistant conductors. These coaches were still all-round musicians, mostly composers. One of them, Marc Antonio Cesti, was a chapel singer besides. To him belongs the honor of having been exported to the Austrian court, where for three years he worked as vice-conductor or, as we would call it today, associate conductor, for Emperor Leopold I. In this position he prepared the performances of his operas, and no doubt he also coached the singers. Soon opera houses were built in other Italian cities — Bologna, Florence, Rome, and Parma. And other Italian composers and conductors held temporary positions in Austria or Germany — Antonio Sartorio who, before becoming vice-conductor at the Cathedral of St. Mark in Venice, was employed by the court of Hanover; Carlo Pallavicino who was first vice-conductor, then regular conductor at the Dresden court; Marc Antonio Ziani, who became imperial court conductor in Vienna.

The operatic center shifted from Venice to Naples, where it remained for a long time. Scarlatti and Jomelli are the main representatives of the Neapolitan school.

If Venice had been very important for the popularization of Italian opera in the central European countries — thus creating operatic coaches in Austria and Germany — the influence of the Neapolitan opera was overpowering. Italian opera companies were playing all over Europe, even in such a far-off city as the newly founded St. Petersburg. Italian singing stars were also performing all over Europe, and some were as temperamental as they are today, requiring conductors and coaches to find a way to handle them. A famous dramatic soprano, Cuzzoni, known to be most difficult, was rehearsing in London with Handel. He gave her the cue to start singing but she did not want to come in. Handel waited a while, then repeated the cue. Again nothing. He got up calmly, grabbed the Cuzzoni, and dragged her to the open window: "Madam, either you will sing or I shall throw you down the three flights. You may be the Devil, but I, I am Beelzebub!" The lady preferred singing to a trip to the nether world.

The great reformer of operatic performances in Paris, Lully, was his own general manager, composer, conductor, and a marvelous trainer of singers and the orchestra. He was the first conductor to use a baton — a heavy cane with which he beat the time on the floor. Quite often he kicked musicians and singers if they did not perform to his taste. And he is said to have smashed a violin over the head of one of his fiddlers. All this, needless to say, took place before the time of the musicians' union.

Mozart rehearsed with his singers at the clavier. He must have been a wonderful coach of his own music, though not all composers have the patience to coach their own works. Mozart, however, had help in the person of the conductor Joseph Weigl, who took over the direction of Le Nozze di Figaro after the first five performances. In Prague, during rehearsals for the first performance of Don Giovanni, it was the Czech conductor Kucharz who helped Mozart rehearse the orchestra. Kucharz did also the first vocal scores for Le Nozze di Figaro and Don Giovanni.

When Zauberflöte was rehearsing in Vienna, Mozart was busy in Prague with the preparations for a gala first performance of Titus. In his absence, the young conductor J. B. Henneberg rehearsed singers and orchestra and did such a good job that Mozart, after conducting the first couple of performances, turned the musical direction of Die Zauberflöte over to Henneberg. This enabled Mozart to appear backstage during the performance and have great fun confusing his singers. At one point he took the glockenspiel out of the hands of the assistant conductor backstage, who was supposed to play it while Papageno onstage went through the motions of shaking his dummy glockenspiel, and played the little bells purposely before the musical cue had arrived, hoping to confuse Papageno. But Schikaneder, Jr., the Papageno, could not be confused. Quickly he ad libbed, hitting his little glockenspiel and shouting to it, "Shut up!" In this way, he and the audience had the last laugh. On the basis of this little story, which was told by Mozart himself, we may call him an assistant maestro in charge of backstage duties.

A similar story, but without Schikaneder's sense of humor, has been credited to Puccini. At a performance of *Tosca* at Covent Garden, he had a whimsical desire to play the backstage bells, a difficult duty feared by all coaches and assistant conductors. Puccini naturally made a mess of it. After the performance, the conductor, Mugnone, stormed backstage, yelling, "Which ass beat the bells tonight?" The chronicler is silent about Mugnone's reaction when he found out that Puccini himself was to blame.

Operatic coaches during the eighteenth and early nineteenth centuries were given positions as Hilfskapellmeister (auxiliary conductors), very much the same as in Austria and Germany today, where the great conductors of our time learned their business as coaches. Although I have no direct proof, I believe that specialization of operatic coaching set in with the tremendous reform that Carl Maria von Weber under-

took in Prague in 1813. He was the first Operndirektor to organize enough piano rehearsals for his artists. For this purpose he certainly needed coaches, who would not have time to do anything else but to rehearse the singers. The first voice coach mentioned in the annals of the Vienna Opera was a certain Johann Coci (presumably a Bohemian) who worked at the opera house from 1849 until 1869. The first conductor of backstage bands in Vienna, Josef Kaulich, worked from 1854 to 1885, the first chorus master from 1849 to 1870, the first ballet coach from 1864 to 1875.

With the complicated productions of Wagner's Ring cycle and others of his operas in Munich and Bayreuth, the golden age of the operatic coach began. The young Anton Seidl, Hans Richter, and many others got their first training from Richard Wagner in Bayreuth. Arturo Toscanini is the exception to the rule: he began as a violoncellist and took over a performance of *Aida* in Buenos Aires in an emergency.

In the past, song coaching was done by the great singers' accompanists, who traveled with them all the year round. Even today, some singers and instrumentalists hire their accompanist on a year-round basis: Franz Rupp for Marian Anderson and Emanuel Bay for Jascha Heifetz, for example. In three hundred and fifty years of coaching, the coach has finally come of age: he occupies an important if not always appreciated position behind the footlights and in the wings of our musical stages. He is also active in his studio, and the most famous opera and concert singers of our time have gone through their training with conscientious coaches.

The Mechanics of Musical Instruments

THE accompanist and coach must first of all know the mechanics of the musical instruments he plays — the piano, the organ, and the small group of keyboard instruments used in orchestras for opera or for choir practice, such as the celesta and the harmonium. It is amazing how little most pianists, even professionals, know about the construction and mechanics of their instrument. A driver of an automobile — in this country — need not know how the motor works; the next mechanic is usually just around the corner. But the ability to repair a motor or an instrument's mechanism is not the only reason for knowing how it works. A driver or a machine operator will handle his machine much more easily and better if he knows all the problems of its construction; he will make it run more smoothly and with more gratifying results to himself and to others. How much truer is this for the musician — the pianist, organist, accompanist, and coach! Knowledge of a piano's anatomy will result in a more varied and finer touch, better pedaling, and more interesting combinations of sound.

The accompanist and coach has not only his own instrument to learn. He should know thoroughly the mechanics and intricacies of his instrumentalist's or vocalist's instrument. The description of each instrument's mechanics could fill a separate book, and very good books are listed in the bibliography, which should be consulted by accompanists and coaches who want to delve into the minute details. I shall try here to give an adequate explanation of the mechanics of instruments — a basic amount of knowledge with which the coach or accompanist will be able to get along.

The working principle of every musical instrument, including the human voice, is the same. Each instrument must have three basic parts without which no useful tone can be produced: (1) the energizer; (2) the vibrator; (3) the resonator.

The energizer. The energizer is the physical source of an instrument's power. It can be inside or outside the instrument and is, of course, always set in motion by man. In a stringed instrument the energizer is the arm of the player who holds the bow in his hand and moves it back and forth to make the strings sound. The pianist uses his finger to depress a key and bring into operation a complicated mechanism; additional effects are originated by his feet. The same system works for the organ: the difference is that the piano is a stringed percussion instrument whereas the organ is a very complicated wind instrument. The human voice, contrary to popular belief, is not a stringed instrument but a wind instrument: its source of power lies in the respiratory system.

The vibrator. The vibrator receives the energy from the energizer and turns it into sound waves. The vibrators of the stringed instruments and the piano are the strings. The human voice has as its vibrator the larynx or voicebox. The vocal cords have a function similar to the lips of the player of a trumpet or trombone. They modify the sound according to the amount of air pressure.

The resonator. The resonator takes over the tone initiated by the energizer and transmitted by the vibrator and modifies its sonority or timbre. Stringed instruments are built to produce a maximum of sonority. The sounding board, the bridge, the quality of the wood, the lacquer, the proportions, the mathematical relations between the different parts of the violin — all these add up to form the resonator. In the piano it is the metal construction of the sounding board, the quality of the material, and many other little elements that make up the resonator. Each organ pipe is an individual resonator, with its own frequency. We call such individual, limited resonators *selective* resonators. In contrast to this, resonators that handle a large number of sounds at once are called *broad* resonators — for example, the stringed instrument's body, the piano's sounding board, and the many resonators of the human body which amplify, modify, and ennoble the voice.

Things become difficult and controversial when we turn to these resonators in the human voice. It is true that the cavities and sinuses of the head contribute to the voice's resonance. But this is only a very small and comparatively unimportant contribution; these cavities are too small to really provide enough resonance. No, the most important determiners of the voice's beauty, intensity, and timbre are the shaping of mouth and throat, the mastering of breath control, the relaxing of muscles — in short, the harmonious interplay of everything known to be the basis of sound vocal technique.

For the purposes of this book, I shall confine myself to discussing the violin as the stringed instrument an accompanist and coach has most frequently to deal with. The violoncello, except for its size and the pitch of its strings, has the same anatomical and physiological properties as the violin; the principles that apply to the violin apply also to the violoncello.

ANATOMY AND PHYSIOLOGY OF THE VIOLIN

Our violin, like all other musical instruments, is a product of evolution. Among its predecessors are the one-stringed rebec and the gigue (giga), which also started out with one string but had three strings by early in the sixteenth century. The gigue gave its name to the modern German Geige (violin). Another forefather is the fiddle of the late Middle Ages; this name is still very popular in the United States. The gigue became the viola da braccio (viola for the arm) in the later sixteenth and seventeenth centuries. A remnant of this name is still preserved in the German name for the viola: Bratsche.

First built as a diminutive form of the viola, the violin reached the climax of its construction early in the eighteenth century in Cremona when its use was changed from mainly playing harmonies and chords to carrying the melody. In the two hundred and fifty years since this culmination in the workshops of Stradivarius, Amati, Guarnerius, and others, the violin has not altered its form. The violin makers of Cremona found the golden mean of its anatomy and physiology, which led to victory for the violin as the leading solo and orchestra instrument.

The energizer. The violin's energizer consists of the player's right arm and hand which draw the bow. Bowing is the breath that makes the string vibrate. Good bowing is therefore a most important requisite for playing the violin. The right arm must be absolutely steady, able to use the full length of the bow up and down on the strings without the slightest interruption and without any tremor or quivering. Playing a long sustained note with one stroke, starting out pianissimo, increasing the sound gradually to fortissimo, and decreasing it again to pianissimo is comparable to a singer's perfect breath control when he is using what is called the *messa di voce.* Though an accomplished violinist should be able to execute such sustained bowing without instruction, the accompanist or coach may be able to improve his string player's technique by detecting faults in the position of arm and wrist, which should always be loose and relaxed, and by noting the path of the bow, which should always be parallel to but not too near the bridge nor too near the end of the fingerboard. Strength and smoothness of bowing come from the wrist and the fingers, not from the arm. The new science of biomechanics has discovered how to achieve the optimum results in the playing of stringed instruments. The stance, the position of the body, and the angle of the bowing arm to the violin are of decisive influence for the energizer, the bowing arm. The accompanist or coach should not try to change the bowing position which the teacher has taught the player but should consult the teacher if he notices that all is not well with the player's bowing technique.

There are quite a few ways of bowing. Each accompanist and coach should know them and be able to decide which bowing the violinist should use for a given phrase. These varieties are:

Legato or connected bowing, meaning that the legato line should not be interrupted, which becomes difficult when several strings are involved. The change from one string to the next and the change of direction of the bowing must happen unnoticeably.

Détaché or detached bowing means nonlegato broad bowing with very short stops between changes of bow (grand détaché), or shorter strokes of the same kind (détaché sec), or strokes in between these two extremes.

Martellé or hammered bowing is an energetic, strongly accentuated way of playing note for note, slightly interrupting the bowing after each note, mostly starting at the nut of the bow.

Staccato bowing is executed by more or less short bowing with continuous change of bow and with definite stops between the changes usually marked by a dot or a point above the note. The bow may or may not leave the string between notes. A light staccato should have "air" between the notes.

Spiccato in the modern sense is a very light, jumpy, but unaccentuated, airy, staccato in or above the middle of the bow. It is especially important for the playing of the classics. Joseph Joachim, the great violinist and stylist, once compared the different spiccato bowings to the clatter of hail or of rain and the falling of snow flakes.

Saltato (sautillé) means the same jumpy staccato but with a clear accent each time the bow attacks the string, each note being very short.

Col legno (with wood) is an effect created by bowing or attacking the strings with the back side — the wooden part — of the bow.

A punta d'arco means with the point of the bow.

Sul tasto (on the fingerboard) playing creates a soft sound.

Sul ponticello (near the bridge) playing creates a loud metallic sound.

Pizzicato means that the string is plucked with one or two fingers, creating a slightly percussive effect of very short duration.

Tremolo means very fast repeated changes of bow on the same note without any established rhythm, sometimes increasing or decreasing in sound.

The length of the bow is used in many different ways. There are whole bow strokes, half bow strokes, strokes at the point of the bow (mostly *piano* since the leverage does not allow for pressure), strokes at the nut of the bow (mostly used for *forte* bowing or strong attacks). The science of bowing is as complicated as the physiology of breathing. Phrases that end piano normally should be ended at the point; crescendo phrases should be finished near the nut. Arpeggio playing will require special mastery in the bowing arm, as will the playing of chords on two or more strings.

Even the left hand of the player can act as an energizer, especially when left-hand pizzicato is required. Sometimes it is combined with a right-hand pizzicato or staccato as in some virtuoso pieces by Paganini or Sarasate.

The vibrator. The bowing arm with the bow energizes the strings which are the vibrators of the violin. The violin has four strings tuned in fifths. They are from left to right the G, D, A, and E strings. These strings are fastened to the violin by the four pegs (1) stuck into the holes of the scroll box (2). The scroll of a violin which forms the end of the neck (3) and the neck are usually made of maple. The pegs have holes into which the ends of the strings are inserted. The strings then lead to the tailpiece, which lies just a little bit higher than the fingerboard (4), so that they can be depressed or stopped by the fingers of the player's left hand. The ebony fingerboard nut raises the strings off the fingerboard. The tailpiece (5) is usually also made of ebony. It has four holes and slits into which the strings are fastened. On their way to the tailpiece the strings are drawn over the bridge (6), which is the conductor of the strings' vibrations to the resonator. The design and the material of the bridge is very important for resonance. It is usually made of maple, rests on two feet, and its thickness tapers at the top, where it is only half as thick as at the bottom. Various curved designs have been cut out of the bridge, all helpful in improving the sound. A bridge may improve or impoverish the sound of a violin. Each violinist will have to search until he finds the right

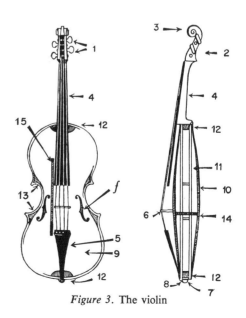

Figure 3. The violin

bridge for his instrument. To return to the tailpiece: its length is also a determining factor in the harmonious sound of a violin. The distance between the bridge and tailpiece is comparable to the distance between the bridge and the pegs of the piano (see p. 27). The tailpiece is attached to the button (7) of the violin by the tailgut (8), usually a thick, colored piece of gut. It should be fastened in such a way that the tailpiece just reaches the small ridge of ebony above the button.

The mute, a small piece of wood, metal, or leather, can be set on the bridge, checking the bridge's motion and thereby softening the sound and lessening the intensity of the vibrations.

The strings are vibrated by the bow and, in addition, by the fingers of the left hand. This action should not be overdone. The speed of the vibrato should not be excessive. Wide vibration is comparable to a shake or tremolo in the human voice. Vibrato should be dense but light. The strings of a violin must never be manhandled; where a *non espressivo* tone is desired the fingers must rest on the strings firmly but quietly.

The player's left hand functions principally to produce the desired pitch. Since the stringed instruments are not well-tempered like the keyboard instruments, any interval is possible. Experience teaches the player to move by half tones, but sometimes quarter tones are necessary to adjust harmonies. The fingerboard of the violin is divided into many positions, all unmarked, of which the first seven are most used. These positions are one tone apart, and the left hand makes the shifts from one to another. This should be done with ease and assuredness. The thumb, which initiates the shift, should lean against the neck of the violin firmly but not too tightly. As in everything else, economy and coordination of movement are essential. In higher positions the distances are shorter, and intonation becomes more difficult. The fingers should not be lifted from the strings, unless it becomes necessary or unless *espressivo* playing requires that each tone be clearly focused. This is quite different from piano technique where the fingers not in use must get out of the way.

Effects produced by the left hand include: *Trills*— Rapidly changing and repeated embellishments between main note and next higher half or whole step. *Double stops*— Simultaneously playing two notes on two strings. *Harmonics*— High tones of ethereal quality, produced by lightly putting the finger at a point on the string that divides it exactly into a half, a third, or a quarter of its length (natural harmonics). Harmonics also can be produced by shortening the string with a finger placed on a particular spot and then lightly touching with another finger a spot above which belongs to one of the natural overtones of the newly created ground tone. *Glissando (slide)*— A more or less slow glide from one tone to another with one finger whereby all tones in between are sounded in passing.

The resonator. The vibrations are transmitted to the body of the violin, its resonator, by the two feet of the bridge. The position of the bridge on the belly is therefore of utmost importance: the back edge of the right foot should be just in front of the front edge of the sound post. The left foot should be just above the center of the bassbar.

The body of a violin, its soundbox, consists of two plates, the belly (9) and the back (10), connected by glue to the ribs or side walls (11) with the help of six blocks with linings (12).

Pine from the south side of the tree—wood that is elastic—is used for the belly. It can be made of one piece if the grain is uniform, but usually two are used. The thickness of the wood is not uniform. The art and skill of the violin maker are apparent in his choice of the right proportions for these measurements (this is known as the graduation of the violin). The proportions of the curves of the arch of the belly are another secret of a well-constructed violin. These curves conduct the sound waves and help to augment and cleanse the sound of ugly by-sounds. Cut into the belly are the sound holes, two f-shaped ornaments which allow outside air to communicate with the air inside the body and increase the flexibility of the middle part of the belly, thereby making it more able to vibrate sympathetically as the strings are sounded.

The back of the violin is usually made of two mirror-image pieces of maple or, rarely, sycamore, glued together in such a way that the grain is symmetrical. The wood used for the back is harder, more resistant, and vibrates more slowly than does the wood that is used for the belly.

The ribs are the sides of the soundbox. They are made of maple or sycamore and supported by the six blocks, with linings consisting of narrow strips of pine. Belly and back are glued to the flat surfaces of the blocks. Two of these serve also as support for the neck and tailpiece. In this way, the body of the violin is finally connected. The edges of the body, which can testify to the mastery of the violin maker when made well, remain to be discussed. The contours of the violin on belly and back are followed by inlaid ornamental strips, the purfling (13), which look like black lines but are actually thin strips of ebony or dyed willow divided by a strip of light wood. A small part of the belly has no purfling; the neck is inserted in the free space. It protrudes at the edge of the violin and is somewhat raised above it. The peg is fastened into a hole drilled into the lower rib and its supporting wood block.

All these parts of the soundbox are visible. Two invisible wooden pieces — the soundpost and the bassbar — are of cardinal importance for the working of the soundbox resonator. The *soundpost* (14), called âme (soul) in French, is made of very old pine. The wood is chosen with regard to the desired tone quality of a particular violin. If the tone quality is to be hard, the soundpost should be made of soft pine, and vice versa. The soundpost is cylindrical and is fitted upright into the body. It serves as resonance conductor between belly and back, so that their vibrations may become attuned to the same frequency. The position of the soundpost is subject to experimentation. It should be somewhere behind the right foot of the bridge and should be wedged in between belly and back, but not too tightly. The soundpost also serves as support for the belly.

The bassbar (15) is a strip of pine about ten and a half inches long, thicker in the middle and tapering off toward the end, shaped to follow the inside curve of the belly with a slight tension. It is glued to the inside of the belly just under a line formed by the G string. The bassbar has three functions. It reinforces the belly against the pressure of the tightly tuned strings, particularly through the increased thickness in its middle part. It helps to facilitate the vibration of the belly. Finally, it increases the resonance, particularly of the lower notes.

The last but by no means least important resonator is the varnish of the violin. Many books have been written about the secret of the old masters' varnish, and with all the facilities of modern chemical analysis, this secret has still not been found. We know only that the Cremona masters used oil varnish made from natural products of trees and plants — resin, turpentine, and possibly linseed oil. Amber, another organic substance, is also found in their varnish. Modern varnish is also usually oil varnish, although in cheaper violins spirit varnish is sometimes used.

The first layer of varnish seeps gradually into the wood. This absorption takes a long time. The other layers serve to protect the instrument and give it visual beauty. This is the reason why so many old instruments look as if they had no varnish at all. The first layer has seeped in, the outer layers have rubbed off through the centuries. Varnish affects the tone; good varnish improves the tone. But varnish alone is not the deciding factor for good resonance in a violin. Though the secret has not yet been explained satisfactorily, good resonance is a combination of wood, varnish, proper dimensions for the soundbox, and all the sympathetically vibrating resonators.

Lastly, a word about the anatomy of the bow. The bow has a long line of ancestors. One of the first and still the best of all bow makers was the Parisian François Tourte (1747–1835). The length of the bow should be about twenty-nine inches. A good bow is made of brazilwood which has good elastic qualities, possibly also of snakewood or ironwood. In the small triangular part at the end of the bow called the *head* is an opening for the knotted bunch of horsehair, which is fastened to it by a wooden plug. The head — called the plaque — is usually protected by ivory, silver, or gold. At the other end of the bow is a piece of ebony called the nut, or frog, into which the horsehair is fastened the same way as into the head. A screw at the end of the frog tightens or relaxes the horsehair. This horsehair should come in a strip of 200 to 250 single hairs. A good bow must have the right balance. The weight of a bow is largely a question of personal taste, but it should be between two and two and a quarter ounces. Silver thread or whalebone covers the part of the bow near the nut, to keep the fingers from slipping.

ANATOMY AND PHYSIOLOGY OF THE PIANOFORTE

The modern pianoforte is the descendant of the harpsichord, clavecin, clavichord, virginal, and clavicymbalum. *Clavis* means key, and the word remains in the German Klavier. The keyboard instruments favored in the baroque period could not produce any contrasts in dynamics worthy of mention. The need, therefore, was to develop an instrument that could clearly produce loud and soft tones. The first to construct such an instrument, by using hammers, was the Florentine Bartolomeo Cristofori (in 1711). He called his instrument the *piano e forte*. His invention was more or less forgotten, but later revived by the German organbuilder Silbermann. Two mechanisms were developed: the Viennese action (with the hammer fastened to the end of the key), and the English action (with the hammer hinged to a special wooden rail).

Beethoven wrote his Hammerklavier sonata in 1818. Until then, composers had written their works for the more modest prototypes of our modern pianoforte.

The nineteenth century brought a lot of improvements, until the main features of our modern piano were established by Steinway and Sons in New York around 1855, using the English action, which proved better for touch and sound. The pianoforte is predominantly a percussion instrument operated by digital levers. Steel wires in high tension are struck by felt-covered hammers and made to vibrate; the vibration is transmitted to the soundboard and resonated there.

The energizer. The piano's energizer is the system of hammer action put in motion by the fingers of the player. The action is constructed in such a way that finest shadings of dynamics and tonal production can be effected by varying the touch. Like the bowing arm and the left hand of the violinist, the arms, hands, and fingers of the pianist produce the desired tonal shade. The pianist's arms and fingers can act as hammers, the fingertips can transmit the most caressing touch. The fingers can crawl or cuddle on the keys to produce a legato. They can fall swiftly and the result will be staccato or martellato. All this is the armament of a pianist — his technique and his touch. Accompanists and coaches must have their technique and their touch professionally perfect. Some pianos will meet particular requirements of touch and technique better than others: Steinways, Bechsteins, and Bösendorfers are the best all-round concert pianos for

brilliance. For the finest shadings of, for example, French impressionistic music, the Blüthner, Erard, and Pleyel may be better. Percussive effects may be best achieved on a Baldwin. But these are fine differences: the principle of construction is the same in all. The accompanist and coach usually will not have his choice of piano; he must be at home at any piano.

The complicated mechanism which transmits energy to the vibrator is called the action, a complex mechanism of three systems of levers or jacks. This is the way a tone is produced: The key (1) which is balanced in the middle by the balance rail (2) will when struck in its front part by the finger rise with its back end. This will also lift the capstan screw (3). The capstan screw lifts the wippen (4) which is hinged to the flange (5) at its rear end. The wippen has a fork-like front end which carries in its axis the jack fly (6), a bell-crank lever. This lever attacks the knuckle (7) on the hammershank (8) and throws the hammer (9) onto the string (10). The hammerhead then strikes the string. But, an infinitesimal moment before the string is struck, the arm of the jack hits against the letoff regulating button (11). This frees it from the knuckle and effects the so-called escapement. Escapement is the ability of the hammer to fall back into its original position after hitting the string and strike again at the slightest touch of the key. This escapement is facilitated by yet another leverage system. The repeti-

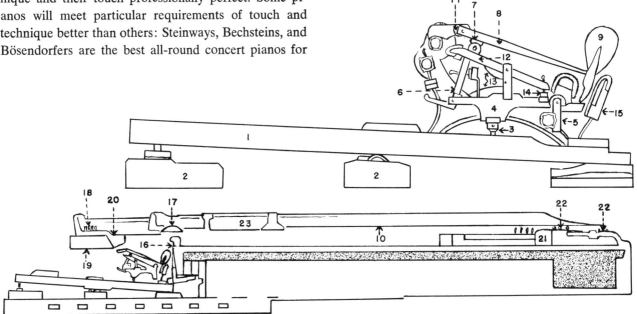

Figure 4. The action of the piano

tion lever (12), supported by a spring (13), holds up the knuckle. The padded front end of the repetition arm, when in use, contacts the drop screw (14) which holds the repetition lever down and out of the way. For the combination of these two leverage systems the expression double escapement has been coined, which characterizes the modern piano action. Hammerhead, shank, and knuckle, when "escaping," fall back on the repetition lever. If the key is held down, the hammerhead is readied for repetition by the back check (15) which is mounted on the key by a wire. A part of the vibrator system is also put under the control of the key. It is the damper system.

The key when struck lifts with its rear end a wooden lever (16) which in its turn lifts a long wire which stretches up through the strings. This wire carries on top the felt-covered damper (17). The damper rises together with the wire and lifts the dampening felt from the strings. Thus the strings may vibrate freely. Upon the return of the key to its initial position, the felt dampens the strings again if it is not lifted independently by the forte pedal (see p. 28).

The modern keyboard of a grand piano consists of eighty-eight keys (seven and a third octaves). The keys are not straight in their entire length. In the back they lead either to the right or to the left in accordance with the way in which strings and metal frame are constructed. The keyboard is mounted on a wooden frame and, by action of the damper pedal (see p. 28) may be shifted a few millimeters, usually to the right. The hammerhead which strikes the strings is felt-covered. With time, the felt becomes too hard and has to be pricked with needles by the piano tuner to soften it. The angle of the hammerhead has a decisive influence on the crispness of the sound. The upright piano is constructed in a very similar if simplified manner.

The vibrator. The pianoforte's vibrators are the strings, made of steel wire. Low tones are produced by long, thick strings, high tones by short, thin strings. All together, there are about two hundred and forty strings on a piano. Of these, about the eight lowest bass keys have single strings covered with a copper loading. Above these are about seventeen bichord (double wire) strings, all of them covered. These twenty-five strings all go in one direction — diagonally to the right. All the other strings lead diagonally toward the left. There are therefore two crosswise-directed divisions of strings, the bass strings crossing diagonally on top of the other strings

(over-strung scale). The other strings are divided into three fan-shaped sections of about twenty-one each. Often only the lowest four notes of the first of these three sections are bichords and all others are trichords.

This is the place to explain the design of the scaling system of a string. The "scale" of the piano (as described by Lawrence M. Nalder in "The Modern Piano," in *Musical Opinion*) is "the succession and co-relation of measurements which govern the size, shape and the internal lay-out of the instrument." Each string is fastened to the tuning pin (18) by being turned around it several times. The tuning pin is made of strong steel and anchored in the wrest plank (19). The piano tuner must turn the tuning pin to tune the string. The wrest plank has to be made of very strong layers of wood so that the tuning pin, even under the strong pressure of the string (an average of 160 pounds per string) does not move.

The capo d'astro bar (20) is made of cast iron. This bar has a pointed lower edge which holds the string down. This point where the string is held down is the actual beginning of the string's sounding part. Between tuning pin and capo d'astro bar, the string is dead or mute. The capo d'astro bar nowadays extends through the treble sections only. For the lower strings, agraffes, or small brass studs, may be used. The string is now able to vibrate when struck by the hammer. Usually all hammers are set in a straight line so that all strings are struck in the same place. This would never give a clean sound if the strings were not of different lengths. The best point of strike is at one eighth of their length for the bass strings and about one fourteenth of their length for the treble strings. The end of the sounding part of the string is determined by the bridge (21), which must conform to the different lengths of strings. It is, therefore, curved. Actually, there are two bridges, one situated further back and elevated for the bass strings, the other for the treble strings. The bridges contain two bridge pins for each string, which press against the strings and end their sounding length. The string is firmly held on the bridge. Like the bridge on a violin, the bridge of a piano is the transmitter of vibrations to the soundboard, to the piano's resonator system. The bridges must be made of hardwood (mostly maple) and are tightly glued to the soundboard. The end of the string is fastened to the hitch pin (22). The part of the string between bridge and hitch pin is dead, but the dead lengths of string vibrate sympathetically. In first-class concert grands, these dead parts, the lengths of which are the result of thorough research, add harmonics to the richness of sound. All fastening devices must be anchored in a very strong frame, to withstand the enormous tension of the strings. This is the iron frame (23), which in its construction must closely follow the scale design of the interior of the pianoforte. The frame, which must be cast of high-quality iron, is divided by several bars which usually break the strings into three treble and one bass section. The circular holes in the back part of the frame have no acoustical function, but are cut out to diminish its weight. Even so, a frame weighs about two hundred and fifty pounds.

The pedals are auxiliary machines which control the vibration of the strings. They also have a definite influence on the sound and color scale which a pianist can create. Most pianos of American construction have three pedals. The forte pedal (at the right) sends a metal bar up to the inside of the keyboard. It activates a wooden bar which in its turn lifts the whole damper system. The strings thus vibrate freely as long as the foot does not leave the pedal. The left pedal is called the soft pedal. It will shift the whole keyboard action slightly toward the right, causing the hammerhead to strike only two strings of the trichords, one string of the bichords. The unstruck string still vibrates sympathetically, with the result that the tone is not only softer but has a different color. The accompanist and coach will have more than ample opportunity to use this pedal. The third, middle, pedal can sustain single tones or chords when used after a key is struck but before the finger leaves the key. This sostenuto pedal, although not widely used by accompanists and coaches, nevertheless has its value. For instance, if organ points should be held in accompaniments, the only way to do so is with the help of the sustaining pedal (see Fig. 5).

Pedaling is an art in itself. I shall discuss its relation to the different styles of music in a later chapter.

The resonator. I have already said that the two bridges of the pianoforte form the connection between vibrator and resonator. They are connected to the soundboard not by means of some kind of feet as in the violin bridge, but rather are glued to the soundboard along their entire length. The soundboard is made of especially selected spruce wood. Like the wood for the bodies of stringed instruments, this wood should come from high and evenly grown trees, i.e., the grain should run parallel and the distance between streaks should be narrow.

Figure 5. Example of the use of the sostenuto pedal, from Debussy's "Proses lyriques"

Boards with parallel grain running diagonally are best suited to forming the soundboard.

The soundboard extends over almost the entire expanse of the pianoforte. The boards are glued together and supported at right angles by wooden ribs or bars. They are scalloped at the end. The soundboard has a slight upward curvature.

But the soundboard is by no means the pianoforte's only resonator. The wooden case in which the action and the string system are enclosed vibrates sympathetically. Good varnish is necessary for protection of the soundboard, to keep the wood from getting damp. Although it is not so important as in old and new stringed instruments, it has some influence on sound and also on the independence of pianofortes from alterations in the temperature and humidity of the atmosphere.

Finally, a word about the piano's acoustics. The strings are tuned so that the octaves are pure, but the octave has been mathematically divided into twelve half steps which do not conform to their natural acoustical impure fractional numbers. Thus, each half step has a certain number of vibrations which has been arrived at by a system of averages. This system of tuning is called the tempered pitch system. In it, tones can be enharmonically substituted for each other. For instance, a G sharp and an A flat on the piano are the same tone, whereas in reality their vibration figures are quite different. In all music accompanied on a piano this tempered pitch must be adhered to by the string player or the human voice. The tempered pitch is likely to ruin the sensibility of a musical ear, and the accompanist and coach will have to constantly retrain his ear to the natural pitches by listening to orchestral music or unaccompanied string or vocal music.

THE CELESTA

The celesta is a small keyboard percussion instrument with a mechanism similar to a pianoforte's action. The celesta, however, has no strings, but rather tuned steel plates or bars, each connected to a wooden resonance body. The steel plates have dampers attached to them. A pedal can lift the dampers and create a kind of swimming sound of fairytale or celestial quality. The keyboard has 25 or 37 chromatically arranged notes. The resonators give the celesta a beautiful, silvery sound. It is not by chance that Richard Strauss in his *Rosenkavalier* used the celesta effect just at the point when Octavian hands the silver rose to Sophie. The celesta cannot be played legato; it is played with a lighter or heavier staccato, as the particular line of music requires.

The celesta is used in many operas besides *Rosenkavalier*; the best known are *Tosca, Louise, Salome, Ariadne, Die Frau ohne Schatten.*

The music for celesta is notated one octave lower than its actual sound. The diapason is so limited that accompanists and coaches must use their own judgment as to which octave they should play a particular phrase in. Jumping from one octave into another should be avoided as much as possible.

ANATOMY AND PHYSIOLOGY OF THE ORGAN

The king of musical instruments, as the organ is rightly called, is a tremendous combination of numerous wind instruments. Its construction is so varied and technically so difficult that a description would far overreach the purpose of this book. Organists must go through years of specialized training. An accompanist or coach who understands the construction of the organ and has mastered the technique of organ playing will not have to burden himself with details. It will be enough to show in this chapter the common principle of energizer-vibrator-resonator, and to discuss the difference between piano and organ technique. Special literature on organs may be found in the bibliography.

The organ is one of the oldest musical instruments. Known in primitive form some three thousand years ago, it found its permanent place in music with the development of polyphony. The Renaissance already had some beautifully perfected organs, but the height of organ construction and organ literature was reached with the baroque era. Our modern organ has been further perfected through innovations in physics. Today we distinguish between pipe organs and electronic organs,

but I shall limit myself to the general principles of pipe organs. The electronic organs found in smaller churches may be easily transported onto any stage where organ sound is required. Mastery of playing them requires additional specialization. Good instruction booklets are available from the firms which build these electronic organs, giving a description of registration and offering shortcuts by way of prearranged sound combinations.

The energizer. Modern organ blowing apparatus has developed from the old bellows system. Instead of the bellows being worked manually, the wind supply is generated electrically, usually with centrifugal fan blowers powered by electrical motors. These blowers build up and transmit pressurized wind. The pressure can be regulated. Wind is stored in the bellows and conductor lines and controlled by regulators. Thus a reservoir of wind is created for sudden outbursts of forte or expansive sound combinations. In larger organs, there is at least one regulator for each manual division, as well as for the pedal. The conductors lead the air into the wind chest. The wind chests (there are separate ones for manuals and pedals) are boxes with holes on top into which the pipe feet are fitted.

Pipes are arranged in sets. Each set or rank of pipes stands on its individual part of the wind chest. The flow of air into the pipes is controlled by two sets of valves working in conjunction with each other. One set is operated by the stop controls, the other by depressing manual

Figure 6. A typical organ console,
with four manuals

or pedal keys. The pressurized wind exists in the chest, but cannot flow into the pipes until two conditions are satisfied: the organist must draw the stop assigned to a given set of pipes and must also depress the manual or pedal keys which control that set of pipes. Releasing the key causes the stream of air to the pipes to cease flowing, and as long as the stop control is still turned on, depressing the keys will produce a sound.

This leads us to a description of the manual and pedal keyboards which at present are encased in one or more consoles. These can be attached to the wind chests or may stand apart. In the latter case the console is connected to the chest or chests by a system of electric cables, carrying current to the magnets which in turn operate the pipe valves and stop valves. Each organ has at least two manual keyboards; larger instruments may have four or five, and there are organs with seven. Keys today perform the simple function of closing an electrical circuit. They require merely a gentle touch — about four ounces of pressure. Here lies one of the major differences between the pianoforte and the organ: the piano is responsive to differences in striking power, but the electropneumatic organ is not, because its keys simply make or break an electrical circuit.

The principal keyboard (manual) is called the Great. The one above this is the Swell. The one below the Great is called the Choir. A fourth manual, higher than the other three, is called the Solo and/or Echo, often used when a colorful solo stop is desired; it is accompanied by a stop played on one of the other manuals. The pipes of the Echo organ are usually at a remote distance and give a mysterious and echo-like effect. Three manuals are adequate for the performance of all the great organ literature. Any manual above the fourth is optional and is often typical of the unnecessary overabundance of movie organs. Each manual has a five-octave range (61 keys).

There is a special keyboard or pedal clavier with keys arranged in a radiating and concave manner so as to be played by the organist's feet. This is called the Pedal. Pedalboard mastery requires years of special study; but the accompanist or coach will not be called upon to play complicated organ pieces with difficult pedal passages. It is enough that he acquire a feeling of complete security in reaching any desired pedal key and also attain a workable legato pedal technique by using a heel-toe-heel-toe movement of the feet.

On the console are the many stops which control the individual voices of an organ. They appear as drawknobs, tilting tablets, stop-tongues, and so on. They are all subject to piston-controlled combination action and their instantaneous change offers no physical difficulty at all. A slight touch of the combination pistons (below the keys) will bring groups of them into action. Any sort of combination of these knobs or tablets can be arranged while playing (or prearranged before playing) by making use of the pistons. This prearrangement makes things easier for the accompanist or coach who may not have the dexterity or the opportunity while playing to manipulate the various stop controls. There are several combination pistons for each manual and some for the pedal. In addition, there may be others controlling the resources of the entire organ. Each of these pistons can be set to turn a prearranged group of stops on or off. The manner of prearranging varies with different builders, but the most desirable system (the capture system) operates as follows: (1) By hand, draw the various knobs, or turn on the various tablets desired. (2) Push in the "master" or "setter" piston. (3) While still holding the setter piston in, push firmly whichever piston you wish to control this particular combination. (4) Release both pistons. From then on, that piston will control the desired combination.

Each stop or set of pipes belongs to only one of several manuals, together with other stops belonging to that manual. To combine the pipes of different manuals, one uses couplers. In a four-manual console there are approximately thirty couplers, at various pitch levels: unison, subunison, and octave. The system of coupling the pipes of different manuals and pedals is well-nigh endless, and its tasteful use requires much experience. The accompanist or coach will use the couplers sparingly. Some of the more frequently used couplers are Swell to Great 8′, Great to Pedal 8′, Swell to Pedal 8′.

The dynamic range of a modern electropneumatic organ cannot be influenced by varying the touch of the fingers on the keys. Legato and staccato effects, of course, can be cultivated. For sudden pianos or fortes one will often have to change suddenly to another manual whose stops have been prearranged at a different dynamic level, or make a rapid change in the stop arrangement of the same manual. A crescendo or decrescendo can be achieved, however, by two means: by using the crescendo pedal or the expression pedal.

The crescendo pedal acts as follows: As the crescendo pedal (or shoe, as it is often called) is depressed, more and more sets of pipes (stops) are called into action, until the shoe is opened to the fullest. At that point the entire organ is almost, but not quite, in action. Total full organ (sometimes called tutti) is achieved by touching a foot or hand piston labeled Full Organ. The greatest potentiality of this crescendo shoe is reached by playing on the Great keys and the pedalboard. The crescendo shoe is wired to the stops in such a way as to bring the softest stop on first, followed by more and more stops. The couplers from the other manuals are also affected and are brought into action in the proper sequence. Artistic organ playing avoids the use of this device in preference to bringing various stops on at will and changing from one manual to another, but it is a great lifesaver in moments of stress, and most certainly there are many of these moments in rehearsals and performances.

The second way of obtaining dynamic expression is by using the one or more expression pedals. With the exception of the Great (which is rarely enclosed) the various divisions of the organ (Swell, Choir, etc.) are enclosed in soundproof boxes. One side of these boxes is open, but is covered with movable louvers, resembling Venetian blinds. The amount of opening of these louvers is controlled by expression shoes, one for each group of louvers. The louvers, called shutters or shades, may be opened gradually, each step augmenting the tone without significantly changing the tone color of the stop combination. The impression on the hearer, however, is not one of continuous increase, but rather of jumps from one grade of dynamics to the next, until the mastery of the expression pedal is complete. But these jumps are not nearly so noticeable as those caused by the use of the crescendo pedal, as the latter actually and distinctly adds on more and more sets of pipes, whereas the swell pedal merely enables such pipes as are playing to be heard more or less. I shall return to these expression boxes when discussing the organ's resonators.

Crescendi and decrescendi as a whole are somewhat foreign to the basic idea of an organ as conceived by the old masters, and are a comparatively late development.

The vibrator. As I have said, the organ is a keyboard wind instrument. The vibrator, therefore, is to be found in the organ pipes, whose construction corresponds roughly to that of the flute, oboe, or clarinet. The organ pipes, like any other wind instrument, act as their own resonators. This function will be discussed later.

There are two main groups of organ pipes, the flue pipes and the reed pipes, or, more simply, whistles and horns.

The flue pipes may be of wood or metal, depending on the sound desired. If it is supposed to be soft and swimming, a soft wood is used. Often even-grained, dry, hard pear, maple, or oak is used, the kind of wood depending on the desired timbre. Most organ pipes are of wood or alloys of tin and other metals, such as lead.

Figure 7. Flue pipe. A. Languid. B. Upper Lip. (Though shown in horizontal position here, the pipe in the organ is vertical.)

While the choice of material is important to the sound of an organ pipe, it is not the only contributing factor. The relation between the length and the diameter of a pipe must also be right. This is called the scale. There are now standard scales which are used in organ pipe construction. The shorter the pipe, the higher its tone. At the interval of an octave the pipe is just half the length it is for a tone an octave lower. The diameter diminishes in a different way: the diameters are usually halved with every seventeenth pipe belonging to a particular system or compass. The most important factor in an organ pipe is the voicing. The mouth of a flue pipe must have the right shape and must be cut at exactly the right height. There are countless variables in the voicing technique.

The sound in a flue pipe is produced as follows: Compressed air enters the pipe (which is set on the chest) through its open foot. It proceeds up through the foot until it reaches a horizontal plate or obstruction called the languid (A). The languid cuts off the passage of the air except through a narrow slit or "flue." The air escapes through the flue and vibrates across the upper lip (B) of the mouth. The construction and position of the upper lip can influence the tone considerably. This is the art of voicing. The upper lip may be straight or arched, blunt or sharp. The opening at the foot of the pipe, the amount of opening in the flue, and the set of the languid are also important.

The escape and play of the air at the mouth, with alternate pressure and vacuum, affects the air in the upper portion of the pipe. This alternate increase and decrease creates a sound wave whose pitch is largely determined by the acoustical length of the pipe.

A pipe of given length can be made to sound an octave lower by closing (stopping) it off at its upper end. This closure creates a wave node, producing only the odd-numbered harmonics, as in a clarinet. The inside air column, unable to escape, has to return downward, which doubles the wave length. The old name for stopped pipes is *gedackt*. They are used extensively in organs. Some pipes are made that are half-stopped. Half-stopped effects can also be obtained by boring a small hole into the side of a stopped pipe at the nodal point. Pipes may be overblown deliberately by increasing the wind pressure. When this is done the fundamental or prime tone disappears and the pipes sound only a harmonic.

The timbre of pipes depends largely on the material, their form, voicing, and their measurements or scales. The more harmonics a flue pipe creates, the clearer will be its sound. Even the thickness of the walls of the pipes is important for the timbre. Some flue pipes taper off at their upper end, which also alters the timbre.

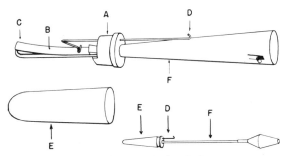

Figure 8. Reed pipe. A. Shallot. B. Brass tongue. C. End. D. Tuning wire. E. Block. F. Stem. (Though shown in horizontal position here, the pipe in the organ is vertical.)

While flue pipes generate string-like, flute-like, and diapason tones, the reed pipes fulfill the function of the single reed woodwind and brass sections of an orchestra. Reed pipes may be made of wood (only the large pipes) or of the metal used in flue pipes. They may be cylindrical, square, or conical, or a combination of these. Their function may be described thus: The base of the pipe contains a short, semi-cylindrical tube closed at the end, the shallot (A), which has a longitudinal opening in the form of a goose beak. Over this opening, a brass tongue (B) is set which covers the opening but is curved away from it at the end (C). Air pressure admitted by the valves in the wind chest makes the free end of the

tongue vibrate toward the shallot and close over it. The length of the tongue is controlled by the tuning wire (D), a crooked staff which can lengthen or shorten the vibrating part of the tongue. There may be other auxiliary ways to control the vibration of the tongue, such as screws, sliding rolls, and so on. The shallot, together with the tongue, is encased in a block (E) that is embedded in the foot, which in turn is set on the chest. The body of the reed pipe starts with its stem (F) which acts as a resonator (see p. 31). The stem, or body, unlike the mouth of a flue pipe, has nothing to do with the initial production of a tone as such; the tongue vibrating over the shallot does this. It is, however, very important for the timbre, strength, and carrying power of the tone. The thickness and form of the tongue, and the scale of the shallot, are the deciding factors in the timbre of a reed pipe. Reed pipes when overblown sometimes sound the decime, or other intervals, according to the shape of the pipes. They are never entirely stopped at the end, but are sometimes partially stopped (half-capped).

Organ pipes are also classified by their length. If you depress the middle C of the keyboard and draw an 8′ stop, you will hear a sound with the same pitch as the equivalent key on a piano. 16′ stops sound one octave lower, 32′ two octaves lower, 64′ three octaves lower than 8′. 4′, 2′, and 1′ stops sound one, two, or three octaves, respectively, higher than the 8′ stops. These sets of pipes with even footage are called unison stops. They consist of either flue or reed pipes.

There are other families of stops, belonging to the flue family, that reproduce a pitch different from the one represented by the key. They are called mutation stops. Their footage is expressed by a fractional number, as for instance, the Fifth, Tenth, Twelfth, Fifteenth. These stops are important for the enrichment of tone. The harmonics of the unison stops are reinforced if mutation stops are used. The third kind of stop in relation to its footage consists of a combination of unison and mutation stops, or combinations of mutation stops among themselves. They are called mixtures.

These mixture stops are made up of several ranks as, for instance, the Cornet: a 5-rank mixture consisting of principal 8′ (C) plus Octave 4′ (C), plus Quint $2\frac{2}{3}′$ (G), plus Octave 2′ (C), plus Third $1\frac{3}{5}′$ (E). All mixtures serve to reinforce upper partials of unison tones and contribute to the brilliance of an organ. In accompaniment they should be used sparingly for they may confuse pitch, especially if the composition is strong in off-unison harmonics.

Pipe systems can also be classified by timbre. These timbre families are built from very diversified specifications and vary from country to country because of acoustical conditions. A typical American or Canadian organ is divided into four different timbres, sometimes placed separately: the Diapason or Principal class, the Flute class, the String class, and the Reed class. Each of these timbres may appear at unison, 16', or 4' pitches. The names of different stops vary, even though the sound may be similar. Different organbuilders use different names, primarily of French, German, and Italian origin. Accompanists and coaches may have to use various makes of organs. A typical three-manual organ may have stop names as in the following tabulation.

Stop	Name	Alternative Names
	Great Organ	
16'	Violone	Principal, Diapason, Gamba, Quintaton, Bourdon, Geigen
8'	Principal	Diapason, Prinzipal, Spitzprinzipal, Geigen
8'	Gemshorn	Spitzflöte, Spitzprinzipal, Flute Conique, Erzähler
8'	Stopped Flute	Bourdon, Gedackt, Stopped Diapason, Bordun, Rohrflöte, Chimney Flute, Lieblich Flöte
8'	Open Flute	Clarabella, Waldflöte, Flute Harmonique, Hohlflöte, Holzflöte, Melodia, Concert Flute, Traverse Flute, Orchestral Flute
4'	Octave	Oktave, Principal, Prestant
4'	Flute	Either of stopped or open flutes above
2⅔'	Twelfth	Quint, Nazard
2'	Fifteenth	Super Octave, Principal
	Mixture IV ranks	Fourniture, Plein Jeu, Harmonics
	Scharf III ranks	Cymbal, Zymbal, Acuta, Zimbel
16'	Posaune	Bombarde, Trumpet, Ophicleide, Fagotto
8'	Trumpet	Trompette, Tromba, Tuba
4'	Clarion	Clairon, Octave Trumpet
	Swell Organ	
16'	Bourdon	Gedackt, Flute Conique, Rohrflöte, Gemshorn
8'	Geigen Diapason	Montre, Principal, String Diapason
8'	Viole de Gambe	Viola, Gamba, Gambe, Viol d'Orchestre, Salicional
8'	Viole Celeste	Voix Celeste, Viola, etc.
8'	Stopped Flute	See *Great Organ*
4'	Principal	Spitzprinzipal, Prestant
4'	Open Flute	See *Great Organ*
2'	Flautino	Flageolet, Octavin, 15th, Piccolo
	Plein Jeu III ranks	Mixture, Cymbale, Cornet
16'	Bombarde	Posaune, Fagotto, Hautbois, Oboe, Trumpet, Bassoon, Waldhorn
8'	Trompette	Trumpet, Tromba
8'	Oboe	Hautbois, Cor d'Amour
4'	Clairon	Clarion, Octave Trumpet
	Tremulant	Tremolo

Stop	Name	Alternative Names
	Choir Organ	
16'	Viola	Gemshorn, Viol, Salicional
8'	Diapason	Principal, Spitzprinzipal, Gemshorn
8'	Open Flute	See *Great Organ*
8'	Stopped Flute	See *Great Organ*
8'	Flute Celeste II ranks	Unda Maris, Aeoline Celeste, Dolcan Celeste, Voix Celeste
4'	Koppel Flöte	Spillflöte, Rohrflöte, Orchestral Flute
2⅔'	Nazard	12th, Nasat, Quint
2'	Blockflöte	Terz, Seventeenth
1'	Sifflöte	Fife, Principal
	Mixture	Carillon, Plein Jeu, Cornet
8'	Clarinet	Krummhorn, Schalmei
8'	English Horn	Oboe, Cor d'Amour
	Tremulant	Tremolo
	Pedal Organ	
32'	Bourdon	Diapason, Principal, Sub Bass
16'	Diapason	Contre-Basse, Principal
16'	Violone	Geigen, Viola, Spitzprinzipal
16'	Bourdon	Gedackt, Quintaton, Bordun
8'	Octave	Principal, Diapason
8'	Cello	Spitzflöte, Bourdon
4'	Super octave	Choralbass, Principal
4'	Flute	Stopped or open, see *Great Organ*
	Mixture IV ranks	Mixture, Fourniture, Acuta, Cornet
32'	Contre Bombarde	Kontra Posaune, Fagotto, Hautbois
16'	Bombarde	Posaune, Waldhorn, Trompette, Bassoon, Ophicleide, Tuba
8'	Trumpet	Trompette, Tromba, Clarion
4'	Clarion	Octave Trumpet, Tromba

The stops can be combined and augmented with the help of playing aids: couplers, combination pistons, swell shutters, crescendo shoes, and tremulants. The couplers are as follows:

Swell to Great	16'		Swell to Swell	16'
Swell to Great	8'		Swell to Swell	4'
Swell to Great	4'		Swell	Unison Off
Swell to Choir	16'		Choir to Choir	16'
Swell to Choir	8'		Choir to Choir	4'
Swell to Choir	4'		Choir	Unison Off
Choir to Great	16'		Swell to Pedal	8'
Choir to Great	8'		Swell to Pedal	4'
Choir to Great	4'		Choir to Pedal	8'
			Choir to Pedal	4'
			Great to Pedal	8'

The mechanicals are as follows:

Six "general" pistons affecting all
　stops and couplers
Six pistons to each manual and pedal
General Cancel
Crescendo Pedal
Swell Expression Pedal
Choir Expression Pedal
Full Organ Reversible Piston

One word about the tremulant aid, a mechanism that shakes the wind in the regulator or wind chest, creating a change in pitch as well as intensity of a whole division or manual. The result may be more or less dense tremolo, full of sentimentality, which is as irritating and painful as the tremolo of a human voice. Our ears are abused by it constantly in movie organs, soap opera music, and at funerals. The tremolo should have no place in serious organ accompaniment, because it diffuses the pitch; or at least it should be used so sparingly that it may be considered negligible.

Organ pipes, since Bach's time, have been tuned in the tempered scale. The pitch is more or less constant, though in summer it may go up somewhat, and during cold weather down slightly. The total variation may be as much as a semitone.

The resonator. There are several resonators in the organ itself. As we have seen, the pipes themselves function as vibrators as well as resonators (see p. 31). They belong to the so-called coupled system of resonators. The column of air in the foot of the pipe carries the wind, just as it is carried in the windpipe of the human body. The shape of the pipe, the material used, and especially the upper part of the pipes reinforce and ennoble the sound. Those reed pipes which give the more brilliant brass colors to the organ have resonators which are inverted cones.

The wind supply is another factor in resonance. As good breath support is necessary for a good singing voice, so a steady amount of air pressure enriches the sound of an organ. The only difference is the organist's inability suddenly to increase or decrease the air pressure (and thus dynamics) of a given pipe except through the use of the swell shutters. These, however, vary only the dynamics, not (significantly) the color of tone. Change of tone color can be achieved by using mixture stops to increase upper partials.

The enclosure of parts of the organ has an important effect on resonance. The shutters open and close the sound (like the "covering" or "opening" of a singer's voice). The fact that some manual pipes are enclosed and some are freestanding is also of great importance. The varying distance from the console and the listener of the pipes for different manuals likewise has a resonance effect. Of course, the auditorium — be it church, concert hall, or theater — helps or hinders the proper resonance. All in all, the matter of resonance in a properly designed organ (while it depends greatly on the acoustics of the building) is not so vital as in a stringed instrument or in the human voice. There are many resonance cavities in the complex anatomy and physiology of the king of instruments. The problems of a proper reverberation period for music of different types, and of means of correcting poor acoustics generally, have been the subject of recent research using both electronic and mechanical devices.

THE HARMONIUM

The harmonium is another keyboard wind instrument, similar in construction to a simple organ. Its much smaller size and less complicated mechanism have popularized it during the last seventy years to the extent of its being used frequently in small churches and chapels, in choir practice, in homes, and backstage in opera houses. The accompanist and coach will be called upon to play the harmonium more or less often and should understand its mechanism. The main difference between the mechanisms of the organ and the harmonium is that the latter has no pipes. The vibrators in the harmonium are thin brass or steel tongues or reeds which, however, are not "beating" or "striking" reeds that close the opening at each vibration, as are organ reeds, but *free* reeds. In vibration they do not completely close the openings in which they are set. Fastened to a rigid piece of metal with an opening in it only at one end, the reeds swing freely through this aperture and return to their former position.

The energizers are again bellows, usually put into action by the action of the player's feet on treadles, which are moved alternately, with a movement of the feet as in bicycling. If more air is needed for more sound (which culminates in the "Grand Jeu," the full sound of a harmonium) the feet must work the treadles faster but always evenly. Wind then rushes into the wind chest and is stored up in a reservoir. Excess wind may escape with the help of a discharge pallet. In the most modern harmonium, air is pumped in electrically, and there is a system of valves shutting off the wind chest from the vibrators. Pulling stops and depressing keys lifts the valves below the reeds; the air energizes the reeds into vibration. Behind each vibrator there are individual channels, air chambers which act as resonators to the reeds or tongues. These channels are built in different ways; their construction gives each tone its particular timbre.

There are two different kinds of harmonium. One is

the European kind, which works on the above-described principle, forcing the wind out through reeds. This harmonium, whose tone is rather strong, bears the German name *Druckluftharmonium* (pressure bellows harmonium). It has some attachments, such as the expression stop which enables the player to produce crescendo and decrescendo by working the treadles in different ways. It also sometimes has a prolongment, a stop similar to the sostenuto pedal on the pianoforte which enables the player to sustain notes. Some of the larger harmoniums of this kind also have a percussion stop which connects the key with an escape action containing a hammer. The reed, at the moment of touch, is struck by the hammer which gives the sound a pianoforte-like percussive quality. The tone of a Druckluftharmonium is crisp and the reaction is fast, but the sound does not resemble an organ's so much as an accordion's.

The other main system of harmonium construction is the so-called American Organ, originating and mostly used in this country. In German, this instrument is called *Sauglutharmonium* (sucker bellows harmonium). Air enters it from above and is sucked through the reeds into the bellows, from which it leaves the instrument. The construction of the reeds in the American Organ is somewhat different than in the pressure harmonium. They are smaller, more twisted, and have a greater curvature. The reed channels, moreover, are always of the same length as the reeds themselves. All these differences in construction help to make the sound of an American Organ more organ-like, nobler, and softer. It does not, however, have the variety of coloring and expression characteristics of the European harmonium. These American Organs are still being built by Estey in Brattleboro, Vermont.

Harmoniums are sometimes made with two manuals and a pedal. Recently, however, this has been abandoned, since electronic organs (of quite different, inferior sound) have taken over the main functions of the harmonium.

The harmonium has a keyboard of five to five and a half octaves, with different stops, bearing different names, for bass and treble. Each functions only on its half of the keyboard. The bass section of a five-octave harmonium starts on F an octave below the staff and ends on B below middle C. The treble section starts on middle C and goes up to D above the staff. Average American organs — which are the ones an accompanist and coach will most frequently play — have 16', 8', and 4' stops. Bigger instruments may add some 2' stops. Here are some of the stops an accompanist and coach may encounter in the bass section: Diapason 8', Echo 8' (softer), Diapason dolce or Dulciana 8' (softer), English Horn or Vox Jubilante 8' (more brilliant), Viola 4', Flute 4', Dolce 4', Sub-bass 16' (usually only an octave), Bourdon 16' (the same, but softer). In the treble section he may find Diapason 8', Melodia 8', Melodia dolce, or Dulciana 8' (softer), Oboe 8' (more nasal), Vox Jubilante 8' (more brilliant), Vox Coelestis 8' (soft), Flute 4', Forest 2'.

There are some auxiliary stops, such as the forte stops, the treble and bass couplers, and the vox humana. This last is nothing but a fan which, by revolving rapidly, gives the tone a vibrating quality, that, however, does not go to the extreme of a shake or tremolo. The harmonium also has two knee attachments: by pushing one of them outwards a crescendo effect can be obtained, similar to the expression shutters of the organ; similarly operated, the other knee lever gradually brings all harmonium stops into play. When both knee levers are fully pushed, the Grand Jeu, the full sound, has been reached.

ORGAN AND HARMONIUM TECHNIQUE

The finger technique for organ and harmonium is approximately the same. Both differ widely from the modern piano technique, although the playing of Bach's and Handel's music on the piano requires a great knowledge of organ technique.

The organ, in general, uses four ways of playing: the legato, the semi-legato or portato, the marcato, and the staccato. Since the organ has not, as has the piano, a damper pedal that can be employed when continued sound is desired, the fingers — and the feet on the pedal keyboard — are alone responsible for tying over notes.

Once a finger leaves the key, the organ tone ceases. In legato playing, the fingering, therefore, is of utmost importance and differs greatly from piano fingering. The accompanist and coach will do well to finger each legato passage or chain of chords before he plays it. There are two principal ways by which a pianist may achieve flawless legato technique: finger or hand substitution and glissando.

In finger substitution, known to the pianist from Bach's music, a silent change of fingers takes place on a key so that the finger first employed is freed to depress yet another key (Fig. 9). In hand substitution, a whole

Figure 9. Finger substitution

chord may be taken over by the other hand in order to enable the freed hand to shift to another manual or to pull a stop. Such shifts may be only temporary. In the example shown in Figure 10, the right hand may return to the chord as soon as its job of pulling a stop is completed. It goes without saying that these substitutions must be made while one hand still firmly presses the keys down.

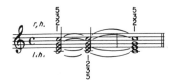

Figure 10. Hand substitution

The glissando may be done with any finger. It is quite easy when it involves changing from a black to a neighboring white key but becomes difficult if full steps are to be tied by legato. Here, as in all organ-playing, the fingers must leave one key completely before touching the next; otherwise, cacophony will result. The same is true for the feet in pedal playing. The accompanist and coach will have a few dreadful experiences before he will be able to play cleanly and clearly (Fig. 11).

Figure 11. Glissandi

It may sometimes be necessary to use different joints of fingers for different tones. Even the position of the fingers on the keys is of importance: sometimes they should slide in toward the rear of the key as far as the neighboring keys will allow, in order to be better prepared for the next legato chord or note. Some substi-

tutions, glissandos, and the sliding technique may all have to be employed in a single musical phrase (Fig. 12).

There is still another technical aid in playing legato on the organ: crossing the fingers, the longer over the shorter. This was standard piano technique up to the time of Mozart, who first employed our modern fingering, 1-2-3-1-2-3-4-5. The polyphony of Bach's time necessitated crossing the fingers whenever possible. A scale then was probably fingered 1-2-3-4-5-3-4-5, or something similar.

Figure 12. Finger substitution, glissando, and sliding in employed in a single musical phrase

The same problems arise in pedal technique: substitution and crossing. Jumps even of a third and more are not at all uncommon. This is done by way of change of heel and toe, of substitution of heel for toe, and by crossing the feet repeatedly. Even a pedal mute glissando is possible and sometimes advantageous.

The semilegato or portato will be employed when a division between notes is desired. It is also advisable to play accompanying figurations portato while playing the melody legato. This will make the melody stand out better, even without different registration. Portato should also be used in rapid passage work; legato would make any fast passage too muddy.

Marcato and staccato are also used in organ playing. Marcato means complete depression of the keys and energetic release of the hand. Notes should not be held for the duration of their actual value, but should be released from one quarter to one eighth of their value earlier. Staccato, technically, means the use of the wrist, which is thrown back after each note. Staccato on the organ is dangerous; it is only too easy to change noble organ sound into barrel organ or jazz organ imitations. The accompanist or coach will not have to employ it often.

One word about the organ bench: the accompanist and coach must be sure that the organ bench is at the right height and the right distance from the keyboards; a relaxed posture is essential for good organ and harmonium playing.

The rest of organ technique — playing on different manuals, registration, use of the swells, and the like — is too complicated to be dealt with here. The accompanist or coach should consult a good school of organ playing. But for simple accompaniments or choir coaching duties, the above hints may suffice.

ANATOMY AND PHYSIOLOGY OF
THE HUMAN VOICE

To start with, I should like to mention two recent publications which present the medical and technical aspects of the vocal apparatus in a way easily understandable to lay persons: Dr. Friedrich Brodnitz's *Keep Your Voice Healthy*, and William Vennard's *Singing, The Mechanism and the Technique*. With the authors' permission I shall follow their line of reasoning.

The energizer. The energizer is the singer's respiratory system. Though normal breathing is through the nose, the relatively small openings of the nostrils would not be sufficient to provide the amount of air necessary for singing. A singer therefore breathes mostly through his mouth. The air passes through the throat into the windpipe, which divides into many larger and smaller branches called bronchi whose ends reach into the lungs, carrying fresh air into the lobes of the lungs. The lungs fill the greater part of the chest cavity and rest on the diaphragm, a muscle that separates the chest from the abdomen. In relaxed position it is dome-shaped. When air is inhaled, the rib cage expands and the diaphragm contracts and flattens downward. This kind of breathing is called lower chest or rib breathing. (There is also the so-called clavicular breathing which affects only the upper part of the chest. It is an "out of breath" state and is too strained to be used in normal singing.) The flattened diaphragm presses on the abdominal organs and these organs protrude and thus expand the belly. This process is called abdominal breathing. Restraining garments, sedentary habits, and other attainments of our civilization lead to the weakening of abdominal breathing in modern people (see Fig. 13).

The downward and outward movement of the upper part of the abdomen under the pressure of the flattening diaphragm is not very great in an untrained body, and is limited in everyone. But it can be developed to its greatest possible limits and thus create more air space in the bottom of the chest cavity. Breathing can and should be trained. Dr. Brodnitz is right in saying that whichever kind of respiration is the weaker should be strengthened through exercise so that both kinds of breathing (rib and abdominal breathing) may be co-

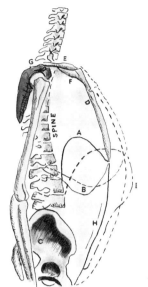

A. DIAPHRAGM
B. RIBS
C. PELVIS
D. STERNUM
E. CLAVICLE
F. FIRST RIB
G. SCAPULA
H. RECTUS ABDOMINIS
I. EPIGASTRUM

Figure 13. Diagram of the chest and abdominal cavity

ordinated. This seems to be the best way for a singer to breathe.

In expiration, the whole process is reversed. The diaphragm relaxes and resumes its dome shape. The abdominal muscles which were relaxed during inspiration, contract and the abdominal organs return inwards and upwards to their original position. Actually, it is not the diaphragm which assures good breath support but the epigastrium—the group of abdominal muscles that in expiration should gradually contract as the sung phrase requires. This procedure should be in direct relationship to the length of the sung phrase. The rib cage returns to its former position. The air is squeezed out of the lungs and proceeds through the bronchi into the windpipe, where it meets the larynx or voicebox (Fig. 14).

This organ is so important for the production of sound that I must describe its anatomy and its functions in detail.

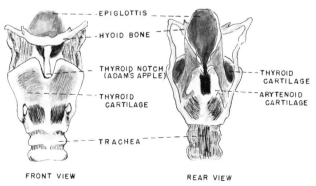

Figure 14. The voicebox

After passing the vocal cords, making them vibrate and thus producing a sound, the air exits through the mouth, thus completing the circle of respiration. If he has time, it is important that the singer should completely rid himself of his stale breath before inhaling again. Otherwise, stale and fresh breath combined may be more than he requires to sing a particular phrase, clogging his thoracic air space and abnormally tightening his whole system instead of allowing for relaxation between phases of normal tension. If there is not enough time to get rid of the stale breath, only such an amount of fresh air should be taken as to fill the need for the forthcoming phrase without clogging the chest cavity. Thus, breath pressure must be regulated: there must be a kind of tidal rhythm of inspiration and expiration. Here, as everywhere else, experience will teach economy.

The vibrator. The larynx or voicebox consists of a number of cartilages. It is closed toward the front and open toward the back, and held in suspension in the throat from above and below by elastic muscles which guarantee that the larynx is rarely hurt by normal impacts. The muscles that hold the larynx in suspension from above are fastened to the hyoid bone at the base of the tongue. The hyoid bone is roughly U-shaped, with the opening pointing toward the back.

The topmost cartilage of the larynx is the epiglottis, whose main function is to seal off the larynx and the trachea during swallowing, so that food moves into the right channel, the esophagus.

The next important cartilage is the thyroid cartilage. Shaped like a shield, again open toward the back, consisting of two wings with a buckle or a notch at its meeting point, this is the "Adam's apple" which can often be clearly seen and distinctly felt. Two pairs of horns protrude from the back ends of the wings of the thyroid cartilage. The upper pair forms the connection to the hyoid bone, the lower pair joins the cricoid cartilage to the larynx. This cartilage looks like a signet ring, the signet facing the back. The cricoid is the lowest cartilage of the larynx and the windpipe starts just below it. On the upper rim of the cricoid there are two small cartilages, the arytenoid cartilages. Each looks like an antique pitcher with a triangular base.

All these, and some other cartilages less important for the layman, are connected to each other by ingenious joints which make possible all kinds of movements, allowing the vocal cords to be lengthened and stretched.

The vocal cords lie horizontally in the larynx. Their front is attached to the inside of the thyroid cartilage, where the two wings meet, a little below the point where the Adam's apple can be felt. In front, the vocal cords lie in fixed position and touch each other. In the rear, they are attached to the anterior corner of the base of the arytenoid cartilages. They lie together when closed and come apart with phonation owing to the complicated shift mechanism of the arytenoids. The space thus created is called the glottis.

But their opening and closing alone does not produce phonation; rather, this is achieved by vibration of the vocal cords. In the larynx is a whole system of complicated muscles. These muscles connect different parts of different cartilages with each other and allow for opening and closing of the cords as well as for the cords' modifications as regards their stretching. Thus, the vocal cords can be shortened or lengthened, thickened or thinned, tensed or relaxed.

At the beginning of phonation the vocal cords are closed and tensed. When enough air pressure is built up in the windpipe, the vocal cords are blown apart; then their inner elasticity brings them together. Together, these constitute a fast rhythmical opening and closing, and the vibration finally produces the sound. Higher pitch is created by faster vibrations of the tensed vocal cords. Greater intensity of sound is created by increased air pressure from the windpipe which makes the vocal cords swing wider. To produce middle (chamber) A, for instance, the vocal cords, like a tuning fork, vibrate 440 times a second. They vibrate, however, not in a straight line but in a rippling, undulating movement, which at no time lets their entire length close.

The Bell Telephone Laboratories' pictures (Fig. 15) taken with a high-speed camera, will show the accompanist or coach how the vocal cords vibrate on a given tone. The sound thus created would be much too weak, however, to be of any use to the singer. It must be augmented and enriched by overtones, which is done with the help of the resonating cavities.

The resonator. The resonators of the human voice are many and varied. The most important of them can change their shape considerably and belong, along with the complex body of a stringed instrument, to the broad type of resonators (see p. 22). I have said earlier in this chapter that the question of resonance in the human voice is highly controversial. Although, with a laryngeal mirror, the vocal cords can be seen in operation, the workings of resonance cannot be seen. Experiments with

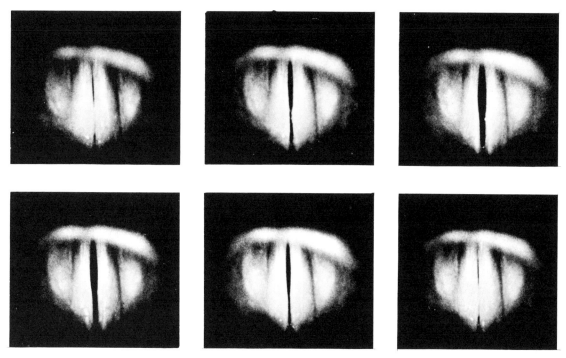

Figure 15. The opening and closing of the vocal cords at a pitch of 350 cycles per second, photographed with Bell Telephone Laboratories' high-speed motion picture camera. Used by permission.

mechanical resonators approximating those in the human body have resulted in startling but not altogether conclusive revelations. The sum of these observations is that the singer's feeling and the placing of a sensation of resonance often have nothing to do with where the resonance is actually taking place. I shall therefore limit myself to enumerating the possible resonators and the resonance cavities of the human voice. In contrast to the wind instruments, the human resonators are shaped in different ways determined by the complicated configuration of surrounding structures.

The resonators not only augment the tone; correctly used, they also enrich the quality, filter and sift it, dampen it by taking away some undesirable overtones, and project it. Resonance starts deep inside the body in the air spaces of the windpipe and the bronchi, particularly for low tones with frequencies up to 250. This should not be confused with chest resonance, a word widely used by teachers, accompanists, and coaches. Actually, the chest is not a good resonator; it is clogged with too many organs, and with too much spongy, sound-absorbing substance to produce a favorable resonance. Chest resonance has nothing to do with chest quality, which is a term for a certain vocal timbre. The trachea

acts as an over-all resonator without having any selective faculty.

The next resonator, working our way upward, is the larynx, above the vocal cords. A small resonator, looking like the collar of the larynx, seems to be especially important for good resonance. Wilmer T. Bartholomew writes in his *Acoustics of Music* that experiments have proved that the particular overtone which gives a voice its "ring"—an overtone of an approximate frequency of 2,800 cycles per second for male and 3,200 for female voices—originates in this collar of the larynx. Be this as it may, the larynx must be counted among the important resonators of the voice.

The next cavity important for resonance is the pharynx, on top of the larynx and extending through the space behind the tongue to the space behind the nose, above the soft palate (velum). The pharynx is undoubtedly very important, especially for ennobling the voice. It can be controlled with exercise and should be kept open at all times. Bartholomew thinks that it contributes mostly to the improvement of the quality of the lower frequencies, up to 600 in the male voice. We see in Figure 16 that the pharynx can be partly shut off by a constricted tongue, which is very undesirable. We see

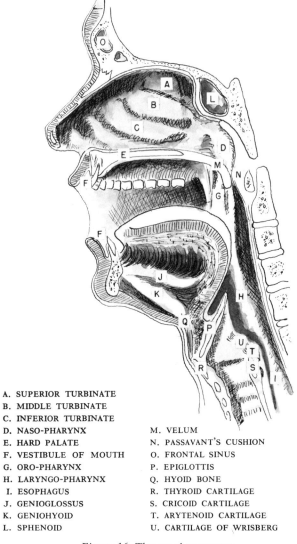

A. SUPERIOR TURBINATE
B. MIDDLE TURBINATE
C. INFERIOR TURBINATE
D. NASO-PHARYNX
E. HARD PALATE
F. VESTIBULE OF MOUTH
G. ORO-PHARYNX
H. LARYNGO-PHARYNX
I. ESOPHAGUS
J. GENIOGLOSSUS
K. GENIOHYOID
L. SPHENOID

M. VELUM
N. PASSAVANT'S CUSHION
O. FRONTAL SINUS
P. EPIGLOTTIS
Q. HYOID BONE
R. THYROID CARTILAGE
S. CRICOID CARTILAGE
T. ARYTENOID CARTILAGE
U. CARTILAGE OF WRISBERG

Figure 16. The vocal apparatus

rate upon later in the chapter about phonetics and diction, I am a partisan of the open throat–open mouth way of singing.

With William Vennard's permission, I am using his illustrations of three mouth positions, adding a fourth one, that of the "smiling" position (see Fig. 17). It is quite evident that only the second position guarantees the freest use of the oral-pharyngeal resonance cavities.

I touch here a dangerous subject — dangerous to the relation between accompanist or coach and voice teacher, a relation I shall discuss elsewhere in greater detail (see p. 185). But it must be said here that the accompanist or coach should know enough about the mechanics of musical instruments to spot the danger signals of wrong production of sound. At certain intermediate and passing stages and in some repair work it may be advantageous to have a singer use the smiling position especially when, as in coloratura singing, swiftness and flexibility are required. But at best this is only following the line of least resistance: this position may make it easier to cover vocal defects, but they will never be remedied in this way. The smiling position means a tight throat and will, sooner or later, result in an exaggerated vibrato, even a shake or a tremolo. In my opinion, the mouth should always be round like an O, and should be elongated on sustained or increased tones by gradually lowering the lower jaw and arching the palate. This goes for increases toward the forte end of the dynamic scale, as well as for decreases toward pianissimo. But the jaw should never get "stuck" or tight. Its motion must be directed by the chewing muscles. I should like to add that in the artist who has attained the highest professionalism in singing even a smiling position may prove valuable for certain emotional or technical effects. But for vocalists at the beginning of their career, I cannot recommend this smiling position.

The nasal cavities are formed by the septum and three shell-like structures encased in walls called the turbinates. Because of the winding bone structure of

also that the velum, if lifted too high, can press against the muscular part called Passavant's cushion and thus shut off the postnasal part of the pharynx. This may not be too bad for resonance, since nasal resonance is desirable only in certain cases (when singing French nasal vowels for instance) (see pp. 71–73).

The most important resonance cavity by far is the mouth. Its shape can be altered in many ways. It also can — and should — form a continuous cavity with the throat, provided the tongue is not in the way. Great care should be taken that the tongue should always be relaxed to allow free passage of the tone. Otherwise, the tone will sound muffled, mouthy, mushy. The position of mouth, tongue, palate, lips, jaw, and teeth will depend mainly on the speech sounds used. But, as I shall elabo-

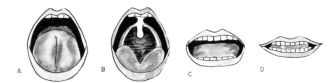

Figure 17. Mouth positions in singing. A. Wrong position: tongue gets in the way. B. Right position: tongue low and grooved. C. Wrong position: mouth too tense. D. Usually wrong position: "smiling" position

the turbinates they have little space for resonance, and the nostrils certainly are not very fit for resonating and enriching the sound. All these cavities are much too small to improve the sound a great deal, and the nasal resonators must therefore be looked upon as rather poor. If used to a great extent, with the pharyngeal and oral resonators constricted, the well-known nasality will result. When this happens, teachers should try hard to get the voice out of the nose. Bartholomew, however, thinks that if nasal resonance is used only sparingly, it will contribute to the so-called head resonance.

The last cavities are the sinuses, four small pairs situated in the region of the cheeks, in the inner nasal region, and behind the eye sockets. Popular — and even professional — belief has it that these sinuses are most important for the production of head tones, but scientific experiments in recent years have proved that the sinuses have no appreciable influence on resonance. This is hard to believe. Singers are very conscious of the sinuses and the head, as such, for head voice placement. The scientific statement that falsetto tones get more resonance and more vibrations in the laryngeal and tracheal parts of the body may be true. But by empiric reasoning, I think that, as minute as the added resonance of the sinuses may be when measured — and how could it be large considering the small size of the cavities? — this small addition of resonance helps to improve the quality of the head tone.

It is true that tone cannot be directed into any resonator just at the will of the singer. Most singers try to place their voices so that they hear them well — so that they feel the vibrations and reverberations. This will always produce a tone which projects inward but not outward. The teacher, the accompanist, or coach will have to tell the singer constantly when the voice sounds best and projects best. With growing experience the pupil will come to know what particular sensation he feels when he produces and places the tone properly according to his teacher's judgment and will be sure he is singing best whenever he feels that particular sensation.

Vocal sounds and vocal technique can be analyzed by scientific methods, and the conclusions will undoubtedly prove right. But science alone will not be able to build a beautiful voice. There are many imponderabilia; call them sympathetic co-resonance of bones; give them unscientific names as all voice teachers do — head voice, chest voice, falsetto, in short, the registers; describe the different spots for placing a voice, high or low larynx,

and so on. A voice teacher's or a coach's language is mainly unscientific, his technical terms are mostly flowery images; each will have to discover what image strikes the imagination of a particular pupil. I am not at all against that. But I am also of the opinion that teachers and coaches ought to know the scientific facts and use them for voice analysis.

The accompanist and coach should frequently confer with the teacher (see p. 185) and discuss the problems and progress of each singer. They also should try to use the same images in order not to confuse the pupil.

CONCLUDING REMARKS

I should like to end this chapter about the mechanics of musical instruments with a few words about my own ideal of tone production both for instrumentalists and for singers.

First of all, perfect coordination of mind and body should be achieved. The fingers and the vocal cords should be able to obey the dictates of the brain, the heart, and the soul. The accompanist and coach can help in achieving this by knowing the technical, anatomical, physiological, physical, and mechanical facts and laws. Energizer, vibrator, and resonator must work closely together, without one of them taking a greater share of the prize than the others.

Secondly, economy in producing a sound is most important for quality. No artist should give more at a particular moment than the music actually requires. Thus, he will never be too tired to put all of himself into the climaxes when all is needed of him. A climax, of course, may happen in fortissimo as well as in pianissimo. Economy is something that very few artists are able to attain by themselves; the accompanist and coach must help them. Economy begins with the artist's stance. The pianist has to have what may be called body feeling: the way he sits at the piano, curves his back, or lifts his hands should not be the same for a Mozart as for a Brahms composition and, as we have seen, there is an optimum position for a violinist where he will expend the least energy to get maximum results. The singer will achieve economy by not artificially tightening his vocal apparatus, by standing erect, by keeping his feet anchored firmly on the ground, and holding his head up — in short, by being free in his body position.

Thirdly, ideal tone production is enhanced by intensity. The accompanist and coach must make it very clear to the artist that soft dynamics do not mean relaxing the energizer, vibrator, and resonator. On the contrary, the softer a sound gets, the more intense it must become. Only in this way does it keep or increase its beauty and carrying power. The pianist's touch in soft dynamics must become more intense, the violinist's or cellist's left hand must become even more expressive, the singer's muscular action must be stronger, his resonance cavities must be used to their full extent. Piano singing produced by lack of intensity is nothing but fakery and must be condemned.

By now, the accompanist and coach should have mastered the knowledge of his and his artists' instruments. But this is only the beginning. The next chapters will take up in detail the various other important ingredients that go into the making of a good accompanist and coach.

Phonetics and Diction in Singing

WHICH is more important, the words or the music? To this day, the old argument has lost nothing of its ardor, its vehemence, its partisanship, and above all its emotional aspects and its question mark.

Truly, which of the two arts is more important when combined in a vocal composition? The question has occupied many great creative artists and many of their utterances about this problem could be quoted. But it may be best to let a great musician take the rostrum. At an age when wisdom and experience become molded into serene impartiality, Richard Strauss undertook to cast this ever-alive question into poetic and musical form. His conversation piece for music, *Cappriccio*, has this problem as its main topic. He lets a poet and a musician argue the question, fight about it, and finally leave it to a beautiful woman of noble heart and soul to solve. Though Strauss leaves the question unanswered — the opera ends without the solution's actually being announced — by his words "music and word are brother and sister" he leaves no doubt in anybody's mind that the fight must end in a draw. In vocal art the word is lifted up and ennobled by the music, the music is made clear and brought into focus by the word. This chapter will analyze the elements of the spoken word and discuss their adjustment to the singing phrase.

It has been said that in vocal art the singing comes from the heart, but the words must be controlled by the intellect. This is only partly true. Both music and words must come from the heart, but both must also be controlled by the brain — not only controlled but brought under a common denominator which could be called the esthetic golden mean.

A word consists of sounds. The science of producing and pronouncing sounds is called phonetics; the enunciation of words and sentences synthesized from sounds is called diction. Spoken and sung sounds fall into the categories of vowels, semivowels, vowel combinations (diphthongs, triphthongs), and consonants.

The popular belief that there are five different vowels has been discarded by the science of phonetics. Of the languages most frequently encountered in vocal literature, Italian has seven vowels, German fourteen, English fifteen, and French sixteen. When we come to vowel combinations and consonants, the confusion grows even greater.

The International Phonetic Alphabet (IPA), created in 1888 and revised in 1951, has a sign for each sound. This alphabet may be too complicated for every singer to learn, but it is a necessity for accompanists and coaches who want to master the intricacies of phonetics and diction for singers. This book will use the IPA because of its definitiveness and because it allows no error and no second meaning of a sound. It will then be up to the individual accompanist or coach to judge the intelligence of his singers and use any method of making the sound clear to them.

The comparative simplicity of Italian, as suggested by its use of only seven vowels, makes it the easiest language to sing. It therefore will be the first language to be discussed and its vowels will form the basis for those of all other languages with which singers should be familiar, at least phonetically.

The accompanist and coach with aspirations must know one Romance language well enough to be able to

Symbol	Italian	French	Spanish	German	English
VOWELS					
[a]	patria	pâle, pas, patte	pan	fahren, Gast	far
[ε]	vendetta, pesca (peach)	tête, mère	escuela, cerca	Bett, Bär	pet
[e]	era, pesca (fishing)	thé	. . .	leben	chaotic (approx.)
[ə]	. . .	vil*le*	. . .	Erd*e*	*a*bout, h*e*rb (approx.)
[i]	si	si	sì	wie, bitte	see, bit
[o]	dove	beau	llorar	wohl	. . .
[ɔ]	cosa	porte, fort	ojo	Sonne	Scotch, fought
[ø]	. . .	peu	. . .	schön	. . .
[œ]	. . .	oeuf, veuve	. . .	zwölf	surf, sir (approx.)
[u]	subito	tout	mucho	gut, Hund	doom, book (approx.)
[y]	. . .	lune	. . .	über, Glück	. . .
[ɑ̃]	. . .	ange, ensemble	. . .	. . .	. . .
[ɛ̃]	. . .	infame, teint	. . .	. . .	. . .
[õ]	. . .	ombre, onde	. . .	. . .	. . .
[œ̃]	. . .	un, humble	. . .	. . .	. . .
SEMIVOWELS					
[w] ...	quando	oiseau, oui	cuando, huelga	. . .	suave, persuasion
[j]	ieri	hier	tib*i*o	ew'ge, Jahr	you, yet
[ɥ]	. . .	puis, huit	. . .		
CONSONANTS					
[b] ...	bene	bien	bueno	Bett	bet
[β]	. . .	. . .	hablar	. . .	love (Southern U.S., approx.)
[ç]	. . .	. . .	yo (in stress)	ich	hue (in stress)
[d]	dormire	dormir	duerme	du	doom
[ð]	. . .	. . .	lado	. . .	this, other
[θ]	. . .	. . .	corazon, cinco	. . .	thunder
[f]	forte	fort	fuerte	fast	fast
[g] ...	gamba	guérir	guerra	gerne	get
[gs]	. . .	exil	. . .	. . .	exile
[ɣ]	. . .	. . .	luego	. . .	. . .
[h]	. . .	haine	. . .	hoch	high
[k]	caro	carte	calidad	kalt	cold
[ks]	. . .	luxe	excavar	Luchs	lax
[l]	lungo	long	leche	lachen	. . .
[ʎ]	figlia	. . .	llamar (Castilian)	. . .	. . .
[j]	. . .	fille	llamar (Mexican)	Joch	yonder
[m] ...	amore	amour	amor	Mann	man
[n]	onda	nez	andar	Name	name
[ɲ]	agnus	agneau	señor	. . .	onion
[ŋ]	angolo	. . .	cinco, tengo	singen	sing
[p]	padre	père	padre	Pore	pour
[r]	rosso	rouge	rojo	rot	red
[s]	sangue	sang	sangre	rasten	see
[z]	sdegno	zèle	rasgar	Sohn	zeal
[dz] ...	zero	. . .	. . .	. . .	adze
[ʒ]	. . .	jour	alli (Argentinian)	Gendarm	vision, measure
[dʒ] ...	giubilo	. . .	. . .	. . .	jar
[ʃ]	sciocco	chaud	. . .	schön	show
[t]	tutto	tout	todo	Tonne	tan
[ts] ...	zio	. . .	. . .	Zahn	Tsar
[tʃ] ...	cielo	caoutchouc	charro	rutschen	church
[v]	verde	vert	verde	warm	vast
[x]	. . .	. . .	gente, jabon	Loch	khan, loch

converse fluently, in addition to thoroughly understanding its phonetical, grammatical, and stylistic intricacies. Since Italian is easier than French, the American coach or accompanist will have fewer difficulties in speaking Italian than French. Besides this complete mastery of one Romance language, a thorough knowledge of another one, as well as of German, is essential. The accompanist or coach must understand these languages from the point of view of all their phonetic and linguistic problems. This seems a very high standard, but we must keep in mind what I said in the introductory chapter about the qualifications and background of an accompanist or coach. If he is able to thoroughly search one language for its philological qualities he will be in a much better position to study and understand other languages. As a famous linguist who was proficient in about sixty-four languages once said: "Only the first six are difficult; after that, everything becomes very easy."

This book is meant for American and English accompanists and coaches. Complete knowledge of English is an assumed prerequisite. Although it is a known fact that English singing diction is frequently massacred by coaches as well as by singers, this book will not undertake to analyze faulty production and enunciation of English phrases. A very good book, *The Singer's Manual of English Diction* by Madeleine Marshall (published by G. Schirmer's, Inc., New York), is available and should not be absent from any accompanist's or coach's studio. Where my experience with singers has led me to different conclusions from Miss Marshall's, my point of view will be offered.

This chapter, then, will make Italian, Latin, French, Spanish, and German singing diction understandable to accompanists and coaches. The problems which will be brought into focus must necessarily be based on the relation of the pronunciation of these languages to the pronunciation of native tongue of teacher and student, namely, English.

I purposely use the term "singing diction." This book is not concerned with speech as such and the elements of speech are treated only as they are related to singing. One of the most widespread errors is that spoken and sung sounds are the same. Nothing is further from the truth. To sing the way you speak may be advisable for popular music, but it would make the voice sound brittle, harsh, and uneven in opera, song, and choral music. The adjustment of phonetics to the vocal phrase is the real problem for any accompanist and coach and the

solution constitutes a very important part of his art. The basic elements of phonetics are nevertheless the speech sounds and this chapter will start with them. Of the speech sounds, the vowels are the simplest.

A vowel is a voiced speech sound which originates in the larynx and passes unhindered through the channel formed by throat and mouth. Different vowels will require different positions of the speech apparatus, but in all vowels the passage through throat and mouth is uninterrupted by obstacles. Obstacles to the speech sounds come into play in helping to form the other speech sounds, the consonants. Vowels' unobstructed passage makes them the foremost carriers of the singing tone. A simple example will illustrate this: The vocalise in its voice-building form in a teacher's studio and in its adaptation as a special vocal art form (see Ravel's or Rachmaninoff's Vocalise) consists entirely of a vowel or vowels. Any examination of singing phonetics and diction must therefore start with the vowel speech sounds; this I shall follow, for each language, with a discussion of semivowels, combinations of vowels (such as diphthongs and triphthongs), and consonants.

CLASSIFICATION OF VOWELS

The vowels can be classified in many ways. The easiest way is to divide them into front, middle, and back, a division based on different positions of tongue and lips. Each vowel can be further divided into a long and closed or short and open vowel. The most natural vowel is the

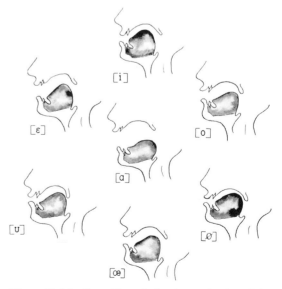

Figure 18. Mouth positions during the production of the principal kinds of vowel sound

a which is the least modified vowel. According to William Vennard, "The pharynx is distended comfortably, the jaw is dropped, the tongue is low and grooved, if possible."

e and i are formed by slight changes of the tongue position, o and u by progressive rounding of the lips.

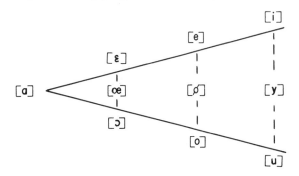

Figure 19. Diagram showing relative positions of Italian, French, and German vowels

Figure 18 shows simplifications of X-rays of tones, as illustrated in G. Oscar Russell's book, *Speech and Voice*. This should help to give the accompanist and coach an idea of the changes in the mouth when different vowels are pronounced. Figure 19 may make the relative position of the Italian, French, and German vowels more understandable. The difference in production between long and short vowels is neglected in Figure 18.

CLASSIFICATION OF CONSONANTS

The consonants are produced by actually putting obstacles in the way of the free flow of the air stream, which deflects, hinders, or interrupts it. If the vowels can be considered the flesh of the sound body, the consonants are the bones that hold the flesh together. There are several possible systems for the classification of consonants.

Some consonants are *voiced*; this means that they carry with them some remnants of voice sound. Others are *voiceless*; they do not contain voice sound at all. You can "hear" the voiced consonants if you cover your ears and softly articulate [b], [d], [g], [v], and [z]. Using the same method, you will "hear" nothing while articulating [p], [t], [k], [f], [s], and [ʃ].

Moreover, the consonants can be classified by the location of the speech apparatus in which they are produced. This most widely accepted classification contains the glottal fricative sound, the [h] which is aspirated in the larynx; the labial sounds, produced by the lips, called bilabials if both lips are involved (p and b) and labiodentals if upper teeth and lower lip are used in producing these sounds (f and v). Bilabials and labiodentals are either voiced (b and v) or voiceless (p and f).

Yet another method of classification takes into consideration the degree of freedom from obstruction of the air stream in forming consonants. If the obstruction is total, we talk of plosives. Their release requires a slight explosion of the accumulated air pressure. Consonants of this type are [b], [p], [d], [t], [g], and [k]. If the obstruction is not complete but leaves a narrow channel open in which the articulated consonants rub against the channel's borders, we speak of fricative sounds, such as [f], [v], [θ], [ð], [ʃ], [ʒ], and [h].

The other consonants cannot be produced without the aid of the tongue. They are therefore called *linguals*. If tongue and upper gum ridge are involved in producing consonants, their name is lingua-alveolars. Such consonants are [d] (voiced) and [t] (voiceless). By slight modification of the tongue (letting some breath escape through a slight contact between tongue and upper teeth) we get the [s] (voiceless) and the [z] (voiced). Further modifications of this are the [ʃ] (voiceless) and the [ʒ] (voiced), produced by withdrawing the tongue a little from the alveolar ridge. [g] (voiced) and [k] (voiceless) are velar consonants, produced by a meeting of the back of the tongue and the soft palate.

Of the nasal sounds, [m] is a bilabial nasal, produced by closing the lips; [n] is an alveolar nasal, made by pressing the forward part of the tongue against the upper gum ridge. [ŋ] is a velar nasal effected by pressing the middle part of the tongue against the hard palate. For all these the velum should be arched, unless a French nasal sound is desired, in which case the velum is somewhat lowered. Those consonants which belong to French or German only will be described in their proper place.

A special discussion is needed for the [l] which is either *dental-alveolar* (as in Italian, French, and German), or more *guttural* (as in English). Some Slavic languages have both of these l's and use different signs for them: ł for the guttural (hard) and l for the dental (soft) [l] in Russian and in Polish.

There are four ways to articulate the [r]. Firstly, it can be flipped by a slight trill of the tip of the tongue against the upper gum ridge. This is the Italian or French (in singing) and English alveolar [r]. Secondly, it can be rolled by a flutter of the soft palate against the back of the tongue. This is the German and Slavic r and with a lesser roll it appears also in the speech of the French, especially Parisians (but should not be used in singing). The third kind of r is the English way of articulating it by curling the tip of the tongue upward and slightly backward toward the region of the alveolar ridge and hard palate and returning very fast to its initial position. The fourth way is typically American, pronounced very sloppily.

The production and pronunciation of semivowels, diphthongs, triphthongs, and consonant combinations will be discussed in the paragraphs concerning the individual languages to which they belong.

Italian Phonetics and Diction

I HAVE said before that the Italian needs only seven different vowel sounds to form words and sentences in his language. These vowel sounds are the purest of any language and the most easily produced. This purity, free from any disfiguring diphthongization, is the main reason for the undisputed position of Italian as the most musical language in the world. Vowels are only infrequently interspersed with consonants. Diphthongization is practically unknown. All this creates the basis for the bel canto style of singing which is predominant today in America. It is quite possible to adjust even French and German words to this style of singing. The seven Italian vowels are shown in Figure 20. Most of these vowels are long. They are short — but not necessarily open — only before a double consonant. This is true only of Italian, which is the sole language where the shortening of a vowel does not automatically mean the opening of that vowel.

Cond[ɔ]tta ell' era in c[e]ppi (VERDI *Il Trovatore*)
Povero Rigol[e]tto (VERDI *Rigoletto*)
Buon giorno, Marc[ɛ]llo (PUCCINI *La Bohème*)

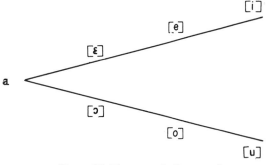

Figure 20. The seven Italian vowels

The [a] *sound.* The pronunciation of the Italian a is similar to the Boston way of saying father. The a is always bright, except when vocal blending asks for darkening or adjustment of the vowel. In producing it the tongue should be relaxed and grooved, its tip lightly anchored on the lower teeth ridge.

a can be either long or short. It is long in an accentuated syllable, before another vowel or a single consonant, and always short if not accentuated, or before more than one consonant.

Āmămi, oh Ălfredo! (VERDI *La Traviata*)
Ăll' ărmi! (VERDI *Il Trovatore*)

a gets a grave accent if it is the final letter of a word and supposed to be stressed. It is always long.

Ăbbiăte cārità! (VERDI *La Forza del Destino*)
Pietà di me, pietà, Signor! (VERDI *La Forza del Destino*)

The [ɛ] *sound.* The [ɛ] corresponds exactly to the sound in the English words *bed, set, letter*. In singing, the [ɛ] is always open when it is the final sound of a word or if it falls on an unaccentuated syllable of a polysyllabic word.

E a parlar[ɛ], mi sforza d'amor[ɛ] (MOZART *Le Nozze di Figaro*)
L[ɛ] d[ɛ]lizi[ɛ] d[ɛ]ll' amor (VERDI *Rigoletto*)

In the following words the final e is *closed*: *chè* (and combinations, such as *perchè, poicchè*, etc.) *tre* (and combinations), *me, te,* and *se* if stressed; *re; nè; mercè,* vendè (and other 3rd person singular forms of the absolute past of verbs on -*ere*).

In accented syllables of a polysyllabic word the e can be either open or closed. This is also true if the e precedes a double consonant. No hard and fast rule can be established concerning where to use open or short e's; the accompanist or coach will have to look up the word in a good dictionary.

Si, v[ε]nd[ε]tta, tr[ε]m[ε]nda v[ε]nd[ε]tta (VERDI *Rigoletto*)

S[ε]mpr[ε] lib[ε]ra d[ε]gg'io foll[ε]ggiar[ε] (VERDI *La Traviata*)

Sometimes words spelled identically have different meanings, depending upon whether the e is pronounced open or closed.

V[e]nti scudi nè da di prodotto (VERDI *Rigoletto*)
La calunnia è un v[e]ntic[ε]llo (ROSSINI *Il Barbiere di Siviglia*)
La l[e]gge, io non la sò (PUCCINI *Madama Butterfly*)
Ei l[ε]gge, non vi parla (VERDI *Otello*)

Some suffixes with e on stressed syllables are short, as in frat-[ε]llo, sor-[ε]lla, -[ε]nte, -[ε]simo, and -[ε]stre.

Att[ε]ndi, frat[ε]llo (VERDI *Rigoletto*)
Buon giorno, sor[ε]llina (DONIZETTI *Don Pasquale*)
De miei boll[ε]nti spiriti (VERDI *La Traviata*)

The e with grave accent is always pronounced [ε], with the exception of the examples above.

The [e] (closed e) *sound.* There are fewer [e]'s in Italian than [ε]'s. The e is closed in some accented syllables of a polysyllabic word, sometimes even before a double consonant.

O monum[e]nto (PONCHIELLI *La Gioconda*)
Povero Rigol[e]tto (VERDI *Rigoletto*)

The sound in *e* or *ed* (and) is always long and closed. Some monosyllabic words and some e's with grave accents have the closed sound. (See note above.)

Eh or deh (exclamation) is closed as the stretching h indicates.

Stressed e's in suffixes are closed, as in diminutives with -etto and -etta, and in forms with -ese, -essa, -evole, -ezza, -mente.

Caro il mio Figar[e]tto (MOZART *Le Nozze di Figaro*)
Susan[e]tta, sei tu (MOZART *Le Nozze di Figaro*)
Cont[e]ssa, perdono (MOZART *Le Nozze di Figaro*)
All' uso Giappon[e]s[ε] (PUCCINI *Madama Butterfly*)
L[ε]gg[ε]rm[e]nt[ε], dolc[ε]m[e]nt[ε]. (ROSSINI *Il Barbiere di Siviglia*)

The contraction de'e (from deve) is pronounced [deε].

Both e and ε sounds may have to be modified toward [ø] and [œ] if the vocal line demands it.

The i *sound.* The i sound in Italian is almost always long and is pronounced in exactly the same way as the vowels in the English words sea, see, relieve, feeling, and key. Double consonants following the i do not shorten it, but final i's are usually short. The i has four different functions. It can be syllabic (dominating a syllable):

V*i*ssi d'arte (PUCCINI *Tosca*)

It can be asyllabic (unaccented):

Po*i* m*i* guidav*i* a*i* fulg*i*di desert*i* (VERDI *Otello*)

It can serve as a semivowel:

è m*i*ele o f*i*ele (PUCCINI *La Bohème*)

It can be mute, and it remains unpronounced in the following combinations: cia, cie, cio, ciù, gia, gie, gio, giu, scia, scie, scio, sciu, glie, glio, gliu:

mi las*cio* reggere prima di cedere farò *gio*car (ROSSINI *Il Barbiere di Siviglia*)

The i is pronounced in scienza, usually spelled scïenza.

Con scenica scïenza (PUCCINI *Tosca*)

ii is pronounced and sung like one prolonged i.

Fug*ii* pur ora da Castel' Sant'Angelo (PUCCINI *Tosca*)

The i in its pure form tends to sound shrill and metallic, especially in top tones. It is advisable to produce the i sound without spreading the lips, or "smiling." The tip of the tongue should again be anchored against the lower teeth ridge. The forward part of the tongue has to arch upward but should not move too high, otherwise it would make the forward cavity of the mouth too small. While the pure metallic i used to be acceptable in provincial Italian opera houses, the great singers of La Scala always modified it toward [e] or [y]. It will be up to the accompanist and coach to discourage spreading the i and to blend it with the rest of the vowels in a musical phrase.

The y in Italian appears mostly in words of Greek derivation and is pronounced like i. It is always a pure vowel and not, as sometimes in English, a semiconsonant.

The [ɔ] (open o) *sound.* The [ɔ] sound in Italian is similar to the English o in provide. It is produced by rounding the lips and lowering the jaw, keeping the cavity of the mouth open and round, and the position of the tongue low. The tendency to diphthongization must be avoided. The lips must be rounded but should not protrude much since this would result in a closed *o*. German equivalents are S[ɔ]nne, R[ɔ]ss; French equivalents are d[ɔ]nner, t[ɔ]rt.

The o in Italian is always pronounced [ɔ] if it is the final sound of a word or if it falls on the unaccented syllable of a polysyllabic word.

Un cert[ɔ] n[ɔ]n s[ɔ] che (VIVALDI "Song")
Or che mi c[ɔ]n[ɔ]scete (PUCCINI *La Bohème*)

In monosyllabic words the o is always pronounced [ɔ], as in non, con, don.

The o in accented syllables of polysyllabic words may be either open or closed. A non-Italian must look up each such word in the dictionary.

La d[ɔ]nna è m[ɔ]bile (VERDI *Rigoletto*)
P[ɔ]c[ɔ], p[ɔ]c[ɔ] (PUCCINI *La Bohème*)

The o is pronounced [ɔ] before ll, mm, nn, rr, ss, or zz. It can be open or closed before tt. "Oh" as an exclamation is pronounced [ɔ].

[ɔ], quant[ɔ] è bella (VERDI *Rigoletto*)

The ò (with grave accent) is also always pronounced [ɔ]. The accent indicates only the stress of the word and does not change the sound.

L'amer[ɔ], sar[ɔ] c[ɔ]stante (MOZART *Il Re Pastore*)
M[ɔ]rr[ɔ] (VERDI *La Traviata*)

The [o] (closed o) *sound.* The [o] has no equivalent in English. All similar sounds, as in cold, low, are diphthongized. The [o] is equivalent to the German so, wo, hoch, or the French eau, or rose. The best way of finding the right production for the [o] is to produce an Italian a and round the lips while holding it. While the lips are gradually rounded, the vowel change runs from a bright [a] to a covered [a] and thence through different shades to an [o]. All these shades of [a] and [o] are important for the singer in blending vowels and evening out vocal coloring.

Another approach for an accompanist or coach to use in showing the English-speaking singer how to produce a pure [o] would be to analyze the production of an English (diphthongized) o, as in no, so. It starts the same way as the pure [o] — with rounded lips. The lips, however, are relaxed as the diphthongization progresses until the sound approaches a [u] (no = no-u, so = so-u). By pronouncing these words very slowly and arresting the rounded lips on the first part without proceeding to the [u] sound, the first part then is the pure [o] sound.

The cavity of the mouth should be fully utilized for the resonance of the [o] by keeping the palate high and the tongue low, the latter again lightly anchored on the lower teeth ridge. The jaw is less dropped than in pronouncing the open o. The o is closed in some accented syllables of a polysyllabic word but a dictionary must be used to determine exactly which o is open and which closed. Sometimes an o is closed even before a double consonant.

C[ɔ]nd[o]tta ell' era in ceppi (VERDI *Il Trovatore*)
BUT: alla l[ɔ]tta (PONCHIELLI *La Gioconda*)
b[o]cca stretta (DONIZETTI *Don Pasquale*)

The word o means "either-or" and like the vocative is always closed.

Il mi[ɔ] bel f[o]c[ɔ], [o] l[ɔ]ntan[ɔ], [o] vicin[ɔ] (MARCELLO "Song")
[O] n[ɔ]tte, [o] Dea (PICCINNI "Song")
[O] mi[ɔ] Fernand[ɔ] (DONIZETTI *La Favorita*)

Stressed o's in suffixes are always closed, as in nouns and adjectives ending in -ore, -oso, -osa, -ione.

Sm[ɔ]rfi[o]sa, malizi[o]sa (MOZART *Le Nozze di Figaro*)
Am[o]re mi[ɔ] (PUCCINI *Madama Butterfly*)
Maledizi[o]ne (VERDI *La Forza del Destino*)

The [u] *sound.* The Italian u is always long, as in the English word doom, but never diphthongized. Its pronunciation creates a difficulty for the English-speaking singer since the written u in English is pronounced like the IPA sounds ʊ or ʌ. And even the oo (as in doom) is articulated further back in the mouth and is always somewhat diphthongized.

The Italian u is a pure vowel and is pronounced forward with rounded and protruded lips (protruded more than in pronouncing a closed o). The lips should be rounded into a pout, almost as if they were about to gently blow away some light object. It is important to impress on the singer the necessity of keeping mouth and throat relaxed as in a closed o position, otherwise the vowel will sound hooty or muffled. The tongue again should be kept low and the jaw be raised more than when pronouncing o. The u in Italian stays long whether it is an initial, medial, or final sound, and even before a double consonant. The grave accent likewise does not change the quality of the u.

T*u*tta la t*u*a trib*ù* (PUCCINI *Madama Butterfly*)
Omai tre volte l'*u*pupa (VERDI *Un Ballo in Maschera*)
Il t*u*tor ricuserà (ROSSINI *Il Barbiere di Siviglia*)
*U*na gran n*u*be t*u*rba il senno d'Otello (VERDI *Otello*)

All these examples contain the u as syllabic vowel. It can also be asyllabic or a semivowel.

L'aura che tu respiri (GLUCK "O del mio dolce ardor")

Questo o quella (VERDI Rigoletto)

SEMIVOWELS

The Italian language has two semivowels (or half vowels), which belong to the class of diphthongs.

1. The i can sometimes become a semivowel — expressed phonetically as [j] and pronounced exactly like the English y in you. In these combinations the [j] can stand before an a, ɛ, o, ɔ, and u sound. It is always a semivowel in its initial form when followed by another vowel as in [jɛri] (with the exceptions of some words of Greek derivation where the i stands for the Greek digamma as in iacinto). i is a semivowel between two other vowels (acciaio), in words ending in -iera, -iere (cavaliere); in verbal forms ending in -iamo, -iate (amiamoci, facciate). In words derived from Latin, such as dieci (from decem), chiaro, obietto, the i also is pronounced as a semivowel.

Siate felici (VERDI La Traviata)
Datemi vostri fiori (MOZART Le Nozze di Figaro)
Diedi i gioielli alla madonna al manto (PUCCINI Tosca)
Al fiume (VERDI Rigoletto)

An e following a [j] is always pronounced [ɛ].

2. The u can also at times become a semivowel — expressed phonetically as [w] — and is pronounced exactly as in the English suave, persuasion. The u becomes a semivowel in combination with q, g, and ng and can thus be found before a, e, i, ɔ. An o following a [w] is always pronounced [ɔ].

[Twɔna] (VERDI Rigoletto)
Quant' anni avete (PUCCINI Madama Butterfly)
Questo uomo fido provederà (PUCCINI Tosca)
Guidatemi all' ara (VERDI Il Trovatore)
Guerra, Guerra (VERDI Aïda)
Sangue, sangue (VERDI Otello)

In all these the accent does not fall on the semivowel but on the preceding or following vowel. The following words have the accent on the i or the u and are therefore not considered semivowels: mío, mía, míe and all nouns with the endings, -io, -ia, and -ie, with the i stressed as in zío, Dío, allegría, osteríe. The separation between the two vowels is called hiatus. This rule is most important for the English-speaking singer who tends to put the accent on the wrong vowel (mió, miá, etc.). Other vowel combinations which do not contain semivowels due to the accentuated i's and u's are: túo, súo, túa, súa, túe, súe, dúe, búe, túi, súi, lúi, cúi, etc.

Musically, the distinction between vowel and semivowel must be very carefully made. Usually the semivowel is expressed by one note only. The note must be divided in such a way that the stressed vowel gets the longer musical value. Figure 21 shows pure vowels of two syllables, and Figure 22 shows monosyllabic semivowels.

Figure 21. Pure vowels of two syllables

Figure 22. Semivowels of one syllable

Italian composers are usually conscious of these pure vowel and semivowel combinations and write their music accordingly, as for instance Puccini in *La Bohème* (Fig. 23). Sometimes, in order to achieve a special effect,

Figure 23. Puccini, *La Bohème*

composers consciously change the rules of pronunciation. A famous example appears in Verdi's *Otello* (Fig. 24) where he changes the semivowel in paziente into a pure vowel to emphasize the slow, undermining, suggestive power of Iago over Otello. Similarly, in the fourth

Figure 24. Verdi, *Otello*

act of *La Traviata*, Verdi treats the word re-li-gi-o-ne as a five-syllable word, stressing thus Violetta's debility. In Desdemona's "Willow Song," he notates as shown in Figure 25. The stress lies on the e, which must there-

Figure 25. Verdi, *Otello*

fore be held longer than the a. The right way of separation is therefore as shown in Figure 26. In the next line,

Figure 26. Verdi, *Otello*

Figure 27. Verdi, *Otello*

the vowels e and a fall on one short note and may therefore be divided equally as shown in Figure 27. Puccini separates i and a in the word nuzïal (Il nido nuzïal dov'è), (*Madama Butterfly*).

DIPHTHONGS

We speak of a diphthong if two vowels appear contiguously in the same syllable. The following vowel combinations are diphthongs if they belong to the same syllable: ae, ai, ao, au, ea, ei, eo, eu, ia, ie, io, iu, oa, oe, oi, ua, ue, ui, uo. These diphthongs are produced by pronouncing each vowel clearly and separately, without tying them together but without a y sound as in English (li-eto, not li-yeto). This is a frequent error and has to be corrected by accompanists and coaches.

Diphthongs in Italian are either vocalic (syllabic vowel plus asyllabic vowel), or semivocalic (semivowel plus syllabic vowel). If the semivowel precedes the syllabic vowel we speak of an ascending diphthong with the accent on the vowel as in words with ia, iɛ, [iɛ], io, iu, ua, [uɛ], ue, ui, uo, [uɔ]; otherwise the diphthong is called descending. The accent always stays on the vowel (ai, ei, [ɛi], oi, [ɔi], au, eu, [ɛu]).

Figure 28. Ways of singing diphthongs

Of the two vowels of a diphthong, one or the other is accented. The musical accent must conform to the phonetic stress. The accented value gets the longest part of the note under which it stands. If the musical note above a diphthong is very short or the tempo very fast, it is to be divided into equal parts. (See Fig. 28.) Similar diphthongs appearing in musical literature are aere, aiuto, lieto.

TRIPHTHONGS

Triphthongs are three contiguous vowels in one syllable. Each of these vowels must be pronounced clearly and separately, connected, however, by a legato. The musical accent must conform to the phonetic stress. The accentuated vowel gets the longest part of the note under which it stands. Triphthongs are formed by the vowel combinations aio, iei, iuo, uai, uia, uoi.

Miei cari, sedete (VERDI *La Traviata*)
Non ti conoscerà, se tu non vuoi (MOZART *Don Giovanni*)

CONSONANTS

The distinction between single and double consonants in Italian is very clear, more so than in any other language. I shall therefore treat them separately.

We have seen in the introductory remarks to this chapter that the consonants can be classified in several different ways. This book is written for accompanists and coaches, as an aid in their work with instrumentalists and vocalists. The chapter about phonetics concerns singers. For this reason, I shall classify the consonants by their degree of singability and shall start out with the voiced consonants, discussing the voiceless consonants afterwards.

The Italian pronounces his consonants just as he pronounces his vowels: clearly and definitely, with a distinct action of the speech apparatus. There is no delaying, no drawl, no muddiness as there sometimes is in English. Unless the vocal line requires some adjustment, the consonants are pronounced crisply, but without the explosive force that characterizes the consonants of some other languages.

Single consonants in Italian are — with the exception of some initial consonants with or without connection with final vowels of a preceding word — pronounced crisply but gently. The singer must not hestitate over them but must continue to the next vowel. No undue stress, no explosion must be added to the consonant. A consonant between two vowels must not interrupt the flow of vocal line.

Voiced consonants are singable to a greater or less degree. In Italian musical diction the voice does not linger on voiced consonants but proceeds to the next vowel, unless emotional, poetic, or onomatopoetic reasons demand a longer pause on the particular consonant.

The m *sound.* Phonetically, the m is a bilabial nasal sound (produced by both lips, with air escaping through the nose). The lips close firmly but without pressure. Standing by itself, a sung [m] amounts to a hum, since no tone can emerge from the mouth. A hum is usually sung piano but can be increased to a modest mezzo forte.

Great care must be taken to arch the velum highly, to give more resonance to the hum. Otherwise, the nasal quality would be increased, as is sometimes necessary in French. An example is found in the Humming Chorus from Puccini's *Madama Butterfly* (Fig. 29).

Figure 29. Puccini, *Madama Butterfly,*
Humming Chorus

In some bel canto phrases where it is essential that the flow of vocal line from vowel to vowel must not be interrupted, the m should be pronounced weakly, the lips not closing tightly. On such rather rare occasions, clarity of diction must be sacrificed for uninterrupted beauty of sound. These exceptions will occur more often in operas than in oratorios or songs (Fig. 30, 31).

Figure 30. Puccini, *La Bohème*

Figure 31. Mozart, *Don Giovanni*

The m between two vowels receives soft stress (amo). The m before or after a consonant receives moderate stress (tempo, calmo).

Amarilli, *m*ia bella (CACCINI "Madrigal Amarilli")
Caro *m*io ben, credi*m*i al*m*en (GIORDANI "Arietta")
Selve a*m*iche, o*m*brose piante (CALDARA "Arietta")

An initial m after a one-syllable word ending in a stressed vowel is pronounced like mm.

a *mm*e il ferro (VERDI *Don Carlo*)
e par che tenti riscattarlo da *mm*e (MOZART *Le Nozze di Figaro*)

Similarly, the m of Maria between vowels in a phrase receives strong stress.

Ave Mmaria (VERDI *Otello*)
Gesùmmaria (LEONCAVALLO *Pagliacci*)

The n *sound.* The n is an alveolar nasal sound, produced by flattening the most forward part of the tongue against the upper alveolar ridge, with the tip of the tongue touching the upper teeth. At the same time the soft palate should be in a raised position to avoid too much nasal sound. Initial n's and n's between two vowels

must be produced this way, but care should be taken not to exaggerate the pressure of the tongue and not to explode the n by a too sudden release of the tongue.

The n is soft between two vowels (lana), and moderate before or after another vowel (mente, Arno).

Tu me*n*ti (PUCCINI *Madama Butterfly*)
E*n*zo adorato (PONCHIELLI *La Gioconda*)
Cruda, fu*n*esta sma*n*ia (DONIZETTI *Lucia di Lammermoor*)
Pro*n*to a far tutto la notte e il gior*n*o, sempre d'i*n*tor*n*o (ROSSINI *Il Barbiere di Siviglia*)

Initial n gets added stress. Final n gets moderate stress.

Tre giorni so*n* che *N*ina (PERGOLESI "Nina")
Il bale*n* del suo sorriso (VERDI *Il Trovatore*)

Again, great care should be taken not to lower the velum too much. This would decrease the size of the resonance cavity of the mouth and increase the nasality of the n.

The n changes its quality when followed by an f or v. It then assumes a slightly nasal sound. If followed by g or k, the n becomes [ŋ]. If preceded by a g, the combination becomes [ɲ].

The ng [ŋ] *sound.* The alveolar n followed by a g or k becomes a new velar sound. It is produced by a meeting of the raised back of the tongue and the lowered soft palate (velum). There should be no pressure and the sound must be produced in the back of the mouth, *not* in the throat. It has a slight nasal quality which should not be overstressed by lowering the velum too much.

The n and the following g or k are not molded together as in the German jung, or the English sing. The tongue simply moves back from the alveolar to the velar position.

Fruga ogni a*n*golo (PUCCINI *Tosca*)
I*n*gannata (PUCCINI *Tosca*)

There are no initial or final [ŋ]'s in Italian.

The gn *sound.* The gn ([ɲ] phonetically) belongs to the n group, although spelled gn in Italian. It is a palatal nasal sound, and is sometimes called a liquid consonant. It is produced by flattening the middle part of the tongue against the hard palate, while the tip of the tongue is anchored against the lower teeth. The uvula is down. In Spanish, the spelling for [ɲ] is ñ, in Portuguese nh. It has no equivalent in English or German. The French spelling is the same as the Italian wherever it appears.

The nearest sound in English would be the ny as, for instance, in canyon.

In Italian, the [ɲ] can stand before any of the seven vowel sounds.

Ogni città, ogni paese (MOZART *Don Giovanni*)
Il feritore? Ignoto (GIORDANO *Andrea Chenier*)
Ma, gnaffe a me, non se la fa (VERDI *La Forza del Destino*)

The stress of the [ɲ] is moderate in the initial position (*gnocchi*), but strong in the middle of a word (*ignoto*).

The l sound. The l is a dental-alveolar voiced consonant, produced by placing the most forward part of the tongue against the upper teeth near the gum ridge. This l is, therefore, produced forward, the breath escaping along the sides of the tongue. It is of the greatest importance that English-speaking singers are taught how to produce a forward l, since they habitually tend to produce the l further back in a more guttural way. This is not good for a forward voice production. After the dental-alveolar placement, the tongue should come down rapidly to the region of the lower teeth in order to form the following vowel, or should proceed to the position of the next consonant, if the l is followed by such a sound. The l can be given different grades of stress. It is soft between two vowels and moderate before or after a consonant.

Non è su lei, nel suo fragile petto (VERDI *Un Ballo in Maschera*)
Il balen del suo sorriso (VERDI *Il Trovatore*)

In the words là and lì, the l receives strong stress.

The initial l is produced so easily that almost all languages use it for illustrating melodies and rhythms, usually followed by an a. In sustained, melodic singing the stress on the l is soft. When expressing rhythmical patterns, the stress on the l becomes moderate or even strong, approximating ll (Fig. 32).

Figure 32. Mozart, *Don Giovanni*

The gl sound. The [ʎ] belongs to the l group, though spelled gl in Italian. It is a palatal-alveolar sound produced initially like the l, but with the center of the tongue pressed against the hard palate. The sides of the tongue are not so free as they are in pronouncing l, and the air passage is thus narrowed along the side of the tongue. In Spanish, [ʎ] is expressed by ll (Sevilla), in Portuguese by lh (orelha). French and German do not have the [ʎ] sound, except in foreign names. Not all sounds spelled gl in Italian are [ʎ]'s. Initial and medial gl's are always in the g class, unless they are followed by i.

Gloria all' Egitto, ad Iside (VERDI *Aïda*)
l' egloghe dei pastori (GIORDANO *Andrea Chenier*)

But: Nella bionda egli ha l' usanza (MOZART *Don Giovanni*)

The [ʎ] before i gets moderate stress.

Ecco i fogli (VERDI *La Forza del Destino*)

The [ʎ] before i followed by a, e, o, or u gets strong stress.

Lo vedremo, veglio audace (VERDI *Ernani*)
Voglio piena libertà (PUCCINI *La Bohème*)
Quest' uomo ha moglie e sconcie voglie ha nel cor (PUCCINI *La Bohème*)

Some initial and medial gli combinations, derived mostly from foreign words, do not take the ʎ sound, as in glicerina, geroglifico, and negligente and in combinations with n (Anglia).

e sopra tutto questo al mio braccio impresso geroglifico (MOZART *Le Nozze di Figaro*)

The v sound. The v is a voiced labiodental fricative sound, produced by putting the upper teeth lightly and loosely against the inside part of the lower lip. The tongue should again be in a low position but should be relaxed, without touching the lower teeth. Thus a narrow opening is effected through which the sound emerges. The v must always be voiced (it must vibrate a little).

The English-speaking singer is prone to neglect the v by failing to bring the lower lip and upper teeth into contact. This should be corrected by the accompanist or coach. The v is stressed softly between two vowels, moderately before or after a consonant.

amò tanto la vita (PUCCINI *Tosca*)
Ernani, involami (VERDI *Ernani*)

In some phrases, as in sù via, ho visto, dove vai, e venti, the v receives strong stress (suvvia, ho vvisto).

Suvvia, spicciatevi (LEONCAVALLO *Pagliacci*)
Non ho visto compar Alfio (MASCAGNI *Cavalleria Rusticana*)

Initial v is stressed strongly in some cases if emphasis is to be given to the word.

è vile, vile (GIORDANO *Andrea Chenier*)

The voiced s sound. This voiced consonant is sometimes expressed by s, sometimes by [z]. It is an alveolar-dental fricative sound produced forward by cradling the tongue upwards, its tip almost (but not actually) touching the center of the upper front teeth. This sound should always be pronounced in a relaxed manner, never hurried. It is equivalent to the s sound in the English word has.

The z in Italian is pronounced in different ways, according to geographical situation. The northern parts generally pronounce it [z]. Tuscany mixes the pronunciation so that it sometimes sounds s, sometimes [z]; the rest of Italy changes the voiced [z] into a voiceless, though softly stressed, s. No over-all pronunciation rule exists. In singing it will be best always to voice the s when the s stands between two vowels or before another voiced consonant, such as b, d, g, l, m, n, r, or v.

Guidatemi al ridicolo oltraggio d'un ra*s*oio (PUCCINI *La Bohème*)
*S*barazzate all' l'istante (PUCCINI *Madama Butterfly*)
Una *s*mania, un pizzicare (ROSSINI *Il Barbiere di Siviglia*)
*S*gomento io non ho (PUCCINI *Tosca*)

The stress is always soft, only very slightly less so before another voiced consonant.

s between two vowels of which the first one belongs to a prefix is treated like an initial s, which is always voiceless. Likewise, the reflexive pronoun si, used as a suffix, has a voiceless s.

Qui nel cor mi ri*s*uonò (ROSSINI *Il Barbiere di Siviglia*)
Ogni sagezza chiude*s*i (VERDI *Rigoletto*)

The b sound. The b is a voiced bilabial occlusive sound. This means that the lips must be closed lightly, remain in this position for a split second — but long enough to effect an occlusion, and open to let the air emerge. The lip muscles must not be tightened.

In Italian singing diction the occlusion must always be light. In all occlusive sounds, voiced or voiceless, preserving the melodic line may force the singer not to effect complete occlusion — in other words, to fake the occlusion. It is up to the accompanist or coach to decide when this should be done.

The b should never be exploded, as it sometimes is in German. It receives soft stress between two vowels and before a consonant, moderate stress after a consonant.

La donna è mo*b*ile (VERDI *Rigoletto*)
Dammi un *b*acio, o non fai niente (MOZART *Le Nozze di Figaro*)
Ed assoporo allor la *b*ramosia sottil (PUCCINI *La Bohème*)
O dolce viso di mite circonfuso al*b*a lunar (PUCCINI *La Bohème*)

In exclamations, the b can be strongly stressed.

Che *bb*ella bambina (PUCCINI *La Bohème*)

The d sound. The d is a voiced dental occlusive sound. The tip of the tongue touches the point where the upper teeth ridge and the hard palate meet. After remaining there for a split second to effect occlusion, the tongue moves on to the next sound suddenly but lightly, with the emergence of some air.

The d between two vowels and before another consonant is stressed softly; it receives moderate stress after another consonant.

Ah, non cre*d*ea mirarti (BELLINI *La Sonnambula*)
Ah, Pa*d*re mio (VERDI *Rigoletto*)
Come, m'ar*d*on le ciglia (VERDI *Otello*)

The d of Dio between two vowels in a phrase receives strong stress.

Ah! Dio! (PUCCINI *Tosca*)

The [dz] (z) sound. The z sound expressed phonetically by [dz] can also be voiceless and is, in that case, represented phonetically as [ts].

The [dz] is a voiced dental semiocclusive sound. Its production starts in the same way as the production of the d and is continued by the sides of the tongue touching the alveolar ridge. In this way air can escape through a narrow passage which explains the classification of the [dz] as semiocclusive. The production is fast, and there should be no hissing; [dz] is a gentle sound.

There is no hard and fast rule to determine when the Italian z is voiced [dz] and when it is voiceless [ts]. Regional differences exist. A good orthophonetic dictionary will have to be consulted in case of doubt.

To students of linguistics I should add that the [dz] usually derives from the Latin voiced d (mediu → meddzo) or from the Greek zeta (as in the Italian dzona). The Latin voiceless t usually changes into an Italian [ts] (martiu → marzo).

An initial z may be voiced as in zero, zara. Likewise, a voiced z can stand between two vowels as in ozono, or it can come after another consonant, as in garza. Even zz can be voiced, as in all verbal suffixes on -izzare, or in words like olezzo. The stress on the initial [dz] and [dz] following another consonant is moderate; [dz] between two vowels gets a strong stress (lo ddzero, Doniddzetti).

Che soave *z*efiretto (MOZART *Le Nozze di Figaro*)
Ei gongolava ar*z*illo, pettoruto (PUCCINI *La Bohème*)

Per tener ben fuori le zanzare, i parenti (PUCCINI *Madama Butterfly*)

The g sound. The g and gh consonant in Italian is a voiced velar occlusive sound produced by the contact of the soft palate with the back part of the tongue. This causes a split second of occlusion which has to be resolved smoothly and without explosion. The tip of the tongue should be anchored against the lower teeth. The accompanist or coach should see to it that the meeting point of tongue and soft palate (velum) is not so far back as to make the g sound guttural.

g in Italian may be pronounced [g] (gone) or [dz] (Joe). It is pronounced [g] before the vowels a, o, and u. It adds the silent h to keep its sound before e and i (ghe, ghi). It is also pronounced [g] before an r and sometimes before an l, as I have said when discussing the gl sound. g and gh have a soft stress between two vowels and before another consonant, and a moderate stress after another vowel.

> Un' agonia (PONCHIELLI *La Gioconda*)
> Ogni borgo, ogni paese (MOZART *Don Giovanni*)
> Scrivo ancor tre righe a volo (PUCCINI *La Bohème*)
> Ora sono di ghiaccio (MOZART *Le Nozze di Figaro*)

The [dʒ] sound. ge or gi ([dʒ]) is a voiced alveolar-palatal semiocclusive sound (as in the English *job*), actually a combination of d and [ʒ] sounds. The tongue takes its position at the alveolar ridge and its center touches the hard palate. The sound which results leaves a small space for the breath to escape. The [dʒ] must be pronounced gently to preserve its full voiced quality. The [dʒ] is expressed in Italian by the letter g in front of an e or i. If the same sound is desired before an a, o, or u, a mute i must be inserted (as in giardino, gioia, giù).

The stress on the [dʒ] is soft between two vowels,

> L'agile mandola nè accompagna il suon (VERDI *Otello*)
> Io gelo (VERDI *Il Trovatore*)
> gira la cote, gira, gira (PUCCINI *Turandot*)
> Dunque in giardin verrai (MOZART *Le Nozze di Figaro*)
> O gioia (VERDI *Rigoletto*)

moderate after another consonant.

> Urge l'opra (PUCCINI *Tosca*)

The j sound. The [j] can sometimes still be found in old Italian scores or books. It is now replaced entirely by i and is either a vowel or semivowel.

> che tai baje costan poco (VERDI *Rigoletto*)

The r sound. The r, because of the various ways in which it can be produced, has a special position in the Italian consonants. In its pure Italian form, it is a voiced alveolar vibrant produced by keeping the tongue forward with the tip against the upper alveolar ridge, and vibrating it by a flutter or roll which, depending on the stress, is repeated from one to four times. The breath escapes over the tongue, not along its sides. The r is sometimes called dental r, sometimes rolled r. It is used by most Italians and is easy for the English-speaking singer to master. The roll of the r must not be overdone. Some Italian singers use the uvular (or guttural) r which is rolled or fluttered against the back of the tongue. It is very difficult to change a student's manner of producing the r, but since the English (though not the American) way is similar to the Italian way, the accompanist or coach should have no difficulties with it. The stress on the r, on the other hand, creates difficulties for the English-speaking singer.

r between two vowels always receives soft stress — one flutter is enough.

Initial and final r and r before and after another consonant are pronounced with moderate to strong stress, mostly the latter. From two to four flutters will be necessary. Italian ears are very sensitive to the pronunciation of the r; a strong r between vowels repels them. The following are examples of soft stress.

> O mio amore (PUCCINI *Tosca*)
> Molto raro complimento (PUCCINI *Madama Butterfly*)

Examples of moderate stress are as follows.

> All' armi (VERDI *Il Trovatore*)
> In dietro, anima scellerata (ROSSINI *Il Barbiere di Siviglia*)
> Ah frate, frate! (VERDI *La Forza del Destino*)

The r fulfills another important vocal function. The trill or flutter enables the singer to shift from one vocal position to another without disturbing the phrase. Such r's act like the neutral gear on a car: it is easy to shift into any position from there.

VOICELESS CONSONANTS

Voiceless consonants contain no trace of singability. In Italian lyric diction the voice does not linger on them but, having sung the preceding vowel, ties the consonant, or group of consonants, to the next vowel.

In Italian, voiceless consonants are never aspirated, as in German or English, unless emotional, poetical, or onomatopoetical reasons require it. In operatic singing, where strong projection is more important than in concert singing, some initial voiceless consonants — mostly f, p, and k — must receive strong stress in order to be heard. English-speaking singers must be constantly reminded of this, because they frequently neglect strong stress on these initial sounds.

The f sound. The f is a voiceless labiodental fricative sound. It is produced like its voiced counterpart (see p. 54). However, the upper teeth and the inside of the lower lip come together with more firmness. The small amount of air must emerge more suddenly, but without an explosion.

The stress on the f is soft between two vowels, and if it precedes another consonant, moderate if it follows another consonant.

> Urna *f*atale del mio destino (VERDI *La Forza del Destino*)
> O mio Rodol*f*o (PUCCINI *La Bohème*)
> Nin*f*e! El*f*i! Sil*f*i! (VERDI *Falstaff*)

Initial f without a preceding vowel in the same word should, as I said before, be stressed strongly in operatic singing.

> Finch'han dal vino (MOZART *Don Giovanni*)
> Credo con *f*ermio cuor (VERDI *Otello*)

The f also receives strong stress after exclamations like ah, oh, o, and deh.

> Ah *f*rate, *f*rate! (VERDI *La Forza del Destino*)

The s sound. The s is a voiceless dental-alveolar fricative sound. It is produced exactly as its voiced counterpart (pp. 54–55) except that the voiceless s is produced by letting out the stream of air suddenly, although with less explosion than a German or English voiceless s.

The initial s in Italian is voiceless before a vowel and before a voiceless consonant.

> Il dolce *s*uono (DONIZETTI *Lucia di Lammermoor*)
> Il *s*uo *s*temma (PUCCINI *Tosca*)
> A te la *s*pada io rendo (VERDI *Don Carlo*)
> *S*fogati, amazzami (MOZART *Don Giovanni*)

s in the middle of a word is voiceless before a voiceless consonant and following any consonant.

> Entrando per gli occhi, mi fe' *s*ospirar (LEGRENZI "Che Fiero Costume")
> Tal pen*s*iero perchè conturba ognor (VERDI *Rigoletto*)

The s receives medium stress at the beginning of a word and before and after consonants.

Like the z, s does not conform to an over-all rule of pronunciation. It varies according to geographical situations. Mese is pronounced [mezɛ] in northern Italy; in Tuscany the pronunciation varies between [meze] and [mesɛ] according to local differences; southern Italy almost always pronounces it [mesɛ] (with soft stress). It may be said, however, that modern diction tends to make the s between vowels voiceless, for instance in some root endings on -es and -os as in gelo*s*o, me*s*e, spe*s*e. But such words as paese and cortese, on the other hand, have the voiced [z].

The words casa, cosa, chiuso, and naso are also usually voiceless, but with very soft stress; otherwise they would sound like cassa, cossa, and so on. Until Italian phoneticists decide on an over-all rule for pronunciation of the s, the accompanist and coach will do well to ignore the regional variations and teach the above rules to their singers.

s between two vowels is voiceless and receives moderate stress in the case of word combinations like offria*s*i, chiude*s*i that stand for si offria, si chiude.

The p sound. The p is a voiceless bilabial occlusive sound. It is produced like the b (see p. 55) but with greater occlusion of the lips. For the operatic singing of initial occlusive voiceless sounds (p, t, k) I advocate slight explosion, since these sounds are sorely neglected by English-speaking singers and get lost in our opera houses and concert halls. They should, however, have a less explosive sound than their German counterparts. The pressure of the lips in forming the p must be firm, the release of air must be without aspiration. No breath should be allowed to escape.

The initial p receives a strong stress, the p between two vowels and before a consonant is stressed softly, p after a consonant receives moderate stress.

> O *p*atria mia (VERDI *Aïda*)
> A*p*erta! Arcangeli! (PUCCINI *Tosca*)
> A*p*rite! A*p*rite! (VERDI *Otello*)
> Em*p*ia razza (VERDI *Aïda*)

Some initial p's in phrasal connections are strongly stressed.

> Fra *pp*oco alla meco verrà (MOZART *Le Nozze di Figaro*)
> E *pp*oi? E *pp*oi? (VERDI *Otello*)

The t sound. The t is a voiceless dental occlusive sound, produced like the voiced d (see p. 55) except that the removal of the occlusion by the tongue has to be effected with more energy, less softness. The t must never be aspirated, like the German t, but a slight explosion of initial t's is recommended to insure clear diction and projection.

The initial t and the t after a consonant receive moderate stress; t between two vowels and before a consonant is stressed softly.

> O *t*erra addio (VERDI *Aïda*)
> Vissi d'ar*t*e (PUCCINI *Tosca*)
> E Silva non ri*t*orna (VERDI *Ernani*)
> Scorsa fu la notte al *t*ripudio (DONIZETTI *Lucia di Lammermoor*)

Some initial t's in phrasal connections receive strong stress, as in sò ttutto, così ttardi.

The [ts] (z) *sound.* This [ts] sound is a combination of the voiceless t and s sounds. It is expressed by the letter z, which in Italian can also be voiced and is, in that case, phonetically represented by [dz].

The [ts] is a voiceless, dental, semiocclusive sound. It starts the same way as the t, but the tongue cannot come down to a relaxed s position. The sides of the tongue touch the upper gum ridge, thus allowing the air to escape through a narrow passage. This is the reason why the [ts] is called semiocclusive. No hissing must occur in the pronunciation of the [ts].

As we said when discussing the [dz], no over-all rule exists concerning whether a z is pronounced voiced or voiceless. A good orthophonetic dictionary must be consulted in each case.

An initial z may be voiceless as in [ts]itto, [ts]io. z between vowels may be voiceless as in vi[ts]io, a[ts]ione, [ɛts]io. Likewise, z may be voiceless after consonants, as in sen[ts]a, Pin[ts]a, an[ts]i, al[ts]ati. The stress varies greatly. [ts] between vowels can be stressed strongly, whereas it receives moderate stress after another consonant.

> Alzati! là tuo figlio a te concedo riveder (VERDI *Un Ballo in Maschera*)
> La mia candida veste nuziale (VERDI *Otello*)

The [k] (c, ch) *sound.* The c and ch sounds expressed phonetically by [k] are voiceless, velar, occlusive sounds, produced like their voiced counterpart, the [g] (see p. 56) except that the contact between tongue and soft palate must be sudden and more firm. No aspiration is permissible and the resulting slight explosion should not be overdone, except on initial [k]'s for reasons of clarity.

The Italian c is pronounced [k] if it stands before a, o, or u. Before an e or i, a silent h is added to effect the same pronunciation, [k]. c before another consonant (l, r) is also pronounced [k].

[k] is stressed softly between two vowels, and before an r or l; moderately after another consonant.

> *C*aro mio ben (GIORDANI "Caro Mio Ben")
> *Ch*i va là (MOZART *Don Giovanni*)
> *Ch*e fai (PUCCINI *Tosca*)
> *C*ome va l'e*c*o della pia *c*ampana (CATALANI *La Wally*)
> Ell' è una mia *c*ugina (MOZART *Le Nozze di Figaro*)
> Per*ch*è me ne rimuneri *c*osì (PUCCINI *Tosca*)
> Mi *ch*iamano Mimi (PUCCINI *La Bohème*)
> È s*c*ritto (VERDI *La Forza del Destino*)

In some phrasal combinations the [k] receives reinforced stress, as in qualche ccosa.

The [kw] (qu) *sound.* The consonant q in Italian appears only in combination with the vowel u and is expressed, phonetically, by the symbol [kw]. The pronunciation corresponds exactly to the pronunciation of the Italian cu.

> *Qu*esto o *qu*ella (VERDI *Rigoletto*)
> *Qu*and' ero paggio (VERDI *Falstaff*)
> Ini*qu*o (VERDI *Rigoletto*)
> Per offrirvi l' ac*qu*a benedetta (PUCCINI *Tosca*)

The stress is soft between two vowels, moderate after another consonant.

The [ks] (x) *sound.* The x is a combination of voiceless k and s sounds. In Italian, it appears only in foreign words, as in Xidias. Usually the x is supplanted by z, s, or ss.

The [tʃ] *sound.* The [tʃ] sound is a voiceless alveolar-palatal semiocclusive sound, corresponding to the ch in the English words chur*ch*, fet*ch*. Its production is the same as for voiced [dʒ] (see p. 56) except that the occlusion and subsequent release have to be somewhat firmer. But there must be no explosion. The [tʃ] sound in Italian is as gentle as its voiceless quality will allow.

[tʃ] is pronounced when a c stands in front of an e or i. If the same sound is desired before an a, o, or u, a silent i has to be interpolated (cia, cio, ciu).

[tʃ] receives soft stress between two vowels, moderate stress after another consonant.

> Ha *c*iascun i suoi gusti (MOZART *Le Nozze di Figaro*)
> Burro e ca*c*io (PUCCINI *La Bohème*)
> Pa*c*e, pa*c*e (VERDI *La Forza del Destino*)
> Scuoti quelli fronti di *c*iliege (PUCCINI *Madama Butterfly*)
> La *c*iurma, ovè (PONCHIELLI *La Gioconda*)

Sometimes a mute i is also put between a c and an e, as in cieca or cielo. The pronunciation is the same as if it were spelled ce.

Cielo e mar (PONCHIELLI *La Gioconda*)

The [ʃ] *sound.* The [ʃ] sound corresponds to the English sh. It is a voiceless alveolar-palatal fricative sound and not a combination of consonants. It is produced by the upward-curled tip of the tongue which approaches but does not touch the hard palate, well back of the upper gum ridge. At the same time, the side edges of the tongue should be anchored against the upper molars and the lips should be rounded but motionless. After this procedure the air stream is gently exploded. [ʃ] is spelled sc before an e and i, and sci before a, o, and u. It is stressed moderately after a consonant and strongly between two vowels and as the initial sound of a word.

Non fate *sc*ene qui (PUCCINI *La Bohème*)
Brutto *sc*imiotto (ROSSINI *Il Barbiere di Siviglia*)
*Sci*agurato! Così del mio cor gioco ti prendi (MOZART *Don Giovanni*)
Siamo all' *asci*utto (PUCCINI *La Bohème*)

A mute i is sometimes interjected between [ʃ] and e, as in scienza (although this word, if spelled sci̇enza, ought to be pronounced [ʃ]i-en-tsa). Otherwise the pronunciation of these words is identical with sce.

The [sk] *sound.* sc before an a, o, and u is pronounced [sk]. If the same pronunciation is desired before an e or i, an h must be interjected before the vowel (sch).

Come *sc*oglio (MOZART *Così fan tutte*)
Ti crucci d'uno *sc*acco (PUCCINI *Manon Lescaut*)
Tu dormi in *sc*uderia (VERDI *Rigoletto*)
La *sch*iena oggi vi prude (LEONCAVALLO *Pagliacci*)
È *sch*erzo, è follia (VERDI *Un Ballo in Maschera*)

The h *sound.* The h in Italian is *always* silent be it at the beginning of a word, in its middle, or at the end, as in ho, hanno, chi, paghi, oh, deh.

Fame non *h*o (PUCCINI *Tosca*)
Ch' *h*ai di nuovo, buffon (VERDI *Rigoletto*)

DOUBLE CONSONANTS

The difference between single and double consonants in Italian is most important. A single consonant is always pronounced gently, with different degrees of stress — soft, moderate, and only sometimes strong. Double consonants are always stressed strongly. Distinctive pronunciation of a double consonant is the only way to mark the difference between similarly spelled words: eco-ecco, caro-carro, fato-fatto, rida-ridda, casa-cassa, pala-palla, nono-nonno, fumo-fummo, quadro-soqquadro, regia-reggia, papa-pappa, libra-libbra, tufo-tuffo, lego-leggo.

Voiced double consonants are ll, mm, nn, rr, gg, ([ddʒ]), bb, dd, gg, zz ([ddz]), ggh, vv; voiceless: cc ([ttʃ]) or cch ([kk]), ff, pp, ss, tt, cqu, or qqu ([kkw]).

Double consonants are pronounced like one prolonged consonant and are not divided into two consonants. Double consonants in Italian shorten the preceding vowel but do not necessarily open closed vowels as they do in German.

CLOSED VOWELS: Povero Rigoletto (VERDI *Rigoletto*)
Sei buona, o mia Mus*e*tta (PUCCINI *La Bohème*)
OPEN VOWELS: Attendi frat[ɛ]llo (VERDI *Rigoletto*)

The voiced double consonants can fulfill an important vocal function. They can carry the vocal line from vowel to vowel. Double consonants give more intensity, impetus, and importance to the words that contain them. While all double consonants are being drawn to the succeeding tone, the voiced consonant ought to receive some portion of singing sound. This holds true especially for the ll, mm, nn, rr, and vv sounds (Figs. 33, 34).

Figure 33. Mozart, *Le Nozze di Figaro*

Figure 34. Verdi, *Rigoletto*

The occlusive and semiocclusive double consonants, voiced and voiceless — bb, dd, gg, pp, tt, cc ([kk]), zz ([tts]), and [ddz], qqu ([kkw]), cc ([ttʃ]), gg ([ddʒ]) — are produced in the following way: the tongue and lips form the double consonant at the end of the preceding tone, *but without pronouncing it.* After a split second, air is exploded gently and the occlusion is ended while the speech apparatus slides over to the succeeding vowel. A minute interruption of the vocal line thus is inevitable but serves to stress the double consonant (Figs. 35–38).

Figure 35. Verdi, *Aïda*

Figure 36. Verdi, *Il Trovatore*

Figure 37. Puccini, *La Bohème*

Figure 38. Puccini, *La Bohème*

There is only one example of a qqu (double consonant with following semivowel) in the Italian language. It appears in the word soqquadro (Fig. 39).

Figure 39. Verdi, *La Forza del destino,* an example of the only qq in Italian

Some Italian words end in l, m, n, and r. If these final consonants are followed by words beginning with the same consonant they will sound like double consonants and should be treated as such.

> Or lasciami a*l l*avoro (PUCCINI *Tosca*)
> Andia*m m*aestro (BOITO *Mefistofele*)
> Disperda il cie*l* [ʎ]i affanni (VERDI *Otello*)
> Vile so*n n*ato (VERDI *Otello*)
> Pe*r r*idurre un geloso allo sbaraglio (PUCCINI *Tosca*)

COMBINATIONS OF CONSONANTS

Combinations of consonants exist in Italian, although it has fewer than any other language. They do not present insurmountable difficulties for the English-speaking singer. Some combinations may be initial, as in words beginning with bl, br, cl, cr; some in combinations of three consonants, as in words starting with sbl, sbr, scl, scr, sdr, sfr, sgr, spl, spr. Other combinations — as in bbl, bbr, ccl, ccr, ddr, ffl, ffr — can be found only in the middle of a word. There may also be combinations of final consonants (l, m, n, r) with initial ones: mc, mgl, ngl, nm, rgl, and others.

In all these combinations of consonants the musical sound falls on the preceding vowel and the combination of consonants is drawn to the next vowel, which receives the next musical sound. Since only a minimum amount of time should be lost in pronouncing the consonant combination in order not to interrupt the vocal line, the accompanist or coach must impress upon the singer the necessity of enunciating these consonant combinations lightly and rapidly.

LIAISON AND SEPARATION

The great majority of Italian words end in vowels. Many words start with vowels. In singing, these final and initial vowels must be connected by liaison. The rules of the liaisons of different vowels are most important and must be completely understood by the accompanist or coach. Musically, these vowel connections are usually expressed by only one note. The reason for this is that the Italian language normally connects vowels, and any Italian does it naturally.

I have shown how to sing diphthongs and triphthongs. Connected vowels are sung very similarly. The stressed vowel gets the greater part of the value of the musical note, the unstressed vowel has to be content with a smaller part.

LIAISONS OF IDENTICAL VOWELS

If two words are connected by final and initial vowels, identical in print if not in sound, the liaison will simply have the effect of a prolonged vowel sound. If the phonetic values of these two vowels are different (one short, one long) the resulting liaison has the sound of the long vowel.

> Bell*a a*dorata (VERDI *Don Carlo*)
> E sento il fang*o o*rdinario in me (VERDI *Otello*)
> Nobili sens*i i*n vero (VERDI *La Traviata*)

In evaluating the length that each vowel receives in combinations of different vowels, one will have to take several elements into consideration. Firstly, if one of the two or more vowels is long and closed, it will receive the greater share of the value of the note and the other vowel or vowels the lesser. Secondly, the length of the musical note will determine whether the longer vowel is prolonged. If the note is very short or the tempo very fast, the time value of the musical note becomes so minute that both vowels may receive the same amount of time. Thirdly, accentuated vowels receive a greater share of the available musical note, unstressed ones a smaller one. Unaccentuated i's before an a, [ɛ], [o], or [ɔ] become half vowels. The vowel of an article is always shortened. The word è is always lengthened.

A few examples may suffice to illustrate these rules. It would be too ponderous to enumerate all possible

A Se il mio sogno si averasse

B Un solo istante i palpiti

C Largo al factotum

Figure 40. Examples of liaisons of two sounds.
A. Verdi, *Aïda.* B. Donizetti, *Elisir d'amore.*
C. Rossini, *Il Barbiere di Siviglia*

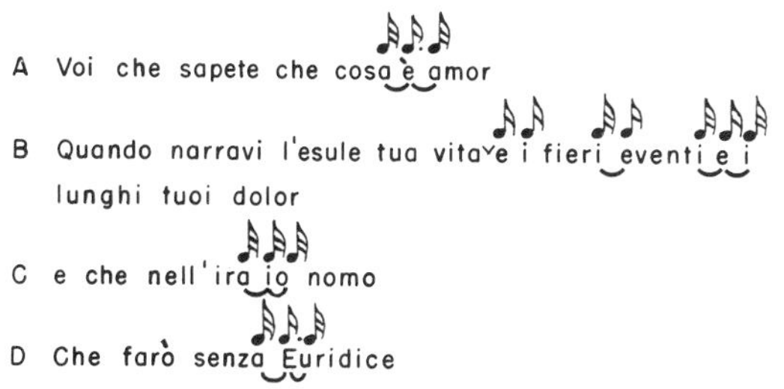

A Voi che sapete che cosa è amor

B Quando narravi l'esule tua vita e i fieri eventi e i
   lunghi tuoi dolor

C e che nell'ira io nomo

D Che farò senza Euridice

Figure 41. Examples of liaisons of three sounds.
A. Mozart, *Le Nozze di Figaro.* B. Verdi, *Otello.*
C. Verdi, *Otello.* D. Gluck, *Orfeo ed Euridice*

combinations which serve as liaisons. Figure 40 shows liaisons of two sounds, Figure 41 liaisons of three.

Sometimes, although rarely, final and initial vowels should be separated. There are several reasons for this. First, punctuation sometimes forces a separation instead of liaison. Generally the composer will write separate notes, but it may happen that he trusts to the understanding of coaches and singers, as in Figure 42. Here the comma as well as the phrasing make the change to the rendering shown in Figure 43 preferable. In Figure 44, the liaison must be interrupted, according to the logical declamation of the sentence and the e has to be separated from the o and tied to i.

U - mi - li e si - len - zio - se, ad u - na te - ne - rez - za

Figure 42. Puccini, *Tosca,* phrase as written

zio - se, ad u - na te - ne -

Figure 43. Puccini, *Madama Butterfly,* phrase as
it should be sung

Io qui mi strug - go e in - tan - to d'al - tra in

bra - ccio le mie sma - nie de - ri - de!

Figure 44. Puccini, *Madama Butterfly*

Secondly, for reasons of phrasing: if a musical phrase is too long, the singer must take a breath somewhere. It may be that must happen where a liaison would otherwise be made (Fig. 45), but here the phrase is simply too long to be sung in one breath. The accompanist or coach is therefore justified in changing the phrase as shown in Figure 46.

e al vo - stro pre - go be - ni - gna - men - te op -

por - re il mio ri - fiu - to.

Figure 45. Puccini, *Manon Lescaut,*
phrase as written

be - ni - gna - men - te op - por - re

Figure 46. Puccini, *Manon Lescaut,*
phrase as it should be sung

Sometimes the separation (hiatus) is optional and depends on the singer's vocal abilities. Rodolfo's and Marcello's duet in Act 4 of *La Bohème* ends as shown in Figure 47. If the singers can muster a beautiful diminuendo on the fermata tone, the vowels could be divided as shown in Figure 48. The breath should be an expression breath to portray the Bohemians' nostalgia and resignation — although not too much time should be lost in breathing. The fermata tone should be held very long, diminish, and end in the finest possible pianissimo. Some conductors, it must be said, frown upon such a change.

Rod.: poi - chè è mor - to a - mor.
Mar.: e a - spet - ta il vil mio   cuor.

Figure 47. Puccini, *La Bohème,* phrase as written

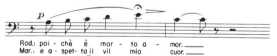

Rod.: poi - chè è mor - to   a - mor.
Mar.: e a - spet - ta il vi - le mio cuor.

Figure 48. Puccini, *La Bohème,* phrase
as it might be sung

Thirdly, strong rhythmic or dramatic impetus may, in very rare cases, force the singer to separate final and initial vowels which would otherwise be connected (Fig. 49). Puccini asks that this be sung "with great passion," drama so strong that the liaison would not do it justice. It is therefore proper to disconnect the two

Figure 49. Puccini, *Tosca*, phrase as written

Figure 50. Puccini, *Tosca*, phrase as
it should be sung

Figure 51. Puccini, *Manon Lescaut*

vowels, divide the eighth note into two sixteenth notes, and breathe between (Fig. 50).

Fourth, in turns or other embellishments that are written on a liaison, the two vowels must be distributed according to natural diction (Fig. 51).

OMISSION AND DISTRIBUTION OF VOWELS

Omission and distribution of vowels are bad habits of teachers and singers. Since the connection of some vowels, especially at faster tempi, is difficult and demands special effort, many coaches simply tell their charges to omit some of the vowels. Such an omission does not conform to the composer's wishes and is almost always avoidable. The only time vowels may (but need not) be omitted is when the abbreviation does not change the meaning of the phrase. Otherwise, omitting vowels or distributing them among different musical notes should be avoided.

Figure 52. A melisma

Figure 53. Same notes, sung on separate syllables

Figure 54. Mozart, *Don Giovanni*, passage as written

All vocal music contains melismas, meaning that more than one musical note is written over one syllable or one vowel. The notation for a melisma shows a connection between the musical notes (Fig. 52). If each note were to be sung on a separate syllable the notation would be as shown in Figure 53. Similarly, in the passage from

Don Giovanni shown in Figure 54, Mozart definitely wanted the liaison on bottead sung on the first of the two sixteenth notes; otherwise, he would have notated as shown in Figure 55. In the same aria, a few measures

Figure 55. Mozart, *Don Giovanni*, passage as
it should not be sung

Figure 56. Mozart, *Don Giovanni*, passage as written

Figure 57. Mozart, *Don Giovanni*, passage as
it should not be sung

Figure 58. Mozart, *Don Giovanni*, passage as written

later, Zerlina should sing the passage as shown in Figure 56, and not as shown in Figure 57. Still later, she should sing the passage as shown in Figure 58. Many singers, even in the best opera houses, sing phrases from this as shown in Figures 59 and 60. There is not the slightest need for such a change. It simply loses Mozart's melismatic pattern of two connected and one separate eighth note in one place and of one separate and two connected eighths in the other place. Examples of this kind of wrong distribution can be found in performances of almost any composer's work, but the offense against Mozart is possibly the worst.

Figure 59. Mozart, *Don Giovanni*, phrase from passage
as it should not be sung

Figure 60. Mozart, *Don Giovanni*, phrase from passage
as it should not be sung

One more example: Puccini, in the third act of *La Bohème*, wrote the passage shown in Figure 61. Some singers separate the first three eighth notes of this phrase, giving each a separate syllable. They like to attack the

Figure 61. Puccini, *La Bohème*

vowel directly, which is definitely against Puccini's intention and can be avoided with a little practice.

I have now described the main features and problems of Italian phonetics and singing diction. As a postscript to this section, I here present two popular Italian arias transcribed into phonetic characters.

PHONETIC TRANSCRIPTION OF MIMI'S ARIA FROM THE FIRST ACT OF "LA BOHEME"

mi kja:manɔ mimi:, ma il mi:ɔ nnome ɛ ʎutʃi:a. la
storja mi:a ɛ bbrɛ:ve. a tela ɔ a seta rika:mɔ in ka:za ɔ
fwɔ:ri. sɔn trankwilla e ʎʎe:ta ed ɛ mmi:o zvagɔ far
dʒiʎʎi e rrɔze. mi pja:tʃʃon kwelle kɔze ke an si doltʃɛ
mali:a, kɛ pparlanɔ d'amo:r, di primave:re, kɛ pparlanɔ
di soɲi e di kime:re, kwelle kɔze kɛ an nnome poezi:a.
lei m'intɛndɛ?

mi kja:manɔ mimi:, il perke: nɔn sɔ. Sola, mi fɔ il
prantsɔ da mme ste:ssa. Non va:dɔ sempre a me:ssa ma
prego assai il siɲor. Vi:vɔ so:la, sole:tta, la in u:na
bjanka kamere:tta gwardɔ su:i te:tti e in tʃe:lɔ. ma
kwandɔ vjen lɔ zdʒe:lɔ il pri:mɔ so:le ɛ mmi:ɔ! il
pri:mɔ ba:tʃɔ dɛll' apri:le ɛ mmi:ɔ! il pri:mɔ so:le ɛ
mmi:ɔ! dʒermɔʎʎa in un va:zɔ una rɔza, ffoʎʎa a
ffoʎʎa la spi:ɔ! Kɔzi: dʒenti:l il profu:mɔ d'un fjor! Ma
i fjor ki:ɔ ffatʃtʃɔ ai mmɛ! non annɔ odore!

Altrɔ di mmɛ nɔn lɛ sapre:i narra:re. sonɔ la su:a
vitʃi:na ke la vvjen fwɔri do:ra a importuna:re.

PHONETIC TRANSCRIPTION OF GERMONT'S ARIA FROM THE SECOND ACT OF "LA TRAVIATA"

di provɛntsa il ma:r il swɔl ki dal kɔ:r ti kantʃello? ki
dal kɔ:r ti kantʃellɔ di provɛntsa il ma:r il swɔ:l? Al
nati:ɔ fuldʒɛ:ntɛ sol kwal desti:nɔ ti furɔ? o rrammenta
pu:r nel dwɔ:l ki:vi dʒɔ:ja a tɛ bbrillɔ, e kɛ ppa:tʃɛ kɔla
sol su tɛ ssplɛndere ankor pwɔ. di:ɔ mmi gwidɔ:!

a il tu:ɔ vekkjɔ dʒenitɔ:r tu non sa:i kwantɔ ssɔffri:!
Tɛllonta:nɔ, di skwallo:r il su:ɔ tetto si kɔpri:. ma ssɛ
alfi:n ti trovɔ ankor, sɛ in mɛ sspɛ:mɛ non falli:, sɛ lla
vo:tʃɛ dɛll' ono:r in tɛ appje:n non ammuti:, di:ɔ
mɛzaudi:!

LATIN PHONETICS AND DICTION

The vocal accompanist and coach, especially those who handle choirs, will frequently encounter sacred or secular Latin texts. There has always been great confusion about the way to pronounce Latin, each country pronouncing it according to its own diction: French Latin sounds thoroughly French; German Latin is pronounced differently in Austria and in Germany; English Latin assumes a very strange twang in the United States; and our English and Irish cousins pronounce it with a distinct accent of their own.

Only during the last few decades has a definite change taken place. Latin pronunciation has been established by the Roman Catholic Church for the whole Roman Catholic world and lay people have accepted the Church's ruling.

The first edict of a pope concerning this matter was issued in 1903. Pius X, who in his "Motu Proprio" had initiated a complete reform of church music, decided also to admonish his priests to pronounce the Latin exactly like the Italian, and, more correctly, like the Roman pronunciation of Italian. These reforms took time to seep down to the lower levels of the Church.

In 1912, Pius X wrote to Louis Du Bois, Archbishop of Bourges, saying: "We learn . . . with real pleasure that this reform has already spread to a number of places and been successfully introduced into many cathedral churches, seminaries and colleges and even into simple country churches. The question of the pronunciation of Latin is closely tied up with that of the restoration of the Gregorian Chant, the constant subject of Our thoughts, and recommendations from the very beginning of Our Pontificate. The accent and pronunciation of Latin had great influence on the melodic and rhythmic formation of the Gregorian phrase and consequently it is important that these melodies should be rendered in the same manner in which they were artistically conceived at their first beginning. Finally the spread of the Roman pronunciation will have the further advantage . . . of consolidating more and more the work of liturgical union in France, a unity to be accomplished by the happy return to Roman liturgy and Gregorian Chant. This is why We desire that the movement of return to the Roman pronunciation of Latin should continue with the same zeal and consoling success which has marked its progress hitherto."

In 1919, the Cardinal Secretary of State, Gasparri, wrote to an abbot in Spain: "In His unending solicitude the Holy Father has not lost sight of the happy and timely initiative taken by you a few years ago by your introduction in your Monastery of the Roman pronunciation of Latin in order to bring about the desired uniformity.

"His Holiness, having resolved to insist on this point in Spain and in other countries, would be very happy to learn what reception has been given to this wise reform . . ."

And on November 30, 1928, Pope Pius XI wrote to the same Louis Du Bois, who in the meantime had become a Cardinal and the Archbishop of Paris:

". . . We also esteem very greatly your plan of urging all who come under your jurisdiction to pronounce Latin *more romano*. Not content like Our predecessors of happy memory, Pius X and Benedict XV, simply to approve his pronunciation of Latin, We, Ourselves, express the keenest desire that all bishops *of every nation* shall endeavor to adopt it when carrying out the liturgical ceremonies." (Italics mine.)

If Latin singing diction is to be exactly the same as Italian singing diction, clearly all phonetic rules for Italian remain valid for Latin. There are, however, a few additional sounds in Latin which must be dealt with briefly.

The y is pronounced as i.

The semivowel [j] is pronounced the same way as in the Italian word ieri which in earlier days was spelled jeri.

The diphthongs ae and oe are pronounced like the Italian [ɛ].

Dies ir*ae*, dies illa solvet saecula in favilla.
C*oe*lum et terrae ([tʃɛ:lum et tɛrrɛ])

The double consonant x [ks] is encountered frequently. It is pronounced like a voiced g and z in initial syllable sounds when it is preceded by an e and followed by another vowel, or when an h or s is interjected between the x and the following vowel.

Domine e*x*audi orationem meam ([ɛgzaudi])

In all other cases the x is pronounced like voiceless k and s.

Gloria in e*x*celsis Deo ([ɛkstʃɛlsis])

The h is a frequent initial sound in Latin, but according to the pope's ruling it must be mute, exactly as it is in Italian.

Some oratorios and operatic works written in Latin use the Greek pronunciation, which is the pronunciation taught in German high schools and colleges. For instance, Stravinsky's *Oedipus Rex* and some of Orff's compositions are expressly spelled in the Greek manner. Since the musical idea was conceived in that way, the accompanist or coach should not Italianize pronunciation.

The following example of phonetic spelling of the "Dies Irae" should suffice to make the *more romano* pronunciation altogether clear to the accompanist and coach.

PHONETIC TRANSCRIPTION OF "DIES IRAE"

di:es i:rɛ, di:es illa, sɔlvet sɛklum in favi:lla: teste da:vid kum sibi:lla. kwantus tremɔr ɛst futu:rus, kwandɔ ju:deks ɛst ventu:rus kunkta striktɛ diskusu:rus! tu:ba mi:rum spardʒens sɔ:num per sepulkra redʒio:num, kɔdʒet ɔmnɛs antɛ tro:num.

mɔrs stupe:bit et natu:ra, kum rɛsurdʒet kreatu:ra, judikanti responsu:ra.

li:bɛr skriptus profɛre:tur, in kwo tɔtum cɔntine:tur, undɛ mundus juditʃe:tur.

ju:deks ɛrgɔ kum sɛde:bit kwidkwid la:tɛt appare:bit, nil inultum rɛmane:bit.

kwid sum mi:zer tunk diktu:rus? kum viks justus sit sɛku:rus.

rɛks trɛmendɛ: majesta:tis, kwi salvandis salvas gra:tis.

salva me, fons pieta:tis.

rɛkorda:rɛ je:zu pi:ɛ, kwɔd sum kau:za tuɛ vi:ɛ nɛ me pɛrdas illa di:ɛ.

kwɛrens mɛ, sɛdisti lassus: rɛdɛmisti krutʃem passus: tantus la:bɔr non sit kassus.

justɛ ju:deks ultsio:nis, do:num fak rɛmissio:nis; antɛ di:em ratsio:nis.

indʒemi:skɔ, tamkwam re:us, kulpa ru:bɛt vultus me:us supplikanti partʃe de:us.

kwi mari:am abzɔlvi:sti, et latro:num ɛgzaudi:sti mi:i kwokwɛ spem dɛdi:sti.

pretʃes me:ɛ non sunt diɲɛ; zed tu bo:nus fak beni:ɲe, ne perɛnni kre:mer iɲe.

intɛr o:vɛs lo:kum pre:sta, et ab ɛdis me sɛkwe:stra sta:tuɛns in partɛ dɛkstra. kɔnfuta:tis malɛdi:ktis, flammis a:kribus addi:ktis, vo:ka me kum benedi:ktis.

orɔ supplɛks et akkli:nis, kɔr kɔntri:tum kwa:zi tʃi:nis, dʒe:rɛ ku:ram me:i fi:nis.

lakrimo:za di:es illa, kwa: rɛsurdʒet ɛks favilla.

judikandus o:mɔ re:us, u:ik ɛrgɔ partʃe de:us.

pi:ɛ je:zu do:minɛ, do:na e:is re:kwiɛm. a:mɛn.

French
Phonetics and Diction

FRENCH is a much more complicated language, phonetically, than Italian. This will become evident to anybody who compares the number of phonetic vowel sounds. There are sixteen such sounds in French, fifteen in English, fourteen in German, seven in Italian.

The English-speaking singer will find the whole group of vowels, as well as the array of velar (nasal) sounds which are so characteristic of the French, difficult to master. Other problems, to name but a few, are the h and r sounds, the semivowels, and the liaisons.

A conscientious accompanist and coach must have a thorough working knowledge of French, the product of long study under qualified observation, and must continue to practice self-observation. As in all phonetic studies, a tape recorder will be very helpful to him. With it, he can not only listen to his own diction but demonstrate faulty pronunciation to a singer and thus make him aware of the correct pronunciation.

Speaking and singing diction are even more different from each other in French than in Italian. The greater number of vowels plus the nasal sounds, the r, and many other French phonetic qualities require adjustment when sung. The intelligent French artist himself sings his language differently from the way he speaks it. As in Italian, the vast number of regional dialects forces the singer to accept a uniform pronunciation. I have chosen the French of the cultured Parisian (not the slang or argot) as the best standard for singing in French. This may be exemplified by the manner of pronouncing the r. For vocal purposes, the nasal sounds must also be adjusted. If the velum is lowered too much, as it is in speaking, the resonance switches from the mouth to the nose and an uneven, exaggerated way of singing

French words results. Moreover open and closed vowels must fit the vocal line, especially in classical music. Nothing is worse than to change vocal color from tone to tone, as spoken diction sometimes warrants.

In general, it may be said that French singing diction conforms to the rules of the Italian bel canto — with the unavoidable exceptions, of course, that result from the peculiarities of the French language. Correct pronunciation of French sounds is indispensable in order to avoid misunderstanding such words as pécheur-pêcheur, poison-poisson, près-prêt-pré, and many others.

VOWELS

The great number of French vowels necessitates a keen ear and a willing tongue. The differences are small. Examples must be well chosen by the accompanist and coach. Special care must be taken to explain to the singer the function of the three written accents.

French linguists differentiate several a's which — for singing purposes — they simplify to an anterior and a posterior sound. This classification is highly misleading, because every singer will associate the word posterior with backward production, which is always undesirable vocally. Every a must be pronounced forward. The difference lies in the position of lips, tongue, and jaw. The spot where a French a should be produced in singing is exactly where the Italian a is situated and the mode of production is the same. (See p. 48.) I shall distinguish, however, between long a and short a.

The long a sound. The a is long in final syllables ending in -ar, -are, -arre, -age, -ave, -asion, -assion, -ation.

Mets-le vite à ton cors*a*ge. Il est fait à ton im*a*ge (DE-BUSSY "Fleurs des blés")

Mais n'apportant de p*a*ssion profonde, qu'à s'adorer (FAURE "Au Bord de l'eau")

It is long and less open in final syllables ending in -ase, -aze, -able, -acle, -asse, and in words like mac*a*bre and s*a*bre when the final r is preceded by a voiced consonant.

C'est l'ext*a*se langoureuse (DEBUSSY song)
De sa dent soudaine et vor*a*ce (DUPARC "Le Manoir de Rosemonde")

In words like place, masse, and chasse, the a is short. This is an exception to the above rule.

Pl*a*ce, pl*a*ce au seigneur Alcade (BIZET *Carmen*)
La nuit qui tombe et ch*a*sse la troupe (DEBUSSY "Chevaux de bois")

â (with circumflex accent) is also long and comparatively closed as in mâtin, pâle, grâce.

In endings on -âmes, -âtes, and -ât the a is short.

a is long but open in nouns and adjectives derived from or composed by the syllable -as, as in l*a*s, l*a*sser, p*a*s (step), p*a*sser, etc.

Tes beaux yeux sont l*a*s, pauvre amante (DEBUSSY "Le Jet d'eau")

In endings on -as of the second person singular the a is short as in tu viendr*a*s.

a is long and rather closed in some words on -as, such as the adverb pas (not), parias, bras, chas.

Je lui disais: Tu m'aimer*a*s.
Aussi longtemps que tu pourr*a*s.
Je ne dormais bien qu'en ses br*a*s (CHAUSSON "Chanson perpetuelle")
Fille du Pari*a* (DELIBES *Lakmé*)

The a is also long in words like casser, classe, tasse, damner, condamner (the m is mute in these last two words).

Que la sort te cond*a*mne (GOUNOD *Faust*)

The a is also long in endings on -ail and -aille, as in taille, bataille, etc.

Aux vautours, il faut la bat*a*ille, pour frapper d'estoc et de t*a*ille (GOUNOD *Roméo et Juliette*)

The word médaille is an exception. Its a is short.

O sainte méd*a*ille (GOUNOD *Faust*)

a followed by a single n or m in the same syllable changes to the nasal [ã].

a's must be sung long but very open before a final r, z, or v, as in rare, sage, cave.

The short a *sound.* The short open a is found in words in which the a has an accent grave as in voilà, là, déjà, holà, etc.

Ils ont fui les longs soirs moroses déj*à* le jardin parfumé (CHAMINADE "Viens, mon bien-aimé")

In endings on -ac, -ak, and -aque.

Et dans les fl*a*ques d'eau retentissaient mes pas (POULENC "Air romantique")
Et ses jambs faisaient clic-cl*a*c (OFFENBACH *Les Contes d'Hoffmann*)

In endings on -at, -atte, -ap, -ape, -appe, -af, -afe, -aphe, -ache.

Votre tourterelle vous éch*a*ppera (GOUNOD *Roméo et Juliette*)
On viendra l'arr*a*cher (MASSENET *Manon*)

Final a's, as in ma, ta, la, va, sera are short and open. The a in monosyllabic words such as car, bal, mal is also short.

Je suis le spectre de la rose que tu portais au b*a*l (BERLIOZ *Le Spectre de la rose*)
Et cependant, c'est m*a*l (MASSENET *Manon*)

The a in août is mute.

The e *sounds.* For singing purposes we have to differentiate between three e sounds with three subtypes (not counting diphthongs and nasal sound combinations). These are the wide-open e [ɛ], the open e [ɛ], the intermediate e [ɛ], the closed e, the weak e [ə], and the mute e [ə].

In French singing diction, the ê and è sounds are not quite the same. The ê sound should be even more open than the open è vowel. Both are expressed phonetically by the symbol [ɛ].

The wide-open e *sound.* The wide-open e is encountered in words spelled with ê (circumflex accent). It is pronounced somewhat like — in an exaggerated way — the English bad. Words pronounced thus are tête, mêler, bête, rêve, naître.

Je r*ê*ve aux amours défunts (DEBUSSY "Nuits d'étoiles")
Ta fen*ê*tre vide où ne brille plus ta t*ê*te charmante et ton doux sourire (CHAUSSON "Printemps triste")

The open e *sound.* The open e is found in words with è (grave accent), as in près, succès, père, mère, also in maire, chaise, etc. It matches exactly the Italian [ɛ] but in a somewhat exaggerated way. Also in monosyllables mes, tes, ses, les, es, when sung; in endings on -et, -ets, -ect.

The conjunction et (and) is an exception. The e is

closed. Similarly, e is closed in some words like Nazareth.

> Du temps de nos pères, des blancs descendirent dans cette île (RAVEL "Chansons madécasses")
> Tes yeux, tes traîtres yeux sont clos (D'INDY "Lied Maritime")
> Qu'elle puisse connaître l'émoi qu'elle fait naître (GOUNOD Faust)

Generally, it can be said that the e in French is always open in words with syllables that end with a consonant whether this consonant is pronounced or just expressed by spelling, with the exception of syllables ending in -ez or -er (which have a closed e).

The wide open and open e's are long before final r, [z], [ʒ], and v when they are pronounced, as in colère, aise, neige, paisible, seize.

> Puis, chez nous, tout heureux, tout aises (BERLIOZ "Villanelle")
> Il neige, il neige (BEMBERG "Il neige")
> Et vous, paisibles vallons, adieu (TCHAIKOVSKY Jeanne d'Arc)

e is short before all other consonants that appear in the same syllable. This is also true for the vowel combinations ai, aî, ei, and ey, which are pronounced like open e's.

The words aile, aime, and baisse are long.

> Je t'aime et meurs, ô mes amours, Mon âme en baisers m'est ravie (FAURE "Lydia")
> Mon bonheur renaît sous ton aile (BACHELET "Chère Nuit")

The intermediate e sound. The intermediate e, still expressed phonetically by [ɛ], is somewhat less open than the [ɛ] in père. Its English counterpart may be found in the words set and bell. In French, it is pronounced when an e is found before two or three consonants, as in descendre, faible, laisser, parfait, merci, peste, permettre, espoir, terminer.

> Bon Saint Michel veuillez descendre (RAVEL "Chanson épique")
> La peste! Décidément vous avez la main leste (BIZET Carmen)

The e is also intermediate in endings on -ec, -ef, -el, -elle, -em, -en, -ex, as in avec, chef, harem, etc., when the final consonant is pronounced.

> Le mien devient un chef fameux (BIZET Carmen)
> Leurs becs sont aiguisés (GOUNOD Roméo et Juliette)

In the word clef the f is mute and the e, therefore, changes into a closed e.

> Voici la clef, je croix (GOUNOD Faust)

The e is also intermediate in Noël.

> Voici Noël petits enfants (WEKERLIN "Voici Noël")

e followed by a single m or n in the syllable changes to the nasal sounds [ɛ̃] or [ã]. The intermediate e is always short.

e in the middle of a word followed by mm, nm, or nn sometimes changes into a short a as in femme, prudemment, indemnite, solenelle. In other such cases the e does not change, as in ennemi, where it becomes intermediate or in ennui where it changes into the nasal [ã] sound.

> Mais viendra le jour des adieux car il faut que les femmes pleurent (FAURE "Les Berceaux")

Faisons, and all imperfect forms such as faisais, have the weak e [ə].

The closed (é) [e] sound. The term "closed e" should not be taken to mean that the throat must close in order to produce it. It is only relatively more closed than the [ɛ]'s. The lower jaw is extended slightly less downward. But the accompanist and coach must take pains to make sure that the singer does not "spread" the sound. The tongue should still be low and the corners of the lips should not be extended outward. This closed e sound exists in English, as in the words chaotic and chaos, but it is difficult for an English-speaking singer, and one hears more faulty pronunciation of this than of any other vowel. This is especially true for verb endings on -er.

German-speaking singers have no difficulty at all with the closed e. It is exactly the same as in the word leben. The Italians use it in their words eh' and deh.

The closed e in French is usually expressed by é (acute accent), as in blé, désir, été.

> Dans ton coeur dort un clair de lune
> Un doux clair de lune d'été (DUPARC "Chanson triste")
> O grands désirs, inapaisés (BERLIOZ "Absence")

The e is also closed in nouns and adjectives ending on -er and -ier where the r is mute.

> J'avais tes cheveux comme un collier noir autour de ma nuque et sur ma poitrine (DEBUSSY "La Chevelure")
> Oh que ton jeune amour, ce papillon léger (FAURE "Les Roses d'Ispahan")

If the r is pronounced, the e changes to an intermediate [ɛ], as in hier, mer, cher, and enfer.

> Elle à la mer, nous au tombeau (DEBUSSY "Beau Soir")
> Le ciel, l'enfer ce que tu veux (PIERNE "A Lucette")

In verb endings of the first conjugation on -er and -ier (parler and prier), the e is also closed.

> Et mes mains sont lasses de pri*er* (DEBUSSY "De Fleurs")
> J'irai dans*er* la Séguédille (BIZET *Carmen*)

If the final r must be sounded because of a liaison, the e before becomes an intermediate [ɛ].

> Les deux oiseaux siffl*er* et chant*er* à la fois (DEBUSSY "Voici que le Printemps")

In endings on -ez, -ied, -ieds, if the final consonants are mute as in nez, assez, croyez, pied, assieds, the e is closed.

> Son pi*ed* sur le clair parquet (MASSENET "Première Danse")

If the final consonant is pronounced, the e changes into an intermediate [ɛ] as in Cortez.

The weak e [ə] *sound.* The weak e has no direct counterpart in English. It is similar to the e sound in herb, but produced more forward and without any trace of the following r. It is also similar to the short ö in German, but it is weaker and less stressed. The weak e is produced with slightly protruding and rounded lips with the tongue's sides curling upward.

The e is weak in syllables ending with e, as in je, te, ce, de, retour, venir, ceci, cela, dehors.

> Va! j*e* t*e* hais (BIZET *Carmen*)
> Carmen! Carmencita! C*e*la r*e*vient au même (BIZET *Carmen*)

If re- as an initial syllable followed by two or three consonants is not a prefix but belongs to the root of the word, the e has the intermediate sound, as in respirer, ressuciter.

The mute e [ə] *sound.* The mute e is only a subtype of the weak e. This also extends to the plural of verbs and adjectives on -es, as in mèr(es), ell(es), and the second person singular and the third person plural of verbs on -es and -ent, as in tu aim(es), ils aim(ent).

Accompanists and coaches must clear up confusion among their pupils about the ending on -ent of adverbs or nouns which are pronounced with nasal en (notablement, moment) and the third person plural endings of verbs which are mute—ils aim(ent), ils aimai(ent), aimèr(ent), aimerai(ent), aimass(ent).

In speech there are many very complicated rules covering when a [ə] should or should not be pronounced—i.e., when it becomes mute. In singing diction these rules become more or less simplified by the way the

composers handle the [ə]. It is most frequently found in endings — mère, elle, porte, j'aime, etc. None of these final e's is pronounced in everyday speech. They must be pronounced, however, in singing if they are placed under a long note or under a note which differs from the preceding note (see Figs. 62 and 63). Otherwise, the

Figure 62. Bizet, *Carmen*, example of a mute e which must be sung

Figure 63. Massenet, *Thaïs*, example of a mute e which must be sung

e is mute. But here a distinction must be made between classical and modern music. In classical music, final e's even on short notes or on the same pitch as the preceding note should still get a very small amount of sound. This sound had best be given to the preceding consonant, as in the carefully spoken English words, soun*d*, la*g*. But even voiceless consonants should receive a little of the mute e in classical music. Weak final e's following another vowel as in poupée, bleue, vie, rue, receive the same treatment; the music will decide whether or not it should become mute (Fig. 64).

Figure 64. Debussy, "Nous n'avons pas de maison"

Things are different in modern music. Here, the final e may be entirely mute if put under the same short note (Fig. 65). Within a sentence, the e which is frequently mute in speaking can also become mute or be elided in singing, mostly in operettas, popular music, or music with a strong colloquial flavor (Figs. 66–68).

Figure 65. Poulenc, "L'Écrevisses"

Figure 66. Offenbach, *Madame L'Archiduc*

Figure 67. Charpentier, *Louise*

Figure 68. Charpentier, *Louise*

Under all circumstances the [ə] must be pronounced in monosyllables which are followed by an aspirated h and cannot, therefore, be connected by liaison, as in le héro. The [ə] is also pronounced lightly before the word rien, as in je ne demande rien. When the [ə] stands between two consonants on one side and one consonant on the other side, it must always be pronounced for euphonic reasons, as in "Voici notre repas," from Massenet's *Manon*.

The mute e may be called elided if not even a trace of it is retained in pronouncing a word. The e is always elided in words like eau, asseoir, tombeau, beaucoup, where the e is only an orthographic relic. The e is also elided when it stands between a [ʒ] sound and another vowel, as in affligeant, geôlier, Georges.

Le geôlier dort (GOUNOD *Faust*)

Final weak e is also elided when a liaison is made from it to another initial vowel.

La mer est infinie et mes rêves sont fous (FAURE "La Mer est infinie")

The eu [ø], [œ] *sounds.* The eu sounds are long and closed [ø], and short and open [œ]. Phonetically, they are not diphthongs but vowels. They are not found in English, but they exist in German as ö. They are produced in a way similar to the [ə] sound. Since their place in the phonetic diagram is halfway between e and o, they should be practiced by vocalizing an o and then protruding and rounding the lips, gradually changing into an [ø]. The same exercise should then be continued beginning with [ə] (with lips slightly less protruded) to an intermediate e (with lips relaxed). The same process may then be reversed — e to ə to ø to o.

The open eu [œ] is produced the same way except for a much larger rounded opening of the mouth and slight dropping of jaw and tongue (Fig. 19).

The closed eu [ø] *sound.* All [ø] sounds are to be pronounced long. This sound, which may also be spelled oeu, can be found in three places.

First, at the end of words (dieu, feu, jeu, peu, queue, bleue), or with a final mute consonant or consonants as in words ending in -eux, oeufs, boeufs, neufs (new), pleut, peut, monsieur, messieurs.

Secondly, it is found in endings followed by consonants

that are pronounced, as in jeûne, and in endings on -euse, -eute, and -eutre.

Ouvre tes yeux bleus ma mignonne (MASSENET "Ouvre tes yeux bleus")
Elle est dangereuse (BIZET *Carmen*)

Déjeune, which is derived from jeûne, is pronounced more open.

Thirdly, eu in the middle of a word is closed and long in words such as deuxième, lieutenant, bleuir, jeudi, meunier, and in adverbs ending in -eusement.

Mon officier n'est pas capitaine; pas même lieutenant (BIZET *Carmen*)
De blé le grenier est plein, le meunier fait sentinelle (PIERNE "Le Moulin")

The open eu [œ] *sound.* This sound is actually an intensified [ə] sound. It may also be spelled oeu. It is found and pronounced short in words where it is followed by the consonants f, g, l, n, p as in neuf (nine), oeuf (see exception in plural forms above), aveugle, seul, peuple, jeune.

Je suis seul! Seul enfin (MASSENET *Manon*)
Mais quelquefois le souvenir du jugement injuste et aveugle des hommes (MILHAUD "A la lune")

If followed by the consonants r and v, eu is still open but long, as in coeur, beurre, leur, sieur, pleure, soeur, oeuvre, fleuve, oeil, deuil.

Dans ton coeur dort un clair de lune (DUPARC "Chanson triste")
Il pleure dans mon coeur comme il pleut sur la ville (DEBUSSY "Il pleure dans mon coeur")

In heureux ([œrø:]), the first syllable is slightly less open than in heure.

Forms of the verb avoir spelled with eu elide the e, such as in j'eus (pronounced [ʒy]), eu ([y]), j'eusse, etc.

J'eus un moment de tristesse (MASSENET *Manon*)

The i *and* y *sound.* The French i, in some cases spelled y, is a closed vowel. That does not mean — I must stress this again and again — that its production by a singer requires closing the throat. There just is no other term that would describe as well the function of some sounds. The i is produced the same way as the Italian i, and the dangers of spreading and of a pushed, metallic sound are the same (see p. 49 for description and production). One could also say that the French i and y are exactly the same as the vowel sounds in the English words sea and key.

There are two kinds of i in French, the long and the

short. Final i's are moderately short, as in ami, si, lit, lys, riz, radis, ici, hardi.

> Nous avons des lits pleins d'odeurs légères (DEBUSSY "La Mort des amants")
> La fauvette dans les vallons a laissè son ami fidèle (BIZET "Vieille Chanson")
> Sur un lys pâle mon coeur dort (DUPARC "Extase")

The i is somewhat longer in pis, puis, minuit.

i is short before consonants except r, [z], [ʒ], [ɲ], and [v], as in pipe, huit, riche, captif, profiter, fils.

> Ah, mon fils (MEYERBEER Le Prophète)
> Profitons bien de la jeunesse (MASSENET Manon)
> BUT: Songe à la douceur d'aller là bas vivre ensemble (DUPARC "L'Invitation au voyage")

î follows the same rules, as in île, huître.

i is long before r, [z], [ʒ], [ɲ], and [v], as in mourir, rire, lyre, brise, vertige, digne, and rive.

> Je ne suis pas digne de vous (MASSENET Manon)
> La voile enfle son aile, la brise va souffler (BERLIOZ "Les Nuits d'été")
> Triste lyre soupire (DEBUSSY "Nuits d'étoiles)

In endings on ie the i is lengthened somewhat by the weak or mute e.

> Allons, enfants de la patrie ("La Marseillaise")

ï in words like haïr means simply a division into two syllables and therefore it remains i.

i followed by a single n or m in the same syllable changes into the nasal [ɛ̃].

The o sounds. o in French may be closed or open, long or short. It may also be spelled au or eau; in these cases it is always long. The French vowel sound o does not exist in English, which diphthongizes the o, but it does exist in Italian and German. (See pp. 49 and 50 for detailed description of production of the two o's.) In French speech the o's are pronounced in a rather guttural way. This must not be done in singing. Forward production is as essential here as anywhere else.

The closed o [o] *sound.* Final [o] is closed and long as in oh, mot, tôt, nôtre, eau, faux, chaud, trop, bravo, repos, un os, des os.

> Un chaud parfum circule, repose ô Phidylé (DUPARC "Phidylé")
> Les eaux sur les grands saules coulent (DUPARC "Au Pays où se fait la guerre")

The word dot has an open o ([ɔ]); the final t is pronounced. In some idiomatic phrases such as pot-au-feu, mot-à-mot, the first o is open.

In the middle of a word the o is closed and long or moderately long in words where it has a circumflex accent (trône), before a [z] (rose, generosité) and when it is followed by the suffix -tion as in emotion, devotion. If expressed by au, the o is likewise closed and long when followed by a consonant other than r, as in cruauté, beaucoup.

> Sourbillonnent dans l'extase d'une lune rose et grise (DEBUSSY "Mandoline")

The closed short o, which exists in Italian as in bocca, is not known in French.

o is closed and long in grossir, dossier, rôtir, odeur, obus, arome, exauce.

> Exauce ma prière (GOUNOD Faust)

The open o [ɔ] *sound.* Initial o is open and short when it has no circumflex accent and is not followed by an s plus vowel, as in orange, hostil.

In the middle of a word it is open and short before all consonants, as in bloc, noce, étoffe, coq, propre, poste, cloche, notre, loge, robe, homme, donne, école, ivrogne, Rome.

> Les cloches tintaient légères et franches (DEBUSSY "Les Cloches")
> Et que les hommes curieux tentent les horizons (FAURE "Les Berceaux")
> Un ivrogne qui dort (OFFENBACH Les Contes d'Hoffmann)

o is open but long in all endings on -or and -orre with or without a final mute consonant, as in abord, encore, tort, abhorre, effort, fort.

> Le bois embaumé semble dormir encore (MASSENET "Les Oiselets")
> Un fort menaçant s'éleva (RAVEL "Chansons madécasses")

o followed by a single n or m in the same syllable changes to the nasal sound [õ]. o followed by a syllable starting with another vowel is frequently closed slightly for reasons of assimilation, as in poème and coalition.

au before an r is always more open than the au would be otherwise, and long, as in aurore, taureau, j'aurai, restaure, mauvais.

> Aussi me trouves — tu toujours à chaque aurore tout en pleurs (FAURE "Le Papillon et la fleur")
> Nous venions de voir le taureau (DELIBES "Les Filles de Cadix")

The name Paul (but not Pauline) has an open au.

The ou [u] *sound.* Ou in French speech is pronounced rather backward. In singing diction, we again revert to the pure bel canto way of production as in Italian. (See p. 50.) It is pronounced as in the English doom, but without the slightest trace of diphthongization. In order to overcome the danger of his singers' sounding hooty or muffled the accompanist or coach should practice with them a closed [o] and progress to the [u] sound without too much change of mouth and tongue position. The u in Italian is always long. It may be long or short in French.

Final ou is long in où (where), cou, etc., and before mute final consonants such as b, bs, d, g, p, t, and x, as in radoub, joug, loup, tout, doux, and also in foule and douce.

Tout doux, monsieur, tout doux (BIZET Carmen)
L'âme du loup pleure dans cette voix (DEBUSSY "Le Son du cor s'afflige")

ou is long in stressed syllables before an r, [z], [ʒ], or [v], as in jour, amour, douze, épouse, rouge, trouve.

Le jour venait, l'astre des nuits pâlit (BIZET "Le Matin")
Belle nuit, o nuit d'amour (OFFENBACH Les Contes d'Hoffmann)
Épouse au front lumineux (CHANSON "Cantique a l'épouse")

ou is short before any pronounced or mute consonant — with the exception of b, bs, d, g, l, r, t, x, v, z, [ʒ] — as in nous, vous, tousse, mousse.

Les roses d'Ispahan dans leur gaîne de mousse (FAURE "Les Roses d'Ispahan")
Vous viendrez avec nous (BIZET Carmen)

The word tous is pronounced in different ways. When it is an adjective the s is mute and the ou long, as in tous les jours, tous les hommes. Where tous is used as a pronoun it is pronounced [tus]. The s is sounded and the ou short.

Ici-bas tou(s) les hommes (FAURE "Ici-bas")
Je vous invite tous (BIZET Carmen)
Et tous s'en vont dans l'ombre et dans la lune (CHAUSSON "Les Heures")

Sometimes a circumflex accent appears on the u of the ou sound, as in coûter, goûter, etc. This does not change the pronunciation of the ou.

The u [y] sound. The u sound does not exist in English or in Italian, though it appears in German. Pronouncing it creates considerable difficulty for the English-speaking singer. The [y] is produced by pursing the lips, rounded for pronouncing an ou (see p. 50 for production of the [u]). The position of mouth and lips is not unlike the preparation for whistling. The tongue is higher than in pronouncing the ou. The accompanist or coach will have to explain the [y] to the singer by describing the position of the lips and by emphasizing the fact that the [y] lies halfway between [u] and [i]. The singer should practice holding one tone while changing from [u] to [y] to [i], at the same time fixing in his mind the exact position for the different sounds.

The [y] is long before r, [z], [ʒ], and [v], as in pur, ruse, déluge, étuve.

L'amour est pur comme la flamme (BEMBERG "Elaine")
Cinq ans! et pas de leçon mais c'est rusé dame (MASSENET "Première Danse")

[y] is short or at best moderately long in most other cases, as in tu, nue, lutte, fut, rue, Jésus, plus, salut, lune.

La lune blanche luit dans les bois (HAHN "L'Heure exquise")
Salut, demeure chaste et pure (GOUNOD Faust)
Aussitôt qu'on aime où est Jésus même (CHARPENTIER "Prière")

The circumflex accent does not change the length of the [y], as in fûmes, fût, flûte.

Et tour à tour nos bouches s'unissent sur la flûte (DEBUSSY "La Flûte de Pan")

Syllables in which the u is followed by n or m are nasalized [œ̃].

In the exclamation chut, the u is almost completely suppressed.

Chut! Le voilà (GOUNOD Faust)

NASAL VOWEL SOUNDS

There are four nasal vowel sounds: [ã], [õ], [œ̃], and [ɛ̃]. These sounds do not exist in English, Italian, or German. They are produced by lowering the velum (soft palate) a little so that the stream of air will partly escape through the nasal passages and partly through the mouth. This lowering of the velum must not be exaggerated because the result would be an ugly nasal sound which would mar language and tone. The position of mouth, lips, and jaw remains unchanged for the nasal vowels. A singer should use as little nasality as is possible. The positions correspond to those for the original vowels, [a], [o], [œ], and [ɛ], which must never lose their identity. Here the n and m are blended into the nasal vowel and are not pronounced by themselves. Sang is pronounced [sã] in French and not [saŋ]. The accompanist or coach must make it clear to the singers that these nasal vowels are not like the English nasal consonants, as in long, sing, where nasality is effected on the n and g sounds. The consonants following a nasal sound must be pronounced as late as possible, as in songer ([sõ:ʒe]).

Figure 69 shows place of the four nasal vowels in simple diagram form. The nasal vowels are either long or moderately long, never really short. Initial nasal vowels should be attacked softly, without any glottal stroke.

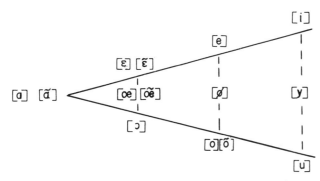

Figure 69. Diagram showing the four French nasal vowels

The [ɑ̃] *sound.* This sound is produced initially the same way as the vowel a. The mouth must be wide open. Then the velum is lowered slightly.

The [ɑ̃] is long when followed by a consonant other than n or m in the next syllable, as in blanche, grande, langue.

> La lune blanche luit dans les bois (HAHN "L'Heure exquise")
> Adieu, notre petite table, si grande pour nous cependant (MASSENET *Manon*)

Damner and bannir are not nasalized.

> Il voudrait en vain de son âme pouvoir me chasser, me bannir (SAINT-SAENS *Samson et Dalila*)

[ɑ̃] is medium long in all other cases, as in banc, temps, dedans, champs.

> Voici venir les temps où vibrant sur sa tige (DEBUSSY "Harmonie du soir")
> Et qu'un tiède frisson court sur les champs de blé (DEBUSSY "Beau Soir")

The words faon and paon elide the o and nasalize the an ([fɑ̃], [pɑ̃]), as, for example, in the title of Ravel's song, "Le Paon."

Initial en is pronounced [ɑ̃] before a consonant other than n or m, as in ensemble and entends.

> Ensemble, relisons (MASSENET *Manon*)
> Je l'entends rire et je vois luire (BIZET "Sérénade")

In ennui, ennoblir, emmener, etc., notwithstanding the double n or m, the pronunciation is [ɑ̃]. Not so, however, in ennemi, or hennir (which also may be pronounced hannir).

Interior en or em is pronounced [ɑ̃] when followed by a consonant other than n or m, as in ensemble, temple, cadence, entente, also in endings on -ention, -entiel.

Final en is pronounced [ɑ̃] when followed by a mute consonant as in temps, souvent, entends.

> Nous avons dit souvent d'impérissables choses (DEBUSSY "Le Balcon")
> Il en est temps encore (GOUNOD *Faust*)

Some words of foreign derivation are nasalized; for such, consult a phonetic dictionary.

The [ɛ̃] *sound.* The [ɛ̃] is produced the same way as the open [ɛ] but with the velum slightly lowered so that nasality is produced.

Initial in sounds are nasalized before a single consonant as in infame, infortune, inconnu, imprégner. These [ɛ̃]'s are long.

> Et de bonheur à l'infortune (MILHAUD "L'Innocence")
> Quelque inconnu (MASSENET *Manon*)

Initial in and im, when followed by a vowel or by another n or m, are not nasalized, as in image, inutile, immense, innovation.

> Dans un sommeil que charmait ton image (FAURE "Après un rêve")
> Devant l'immensité ton extase s'éveille (FAURE "Rencontre")

The word hymne is also not nasalized.

Exceptions to the above rule are immangeable, immanquable, which nasalize the initial im.

Interior in sounds are nasalized before a consonant other than n or m, as in crainte, vainqueur, Olympia, nymphe, timbre. They are always pronounced moderately long.

> L'Amour vainqueur et la vie opportune (FAURE "Clair de lune")
> Je vous présente ma fille Olympia (OFFENBACH *Les Contes d'Hoffmann*)

Final in sounds in any of the above-listed spellings are nasalized with or without a terminating consonant, as in faim, thym, rein, saint, cinq, main, lynx, point, poing. They are of medium length.

> Ne les déchirez pas avec vos deux mains blanches (DEBUSSY "Green")

Et le *poing* sur la hanche (DELIBES "Les Filles de Cadix")

In endings on -ien or -ient, the en sound is pronounced [ɛ̃], as in mien, tien, chien, bien, païen, récipient, moyen, chrétien, viens, tiens.

Comme un ch*ien* l'amour m'a mordu (DUPARC "Le Manoir de Rosemonde")
V*iens* mon bien-aimé (CHAMINADE "Viens mon bien-aimé")

Words ending in -ienne are not nasalized, as in Vienne, ancienne, ils viennent, etc.

The [ɔ̃] *sounds.* The [ɔ̃] sound is produced like the regular closed o (see p. 50), with nasalization by a slight lowering of the velum. It is important that the lips should be rounded and protruded, otherwise it may sound too much like [ɑ̃].

Initial on or om sounds are long, and are nasalized before a single consonant as in ombre, onde.

Comme s'en va cette *on*de (DEBUSSY "Beau Soir")
C'est l'*om*bre que j'embrasse (SAINT-SAENS "La Solitaire")

Interior on sounds are likewise nasalized before a consonant other than n or m as in monde, songe, tombeau, comte, compter, rompu, longue, blonde, honte. In these cases the on sounds are long.

In monosyllables or final syllables the on is also nasalized and is of moderate length, as in mon, fond, long, réponds, talon, applombe, romps, compt.

Le *long* du quai les grands vaisseaux (FAURE "Les Berceaux")
Ah, rép*ons* à ma tendresse (SAINT-SAENS *Samson et Dalila*)

The word monsieur is pronounced [məsjø]; the n is mute. For pronunciation of paon, faon, see page 72. For pronunciation of messieurs, see page 69.

On and om before another n or m are not nasalized, as in donner, bonne, nommer, en somme, omnipotent, calomnie. In the last two cases the m is mute. (See p. 77.)

En s*om*me, un vrai gentilh*om*me (GOUNOD *Faust*)
D*on*ne (GOUNOD *Faust*)
Infâme cal*om*nie (MASSENET *Manon*)

The [œ̃] *sounds.* The production of the [œ̃] sound corresponds to the [œ] (see p. 69), with slightly lowered velum. It is important that the sound be kept open. The [œ̃], like the [œ], creates difficulties for the English-speaking singer. These sounds must be practiced thoroughly, if possible with the help of a tape recorder.

Initial un is only moderately long. It is nasalized in the article un, but not in une.

C'était *un* ange, *un* ange (GOUNOD *Faust*)

Interior um and un are nasalized and long before a consonant, as in humble, lundi, défunte, etc.

Et qu'à vos yeux si beau l'h*um*ble présent soit doux (DEBUSSY "Green")
Comme au temps des déf*un*ts amours (CHAUSSON "Nos Souvenirs")

Final un is always nasalized and moderately long, as in chacun, brun, jeun.

Chac*un* se paie un sou de dimanche (DEBUSSY "Chevaux de bois")
C'est un beau br*un* (CHARPENTIER *Louise*)

There is only one nasalized word ending in -um: parfum.

Le parf*um* en est fort (BIZET *Carmen*)

Other words ending in -um, such as rhum, album, are not nasalized.

The word punch, for no obvious reason, is pronounced ponch (pɔ̃ʃ).

Allumons le p*unch*! (OFFENBACH *Les Contes d'Hoffmann*)

SEMIVOWELS

Semivowels are vowel combinations. The French language has three, expressed phonetically by [w], [j], and [ɥ]. Although they might in speech be called semiconsonants, in singing they are nearer to vowels. The overall rule for semivowels is the following: when in ordinary spelling i, y, o, and ou are preceded by a single consonant and followed by a vowel, they turn into semivowels. However, the combinations oi, ieu, and ui become semivowels even in initial form or if preceded by more than one consonant. All semivowel sounds are extremely short. As in Italian music, the French composers show by their way of writing when a vowel combination should be sung as a semivowel and when it should be separated into ordinary vowels. If words containing them are put under a single note they definitely must be sung as semivowels. If two or more notes are given to them they lose their semivocalic character. The following individual rules must therefore be checked against the words in a given song, opera, or choral work.

The [w] *semivowel.* This sound exists in English in words like suave, language, and persuasion, and is pronounced in the same manner. In French, the [w] is pronounced in vowel combinations of o and i, as in oiseau, soit, trois, droite, bois, croix.

> Aimable *oi*seau lui disait-il (BIZET "Vieille Chanson")
> B*ois* frissonants, ciel ét*oile* (CHAUSSON "Chanson per-petuelle")
> Je b*ois* à la Stella (OFFENBACH *Les Contes d'Hoff-mann*)

The [w] must be pronounced very quickly, giving almost the entire full value of the musical note to the following vowel. There must not be any separation (Fig. 70). This gliding from the semivowel to the vowel creates a difficulty for the English-speaking singer and should be thoroughly explained to him; he should also practice all the semivowels on notes of different lengths.

Figure 70. Pronunciation of the semivowel w

A circumflex accent on the second part of a semivowel lengthens it, as in cloître, croître.

> On sent croître ton amour dans la nuit
> Du vieux cloître ou s'en va se becquetant (FAURE "Dans les ruines d'une abbaye")

Words ending in oie, oye, have the [w] followed by a weak e, as in joie, proie, oye.

The English vowel y must never be interspersed between semivowel and mute e. Joie is pronounced [ʒwə] and not [ʒwjə].

[w] is also pronounced in combinations of o with in, int, and ins, as in loin, point, moins, poing. In all these cases the in sounds are nasalized. The pronunciation of moins, for instance, is [mwɛ̃].

> Je bois à la j*oie* (RAVEL "Chanson à boire")
> Comme une fleur l*oin* du soleil (BIZET "Absence")

[w] is also pronounced in vowel combinations of ou with a, e, and i, according to the above general rule, as in louange, oui, louis, etc.

> *Oui* je suis dans son boudoir (THOMAS *Mignon*)
> Roi du ciel et des anges je dirai tes l*ou*anges (MEYER-BEER *Le Prophète*)

The singing of the ou as [w] in these cases depends largely on the music. If the composer gave two or more notes to the ou plus vowel combination it retains its original vowel quality (Fig. 71, 72).

Ou followed by a, e, or i and preceded by two consonants always retains the original vowel form, as in éblou-ir, trou-ait, prou-esse.

Figure 71. Charpentier, *Louise*, pronunciation of the semivowel [w]

Figure 72. Massenet, *Manon*, pronunciation of the semivowel [w]

The words moelle and poêle and their forms are pronounced [mwal], [pwal].

The [j] *semivowel.* This [j] sound has its parallel in the English y, as in you. In French it is called the yod and is very common. But in poetry and musical lyrics the composer will decide whether one or more notes should be given to the syllable containing the [j]. If one note is given a semivowel must be sung; if two notes, the syllable is divided into two parts and retains the original vowel. The above-mentioned general rules apply.

The [j] is pronounced in words with ia, iai, ian, as in diamant, diable, biais, étudiant.

> Scintille, d*ia*mant (OFFENBACH *Les Contes d'Hoff-mann*)
> Cette vieille impitoyable, de force ou de gré, je crois, allait épouser le d*ia*ble (GOUNOD *Faust*)

In words with ie, iè, ieu, as in pied, nièce, riens, dieu, etc., the [j] is pronounced.

> Ses p*ie*ds se font légers et ta voix endormante (HUE "Nuits d'été")
> Et bénissez le nom du D*ieu* saint de nos pères (SAINT-SAENS *Samson et Dalila*)

In words with i and weak e the pure vowels must be pronounced. Great care should be taken not to inter-ject a [j].

> Je suis encore tout étourd*ie* [eturdi:ə] (MASSENET *Manon*)
> La mer immense et la prair*ie*, choeur immortel: Di-vine éternelle harmon*ie* (BIZET "Le Matin")

In words with io, iou, iu — passion, opium — the [j] is pronounced.

> Mais n'apportant de pass*io*n profonde qu'à s'adorer (FAURE "Au Bord de l'eau")

If, according to the above general rules, two consonants precede the i vowel combinations, they retain their pure vowel form, as in tri-omphe, pri-ère, cri-ant, etc. However, the [j] is used to connect the two syllables. The right pronunciation is therefore [trijõfə], [prijɛrə], [krijã].

O toi, Dieu de lum*ière*, comme aux jours d'autrefois exauce ma pr*ière* et combats pour tes lois (SAINT-SAENS *Samson et Dalila*)

The forms of the verb rire and lier, although they begin with only one vowel, follow the same rule, as in rions, liez, riant — pronounced [rijõ], [lije], [rijã].

Et nous étions l*iés* pour toujours ainsi (DEBUSSY "La Chevelure")
Ah! Ah! R*ions* de sa fureur (SAINT-SAENS *Samson et Dalila*)

If a y stands between two vowels, it is divided orthographically into two parts, the first becomes [wa], [ɛ], or [ɥ] and is attached to the preceding vowel; the second becomes [j] and is drawn to the following vowel, as in rayon, aiyant, voyez, essayer, payer, royal, fuyant. These words are pronounced [rɛjõ], [ɛjã], [vwaje], [ɛsɛje], [pɛje], [rwajal], [fɥjã].

Il faut p*ayer* (BIZET *Carmen*)
Qu'un r*ayon* de soleil ne doit jamais tarir (MASSENET *Le Cid*)

ay, orthographically, is also divided into two parts at the end of words like pays, abbeye, paysan, and paysage, pronounced [pɛi:], [abɛi:ə], [pɛizã:], [pɛiza:ʒə]. The semivowel [j] should *not* be added.

Connais-tu le p*ays* (THOMAS *Mignon*)

y by itself or as an initial sound before a vowel is pronounced like [j], as in il y a [ilja]. As an initial sound it appears mostly in words of foreign derivation, hardly ever used in the vocal literature.

At this point it is necessary to discuss the so-called l mouillé, the liquid l, which turns into the semivowel [j]. This sound is used in combinations -ail, -aille, -eil, -eille, -euil, -euille, -ouil, and -ouille, as in travail, bataille, soleil, vieille, deuil, feuille, accueillir, fenouil, bouillon.

Comme un ange blond sous le clair sol*eil* (RAVEL "Chanson des cueilleuses de lentesque")
Le d*euil* est sans raison (DEBUSSY "Il pleure dans mon coeur")
Aux vautours il faut la bat*aille* (GOUNOD *Roméo et Juliette*)

Words like cercueil, orgueilleux, cueillir are pronounced [sɛrkœj:], [ɔrgɛjø:], [kœji:r]. These words are met with very often in vocal literature.

Et nous n'irons plus courir, et c*ueill*ir les lilas en fleur (CHAUSSON "Le Temps des lilas")
Dans le cerc*ueil* de blanc capitonné (CHAMINADE "L'Anneau d'argent")

In the word aile the l is not liquidized.

Most words ending in -ille also are pronounced with the [j] as in famille, briller, fille, oreilles, séguédille.

Occupez mon or*eille* par vos accents prolongés. Le vent du soir se lève, la lune commence à br*iller* au travers des arbres de la montagne (RAVEL "Chansons madécasses")
C'est une brave f*ille*, qui fait l'honneur à la fam*ille* (MASSENET *Manon*)

The ll is not liquid, and therefore not pronounced [j] in ville, mille, tranquille, illustre, and their derivatives.

La chère musique de la grande Vi*lle* (CHARPENTIER *Louise*)
Soit, monsieur, mi*lle* pistoles (MASSENET *Manon*)

The proper noun Séville should actually be liquidized, for instance when it rhymes with séguédille. But when it is rhymed with ville one gives it the ordinary ll sound.

Près des remparts de Séville ([Sevijə]), chez mon ami Lillas Pastia, j'irai danser la Séguédi*lle* et boire du Manzanilla (BIZET *Carmen*)
BUT: Tu vas, m'a-t-elle dit, t'en aller à la vi*lle* [vilə].
La route n'est pas longue, une fois à Séville [sevilə].

Some proper names such as Villon and Milhaud may be pronounced with [j], but the ordinary pronunciation is just as correct.

The liquid l sound [j] is not related to the Italian [ʎ] sound, spelled gl.

The [ɥ] *semivowel.* This sound has no equivalent in any other language. The difficulty it creates for English-speaking singers can only be overcome by concentrated practice. It is a combination of the u ([y]) and i with the a, [e], [ɛ], [ɛ̃], [œ] or [õ] sounds but the [y] part is of extremely short duration and glides immediately into the i.

In producing the [ɥ], the lips must be rounded and protruded very far, as for the French u (see p. 71), then suddenly withdrawn and changed into a slightly spread position. This is the only occasion where I recommend even slight spreading; otherwise the semivowel will sound indistinct. The [ɥ] semivowel is not related to the Italian ui, as in lui, which consists of two pure vowels of which the first is longer. In French, the u is very rapid and the i gets the full value of the note, similar to the oi ([w]) (Fig. 73).

puis [(p)yi:)] = [py-i:]

Figure 73. The semivowel [ɥ]

Most [ɥ]'s appear in the ui combinations, with preceding single consonants, as in nuit, lui, suis, détruire, puisque, puissant, ennui.

> Je suis, je suis le cri de joie (LALO "La Chanson de l'alouette")
>
> Chère nuit aux clartés sereines (BACHELET "Chère Nuit")

[ɥ] is also pronounced in combinations of [y] with a, [e], [ɛ], [ɛ̃], [œ], and [ɔ̃], preceded by a single consonant, as in nuage, suaire, insinuant, juin, respectueux, concluons.

> Ô Juin, étincelle enivrée (FAURE "Nell")
>
> En suivant le nuage clair que la pipe jette dans l'air (OFFENBACH Les Contes d'Hoffmann)

If a weak e follows a [ɥ], as in pluie, the music determines whether it is pronounced or mute. When it is pronounced, however, no additional semivowel [j] must be added.

> Ô bruit doux de la pluie (DEBUSSY "Il pleure dans mon coeur")

Some words with syllables starting with two consonants do not take the [ɥ] sound, but retain the pure vowel sounds, as in cruelle, truelle, bruire (but [brɥ:] for bruit), bruyant.

> Cruelle destinée! (GOUNOD Faust)

In concluding the section about semivowels I want to emphasize once more that it is up to the poet and composer to decide when semivowels are to be sung. May Laird-Brown, in *Singers' French*, gives a few examples from French music for avoidance of semivowels which could be extended ad libitum:

> nu-a-ge (OFFENBACH Les Contes d'Hoffmann)
> su-a-vi-té (DEBUSSY "Romance")
> dé-fi-ance (HALEVY La Juive)
> mari-age (BIZET Carmen)
> radi-eux (GOUNOD Faust)
> mélodi-euse (MASSENET Herodiade)
> ru-ine (OFFENBACH Les Contes d'Hoffmann)

CONSONANTS

The intensity with which French consonants are to be pronounced in singing lies somewhere between the German explosiveness and the American-English underplay. It conforms in general to the crispness and gentleness of the Italian consonants. There is, however, one big difference: double consonants in French receive no additional stress; they are pronounced and sung like single consonants. For this reason I shall not discuss them separately. French consonants are sometimes pronounced, sometimes mute. The numerous rules and exceptions to the rules will form the bulk of this chapter. For the definition and production of French consonants I shall refer to the Italian wherever they coincide and write about them separately wherever they differ.

The h sound. One of the cardinal differences between the Italian and the French consonants is the treatment of the h, which is always mute in Italian, whereas in French it may be either mute or aspirated. The first kind are only spelling conventions, the second kind are consonants of the glottal fricative class. The great majority of French h's are mute; the aspirated h interests us here. The initial mute h lends itself to a liaison (see p. 84). The initial aspirated h must never be tied to the preceding word but must be separated by a hiatus (see p. 84). h in combination with gh, kh, lh, nh, rh, and th may be interior or final; it is of course also mute and does not change the pronunciation of the preceding consonant. The pronunciation of the ch will be discussed in connection with the c (see p. 79).

One hard and fast rule determines when initial h is mute and when it is aspirated, but this rule requires so much philological background that it may well remain a theory for accompanists and coaches: the initial h is always mute in words of Greek or Latin origin. Most aspirated h's come from Teutonic words, though they are sometimes hardly recognizable as such.

The aspirated h sound. The aspirated h is found almost exclusively as an initial consonant. The only exception is the final h of exclamations like oh! and ah! which will get slight aspiration or breathiness when expressing real emotion.

> Je suis perdue! Oh! Oh! (DEBUSSY Pelléas et Mélisande)

Initial aspirated h is strongly aspirated in words of violent emotion, such as ha! haine, haineux, je te hais. The pronunciation corresponds to the violence of an English exclamation like Oh, hell!

> Je te hais! (BIZET Carmen)

In all other instances, the h is aspirated more or less gently — less gently in words that still have emotional impact (honte, honteux), more gently in all others. A gently aspirated h corresponds to the h in the English words home, humble. The aspirated h's are numerous. I list those most frequently found in French vocal literature (for words not contained in this list, a dictionary may be consulted): Ha!, hache, haie, haine, haineux, haïr, haler, halte!, hameau, hanche, hardi, harceler, harasser, harpe, hasard, hâte, hâter, haut (and derivatives), Hé!, hennir, héros (but *not* héroïsme, héroïne, héroïque), hideusement, Holà!, honte, honteux, honni, horde, hors, houille, houle, hourra!, Hue, huche, huit, huguenot, hurler.

> Déesse charmante *h*âtes toi (MILHAUD "L'Aurore")
> Paraît liste fringant et les poings sur les *h*anches (DEBUSSY "Voici que le printemps")

The h in hélas is thought to be mute. There are, however, some teachers of phonetics who will break their lances for an aspirated hélas! Huit is also aspirated in its derivatives, such as huitième, but not when it is the second word in combinations like dix-huit, vingt-huit.

The m and mm sounds. For definition and production see page 52. The vowel preceding an m must never be nasalized except in the cases where am, em, om, and um stand for [ã], [ɛ̃], [õ], [œ̃] (see pp. 71–73). The final m is always nasalized with the exception of a few words of foreign origin like harem, intérim, album, Jérusalem, etc. A vowel preceding an m which is followed by b or p is combined with the m into a nasal sound, as in jambe, simple, nymphe, compte (also, as an exception, comte).

> Les satyres et les ny*m*phes aussi (DEBUSSY "Le Tombeau des naïades")
> Cependant l'excellent docteur Bolonais cueille avec lenteur des si*m*ples (DEBUSSY "Fantôches")

The prefix em is nasalized [ã] if followed by another m, as in emmener.

In the mn combination, the m is assimilated to the n, as in the words damner, automne. Damner, for instance, is pronounced [dane:].

> Que le sort te conda*m*ne (GOUNOD *Faust*)
> Mais le vent d'auto*m*ne qui brame (CHAUSSON "La Dernière Feuille")

Modern diction pronounces both m and n in the following words: indemnité, calomnie, hymne, omnibus, Agamemnon, Clythemnestre.

The n and nn sounds. For definition and production see page 53. The syllables an, en, in, ain, ein, oin, on, un are nasalized (see pp. 72–73). A few endings on -en in words of Latin origin are not nasalized, as in éden, hymen. Final syllables with the above sounds followed by c, g, d, t, and s are also nasalized, as in banc, poing, quand, point, gens.

> Qua*n*d ton regard tomba sur moi (CHAUSSON "Le Chasme")

Et ce jeu nouveau pourtant poi*nt* ne l'embarasse (MASSENET "Première Danse")

nn, always pronounced like a single n is not nasalized with the exception of ennoblir, ennui.

> L'année en vain chasse l'année (DEBUSSY *L'Enfant prodigue*)
> NASALIZED: Dans l'immortel e*nn*ui du calme sidéral (FAURE "L'Horizon chimérique")

The gn sound. For definition and production, see page 53. Some words containing this consonant, which is called n mouillé in French, are agneau, compagnie, magnifique, montagne, digne.

> Je ne suis pas di*gn*e de vous (MASSENET *Manon*)
> Que de vallons et de monta*gn*es (BERLIOZ "Absence")

For exceptions, see page 82.

The l and ll sounds. For definition and production, see page 54. There are two kinds of l in French, the normal l and the liquid l (or l mouillé). Rarely, the l is mute. The normal l is to be found as an initial, interior, or final sound.

l is normal in endings in -al, -el, -eul, -ol, -oil, as in bal, ciel, seul, col, voile, and in the middle of words in connection with the same vowel combinations.

> Si vous me disiez que l'ennui vous vient du cie*l* trop fleuri (RAVEL "Chanson romanesque")
> Passe, passe dans un rayon tremblant en voi*l*e blanc (BERLIOZ "Au Cimitière")

l is normal in combinations of -oul and -ul as in foule, brûler, with the exception of pou(ls), sou(l) and cu(l) where the l is mute.

l in combination with -il is mostly normal, as in mil, fil, subtil, île, péril. It is mute in some words, such as genti(l), fusi(l), nombri(l), but liquid in some similar ones, such as gentilhomme, gentille.

> Du mal en masse et du bien en fou*l*e (DEBUSSY "Chevaux de bois")
> D'un sillage d'argent des *î*les de la sonde (FAURE "Les Matelots")
> But: En somme, un vrai genti*l*homme (GOUNOD *Faust*)

The l in fils is mute, the i is short, and the s is stressed [fis]. The l is normal in the word aile.

Combinations with -il in the middle of a word are always normal when followed by another vowel, as in milieu, poilu, filial, fusilier, sommelier (but fusiller and sommeiller which are spelled with double l have the ll liquidized).

> Au mi*l*ieu notre barque fuit (LEROUX "Le Nil")

ll is normal in combinations of -all, -ell, -oll, -ull, as in salle, quelle, folle, Lully.

Quelle belle vie! (CHARPENTIER *Louise*)

A few words with -ill have the normal l. These are ville, mille, tranquille and their derivatives (see p. 75).

Liquid l *and* ll. These sounds have been discussed thoroughly on page 75 in connection with the semi-vowel [j].

The v *and* f (ff) *sounds.* For definition and production see pages 54 and 57. w and ph are pronounced [v] and [f] (as in Wagram, Phidylé). The voiced v is entirely regular and appears in words like voilà, revoir, rêve, etc.

Dites lui qu'il est ma pensée et mon rêve (DUPARC "Au Pays où se fait la guerre")
Je mourrai — mais je veux la revoir (GOUNOD *Roméo et Juliette*)

Voiceless f and ff as an initial or interior sound is always pronounced as in famille, effet, affaire.

Voilà l'affaire (MASSENET *Manon*)
Et dans la pieuse famille (DEBUSSY *L'Enfant prodigue*)

Final f is also almost always pronounced as in chef, boeuf, oeuf, attentif.

Le mien devient un chef fameux (BIZET *Carmen*)
L'air attentif passe sans bruit (MASSENET *Hérodiade*)

f in clef is mute (see also p. 67). In chef d'oeuvre the f is elided. The plurals oeufs and boeufs have the f and s muted.

Voice la clef, je crois. (GOUNOD *Faust*)
On ramenait les grands boeufs roux (DEBUSSY *L'Enfant prodigue*)

Cerf and cerfs, appearing in older poetry and music, should also be pronounced with a mute f.

The [z] *sound.* For definition and production of z see pages 54, 57. The voiced s in French can be spelled either s or z.

z is always pronounced initially, as in zèle, zone, Zuniga.

Vous montrez trop de zèle (MASSENET *Manon*)
Un zéphir vient ternir (WEKERLIN "Bergerettes")

Interior z is also always pronounced, as in bronzé, onzième, gauze.

Azaël, Azaël, pourquoi m'a-tu quittée? (DEBUSSY *L'Enfant prodigue*)
Atteindre ton azur fidèle son beau ciel nacré (SAINT-SAENS "Désir de l'Orient")

Final z is pronounced in gaz and fez. Otherwise it is mute as in voyez, aimez, nez, riz, chez.

Lorsque ses doigts tressent la natte, ou lorsqu' assise auprès du riz (RAVEL "Chansons madécasses")
Voyez-vous toujours en vos songes d'or (CHAUSSON "Amour d'antan")

For the pronunciation of proper names ending in z, like Dumouriez, consult a phonetic dictionary.

Interior s between two vowels of which the first one is not a nasal vowel is pronounced [z], as in visage, raison, résumer, rose, présage, désarmer, réserver, cousin.

Volupté enfin s'aperçu ton visage (HUE "Volupté")
Il pleure sans raison dans ce coeur qui s'écoeuré (DEBUSSY "Il pleure dans mon coeur")
Fâcheux présage (GOUNOD *Faust*)

s followed by a vowel and preceded by a-, anti-, co-, contre-, entre-, para-, or pro- is pronounced [s] as in aseptique.

s is voiced [z] in combination with trans-, notwithstanding the nasal vowel, as in transition, transaction, etc., and in Alsace, balsamique, Israël.

Israël, romps ta chaîne (SAINT-SAENS *Samson et Dalila*)

s is pronounced [z] before the voiced consonants b, d, g, j, and v, as in sbire, disgrace, disjoindre, and svelte, and in endings on the -isme and -asme.

Les grands jets d'eau sveltes parmi les marbres (FAURE "Claire de lune")

s is pronounced [z] in subsister. s in liaisons is mostly pronounced z (see p. 87).

The s (c, ç) *and* ss *sounds.* For definition and description see page 57.

Initial s is voiceless [s], as in séance, sans, soif.

Partir, nous séparer? Sans doute (BIZET *Carmen*)

But, as mentioned above, when initial s stands before a voiced consonant it changes into [z].

c and sc before e or i are pronounced [s], as in scène, conscience, resusciter, cygne, ceçi, cela.

Ah, cela ne peut être qu'un cierge (CHARPENTIER "La Chanson du chemin")

An intensified [s] should be pronounced in the words transcendant, lascif, rescinder.

Interior s is always pronounced [s] before a consonant other than b, d, g, j, and v, as in lorsque, espérer, distance, estomac.

Mon coeur comme un lys plein s'épanche et je n'ose plus ésperer (DUPARC "Au pays où se fait la guerre")

Lorsque tu parais ange si doux (RAVEL "Chanson des cueilleuses de lentisque")

Interior s or c is pronounced [s] before a vowel if preceded by a consonant as in versez, valsez, arcières. Also in combination with abs-, obs- and subs- (with the exception of subsister) as in obsolète, absolumment, subséquent.

Valsez, valsez toujours (GOUNOD *Faust*)
Ce n'est pas là ton dernier mot? Absolumment (BIZET *Carmen*)

Interior s or c is pronounced [s] between two vowels if the first one is a nasal vowel, as in dansez, linceul, penser, insister.

Sur moi la nuit immense s'étend comme un linceul (BERLIOZ "Sur les lagunes")
J'irai danser la Séguédille (BIZET *Carmen*)

s is pronounced [s] in susurrer.

c is pronounced [s] as in reçu. ss is always pronounced [s].

Final s is usually mute after a vowel. Exceptions are as (ace), hélas, some names like Pelléas, jadis, fils, lys — but the last is pronounced with mute s in fleur de lis in older poetry; os (in singular form); tous, if used as a pronoun; plus, if followed by que and not preceded by pas or autant, as in La Plus que lente (but: pas plu(s) que lente); plus also if it means the arithmetical term; sens; Saint-Saëns.

Plus in liaison assumes the z sound, as in de plus en plu(s).

Enveloppe-moi du silence argenté des lys (CHAUSSON "Sérénade")
Tes baisers pénètrent jusqu'à l'âme, tes caresses brûlent tous mes sens (RAVEL "Chansons madécasses")

Final s after a vowel is always pronounced in Greek or Latin words and names: Barrabas, de profundis, Laïs, Thaïs, cosmos, and others.

Final s is always mute if preceded by a mute consonant as in la(cs), me(ts), tem(ps), remor(ds). The sole exception is fi(l)s.

Ah, mon fils (MEYERBEER *Le Prophète*)
Le temps des lilas et le temps des roses (CHAUSSON "Le Temps des lilas")

Final s is also mute if preceded by an r, as in alor(s) and toujour(s), with the exception of the words mars, moeurs, and ours (unless found in old poetry).

s sounds in names of persons and places are pronounced in various ways; consult a dictionary.

The [ʒ] *sound.* This sound is a voiced alveolar-palatal semiocclusive sound which has no equivalent in Italian or German. It corresponds to the s in the English word measure and is produced the same way.

The [ʒ] sound is expressed by the French j or g in the combinations ge, geo, and gi. The [ʒ] never appears as a final sound. Spelled with j it is always followed by a vowel, as in joli, jaloux, ajouter, déjà.

Voulez-vous qu'icy je demeure demi mort tremblant et jaloux (MASSENET "Sérénade de Molière")
Ils ont fui les longs soirs moroses, déjà le jardin parfumé (CHAMINADE "Viens mon bien-aimé")

Spelled with a g in combination with e and i it may be initial, interior, or final, as in gentil, Geneviève, Gérard, girasol, gymnase, argent, large, mangé, mangeait, ange, rougissant, réagit.

Le cher anneau d'argent que vous m'avez donné (CHAMINADE "L'anneau d'argent")
Un ange est venu dans ma solitude (BEMBERG "Un Ange est venu")

e in combinations of gea and geô is elided, as in vengeance, geôlier (see p. 69).

The ch [ʃ] *sound.* For definition and production see Italian sce, sci, page 59. It must be aspirated somewhat more firmly than its Italian counterpart. This sound corresponds to the English sh. It appears as an initial sound before a vowel, as in chat, chant, chère, chimère, schisme, chaud, chut, chérif, chèrubin.

Chère nuit aux clartés sereines (BACHELET "Chère Nuit")
Elle veut de ses chants peupler l'air froid des nuits (CHARPENTIER "La Cloche fêlée")

In most words of Greek or Latin origin, the initial ch is pronounced k, as in chaos, choeur, chrétien (see p. 82 for more detailed description).

Choeur [kœːr] immortel! Divine éternelle harmonie (BIZET "Le Matin")

Interior ch is pronounced [ʃ] in French words before a vowel, as in acheter, niche, sécher, échapper, Sancho, Don Quichotte.

Je veux sécher tes larmes (SAINT-SAENS *Samson et Dalila*)

In most words of Greek or Latin origin interior ch receives the [k] sound. But words of Greek or Latin derivation keep the [ʃ] sound before a weak e (archevêque, brioche); in some cases before an i; in words with the prefix archi- (archiduc); and in the names Rachel, Michel, Psyché.

Bon Saint Mi*ch*el qui me daignez choisir (RAVEL "Chanson épique")

Ra*ch*el, quand du Seigneur (HALEVY *La Juive*)

Je suis jaloux, Psy*ch*é, de toute la nature (PALADILHE "Psyché")

Interior ch is pronounced [ʃ] in all words ending in -archie, -machie, -chin, -chine, -chique, -chisme, and -chiste, as in machine, catéchisme.

Ch before the consonants l, m, n, and r is always pronounced [k].

Words of Italian origin with ch receive the [k] sound.

Final ch is very rare. It is pronounced in punch, lunch, tarbouch.

Allumons le pun*ch* (OFFENBACH *Les Contes d'Hoffmann*)

The b *and* bb *sounds.* For definition and production see page 55. bb is always pronounced like a single b. Initial b appears in a multitude of words, such as bête, bal, Bacchus, bière, bruit.

Je suis le spectre d'une rose que tu portais hier au *b*al (BERLIOZ "Le Spectre de la rose")

D'aller ainsi dans ce cirque *b*ête (DEBUSSY "Chevaux de bois")

Interior b is always pronounced, be it before a vowel or a consonant, as in robe, tombe, ombre, obstine, absolumment, abbé.

Sous la tom*b*e elle emporte mon âme et mes amours (BERLIOZ "Sur les lagunes")

La seule om*b*re qu'on ait c'est l'om*b*re du vautour (CHAUSSON "La Caravane")

Final b is mute in French words and their plurals as in aplomb, plombs.

Final b is pronounced in foreign words and names like club, Jacob, Moab.

The p *and* pp *sounds.* For definition and production see page 57. pp is pronounced like p. Initial p appears in many words: péril, pas, partir, pleurer, pitié.

O mère du verbe incarné: *p*itié, *p*itié! (MASSENET "Souvenez-vous, Vierge Marie")

Entends ma voix chanter, entends ma voix *p*leurer dans la rosée (FAURE "Chanson Toscane")

Initial p is also pronounced in the ps combination, as in psaume, psychologie, Psyché.

Interior p is always pronounced, be it before a vowel or before a consonant, as in rompre, opportun, applique, symptome.

Et pour fuir la vie im*p*ortune (DUPARC "Chanson triste")

Qui se ré*p*and dans l'air chargé d'ivresse (CHAUSSON "Printemps triste")

Interior p before a t is mute only in the following words: ba(p)tisme (and all derivations of it), se(p)t, se(p)tième (but not in its derivations such as septembre), exem(p)ter (and derivatives except exemption), com(p)te (and its derivatives), prom(p)titude, dom(p)ter (and its derivatives).

Mais ce qui dom*p*tait mon esprit (CHAUSSON "Le Charme")

Final p is quite rare and mute in French words such as loup, beaucoup, trop, champs, camp, galop, drap, and their plurals.

In cap, cep, hip, hop, houp, and in foreign words such as stop and group, the p is pronounced.

Final p is mute in the words rom(ps), cor(ps), exem(pt), tem(ps), printem(ps).

Lève toi, lève toi, le printem*p*s vient de naître (BIZET "Chanson d'avril")

Le tem*p*s des lilas et le tem*p*s des roses ne reviendra plus à ce printem*p*s-ci (CHAUSSON "Le Temps des lilas")

ph is pronounced f (see p. 78).

The d *and* dd *sounds.* For definition and production, see page 55. dd, which is very rare, is pronounced like d, as in addition and adition, pronounced alike.

Initial d offers no difficulty. It is pronounced crisply but without any explosion in dans, dormir, doux, depuis.

Mais la vague légère avec son *d*oux refrain (FAURE "Les Matelots")

*D*epuis le jour (CHARPENTIER *Louise*)

*D*ans les bois l'amoureux myrtil (BIZET "Vieille Chanson")

Interior d is pronounced before vowels and consonants, as in adosser, jeudi, mademoiselle, rendre, adversaire, adjoindre, admirer, sourde.

Pour ren*d*re le juge propice (FAURE "La Rançon")

Laisse ta mante lour*d*e et ton manchon frieux (BIZET "Chanson d'avril")

J'aime qu'on m'a*d*mire (MASSENET "Première Danse")

Final d is mute in all French words and their plurals. These words usually end in -and, -end, -aud, -oud, -ard, -erd, -ord, and -ourd, as in brigand, défends, chaud, regard, perds, accords, lourd.

Lour*d* d'une tristesse royale (CHAUSSON "L'aveu")

Quan*d* ton regar*d* tomba sur moi (CHAUSSON "Le Charme")

In some words of foreign origin the d is sounded, as in sud, Cid, David.

The t sound. For definition and production, see pages 57–58. tt is pronounced like single t.

Initial t or th is always pronounced t decidedly but without explosion, as in tabac, tort, tiens, tu, théâtre.

> Qui le *t*ient si longtemps, mon Dieu (DUPARC "Au Pays où se fait la guerre")
> Mais ce soir, *t*out a l'heure au *th*éâtre (OFFENBACH *Les Contes d'Hoffmann*)

Interior t is pronounced [t] before the vowels a, e, o, u, and the nasal vowels, as in détacher, hâter, atone, partout, actualité, attends, rotond.

> Me recompensent de l'at*t*ente (DUPARC "Phidylé")
> Hâ*t*e toi (GOUNOD *Faust*)

Interior t is pronounced [t] if spelled th, as in sympathie, gothique, etc.

Interior t is pronounced [t] between a vowel and a consonant as in pupitre.

Interior t is pronounced [t] between two consonants, if the second is an r, as in astral. Otherwise, the sequence of three consonants is difficult for a Frenchman to pronounce. The t is therefore usually elided as in as(th)me, is(th)me, etc.

The ti *group.* Interior ti is pronounced [si], except after s as in question, modestie, bestial.

> Et quelle modes*tie* (GOUNOD Faust)

The ti in the words étiage, châtier, and chrétien is also pronounced [ti]. These words were spelled with an s in old times (chréstien).

Ti is also pronounced [ti] in the forms of the verb tenir and its composites, as in contient, maintiendrai, soutien.

> Je veux un trésor qui les con*tie*nt tous (GOUNOD *Faust*)
> Je te sou*tie*ns de toutes mes forces (POULENC "Nous avons fait la nuit")

Interior ti is pronounced [ti] in the endings on -tions of verbs, as in étions, partions, chantions, mentions, portiez, mentiez.

Interior ti is pronounced [ti] in the feminine endings of the past participle of verbs ending in -tir, as in partie, sortie.

> Elle est par*tie* (GOUNOD *Faust*)
> Et nous é*tie*ns liés pour toujours ainsi (DEBUSSY "La Chevelure")

Interior ti is pronounced [ti] in the words pitié, moitié, amitié, antienne, sortie, ortie.

> Pitié, pi*tié* pour mon martyre (CHAMINADE "Rosemonde")
> Dont s'exhale l'humble an*tie*nne (DEBUSSY "C'est l'extase langoureuse")

Interior ti is pronounced [ti] in endings on -ique, such as poétique, prophétique; also in adjectives or nouns that end in -tier, -tière, like entier, charcutier, tabatière.

> Le monde en*tie*r pour se cacher (POULENC "Je n'ai envie que de t'aimer")
> Cette taba*tie*re a son secret (LIADOFF "Une tabatière à musique")

The final t sound. Final t with or without the plural s is generally mute, as for example in petit, saint, concerts, meurt.

> Mon âme meur*t* de trop de soleil (DEBUSSY "De Fleurs")
> Peti*t* père, peti*t* père (DEBUSSY *Pelléas et Mélisande*)

In the following words the final t is pronounced: fat, mat, pat; in the Latin words fiat, stabat, vivat; in the word soit, if it stands by itself; and also in net, fait, if the word is accentuated as in au fait (but never when it appears in its plural form); and finally in dot, chut, zut, luth, rut, brut.

> Soi*t*: on paiera! (BIZET *Carmen*)
> Mon vieux lu*th* s'éveille (THOMAS *Mignon*)

Final t is pronounced after the consonants c, p, and s, as in abject, succinct, rapt, abrupt, transept, est (east), ouest.

The final t in the singular verb est (is) is always mute.

Finally, final t is pronounced in the numerals sept (the p is mute; see p. 80) and huit, and their combinations, such as vingt-sept, dix-huit, if they stand by themselves or are not followed by a consonant; the t of vingt is also pronounced by liaison in the number vingt et un.

> Le voilà, le beau Ving*t*unième! (DONIZETTI *La Fille du régiment*)
> Elle avait trois lys à la main et sep*t* étoiles dans les cheveux (DEBUSSY *La Damoiselle élue*)

The g sound. For definition and production see page 56. gg is pronounced like single g. Exceptions are the words suggérer, suggestion, suggestif, which are pronounced [sygʒere, sygʒestiõ, sygʒestif].

Initial and interior g is pronounced [g] before an a, o, ou, u, [ɑ̃], and [õ] as in galant, agonie, goût, figure, brigand, gonfler.

Je t'adore, brigand! (OFFENBACH *La Périchole*)
Ainsi ton *g*alant t'appelle (GOUNOD *Faust*)

g before e and i is pronounced [ʒ] (see p. 79). Words of Teutonic origin, however, retain the g in French: Gerolstein, Peer Gynt.

Gu before e and i is pronounced [g], as in guérir, guerre, guider, ligue, guitare.

Et les anges venus à notre rencontre chanteront, s'accompagnent de leurs *g*uitares (DEBUSSY *La Damoiselle élue*)
Que peut-être je *g*uérirai (DUPARC "Chanson triste")

Exceptions are the word arguer, where the u is pronounced [argye]; a few words such as aiguë, ambiguë, exiguë where the mute e has the hiatus sign [εgye]; also in nouns ending in -uité, such as oxiguité.

Words with -gui can also be combinations of g with the semivowel [gɥ] (see p. 76).

Words with -gua are pronounced [gwa], as in alguazil, jaguar.

Initial and interior g is pronounced [g] before all consonants with the exception of n, as in gloire, dogme, grand.

Le long du quai les *g*rands vaisseaux (FAURE "Les Berceaux")
*G*loire immortelle de nos aïeux (GOUNOD *Faust*)

Initial and interior g before n is almost always pronounced [ɲ] (see p. 77). There are, however, exceptions. Words of Greek origin with gn, such as gnome, physiognomie, diagnostic, are not liquidized. Also the words stagnant, stagnation, agnat, magnat are not liquidized.

Magnolia used to be liquidized, but for euphonic reasons it now has the [gn] sound. On the contrary, the words agnus and magnificat, which formerly had the [gn] sound, should be liquidized because of the Pope's ruling about the correct pronunciation of Latin.

Le livre vieux qui se déplie du Ma*g*nificat ruisselant (RAVEL "Sainte")

Final g, as in sang, poing, long, longtemps, vingt and derivatives, joug, and doigt, is never pronounced.

Des rivières de san*g* vont être répandues (BERLIOZ *L'Enfance du Christ*)
Et son petit doi*gt* coquet relève sa robe (MASSENET "Première Danse")

In foreign words, the final g is pronounced, as in zigzag.

Zig, zig, zag (SAINTS-SAENS "Danse macabre")

The k sound. For rules of definition and production see page 58. cc is pronounced [k]. Initial k appears in a very few foreign words, such as képi, kilogramme. Initial [k] is pronounced in words starting with c before the vowels a, o, ou, u [ã], [õ], and [œ̃], and all consonants, as in carillon, cortège, cueillir, couler, coeur, cuisine, candeur, comte, claque, cric-crac.

où l'on *c*ueille à pleine main (FAURE "Rêve d'amour")
Ils voient *c*ouler les ans (DEBUSSY *L'Enfant prodigue*)
Elle ne *c*royait pas dans sa *c*andeur naïve (THOMAS *Mignon*)

Interior [k] follows the same rules, as in reculer, accabler, occasion, Bacchus, aucun, acclamer, éclat, écraser, artistique, ecclésiastique.

qui ne se prend à au*c*un piège (POULENC "Le Garçon de Liège")
Et sous les fleurs, é*c*rasée (DELIBES *Lakmé*)

Interior c is pronounced g in the word second and all its derivatives.

ch followed by a, o, u, l, m, n, and r is pronounced k in many words of Greek origin, such as chorus, Chérubini, écho, orchèstre, Christ, chrétien (see also p. 79).

De la joie frais é*ch*os mêlés au vent qui frissonne (FAURE "Dans les ruines d'une abbaye")
Alors je demanderai au *Ch*rist notre Seigneur (DEBUSSY *La Damoiselle élue*)

Note: ch before the vowel i is sometimes pronounced k as in brachial, orchidée (see also p. 79). For pronunciation of c and sc before e and i, see page 79.

cc before e or i is pronounced [ks] as in acceleration, accident.

A*cc*eptez cet air de guitare en échange d'un bon repas (SEMET "Sérénade Gil Blas")

The c in combinations of ct is pronounced [k] as in instinctif, action, tact, direct, respectueux.

Des fous que tu respe*c*tes, des simples où tu te baignes (POULENC "Nous avons fait la nuit")

ct is mute in respe(ct), aspe(ct), instin(ct).

Final [k] is pronounced after a vowel other than a nasal one as in lac, sac, cognac, bec, sec, avec, Abimelech, Calpack, Klein Zach, Eisenach. This rule holds true also for the plurals, with the exception of la(cs).

Et j'ai sur le be*c* . . . un bon coup se*c* (MONSIGNY *Le Roi et le fermier*)
Il était une fois à la cour d'Eisena*ch* un petit avorton qui se nommait Klein Za*ch*! (OFFENBACH *Les Contes d'Hoffmann*)

Final c after a nasal vowel is mute as in banc, flanc, tronc.

> Comme ils vont du fer de leur lances harceler le flanc des taureaux! (BIZET *Carmen*)
> Vite, à mon banc de pierre! (MASSENET *Manon*)

The word donc presents difficulties. It is pronounced [dõk] (with a slight [k]) if it stands at the beginning of a sentence as in "Donc c'est fini"; and also if it is used in the sense of a logical conclusion as in "Je pense, donc je suis," or if it is underlined by stress; also before a vowel, usually tied to it by liaison.

> Dieu! où donc est elle? (HALEVY *La Juive*)

The c in donc is not pronounced before a consonant and at the end of a phrase.

> Vous êtes don(c) sorcier? (GOUNOD *Faust*)
> Tu ne m'aimes don(c) plus? (BIZET *Carmen*)

Words with q are pronounced like [k] as in coq, cinq, inquiet, question, tranquille, Quinquin, quand, que, qualité.

> Cinq ans et pas de leçons! (MASSENET "Première Danse")
> Sois sage ô ma douleur et tiens-toi plus tranquille (DEBUSSY "Recueillement")

qu is sometimes, but rarely, pronounced [kw], as in quatuor, obséquieux, loquace.

The x sound. The x is a combination of several sounds, its pronunciation depending on the succeeding vowel. Initial x is rare but always pronounced [ks] as in xylophone.

Interior x is pronounced [ks] as in axe, fixer, maxime, extase, exquise, luxe.

> C'est l'extase langoureuse (DEBUSSY "C'est l'extase langoureuse")
> C'est l'heure exquise (HAHN "L'Heure exquise")

Interior x is pronounced [s] in soixante, dix-sept, Bruxelles.

Interior x is pronounced [z] in deuxième, sixième, dixième, dix-huit, dix-neuf, six heures, deux hommes.

x in the prefix ex, followed by s, ce, or ci is pronounced [k], as in excellent, exciter, excentrique.

> Cependant l'excellent docteur Bolonais (DEBUSSY "Fantoches")

x in the prefix ex-, followed by a vowel or a mute h, is pronounced [gz], as in exalter, example, exhaler, exil, existence, exotique, exubérant, exaucer.

> S'exalte et se brise comme la mer (D'INDY "Lied maritime")

> Comme un prince acclamé revient d'un long exil (DEBUSSY "Voici que le printemps")

In the word execrable, the x is pronounced [ks].

Final x is usually mute, as in deux, doux, faux, aieux, heureux, paix, prix, croix.

> Il est doux, il est bon (MASSENET *Hérodiade*)
> Aux important la paix (DEBUSSY "Recueillement")
> Deux éclats tombés des cieux (DEBUSSY "Fleurs des blés")

The x in six and dix is mute, but it is pronounced [s] before the names of some months, as in six avril, dix octobre, and, for instance, in phrases such as j'en ai six.

Final x is pronounced [ks] in a few words of foreign origin, such as sphinx, lynx, syrinx, lux.

> Sphinx étonnant, véritable sirène (MASSENET *Manon*)
> Pour le jour des Hyacinthies il m'a donné une syrinx (DEBUSSY "La Flûte de Pan")

The r sound. In pronouncing the French r we encounter the same problems as in Italian or German, with the addition of yet another. The so-called Parisian r is widely used in speech. It is produced by relaxing the tip of the tongue toward the lower teeth, at the same time lifting the back of the tongue toward the palate. In this way, a sound is produced which is not unlike a soft guttural German ch. In singing, however, this Parisian r is never used — at least not by serious interpreters of French vocal art music, because it distorts the vocal line and muddies the enunciation. (For definition and production, also for more detailed discussion of the various r's, see pp. 46–47.) With the Parisian r eliminated, there remain the two other kinds: the dental or rolled r, and the uvular or guttural r. The former is the one mostly used by French singers. It is a common mistake of many English-speaking singers who want to appear more French than the French singers themselves, to employ the Parisian r. The accompanist or coach, however, ought to insist on the dental rolled r.

rr is pronounced like a single [r], but a longer roll on emotionally stressed words with rr, such as terreur, terrible, horreur, erreur, may be excused.

Initial r presents no phonetic problems. It is encountered in a multitude of words — rare, rose, rire, rouler, rond, rue.

> Et les soirs au balcon voilés de vapeur rose (DEBUSSY "Le Balcon")
> Sur votre jeune sein laissez rouler ma tête (DEBUSSY "Green")

Interior r is always pronounced after a vowel and

usually also after a consonant as in partir, fermer, glorieux, furieux, mercredi, arracher, courroux, corriger.

> Il est à moi! C'est mon esclave. Mes frères craignent
>   son courroux (SAINT-SAENS *Samson et Dalila*)
> Glorieux il se promène avec une allure de prince indien
>   (RAVEL "Le Paon")

r before mute e and after a consonant often tends to be elided or sounded very lightly, as in notre, votre, ordre, être, libre, quatre, maître. But this exception pertains mostly to everyday speech. Composers of songs usually see to it that a separate note is allotted to the syllable -tre of, for instance, no-tre.

> No-*tre* métier, no-*tre* métier est bon (BIZET *Carmen*)
> Oui, mon maî*tre* (OFFENBACH *Les Contes d'Hoff-
>   mann*)

Final r with or without the plural s is regularly pronounced, as in clair, zéphir, amour, trésor, hier, fier, chers, mer, ver, vers, hiver, coeurs, toujours.

> Voici l'hive*r* et son triste cortège (FAURE "Charité")
> Je rêve aux étés qui demeurent toujou*rs* (FAURE
>   "Ici-bas")

Final r is silent in infinitives of verbs ending in -er, and in nouns and adjectives ending in -ier.

> Chante(*r*), aime(*r*) sont douces choses (MASSENET
>   *Manon*)
> Viens te couche(*r*) sur mon coeur (CHAUSSON "Can-
>   tique à l'épouse")
> Telle aussi mon âme eut voulu mourir du premie(*r*)
>   baise(*r*) (CHAUSSON "Le Colibri")
> Cavalie(*r*) pâle au regard de velours (SAINT-SAENS
>   "La Solitaire")

Final r is also mute in nouns and adjectives ending in -cher or -ger, such as danger, léger, gaucher, rocher.

> Oh, que ton jeune amour, ce papillon lége*r* (FAURE
>   "Les Roses d'Ispahan")
> Dans mon premier dange*r* je veux dire ton nom (BIZET
>   *Carmen*)

Final r followed by a mute consonant changes the r from mute to pronounced, as in par(s), per(d), dor(t), cor(ps), bour(g).

> Il pe*rd* la tête (BIZET *Carmen*)
> Vieux bou*rgs*, jeunes maîtresses (GOUNOD *Faust*)
> Oh, quand je do*rs* (LISZT "Oh, quand je dors")

THE LIAISON

We have arrived at the concluding section about French singing diction; liaisons are the most complex aspect of French singing diction. Except for a few established rules, they are controversial, even among French-

men. The evolution of the French language has not bypassed the liaisons; on the contrary, their use is proof that style and taste are in continuous flux. It is no exaggeration to say that liaisons which were made thirty to forty years ago have been abolished and are scoffed at today. My colleagues and I were dumbfounded when the venerable octogenarian conductor Pierre Monteux, an undisputed master of French musical culture, upon returning to the Metropolitan Opera after an absence of nearly forty years, changed a sizable part of the established liaisons in the operas he conducted. It took some time and thought to find the explanation: his way of treating the liaisons evidently represented the style and the taste of his youth, fifty or sixty years before, and was the result of his intimate personal and artistic knowledge of French composers, starting as far back as Massenet.

The style of a performance—as I shall elaborate on later—is the product of three influences: the inherent style of a composition, the taste and musical practice of the age in which it is written, and the taste and practice of the age in which it is performed. This is also true of the practical use of French liaisons. Apart from the few established rules, it is mainly a matter of taste and culture. There is no highest authority to fall back upon. I do not claim to be by any means infallible. All I can do is to make accompanists and coaches conscious of the difficulties and to give them the rules, as well as the logical and esthetical reasons for the treatment of the liaisons in this chapter. Undoubtedly, the deeper the accompanist or coach descends into the well of the French language, the easier he will find it to solve the intricacies of the liaisons.

A liaison is the connection of the final mute consonant of one word and the initial vowel or semivowel or mute h of the following word. Of course, pronounced final consonants are also linked to the following vowel but one does not really call these liaisons. Many more liaisons are made in music and poetry than in everyday language. Rules for liaisons can be divided into three categories: where liaisons must not be made; where liaisons must be made; where a liaison is optional and the handling of it depends upon the taste and preference of the artist or teacher.

Forbidden liaisons. No liaison must be made before an aspirated h.

> Que j'admirais de tous mes yeux, les | hameaux, les
>   grands bois, la plaine (MASSENET *Manon*)

Et si je puis braver les | haines sacrilèges de l'ennemi triomphant (DELIBES *Lakmé*)

Liaison is to be avoided between words separated by punctuation marks.

Et tous deux, | oubliant le nom qui les outrage (GOUNOD *Roméo et Juliette*)

Si vous voulez, | amis, on peut la consulter (GOUNOD *Mireille*)

Wherever a liaison could produce misunderstanding of words for grammatical reasons, or where a liaison would change the meaning of a word or phrase, it must be avoided.

Dans les lianes posée et sous les fleurs, | écrasée elle attend des gens heureux (DELIBES *Lakmé*)

The word et is never connected by liaison to the following word.

Et | il écoute, point d'alarme dehors (RAVEL "Le Grillon")

Il le vise du bec, et | il plonge tout à coup (RAVEL "Le Cygne")

Liaison must never take place between the words oui, huit (numeral), onze, or the exclamations oh and ah and the final consonant of a preceding word. Dix-huit and vingt-huit use the liaison.

The mute final consonant of a noun or pronoun in the singular should not be tied over to its verb by liaison except for euphonic or musical reasons — if, for instance, the absence of a liaison would leave two vowels of identical or very similar kind unconnected.

Obéissons, quand leur voix‿appelle (MASSENET *Manon*)

Without liaison the [wa] and [a] would sound very unpleasant. This rule is to be taken with a grain of salt, anyway. In fast musical declamation, fluency will demand liaisons whether or not they are grammatically correct.

In phrases like mot‿à mot, nuit‿et jour, de temps‿en temps, liaison is made.

Il veille et nuit‿et jour mon front rêve enflammé (WIDOR "Albaÿde")

Nouns ending in a nasal vowel are not to be connected by liaisons.

Le printemps | est venu, ma belle (BERLIOZ "Villanelle")

Adjectives and adverbs ending in a nasal vowel are tied over by liaison with the exception of chacun, selon, environ, and quelqu'un, which are never tied over.

Chacun | à son gout (JOHANN STRAUSS *Die Fledermaus*)

No liaison should be made between the pronouns ils, elles, and on, placed after the verb in a question, as in sont-elles | arrivées?

Whenever a rest or a hiatus interrupts the flow of the musical phrase the liaison must not be made unless the tempo is very fast or unless a liaison helps the vocal line (in Figs. 74, 75, and 76 no liaison is made).

Figure 74. Saint-Saëns, *Samson et Dalila*

Figure 75. Bizet, *Carmen*

Figure 76. Offenbach, *Les Contes d'Hoffmann*

Required liaisons. Most liaisons are made between words belonging to the same phrase in a sentence. There must be some logical or musical connection between the words. If this connection exists, and if none of the rules which prohibit a liaison applies, the words should be linked.

Liaison is made between articles or pronouns such as les, des, ces, un and the following noun or adjective.

Cette rose c'est ton haleine, et ces‿étoiles sont tes‿yeux (DEBUSSY "Nuit d'étoiles")

Tout mon bonheur s'est envolé sur les‿ailes de la fauvette (BIZET "La Vieille Chanson")

Liaison is made between personal pronouns and the verbs to which they belong.

Vous‿arrivez fort mal (BIZET *Carmen*)

Ils‿accouraient, nuit‿et jour (HAHN "Si mes vers avaient des ailes")

Liaison is made between on and tout and the verb to which they belong; also between verbs and the words to which they belong in the question form.

Entre nous, tout‿est fini! (BIZET *Carmen*)

Et que l'on‿ait été par vous‿abandonné (MASSENET "Souvenez-vous, Vierge Marie")

Liaison is made between possessive, indefinite, and qualifying adjectives and the word to which they refer. Also between numerals and the word to which they refer.

Dans nos deux esprits ces miroirs jumeaux (DEBUSSY "La Mort des amants")

Ouvre au matin tes ailes (RAVEL "Chanson de la mariée")

Liaison is made between dont, quand, soit . . . soit, tant . . . que, tout, très, bien, quant à, and the words that follow them.

Soit par hasard soit à dessein (BIZET "La Vieille Chanson")

Quant à toi beau soldat, nous sommes manch(e) à manche (BIZET *Carmen*)

Liaison is made between prepositions and the words which follow them.

dans un pays lointain (CHAUSSON "Chanson per-pétuelle")

Ah, sans amour, sans amour s'en aller sur la mer (FAURÉ "Chanson du pêcheur")

Liaison is usually not made between vers (toward) or hors and the words that follow them except for euphonic reasons.

Pourquoi n'irai-je pas vers elle? (GOUNOD *Faust*)

Liaison is made between the third person singular or plural of avoir and être and the following word; also between auxiliary verbs and the infinitive which follows.

Les lys ont enfermé leur coeur (MASSENET "Cré-puscule")

Il eut en échange un baiser d'adieu (GOUNOD *Mireille*)

Liaison is made between two adverbs.

Il n'est pas encore mort (GOUNOD *Faust*)

Optional liaisons. Actually, all liaisons which are not expressly forbidden by the rules can be made, but sometimes taste and understanding require that they should not. In such places liaisons are optional, sometimes doubtful. No rules can be established. Euphony, the musical line, and, last but not least, the period in which the particular piece was composed are the criteria; of course, whatever we choose will be permeated with the taste of our time. In classical French music, liaisons are numerous. In modern music the tendency is toward fewer liaisons, though speed and fluency are conducive to making them.

I shall give but one example to illuminate the problem (Fig. 77). This "Je dis, hélas" has been the subject of

constant discussion among coaches. Partisans of the liaison claim it should be made notwithstanding the comma, because the melodic line requires it. Their adversaries fight against liaison, maintaining that the comma rules it out completely. I side with the latter group, not only because a slight break before the exclamation hélas is helpful to underline Micaela's plea, but also because I think the analogy with the first "Je dis" makes a separation desirable. But I realize that adherents of the unbroken legato line have the right to insist on their way of handling this phrase.

Specific rules for liaison. I have discussed the grammatical, esthetical, and musical rules for liaisons. Now we shall see how the different mute consonants are treated when tied over to the following vowel. In singing, it is extremely important to pronounce consonants tied over by liaison as late as possible and as gently as possible, and to lose only a minimum of time on them before gliding over to the following vowel.

b does not lend itself to a liaison.

Mute c is not tied over, as in blanc et noir.

The adjective franc and the noun porc can be linked to a following vowel.

Mute d of nouns is not likely to be linked by liaison.

Par un grand froid | au bois j'étais seulette (CHAR-PENTIER "La Petite Frileuse")

d is linked over in inverted verbal forms when the verb comes before its subject, or in adjectives when followed by their qualifying nouns, as in un grand écrivain.

The d of quand is tied by liaison.

Quand il eut achevé (DEBUSSY "La Chevelure")

The d in liaisons of quand, grand, and second is pronounced like a soft t, as in un grand ami ([grãt ami:]).

Le grand astre torrentiel (CHABRIER "Les Cigales")

In the combination rd the mute d is not apt to be tied over; instead, the r is linked.

Je ne pus d'abor(d) en répondre (CHAUSSON "Le Charme")

No liaisons are made with the f. The word neuf, however, can be tied by liaison. The f in this case is pronounced v, as in neuf heures ([nœv œ:r]). For euphonic reasons one would pronounce neuf enfants ([nœf ãfã]).

There is no unanimous opinion about the ability of the final g to be tied over by liaison. In nineteenth-century music, however, a liaison is preferable, as in sang (h)umain, if not expressly prohibited by one of the

Figure 77. Bizet, *Carmen,* undesirable liaison

above general rules. g in liaison is pronounced like a soft k. The words coing, poing, and seing are not apt to be linked by liaison.

Mute l is not tied over by liaison. The word gentil can be tied over but the l is in that case liquidized. Sonorous final l and liquidized l and ll are, of course, always tied over.

Sous le mol abri de la feuill(e) ombreuse (FAURE "Nell")

Liaison is never made with m.

The nouns ending in -an, -ien, -yen, -in, -ain, -oin, -on, -in cannot be linked to the following vowel.

Que ce vin | est mauvais (GOUNOD Faust)

The situation becomes complicated, however, in the case of adjectives, pronouns, prepositions, and adverbs. The words ancien, certain, hautain, humain, lointain, moyen, plein, prochain, soudain, souverain, vain, vilain before a noun are tied over by liaison. But they lose their nasal quality, as in vain espoir ([vɛn ɛspwar]).

De quelque lointain Angélus (CHABRIER "Les Cigales")

If the adjective is not followed by a noun the liaison does not take place, as in vain | et faux.

Bien, combien, and rien are apt to be tied over if tied to the following word logically, but they keep their nasal quality.

Nous n'avons rien à nous dire (DEBUSSY "La Flûte de Pan")

Adjectives ending in -in are not denasalized because if they were they would assume the feminine ending -ine. An exception is the word divin.

Oh! Sois béni divin enfant (BERLIOZ "L'Enfance du Christ")

Adjectives ending in -an do not adapt to liaison. En as pronoun, adverb, or preposition is subject to liaison.

Mon, ton, son, bon are tied over by liaison, but are denasalized.

Mon amour quand tu berceras mon triste coeur et mes pensées (DUPARC "Chanson triste")
Mon bonheur renaît sous ton aile (BACHELET "Chère Nuit")

On is subject to liaison without denasalization.

Ce bouquet eut le sort des choses qu'on oublie (MARTY "Fleurs fanées")

Words ending in -un are liable to liaison, but are not denasalized, because they would assume the feminine ending -une.

Sous ta fenêtre un autre chante (CHARPENTIER "A Mules")

Un is not tied by liaison in the phrases: un et trois, un ou deux, un et un. The liaison is made when the noun is multiplied by un, as in vingt et un ans. In the expressions un à un, l'un ou l'autre, l'un avec l'autre, l'un et l'autre, l'un après l'autre, the liaison is optional.

Je les écouté, un à un (HUE "Les Clochettes des muguets")

p does not lend itself to liaison.

For q, see c.

Le coq a chanté (SAINT-SAENS "Danse macabre")

Nouns ending in -er and -ier are not tied over if the following word is an adjective or a verb.

De blé le grenier | est plein (PIERNE "Le Moulin")

Adjectives ending in -er, if followed by a noun, are liable to liaison, as in premier ami.

Verbs ending in -er are subject to liaison, especially in music.

In all liaisons, the r must be pronounced very softly, the singer immediately gliding over to the following vowel.

We must distinguish between s as singular ending and the plural s. In almost all liaisons the s is pronounced voiced z.

The singular s. Nouns are usually tied over.

Par ton printemps embaumé (DUVERNOY "Douces Larmes")

Adjectives are also tied over.

Pour que tu sois la plus aimée (PALADILHE "Les Trois Prières")

Verbs are mostly tied over.

Viens auprès de ma couche (LISZT "Oh, quand je dors")

Verbs in the second person singular ending on -es are not subject to liaison, as in Tu chantes | à l'opéra.

Some verbal endings of être do not lend themselves well to a liaison, especially those ending in -es or -s, as in Tu as | aimé.

Prepositions like dans, des, sans, chez, sous, après, depuis are linked to the next word.

Après un rêve (FAURE "Après un rêve")
Et vais me mirer dans un flot (LALO "La Chanson de l'alouette")

The adverbs plus, moins, très, assez, puis, autrefois, parfois, longtemps and the words pas, plus, jamais are likewise linked over to the next word.

N'est-il plus‿un parfum qui reste (DEBUSSY "Romance")

Qui n'est pas‿aimé perd le moi de Mai (CHARPENTIER "Prière")

Mais may or may not take the liaison, depending upon punctuation and musical phrasing.

Mais‿en attendant qu'il vienne (BIZET *Carmen*)

Mais, ô mon bien‿aimé (SAINT-SAENS *Samson et Dalila*)

ss keeps the [s] sound in liaisons.

The words fils, jadis, lys, which were tied over with the [s] sound in former times, now tend to change the sound to [z] in liaisons.

The plural s. Most plural forms are subject to liaison. Where the plural s follows another mute consonant, the s is tied over.

Voyez les! regards‿impudents (BIZET *Carmen*)

Words in singular form link the r.

Le discour(s)‿est très net (BIZET *Carmen*)

The verbs (je) pars, (tu) sors, tie over the r.

Toujours, hors, vers, envers follow the same principle, as in ver(s)‿un monde meilleur.

Et nous étions liés pour toujour(s)‿ainsi (DEBUSSY "La Chevelure")

In words with plural s a liaison is usually made with the s ([z]), as in plusieurs‿enfants.

Splendeurs‿inconnues, lueurs divines‿entrevues (FAURE "Après un rêve")

In endings with ts, the s is linked to the next word.

In general the t is tied over by liaison.

Mais ce que serait cet‿émoi (CHAUSSON "Le Charme")

The conjunction et is never subject to liaison with the following word.

In endings with rt, the r is linked to the next vowel.

De chaque branche par(t)‿une voix (HAHN "L'Heure exquise")

O sor(t)‿amer, ô dur(e)‿absence (BERLIOZ "L'Absence")

The adverb fort ties the t over, as in fort‿aimable. Likewise the t is subject to liaison in interrogative phrases.

For reasons of euphony the t is tied over in:

Cela ne sert‿à rien (BIZET *Carmen*)

ct endings tie the t over.

In the words aspect, respect, suspect, and circonspect, the c ([k]) is tied over, as in quel aspec(t)‿affreux. This, however, is an antiquated rule. Today, both c and t tend to be mute.

The x is subject to liaison. It assumes the sound [z].

La paix‿est faite (GOUNOD *Faust*)

Des bons vieux‿airs très connus (MASSENET "Première Danse")

The x in the word noix is never linked.

The z sound, too, is tied over, as in restez‿avec moi.

Laissez‿un peu, de grâce (GOUNOD *Faust*)

The z in the words nez and riz in the singular is not subject to liaison, as in ne(z) à ne(z); in the plural form it is tied over.

PHONETIC TRANSCRIPTION OF CAVATINA FROM GOUNOD'S "FAUST"

kɛl trubl ɛ̃kɔny: mə penɛ:trə? ʒə sɑ̃ lamu:r sɑ̃pare: də mɔn ɛ:trə! o margəri:tə, a tɛ pje mə vwasi:!

saly:! dəmoerə ʃast‿e pyrə, u sə dəvi:nə la prezɑ̃:sə dyn‿a:m‿inɔsɑ̃:t e divi:nə! kə də riʃɛ:s ɑ̃ sɛtə povrəte:! ɑ̃ sə redwi:, kə də felisite:! o natyrə, sɛ la kə ty la fi si bɛlə!

sɛ la kə sɛt‿ɑ̃fɑ̃ a dɔrmi su tɔn‿ɛ:l, agrɑ̃di: su tez jø. la kə tɔn alɛ:nə ɑ̃vəlopɑ̃: sɔn‿a:mə, ty fiz‿avɛk‿amu:r epanui:r la fam‿ɑ̃ sɛt‿ɑ̃ʒə de sjø! sɛ la! wi, sɛ la!

PHONETIC TRANSCRIPTION OF FAURE'S "LES BERCEAUX"

lə lõ: dy ke:, lɛ grɑ̃: vɛso:, kə la hu:l‿ɛ̃klin ɑ̃ silɑ̃sə, nə prənə pa: gard‿o bɛrso:, kə la mɛ̃ de famə balɑ̃sə. mɛ vjɛ̃dra: lə ʒu:r dez‿adjø, kar il fo kə lɛ famə plørə, e kə lez‿ɔmə kyriø: tɑ̃tə lez‿ɔrizõ: ki lørə!

e sə ʒu:r la lɛ grɑ̃ vɛso:, fɥɑ̃ lə pɔ:r ki diminyə, sɑ̃tə lər masə rətəny:ə pa:r la:mə de lwɛ̃tɛ̃: bɛrso:.

7

Spanish
Phonetics and Diction

As IS true of all other European languages, the variety of Spanish dialects is great, extending not only to the frontiers of the Iberian peninsula but to Central and South America as well. The cultured singer of Spanish music will restrict his diction to two main dialects. When he sings songs written in Spain or by Spanish composers and poets he will employ the Castilian pronunciation. When he sings Spanish music from the Western hemisphere he will use a somewhat different pronunciation. And even here, the diction varies: Argentinians or Chileans pronounce certain sounds quite differently from, for instance, Mexicans.

But for all practical singing purposes, the accompanist or coach will have to teach Castilian Spanish and the Mexican variety. The vocal literature used in concerts in the United States is not overly rich. One will encounter principally songs by de Falla, Turina, Obradors, Niñ, and Granados; Mexican songs by Ponce and Revueltas; and the large array of folk songs of Central and South America.

Spanish phonetics differ from their Italian counterpart in only a few respects. I shall therefore limit myself to discussing the sounds characteristic of Spanish. At the end of this chapter I shall transcribe phonetically one Castilian Spanish and one Mexican song.

VOWELS

In singing, all Spanish vowels are pronounced like the Italian vowels. This rule is also valid for vowels which may be pronounced differently in spoken Spanish, such as the a (akin to the French a).

The e and o vowels are usually open, but not quite so open as the Italian [ɛ] and [ɔ]. I shall, however, use these signs in Spanish phonetic transcriptions.

The y when it stands by itself is pronounced like an Italian i.

SEMIVOWELS

Spanish has the [w] and the [j] semivowels. The semivocalic pronunciation is used when i, y, or u stands before a more open vowel.

Cualquiera que el tejado (DE FALLA "Seguidilla murciana")
Voy a partir al puerto donde se halla la barca (PONCE "Voy a partir")
Clavelitos, que vienen de Granada (VALVERDE "Clavelitos")
Yo no sé qué siento (DE FALLA El amor brujo)

DIPHTHONGS

Spanish has diphthongs like German. The two vowels need not be sung separately as in Italian, but are connected in a diphthongal sound, as in aire, auto, oiga.

Así que el baile empieza, si hay donaire (GRANADOS Goyescas)
La mi sola, Laureola (OBRADORS "La mi sola, Laureola")
Cuando estoy a tú lado (MEXICAN FOLKSONG "Yo no sé si me quieres")

CONSONANTS

Consonants that cannot be found in Italian are j, x, z, and b, d, g, in some positions and combinations.

The voiced occlusive sounds b, d, and g keep their occlusive quality as initial consonants, as in beber, decir, gato, and as interior sounds when they are preceded by an m or n, or, in the case of the d, also by an l.

These occlusive sounds change into voiced fricative sounds in so-called weak positions, i.e., as interior sounds. The b (phonetically expressed by [β]) in this case is pronounced as a lazy v, as an American from the South would pronounce it in love. The lips make a slight effort to close, but never quite effect the occlusion.

Y yo, como soy tan po*b*re (NIN "El vito")
Luz de mis ojos, si luz no hu*b*iera, Ha*b*ias de ser (MEXICAN FOLKSONG "Carmela")

D [ð] in an interior (weak) position is a voiced dental fricative produced and pronounced like the th in the English words the, other, this, as in lado, desnudo. As final sound, the d becomes very soft and indistinct.

Pue*d*e que en el camino nos encontremos (DE FALLA "Seguidilla murciana")

Interior g [ɣ] before a and o and a consonant other than m or n receives a weak velar fricative voiced sound. It is produced the same way as the Italian g (see p. 56), but occlusion is not effected. The back part of the tongue and the soft palate never quite connect, as in analogo, luego.

Vivir lejos de tu ve*g*a (BARIERA Y CALLEJA "Granadinas")
Desengañémonos ya, mal pa*g*ado pensamiento (NIN "Desengañémonos ya")

The g in Spanish can stand for several other sounds as well. Before an e and an i, it becomes a voiceless velar fricative sound similar to the ch [x] in the German ach, or the Scottish loch (see p. 107 for production). The only difference is that the Spanish ge or gi sounds are produced slightly more forward, in the velar section of the mouth, not in the uvular, guttural spot. They are therefore not so explosive or so strongly stressed as their German equivalents.

No se te vaya a escapar y te vaya a ti aco*g*er (OBRADORS "El molondrón")
Olas *g*igantes que os rompeis bramando (TURINA "Tres poemas")
Más toreo y más *g*itano (OBRADORS "Canción del café de chinitas")

The gu sound is pronounced [g] before an e or i, or a consonant, and [gw] before an a or o.

Le juyes, y te persi*gu*e (DE FALLA El amor brujo)
Pre*gu*ntale al manso rio (MEXICAN FOLKSONG "Preguntale á las estrellas")
Acaso al rey del día *gu*arda rencor (GRANADOS Goyescas)

Gü before an e or i is pronounced [gw].

Y hay que ver las coces que le dió mi "a*gü*elo" (OBRADORS "El molondrón")

Spanish y [j] is pronounced like the English y in you except when it stands by itself (see p. 89). In strong emotion it may become a fricative like the ch in the German ich.

Spanish j in all positions is pronounced [x], as in Juan, hijo, mujer. As final sound it tends to disappear, as in reloj.

A la *J*ota que hay muchas palomas (NIN "A la jota")
Las azoteas y calles hierven de curioso pueblo, que en él fi*j*ando los o*j*os (TURINA "Romance")

qu before an e or i is pronounced [k], as in queso, quedar, quien.

Spanish c before a, o, or u is pronounced [k], as in comer, casa, cuyo.

El *qu*e las moriscas lunas llevó glorioso a Toledo y torna con mil *c*autívos y *c*argado te trofeos (TURINA "Romance")

cu before another vowel is pronounced [kw], as in cue, cui, cuerpo, cuidado.

*Cu*alquiera que el tejado tenga de vidrio (DE FALLA "Seguidilla murciana")
Dame Amor besos sin *cu*ento (OBRADORS "Al amor")

c before an e and i is a voiceless dental fricative [θ], as in cinco, diciembre. It is pronounced like th in thorn, wrath.

Por menos pre*c*ios se vende (DE FALLA "El paño moruno")
Duérmete, lu*c*erito de la mañana (DE FALLA "Nana")

This is true only of Castilian Spanish. In Mexican Spanish c before e or i is pronounced [s], as in French. Southern Spain — Andalusia in particular, home of the most beautiful folk songs — pronounces c as the French and Mexicans do. It is therefore quite justifiable to sing many of the de Falla, Turina, Granados songs in this way.

ch in Spanish is pronounced like the Italian [tʃ], as in charro, ancho.

Guarda quizás su pe*ch*o oculto tal dolor (GRANADOS Goyescas)
Como la man*ch*a oscura orlado en fuego (TURINA "Rima")

Spanish ñ (as in doña, señor) is simply a way of indicating that palatal nasal sound is required. It corresponds to the Italian and French gn [ɲ].

ng and nc (as in ningun, nunca) — [ŋ] — are pronounced as in the German words singen, Anker, or the corresponding English words sing, anchor.

ll (as in llamar, allegar, allí) — [ʎ] — is the Spanish

equivalent of the Italian gl. In singing, the ll is pronounced somewhat weaker than in speaking.

> Alma sintamos! Ojos *ll*orar! (NIN "Alma
> sintamos")
> "Madre, á la ori*ll*a" (DE FALLA "Canción")

ll in Central America is pronounced like the liquidized ll in the French word fille.

Whereas the word llamar in Castilian Spanish is pronounced [ʎamaːr], its Mexican pronunciation is [jamaːr].

The single Spanish r is produced exactly like the Italian r, and pronounced somewhat more strongly. r between vowels and as a final sound is weak, as in pero, mujer. This last sound is different from the Italian final r, which is always strong.

Initial r, r after an n or s, and rr (as in rosa, garra, arbol, honra) are pronounced very strongly, much stronger than their Italian counterparts.

> Antes de que *r*ompa el día (OBRADORS "La madruga")
> A*rr*ieros semos (DE FALLA "Seguidilla murciana")

s in Spanish (as in soy, estoy, rosa, más) equals the Italian voiceless s.

> Agua qui*s*iera *s*er luz y alma mía (TURINA "Anhelos")
> *S*oy má*s* valiente que tú (OBRADORS "Canción del café de chinitas")

s before a voiced consonant takes on the voiced sound, as in rasgar [rrazgar].

Spanish z equals the sound of the c ([θ]) before e or i, as in zapato, hizo, diez.

> ¿Corazón, porque pasais? (OBRADORS "¿Corazón porque pasais?")
> Tres morillas tan lo*z*anas (OBRADORS "Tres morillas")

In American Spanish the z is pronounced like the voiceless Italian s.

Spanish h is silent. Hu before vowels is pronounced [w] as in huelga, huevo.

The Spanish x is pronounced [ks] as in inextinguible, exhalar. In South American Spanish the j sound is now mostly spelled with an x and pronounced [x], as in Mejico-Mexico.

Many Mexican proper names of Indian origin, such as Xochimilco, Tuxpan, Ixtapan, contain an x. There is no set rule for pronunciation of these names. For instance, Xochimilco is pronounced [sɔtʃimilkɔ], Oaxaca [ɔaxaka], Tuxpan [tukspan].

DOUBLE CONSONANTS

All double consonants in Spanish are pronounced strongly and explosively as in Italian. Liaisons and separations in Spanish singing diction are made the same way as in Italian.

PHONETIC TRANSCRIPTION OF CASTILIAN SPANISH: "SEGUIDILLA MURCIANA" FROM THE SEVEN NATIONAL SONGS BY MANUEL DE FALLA

kwalkjɛra kɛ‿ɛl tɛxaðɔ tɛŋga dɛ viðrjɔ. nɔ dɛβɛ tirar pjɛðras al dɛl vɛθinɔ. arrjɛrɔs sɛmɔs. pwɛðɛ kɛ‿ɛn ɛl kamiːnɔ nɔs ɛnkɔntrɛmɔs!

pɔr tu mutʃa inkɔnstanθja jɔ tɛ kɔmparɔ kɔn pɛsɛta kɛ kɔrrɛ dɛ manɔ ɛn manɔ; kɛ al fin sɛ bɔrra, i krɛjɛndɔla falsa naðjɛ la tɔma!

PHONETIC TRANSCRIPTION OF MEXICAN SPANISH FOLKSONG: "PREGUNTALE A LAS ESTRELLAS"

prɛguntalɛ‿a las ɛstrɛjas, si nɔ dɛ nɔtʃɛ mɛ vɛn jɔraːr, prɛguntalɛ si nɔ buskɔ, para aðɔrarrtɛ la sɔlɛðad. prɛguntalɛ‿al mansɔ riɔ si ɛl jantɔ miɔ nɔ vɛ kɔrrɛr. prɛguntalɛ‿a tɔðɔ‿ɛl mundɔ si nɔ‿ɛs prɔfundɔ mi paðɛsɛr.

ja nunka duðɛs kɛ jɔ tɛ kjɛrɔ, kɛ pɔr ti mwɛrɔ lɔkɔ dɛ‿amɔr; a naðjɛ amas, a naðjɛ kjɛrɛs, ojɛ las kɛxas dɛ mi amɔr.

prɛguntalɛ‿a las flɔrɛs, si mis amɔrɛs lɛs kwɛntɔ jɔ, kwandɔ la kajaða nɔtʃɛ sjɛrra su brɔtʃɛ, suspiːrɔ jɔ, prɛguntalɛ‿a las aːvɛs, si tu nɔ saːβɛs lɔ kɛ‿ɛs amɔr, prɛguntalɛ‿a tɔðɔ‿ɛl praːðɔ, si nɔ‿ɛ lutʃaðɔ kɔn mi dɔlɔr.

tu bjɛn kɔmprɛndɛs, kɛ jɔ tɛ kjɛrɔ, kɛ pɔr ti mwɛrɔ, sɔlɔ pɔr ti; pɔrkɛ tɛ kjɛrɔ bjɛn dɛ mi viːða, sɔlɔ‿ɛn ɛl mundɔ tɛ kjɛrɔ‿a ti.

8

German
Phonetics and Diction

THOUGH we are confined in Italian and French to tradition and experience as our supreme law for phonetics and diction, we can base our rules for German diction on an officially sanctioned publication, *Deutsche Bühnenaussprache-Hochsprache*, by Theodor Siebs, which was published and republished at the initiative of the Association of German Theatrical Stages and the German Actors Union. It numbers among its contributors the foremost experts in phonetics and stage diction, and deals with singing diction as well. The accompanist or coach who wants to give his pupils an authoritative account will do well to own the book. My experience with German diction has at almost all points been supported by this book. I base this chapter on it and will deviate only where adjustment to singing is necessary.

The vowels in German are, as in the Romance languages, the main elements on which the tones are built. They must be sung clearly, without any trace of diphthongization, unless coloring, covering, or blending of tones into vocal phrases warrants a certain adjustment. In German, as in the Romance languages, the tones are sung on vowels, the consonants following them being drawn to the next vowel. There is a widely held misconception that German is the language of harsh consonants. The old Wagnerian school and some singers of the past, who stressed consonants in a heavy Teutonic fashion have done great harm to the singing of German. As in many other musical fields, our taste has changed here, too. Today we prefer German to be sung according to the principles of the classical Italian school of singing, giving full rights to the onomatopoetical power of consonants, but with the diction based primarily on pure articulation of vowels.

THE A VOWEL

There are only two a's in German, the long a as in Rat and Fahrt, corresponding to the English word father, and the short a as in Mann and Sache, corresponding to the second a in the English exclamation aha!

The long a sound. a in German is long when it is spelled aa or ah, as for instance in Aar, Paar, Saal, Fahrt, Wahn. Phonetically, it is expressed by the symbol [a].

Wahn, Wahn, überall Wahn (WAGNER *Die Meistersinger von Nürnberg*)
Woher ich kam der Fahrt (WAGNER *Lohengrin*)

It is long when it forms the end of a syllable, as in da, ja, Vater, graben, tagen.

Walvater harret dein (WAGNER *Die Walküre*)
Nur hurtig fort, nur frisch gegraben (BEETHOVEN *Fidelio*)

When a stands in front of a single consonant in the same syllable, as in kam, war, Grab, Schwan, it is long.

Nun sei bedankt, mein lieber Schwan! (WAGNER *Lohengrin*)
Ein Stündlein wohl vor Tag (WOLF "Mörike Lieder")

The a in some words to which the above rules appear to apply is short: ab, Ungemach, Walfisch, am, Bräutigam, Garten, hart, das, was, du hast, er hat, Monat, Klatsch.

Wie wehr ich da dem Ungemach (WAGNER *Die Meistersinger von Nürnberg*)
Ich muss hier warten (RICHARD STRAUSS *Elektra*)

The short a sound. a is short in front of more than one consonant, as in bald, Land, Rast, warten, lassen, and before sch, as in rasch, Fasching.

a before ch and ss is usually short, as in Bach, wachen, nass.

> Warte nur balde ruhest du auch (SCHUBERT "Über allen Wipfeln ist Ruh")
> Warten lassen (RICHARD STRAUSS *Der Rosenkavalier*)

It assumes the long sound, however, in some cases, as in brach, Frass.

Some words to which the rules for short a's apply have the long a. These are exceptions, expressly created by the committee of experts who regulated German pronunciation. Such words are ihr habt, gehabt, Gemach, Schmach, Jagd, Walstatt, Schicksal, achtsam, Papst, dankbar, Arzt, Art, Heirat.

> Erhebe dich, Genossin meiner Schmach (WAGNER *Lohengrin*)
> Auf der Walstatt seh'n wir uns wieder (WAGNER *Die Walküre*)
> Noch wie mein' Nam' und Art (WAGNER *Lohengrin*)

The e sounds. There are four kinds of e in German: the long closed e, the long more open e, the short open e, and the weak e. All these sounds can be found in the languages discussed above.

The long closed e [e] *sound.* This sound corresponds to the French é, or the e in the English words chaos and chaotic (for description and production see p. 67).

e is long and closed when spelled ee or eh, as in See, fehlen, or when it is itself a syllable.

> Angelehnt an die Epheuwand (WOLF "An eine Aeolsharfe")
> Unsere Liebe muss ewig bestehn! (BRAHMS "Von ewiger Liebe")
> Ich such' im Schnee vergebens nach ihrer Tritte Spur (SCHUBERT "Erstarrung")

e is long when it is the last letter of an accentuated syllable, as in Leben, heben, beten.

> Was vermeid' ich denn die Wege (SCHUBERT "Der Wegweiser")
> O wie selig seid ihr doch, ihr Frommen (J. S. BACH "Song")

When followed by a single consonant in the same syllable, as in schwer, wer, wem, e is long.

> O wüsst ich doch den Weg zurück! (BRAHMS "Song")
> Wer in die Fremde will wandern, der muss mit der Liebsten gehn (WOLF "Heimweh")

e in word forms contracted by elision of another vowel is pronounced long and closed, as in gebt (which comes from gebet).

> Gebt eu're Eifersucht nur hin, zu werben kommt mir

nicht im Sinn (WAGNER *Die Meistersinger von Nürnberg*)

Some e sounds have been declared long and closed by agreement of the committee of experts (see p. 92), such as Krebs, nebst, Erde, Herd, Pferd, werden, Schwert, Erz, stets.

> Ein Schwert verhiess mir der Vater (WAGNER *Die Walküre*)
> Wes Herd dies auch sei (WAGNER *Die Walküre*)
> Die liebe Erde allüberall blüht auf (MAHLER *Das Lied von der Erde*)

The long, more open ä [ɛ] *sound.* This sound corresponds to the French è (for description and production see p. 66).

ä is long, but more open when it is spelled äh, as in Ähre, Fährte.

> Früh, wann die Hähne krähn (WOLF "Das verlassene Mägdlein")
> Die Luft ging durch die Felder, die Ähren wogten sacht (SCHUMANN "Mondnacht")

ä is long and more open when it ends a syllable, as in Träne, Täler.

> Träne auf Träne dann stürzet hernieder (WOLF "Das verlassene Mägdlein")

When it is followed by a single consonant in the same syllable, as in Bär, spät, ä is also long and more open.

> Aus alten Märchen winkt es hervor mit weisser Hand (SCHUMANN "Aus alten Märchen")

ä is also long and more open before a ch or an ss, if closely related or lengthened forms have the long vowel, as in Gespräch, Gefäss.

> Drin ein Gefäss voll wundertätgem Segen (WAGNER *Lohengrin*)

Some ä sounds have been established long and more open by agreement (see p. 92), as in Städte, zärtlich, Rätsel.

> Beschirmte Städt' und Burgen liess ich bau'n (WAGNER *Lohengrin*)

The short open e sound. This vowel corresponds exactly to the sound in the English bell and held, or the Italian [ɛ] (for description and production see p. 66).

e or ä is short and open when it appears before more than one consonant or before a ch, as in Held, hält, Nächte, schlecht, Bett.

> Ich habe keine guten Nächte! (RICHARD STRAUSS *Elektra*)
> Behalt ihn, Held! (WAGNER *Götterdämmerung*)

Some exceptions exist: e is short and open in weg, Herzog, Vers, Herz, es, des.

> Was drängst du denn so wunderlich, mein Herz, mein Herz? (SCHUBERT "Die Post")
> Doch will der Held nicht Herzog sein genannt (WAGNER *Lohengrin*)

The weak e [ə]. The sound corresponds to the French weak e. (For description and production see p. 68.)

e is pronounced [ə] in unaccentuated initial, medial, or final syllables, as in Gerede, Ebene, alle.

> Geh, Geliebter, geh' jetzt! (WOLF *Spanisches Liederbuch*)
> Tiefe Stille herrscht im Wasser (SCHUBERT "Meeres Stille")

This weak e appears in many unaccentuated final syllables on -er, -el, -en, -em, as in jeder, jeden, jedem. The English-speaking singer has great difficulty in pronouncing these e's weak. Thorough study of the above rule should suffice to remedy this difficulty. The pronunciation of the word sister may also be used to help in explaining.

Figure 78. Weber, *Der Freischütz*, German "weak e"

Figure 79. Mozart, *Die Zauberflöte*, German "weak e"

Although there is no mute e in German (see p. 68), it is sometimes advisable for vocal reasons to interpolate it between two consonants, especially if they are of the same kind. The singing line may otherwise be in danger of being broken by the harshness of the consonants, as illustrated in Figure 78 (between wohl and lacht) and Figure 79 (between nicht and der).

THE I SOUNDS

There are two kinds of i sounds: the long closed i and the short open i.

The long closed i [i] *sound.* The long closed i corresponds exactly to the English e in me, see, sea. In German the long closed i appears in words like dir, wir, wider, Lid, Nische. It can also be spelled ie, as in die, Miete, Lied, or ih, as in ihr (for description and production see p. 49). In German, as in Italian, it is most important that the tongue is low and grooved while pronouncing an i sound.

> Auf *ih*rem Leibrösslein, so weiss w*ie* der Schnee (WOLF "Der Gärtner")
> S*ie*h Tam*i*no, d*ie*se Tränen fl*ie*ssen, Trauter, d*ir* allein! (MOZART *Die Zauberflöte*)

The short open i *sound.* The short open i corresponds to the English i in words such as tin, in, bin. In German it appears in all words that are not covered by the above rules for the long closed i. That means i is pronounced short if it stands in front of more than one vowel, as in Tisch, Kind, bitte.

> Am fr*i*sch geschn*i*ttenen Wanderstab (WOLF "Fussreise")
> Des H*i*mmels Segen belohne d*i*ch! (MOZART *Die Entführung aus dem Serail*)

Some words do not conform to the above rules: in vierzehn, vierzig, viertel, the i should be long but has been declared short (see p. 92) (but not in vier and Vierteil).

THE O VOWEL AND Ö UMLAUT

There is a great variety of o and ö sounds in German. Some have equivalents in English.

The long closed o [o] *sound.* For description and production, see page 50. German o is pronounced long and closed when it is the final sound in a syllable as in so, wo; or if the o stands in front of a single consonant, as in rot, holen; and also in some words containing an o followed by a ch or an ss, like hoch or gross, bloss, Stoss. There are, however, comparatively few of these words. This kind of o can also be expressed by oo, as in Moos, or oh as in Lohe.

> Wie ich hinaus v*or*'s T*or* gekommen (WOLF "Auf einer Wanderung")
> Ein St*o*ss — und er verstummt! (BEETHOVEN *Fidelio*)
> Ein Wälsung wächst dir im Sch*o*ss (WAGNER *Die Walküre*)
> Dämmert der Tag? Oder leuchtet die L*o*he? (WAGNER *Götterdämmerung*)

The o in Obst, beobachten, Obacht, Mond, Montag, Ostern, Trost, Kloster is long.

> Der M*o*nd steht über dem Berge (BRAHMS "Ständchen")
> Ein Kl*o*ster ist zu gut! (RICHARD STRAUSS *Der Rosenkavalier*)

This pure closed o does not exist in the English language, where it is always diphthongized as in no, oh, cold, blow.

The short open o [ɔ] *sound.* For description and production, see pages 49–50. Short open o stands in front of more than one vowel as in kommen, rollen, kosten.

Sometimes also before ch or ss, as in doch, Ross, etc. (consult an orthophonic dictionary).

Du holde Kunst (SCHUBERT "An die Musik")
Er kommt, er kommt, o Wonne meiner Brust! (COR-
NELIUS Der Barbier von Bagdad)
Am leuchtenden Sommermorgen (SCHUMANN "Am
leuchtenden Sommermorgen")

There are again a few exceptions, where the o instead of being long has been declared short by the above-mentioned committee of experts: ob, Hochzeit, vom, von, Ost, Osten, erloschen, gedroschen.

Nach Osten weithin dehnt sich ein Wald (WAGNER
Die Walküre)
Und als das Korn gedroschen war (MAHLER "Das ir-
dische Leben")

In English, this short open o is found only in unstressed syllables as, for instance, in omit, or the o sound in words that start with the prefix pro- (provide is an example).

The accompanist or coach must be careful to correct any tendency on the part of the singer to pronounce the o toward the darkened a, unless the melodic line warrants it.

THE Ö UMLAUT SOUNDS

These sounds, phonetically, stand between o and e. They can be found long and closed, or short and open. They must be formed by protruding, completely rounded lips. For description and production see page 69.

The long closed ö *[ø] sound.* For description and production, see page 69. [ø] must be pronounced like the long closed eu or oeu in French, as in eux or heureux. It has no real equivalent in English. The nearest approximation can be found in the words learn and herb, but these words are produced with a more open sound. In order to approach and reach the sound of [ø], the lips must be completely rounded and close together and the opening of the mouth must be small, until the real long closed ö sound is perfected.

ö is long and closed when it forms a syllable by itself, as in Öde, or when it is followed by a single consonant, as in Öl and König. Also it is long and closed if it is preceded or followed by an h, as in Höhle and Möhre, or if its singular form contains a long closed o, as in Schösse (Schoss), Stösse (Stoss).

Der öde Tag zum letztenmal! (WAGNER Tristan und
Isolde)
O König, das kann ich dir nicht sagen! (WAGNER Tris-
tan und Isolde)

In einer Höhle hütet er Fafners Hort (WAGNER Die
Walküre)
Höchstes Vertrau'n hast du mir schon zu danken!
(WAGNER Lohengrin)

There are a few exceptions where the ö, although followed by more than one consonant, must be pronounced long, as in Gehöft, Behörde, Börse, trösten, Österreich, rösten.

Nun Herr, wess soll ich mich trösten? (BRAHMS Ein
deutsches Requiem)
Dem Ahnenspiegel Österreichs (RICHARD STRAUSS
Der Rosenkavalier)

The short open ö *[œ] sound.* For description and production, see page 69. Open ö likewise has no equivalent in English; it corresponds to the open eu in the French coeur.

In German, ö is pronounced short and open wherever it stands before more than one consonant, as in Söller or Wölfe, and also before sch as in Frösche, or in front of ch or ss if the singular of the word has a short open o, as in Köche (Koch), Schlösser (Schloss).

Der Herr auf seinem Rösseli sagt zu der Frau im
Schlösseli (MAHLER "Um schlimme Kinder artig zu
machen")
Löschet sie, immerzu (BRAHMS "Vergebliches Ständ-
chen")
Ein Wölfing kündet dir das! (WAGNER Die Walküre)

The following exercise for English-speaking singers might be helpful: the singer should pronounce the word her in English, then go over to pronouncing the same word with a long closed ö in German by protruding and rounding his lips and making the mouth smaller. In this way he would arrive at an approximate pronunciation of the word hören. The opposite should be done if an open ö is desired; the lips should still be protruded and rounded but the mouth should be opened further. In this way we might arrive at the word Hörner. With these exercises, a singer could learn the correct ö sounds in a short time. Some accompanists or coaches mark with *er* the spots in songs and arias which contain ö's. This leaves too much room for misunderstanding. It is always better to make the singer conscious of the right pronunciation by means of the above exercise and the phonetic explanation of what happens to mouth and lips. Of course, the use of a tape recorder will also help to alleviate the troubles of the English-speaking singer.

The u *vowel and* ü *umlaut sounds.* For description and production of u, see page 50. No other vowel creates such difficulty for the English-speaking singer. The u sound in English is pronounced farther back in the mouth than the Italian or German u. Besides, in English it is never pure but is always diphthongized to sound like yu or ui.

This is the right way of pronouncing a pure u: the lips must be rounded into a pout, closing them much more than for the o sound while relaxing the throat all the time. The singer should be made conscious of the fact that the u must be pronounced at the very tip of the lips. The lips are rounded into a circle almost as if they were about to gently blow away a light object.

The long closed u [u:] *sound.* For description and production, see page 50. Long closed u stands in open syllables like du; or if the u precedes a single consonant as in Zug, Mus; and if followed by an h as in Schuh; and sometimes before ch and ss, as in Buch and Fuss.

> Sch*u*hmacher und Poet daz*u* (WAGNER *Die Meistersinger von Nürnberg*)
> Ein altes B*u*ch, vom Ahn' vermacht (WAGNER *Die Meistersinger von Nürnberg*)

Exceptions agreed upon are flugs and Geburt and words with the prefix ur- (as in Urwald, Urfehde). Also in Schuster, Wust, husten, pusten, Russ.

> Vor allem Volk ward *U*rfehde geschworen (WAGNER *Tristan und Isolde*)
> Der Sch*u*ster schafft doch stets mir Pein! (WAGNER *Die Meistersinger von Nürnberg*)

The short open u *sound.* For description and production, see page 71. u is pronounced thus when followed by more than one consonant, as in Brust, Mutter, or by sch, as in Busch, and also when followed by a ch or ss, if related forms have a short vowel, as in Bruch, Bucht, Schuss, muss.

> Füllest wieder B*u*sch und Tal (SCHUBERT "An den Mond")
> Wann der silberne Mond d*u*rch die Gesträuche blinkt *U*nd sein schlummerndes Licht über den Rasen streut *U*nd die Nachtigall flötet, Wandl' ich traurig von B*u*sch zu B*u*sch (BRAHMS "Die Mainacht")
> Sandvike ist's, genau kenn ich die B*u*cht (WAGNER *Der Fliegende Holländer*)

This short open u does not appear in Italian diction. It must be pronounced forward, without the slightest tension of the throat. The lips are again rounded, but slightly more open than in pronouncing the closed long u. The short open u can be illustrated in English by the words put, foot, good, book, provided that every trace of diphthongization is avoided.

THE Ü UMLAUT SOUNDS

For description and production, see page 71. The ü is the same sound as the French u. It should not present any difficulties for singers who have already mastered French phonetics.

There are two kinds of ü's in German: the long, closed ü, and the short, open ü.

The long closed ü [y:] *sound.* This umlaut is pronounced in open syllables or before single consonants, as in Tür, müde, schwül, also before an h as in führen, fühlen. Again before a final ss in süss, or if the root of the word contains a long closed u, as in Füsse (Fuss), büssen (Busse); also before a ch if the root of the word contains a long, closed u, as in Bücher (Buch), Flüche (Fluch).

> Ein B*ü*sser ist's (WAGNER *Tannhäuser*)
> Ich träumte von bunten Blumen, so wie sie wohl bl*ü*hen im Mai, Ich träumte von gr*ü*nen Wiesen (SCHUBERT "Frühlingstraum")
> Wird's nicht zu k*ü*hl? 's war heut' gar schw*ü*l (WAGNER *Die Meistersinger von Nürnberg*)

Exceptions agreed upon by the committee of experts (see p. 92) Brüche, Gerüche, Küche, Sprüche, where the ü is short and open.

> Kannst du dein Spr*ü*chlein, so sag' es her! (WAGNER *Die Meistersinger von Nürnberg*)
> Was Fein's aus der K*ü*ch' (WAGNER *Die Meistersinger von Nürnberg*)

The short open ü [y] *sound.* This sound is pronounced if the ü stands in front of more than one consonant or before sch or ss, as in stürbe, nüchtern, Glück, rüsten, Büsche, Gelübde, gebürtig.

> Doch st*ü*rbe nie seine Liebe, wie st*ü*rbe dann Tristan seiner Liebe? (WAGNER *Tristan und Isolde*)
> Wenn Dein Gel*ü*bde dich bindet mir zu schweigen (WAGNER *Parsifal*)
> Zu mir, du Ged*ü*ft! Ihr D*ü*nste, zu mir! (WAGNER *Das Rheingold*)

There are only a few exceptions, such as düster and wüst, that according to the rules would have the ü short, but are pronounced by agreement with a long closed ü.

> Ein w*ü*stes Gesicht wirrt mir wütend den Sinn! (WAGNER *Götterdämmerung*)

THE Y [y] SOUND

The y in German (pronounced ypsilon) in the middle of a word is always pronounced ü. It appears only in words of Greek derivation. There are two y's, analogous to the two ü's. Since there are comparatively few words with y in German operatic or lied literature it might suffice here to mention a few examples and mark the pronunciation.

The y is pronounced a shade higher (approaching the i) than the ü.

> Will suchen einen Zypressenhain (SCHUBERT "Die liebe Farbe")
> Freude schöner Götterfunken, Tochter aus Elysium (BEETHOVEN Ninth Symphony)
> Zurück, Tochter Babylons! (RICHARD STRAUSS *Salome*)

THE DIPHTHONGS

The diphthongs are combinations of two vowels or of umlaut and vowel which in German speech are pronounced as one unit, very much as in English. They require a change of mouth, lip, and tongue position in the very short time that the pronunciation of the diphthong takes. Such a quick change is not in the interest of uninterrupted bel canto singing. If too many changes of positions of the vocal apparatus have to be made — not only within a word, but even within a syllable — the vocal phrase will be broken and the tone will sound unsteady. For this reason, the German diphthongs must be sung differently from the way they are spoken. The first vowel of the diphthong has to be held longer than the second. The singer should proceed to the second vowel of the diphthong just before the following consonant or vowel. There is a definite difference between the Italian (Fig. 80) and the German (Fig. 81) way of singing in this respect. Italian has no diphthongs; it gives equal weight and length to each of two successive vowels. On long notes the first part of the diphthong should be held longer; the second part always stays the same: it should be short and pronounced late.

Figure 80. Verdi, *Aïda,* Italian diphthong

Figure 81. Schumann, "Im wunderschönen Monat Mai," German diphthong

This rule may completely contradict the old way of German singing which can still often be heard, even from very prominent German singers. But as I have said before, our taste has returned to the uninterrupted, evenly produced vocal line of the Italian bel canto, modified

for each language, but basically unchanged. No principle of clarity of diction need be broken in following this rule. As a matter of fact the ear — and the heart — will comprehend vocal music much more clearly if singing is built on the beauty of an uninterrupted flow of vocal line.

There are only *three different diphthongs* — ai, au, and eu — in German, although different ways of spelling make them seven.

The ai *diphthong sounds.* The ai diphthong may also be spelled ei, ay, or ey. In speaking or singing, it is not divided into the vowels a and i, but always into a comparatively bright a and a very short, closed e, as in Leib (sung [la:ep]). In analyzing the motions of tongue and lips one will find that the singer does not lift the tongue from the a position to the i position, but after reaching the closed e position will slide over to the next consonant or vowel.

Some examples of the ai spelling are Maid, Mai, Saite, Waise. The ei spelling (pronounced exactly the same way) includes such words as Leib, Seite, Weise. The ay and ey spelling, used in older times (some of it can still be found in old editions of vocal scores or lieder anthologies), is now restricted to names of people and places.

The English equivalent for all these diphthongs is the simple i as in life.

There are a few words (Kain, Mosaik) in which the ai is not a diphthong, but belongs to two different syllables. They are hardly ever found in the German vocal literature.

In exclamations or onomatopoetical words — hei; tandaradei; ei, ei; ai, ai — the second vowel is an open i and gets more stress than the a.

> Ei, ei, wie fein! (MOZART *Die Zauberflöte*)
> Ai, ai, ai, der Dieb! (RICHARD STRAUSS *Ariadne auf Naxos*)
> Hei! Siegfried gehört nun der Helm und der Ring! (WAGNER *Siegfried*)

The au *diphthong sound.* The au diphthong when sung consists of the vowel a, which is open, and a closed but very short o, as in Maus (sung [Ma:os]). The tongue, and especially the lips, move from the a forward to the u, but before reaching it stop at the closed o and slide from it to the next consonant or vowel.

> Weck' ich ihn nun *auf*? (WOLF *Spanisches Liederbuch*)
> Das Wasser r*au*scht, das Wasser schwoll (SCHUBERT "Der Fischer")
> Ich sch*au*' dich an, und Wehmut schleicht mir ins Herz hinein (SCHUMANN "Du bist wie eine Blume")

The English equivalent is the diphthong ou or ow, as in house, now.

There are cases in German where for poetical or onamatopoetical reasons the above ao rule should be broken and the a and the u in the diphthong given their full values. If, for instance, the dreaminess of the word Traum is intended to be stressed, the word should be sung Tra-um (with a very closed, not too short u). Or the word raunen, which means something like to mumble secretively, should be sung ra-unen.

Und wie in Tr*au*me r*au*nt er das Wort (WAGNER *Götterdämmerung*)
Lieb' und Leid! Und Welt und Tr*aum*! (MAHLER *Lieder eines fahrenden Gesellen*)

The inherent musicality of the au diphthong may be illustrated by the fact that in one of the most musical and singable languages, Finnish, the root for the very words for singing and song is laul.

In an exclamation au! (exclamation of pain) the second vowel is a u and gets more stress than the a.

The eu *diphthong sounds.* The eu sounds may also be spelled äu, occasionally even oi or oy. These diphthongs consist of an open o and a very short, closed ö, as for instance in Treue. Tongue and lips should move from the open o as if they wanted to attain a closed ü (by rounding the lips), but on reaching the closed ö, they should slide to the next consonant or vowel.

Auf, auf, mein Herz, mit Fr*eu*den nimm wahr, was h*eut*' geschicht! (J. S. BACH "Auf, auf! mein Herz, mit Freuden")
Niederwallen auch die Tr*äu*me, wie dein Mondlicht durch die R*äu*me (SCHUBERT "Nacht und Träume")

In exclamations like hoi and hoiho, the second vowel is an open i and gets more stress than the o.

Hoiho, Hagen! (WAGNER *Götterdämmerung*)

Wherever the u after an e or ä belongs to a final syllable, as in Te Deum, Jubiläum, no diphthong ought to be sung.

THE CONSONANTS

Nowhere has there been so much sinning against the musicality of a language than by the exaggeration of the German consonants. Their so-called harshness has been the basis of many a comedian's repertory and the laughingstock of many an audience. It must be said that some of the worst sinners are to be found among the German singers themselves. This came about mostly as a result of the development of the Wagnerian Sprechgesang, the whole old style of overdeclaiming, overplaying poetry.

In our time of underplaying (not to be confused with underprojecting), these singers' sounds hurt our ears and create the unfortunate impression that German is ugly. That this is not so can be best realized when one listens to the the great past and present interpreters of lieder like Lotte Lehmann, Elisabeth Schumann, Richard Tauber, Elisabeth Schwarzkopf, Hans Hotter, and Dietrich Fischer-Dieskau. All these singers build their art entirely on diction, using the finest shades for expressing the deepest emotions. Certainly for dramatic effects cruder means must be used, but this is true in any language.

Quite a few languages have been termed "unmusical": German and Czech because of their accumulation of consonants, English because of its many diphthongs and even triphthongs, Dutch and Hebrew or other Semitic languages because of their abundance of gutturals. I should like to take this occasion to break a lance for the singability of any language. True, the ones richer in vowels will sound more pleasant to our ears, which are generally trained to enjoy the Italian vocal style. But any language can be made to sound beautiful, and who would close his ears to the charms of a Schubert lied, an old English ballad, an aria from Smetana's *The Bartered Bride* in its original language, or a simple Hebrew shepherd's song?

The following discussion of German consonants will, I hope, definitely prove that they are singable and not offensive to the ear.

SINGLE CONSONANTS

The h sound. The h sound is always aspirated at the beginning of a word like halten or Herr, and when it appears in the middle of a word as the first letter of the syllable which forms the root of the word or is derived from it as in behalten, verhindern, Walhall, Johannes, also in some names such as Beethoven (Bethofən).

Beh*a*lt' ihn *H*eld! (WAGNER *Götterdämmerung*)
*H*err, lehre doch mich (BRAHMS *Ein deutsches Requiem*)
Folge mir, Frau! In Wal*h*all wohne mit mir! (WAGNER *Das Rheingold*)
Nero, der Kettenhund (WEBER *Der Freischütz*)

The h in the middle of a word is also aspirated in exclamations like aha, oho, hoiho, hehe, hihihi, and in some words like Ahorn and Uhu.

*H*a*h*a! Da hätte mein Lied mir was Liebes erblasen! (WAGNER *Siegfried*)
*H*oiho! *H*agen! (WAGNER *Götterdämmerung*)

In all other cases the h in the middle of a word is mute and used only to elongate the vowel and close it as, for instance, in all words with ah, äh, eh, oh, öh, uh, and üh, such as Fahrt, Fährte, Ehe, sehen, wehe (pronounced [veə]), Lohe ([loə]), Föhre, Ruhe ([ruə]), rühmen.

> Ru*h*e, meine Seele! (RICHARD STRAUSS "Ruhe meine Seele")
> Woher du kommst der Fa*h*rt (WAGNER *Lohengrin*)
> Wie ein guter Hund auf einer guten Fä*h*rte! (RICHARD STRAUSS *Der Rosenkavalier*)

The h after t or r (th, rh) is always mute and does not change the pronunciation of t or r. These forms are relics of the older way of spelling which can still be found in many editions of songs. Needless to say, the th has no relation to the English th. Words with th are Walther and Thron; among words with rh is Rhapsodie.

An h following a p forms the combination of consonants which is pronounced f, as in English.

In strong emotion the h is aspirated with more energy than usual.

> du *H*und! (you *d*og!)
> *H*immeldonnerwetter! (*H*ell!)

THE VOICED CONSONANTS

As in all other languages, some consonants are singable in German and, indeed, sometimes sung on, thus serving to stress the emotional, poetic, or onomatopoetic possibilities of a word. These consonants can be sustained on musical tones passing through the whole diapason of the human voice. Singable consonants in German are, for all practical purposes, m, n, ng, l, w, s, j, and, to some extent, r.

The m *sound.* For description and production, see page 52. m may be initial, medial, or final. It is sung exactly as an Italian m would be, whether it is connected with vowels or other consonants. The m must be finished without being exploded, otherwise we should get the effect of a double m as in the Italian word mamma, where this explosive action is indicated. If, however, the m is the final sound of a word as in kam, it may sometimes be right to stress it by adding a mute e (see p. 94); otherwise the m may be lost. But this device should be used only where absolutely necessary (in big theaters or concert halls, where the necessity for projection may dictate it). Final m followed by an initial m will usually be connected without explosion and will sound like the single m as, for instance, in Am Montag, Komm morgen, nimm mich hin.

> Ein *M*ägdlein sass a*m M*eerestrand (BRAHMS "Treue Liebe")
> Du *m*eine Seele, du *m*ein Herz, du *m*eine Wonn', o du *m*ein Schmerz! (SCHUMANN "Widmung")
> Die Nacht war kau*m* verblühet (FRANZ "Sonntag")
> *M*ein Held, *m*ein Retter, nim*m m*ich hin! (WAGNER *Lohengrin*)

In some bel canto phrases where it is essential that the vocal line from one vowel to the other must not be disturbed it is necessary to pronounce a very weak m. For further description and examples, see page 53.

The n *sound.* For description and production, see page 53. n may be an initial, medial, or final consonant. For initial n's or n's between two vowels the pronunciation is the same as in Italian, but care should be taken not to exaggerate it, and the tongue should not be released explosively.

For final n's the same rules should be followed as for the final m. It may sometimes be necessary to explode the final n, adding a mute e, in order to stress the sound adequately.

> Leise flehe*n* mei*n*e Lieder durch die *N*acht zu dir (SCHUBERT "Ständchen")
> Fleuch', *N*achtigall, i*n* grüne Finsternisse, i*n*s Haingesträuch (BRAHMS "An die Nachtigall")
> Dann flieht der Schlaf vo*n n*euem dieses Lager (BRAHMS "An die Nachtigall")

If n comes before another consonant, especially before m, f, p, b, k, or g, the singer must first complete the n, and then continue to the next consonant, as in a*n*merken, sa*n*ft, a*n*prangen, u*n*brauchbar, u*n*klar, a*n*genehm.

> Von Liebe sa*n*ft bedeckt! (BRAHMS "O wüsst ich doch den Weg zurück")
> Rosendüfte wehen in dieser dumpfen Felse*n*kluft (SCHUBERT "Ave Maria")
> Bei dem a*n*genehmsten Wetter singen alle Vögelein (WOLF "Der Scholar")
> So stolz, so keck, so schade*n*froh (SCHUBERT "Die böse Farbe")

The ng [ŋ] *sound.* For description and production, see page 53. The effect of this sound is to mold n and g into one sound, as in jung, streng, lang, Junggesell. The g must not be audible as a separate sound.

> O liebliche Wa*ng*en ihr macht mir Verla*ng*en (BRAHMS "O liebliche Wangen")
> Ein Ju*ngg*esell muss es sein (WAGNER *Die Meistersinger von Nürnberg*)
> Ich hör meinen Schatz, den Hammer er · schwi*ng*et (BRAHMS "Der Schmied")

The ng sound does *not* change if it stands in the middle of a word, as in jünger, jüngst, strenger, länger, Engel, Finger, singen. In English, the g is pronounced in many similar words; in German, it is always unpronounced. The accompanist or coach must see to it that this rule is strictly observed, otherwise the result will be a diction which is not German.

The [ŋ] sound is also used when a single n stands in front of a final k as in Dank ([daŋk]), sink, funkeln.

> Und mit gese*n*ktem Haupte erwartet sie träumend die Nacht (SCHUMANN "Die Lotosblume")
> O si*n*k hernieder, Nacht der Liebe! (WAGNER *Tristan und Isolde*)
> Eine Mühle seh' ich bli*n*ken (SCHUBERT "Halt!")
> Habe Da*n*k! (RICHARD STRAUSS "Zueignung")

When an n is followed by a g and a full-voiced vowel, as in Ungarn, the g is pronounced in addition to the ng as in [uŋgarn], (but not in [un-gɛrn]). In this case, the pronunciation of Ungarn is about the same as in the English longer.

The so-called Bayreuth tradition of pronouncing Ring like rink is probably based on a momentary whim of Richard Wagner's during rehearsal and should be disregarded by today's accompanists and coaches.

The ng sound must not be confused with the French nasal an, on, or en sounds where the n is nothing but a nasal resonance sound (see p. 77).

The 1 sound. For description and production, see page 54. German 1 is pronounced forward, like the Italian and French 1. It can appear as an initial, medial, and or final sound, as in Liebe, kalt, Röslein, Veilchen, Wahl.

> Ich *l*iebe dich, so wie du mich (BEETHOVEN "Ich liebe dich")
> Ein Vei*l*chen auf der Wiese stand (MOZART "Das Veilchen")
> Ja ja, ein Meister meiner Wah*l* (WAGNER *Die Meistersinger von Nürnberg*)

Whether the 1 precedes a vowel or a consonant or a group of consonants, it must always be pronounced forward and be stressed fully before the tongue continues to the next sound, as for instance in Hälfte and Halstuch.

> He*l*ft mir, ihr Schwestern! (SCHUMANN "Helft mir, ihr Schwestern")

The 1 can be exploded very easily and therefore serves as the main consonant to demonstrate rhythms (tra la la, la la la, or fa la la). Depending on the length or shortness of tone required, the 1 should be sung on (lall-lall-lall)

or passed over (la-lla-lla). But each new initial l must be exploded freshly in the above rhythmical phrases. (See Fig. 82, 83.)

Figure 82. Mozart, *Die Zauberflöte*

Figure 83. Wolf, *Der Corregidor*

The w [v] sound. For description and production, see page 54. w in German is akin to the Italian, French, and English v. It must vibrate and not be similar to the voiceless f where air is simply blown or exploded.

The w is always pronounced the same way whether it is an initial (wahr, Wort) or medial (gewöhnen, schwarz, Schwefel) sound.

> *W*ahn, *W*ahn, überall *W*ahn! (WAGNER *Die Meistersinger von Nürnberg*)
> *W*ir *w*andelten, *w*ir *zw*ei zusammen (BRAHMS "Wir wandelten")
> Ein Tännlein grünet *w*o, *w*er weiss, im *W*alde (WOLF "Denk'es, o Seele!")

It can be more or less accentuated, according to the lyrical or dramatical impact of the word.

Some words of foreign origin written with an initial v are pronounced like w, as in vehement, Violine, etc.

> Gibt gar nichts auf der Welt, was mich so enflammiert und also *v*ehement verjüngt (RICHARD STRAUSS *Der Rosenkavalier*)
> *V*ictoria, *V*ictoria! Der Meister soll leben! (WEBER *Der Freischütz*)

Final w in some names which end on ow (of slavic etymology) is mute; this is true in Bülow ([bylo]) and Flotow.

The voiced s [z] sound. For description and production, see pages 54–55. German s can be voiced or voiceless. The voiced s is used (1) if it is an initial sound, as in Sand, Segen, so, Salome, Sachs; (2) if it appears between vowels in the middle of a word, as in Rose, Hase, Husar; (3) if it appears between an m, n, l, or r on one side and a vowel on the other side, or after a prefix as in Amsel, unser, Ab-sicht; (4) when a word ends with -sal or -sam, as in Schicksal, langsam.

> Wir *s*assen *s*o traulich bei*s*ammen (SCHUBERT "Trä-
> nenregen")
> *S*elt*s*am ist Juanas Wei*s*e (WOLF *Spanisches Lieder-
> buch*)
> Hieher Maid, in un*s*'re Macht! (WAGNER *Das Rhein-
> gold*)

Many German dialects, especially the southern ones like the Austrian and the Bavarian, do not use the voiced s where it is indicated by the above rules. For this reason, one can hear famous singers "mispronounce" lang-ssam, Ssalome, etc. The accompanist or coach should stress the above rules to the English-speaking singer. Words derived from Greek or Latin have the initial soft s. The voiced s sound is not too pleasant musically if overstressed. Therefore, it should always be sung softly and the tongue should not remain in the voiced s position any longer than is required for clear diction.

The j sound. The j in German is a voiced palatal frica-tive sound produced by curving the sides of the tongue upward so that they touch the hard palate lightly. The tip of the tongue is curled downward and anchors itself against the ridge of the lower teeth. It corresponds to the English y in you, yore, yard, yes. In German the j is used mostly as an initial sound as in ja, Jahr, jeder, Jugend.

> Mein Lieb ist ein *J*äger (BRAHMS "Der Jäger")
> Von *J*asmin und weissen Lilien sollt ihr mein Grab
> bereiten (WOLF *Spanisches Liederbuch*)
> Alljährlich naht vom Himmel eine Taube (WAGNER
> *Lohengrin*)

It is important to pronounce the j as one consonant and not as a semivowel or semiconsonant (see p. 51).

The gn [ɲ] and ll [ʎ] combinations. When a German pronounces a French, Italian, or Spanish proper name the [ɲ] and the [ʎ] combinations are pronounced exactly as in their original languages (see pp. 53, 54, 90). Ex-amples: Se*villa*, Bro*gn*i, Ca*gli*ostro, Do*ñ*a.

The r sound. The r is one of the most important and interesting sounds in German singing diction. It can make the language unnecessarily harsh, if overstressed, or mushy if not projected enough. Different German-speaking regions have different kinds of r's which the singer born in a particular region can change only with the utmost patience and energy. For description and pro-duction of the different r's see pages 56 and 83.

We differentiate in German between a rolled and a

flipped r. The rolled r is produced in the throat by the tongue held loosely in low position. This r may be rolled once or more often, until it approaches a throaty trill. The more it is rolled, the harsher the sound will be-come. The flipped r is the kind used in British English. It is recommended in most cases, because it will present fewer difficulties to the English-speaking singer than the rolled r.

The accompanist and coach must train his charges to forget entirely about the American r except in the end-ings discussed below.

Vocally speaking, the r has a very important func-tion. It facilitates interval leaps and connection of vocal positions as the neutral gear in an automobile facilitates smooth shifting. It enables the singer to shift from one position into the other without mishap. Because of its voiced quality it will not interrupt the vocal line and will guarantee smoothness of execution.

> Und die T*r*eu', 's wa*r* nu*r* ein Wo*r*t (BRAHMS "Sap-
> phische Ode")
> B*r*ich entzwei, mein a*r*mes Herze (J. S. BACH "Brich
> entzwei, mein armes Herze")
> Nach F*r*ankreich zogen zwei G*r*enadie*r*', die wa*r*en in
> *R*ussland gefangen (SCHUMANN "Die beiden Gren-
> adiere")

The r requires very little breath. Because of this, singers will find it convenient to relax on the r for a split second when singing long phrases. The r must be sung clearly, even if successive or consecutive conso-nants require a rapid shifting of tongue and lip positions, as in Forst, Marktschreier, etc.

> Von Hetze und Ha*r*st einst keh*r*ten wir heim (WAGNER
> *Die Walküre*)
> Mich dü*r*stet! (WAGNER *Götterdämmerung*)
> Der Ma*r*kt beginnt, die Glocke schallt (FLOTOW
> *Martha*)

rh in German words (as in Rheingold) is pronounced like a normal r.

Words ending in -er, -em, -en and -el. These unac-cented final syllables require special mention because there is so much confusion about them in the minds of English-speaking singers. They think, for instance, that German diction necessitates a very hard pronunciation of the -er endings, with the result that the words sound more Russian than German. The unaccented final syl-lables all have a weak e ([ə]). The r in the -er combi-nations is equivalent to the American r, as in sist*er* or bett*er*. No flipping or rolling must be permitted. Words with these endings are very numerous: a few are Leder, besser, länger, Wunder.

> Täts't besser, das Leder zu strecken (WAGNER *Die Meistersinger von Nürnberg*)
> O hehrstes Wunder! (WAGNER *Die Walküre*)

This rule is also valid for the unaccented final syllable of the first part of a composite word, as in wunderbar, Wasserstrahl, etc.

The weak e (ə) must also be sung in the corresponding unaccentuated syllables on em, en, and el.

> Guten Abend, mein Schatz, guten Abend, mein Kind! (BRAHMS "Vergebliches Ständchen")
> Wie, welchen Handel hätt' ich geschlossen? (WAGNER *Das Rheingold*)
> Ewige Freude wird über ihrem Haupte sein (BRAHMS *Ein deutsches Requiem*)

The b sound. For description and production, see page 55. Initial b's of words or syllables are sung with a slight explosion which will bring out the voiced quality of the b, as in Baum, bergen, Bild, Liebe, Stube.

> Wo in Bergen du dich birgst (WAGNER *Die Walküre*)
> Es grünet ein Nussbaum vor dem Haus, duftig, luftig breitet er blättrig die Äste aus (SCHUMANN "Der Nussbaum")
> Bedeckt mich mit Blumen, ich sterbe vor Liebe! (WOLF *Spanisches Liederbuch*)

The b has only the slightest amount of voicedness and is pronounced very softly at the end of a syllable ending in -lich, -lein, -ling, -nis, -sam, -sal, as in lieblich, Knäblein, Erlebnis, Labsal.

> O liebliche Wangen, ihr macht mir Verlangen! (BRAHMS "O liebliche Wangen")
> Als Büblein klein an der Mutter Brust (NICOLAI *Die lustigen Weiber von Windsor*)
> Der Mutter Erde lass' das ein Labsal sein! (WAGNER *Götterdämmerung*)
> Schau, wie das Knäblein sündelos frei spielet auf der Jungfrau Schoss! (WOLF "Auf ein altes Bild")

The b becomes voiceless, hard, and aspirated and approximates a p between a long vowel and a consonant in the same syllable as in giebst, Obst, lebt, liebt.

> Doch ihr setztet alles auf das jüngende Obst (WAGNER *Das Rheingold*)
> Die Lilie soll klingend hauchen ein Lied von der Liebsten mein (SCHUMANN "Dichterliebe")
> Und die einsame Träne bebt (BRAHMS "Die Mainacht)

The b in ebnen and übler is voiced and soft. These words in the old spelling contained an e (ebenen, übeler).

Final b is always voiceless, hard, and aspirated if it appears at the end of a word or a syllable. There are, however, two shades of aspiration to be considered.

First: after a long vowel or after r or l, the b approximates a p, which means that the aspiration or explosion is moderately strong, as in Grab, stirb, halb.

> Mein Lieb ist ein Jäger (BRAHMS "Der Jäger")
> Denn solchem grossen Sarge gebührt ein grosses Grab (SCHUMANN "Dichterliebe")

Second: after a short vowel, the b is always pronounced explosively and aspirated exactly like a p, such as in ab, ob, Trab, also in abnehmen, abfahren, and also in the word Abt.

> Bergab gleitet der Weg (SCHUBERT "An Schwager Kronos")
> Rassle den schallenden Trab! (SCHUBERT "An Schwager Kronos")

It is important to remember that the final b in German differs sharply from the final b in English which is sung soft and voiced. The German final b is always voiceless, hard, and must be pronounced like a p.

The d sound. For description and production, see page 55. Initial d (in words or syllables) is always voiced, as in du, da, die, doch, reden, Flieder. It is sung with a more or less strong explosion, depending on the meaning or the accent of the word, but it must always be voiced; otherwise it would sound like a t.

> Du da, Loge! sag' ohne Lug (WAGNER *Das Rheingold*)
> Wie duftet doch der Flieder (WAGNER *Die Meistersinger von Nürnberg*)

The d is almost voiceless, but soft at the end of a syllable before endings on -lich, -lein, -ling, -nis, -bar, -sam, such as in freundlich, Rädlein, Fremdling, verwundbar, friedsam.

> In ein freundliches Städtchen tret' ich ein (WOLF "Auf einer Wanderung")
> Wie friedsam treuer Sitten getrost in Tat und Werk (WAGNER *Die Meistersinger von Nürnberg*)
> Doch endlich ward dem Diebe die Zeit zu lang (SCHUBERT "Die Forelle")

The d is voiceless, hard, and aspirated between a vowel and a consonant in the same syllable, approximating a t, as in du ludst.

The d is voiceless, hard, and explosive at the end of a word or a syllable. This can happen either after a long vowel as in Rad, or after a short vowel plus r, l, m, n, as in Wald, Hemd, Hand.

The final d approximates a t. The aspiration or explosion is moderately strong, as for example in Ba*d*, Fä*d*chen, Lie*d*.

> Du denkst mit einem Fä*d*chen mich zu fangen (WOLF "Du denkst mit einem Fä*d*chen mich zu fangen")
> Meine Laute hab ich gehängt an die Wan*d*, hab sie umschlungen mit einem grünen Ban*d* (SCHUBERT "Pause")
> So war*d* es uns verhiessen (WAGNER *Parsifal*)

In such cases the d *approximates* the t: it is not quite the same as the t, which is exploded much more strongly, but it must be completely voiceless.

The d in words like Wandrer, handle, wandle, Redner, and Adler is voiced and soft. The reason for this is the elimination of an e in the modern spelling of the words. (The earlier spellings were Wanderer, handele, and so forth.)

> Wan*d*rer nennt mich die Welt (WAGNER *Siegfried*)
> Ihr E*d*len mögt in diesen Worten lesen (WAGNER *Tannhäuser*)

It is important to remember that the final d in German differs sharply from the final d in English, which is sung soft and voiced. The German final d.is always hard and voiceless and must be pronounced like a t.

The g sound. For description and production, see page 56. Initial g is sung with a more or less slight explosion, the degree of which depends upon the intensity or the accent of the word, as in Gabe, legen, Geliebter, gleich, gegangen.

> Dem Vater *g*rauset's, er reitet *g*eschwind (SCHUBERT "Erlkönig")
> *G*ibt das *G*eleit der *G*eliebten nach Haus (BRAHMS "Von ewiger Liebe")

Care has to be taken to make the singer conscious of the voiced quality of the g; otherwise it would sound like a k.

g is always soft and voiced at the end of a syllable before the endings -lich, -lein, -ling, -nis, -bar, -sam, as in mö*g*lich, Vö*g*lein, Fei*g*ling, Wa*g*nis, unsa*g*bar.

> Mit Nä*g*lein besteckt (BRAHMS "Wiegenlied")
> Dank, liebes Vö*g*lein, für deinen Rat! (WAGNER *Siegfried*)

For ng ([ŋ]) before the above endings, see page 100 (as in langsam [laŋza:m]).

The g becomes voiceless and hard between a vowel and a consonant in the same syllable approximating a k, as in regt, liegst, logst, beugt.

Was doch heut Nacht ein Sturm gewesen, bis erst der Morgen sich gere*g*t! (WOLF "Begegnung")

The g is voiceless, hard, and explosive at the end of a word or a syllable. This may happen either after a long vowel or after a short vowel and an r or l. The g then sounds like a k and must be sung aspirated (explosive) and strong, as in Ta*g*, la*g*, Betru*g*, Ber*g*, Bal*g*, Bur*g*.

> Die Ähren wo*g*ten sacht (SCHUMANN "Mondnacht")
> Ein Stündlein wohl vor Ta*g* (WOLF "Ein Stündlein wohl vor Tag")
> Betru*g* auch hier! Mein die Hälfte! (WAGNER *Tristan und Isolde*)

The g in words like se*g*nen, leu*g*nen, or in names like Po*g*ner, Pe*g*nitz, Wa*g*ner, is *voiced and soft.* The reason for this is again that in earlier centuries these words were written with an e (Wagener), which was eliminated later as the language developed. The same is true for final ge, when the e is replaced by an apostrophe, as in Gefol*g*', Gehe*g*', le*g*'.

> An der Pe*g*nitz hiess der Hans (WAGNER *Die Meistersinger von Nürnberg*)
> Freund Po*g*ners Wort Genüge tut (WAGNER *Die Meistersinger von Nürnberg*)
> Zei*g*' her, 's ist gut (WAGNER *Die Meistersinger von Nürnberg*)
> Le*g*' dich zu Bett (WAGNER *Die Meistersinger von Nürnberg*)

Special rules for endings on -ig. If a word or a syllable ends in -ig, or if the syllable is followed by a consonant, the g is pronounced like a soft ch [ç] (see pronunciation of ch on p. 106), as in Köni*g*, ewi*g*, freudi*g*, Trauri*g*keit.

> Und neu besänf*t*i*g*t wallt mein Blut (BEETHOVEN *Fidelio*)
> Helft mir, ihr Schwestern, helft mir verscheuchen eine törichte Ban*g*i*g*keit, dass ich mit klarem Au*g*' ihn empfange, ihn, die Quelle der Freudi*g*keit (SCHUMANN "Helft mir, ihr Schwestern")
> Trauri*g*keit ward mir zum Lose (MOZART *Die Entführung aus dem Serail*)
> O Köni*g*, das kann ich dir nicht sagen (WAGNER *Tristan und Isolde*)

If another soft ch appears in the same word, the ig, for euphonic reasons, retains its original pronunciation, as in Köni*g*reich.

> Und wär's die Hälfte meines Köni*g*reichs! (RICHARD STRAUSS *Salome*)

It is a rule in German stage pronunciation to soften the g in words with poetical apostrophes, as in ew'ge, sel'ge, etc. In these cases the ge is pronounced like the semivowel [j], as in [evjə], [zeljə]. I do not, however, recommend following this rule in singing diction. It would weaken the vocal intensity.

Ew'ge ([evjə]) Götter! (WAGNER *Lohengrin*)
Den sel'gen Göttern, wie gehts? (WAGNER *Das Rheingold*)

It is important to remember that the final g in German differs sharply from the final g in English which is sung soft and voiced. The German final g is always hard and voiceless and must be pronounced like a k.

THE VOICELESS CONSONANTS

The voiceless consonants, especially when at the end of a word, create a problem for the English-speaking singer which the accompanist and coach can easily solve. He must impress on the singer that these final consonants must be pronounced absolutely voicelessly, that they have nothing to do with an actual singing tone but are exploded after the vocal sound has come to an end. This will give the singer a welcome opportunity to get rid of his residual breath, since it can be used for the projection of the p, t, k, f, s, etc., or their combinations. Words for which the above is true are knapp, schlappt, klappt, Tat, Stück, Takt, Saft.

Seht hier, wie's schlapp*t* und überall klapp*t*! (WAGNER *Die Meistersinger von Nürnberg*)
Luf*t*, Luf*t*! Ich ersti*cke*! (WAGNER *Tristan und Isolde*)
Glü*ck* das mir verblieb (KORNGOLD *Die tote Stadt*)

The p *sound.* For description and production, see page 57. p can be an initial, medial, or final sound; the pronunciation remains the same. There is not much difference between the English and the German p except that the latter is exploded somewhat more strongly.

Von der Strasse her ein *P*osthorn klingt (SCHUBERT "Die Post")
Das knos*p*et und quillt und duftet und blüht (BRAHMS "Es liebt sich so lieblich im Lenze")

The t *sound.* For description and production see page 57. The sound may also be spelled th or dt, as in Thron, Stadt. The pronunciation stays the same. It does not make any difference whether the t, th, or dt is initial, medial, or final. The t sound is almost identical with the English t, except that it must be sung with more intensity and stronger explosion.

Am fernen Horizon*te* erschein*t*, wie ein Nebelbild, die Sta*dt* mi*t* ihren Türmen, in Abenddämm'rung gehüll*t* (SCHUBERT "Die Stadt")

Heb' auf dein blondes Haup*t* und schlafe nicht (WOLF *Italienisches Liederbuch*)
*Th*üringens Fürsten, Landgraf Herrmann, Heil! (WAGNER *Tannhäuser*)

The k *sound.* For description and production see page 58. k can appear in different spellings and combinations, such as ck, x (k + s), chs (k + s), qu (k + w). The pronunciation always stays the same, whether the different spellings of the k are initial, medial, or final.

The k sound is almost identical with the English k, c, ck, qu, and ch sounds, except that it must be sung with more intensity and stronger explosion. In some places of strong emotion, the k, in German, can be aspirated in such a way that an h may be audible after it.

Verwittert Stein und *K*reuz', die *K*ränze alt (BRAHMS "Auf dem Kirchhofe")
Es *k*lingen und singen die Wellen des Frühlings wohl über mir; und seh' ich so *keck*e Gesellen, die Tränen im Auge mir schwellen (SCHUMANN "Frühlingsfahrt")
Ich will dem *K*ind nur den *K*opf abhaun! (WAGNER *Siegfried*)
Lo*ck*et nicht mit Liebesgaben (WOLF "Verborgenheit")
An der *Q*uelle sass der *K*nabe (SCHUBERT "Der Jüngling am Bache")

qu in German is not related to the semivowel qu in Italian. It is a [kv] combination.

k before n, as in Knabe, must be pronounced, unlike English where it is mute.

The f *and* v *sounds.* For description and production see page 57. f and v are pronounced alike, as in Feind, Vater, Veilchen, Frevel, schlafen, brav. Concerning the pronunciation of the v like w in some words of foreign origin, see page 100.

Ein *V*eilchen auf der Wiese stand (MOZART "Das Veilchen")
Bin *F*reund und komme nicht zu strafen. Sei guten Muts! ich bin nicht wild, sollst san*f*t in meinem Armen schlafen (SCHUBERT "Der Tod und das Mädchen")
Zu spät kam ich, und kehre nun heim, des *f*lücht'gen *F*revlers Spur im eig'nen Haus zu erspäh'n! (WAGNER *Die Walküre*)
Der Herr Gra*f* sind au*f* und da*v*on (RICHARD STRAUSS *Der Rosenkavalier*)

The v in David and Eva is sung like f, although about ninety per cent of German singers pronounce it mistakenly as w ([v]) (this is southern German dialect). The f may also be spelled ph in some words of foreign origin (Photo, Symphonie). The pronunciation stays the same whether the f, v, or ph appears as the initial, medial, or final sound. The f sounds are almost identical with the English f, gh (as in enough), or ph sounds, except that they must be sung with more intensity and explosion of air.

The pf *combination.* The pf combination warrants a special paragraph since its execution is very difficult for English-speaking singers. The lips must first be closed tightly for the p, then the upper teeth must come down for the f sound. The p must be aspirated, but the explosion of air takes place only after the f sound as in Pferd, Apfel, Kopf. The singer should be taught to be very conscious of both sounds, first by pronouncing them separately p . . . f, then by combining them in a slow and gradually increasing speed.

At the right tempo one will observe that the lower lip curls inward right after the p has been pronounced so that the upper teeth encounter the lip in place for the aspiration.

Gold'ne Ä*pf*el wachsen in ihrem Garten (WAGNER *Das Rheingold*)
Mit Näglein besteckt, schlü*pf* unter die Deck' (BRAHMS "Wiegenlied")

The voiceless s *sound.* For description and production see page 57. Its English equivalent is the s or c (as in race). The difference between the voiced and the voiceless s is the same as between the words buzz and hiss.

The voiceless s in German may also be spelled ß especially in the older spelling and after a long vowel, but there is no difference in the way of pronouncing it.

The voiceless s is pronounced (1) at the end of a word or a syllable, as in das, Haus, Häus-chen, loskommen, etc.; (2) when the spelling ß is used, as in Fuß, Muße, mäßig, grüßen; (3) in the middle of a word after consonants other than r, l, m, and n, as in Erbse, sechse, rülpsen. The pronunciation does not change whether the voiceless s stands at the beginning, the middle, or the end of a word. The singer should be warned not to explode it too vehemently, otherwise an ugly hissing sound would result.

Knu*s*per, Knu*s*per, Knäu*s*chen, wer knu*s*pert mir am Häu*s*chen? (HUMPERDINCK *Hänsel und Gretel*)
Eine Stra*ß*e muss ich gehen, die noch keiner ging zurück (SCHUBERT "Der Wegweiser")
Sech*s*e treffen, sieben äffen! (WEBER *Der Freischütz*)

Words derived from Italian and French have the initial voiceless s, as in Santa, Sire, etc.; but if the word has lost its relation to a foreign language, the initial s becomes voiced, as in Sankt ([zaŋkt]).

Jährlich am *S*ankt Johannistag (WAGNER *Die Meistersinger von Nürnberg*)
*S*ankta Justizia, ich möchte rasen! (LORTZING *Zar und Zimmermann*)

The st *and* sp *combinations.* Whenever an st or sp appears in the middle or at the end of a word, it is pronounced as written, st and sp, as in bester, hasten, Leiste, Gast, Ost, Wespe, lispeln.

st and sp at the beginning of a word or after a prefix is pronounced sht and shp ([ʃt, ʃp]). See page 106.

The z *or* c [ts] *combinations.* The German z is phonetically a combination of t and voiceless s. It can either stand by itself, as in Zahn, Zeit, Scherz, spazieren, Mozart, or may be spelled ts (after a long vowel) or tz (after a short vowel), as in Rätsel, putzen, Satz, Schatz, Trotz. The German z and c bear no relation to their Italian, French, or English counterparts.

Erklär dies Rä*ts*el, täusch' mich nicht! (MOZART *Die Zauberflöte*)
Guten Abend mein Scha*tz*, guten Abend mein Kind! (BRAHMS "Vergebliches Ständchen")

The c is a combination of tse, tsa, tsee, and appears only in words of foreign origin, as for instance in ecce [ɛktsɛ], Cäsar [tsɛːzar], Citrone [tsitroːnə]. [ts] is produced by bringing into contact the forward part of the tongue and the hard palate, well back of the upper gum ridge. Aspiration or explosion, as in all other consonant combinations in German, takes place after the second consonant. In connecting final and initial z, both must be pronounced according to the above rule, as in Herz zerstach.

Der jubelnd er das Herz *z*erstach! (WAGNER *Tannhäuser*)

The x [ks] *sound.* The x is phonetically a combination of k and voiceless s. It may also be spelled chs. It is produced by a fast shift of the tongue from the first to the second consonant, the aspiration or explosion taking place after the s. Some words spelled with x or chs are Axt, Hexe, sechs, Luchs. For general problems arising from the enunciation of voiceless final consonants in singing diction, see page 104.

The sch [ʃ] *sound.* For description and production see page 59. The English equivalent of sch is sh; the sch should therefore present no difficulties to the English-speaking singer. Words with sch are numerous: Schatz, Schule, Esche, rasch, Fisch.

> Ich hör meinen *Sch*atz (BRAHMS "Der Schmied)
> Mit *Sch*miegen und Wenden mir *sch*lüpft's an die Brust (WOLF "Erstes Liebeslied eines Mädchens")
> Welch' ein Strahl bricht aus der E*sch*e Stamm! (WAGNER *Die Walküre*)
> In einem Bächlein helle, da *sch*oss in froher Eil, die launi*sch*e Forelle vorüber wie ein Pfeil (SCHUBERT "Die Forelle")
> Wandl' ich traurig von Bu*sch* zu Bu*sch* (BRAHMS "Die Mainacht")

s with the diminutive ending -chen is not fused into sch, but remains a voiceless, hard s, as in Häus-chen, Füss-chen.

> Knusper, Knusper Knäu*s*chen, wer knuspert mir am Häu*s*chen? (HUMPERDINCK *Hänsel und Gretel*)

The initial st[ʃt] *and* sp[ʃp] *combinations.* These sound combinations are pronounced like the English sht and shp. This also holds true for st and sp after a prefix, as in Stolz, Stand, an-stehen, Spott, spassig, aus-spielen. The aspiration or explosion takes place after the t or the p, respectively.

> Ein *St*oss — und er ver*st*ummt! (BEETHOVEN *Fidelio*)
> In ein freundliches *St*ädtchen tret' ich ein, in den *St*rassen liegt roter Abendschein (WOLF "Auf einer Wanderung")
> Treibe nur mit Lieben *Sp*ott, Geliebte mein (WOLF *Spanisches Liederbuch*)
> Ver*sp*rochen? nein das geht zu weit! (BEETHOVEN *Fidelio*)

Initial st and sp in foreign words is pronounced [ʃt, ʃp] only if the word has become part of the German language, as in Spanien (ʃpa:ɲɛn), Statue (ʃta:tuə).

> Als wären Sie die *St*atue auf Ihrer eig'nen Gruft (RICHARD STRAUSS *Ariadne auf Naxos*)
> Und keine *sp*anische Tuerei! (RICHARD STRAUSS *Der Rosenkavalier*)

st and sp within a foreign word are always pronounced st and sp, as in Restaurant, Aspekt, konspirieren.

The soft voiced [ʒ] and [dʒ] (pronounced in English zh or dzh) appear only in foreign words spelled with g in French, as in genie ([ʒeni:]), or with the g in Italian, as in adagio ([ada:dʒɔ]) or with g or j in English, as in gentlemen or jazz.

The tsch [tʃ] *sound.* For description and production see page 58. This sound is not a combination of consonants but a genuine single consonant which appears in the middle or at the end of German words such as lutschen, hätscheln, Kutsche, etsch. It corresponds to the English ch, as in *ch*urch, or tch as in fe*tch*, hi*tch*. It is produced and sung just like its English equivalent, or the Italian cia-, ce-, ci-.

> Kla*tsch*t der Regen auf die Blätter, sing' ich so für mich allein (WOLF "Der Scholar")
> Ich pei*tsch*e die Wellen mit mächtigem Schlag (SCHUBERT "Der Schiffer")

In singing diction even words with t as the final sound and sch as the initial sound of a syllable are pronounced [tʃ], as in Botschaft, rechtschaffen.

The two ch sounds. I have left until last these ch sounds, which cause the English-speaking singer considerable difficulty. Singing them is not, however, an entirely hopeless undertaking. The accompanist or coach can correct faulty pronunciation by insisting that the singer find the position in his speech apparatus where these sounds must be produced.

The ch sounds are not combinations of consonants but regular single consonants, although they differ greatly from each other.

The soft ch [ç] *sound.* The soft ch is a palatal voiceless fricative, produced like its voiced counterpart, the j (see p. 101), except that air is aspirated — but not exploded too violently. There is no English equivalent of this palatal ch. The singer should practice it by saying h as in hue and suddenly aspirating the h until it becomes a soft ch. The resulting sound will approximate very closely the palatal ch of the German.

Soft palatal ch is pronounced whenever ch stands after ä, e, i, ö, ü, ai, ei, äu, eu, as in Bächlein, sprechen, Licht, höchstes, flüchtig, Reich, feucht.

> Ich hört' ein Bä*ch*lein rauschen (SCHUBERT "Wohin")
> Hö*ch*stes Vertrau'n hast du mir schon zu danken (WAGNER *Lohengrin*)
> In ein mildes, blaues Li*ch*t (RICHARD STRAUSS "Traum durch die Dämmerung")
> Nun schuf mi*ch* Gott zum rei*ch*en Mann (WAGNER *Die Meistersinger von Nürnberg*)

Soft ch is pronounced after an l, r, n, as in welcher, Storch, mancher.

> Da klappern die Stör*ch*e im lustigsten Ton (WOLF "Storchenbotschaft")
> Redet so viel und so man*ch*erlei (BRAHMS "Von ewiger Liebe")
> Denn sol*ch*em grossen Sarge gebührt ein grosses Grab (SCHUMANN "Dichterliebe")

Soft ch is also used in the diminutive ending -chen, as in Häns-chen, Mäus-chen, Lüft-chen.

Hänschen klein geht allein in die weite Welt hinein (German folk song)

Wehe Lüftchen, lind und lieblich (BRAHMS "Botschaft")

The ig ending is pronounced like the soft palatal ch (see p. 103).

In some words of Greek or Teutonic origin the initial ch is soft and palatal, as in China, Chemie; but this will hardly ever be encountered in songs or operatic literature.

The hard ch [x] sound. The hard ch is a uvular voiceless fricative produced in the throat by anchoring the tip of the tongue against the lower gum ridge and rubbing the back part of the tongue against the back of the soft palate. This guttural ch which is usually transcribed kh in English corresponds very closely to the Scottish ch as in loch. The ch in German is pronounced gutturally whenever it stands after an a, o, u, or au, as in brach, Loch, hoch, Fluch, Rauch.

Ich musste auch hinunter mit meinem Wanderstab. Hinunter und immer weiter, und immer dem Bache nach (SCHUBERT "Wohin")

So will mir doch die ganze Woche das Lachen nicht vergeh'n (BRAHMS "Sonntag")

Wie durch Fluch er mir geriet, verflucht sei dieser Ring! (WAGNER *Das Rheingold*)

The combination chs is pronounced ks, as in wachsen, sechs, Ochs (see p. 105).

Initial ch in foreign words is mostly pronounced like a k, as in Cherubin, Chloë, Christus, Chor.

Ich war bei Chloë jüngst zu Gast (MOZART "An Chloë")

Edler Täufer! Christs Vorläufer! (WAGNER *Die Meistersinger von Nürnberg*)

THE DOUBLE CONSONANTS

The following double consonants exist in the German language:

Voiced		*Voiceless*	
mm	bb	ff	pp
nn	dd	ss	tt
ll	gg	kk (ck)	
	rr		

Siebs urges that double consonants be pronounced exactly like single ones. He considers double consonants to be only orthographically, not phonetically, different from their single counterparts. The rule then would be the same as for the pronunciation of French double consonants. This may be valid for stage pronunciation, but we will find that it is too simple to be useful for German singing diction.

One thing is certain: the vowel before a double consonant is invariably a short open one. This distinguishes German pronunciation from the pronunciation of Romance languages (see p. 59), where closed vowels stay closed even before a double consonant. Voiced double consonants similar to the Italian ones give more intensity, impetus, and importance to the words which contain them. This may be illustrated by a few examples (Figs. 84–87). The double consonants in the accom-

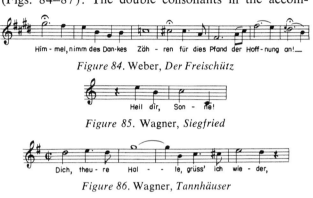

Him - mel, nimm des Dan-kes Zäh - ren für dies Pfand der Hoff - nung an!__

Figure 84. Weber, *Der Freischütz*

Heil dir, Son - ne!

Figure 85. Wagner, *Siegfried*

Dich, theu - re Hal - - le, grüss' ich wie - der,

Figure 86. Wagner, *Tannhäuser*

O Herr!

Figure 87. Beethoven, *Fidelio*

panying list must be sung with much greater intensity than their single counterparts. In a two-syllable word the vowel of the first syllable gets the full tonal value. The double consonant is pronounced and sung at the beginning of the second syllable.

Single	*Double*
Himbeere	Himmel
sondern	Sonne
Halm	Halle
heran	Herr
Rebell	Ebbe
Widmung	Widder
bald	Ball

Figures 84–87 should suffice to make the point that voiced double consonants in German can make the words containing them more expressive, and that they should therefore be more accentuated than single consonants — particularly when dramatic situations or poetic alliterations require special stress. In Figure 84, the invocation of heaven will become more intense if the voice, after scaling the very difficult i sound on a high note, underlines the mm. The same feeling of grandeur and dignity will be achieved by emphasizing the nn in Figure 85, Brünnhilde's invocation of the sun, her first words after her awakening. Jubilation and inner excitement will

carry Elisabeth's entrance in Figure 86 if the soprano gives impetus to the double ll in Halle.

In Figure 87, the stressing of the double rr in Herr will convey to the audience the mixture of emotions in Rocco's plea to Pizarro not to command him to murder the imprisoned Florestan. It is a deeply felt pleading, a feeling of impotence to resist Pizarro, and even a suppressed outcry of rebellion against him — all expressed in the one rr.

This is one of the many times when technical and interpretative problems overlap. Siebs had only the technical side of diction in mind when he concluded that single and double consonants should be pronounced alike. To be sure, double consonants must not be overstressed, with the effect of caricaturing the language. The accompanist and coach will have to show the singer the golden middle road of esthetic taste.

THE VOICELESS DOUBLE CONSONANTS

The voiceless double consonants are not much different from the voiceless single consonants. However, a longer pause between forming and exploding the consonant while diminishing the flow of breath (see p. 59) and a somewhat more violent explosion whenever the music asks for it will help to underline the innate drama of words containing double consonants (Fig. 88).

Figure 88. Richard Strauss, "Ständchen," example of voiceless double consonants

Auch der Küsse Duft mich wie noch nie berückte, die ich nachts vom Strauch deiner Lippen pflückte (BRAHMS "Sapphische Ode")

One word about double consonants before other consonants, as in Schlepptau, Schiffsnetz. In such cases the explosion or aspiration of the double consonant is diminished first and intensified only on the last consonant of the group. About the singing of double consonants which belong to different syllables of a word, as in kom-men, ren-nen, bak-ken, see page 107. Although we form the consonant at the end of the preceding syllable it never must be exploded or intensified until we come to the second syllable (Fig. 89, 90).

Figure 89. Mozart, *Die Entführung aus dem Serail*

Figure 90. Weber, *Der Freischütz*

COMBINATION OF CONSONANTS

Some combinations of consonants create difficulties for the English-speaking singer, perhaps more for psychological reasons than for technical ones. The most common of these combinations is the *sts*, as in er ist's. The English-speaking singer is prone to disregard pronunciation of the final s, forgetting that there are scores of words in English that contain the same combination of consonants, such as lists and beasts. In all cases of conglomeration of consonants with ts it is advisable to practice singing the preceding consonants, then adding the voiceless ts with the residue of the breath. Some words containing these combinations are Er is-ts, nich-ts, mach-ts, durchziehen, vier-zig, sech-zig, lock-ts, Exzess (but furchtsam with voiced s).

Frühling, ja du bi*st's*! (WOLF "Er ist's")
Mein Brusttuch, schau, wohl lie*gt's* im Ort (WAGNER *Die Meistersinger von Nürnberg*)
Wer glau*bts*? und meiner ward es nicht auf dieser ganzen Reise (SCHUBERT "Der greise Kopf")

Other difficult combinations containing st and sp are, for instance, ve*rstr*eut, ve*rspr*ochen, du*rchspr*echen, du*rchstr*eifen. In these last two, the palatal ch should first be established before tongue and lips continue to the str and spr.

Ve*rspr*ochen? nein das geht zu weit! (BEETHOVEN *Fidelio*)
Einsam zu Ross, ohne Ruh' noch Rast, du*rchstr*eift' er als Wand'rer die Welt (WAGNER *Götterdämmerung*)

Other difficulties with combinations of consonants may also be surmounted by first dividing them into two or more units, establishing correct pronunciation for each of them in turn, and then combining them.

CONNECTION OF CONSONANTS

Two or more consonants of the same or of different phonetic groups may have to be connected for musical reasons between two words, or inside the same word, unless they are separated by musical pauses. Certain empiric rules exist. Knowing them will make the work of accompanists and coaches much easier.

Final and initial consonants of the same kind (homorganic) may be found in one word, or in two words, such as in Auf-führung, Schiff-fahrt, Still-leben, hin-neigen, viel lieben, auf Flügeln. These homorganic consonants are, of course, not double consonants. They are connected by pronouncing the final one, then reducing the aspiration during a split-second pause, and then intensifying the aspiration with the start of the following initial aspiration.

> Auf Flügeln des Gesanges (MENDELSSOHN "Auf Flügeln des Gesanges")
> Die Stadt mit ihren Türmen, in Abend-dämm'rung gehüllt (SCHUBERT "Die Stadt")
> Und wüssten's die Blumen, die kleinen, wie tief verwundet mein Herz (SCHUMANN "Dichterliebe")
> Wie bitter sind der Trennung Leiden! (MOZART Die Zauberflöte)

The final consonant may be voiceless, the initial one voiced, as in aus-sehen, Bass singen, auf-wenden. Connect these consonants by pronouncing the first one voicelessly, releasing the flow of voice on the second one.

Similar but not homorganic consonants must *not* be connected, as in aus-streuen, aus-sprechen. Each consonant must be pronounced clearly.

Special importance must be given to the connection of final and initial plosive sounds and final plosive sounds with initial consonants of different phonetic classifications. Into the first category fall the t-t, d-d, t-d, d-t, b-b, b-p, b-d, b-g, b-k, b-t, k-d, k-k, k-g, k-t, t-b, t-p, t-g, t-k, g-b, g-d, g-g, g-k, g-p, g-t connections. These and other similar connections are encountered very frequently in vocal literature.

> Ihr hoher Zweck zeigt deutlich an (MOZART Die Zauberflöte)
> Mein Schatz hat kein Band und kein Stern (SCHUMANN "Die Soldatenbraut")
> Wie Frühlingsblumen blüht es, und schwebt wie Duft dahin (BRAHMS "Wie Melodien zieht es mir")
> Sein frevler Mund tat es kund (WAGNER Tannhäuser)
> Gedenk' der beschildeten Frau! (WAGNER Götterdämmerung)
> Dem nur in Maienwonne die zarte Kost gedeiht (WOLF "Citronenfalter im April")

In all these cases connection is effected by keeping the plosive position for final and initial consonants, not exploding the final sound, concentrating on the consonant during the little pause, and exploding the following initial sound well.

The same rule of exploding only the second sound is valid for connecting final plosive sounds and initial consonants of a different phonetic category. These connections may take place between the following consonants:

b-f, b-l, b-n, b-m, b-s, b-w, t-f, t-j, t-l, t-m, t-n, t-r, t-w, g-f, g-j, g-l, g-m, g-n, g-r, g-s, g-w, as in abfahren, ablehnen, Abwege, entfernen, entlehnen, entwöhnen, wegfahren, wegnehmen, Wegweiser, etc.

> Frühling lässt sein blaues Band (WOLF "Er ist's")
> Doch an andres denkt mein Herz (WOLF Spanisches Liederbuch)
> Ins Land hinabzublicken, das nebelleicht zerinnt (SCHUBERT "Der Alpenjäger")
> Ich weiss ja doch, du liebtest, allein du liebst nicht mehr! (BRAHMS "Du sprichst, dass ich mich täuschte")

Initial voiced consonants ought to keep their voiced quality to some extent.

LIAISON AND SEPARATION

The glottal stroke. The liaison in German singing diction was taboo in Wagnerian and early post-Wagnerian times. According to my tenet, however, that the German language can be made to sound more beautiful by following a vocal bel canto line, liaisons are permissible and often even preferable.

When the separation of words becomes essential, the English-speaking singer and especially the American and English voice teacher resists using the so-called glottal stroke. Glottal stroke is a violent compression of the vocal cords which explosively releases stored-up air (see also p. 38). A glottal stroke is used for certain types of violent attack of tones which start with a vowel. This sounds very dangerous and indeed is, if overdone. There are, however, two kinds of glottal strokes: (1) The vehement one, which should never be used because it can actually hurt a voice and create hoarseness by thickening the vocal cords and, in extreme cases, even developing nodes on the vocal cords. (2) The gentle one, which will never hurt a singer who has enough vocal technique to be prepared for professional work on concert or operatic stage.

As a matter of fact, gentle glottal strokes are regularly employed in any kind of staccato singing. There are several situations in which final consonants and initial vowels or one and the same final and initial vowel must be separated: (1) if a word must be isolated for euphonic reasons; (2) if rhythmic or dramatic emphasis warrants it; (3) for clarity of diction, especially in lieder or choral works or passages; (4) to avoid misunderstanding words.

The artist who studies lieder is more likely to use slight glottal strokes than the singer of classical German operatic music. The lied is built entirely on the word. Each shade, be it as soft as can be, must be brought out. The music must paint, color, and embellish the word. Therefore, slight separation between words is essential, unless the vocal line demands an unbroken legato. In Wagnerian operas more glottal strokes are warranted for alliteration and dramatic emphasis than in other German operas. However, his feeling for vocal line will have to guide the accompanist and coach. I cannot warn strongly enough against chopping up phrases and melodies for the sake of exaggerating the misunderstood German diction.

Figure 91. Weber, *Der Freischütz*

Figure 92. Weber, *Der Freischütz*

Figure 93. Wagner, *Lohengrin*

Choral works or passages, because of the masses of voices that are employed in them, will tend to become muddy if the diction is not very clear. Here the separation of consonants and vowels is an important part of choral technique. In Agathe's cavatine from *Der Freischütz* (Fig. 91) we can prove the necessity for a liaison and separation on the same lyrics. Here the melodic line asks for liaison in accordance with the same phrase at the beginning of this aria: Und ob die Wolke sie verhülle. The legato is indicated by the violoncello melody during the introduction (Fig. 92). In the next line the musical phrasing asks for separation.

In the example from *Lohengrin* (Fig. 93), the words mein and Ohr must be separated; otherwise, the sense-

less connection "nohr" would result. The same happens in the phrases "mein/Aug' ist zugefallen" and "sank/in süssen Schlaf."

Detailed analysis of the liaison-versus-separation fight would fill a whole book. The above-cited rules and examples will have to suffice. The accompanist and coach must have enough cultural and musical background and knowledge of style — in other words, artistic taste — to decide in each case which approach to use.

PHONETIC TRANSCRIPTION OF GERMAN ARIA: "ELSA'S DREAM" FROM "LOHENGRIN" BY RICHARD WAGNER

ainza:m in trybən ta:gən ha:p iç tsu: gɔtt gəflet, dəs hɛrtsəns ti:fstəs kla:gən ɛrgɔss iç im gəbet, da: draŋ aus mainəm ʃtønən ain laut zo kla:gəfɔll, der tsu: gəvaltgəm tønən vait in di: lyftə ʃvɔll. iç hørt i:n fɛrnhi:n hallən, bis kaum main or er tra:f; main aug ist tsu:gəfallən, iç zaŋk in zyssən ʃla:f.

in liçtər vaffən ʃainə, ain rittər na:tə da:, zo tu:gəntliçər rainə iç kainən nox ɛrza:. ain gɔldən hɔrn tsur hyftən, gəlenət auf zain ʃvert, zo tra:t er aus dən lyftən tsu: mi:r, dər rɛkkə vert. mit tsyçtigəm gəba:rən ga:p trøstuŋ er mi:r ain, dəs rittərs vill iç va:rən, er zɔll main ʃtraitər zain!

hørt, vas dem gɔttgəzantən iç bi:tə fyr gəvɛ:r, in mainəs fa:tərs landən di: kronə tra:gə er, miç glykkliç zɔll er praizən nimmt er main gu:t dahi:n, vill er gəma:l miç haissən, geb iç i:m, vas iç bin!

PHONETIC TRANSCRIPTION OF GERMAN LIED: "WOHIN" BY FRANZ SCHUBERT

iç hørt ain bɛçlain rauʃən vol aus dem fɛlzənkvɛll, hinap tsum ta:le rauʃən zo friʃ unt vundərhɛll. iç vais niçt vi: mi:r vurdə, niçt, ver den ra:t mi:r ga:p, iç musstə aux hinuntər mit mainəm vandərʃta:p. hinuntər unt immər vaitər, unt immər dem baxə na:x, unt immər friʃər rauʃtə unt immər hɛllər der bax.

ist dass dɛnn mainə ʃtra:ssə? o bɛçlain ʃpriç, vohi:n? du: hast mit dainəm rauʃən mi:r gants bərauʃt den zinn. vas za:g iç dɛnn vɔm rauʃən? das kann kain rauʃən zain; es ziŋən vol di: niksən ti:f untən i:rən rain.

las ziŋən, gəzɛll, las rauʃən, unt vandrə frøliç na:x! es gen ja mylənrɛ:dər in jedəm kla:rən bax.

Elements of Musical Style

MUSICAL style belongs to the branch of philosophy called aesthetics and, in particular, to musical aesthetics. Though theoretical speculation about this subject does not lie within the scope of this book, a few basic concepts will have to be explained briefly.

Music consists of musical matter cast into form. Musical matter, in turn, is *all* the musical sounds which, combined and taken together, give us an audible sensation of music. The smallest unit is the single tone, which can be augmented by loudness or by duplication in instrumentation, and also coupled with other tones so as to form intervals, chords, consonances, dissonances, and melodies. These combinations follow different patterns of changes — called rhythmic patterns — of heavy and weak accents.

But there cannot be any music without form. Even the music of the most primitive people has its form. Without form, music would sound like an infant's senseless babbling. True, musical form cannot be directly perceived by any of our senses; but it can be understood and appreciated by our aesthetic sense — our sense of beauty and harmony in art. There exists a variety of musical forms: some were used more in the past, some are still employed by composers today. The study of musical form is a very important phase of general musical study — a phase no accompanist or coach can bypass. It is just as basic as the study of harmony and counterpoint. Musical form is so closely connected with and related to musical style that one could say form is a special aspect of style.

A music student in the United States starts his theoretical study with music appreciation and then spends a year or more on harmony and additional time on counterpoint and form. In such a course, the study of musical style is very much neglected — and yet style is the aesthetically most beautiful quality in music. Understanding style leads to the fullest appreciation of music and to the ability to recreate music properly.

What does this mysterious term "style" mean? What is the importance of style for the creation and recreation of music?

The definition of style is controversial. Thus far it has been impossible to define style unequivocally. Webster mentions fourteen different meanings, the *American College Dictionary* seventeen. For our purposes, two of Webster's definitions seem to fit: First, "Style is a characteristic mode of expression, as of a nation, period, person, or school." Second, "Style is a distinctive or characteristic mode of presentation, construction or execution in any art, employment, or product, especially in any of the fine arts." Grove's dictionary completely evades a definition of musical style. *The Harvard Dictionary of Music*, edited by Willi Apel, says: "Musical style means 'characteristic language' or 'characteristic handwriting' particularly with reference to the details of a composition, as distinguished from its large outlines, i.e. form." Leonard B. Meyer, in his *Emotion and Meaning in Music*, gives a still different definition of style. He begins by analyzing what he calls style systems, "by which term something analogous to language has been meant. . . . By style, as distinguished from style system, is meant the more particular variants and modifications of a style system made at different epochs within a culture or by different composers within the same epoch. Thus Bach and Beethoven represent different styles within a single style system, while Mozart and Machaut employ different style systems."

By now the reader must be profoundly confused. And

yet these different definitions will serve to give a clear picture of what musical style is.

First of all, there are several kinds of musical style, depending upon one's approach. There are the style of a period: Renaissance or baroque; the style of a nation: French or Russian; the style of a composition: homophonic, polyphonic, operatic, or symphonic; the style of a musical medium: instrumental or vocal; the personal style of a composer: Mozart or Stravinsky.

Another way of grouping styles has been set forth by Käthe Meyer in *Zum Stilproblem in der Musik*. She finds three important molders of style: social influences, which produce, for example, the music of royal courts or folk music; national influences; and religious and ethical influences. All these are included in Webster's first definition.

These styles are more or less innate in the music in which they appear. For our purposes, period style, national style, and personal style are the most important. Contemporary composers, through their notations and remarks in the scores, tell us exactly the style in which they want us to perform their works. But this is a comparatively recent innovation: before the late nineteenth and the beginning of the twentieth century, the composers themselves said very little. Musicians must therefore study source materials — the works of the old theoreticians, the history and sociology of the period, the biographies and techniques of composition of individual composers, and so on.

It is not too much to say that in order to grasp the style of, for example, Schubert, not only Schubert's songs, but also his orchestral works, chamber music, and sacred compositions must be studied. Otherwise, the accompanist and coach will never get a clear picture of Schubert's style and he will not be able to master his accompaniments. This also means studying the composer's *original* scores, not the usually incorrectly edited ones. When a score is published in an edition revised by a conscientious musician — Max Friedländer in the case of Schubert's lieder, for instance — the accompanist and coach will have nothing to worry about. But all too often editions appear whose editors apparently simply want to be different, and do not understand much about style. Rather than study such a bad edition, the accompanist and coach must go to the source. He must look at the original score in a good music library.

The last few paragraphs should have served to make it clear that there is not only an innate musical style but also a performance style. A Bach Passion, for instance, was performed in completely different styles by Bach himself, by Mendelssohn a hundred years later, and by, let's say, Leopold Stokowski yet another century later. Moreover, there is not only the performance style of the period in which a composition is written — which may be different from the innate style in which it was conceived, being either too modern or too old-fashioned — but there is also the style of the time in which the performers live. We, the musicians of today, live in a period of a certain musical style (or lack of style, if you wish). We cannot perform without introducing some of the style of our day into our performances. This fits Webster's second definition. We try to stick to the original style; this is called following tradition. But how many cycles of change of style, how many generations have passed through the revolving doors of time!

Tradition is the total of authenticity plus all kinds of accretions, good and bad, that have been added over the years. Gustav Mahler once said, "What they call tradition is nothing but sloppiness." These words sound like a declaration of war against traditionalists; they are really not that bad. Mahler was only fighting the bad taste of many who set themselves up as the guardians of tradition. Studying composers' lifeworks and returning to the source whenever possible, combined with a sound over-all cultural and musical background, will enable one to recreate the genuine tradition, the innate and the original performance style of a composition. Naturally, we cannot but add to these the performance style of our own time. The Bach Passions, for instance, were originally performed by an orchestra of eighteen and by a chorus even smaller. Our large concert halls of today require an adjustment of the proportions of modern orchestral and choral sound for the musical style of Bach's works and times.

Styles are cyclical. Just as there are many different streams of philosophical, political, social, and religious thought in any given age, so there are as many different musical styles. No contemporary will be able to decide which style will eventually give his age its name, though he can make a guess by comparing the music of a period with its architecture, painting, and literature. As a rule, music is not the first of the arts to establish a style characteristic of its age. Only future generations can recognize what style governed our age.

The cyclical pattern operates as follows: even when

one style is at its height, many deviations, additions, and counter movements are simultaneously at work; eventually they will cause the style to decline and to disintegrate. The height of any stylistic period may be called its classical phase; every style goes through such a period. But slowly, the counter movements, at first unrecognized and unobserved, grow stronger, become better and better known, and finally become dominant as the new style of a new age. For a while this new style is universally accepted as the age's single means of expression. But before long, dissenting creations deviate from it and break its rules. The antithetical phase of the classical stage of any style may be called the romantic phase. The basic difference between the two stages of an epoch is this: the classical phase is an expression of objectivity, whereas the romantic phase is highly subjective. Objectivity in this respect may be defined as the faculty to express oneself without distortion by personal emotions, giving full weight to clearness, symmetry and poignancy of form, mastery of architectural proportion. The subjectivity of the romantic phase, on the other hand, means the passionate expression of the innermost emotions, resulting in the loss of formal clearness and compactness and architectural proportion. Translated into the language of performance style objectivity means Werktreue — faithful adherence to the work as it was written. Subjectivity, on the other hand, means freer treatment of the work — changing its letter to the spirit which moves the recreative artist during performance.

Each age has these two mainsprings of style. In 1909, for instance, the two greatest conductors of the first half of the twentieth century were active at the Metropolitan Opera: Gustav Mahler (a foe of traditionalism and one of the most subjective conductors of his time) and Arturo Toscanini, who, in conducting Italian and Wagnerian music, established himself as a guardian of objectivity. Twenty years later, the same opposing positions were taken respectively by Wilhelm Furtwängler and Otto Klemperer. The pendulum of style always swings back and forth between objectivity and subjectivity. Or, in the words of Curt Sachs, who divides cycles of musical style into phases and uses the terms ethos, serenity, and classicism for my objectivity and pathos, passion and romanticism for my subjectivity: "Every cycle starts on an ethos phase and ends on a pathos phase. Every phase develops from ethos to pathos" (*The Commonwealth of Art*) — meaning that the pendulum

swings from one extreme to the other as many times as there are phases in a cycle of musical style.

The accompanist and coach must constantly weigh the musical material stylistically, seeking in performance to find the proper balance between innate style, original performance style, and today's performance style. According to Bücken and Mies in their "Grundlagen, Methoden und Aufgaben der musikalischen Stilkunde," style in music is the sum of many components or elements (Stilmomente) in constantly recurring formations. The term "Stilmoment" is appropriate to a situation in which rhythmic, melodic, harmonic, and expression patterns and patterns of form, recur again and again in a single composition, in the total work of a composer, or in an age. Style is the sum of all Stilmomente. Some of these components or elements are of the highest importance in forming and characterizing a style. I shall discuss them in the following sections.

TEMPO

The first thing an accompanist and coach approaching a piece of music must consider is the tempo. Immediately, the question arises: Does a right tempo exist? In answering this question in the affirmative we must apply the categories of the preceding section: a composition has an innate tempo, which the composer had in mind when he wrote it. The same piece has a performance tempo which may have been different from the innate tempo, even when the composer himself played or conducted his music. Finally, there is today's performance tempo, which again may be a slight modification of the innate tempo.

Thus we see that the "right" tempo is subject to alteration. When regular tempo was first employed during the late era of mensural notation in the fifteenth and sixteenth centuries (before that time the relative values of the notes had been established, but the tempo itself was improvised), the unit of time was the beat of the human heart or pulse. This unit of time was first mentioned in 1596 by the Italian theoretician Ludovico Zacconi. In the seventeenth century, several writers elaborated on the problem of tempo, giving us a pretty good picture of the feeling about the subject before Bach's time. The most important treatise about tempo was written by Johann Joachim Quantz in 1752: *Versuch einer Anweisung, die Flöte traversière zu spielen* (Essay of Instruction on How to Play the Transverse Flute). His book takes into consideration the musical style of the period of Bach and Handel. And at about the same time, Leopold Mozart published his *Gründliche Violinschule* (Thorough School for the Violin), giving useful hints about tempo. Wolfgang Amadeus Mozart himself has given us some very valuable information about the tempi that he desired.

With the advent of Beethoven, the metronome — which had been anticipated earlier by some astonishing if simple inventions — was introduced as an objective yardstick for determining the right tempo. We know today that even the metronome's use was, and is, far from reliable. We see that some living composers, when they play or conduct their own music, take different tempi from those indicated by their own metronome markings. This makes us realize that tempo depends upon human elements — age, emotions, physical health, temperament — and in general upon the tempo of life, which is different in different countries.

It is indisputable that youth will take faster tempi than older people. The very old, however, may take tempi faster *or* slower. We have a good means of comparison in contemporary recordings. In his old age, Toscanini conducted the same pieces much faster than he had twenty or thirty years before. The opposite happened with Furtwängler: his interpretations became much slower during his last years. Psychological and physical reasons can be adduced for these changes in choosing the "right" tempo.

It is another indisputable fact that performance tempi in America are faster than in Europe. European guest conductors have often been criticized for taking tempi too slow, just as our artists have been criticized in Europe for being much too fast. American pulses do not beat any faster than European pulses; but the tempo of working and living in America is faster and it is understandable and justifiable that we unconsciously transfer this speed to our musical tempi.

Besides the human temperament, there are other reasons why one and the same piece of music may be conducted, played, or sung faster or slower — even for today's style of performance. Curt Sachs summed these up in his *Rhythm and Tempo*. *Orchestration*: The same piece scored in different ways may be taken slower or faster according to the sound masses of the orchestration. A song will be faster with piano accompaniment, but somewhat slower with orchestra. The richness of orchestral sound takes more time to unfold than the comparatively dry sound of a piano. *The range of the human voice*: A bass or alto will sing the same piece a little slower than a tenor or soprano because of the comparatively slow attacking faculty of the lower voice ranges. *The density of orchestral setting*: A monophonic setting will be taken faster than a complicated polyphonic setting of the same melody. Large masses of musical instruments, or choral voices, will necessitate slower tempi than smaller groups. *The acoustics of concert halls, theaters, churches*: The presence of echoes warrants a slower tempo. And, finally, a very timely and important observation: live performances with visual impression can stand slower tempi than mechanical reproductions without. Most recordings are faster than live performances — the pauses are shorter.

All these undoubtedly contribute to variations in tempo. Yet the most important influence is human and psychological. Tempi will be faster or slower according to the mood, feelings, and physical condition of performers and listeners. I have myself tested this many times by listening to the same record, playing mechanically at exactly the same speed; sometimes the tempi sounded too fast to me, sometimes too slow, sometimes right, depending upon my momentary disposition.

Pre-Bach tempo. The signature for a slow four-beat bar during the early period of mensural notation in the fourteenth century was the so-called tempus imperfectum (Fig. 94A), for the three-beat the tempus perfectum (Fig. 94B). During the later part of the period the unit for a beat was no longer the breve (Fig. 94C), but the semibreve (Fig. 94D). In accordance with this, the time signatures also changed: for tempus imperfectum from that shown in Figure 94A to that shown in Figure 94G, and for tempus perfectum from that shown in Figure 94E to that shown in Figure 94F. The new faster tempo unit was called alla breve.

Figure 94. Time signatures, period of mensural notation

These old time signatures are important to us, for three hundred years later Haydn, Mozart, Beethoven, and even Schubert still employed them, not always as the indication of a certain tempo, but often as a hint of which note value should be taken for the basic unit or pulse of a piece. The old theoreticians gave the average beat as 72–76 strokes a minute. In Quantz's time it had progressed to 80 strokes, and Henry Purcell, in a work published in 1696, after his death, gave indications for the tempi of his works as shown in Figure 95. But he frequently contradicted himself in the time signatures of his actual compositions. As a rule, however, the time signatures and relations shown in Figure 95 are about right for his period.

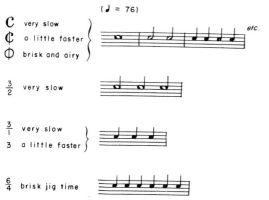

Figure 95. Purcell's indications of tempo

The accompanist and coach will apply the information in Figure 95 to the works of the Elizabethan lutenists and to Purcell's own works. Of course, all of these descriptions of tempo are approximate. In vocal compositions the content and the emotions to be expressed will determine the tempi.

From Purcell's time on, treatises about time signatures and tempo relations appear more and more frequently until they reach a methodical, if too formalistic, basis in 1752 in Johann Joachim Quantz's book. Quantz was King Frederick of Prussia's flute teacher. Born in Germany, he studied in Italy, lived for a time in London, and knew intimately the music of his period, including Bach's and Handel's. His explanations of tempo, as given in the accompanying list, though on the conservative side, offer the most authentic yardstick for the performance of the music of the first half of the eighteenth century.

Common Time

Presto, Allegro assai . . . . ♩ = 80, ♪ = 160
Allegro moderato, Poco allegro,
   Vivace, Allegro . . . . ♩ = 60, ♪ = 120
Allegretto . . . . ♩ = 80
Adagio cantabile . . . . ♪ = 80
Adagio assai . . . . ♪ = 40

Alla breve Time

Allegro . . . . ♩ = 160
Allegretto . . . . ♩ = 80
Adagio cantabile . . . . ♩ = 80
Adagio assai . . . . ♩ = 40

From Quantz's directions, we learn that the presto and allegro assai were taken very fast, almost faster than we are used to hearing them today, and that the vivace, surprisingly, is counted among the not so fast allegro tempi. The lack of an instrument to measure the time makes it difficult for Quantz to explain the fast 3 beat: he says that in a 3-4 allegro with runs of sixteenths or eighth triplets the tempo should be determined by a pulse beat on the first and third quarters of the first measure and the second quarter of the second measure (Fig. 96). If there are no more than six notes in a measure, one pulse beat per measure, Quantz says, should be the right speed (Fig. 97). For presto this must be accelerated so that a dotted half note equals 120. In 3-4 adagio cantabile, if the eighth is the basic unit, the eighth note equals 80. Similarly for arioso in 3-8 time. In arioso 3-4 time, a quarter note equals 80. In adagio assai, mesto, or lento the quarter note equals 40. In a Siciliana in 12-8 time the eighth note equals approximately 120.

Figure 96. Quantz's 3-4 allegro with triplets

Figure 97. Quantz's allegro with no more than
six notes to a measure

Quantz distinguished among instrumental music, where he wants his directions followed; vocal music, where meaning and emotion dictate modification of the above tempi; church music, which he wants to be taken more moderately than instrumental music to underline the holiness of church services; and dance music.

His directions for dance tempi are related to the Bach suites and partitas as well as to many other court dances of his time. The list on page 116, adapted from Dolmetsch's *The Interpretation of the Music of the XVII and XVIII Centuries*, shows that most of Quantz's dance tempi are on the fast side. We must not accept them at face value but try to adjust them according to the era of a particular composition. The music of the seventeenth century, until about fifty years before Quantz published his treatise, certainly has been performed slower. This can readily be deduced from the technical limitations of the musical instruments used at the time. Apart from this, we are astonished in particular cases by Quantz's slow tempo for the courante, and the fast tempo for the

Entrée, Loure, Courante . . . . ♩ = 80
Sarabande . . . . ♩ = 80
Chaconne . . . . ♩ = 160
Passecaille . . . . ♩ = 180
Musette . . . . ♪ or ♩ = 80
Bourée, Rigaudon . . . . ♩ = 160
Gavotte . . . . ♩ = 120
Rondeau . . . . ♩ = 140
Gigue . . . . ♩ = 160
Minuet . . . . ♩ = 160
Passepied . . . . ♪ = 180
Tambourin . . . . ♩ = 180
March alla breve . . . . ♩ = 80

English sarabande and the minuet. But we must realize that the metronome figures in the tabulation are for actual dances; for concert performances the time would be altered. The courante (the name means running dance) would be somewhat faster, the sarabande, because of its solemn court character, slower. The minuet has undergone a change during the years. It was rather fast in Bach's time, a little slower — but not much — in Haydn's, until it reaches the familiar tempo of Mozart's and Beethoven's minuets. Beethoven, however, changed most of his minuets to the scherzo form which is considerably faster than the so-called classical minuet of Mozart's time. By that time the minuet had advanced to stately court-dance proportions, its more popular aspects being taken over by the German Dance and, still later, the waltz. Altogether, it must be said that Quantz's system is too rigid for practical use. Surely tempi in his time fluctuated more than just between 80 and 160 pulse beats. His system should be taken with a grain of salt; its importance is only relative.

Tempo in Bach's and Handel's times. J. S. Bach and other composers of his time left us very much in the dark about their tempi. Bach rarely marked the tempo of a piece, especially in his later works. And still, to his pupils and contemporaries his intentions were absolutely clear, so he must have expressed the tempo in some way. One need not assume the existence of secret code: the structure of each piece itself contains the intended tempo. Three suggestions can be made for establishing the right tempo for the performance of Bach and Handel. The time signature and the smallest note value used in a piece are good indications of the intended tempo; there is a definite relation between smallest note value and tempo. The tempo indications (adagio, allegro) in combination with the time signatures establish the intended tempo and set the performance tempo. The instrument

for which Bach wrote a piece or the instrumental style in which he wrote it limits the tempo. Organ music could not be played so fast as harpsichord or clavichord music. Bach also wrote a number of pieces in the style of lute preambles, for instance the famous C major Prelude (Volume I of the *Well-Tempered Clavichord*), where the tempo again depends on the possibilities of the particular instrument, in this case the lute. This is the general outline; Fritz Rothschild elaborates on the first point above in *The Lost Tradition in Music. Rhythm and Tempo in J. S. Bach's Time.*

Time signatures. Bach's time signatures designate the number of beats (Rothschild calls them "structure beats") to a bar. In common time the whole note receives four such beats, one for each quarter note. If 16th notes other than ornaments appear in a piece in common time, the tempo must be slow, somewhere near our adagio tempo. If the shortest notes in a piece are eighth notes, the tempo is considered fast. If quarter notes are the smallest values in a piece in common time, there are only two beats to a bar. Rothschild's schema for common time prescribes that if whole notes, half notes, quarter notes, eighth notes, and sixteenth notes appear in the slow movement of a piece, a quarter note = 40-60. If whole notes, half notes, quarter notes, and eighth notes appear in the fast movement of a piece, a quarter note = 80–120. If only whole notes, half notes, and quarter notes appear, then a quarter note = 80–120.

Rothschild's book is very interesting, but it does not contain the solution to our problem. Like all "discoverers," he tried to bend everything to fit his scheme — in this case, he attempted to bend all of Bach's music. This does not work. Nevertheless, some of his ideas are well thought out and applicable to some of Bach's tempi.

The alla breve sign in Bach's and Handel's times did not necessarily mean a tempo twice as fast as common time, but only gave a different meaning to the note values. If a breve is the longest note in a piece marked with the alla breve sign, it gets four beats, the whole note two beats, and the half note one beat. The tempo is slow. If the whole note is the largest unit of the piece and sixteenth notes also appear, the tempo is slow, but the whole note gets only two beats. If eighth notes are the smallest units, the tempo is fast.

If the term "alla breve" was used by the composer in connection with the alla breve sign, the tempo really was intended to be fast, and the value of the notes was half what it would have been with a common time signature. The term "alla breve" was also used in connection with the common time signature. Here again, the smallest note value will decide the relative tempo. The 2 and 1 signatures can also be found in music of that time: the first means two beats to a measure and the use mostly of half, quarter, and eighth note values, with a tempo slightly faster than common time and fast if the eighth note is the smallest unit; the second means one beat to a measure, usually with half note and quarter note values and a tempo the same as with the 2.

2-4 time is encountered frequently; it appears with quarter, eighth, and sixteenth note values, and has two beats to a measure.

3-2 time means three beats to a measure, with half, quarter, eighth, and sometimes sixteenth notes appearing in a piece. The tempo is slow. If only half and quarter notes appear, the tempo is fast — this holds true even if an eighth note appears occasionally in such a piece. If only half notes are written, the tempo is also fast.

3-4 time with a sixteenth note as the smallest unit is slow, with an eighth note as the smallest unit faster, and with a quarter note as the smallest unit fast.

3-8 time with a thirty-second note as the smallest unit is slow, with a sixteenth faster, and with an eighth fast.

6-4 time with a sixteenth note as the smallest unit is slow, with an eighth faster.

6-8 time with a sixteenth note as the smallest unit is faster, with an eighth fast.

9-8 time with a sixteenth note as the smallest unit is faster, with an eighth fast.

12-8 time with a sixteenth note is faster, with an eighth fast.

3-16, 6-16, 12-16, and 24-16 time with a sixteenth note as the smallest unit are all fast tempi.

TEMPO INDICATIONS IN CONNECTION
WITH TIME SIGNATURES

We know two kinds of tempo indications, one the actual tempo indication (adagio, allegro, presto), the other a modification made by adding an adjective which contains a hint of the emotion desired (andante flebile, allegro commodo).

In Bach's and Handel's times the actual tempo indications modified the time signatures. Most of the "emotional" or "character" adjectives came later — at the time of the so-called Affektenlehre, around the middle

of the eighteenth century. The tempo indications still used all over the world originated in Italy. Sometimes the French and German composers had a slightly different idea about the meaning of these tempo indications, but on the whole, tempo indications meant the same thing wherever they were used.

Leopold Mozart, in his *Thorough School for the Violin*, gives us a great number of these indications. They are — from slow to fast — grave, largo, larghetto, adagio, lento, adagietto, andante, andantino, moderato, allegretto, allegro non troppo (or moderato), allegro, molto allegro, allegro assai, vivace, presto, presto assai, prestissimo.

In Bach's and Handel's times the adagio was slower than the largo in Italy, faster in France. Andantino is understood differently by different composers, even in modern times. Some, following Leopold Mozart, use it to denote a slightly faster tempo than andante; others hold that it is slower than andante.

The following are a few of the combinations of time signature and tempo indications, along with the supposed beat and metronome figures.

Adagio, common time, quarter, eighth, and sixteenth notes, 8 beats: eighth note = 40–60.

Adagio, common time, quarter and eighth notes, 8 beats: quarter note = 40–60.

Adagio, 3-2 time, half, quarter, and eighth notes, 6 beats: quarter note = 40–60.

Adagio, 3-2 time, half and quarter notes, 6 beats: half note = 40–60.

Adagio, 3-4 time, quarter, eighth, and sixteenth notes, 6 beats: eighth note = 40–60.

Adagio, 3-4 time, quarter and eighth notes, 6 beats: quarter note = 40–60.

All of these are Italian adagios. The same figures are valid for the French largo.

The Italian largo was played with the following tempi.

Largo, common time, quarter, eighth, and sixteenth notes, 8 beats: quarter note = 40–60.

Largo, common time, quarter and eighth notes, 8 beats: quarter note = 80–120.

Largo, 3-2 time, half, quarter, and eighth notes, 6 beats: half note = 40–60.

Largo, 3-2 time, half and quarter notes, 6 beats: quarter note = 40–60.

Largo, 3-4 time, quarter and eighth notes, 6 beats: quarter note = 80–120.

The same figures are valid for the French adagio.

Our principal tempo indications — allegro, allegretto, and andante — are based on the Affektenlehre which, in baroque times, gained more and more popularity. Allegro means gay; andante means walking. These were character indications and not simply indications of tempo like adagio or presto.

The combination of tempo indications with modifying adjectives, based on the Affektenlehre, led to further modifications of tempo. Such combinations are, for instance, allegro moderato, allegro ma non tanto, allegro assai, allegro molto. Another group of adjectives could also change expression during a composition by such directions as lugubre, doloroso, mesto, lagrimoso, maestoso, amoroso, scherzando, con brio, and so on. Soon these flowery adjectives combined with tempo indications to form terms like andante amoroso, andante mesto, allegretto scherzando, allegro maestoso, and allegro con brio. Naturally the tempi in all these cases must be modified according to the expression conveyed.

With the discussion of these emotional tempo modifications we are already trespassing on the preclassical and classical periods of music, the rococo age. Before we look any further into this we will have to dwell a little upon the third factor in establishing the right tempi for Bach's and Handel's music: the different qualities of their instruments, of scoring, of acoustics.

In his research the accompanist and coach must ascertain whether the baroque masters scored a particular piece for organ, harpsichord, or clavichord. Many numbers in Bach's Passions and cantatas he scored with the organ in mind. The lack of agility of baroque organs necessitates tempi some shades slower than might ordinarily be taken. The dimensions of churches and the echo in them, which make fast passages fuzzy, also preclude extremely fast tempi. From the fact that Bach's cantatas were written for and performed in churches we may deduce that the cantata tempi were also on the moderate side. The few strings he used certainly could just barely fill the acoustic space of St. Thomas in Leipzig.

Harpsichords were the concert grands of the baroque era; rich chords and rapid passages could be wrought on them, so the tempi may have been fluent. The same holds true for the clavichord, the intimate instrument of the drawing room — the spinet of the baroque era. Wind and brass instruments, although poorly equipped with valves, were apt to be played with great brilliancy, thanks to the highly developed lip technique of the musicians; the tempi did not have to be slowed down for their sake.

A different situation existed in regard to the stringed instruments. The curved bow used in baroque times allowed a very rapid connecting of complicated chords, but passage work could not be executed quite that fast, and, of course, not so loudly as with the modern bow. A number of Bach and Handel compositions were conceived with the idea of a lute's executing them, or, at least, with the idea of a keyboard instrument's imitating a lute. Chord arpeggios could be played very fast; passages, on the other hand, somewhat slower. And last, but not least, this is the place to mention Philipp Emanuel Bach's dictum that the right tempo may be determined best by looking at the smallest and fastest notes and figurations. Their clear execution will determine the right tempo for the whole piece.

All this does not mean that changes of tempo should occur during a musical piece. But the accompanist and coach, when thinking about the "right" tempo for a Bach or Handel composition, should consider all the aforesaid factors and then make up his mind which tempo to follow through the whole piece. In choosing the right tempo he will also have to decide between the subjective (romantic) and objective (classicist) way of performance. I decidedly favor objective playing of baroque music, especially Bach and Handel.

Haydn's and Mozart's tempi. The age of rococo and early classical music presents us with the problem of determining the right tempo by combining the time signatures of the baroque period with the burgeoning practice of modifying tempi on the basis of the Affektenlehre.

Time signatures in themselves become insignificant. They still present quite a few riddles to us, especially in the use of the alla breve sign, which had not yet exclusively become a symbol for a lively tempo. But the riddle is easier to solve if we consider the additional information given to us by the tempo modifications of the Affektenlehre. This doctrine or "applied theory of emotions" stems from antique times. It means the further explanation of the mood of a musical piece by adjectives added to the main time signature. (Affekt here means emotion rather than affection.) Mood, of course, is the underlying meaning of the whole composition; emotions are smaller units of expression that may change several times within a piece without disturbing the over-all mood. All kinds of joyous or lugubrious emotions may be found in a Haydn or Mozart work written under the influence of the Affektenlehre. To a certain extent this is a notable enrichment of musical expression. It may, in the end, be so systematized as to become static and lead us into program music, something that was very far removed from the mind of composers of the rococo period. We may find some program music, written under the influence of the doctrine of emotion in the baroque era: Vivaldi's "The Seasons," for example, or J. S. Bach's "Capriccio on the Departure of a Beloved Brother." But such works are exceptions rather than the rule.

The Affektenlehre also necessitated the use of a relative tempo as opposed to an absolute initial tempo, meaning that tempi could be slowed down or speeded up within a piece. Ritardando and accelerando play a very important part in classicist music. Leopold Mozart's remark that "Every tempo, gay or slow, has its shades" states perfectly the need for relative tempo. But now I must linger over Haydn's and Mozart's absolute tempi.

Stringed instruments had been perfected, straight bows were now used. Wind and brass instruments still relied on a lip technique of a perfection unheard today. The construction of keyboard instruments other than the organ took a great step forward. Mozart, for example, on his travels through Germany, encountered a pianoforte newly constructed by Stein, and speaks very well of it in his letters. In opera, light coloratura voices with great agility took the place of the old castrati voices. Slowly, the number of musicians in orchestras grew. All this enabled the classicist composers to think, write, and play at a much faster tempo. We know how astonished Mozart was when he heard the famous Muzio Clementi play his presto and prestissimo sonata movements; Mozart complains that Clementi played them all in four-quarters-to-a-measure allegro tempo. Mozart himself is known to have played his fast tempi really fast, but with the utmost clarity. Of course, the fingering he employed (see p. 36) helped considerably. On the other hand, we must take his contemporaries' reports with a grain of salt. It is a well known psychological fact that very rhythmical and clean playing gives the impression of a faster tempo than more rapid but fuzzy and unrhythmical playing. Mozart himself said: "It is much easier to play a passage quickly than slowly. In the swift passages you can miss notes without anyone's noticing it, but is it beautiful?"

The allegro and the andante now become the main moderately fast and slow tempi, the grade of which have to be determined by the adjectives following them or by the mood of the piece. Richard Wagner advocated playing Mozart's allegros as fast as possible. Richard Strauss comments on this: "Yes, but not twice as fast as possible." Strauss suggests $\quarternote = 136$ for the first-act finale (D major) of *Così fan tutte*, and $\quarternote = 128$ for the second-act finale (E♭ major) of *Le Nozze di Figaro*. In the slow tempi we must distinguish between the cantabile and the assai. Adagio cantabile, for instance, is almost twice as fast as adagio assai.

Geography also influences tempo modifications. A classical andante in Berlin was played slower than in the more Italianate, more southern Vienna. As a matter of fact, a contemporary of Mozart, the poet and musical author Christian Friedrich Daniel Schubart, wrote in 1806 that performance style in Naples means splendor, in Berlin — exactness, in Dresden — gracefulness, and in Vienna — comic-tragic style. Haydn and Mozart were very conscious of the difference between the cantabile and the assai types. A Mozart adagio with a definite singing melody must not be taken too slowly. Confusion reigns about the place of andantino and larghetto in the scale of tempo indications. Larghetto is universally faster than largo. Andantino is thought by many to be slower than andante; this, even today, is the prevailing Italian practice. The Viennese classicist school puts the andantino between andante and allegretto. The accompanist and coach in encountering the term andantino will have to decide which of the two rulings to follow. In general, I would advocate that in music of the classicist era the andantino be played as a lighter, diminutive form of the andante, therefore somewhat faster. Taking the moderato as the center of the tempo scale of the classicist masters, the positions of the other most frequently encountered tempi would be as follows:

Grave
Largo
Larghetto
Adagio
Lento
Andante
Andantino
Moderato
Allegretto
Allegro ma non troppo
Allegro
Molto allegro
Allegro assai
Vivace
Molto vivace
Presto
Prestissimo

In Mozart's scores we more and more often find the German equivalent of Italian tempo indications, as well as some very unorthodox ones based on the Affektenlehre: "Scherzhaft" (scherzando), "Mässig, gehend" (moderato, andante), "Traurig, doch gelassen" (sadly but calmly), "Gleichgültig und zufrieden" (indifferently and contentedly). The interpreter is thus given an exact description of the music's prevailing mood, together with its tempo.

If the classicist masters invented new tempo indications, they were quite conservative in their use of time signatures. The most conspicuous relic of the old times is the use of the alla breve sign without regard for the actual speed or slowness of the tempo. Alla breve to them meant only that the accents should fall on the first and third beats of a bar, even if the tempo was very slow. There are instances in Haydn's and Mozart's works where an alla breve, coupled with a largo or adagio tempo indication, at times must be conducted in eight — in the famous largo introduction to Haydn's *Creation*, for instance, which presents quite a problem to our modern interpreters. Again, Mozart marks his grandiose B♭ major mask trio in the first-act finale of *Don Giovanni* adagio with an alla breve sign, but it would be a great stylistic mistake to speed up the adagio because of the sign. We may assume that Mozart, like Haydn in his Largo, still had in mind the assai modification rather than the cantabile. This would mean an approximate ♪ = 80 tempo according to Quantz's theories, well known to the classicist composers. Haydn's adagios are uniformly slow; his minuets, on the other hand, are not yet stately court dances like Mozart's minuets: they still warrant a faster, baroque-type tempo. When we analyze the classicist masters' alla breve notation, we must keep in mind that it is never a tempo indication, but always a clue to phrasing (two accents to a measure in allegro, allegretto, and andante; four accents to a measure in adagio). Even if the conductor subdivides, as he sometimes must, the adagio assai types, the accents must fall only on the main beats.

On the basis of the aforesaid, and keeping in mind the difficulties that the alla breve sign presents us with today, I shall now take up some of Mozart's disputed alla breve pieces and discuss their performance tempo (a musicologist's thesis or pamphlet about the alla breve problem in the classic and romantic ages is long overdue).

Le Nozze di Figaro
No. 16, duet. Andante, four beats to a measure, accents on 1 and 3 only, quarter note = 104–108.

No. 25, Basilio's aria. Andante, four beats to a measure, accents on 1 and 3 only, quarter note = 116–120.

Don Giovanni
Overture. Andante; four beats to a measure, accents on 1 and 3, except in measures 15 and 16, where accent is on 2 and 4; quarter note = 68–72.

No. 1, trio of three bass voices. Andante, four beats to a measure, accents only on 1 and 3, quarter note = 80–84.

No. 9, quartet. Andante, four beats to a measure, accents only on 1 and 3, quarter note = 84–88.

No. 14, finale, trio in B♭ major. Adagio, eighth note = 88–92.

No. 18, Don Giovanni's aria. Andante con moto, beat four quarters to a measure, quarter note = 108–112. Tempo corresponds to 4-4 allegretto.

No. 20, sextet. Andante, four beats to a measure, accents on 1 and 3, quarter note = 96–100.

No. 22, Ottavio's aria. Andante grazioso, rather fluent four beats to a measure, quarter note = 88–92.

No. 26, finale, orchestral quotation from Le Nozze di Figaro. Moderato, tempo corresponds to 4-4 allegro in the original aria of Figaro, quarter note = 112–116.

No. 26, entrance of the Commendatore. Andante as in overture, quarter note = 68–72.

No. 26, G major. Larghetto, corresponds to andante sostenuto; beat four quarters to a measure — in some measures beat eighths; quarter note = 66–72.

Così fan tutte
Overture. Andante, four beats to a measure, accents on 1 and 3 only, quarter note = 76–80.

No. 6, quintet. Andante, four beats to a measure, accents on 1 and 3 only, quarter note = 88–92.

No. 8, soldiers' chorus. Maestoso; lively four beats to a measure, like the marching tempo of Italian soldiers; quarter note = 116–120.

No. 29, duet. Adagio; calm four beats to a measure; first measure may even be in eighths, eighth note = 104–108, the following con moto in four; quarter note = 104–108.

No. 29, A major. Andante, four beats to a measure, accents on 1 and 3 only, quarter note = 120–126.

No. 31, finale, sixteenth scene, chorus. Andante, four

beats to a measure, accents on 1 and 3 only, quarter note = 100–104.

No. 31, last scene. Andante, fluent four beats to a measure, accents on 1 and 3 only, quarter note = 104–108.

Die Zauberflöte

No. 8, finale. Larghetto, calm four beats to a measure, quarter note = 84–88.

No. 8, Tamino's aria. Andante, calm four beats to a measure, quarter note = 88–92.

No. 9, march of the priests. Andante, very calm four beats to a measure, quarter note = 76–80.

No. 9, chords of the priests' trumpets. Adagio; do not beat full measure but think of an eighth note = 84 (about); the best way is just to give the upbeats before the chords.

No. 18, chorus of the priests. Adagio, very dignified and noble four beats to a measure, quarter note = 66–68.

No. 19, trio. Andante moderato, a highly problematic tempo indication, probably meaning that the tempo should lie somewhere between andante and moderato, quarter note = 96–106.

No. 21, finale. Begin andante, four beats to a measure, quarter note = 88; but modifications are necessary at Pamina's entrance and at her attempted suicide.

No. 21, choral variations of the two armed men. Adagio, very deliberate four beats to a measure, quarter note = 69–72; from Tamino's entrance on, faster, quarter note = 96–100 (about); from allegretto, quarter note = 104–108.

No. 21, three genii saving Papageno. Allegretto, half note = 84–88 (about).

No. 21, entrance of the Queen of the Night and her ladies. Più moderato (than preceding allegro), two, sometimes four beats to a measure, half note = 72–76 (about).

The metronome. It is at this point in our search for the right tempo that the metronome becomes of paramount importance. We have seen that crude measurements of time had existed for centuries, based largely on the human heartbeat. But history dealt out the honor of having constructed and marketed the first mechanical instrument to measure musical time to Johann Nepomuk Mälzel, born in Bavaria in 1772. Mälzel was a mechanical wizard; he also invented and built several ingenious mechanical combinations of musical instruments. His metronome is based on a swinging pendulum which may be slowed or speeded up by a sliding lead weight. The higher the weight on the pendulum, the slower the tempo; the lower, the faster. Each swing is accompanied by a sharp click or a bell tone. Behind the pendulum is a numbered scale with figures showing how many swings the pendulum will make during one minute when the weight is set at a particular point on the scale. The tempo indications on the scale (adagio, andante, and so on) do not correspond exactly to the scale figures.

In its very beginnings, the metronome, then called the chronometer, was constructed differently: a lever arm fell on a little anvil to beat the time. Other early metronomes had the pendulum attached to a string. Today, the metronome is electrical and one being marketed looks like a stopwatch. It may be interesting to note that Mälzel moved first to Paris and then to the United States, where he lived in Philadelphia. But even this mechanical paradise did not satisfy the unruly man. He decided to go to South America and died on the way in 1838 on board an American brig.

Beethoven was very enthusiastic about the metronome and encouraged Mälzel. Although the two had a falling out about money, they became friends again in 1817. Beethoven and Salieri, the most famous composers of the day, wrote articles in the musical journals highly praising the new invention. Salieri provided metronome markings for some works by Gluck and Haydn, and in 1817 Beethoven had already started to metronomize quite a few of his works — his symphonies, many string quartets, a piano sonata, and so on — and continued to do so until 1819.

After all this evidence one would think that the importance of the metronome for the indication of tempo had been established for all times. But this is far from true. Beethoven himself grew disenchanted with the metronome's purely mechanical quality. We know that he metronomized his Ninth Symphony twice (one copy had been lost and he had to metronomize another one); the two sets of figures for the same music are different! In 1826, Beethoven wrote to his publisher, Schott und Söhne, in Mainz: "The metronome figures (the devil take all mechanisation) will follow." Another expression of Beethoven's disgust with the metronome that has come down to us is: "It is all stupid, one must feel the tempi." And he hit the nail on the head when he wrote on the manuscript of his song "So oder So" (Nord oder Süd! Wenn nur im warmen Busen . . .): "100, according to Mälzel. But this must be understood only for the first measures, for feeling also has its tempo and this cannot be entirely expressed by this figure." This is like what Richard Strauss said when I long ago played his *Intermezzo* in his presence. "Why do you play it so fast?" he asked. My answer: "I am trying to play it exactly according to your metronome markings." He retorted: "Look, the metronome is only valid for the first bar!" I have never forgotten these words and Strauss's criticism has been extremely valuable for my whole musical development.

No musical composition has a fixed tempo throughout, with the exception of musical imitations of mechanical inventions, such as the perpetuum mobile and the musicboxes and musical clocks. And, of course, music for ballroom dancing also has a steady tempo.

In his pamphlet *Tempo and Character in Beethoven's Music*, Rudolf Kolisch, the eminent string quartet player, valiantly defends the correctness of Beethoven's metronome figures. But he emphasizes that the figures alone do not suffice; they must be brought into relation with the metric unit of a piece and its character. I shall return later on to Kolisch's article in discussing Beethoven's tempi.

If we take the metronome figure as an *indication* of the speed of a piece, but do not follow it slavishly, giving more importance to the music's character, it will remain an invaluable aid to a composer's intentions. That Beethoven really did away with tradition is amply proved by his designation of new characterizing indications in either Italian or German, such as molto legato, dolce, espressivo, Ermattet klagend, Nach und nach wieder auflebend, Beklemmt, Langsam und sehnsuchtsvoll, Etwas lebhaft und mit der innigsten Empfindung, and so on. Some of his indications of tempo and expression have mistakenly been taken as evidence of program music. There is, of course, no serious composition without an inner program; even if its goal is to express the lack of a program — the absoluteness of music — this goal is itself a program. But this is quite different from a composition with an external program, composed only for commercial reasons, as for instance Beethoven's "Wellington's Victory" music. He used the names of feelings to give his interpreter a clear picture of the wanted expression. Expression, then, is the key to all Beethoven's tempi. He finally mixed every possible old Italian and German tempo indication with expressive adjectives and combined them with metronome markings. Thus he hoped to make his intentions completely clear.

But the burning flame in Beethoven was not properly nourished even by all this. After a while he realized that metronome marks cannot be followed too pedantically. His correspondence (1825–1826) with his publisher, Schott und Söhne, shows clearly and even pathetically how hard he tried to metronomize his *Missa Solemnis*. He never got the job done. His belief in the usefulness of metronomical figures changed from day to day. Late in 1826, already sick and only a few months from death, he wrote his publisher: "The metronome figures will follow shortly. Do wait for them. In our century such things are definitely necessary. I have letters from Berlin that the first performance of the [Ninth] symphony took place among enthusiastic approval which fact I mainly ascribe to the metronomization. We hardly can have tempi ordinari any more, having to adjust ourselves to the ideas of a full genius."

We can readily see that Beethoven believed in the metronome as an aid in the performance of his works, even if he at times rebelled against its use. The situation becomes quite different if one compares his metronome figures with reality: some of the tempi he suggests seem impossibly fast. Many reasons have been adduced for this. I believe that the only valid reason lies in human nature and human temperament. Beethoven was definitely the choleric type. He conceived and felt his tempi faster than he afterwards liked to hear them in actual performance. Many of us realize that in humming some music or even singing it at home we will take faster tempi than we would in a concert (see p. 174). Besides, our temperament changes constantly. When we "get our adrenalin up" we think, move, and play faster; when we calm down we are surprised at the speed at which we have been driving ourselves. In listening to the same record several times but on different days we shall find that the tempo seems just right one day, too fast for our taste the next day, and too slow the third. The variations are not in the mechanical record, but in us. We shall therefore forgive Beethoven his metronomical uncertainty; it happens all the time and is the best argument against overemphasis on the metronome.

After Beethoven, the metronome's career had its ups and downs. Schubert certainly knew about it, although he does not seem to have met Mälzel; Schubert did not personally metronomize his works, but some eighteen of his songs were published during his lifetime with metronomical marks which he must at least have acquiesced in. Weber used metronome marks a great deal; but in a letter to a Prague conductor about a performance of his *Euryanthe* he wrote: "Experience has taught me that too precise indications as to time and expression are apt to caricature the composer's intentions. There is no slow movement in which there may not occur the necessity of an accelerando, there is no presto in which passages may not be found requiring ritardando. These things must be felt in our own heart, and if wanting there, neither the metronome nor my imperfect and — according to my own experience — almost superfluous annotations will give much assistance." Mendelssohn gives tempi by metronome; they are not to be taken for a piece's initial tempo, however, but rather as the tempo of its climax.

Schumann's metronome marks are unplayable. They are much too fast, because of his mental condition: his poor brain raced and raced, and nobody's fingers could catch up. With prophetic foresight he said: "Only the internal beat of movement is important. The fastest allegro of a phlegmatic is slower than the slowest allegro of a sanguinic." Well, Schumann unfortunately was much worse than a sanguinic!

Wagner and Brahms, disgusted with the merciless ticking of the metronome, abandoned it early in their careers. In his *Aufführungspraxis für "Tannhäuser"* Wagner wrote: "As to the tempi of entire works in general I here can only say that if conductor and singers are to depend for their time-measure on metronome marks *alone*, the spirit of their work must stand indeed in sorry case."

The composers of the late nineteenth and the twentieth century made ample use of the metronome. Verdi, for instance, provided metronome marks for all his operas, and these tempi seem more or less reliable to a musician's ear. Toscanini followed them almost implicitly, and did the same with Puccini's marks, some of which seem exceedingly slow — but Toscanini kept to them with an iron will. I have already cited Richard Strauss's opinion of the metronome. Mahler's marks are very realistic and easily followed. Stravinsky is said to have an infallible feeling for the right metronome marks; but I have witnessed errors in his judgment during rehearsals of *The Rake's Progress*, and a recording of it which he himself conducted has slower tempi than his marks dictate. Béla Bartók is said to have been another "absolute" expert about metronomization. Asked about a certain metronome mark, he would immediately beat the tempo and when checked would invariably prove to be right. Sibelius put exact metronome marks on all his

symphonies, but he also said: "The right tempo is the one the artist feels."

Only a few years ago, in 1957, a system of codification of metronome signs in relation to tempo indications and metric units was proposed by Robert Dussaut, a Frenchman, winner of the Rome prize. This system, approved by the Academy of Fine Arts in Paris, proves a useful theoretical help; but again it mechanizes the application of the metronome. Many French composers of today, however, are in accord with this mechanization, as, for instance, Poulenc who in his "Air romantique" wants "respecter strictement le mouvement métronomique."

I now return to the tempi of the classical school.

Beethoven's tempi. As in all the other elements of his music, Beethoven's revolutionary genius shows itself clearly in his tempi. He followed in the footsteps of Haydn and Mozart, using their time signatures, tempo indications, and, in general, their modifying or characterizing adjectives; but this was nowhere near enough for Beethoven. Once he felt certain that the metronome would unequivocally express his choice of tempo, he wanted to do away altogether with such traditional tempo indications. In a letter to Ignaz von Mosel in 1817 he says: "What can be more absurd than an allegro which once and forever means gay. How often are we so far removed from this conception of the tempo indication that the piece itself expresses the very opposite of the indication? As far as these four main tempo indications are concerned . . . we gladly do away with them. It is different with the terms indicating the character of the piece — these we cannot abolish, since time is really only the body of a piece but the characterizing words point to its spirit. As far as I am concerned I have long thought of abolishing these illogical designations allegro, andante, adagio, presto; Mälzel's metronome gives us the best opportunity for it. I give you my word here that I shall not use them again in my recent compositions." Beethoven kept his promise for a time, but returned to the tempi ordinari later on. Most of his special relationship to tempo has already been treated above; it remains only to discuss some typical Beethovenish tempi and give hints as to their execution.

Beethoven's tempo scale starts at prestissimo, and then moves up to presto con fuoco, presto agitato, presto, vivacissamente, assai vivace, vivace, vivace ma non troppo, and many different kinds of allegro. The fastest of these are the allegro vivace and the allegro molto. Then come allegro assai, allegro con brio, allegro, allegro ma non troppo, allegro moderato. We know from contemporaries that Beethoven, at least in his youth, played his prestos at very high speed. His playing became progressively muddy later on, no doubt because of his waning hearing.

Further up the scale are the allegrettos. The unusual tempo indication allegretto vivace is found a couple of times. Once, coupled with an alla breve sign, it presents a veritable riddle. The place is the chorus of the returning prisoners in the first-act finale of *Fidelio*. The most divergent tempi have been taken here by different conductors. Toscanini used to underline the vivace indication and beat it in two! By way of contrast, I should like to quote Bruno Walter, who — when I asked him what tempo I should prepare this particular chorus in — answered: "Just make it sound like a Volkslied." This, to me, seems absolutely right: the allegretto is the tempo indication, the vivace means only that there should be inner commotion, in accord with the melancholy lyrics. The alla breve sign means that there should be only two accents in a measure; but the conductor should certainly beat it in four.

Another rare tempo indication is the allegretto agitato. Then come the normal allegretto, allegretto ma non troppo, poco allegretto. These last, according to Rudolf Kolisch, are already on the borderline between allegretto and andante. This is also true for andante piuttosto allegretto, andante scherzoso, più allegretto, and andante quasi allegretto. Beethoven realized that andantino may be meant to be slower or faster than andante (see p. 119). In a letter to Thomson, a publisher in Edinburgh, for whom Beethoven wrote his adaptations of Scottish and Irish folk songs, he said: "If in the future there will be some andantinos among the tunes that you will be sending me, I ask you to notify me whether such andantino is meant to be slower or faster than andante, since this term — like many other musical terms — is of such an uncertain meaning that sometimes andantino approaches an allegro and sometimes is played almost like an adagio." Beethoven himself hardly ever marked any of his compositions andantino. His song "An die Geliebte" is marked andantino poco agitato, which makes it faster than andante. A few bars before the start of the grave-digging music after the melodrama in *Fidelio* are marked andantino. This is open to interpretation: I personally think that it is a transition from the allegro to the following andante con moto.

Beethoven's andante category has many subdivisions, from faster to slower: andante con moto, andante ma non troppo, andante, andante cantabile, andante espressivo, andante sostenuto. In all of Beethoven's compositions we find only one andante 4-4 (string quartet, opus 130) and one andante 12-8 (Sixth Symphony). Most of Beethoven's andantes are in 2-4, 6-8, or in triple time. The lento or lento assai lies between slow andante and adagio. The larghetto is somewhat faster than adagio, almost like a slow andante. The difference lies in the more subdued characterization. His adagios are slow, according to Wagner even very slow. The adagio scale: adagio un poco mosso, adagio ma non poco, adagio, adagio cantabile, adagio sostenuto. The largo is slower than the adagio. We find some largo con espressione, largo e mesto, largo, largo assai. Finally, the grave is Beethoven's slowest tempo indication (piano sonata, opus 13, "Pathétique").

I cannot stress often enough that the right tempi for Beethoven must be deduced from his Italian or German tempo indications, his explanatory indications of expression, his time signatures, his metronomic markings — where available — and above all from the inherent mood of a piece. The form in which the piece is composed is also of great importance in determining the tempo. First-movement allegros in sonata form are not so fast as last-movement allegros in the same form. Beethoven's minuets are rarely of the classical (Mozartian) kind. He developed the scherzo — inherited from Haydn — which he first did not distinguish by name from the minuet. Only in later compositions did he call them scherzos. But the scherzo tempo is decidedly faster than the minuet. The metric unit in scherzos is almost always the dotted half note (whole bar), as against the quarter-note metric unit (three to a measure) for the minuet. None of the tempi applicable to Beethoven's songs, violin concerto, two romances, *Fidelio*, *Missa Solemnis*, masses, and minor choral works — the music most likely to be encountered by an accompanist or coach — will prove enigmatic. But Beethoven's whole complex life work must be studied and digested if the right style is to be grasped and mastered.

The tempo of the romantic composers. Franz Schubert stands on the borderline between the classic and romantic movements, reaching into both, as does Beethoven. As far as his tempi are concerned, we will do well to realize that his time signatures still follow the old tradition and must not be interpreted as if they were our modern symbols. We encounter, for instance, such an atavistic signature as ₵ Ɔ (in his G♭ major Impromptu) which, according to the old sources, is the sign for a double quickening of the ₵. Only twenty-five or thirty years later, Chopin would have used 4-4, and would have written all the arpeggios in small notes. The effect would have been the same. The alla breve sign alone, in Schubert's works, must be understood as it is in the other classicists' compositions, as indicating the accents rather than the tempo. In one of his most famous songs, "An die Musik," Schubert notates ₵ Mässig (moderato). It would be wrong to speed up this wonderfully warm and noble declaration of Schubert's artistic creed because of the alla breve sign. It must be treated simply as a 4-4 moderato, flowing naturally, without any tension; then it will convincingly convey Schubert's thanks to the goddess of music. The same time signature and indication appear in the song "Des Baches Wiegenlied." A real alla breve tempo would spoil the lullaby mood, just as a too slow tempo would wreck the πάντα ῥεῖ feeling, the eternal flow of the water. Similar examples may be found in "Gefrorne Tränen," "Ihr Bild," "Am Meer," "Die Taubenpost," "Der Wanderer," "Der Tod und das Mädchen" to mention only a few of the best-known songs.

Schubert proved a real adherent of indications of expression. Not only did he write his songs' tempo indications in German — no doubt to make them more understandable to his Viennese public, which often consisted of dilettantes — but he also added explanations such as "Mit Liebes-Affekt," "Mit heiligem Jubel," "Mit schwärmerischer Sehnsucht." In his orchestral works he kept to the traditional Italian tempo indications. We shall return to Schubert when we take up lied style in particular.

Mendelssohn, Wagner tells us, favored fast tempi, remarking "that he thought most harm was done by taking a tempo too slow, and that on the contrary, he always recommended quick tempi as being less detrimental"; Wagner was of course against this speed and accused Mendelssohn of "ending every allegro as an undeniable presto."

Robert Schumann's tempi are problematic. He made ample use of the metronome, but as we have already seen his tempi are in part unplayable because they are much too fast, which in turn was the result of his mental condition. His time signatures are less influenced by tradition than Schubert's. His tempo indications are mostly German and, to some extent, relative. One of them (the piano sonata in G minor), for instance, says "so schnell

wie möglich" (as fast as possible), topping this toward the end with a "noch schneller" (still faster) marking. In contrast to these fast tempi, Schumann occasionally used some archaic time signature, such as C Ɔ in his song "Zu Augsburg steht ein hohes Haus." This time signature, which corresponds to our 4-2, can be also found in Brahms's *Ein Deutsches Requiem*.

I must digress again in order to explain the so-called relative tempo which is the soul and body of the romantic school, although it had been known and used since the baroque period and even before. I am speaking of the rubato — "robbed tempo." Time is "stolen" or "robbed" from one part of a phrase and given back in another. The foremost champion of the rubato was Chopin, one of the most inventive and interesting of the romanticists. Although he does not directly concern us in connection with accompanying or coaching — he wrote only a few songs and only a couple of seldom-played pieces for violoncello and piano, his output being largely music for pianoforte, solo or with orchestra — the study of his style is very gratifying to any musician, and the dance accompanist and coach might have to play Chopin's music in ballet classes or dance recitals. I said at the beginning of this chapter that each age had its classic and romantic periods. Even Bach and Handel used relative tempi occasionally and sparingly, mostly in the form of ritardando or accelerando. This, however, has no connection with the romantic performance of a Bach or Handel work by — let's say — Mendelssohn or Schumann, or, in our time, Furtwängler or Stokowski. The rubato was not at all unknown to Mozart. In a letter to his father (October 24, 1772), he wrote: "In tempo rubato in an adagio, they can not comprehend that the left hand does not know anything about it. With them, the left hand gives in." This is very enlightening. We learn from it that Mozart's left hand played the steady beat while his right hand deviated from it at certain times when it fitted the music. It is an interesting sidelight that Chopin, some fifty years later, stressed the importance of steady beat in the left hand against the rubato right hand in about the same words as Mozart's. As far as ritardando and accelerando are concerned, Mozart was a true follower of the so-called Mannheim style of brilliant accelerando in orchestral passages, especially toward the close of a movement (see p. 133). Beethoven, in his later years — the period of his growing predilection for romanticism — is said to have played his compositions with a great deal of rubato. He does not use this word in his terminology but he transcribes it by using different indications in a phrase, such as first accelerando, then ritardando, then a tempo. His contemporary, Josef Czerny, has left us a set of rules for ritardando (as cited in F. Dorian's *History of Music in Performance*). Ritardando is indicated under the following conditions

1. At the return of the principal subject.

2. When a phrase is to be separated from the melody.

3. On long notes strongly accented.

4. At the transition to a different time.

5. After a pause.

6. On the diminuendo of a quick lively passage.

7. Where the ornamental note cannot be played a tempo giusto.

8. In a well-marked crescendo serving to introduce or terminate an important passage.

9. In passages where the composer or the performer gives free play to his fancy.

10. When the composer marks the passage espressivo.

11. At the end of a shake or cadence.

The relative tempo, after acquiring its greatest importance during the romantic era, never again lost its significance. Today's composers, by their markings, tell us exactly where and how they want their compositions executed. The foremost adherent of the relative tempo, Puccini, tells us in almost every measure how we are supposed to execute the rubato. It is interesting to see how many different ways of marking the rubato he employs, hardly ever using the term itself. Our modern absolute and relative tempo signatures, indications, and changes were adopted around 1850 and have kept their validity ever since. Richard Wagner said in his pamphlet *About Conducting*:

"The whole duty of a conductor is comprised in his ability always to indicate the right tempo. His choice of tempi will show whether or not he understands the piece. . . . Haydn and Mozart made use of the term andante as the mean between allegro and adagio and thought it sufficient to indicate a few gradations and modifications of these terms. . . . In my earlier operas I gave detailed instructions as to the tempi and indicated them — as I thought — accurately, by means of the metronome. Subsequently, whenever I had occasion to protest against a particularly absurd tempo, in 'Tannhäuser' for instance, I was assured that the metronome had been consulted and carefully followed. In my later works I omitted the metronome and merely described

the main tempi in general terms, paying, however, particular attention to the various modifications of tempo."

Although we are now able to measure time to an unheard-of degree of infinitesimal exactness, we have, luckily, not succeeded in forcing music into the straitjacket of mechanization. Although recordings made before the invention of the long-playing discs sometimes distorted composers' and interpreters' intentions because of the necessity to speed up performances to fit the time limit, we now may listen to "mechanized" music of absolute interpretative truth. It is only fitting that this section should end with the dictum of the wise old theoretician Johann Mattheson (from his *Der vollkommene Capellmeister*): "The true movement of a musical work is beyond words. It is the ultimate perfection of music, accessible only through eminent experience and talent."

RHYTHM

While there are seventeen possible definitions of tempo, there are more than fifty meanings for rhythm. The definition with the widest appeal comes from Plato, who called rhythm an "order of movement." Movement must be understood as movement of time, the flowing of time which the Greek root ῥεῖν implies. It does not mean, however, movement of melodic units. Melos may be completely absent from rhythm. Some contemporary compositions by Carl Orff, for instance, contain constant rhythmic repetitions of chords or tone clusters which may be very expressive because of their steady rhythmic power. Rhythm is necessary to the esthetic enjoyment of music; without rhythm, any musical piece would be boring. All our occidental rhythmic patterns are based on the classic meters, the iambus, the trochee, the dactyl, the anapaest, the amphibrach, and their sometimes very complex combinations.

We are not concerned here, however, with the theoretical definitions of rhythm, but with the practical performance style of rhythm in the different ages. One thing is clear: rhythmic execution is most important for the vitalization of a musical piece. Strong rhythmic execution energizes and enlivens music; weak rhythm emasculates it and makes us listeners feel bored, unsatisfied. Definite rhythm, therefore, is just as important as the right tempo. In fact, rhythm and tempo are interrelated. Good rhythm will make a piece seem to flow faster; the tempo, therefore, may be more deliberate. Weak rhythm tends to slow down music. This is the reason why so many interpreters take a composition at top speed. They do not have a strong rhythmic feeling and try to compensate for this lack by hurrying the music. Rhythm — always referred to here in terms of our occidental music — was not the same at all times.

For our purposes, it will suffice to start the discussion of rhythm with the time from 1600 to 1750 — the period ending with the deaths of Bach and Handel. The baroque age put great importance on the upbeat, the entrance of music on the weak accent. This is a rhythmical innovation as compared with earlier music. While the study of upbeat and downbeat plays a most important part in the story of phrasing, it also has a definite rhythmical connotation. Music starting on an upbeat has a definite rhythmic drive; it is dynamic and strong. Pauses resulting from an upbeat start must be given their full value. Pauses, rests, or fermatas belong to the style unit of rhythm as well as to the style units of tempo, phrasing, and articulation. Although a rest is not movement and therefore does not conform to Plato's definition of rhythm, it helps to underline the beginning of a new rhythmic phrase, thus silhouetting rhythm against the tapestry of the musical weave. Shorter pauses became more and more common as the centuries went by. Finally, there are minute interruptions in the musical line — suspensions and hesitations that are invaluable to us in our understanding of the psychological background of an instrumental or vocal piece. Especially in Wagner's music do we find these small interruptions that lead to syncopated rhythms (see also p. 211).

Returning to the baroque age, we find that the ever-growing influence of secular music, especially of dance forms with their different rhythms, contributed greatly to the increasing perception of the aesthetic beauty of rhythm. Some of these dance rhythms kept their character throughout the ages, some crept into symphonic and operatic works unnamed but clearly recognizable as, for instance, the triple rhythm of the gagliarda, known also as chaconne or sarabande rhythm, with its heavy accent on the second quarter (Fig. 98) or the minuet, which

Figure 98. The gagliarda rhythm

later developed into the scherzo, the German dance, and the waltz. Medieval polyrhythms vanished during the baroque period and made room for clearly understood but not clearly notated rhythmic combinations. This lack of adequate notation led to the most outstand-

ing rhythmic characteristic of the baroque age, rhythmic alteration. Rhythms had to be played differently from the way they were notated. This is nothing new to us: we need only think of the difference between jazz notation and the way it is actually played or sung; the rhythms in the upper voices are supposed to be off-beat, the only steady beat being kept by the bass and the percussion instruments. François Couperin said in 1717: "We play differently from what we write." All the old theoreticians, Quantz and Philipp Emanuel Bach, for example, were giving considerable space to the alteration of rhythms. Since we recognize in Quantz the theoretical source for Bach's and Handel's performances during their lifetimes, we can safely accept his description of altered rhythm.

Quantz remarks that sixteenth and smaller notes following a dotted note are played faster than notated (Fig. 99). The same principle must be followed if the short note comes before the dotted note (Fig. 100). This

Figure 99. Quantz's suggestions for playing sixteenth and smaller notes after a dotted note

Figure 100. Quantz's suggestion for playing short note before a dotted note

rule of lengthening the dotted note and shortening the note after the dot extends to combinations of triplets and dotted notes (Fig. 101). The sixteenth notes should be played well after the third note of the triplet as shown in Figure 102. In 6-8, 9-8, or 12-8 time the eighth note in the lower voice must be played simultaneously with the third eighth of the upper series of three (Fig. 103).

Figure 101. Triplets and dotted notes

Figure 102. Lower voice with dotted notes as it should be played against the triplets in Figure 101

Figure 103. Eighth notes in lower voice against three
eighth notes in upper, 9-8 time

Figures 99–103 show that double dots are practically
nonexistent in the notation of the baroque masters. The
altered-rhythm rules take care of this deficiency. If pieces
with this kind of dotted note were played on a harpsichord, common sense required the interpreters to lift
the finger from the key and observe rests instead of continuing to depress the key, which would not continue
to sound on the brittle keyboard instrument. Therefore,
the phrase in the third part of Figure 99, for instance,
would be played as shown in Figure 104. Quantz says
that short notes before or after dotted notes in a slow
alla breve or ordinary 4-4 beat should be played as
shown in the second line of Figure 105.

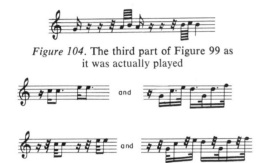

Figure 104. The third part of Figure 99 as
it was actually played

Figure 105. Short notes after dotted notes in alla breve or
4-4 time as written (above) and as Quantz prescribes
that they be played (below)

Even stringed and wind instruments should stop before a dotted note and observe a tiny pause, thus aiding
the plasticity of the phrase. The same is true for the
singing voice. This rule should not only be followed for
the music of the baroque age but whenever strong
rhythm, plasticity, and better understanding of the words
is desired. Here rhythm and expression combine to attain
the goal of clarity and poignancy. Some well-known
phrases from Bach's and Handel's works should, therefore, be interpreted in this way, and many of Gluck's
rhythms are of this kind. An even later example is Donna
Elvira's aria (No. 8) in Mozart's *Don Giovanni*, written
in the manner of Handel. The sixteenth after the dotted
note must always be sounded later and shorter.

The baroque masters frequently wrote ternary rhythms
in binary measures, or, as we would say today, three
against two. Arnold Dolmetsch, in his *The Interpretation of the Music of the XVII and XVIII Centuries*,

gives an interesting example from the D major concerto
for flute, violin, and harpsichord by J. S. Bach, which,
he says, should be played as in Figure 106, second line.

So much for Bach's and Handel's rhythmic style.

Figure 106. Passage from Bach's D major concerto for
flute, violin, and harpsichord as written (above)
and as Arnold Dolmetsch says that it
should be played (below)

We possess a very good source book about the performance practice of the early opera composers, the
Florilegium, by George Muffat, a pupil of Lully. In his
preface to this collection of music (published in 1695
and 1698), Muffat shows that passages consisting of
eighth or sixteenth notes were never played evenly, but
always as if dotted, as in Figure 107, second line. As
early as 1601, Caccini, whom we met as the founder
of the Nuove Musiche, gave some examples of the same
sort. Figure 108 shows how these were written (above)
and how they were executed (below).

Figure 107. Seventeenth-century sixteenth notes as written
(above) and as played (below), according to George Muffat

Figure 108. Seventeenth-century sixteenth notes as written
(above) and as executed (below), according to Caccini

Quantz explains this rule as being necessary to stress
strong beats that he calls "capital notes" more than weak
beats called "passing notes." Exceptions to the rule, however, are fast passages where this rhythmic alteration
could not be heard. A rhythm just the opposite of this
altered rhythm can be found in the baroque age, and,
of course, in later music: it is the so-called Scotch
snap (Fig. 109). The rule of the altered rhythm makes

♩♩♩   ♫♩.

Figure 109. Typical altered rhythm and its reverse, the
Scotch snap of the baroque period

a faster (syncopated) note obligatory. But this change is minute and metrically not measurable. We find this Scotch snap or, as it is also called, the Lombardian manner, not only in Scotch tunes but also in Hungarian and Slovak folk music.

The accompanist and coach will find that he can and should apply the rules about alteration of rhythm in a number of cases; other cases may not yield to them. Since altered rhythms, especially the double dotted notes, were very popular in French music — although no way was found to notate them — Bach's French-style compositions should certainly be altered according to the rules. His other compositions, as well as Handel's works, should be treated with great care in this respect. Some *slight* prolongation of dots may be in order, but smooth sixteenth rhythms, such as those in the C major prelude of the first volume of the *Well-Tempered Clavichord*, should not be made to sound bumpy by the altered rhythm.

Eventually, the rhythmic alteration faded away with the advent of a more effective system of musical notation. In Haydn's and Mozart's music we find no need to alter any rhythm, although dots usually were held longer than written. Leopold Mozart wrote that even single dots ought to be lengthened — that this would make the performance livelier. He also seems to have been the first to advocate the use of the double dot. Neither Haydn nor Mozart is very difficult to deal with when it comes to rhythm. Of course they must be played very rhythmically, and their dance rhythms especially offer us ample occasion for enlivening a performance with vivid accents. One example of polyrhythmics in Mozart's music should be mentioned here. It happens in the famous ballroom scene of *Don Giovanni*, when the stately 3-4 court minuet is joined by a 2-4 and later by a 3-8 rhythm, depicting two different kinds of peasants' dance.

If Haydn and Mozart were more interesting than Beethoven in their audacious harmony, the latter left them far behind in rhythmical inventiveness. As a matter of fact, Beethoven was in his age as great an iconoclast and innovator of rhythm as Stravinsky is in ours. Rhythms of three against two, syncopated rhythms, and rhythmic shifts are to be found in almost every one of his works. Who else would have dared build an en-

tire symphonic movement on the bold rhythm ♪ ♪♪♪|♩? Beethoven's dactylic rhythms (♩.♪♩) are among his most characteristic. A discussion of his rhythmical innovations could itself fill a book. Beethoven's genius is never clearer than in his rhythms and accents. The accompanist and coach must stress both to the full extent of their musical power.

The romantic school employed the rhythms that had been unchained by Beethoven. They continued to develop rhythmical freedom, but tended more toward fanciful diffusion than toward concentrated poignancy. Marching rhythms and dance rhythms came of age and attained respectability. The line of marches leads straight from Mozart's "Non più andrai" or his wedding procession in *Le Nozze di Figaro*, to Beethoven's "Ruins of Athens" and his soldiers' march in *Fidelio*, to Mendelssohn's wedding march, to Schubert's military marches, to Chopin's Funeral March, Liszt's *funérailles*, Berlioz' Hungarian march, Wagner's entrance of the guests from *Tannhäuser*, and on to the innumerable operatic triumphal and other marches by French and Italian composers. One must mention Weber's contribution to dance rhythm. Besides polonaises, he not only used the "Ländler," progenitor of the waltz (his peasants' dance in *Der Freischütz*), but he wrote a brilliant waltz — almost of the much later Viennese type — in his "Invitation to the Dance." Weber is also important to us as one of the first composers to use a Chinese scale and Chinese rhythms (albeit simple ones) in his *Turandot*. Other oriental rhythms had already been introduced successfully by Gluck, Mozart, Beethoven, and many others. The Turkish invasion of 1683 that almost conquered Vienna had not only left its mark in the Viennese coffeehouse but also in a flood of "janissary" music. Spanish dance rhythms (fandango) were used by Gluck, taken from him by Mozart, continued by Weber, and brought to a climax by Chopin in his bolero. Chopin is not only the masterly composer of the classic mazurka, the polonaise, but of the drawing-room waltz, inherited from Schumann's "Carnaval" and other piano pieces.

I have left the discussion of the waltz to the end of the section about the dance rhythms of romantic composers because of its importance to every musician and music-lover. We have seen that the waltz originated in the minuet. When the minuet became a court dance and a symphonic form, ballroom and folk dancing had to find some other similar form. The German dance and contra-dance of our classic masters, Mozart, Beethoven, Schubert, and others not only brought them sorely needed money, but considerably enriched the ballroom dancing season in Vienna. The peasants danced the broader, more gemütliche type, the Ländler, which is always beaten in three with accents on every quarter note. The German dances and the contradances soon became faster again, this time leading to the above mentioned Salon-walzer, the drawing-room waltz of Chopin with even accents, beaten in one. His mazurkas look and sound like waltzes, but a very strong accent on the third beat distinguishes them from their Viennese cousins. The Ländler was continued by the elder Johann Strauss and Lanner and, in part, by Johannes Brahms.

Johann Strauss the younger is unquestionably the greatest waltz composer of all time. He imbued the traditional 3-4 rhythms with mood, expression, and feeling for the beauty of the Austrian landscape. He certainly elevated the ballroom waltz to high art. His "Tales from the Vienna Woods," "Village Swallows from Austria," "Voices of Spring," are not just waltzes, but marvellous paintings of nature and expressions of feeling. The Viennese waltz has a lilt of its own. Its rhythm is very difficult to notate, and actually bears no relation to the ordinary one-two-three beat.

Figure 110. Notation for the Viennese waltz

I have tried in Figure 110 to give an approximate notation, knowing full well that it may sound clumsy in the hands of a non-Viennese musician. The accompanist and coach must be very careful not to extend the 3-4 beat into a 4-4 beat, misunderstanding the faster first and the slower second beat. The upbeat at the beginning of a waltz or a waltz period is always retarded. Sometimes, as for instance in the "Tales from the Vienna Woods," the whole first part is slower, the full waltz tempo being reached only at the beginning of the second period. The reasons for these slowings down must be sought in the character of a particular waltz. The whole waltz consists of several waltz numbers separated by short introduc-

tions. Each waltz number, if played or sung in concerts and not for dancing, has a slightly different tempo. Some of the lengthy repeats may be omitted. The introduction and coda of a waltz have tempi that again depend on the underlying mood. Needless to say, for ballroom dancing the tempo has to be strict.

Schumann, Chopin, Liszt, and Brahms were very inventive in creating complicated polyrhythms. A new rhythmic vista was opened with the appearance of national rhythms such as the Hungarian (Liszt, Berlioz, Brahms), the Czech (Smetana, Dvořák), the Russian (Glinka, Tchaikovsky), and the many oriental rhythms, introduced mainly by the national Russian school of Mussorgsky, Borodin, and Rimsky-Korsakov. These oriental rhythms appear in many forms, some of them using the irregular 5-4, 7-4, 11-4 meters, as for instance the song of the parakeet from Mussorgsky's *Boris Godunov*, the final chorus of *Sadko* by Rimsky-Korsakov in 11-4, or Mussorgsky's promenade in his "Pictures at an Exhibition" which also adds up to an 11-4 rhythm. Many irregular rhythms, however, are just combinations of $3 + 2$, $2 + 3$, or other regular beats. Among them are Wagner's music for Tristan's feverish visions and Tchaikovsky's gracefully frisky tune in the second movement of his Sixth Symphony. Similarly, Richard Strauss's *Der Rosenkavalier* contains some $3 + 4$ and $4 + 3$ combinations.

Coming now to contemporary music, we find genuine irregular rhythms in Ugro-Finnish folk music as used by Sibelius and Bartók. The great smasher of traditional music, Igor Stravinsky, in his early revolutionary period, does not recognize rhythm as we know it, but only accents. He puts the bars where he wants an accent to be played. In his opera *Mavra* no two successive measures have the same rhythm. Similar rhythmic complexities may be found in his "Sacre du Printemps" and many of his other works. I have known conductors who, instead of learning the immensely complicated rhythms, have shifted the bars in order to make the measures regular. The effect was, of course, that all accents were wrong. Other modern composers — Eric Satie, for example — dispensed completely with bars in some of their works, bringing the rhythm back to the free notation of medieval times. And the end is not yet in sight. Jazz, Latin American rhythms, and African jungle drumbeats are entering our art music. Some of the so-called experimental jazz, integrating some or all of these elements, is really fascinating. As far as rhythm is concerned, we have the good fortune to be living in a rich, productive period.

DYNAMICS

By musical dynamics we mean the gradation of loudness. Dynamics is one of the most important means of expression and one of the pillar elements of style. A whole scale of gradations exists, the soft tone on one end and the loud tone on the other — the piano and the forte. These two can become antagonists, set against each other to create contrasting dynamics. A musical effect may also be achieved by starting out at one extreme of the dynamic scale and, running gradually through the intermediate dynamic points by way of crescendo or diminuendo, finishing at the other end.

The terms p, pp, f, and ff became known around the year 1600. Father Mersenne, a French theoretician, recommended in 1636 that eight shades of intensity be used. Our crescendo and diminuendo, as well as their hairpin symbols, are of comparatively recent origin, appearing first in the eighteenth century. This does not mean that crescendo and diminuendo had not been taught before. Caccini, the founder of the epoch of the Nuove Musiche (see p. 12) repeatedly asked for swelling and diminishing of vocal strength. Domenico Mazzocchi, a Roman composer of the 1630's, seems to have been the first one to use the sign C for crescendo and then diminuendo on one long-held tone. In a vocal line this would be equal to the "messa di voce," an effect very much favored by the Nuove Musiche.

The theory and importance of dynamics had at that time already been confirmed by Pope Marcellus, who in 1555 gave instructions to his Sistine choir about the right way to sing sacred music. Such music, he admonished them, "must be sung in a suitable manner with properly *modulated voices* and so that everything can be both heard and understood properly" (translation by Frederick Dorian, appearing in *The History of Music in Performance*). This has to do only with vocal music, of course, and makes it clear that the emphasis should be on understandability and on the lyrics' meaning. We shall see shortly that this principle has to be followed in the performance of all vocal music including that of Bach and Handel.

Dynamics of the baroque age. Starting again with the baroque age, we find that Bach and Handel marked their compositions with piano and forte, sometimes even with pianissimo and fortissimo. All dynamic signs appear relatively seldom and, of course, never in all parts of a full score, usually only in the part of one instrument or in the voice part. Bach never used mezzoforte, and neither master employed the crescendo-decrescendo or diminuendo symbols. This has led to a schism between objective and subjective performers. The first claim that only contrasting dynamics should be played in Bach's and Handel's works; they are adherents of the so-called architectural dynamics or terrace dynamics. The subjectivists hold that Bach and Handel had human feelings like any other mortals, and thus could not restrict voice or instruments from swelling and diminishing the flow of sound in accordance with physiological need for air and the psychological striving for expression. We may call these dynamics emotional dynamics.

In my opinion, both groups are equally right and wrong, subject to several important points of view. These great masters of polyphony got their dynamic effects by the architectural buildup of different voices (not necessarily human voices). The entrance of each new voice would enrich the dynamics, without tonal strength's being added by the interpreter. The importance of the leading voices in comparison with the contrapuntal voices necessitated different dynamics in the same measure or group of measures. This was easily done on an organ or on a harpsichord. Leading voices were played on one manual, the counterpoint on the other manual with less prominent sound. If Bach and Handel wanted a still greater buildup, they could double the bass or draw out all the stops. This increase in sound is sudden, and has nothing to do with crescendo-decrescendo. Moreover, the organ and harpsichord did not have facilities for emotional dynamics.

The echo effect was a means of expression frequently found in baroque music. After a loud passage, the same passage was repeated softly as an echo. Organs, harpsichords, and clavichords were equally suited to the production of the echo effect. But stringed instruments and voices could do the same. The violinists of the baroque age, for instance, would increase the curvature of their bows for such an effect. Architectural dynamics are, therefore, absolutely right for the two great masters' organ and harpsichord works.

Besides this angular, jagged way of composing, Bach very much loved the sound of the intimate clavichord, where he could vary the sound by changing the finger pressure. Albert Schweitzer calls this aspect of Bach's music detail dynamics or declamatory dynamics, because it follows the declamatory cadence of musical language. But even these detail dynamics, though they are on a smaller scale than the dynamics of an organ composition and allow for finer shadings, are not to be thought of as permitting crescendo and diminuendo.

Bach knew and played one of the first pianofortes, which Gottfried Silbermann had built in 1733. Bach liked its general sound, but remarked that the treble sounded too weak. He must have realized that crescendo and diminuendo could — if only in a crude way — be executed on this pianoforte. That he did not endorse it enthusiastically is another proof that the hairpin dynamics were foreign to his artistic makeup. For Bach's and Handel's keyboard compositions, therefore, there can be only one way of dynamic treatment, the architectural or terrace dynamic style which makes their works sound greater, clearer, more majestic, and at the same time simpler than the subjective romantic way ever could.

To achieve accentuation of principal voices without stressing secondary voices, accompanists and coaches should first practice each voice separately from beginning to end and then put the voices together with only one voice at a time forte, all others piano. Do this first with one hand alone, then with both hands. You will gradually acquire the necessary independence of finger dynamics to play each voice loud or soft at will, and thus be able to stress the leading voices without increasing the dynamics of the others.

Let us see now how the question of dynamics fares with regard to Bach's and Handel's instrumental and vocal works. In their works for one instrument with keyboard accompaniment, and in their sonatas, Bach and Handel were both frugal with their dynamic signs. We may assume that no great emotional dynamics, meaning crescendo-diminuendo, were intended for these works. But there were some homophonic movements or parts where the addition of instrumental voices could not produce the intended buildup. We may safely assume that the baroque interpreters did not neglect to add light and shade to their cantilena. This is an artistic and even physiological requirement; otherwise the music would sound mechanical, uninspired, boring. A small amount of gradation of shading must have taken place. Quantz (quoted in Dolmetsch's *The Interpretation of the Music of the XVII and XVIII Centuries*) says, "You must continually oppose light and shade, for you will certainly fail to be touching if you play always either loud or soft — if you use, so to speak, always the same color,

and do not know how to increase or abate the tone when required. You must therefore use frequent changes from forte to piano." Grove's *Dictionary of Music and Musicians* calls this "inner" kind of dynamics transient light and shade. I would like to coin the term vitalizing dynamics for this kind of implantation of subtle shadings. They will enliven a piece of music, but they never must be exaggerated lest a very much romanticized treatment result.

These vitalizing dynamics are even more important for Bach's and Handel's vocal compositions. The human voice cannot but fill its tones with a constant small fluctuation of dynamics. It would be quite unnatural to keep a voice to a steady piano or a steady forte, and it would be well-nigh impossible to achieve this for any length of time. Furthermore, vocal music has its own laws, dictated by the words and their meanings. Growing emotion in the text will have to be accompanied by growing emotion in the singing. Here again I want to warn against sentimentalizing the two masters' music. Simplicity and economy of expression will create the deepest impression.

In choral and big orchestral works, in operas, passions, oratorios, cantatas, the Brandenburg concerti, the "Art of the Fugue," the "Musical Offering" — to speak of only some of the greatest of the two masters' works, superpersonalization takes the place of personalization. And, since choral and orchestral masses are better suited for big architectural moldings, terrace dynamics seem to me the best way of expression. Of course, the great vocal compositions contain homophonic arias, duets, and so on, as well as polyphonic numbers. These homophonic excerpts should be performed with vitalizing dynamics. Chorales should be done in one dynamic shade only. Whenever the text asks for it, repeats should be done, using echo effects. Emotional dynamics are not proper here. I should like, however, to distinguish Bach and Handel once again. Handel, the more Italianized master, can stand more ups and downs of dynamics of the kind that Caccini and Geminiani had asked for. His concerti grossi, for instance, scored entirely for strings, must make use of the light and shade dynamics, as this is natural for stringed instruments. A Handel opera can be performed with more shadings of dynamics than can a monumental, upward-striving edifice by Johann Sebastian Bach.

The homophonic Italian and French school of the baroque age made more use of the crescendo-diminuendo dynamics than Bach and Handel. Geminiani and Rameau used some symbols that came close to the hairpin signs. The "messa di voce" was very popular and singers reached great virtuosity in it. This movement created the soil in which the emotional dynamics of the preclassical and classical periods could grow.

Dynamics of preclassical and classical times. Philipp Emanuel Bach knew the style of crescendo-diminuendo music very well. He was in favor of a harpsichord with pedal stops that enabled the performer to change dynamics gradually, and he also used the words crescendo and diminuendo in some of his music. But the highest point of this style is reached with the advent of Jomelli, Stamitz, and the Mannheim school. We have seen that the crescendo-diminuendo dynamics originated in the Italy of the seventeenth century. The Neapolitan composer Niccolò Jomelli (1714–1774) heard the crescendo manner used in performances in Italy and made it his own. When, in 1753, he was made a conductor at the court of Württemberg in Stuttgart, he brought with him the elaborate scheme of crescendo-decrescendo musical effects. From his performances, which were greeted with great enthusiasm by the German public, the technique made its way to neighboring Mannheim, where the conductor of the local orchestra, the Bohemian J. W. Stamitz (1717–1757), made it the most outstanding musical feature in Central Europe. The English musical writer Charles Burney heard the Mannheim orchestra in 1772 and could not find praise enough for the overwhelming impression of its crescendos and diminuendos. The Mannheim palette of dynamics must have sounded quite stupendous to contemporary audiences. And the final crescendo of a symphony composed in the Mannheim style, with its long runs by all instruments from pianissimo to fortissimo, could not fail to win over the leading German composers of the day. Stamitz used the crescendo — and, to a lesser degree, the decrescendo — without changing the rhythm. He did not accelerate when getting louder nor slow down when making a diminuendo. The trick of the famous Mannheim crescendo consisted in increasing dynamics in the whole orchestral body at once, not by adding different groups of instruments starting out with pp. It is an old maxim that pianissimo never sounds better than when played by the full orchestra.

Mozart, who heard the orchestra several times under Stamitz's successor Christian Cannabich, learned a great deal from the Mannheim range of dynamics. A good example of his use of the crescendo-decrescendo is the end of the overture to *Figaro*, when the whole orchestra starts pianissimo and builds up to a jubilant fortissimo. The Mannheim style had an equally strong influence on Beethoven and on a whole group of preclassical masters such as Dittersdorf and Boccherini. Haydn was the one great classicist master who subscribed to the Mannheim effect only hesitatingly. He still preferred the architectural dynamics of contrast between his wind and string groups. The first orchestra to incorporate the new dynamic ideas of Mannheim was the Paris orchestra. Alfred Einstein writes in his *Mozart*: "The two best orchestras of the world in this period — the Mannheim orchestra which really was unsurpassed and the Paris orchestra which at any rate claimed to be — to some extent owed their development to the symphonic works of Johann Stamitz, while to some extent the works in turn owed their origin to the existence of the orchestras. And it is true that the symphonies of the 'Mannheim School' were concerned above all with exhibiting the qualities of the Mannheim orchestra: its precision, its skill in making the most sudden changes in expression, its excellence in passages bringing out particular groups of wind instruments, and finally its famous crescendo which consisted in raising a motive from the level of pianissimo to that of fortissimo until it finally exploded in a noisy tutti. The beginning of the allegro of Beethoven's Leonore Overture and the scherzo of his Fifth Symphony are the purest, most idealized, and most meaningful examples of the Mannheim crescendo."

Dynamics were assumed to express certain emotions. Light, happiness, jubilation, scorn, and hate, for instance, are connected with forte. Shade, night, fear, and tenderness are expressed by piano. This, of course, is only the usual way of expressing emotions. Very strong emotions, such as inner happiness or extreme hate, may also be expressed by the contrasting dynamics of pianissimo. Deep fear or panic may be impressed on us by forte. It all depends on whether an emotion is felt outside or inside. At the time of Haydn and Mozart the dynamic scale runs something like this: pianissimo, piano, mezzopiano, mezzoforte, forte, fortissimo. Later, ppp and fff were added. Eventually there were to be pppp and even ppppp especially in Verdi's late operas; but these are mainly relative, meaning the utmost pianissimo possible. The crescendo and decrescendo signs became abundant. Other expressive nomenclatures of dynamics were morendo (dying out), susurrando (whispering), smorzando (abating), rinforzando (reinforcing, growing louder), and others. Hans von Bülow's bon mot "Crescendo means piano, decrescendo means forte" is absolutely true. The beginning of a crescendo is still soft, the beginning of a decrescendo is still loud.

Haydn, Mozart, and Beethoven did not necessarily mark all their parts with dynamic signs. In Mozart's operas, for instance, one does not always find dynamics in the voice line; the dynamic notation of the orchestra is in all cases applicable to the voice. Whenever there are sudden pianos in the orchestra, an effect that was a favorite with Mozart and Beethoven, the voice must sing exactly the same sudden piano. Very frequent is the use of a forte-piano. This means that after a definite attack in forte the dynamics have to be immediately taken back to piano. When exactly this has to be done depends on the length of the note above or under which the sign stands. In a whole or half note one may hold a quarter or an eighth note, respectively, forte and the rest piano. In shorter note values the piano takes effect immediately. These piano subito–forte subito effects belong to the category of negative musical accents as much as to dynamics. They may be important landmarks of phrasing, as well as sudden surprising changes of dynamics. The accompanist and coach must see to it that a sudden piano is really done on the note under which the sign stands, even if the piano's note falls on a syncopated note or an off-beat.

Besides these negative accents there is a whole group of positive accents that ask for sudden accentuation of mostly single tones or chords. They can be expressed by a variety of symbols, mostly abbreviations, which help to avoid misunderstandings as to which note or chord they apply to. Such symbols are >, ∧, ′, sf, sfz, fz, ffz, sffz, all emanating from forzato or sforzando. In more recent music, even rfz or rinforzando are sometimes to be found among the sudden accents. All these accents are relative. Their execution requires variation of dynamics in accord with the dynamics of the whole phrase. In a piano phrase, a sf should not be played louder than a mezzoforte, in pianissimo not louder than a mezzopiano. This rule is especially important for Haydn's and Mozart's music where the accent is not always a dynamic, but frequently a melodic accent. In such music it may be found marked sfp. This melodic accent that can be executed really well only in instrumental or vocal lines, not on the pianoforte, should come *after* the attack has been effected. Harshness is thus avoided and the sforzato func-

tions as a melodic intensification — a crescendo, so to speak — of a single, usually longer-held tone or chord. These melodic accents are often misunderstood, and when they are Haydn's and Mozart's music takes on a meaning that we actually find in Beethoven's works: the harsh, cutting, desperate, stubborn, roaring expression accent.

I have said before that Beethoven's genius never revealed itself more clearly than in his tremendous rhythmic originality. I now enlarge this statement to include Beethoven's dynamics. No other composer before him and only a very few after have ever made full use of the rich scale of dynamics at a composer's command. What makes Beethoven's dynamics such a gigantic wrestle with the elements is the almost neverending tension he was able to pack into them, and the sudden explosions that followed this tension. Take, for example, the measures of transition between the scherzo of his Fifth Symphony and the last movement. Through 42 measures there is a whispering pianissimo that keeps us chained to our seats, followed by a sudden, short increase through 8 measures, leading in turn to the explosion of the C-major beginning of the last movement, which makes us want to jump up. Or consider the above-mentioned beginning of the allegro of the Leonore Overture Number 3: 28 measures of tension and 54 measures of discharge. Here is the Mannheim crescendo uplifted into nobility by being richly imbued with inner life and expression.

According to Beethoven's friend Schindler, the composer wanted his rhythmic accents to be played forcefully, the melodic accents to be treated as the situation warranted. The changing notes of the interval of the small second he always accented, even in a cantabile. All this made Beethoven's piano playing sound very poignant and characteristic, far from the smooth, flat playing of others. He was against all miniature painting in musical interpretation and demanded forceful expression everywhere. Louis Spohr tells us that he saw Beethoven conduct, which must have been a strange sight. Beethoven communicated all expression marks to the orchestra by strange movements of his body. For a sforzando, he suddenly flung his arms apart with great vehemence. At a piano he bent down — the softer he wanted the sound the lower he bent. For a crescendo he straightened up, and when forte was reached he leaped into the air. I do not cite this description to prove that Beethoven was a bad conductor but to show

how intensely, even physically, he felt his dynamic requirements.

Intensity of dynamics is an absolute necessity in performing Beethoven's works. This intensity has never been excelled by any composer since. Orchestration has since become more sophisticated, and orchestras and choral groups are larger, but so are opera houses and concert halls. The double and triple fortissimos of later composers have never surpassed the strength of Beethoven's dynamic scale. Three composers trod in Beethoven's footsteps, as far as variety and importance of dynamics are concerned — Berlioz, Brahms, and Wagner — but none added anything really new. A movement that held dynamics very high on its shield was the French golden age of music with its suppressed dynamics, celebrating orgies of reticence and of softest shadings. A contemporary successor to this introspective use of dynamics was the twelve-tone composer Anton von Webern, whose sounds are often so soft that they become almost inaudible. This is exactly what he wanted; the mere hint of a feeling satisfied his fine sense of musical restraint.

MUSICAL PHRASING AND ARTICULATION

The art of phrasing is as old as speech and language. Phrasing is the punctuation of speech. To be understandable, language, particularly musical language, must be phrased according to its structure. This is done with the aid of caesuras, interruptions, pauses, holds, fermatas, which take the place in music of the periods, commas, colons, and quotation marks of written speech. Phrasing gives meaning to the melodic line, and also serves to enhance its expression. Wrong phrasing is comparable to wrong punctuation in a speech that makes the whole speech cryptic or even senseless. But even a speech that has all its punctuation right and every breath in its proper place may be unimpressive if the diction or articulation is not correct. Such a speech will become muffled, its expression will pale, and it will make no impression on the listener. Clear articulation is an important element of style. Most textbooks regard phrasing as the sum of structural phrasing (or "punctuation") and articulation phrasing, but I should like to take an exception to this. Articulation is in its own right an element of style; I shall use the term phrasing only for the punctuation or structural phrasing and treat musical articulation as a separate element of style.

Phrasing and articulation have only two musical signs in common, although their significance is different. These are the slurs and the breath marks. Accentuation by rhythm and dynamics is part of articulation. Rhythm, dynamics, phrasing, and articulation are closely connected. This interplay of style elements will greatly enhance the elasticity of interpretation through the choice of the right tempo. The total of tempo, rhythm, dynamics, phrasing, and articulation will create the right expression of a piece, its right mood, and the right style.

What is meant by "musical phrase"? It means what "sentence" means in the realm of language. A sentence is subdivided by commas, semicolons, dashes, and colons; a musical phrase is subdivided and ended by pauses, caesuras, holds, fermatas. Not all of these subdividing signs are written down. Often we shall have to use our own judgment and knowledge of style to find separations that will make the musical phrases clear and understandable. This is where the real art of musical phrasing becomes overwhelmingly important for correct interpretation.

Vocal music had separation marks as early as the seventeenth century. Couperin was among the first to use signs to make phrasing understandable, using an elevated comma to mark the end of a melody or a phrase. The interruption thus indicated must be very slight, almost unnoticeable. Johann Mattheson distinguishes between complete commas and suspended commas, the latter to be felt without being notated. Most of these commas were breath marks which may or may not have contributed to musical phrasing. Breath marks are often also marks to aid in clear articulation, of which I shall speak later.

Musical phrasing consists of two elements: separation and unification. Separation marks are all kinds of pauses — breath marks in places where the logical phrase comes to an end, hiatuses, and caesuras. The end of a phrase may be marked especially by a pause, a hold, or a fermata or corona. The unification marks are of two kinds: the slurs or ligatures and the vertical stroke that marks the end of a phrase. The trouble with slurs as phrase marks is that they are logical only in a legato phrase. A phrase, however, may be articulated staccato or have a number of different articulation marks. In such cases, a ligature as phrasing sign may confuse or even change the composer's intention. I am, therefore, in favor of the ′ sign as phrasing mark wherever phrasing must be made clear.

Many times phrases intertwine or overlap, and the

really difficult problem is to recognize where one ends and the next begins. Great sins have been committed by musical writers such as Hugo Riemann, who tried to establish a single way of explaining musical phrasing. He is often right and gives us very valuable information; he sometimes accommodates the music to his theory. But he and other theoretical writers such as Heinrich Schenker were more concerned with the importance of phrasing to the musical form and less with the importance of phrasing to the clarity of a composition or its expression. I have said before and I must say over and over again: Knowledge of the different elements of musical style is the best guide for finding the right style. And the accompanist and coach will have to acquaint himself thoroughly with a composition's innate style, its style of performance in the composer's time, and its contemporary style of performance if he is to solve the ticklish problem of musical phrasing.

We have and have had since the Middle Ages plenty of breath signs for vocal — mostly choral — compositions. We are also in little doubt about the other separating marks — pauses, holds, and fermatas. The one rule I should like to establish in regard to separating and prolonging marks is this: *pauses and holds are music.* They are an integral part of the score and must never be neglected or shortened. It is better to shorten a note before a pause in order to achieve a clear separation of phrases than it is to shorten the pause itself. A fermata or corona lengthens the note over which it is put by half the note's value. At the end of a piece, the fermatas may be held longer, and the same is true of the last fermata in a chorale. The fermata at the half period, however, should get only the regular lengthening. Some musicologists hold that chorale fermatas were nothing but reading guides to make things easier for the church congregation. But today the fermata is meant to express a definite hold.

We can only grope in the dark, however, about the old masters' intentions with respect to the unification of phrases, in vocal as well as instrumental music. The old masters, Bach and Handel included, either were their own interpreters or had their music performed by their pupils, which meant that they never needed a score marked with phrasing.

We must distinguish between two kinds of slur bowing: for expression and for articulation; the latter usually cover groups of two, three, or four notes. There is a third, purely technical kind of slur or bowing mark that is employed in notation for strings and winds. If

Figure 111. Legato slur, with separation portato or appoggiato

a string or wind player sees two or more notes of the same pitch under one slur (Fig. 111A) he will not sound the notes separately unless they are also marked with dots (Fig. 111B) or short horizontal lines (Fig. 111C) above the notes. We call this legato with separation portato or appoggiato. Technical slurs belong to articulation. Of course phrasing slurs (musical) and articulation slurs (technical) may often be one and the same.

Much confusion has always reigned about the right application of slurs, and phrasing slurs and articulation slurs are employed rather haphazardly by otherwise very conscientious composers. Among the keyboard instruments it is mainly the organ that suffers from this confusion. If an organ piece is not specially marked, the right phrasing will be hard to find. Because of the legato character of organ music, legato phrasing will be acceptable in the absence of special phrasing indications. But in leaps and in the connection of full chords it may not be possible to keep the legato phrasing. Repeated touching of the same keys will have to be effected legato unless the composer asks for separation by markings or by certain indications such as dynamic changes or changes of manuals.

If legato phrases start with upbeats, the phrasing slurs probably will go from one upbeat to the next. But this is by no means an invariable rule: some composers will vary their phrases in order to make the music more interesting or to avoid the obvious. We shall see this later when we look into Mozart's phrasing. The upbeat phrasing theory as the one and only rule is one of Riemann's worst errors. Another is his plucking apart larger phrases and subdividing them into smaller units. It may be good to *feel* and to *know* that a large phrase consists of many smaller ones, but if one makes all these small phrases apparent by accenting their beginning, the larger phrase will be broken and a nervousness will enter the performance. Instead of a synthesis of phrase elements we would get an analytical execution of the work.

Musical articulation is as old as phrasing. In fact, it was and is even today thrown into one pot with phrasing without any differentiation's being made. I already have made clear the difference between these two. The characteristic features of articulation stem from its being based primarily on instrumental music and in particular on the melodic lines of the stringed instruments. As a matter of fact, for a long time articulation was notated only in instrumental music. Herrmann Keller, in his *Die Musikalische Artikulation, insbesondere bei Johann Sebastian Bach*, sums up the main tasks of articulation:

"1. To connect or to tear apart the melodic line through either legato or staccato.

"2. To give meaning to the melody by either grouping together individual relations or by setting them apart from each other."

Connecting a melodic group is of course done by legato playing with or without special legato slurs. The separation of melodic groups has to be done by staccato or by small pauses; the difference between these two is that pauses may destroy a melodic line by completely interrupting it, whereas staccato will never do this. Staccato simply means that a tone is not sustained to its full value; the melodic line will continue. There are a few intermediate steps between legato and staccato: the legato, portato, or appoggiato; the portato or stentato; the nonlegato, which has no special marks at all; the mezzo staccato. Staccato may be either expressed by dots or by wedge-shaped marks (Fig. 112). In the latter case the staccato becomes a hammered staccato (martellato). Other articulation signs or technical slurs may be found on pages 141–142. Musical phrases may be longer or shorter than articulation groups. Figures 113 and 114 are a couple of examples.

Figure 112. Musical articulation: legato, portato, or appoggiato; portato or stentato; nonlegato; mezzo staccato (above); staccato (below)

Figure 113. Wagner, *Parsifal*

The beginning of the prelude to *Parsifal* has a long phrasing ligature which does not even come to a stop before the two F's in the second measure. Usually the same notes following each other are disconnected by markings, otherwise the player may not sound them twice. Wagner, however, ends his ligature before the C in the last measure, although the musical phrase ends on it and not before. Phrasing the melodic line into

smaller units will necessitate different marks which I show in Figure 113 by means of vertical strokes.

The articulation bowings must take into consideration the technical prowess of the string players. The usual changes of bow are given by dotted ligatures. The problem is different for the wind players who have the same theme to play. Their breath will suffice to phrase it as Wagner marked it.

Examples for very discriminating articulation phrasings may be found in Brahms's compositions. Let us, for instance, take the secondary theme of his Third Symphony's first movement (Fig. 114). Brahms evidently wants clarinet and bassoon to accentuate very lightly — he marks the melody with grazioso and mezza voce — each group of threes in the 9-4 beat, probably in order to underline the waltzlike character of the melody. The musical phrases marked with vertical strokes are longer. This example brings us face to face with two more characteristic details of articulation: minute accents and the Abzug.

Figure 114. Brahms, Third Symphony

As in speech, the voice or the musical instrument, at the beginning of a new articulation group, must start with an ever so slight accent. If this accent is to be made with determination, a special dynamic mark will probably be written in. In the absence of such a mark, the accent must be very soft — minute — effected merely by an ever so slight vocal emphasis, a change of bowing in stringed instruments or a slight tongue attack in wind instruments. The pianist will have to lift his fingers lightly from the keyboard just before the new articulation phrase and start it with a slight accent; the lifting of the finger may have to be combined with an almost unnoticeable diminuendo. This articulation technique had already been described by writers of Mozart's time, such as Sulzer, who must still have known the old Johann Sebastian Bach tradition. A very slight pause between articulation groups — not even large enough to be expressed by any kind of marking — may also be an additional aid in achieving plasticity of articulation.

One of the most useful directives, at least as far as the classical school is concerned, was given me in Vienna: "Let there be air between the notes" or "There must be daylight between the notes." Translated into our terminology this means that infinitesimal pauses between articulation groups will shade them off, and aerate them, and enhance the plasticity. This is very important especially in the case of groups of two notes under an articulation slur; the second note should be given slightly less value. In German this is abgezogen (from the noun Abzug) or abgeschliffen. There is no single word in the English language to fit this meaning except the much abused "slur." We can say that a legato mark over two notes necessitates shortening the second note and lightening it by a slight diminuendo. Our classicist masters made frequent use of the Abzug nuance; their ways of writing it are shown in Figure 115, the third being the most common. The Abzug is mostly used where two sixteenth notes follow each other and where a certain characterization is intended. In *Don Giovanni*, for instance, Zerlina sings as shown in Figure 116; here the Abzug must be made. Later, the same Zerlina, on the other hand, sings as shown in Figure 117. Here the groups call for legato singing in accordance with the meaning of words and musical phrase. From Mozart's instrumental music I shall only give one example from among many, the beginning of the finale from his G minor Symphony (Fig. 118).

Figure 115. Classicist masters' ways of writing the Abzug

Figure 116. Mozart, *Don Giovanni,* example of Abzug

Figure 117. Mozart, *Don Giovanni,* no Abzug

Figure 118. Mozart, G minor Symphony

In Vienna, these articulation groups are definitely played with "air between the notes." Perhaps the best proof may be furnished by Mozart's different markings of the same melody. In Cherubino's Canzonetta (*Le Nozze di Figaro*) the oboe plays as shown in Figure 119. When Cherubino sings the same phrase, Mozart notates as shown in Figure 120. The execution is of course the same — with "air between the notes."

Figure 119. Mozart, *Le Nozze di Figaro,* oboe phrase

Figure 120. Mozart, *Le Nozze di Figaro,* same phrase sung by Cherubino

After these general remarks about musical phrasing and articulation, I shall now briefly take up their application by the baroque masters. I have already said that the baroque masters did not have to make their phrasing evident by separating and enjoining marks, because the music was played by the master himself or by pupils who knew his intentions. We can, however, come to a few plausible conclusions about baroque phrasing when we study their works. First of all, the organ or harpsichord fingering in Bach's and Handel's times makes it clear that long slurs could not have been the taste of the time. Since the thumb was hardly ever used in fingering, the passages could not have been smoothly connected. The way these baroque masters connected passages in their keyboard compositions made for separation of phrases rather than for linkage. Bach and Handel also indicated their phrasing by the way they change from one manual to the other. We are justified in using a similar manner of phrasing in their vocal and instrumental works. Their phrasing is usually, though not invariably, from upbeat to upbeat. Here, I want to warn once more against plucking phrases apart by subdividing them too obviously into smaller groups. Phrases may be subdivided unnoticeably. Schweitzer calls this "secret phrasing." It would be interesting to know whether Schweitzer, today, has changed his concept of exclusive upbeat phrasing which he conceived under strong influence of Riemann's theory. In baroque fugato pieces, especially in fugues, the various voices may be phrased differently in order to enhance the plasticity of the polyphonic weave.

The change between legato, staccato, and portato, and the various slurs of short melodic or contrapuntal groupings belong to articulation rather than to phrasing. When we hear Bach's and Handel's phrasing discussed we may safely assume that articulation and accentuation are meant. The many pages dedicated to phrasing in Schweitzer's monumental *J. S. Bach* contain detailed suggestions about Bach's musical diction, i.e., his articulation. Schweitzer gives two principal rules for Bach's articulation: (1) Notes must be played staccato (or portato), if they follow each other in characteristically wide intervals. Schweitzer includes in this category all "leaping" themes. (2) Staccato is indicated if an even motion of a voice is interrupted by an uneven or zig-zagging motion.

Bach marked many of his compositions with legato bowing or staccato dots, using a great variety of combinations, the most frequent of which are shown in Figure 121. Bach meticulously marked the parts of his Brandenburg concerti, of the B minor Mass, of the Christmas Oratorio, of the St. Matthew Passion, of many cantatas. His articulation is an open book for those who have thoroughly studied the source material — the original scores.

Figure 121. Example of Bach's articulation

Handel took more care with dynamic signs than with phrasing and articulation marks. We must keep this in mind when we try to perform a Handel composition. Beware, however, of impossible Handel editions such as the ones by Seiffert or Oskar Hagen that romanticize the baroque grandeur of Handel's musical language.

Phrasing and articulation of the classicist masters. As we have already seen in the general discussion of phrasing and articulation, the notation of articulation took a decisive step forward during the preclassical and classical age. Important to its development were the abolishing of the figured bass and the composers' tendency to make their intentions clear to any interpreter. Musical script came of age and became so binding that it usually allowed but one interpretation. Whereas the composers of the baroque era were their own interpreters or let their best pupils play or direct their works, the classicist masters wrote their music for a much larger group of performers, in the home as well as on the concert stage. Indications, therefore, had to be much more detailed. Besides, the more individualistic the time became — as the broad stream of the baroque became the playful rococo and then culminated in Beethoven's highly personal style — the more urgent grew the need for unequivocally-marked articulation.

The dividing component, phrasing, was also stressed more and more by clearer breath marks and instrumental bowing marks. The other components of phrasing, however, the unifying slurs, were still scarce in Haydn, Mozart, and even Beethoven. Only when these masters asked for phrasing that differed from the ordinary did they make a special effort to notate it. The often-cited passage from Mozart's A minor Rondo (K. 511) may

Figure 122. Mozart, A minor Rondo

serve as an example (Fig. 122). In his manuscript, Mozart first used the conventional way of phrasing in ending the phrase on G sharp as I have indicated by a dotted bow. Later, he crossed out this bow sign and let the phrase run to the end of the measure, thus undoubtedly creating a headache for Hugo Riemann. But it is this irregularity of phrasing that makes Mozart's, Haydn's, and Beethoven's works so interesting to us. It is as if a new, unknown spice had been added. Notice further in Figure 122 how Mozart divided his phrase into short phrases by means of rests.

When it came to vocal melismas or espressivo coloraturas, Mozart and Beethoven loved to write the longest possible phrases. Take, for instance, Donna Elvira's aria "Mi tradì" from *Don Giovanni* or the immense sweep of expression in the legato passages in Leonore's aria from *Fidelio*. The composers were able to write long phrases because the singers of their era had perfect breath control. Most singers today have difficulties with these long phrases, and the accompanist and coach is fully justified in putting in auxiliary breath marks and in repeating words. These long coloraturas are derived from Bach's and Handel's melismas, the execution of which *come scritto* is an almost impossible feat today. The classicist masters made phrasing most intriguing by having phrases overlap and intertwine. By means of this artistic device they avoided a tiring repetition of regular phrases of four or eight measures, the so-called periods. Some contemporary critics shook their heads at such liberties. But the irregularity of phrasing increases our interest and our enjoyment of the music.

The classicists' phrasing must be studied thoroughly. They employ very few phrasing bows that can serve as explanation of intentions of phrasing. Most of the bow marks are short and refer to articulation rather than to phrasing. Beethoven's Violin Concerto has bowing marks as shown in Figure 123. The violinist should fol-

Figure 123. Beethoven, Violin Concerto

low these by changing the bow as prescribed by Beethoven, but the change should be unnoticeable, so that the musical phrase continues for four measures with a slight subphrasing after two measures. Moreover, Beethoven was rather sloppy in his phrasing notations if and when he used them. He was not at all consistent, and neither were his copyists, who had their hands full trying to decipher his hieroglyphics.

As I said before, the classicist masters' articulation marks are manifold and most sophisticated. There is a continuous interplay of legato and staccato, of dots and wedge-shaped signs, of portato and Abzug patterns. Mozart, especially, went out of his way to make his articulation as colorful and varied as possible. It is amazing how articulation may influence accents and meter. In Mozart's gigue for piano (K. 574), for instance, the effect of irregularly spaced Abzug slurs approaches a rhythmic pattern which is very near to our American jazz syncopation (Fig. 124). Mozart's treatment of articulation is probably the finest, most detailed, and most irregular of all the classicist composers.

Figure 124. Mozart, gigue for piano, K. 574

Beethoven, though he differentiates no less in his articulation, puts it entirely to the service of expressing his innermost personal feelings. His staccato is more biting than Mozart's. His strong fist, always raised against fate's scurrilous attacks, differentiates in great detail between the dots and the wedge-shaped signs (see Fig. 112). His letters and conversations prove that he was very conscious of the different sounds of staccato and very insistent on the correct application and execution of the signs.

The phrasing and articulation of romanticists, neoclassicists, and contemporary composers. After the peak that phrasing and articulation reached during the classical age of music, a reaction set in with the appearance of the romanticists. Other ingredients of music were refined and became more important, especially the feeling for harmony, which found its first audacious representative in Schubert and reached a climax with Chopin. Dynamics developed greatly as the nineteenth century grew older; with forms becoming smaller and less concise, dynamic shadings assumed more and more importance. But the loosening of form that took place during the years from 1830 on could not but impoverish

phrasing and articulation. Nothing new was added; regularity was replaced by the rule that the more irregular phrases were, the more interesting the composition would become. True, the phrasing slurs were notated with more care; the portato articulation in Schumann's and Chopin's works becomes more refined; the light, elfin-like staccato of Mendelssohn represents a new musical development which we may call an attempted suspension of gravity. But all in all, the years from 1830 to 1850 were not too abundant as far as phrasing and articulation are concerned. It was left to the two antipodes Brahms and Wagner to re-establish the importance of these two elements of style.

Brahms is undoubtedly one of the most interesting if most cryptic masters of phrasing. He writes long phrases, but he does not notate them. His slurs are derived from the stringed instruments' changes of bow. Furthermore, in most cases he ends a ligature on the first of two like notes, whether or not phrasing or articulation warrants it. This technique of notation stems from his fear, acquired through his experiences with string and wind players, that the second tone would not otherwise be sounded separately. A good example of this may be found in Brahms's A flat major Waltz (Fig. 125).

Figure 125. Brahms, A flat major Waltz

In general, it may be said that Brahms's phrasing and articulation continue where Beethoven's left off. The accompanist and coach will have to unite Brahms's short phrases to longer phrase periods, will have to extend articulation slurs whenever necessary, and, furthermore, play Brahms's staccatos with a certain roughness and strength. Hardly ever is Brahms dainty or downright happy. His happiness is almost always somewhat muted. Brahms's predilection for a wide bass range expresses itself in jumps and wide arpeggios and chords. These bass figurations should be connected by legato, or, when the notes lie too far apart, by pedal. Figure 126 is an example from Brahms's "Meine Liebe ist grün."

An unbelievable richness of phrasing and articulation may be found in Wagner's operas, especially his later ones, starting with *Tristan und Isolde.* We have already

Figure 126. Brahms, "Meine Liebe ist grün"

seen (p. 137) how long Wagner's phrases can be. The expression "infinite melody" has been used to describe phrases like the one at the beginning of the prelude to *Parsifal*. Wagner is always most meticulous in writing pauses when he wants separation of phrases. These must not be confused with his small pauses after short phrases that guarantee plasticity of articulation and the stressing of words, as well as psychological aspects such as sudden inhibitions in speech, expressed by syncopated notes (see p. 211). From the wealth of Wagner's long phrases I would like to give just two more examples from *Tristan und Isolde*, one played by the clarinet (Fig. 127), the other (Fig. 128) played by the second violins, showing that Wagner marks phrasing slurs and articulation bows at the same time.

Figure 127. Wagner, *Tristan und Isolde*,
clarinet passage

Figure 128. Wagner, *Tristan und Isolde*, same
passage for second violins

Understanding the phrasing of Italian opera up to and including Puccini must come from following the vocal line. Phrasing comes very naturally to an Italian vocalist of good musical breeding, notwithstanding the fact that breath at times has to be taken within a phrase. Perhaps the greatest Italian composer of long and beautiful phrases is Bellini. His melodies are so pure that they leave no doubt about their phrasing. It may be enough to mention his "Casta Diva" from *Norma* to prove the point.

But in notating vocal phrases, Italian composers are not much concerned with exactness. They leave the phrasing to their interpreters. Verdi is very sensitive when it comes to articulation, even if he is not always consistent in using articulation signs in his instrumental and vocal melodies. In Desdemona's Ave Maria from *Otello*, for instance, he marks the first violin part as shown in Figure 129, whereas the voice line is as shown in Figure 130. The instrumental melody has the long

Figure 129. Verdi, *Otello*, first violin part

Figure 130. Verdi, *Otello*, same passage for voice

phrasing slurs and portato articulation signs; the voice line has only the short articulation slurs plus the portato marks. Verdi knew that his singers would know how to phrase this melody. Actually, it is an especially difficult phrase for a soprano, starting with the low E flat which Verdi wants to have connected with the following C by a portamento. Only sopranos with excellent breath support and control would be able to sing the whole phrase in one breath; others may have to take the auxiliary breath I have marked with a hiatus mark in Figure 130. The portato dots in Verdi's operas are of utmost importance and must not be neglected. They form an integral part of his articulation style. In the fourth act of *Il Trovatore* Azucena sings between dreaming and waking as shown in Figure 131. The second period of eight measures is notated as shown in Figure 132. Verdi's articulation bows change with every measure. We would phrase the first period (Fig. 131) in groups of two measures from pause to pause. For the second period (Fig. 132) Verdi puts portato dots in some but not all measures. We may deduce from this that he wants Azucena to appear weaker the second time she sings the melody, to recover some of her strength with the words "in sonno placido," but to sink back into her dreams with the words "io dormirò!"

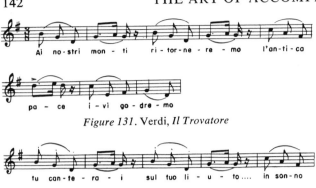

Ai no-stri mon - ti ri-tor-ne - re - mo l'an-ti-ca

pa - ce i - vi go-dre-mo

Figure 131. Verdi, *Il Trovatore*

tu can-te-ra - i sul tuo li - u - to.... in son-no

pla - ci-do.... io dor-mi - ro!...

Figure 132. Verdi, *Il Trovatore*

This example from *Trovatore* is not too difficult to fathom. Sometimes, however, Verdi's portato dots do not fit any such psychological explanation. I personally believe that in such cases Verdi wants to tell us to stress the words even in a long bel canto phrase, by separating them — but not the tones — lightly under a vocal legato singing line. If Verdi wants a more pronounced separation of syllables, but still under one vocal legato line, he uses small pauses. Germont in *La Traviata* sings first the passage shown in Figure 133, and a few measures later the passage shown in Figure 134. In these meas-

Un di, quan-do le ve-ne-ri il tem-po a-vrà fu -

ga - te

Figure 133. Verdi, *La Traviata*

Ah dun-que, dun-que sper-da - si

Figure 134. Verdi, *La Traviata*

ures we find articulation pauses, legato slurs over two and four notes, extreme legato, and legato portato — showing how particular Verdi was in his articulation requirements. Still, he sometimes creates problems for us, as, for instance, with his portato marks in Germont's aria "Di Provenza," for which my only explanation is the above-mentioned stress on the words.

The French impressionists, in their search for *clarté*, made phrasing and articulation even more important than did their predecessors. Their over-all concern was with the truthfulness and the realism of musical declama-

tion. The words of a song, an opera, or a choral composition had to be rendered with all the natural inflections of the spoken word. Their phrases are short, their articulation marks very elaborate, their shades innumerable. In opposition to impressionism, Mahler and Richard Strauss preferred sweeping phrases and articulation marks that had not often been used before, such as caesuras, elevated commas, sudden holds, long and overlong fermatas. Mahler even gave directions as to the length of pauses between the movements of his symphonies. In his Second Symphony he requires a pause of "at least five minutes."

The modern composers, such as Stravinsky, Bartók, Schoenberg, and Berg, found new ways of expressing phrasing and articulation — too many to be discussed in this chapter. Suffice it to mention here that Alban Berg in his *Wozzeck* ends an act with a general pause (fermata) and starts the next act with another one. He requires from the conductor the strict conducting of these empty bars after the music has come to an end and before it begins again. For Berg, the music goes on in stillness, and the audience's attention must not cease with the last bar of sound. Stillness is also sound, and pauses are music.

ORNAMENTATION

The story of ornaments is just as tricky and ambiguous as the stories of tempo, rhythm, dynamics, phrasing, and articulation. During the time that marks the beginning of interest for our purposes — the baroque era — ornamentations were extremely complicated. No two theoreticians of the period agree exactly on their execution. In different countries, ornaments were notated and executed differently. Their popularity in those days is easily understandable if one looks at baroque architecture and painting. The scrolls of a baroque church and the curves and movements in baroque paintings express the spirit of the times as do the ornaments in baroque music. The term "embellishment" proves that the ornaments were a means of expressing the baroque feeling.

But there is yet another, more practical reason for the abundance of ornaments in baroque and rococo times. The harpsichords, clavichords, and lutes that had just come of age were unable to sustain notes. To make notes sound as if they belonged to a continuous melodic line one had to sound them at least twice and often many times in succession. This would have been impossible by simply repeating them if a legato line was required.

Therefore, composers had to use mordents, turns, and trills, playing around the main notes and returning to them.

But not only was the melodic line to be made more interesting: ornaments were also a necessity for deviations from the pure harmonic structure, thus spicing the monotony of harmony. Not daring to write notes on heavy beats that were foreign to accepted harmonies, composers got them in clandestinely by writing them as small notes that were nevertheless to be sounded on heavy beats. If the conservative ear was offended, at least the eye reading the music would not be. The principal harmonic seasonings were the appoggiaturas, especially the long ones. Besides changing melody and harmony, appoggiaturas also wrought a change in the rhythm of their particular phrases, as we soon shall see.

Since the appoggiaturas constitute a most important element of style not only for the baroque era but also for the classic and romantic period, a detailed analysis is absolutely essential. The execution of all other ornaments became more or less fixed during Haydn's and Mozart's lifetimes. But the execution of the appoggiaturas of Mozart and Schubert are, even today, a matter of conjecture, or, at best, of uneasy hesitation among musicians.

The number of serious theoretic writings about ornamentation is not large, and we must keep in mind that these writings portray the execution of ornaments during the last few years before their publication. The most authoritative work by Philipp Emanuel Bach, for instance, cannot be taken literally as giving correct data for the execution of his father's ornaments. A renegade, he represents the preclassical period; his explanation of the ornaments is of value principally for that time. If we want to know more about J. S. Bach's ornaments we should consult Johann Joachim Quantz's *Essay of Instruction on How to Play the Transverse Flute* (Berlin, 1752), which is more old-fashioned than the work of Philipp Emanuel Bach. Luckily, we have Johann Sebastian Bach's own manner of execution of ornaments, written down by him for his son Wilhelm Friedemann (see illustration on p. 144). We shall do well to follow his indications when we are concerned with ornaments in his works.

Handel's ornaments should be treated, on the whole, like Bach's embellishments. His Italian oratorios and operas, however, can stand more appoggiaturas than Bach's more northern works. Anglo-Saxon performances

have romanticized *The Messiah* to such an extent that ornaments and especially appoggiaturas are sung and played in it much too frequently; greater discrimination will help to clear unnecessary doodads from *The Messiah*.

Philipp Emanuel Bach's execution of ornaments is still valid for the Mozart era and, in part, much later. Leopold Mozart's *Thorough School for the Violin* is a valuable contribution. We may safely assume that his son accepted his teachings, just as he accepted and admired Philipp Emanuel Bach's theoretical knowledge.

The next stage in the teaching of ornamentation is reached with D. G. Türk's *School for the Pianoforte*, published in 1789. Türk used the Mozart ornamentation technique, and forms the bridge between him and Beethoven's somewhat more simplified use of ornaments. The most progressive writers who were still contemporaries of Mozart were J. A. Hiller, whose explanations of appoggiaturas in 1780 are especially valuable, and Muzio Clementi. Beethoven's mature theory of the use of ornaments may be found described in the books about piano by J. N. Hummel and J. B. Cramer, leading virtuosos in their day. Both were also contemporaries of Schubert. These authors were the last who had something new to say about ornamentation. During the 1830's, the modern manner of executing ornaments won out over the remnants of the baroque and rococo eras. And no significant change took place thereafter; the ornaments of all composers up to our time hold no more secrets for us.

THE APPOGGIATURA

All old theoreticians recognized the importance of appoggiaturas. Philipp Emanuel Bach treated them at the beginning of his chapter about ornamentation. It is to be regretted that we do not have a modern English word for these ornaments. In earlier English, they were called backfalls, forefalls, and half falls. What we call appoggiatura or, in French, *port de voix*, has two different names in German, the *Vorschlag* and *Vorhalt*. This latter term, if used in terms of harmony, may be called suspension. The old school, however, made no difference between these two terms so that our sole term appoggiatura may be justified after all.

This most common of the whole group of ornaments is also the most disputed one. Musicologists and conductors fought bitter battles about the performance of the appoggiaturas. What I said about today's performance style's being antagonistic to yesterday's and tomorrow's is especially true for the appoggiaturas. My personal opinion is that the coach and accompanist should know the rules established by writers of various times. But knowing the rules is not enough. One must sense where exceptions should be made. The expression inherent in the music ought to be the guiding light for the execution of appoggiaturas.

There are different kinds of appoggiatura: long and short ones; appoggiaturas from above and from below; appoggiaturas that start on the beat of the main note and others, passing ones, that fill out the time between the main notes and therefore start before the beat. Appoggiaturas that start on the beat of the main note have to be played or sung louder than the main note. In each case a diminuendo must be effected. Appoggiaturas from below usually repeat the preceding note. There is considerable confusion about composers' notation of appoggiaturas. The notations shown in Figure 135A, for

Figure 135. A. Long or short appoggiaturas.
B. Long appoggiaturas

instance, may be long or short; whereas those shown in Figure 135B are unequivocally short and have existed only since Mendelssohn and Berlioz. I shall deal separately with appoggiaturas in concerted numbers and in recitatives.

APPOGGIATURAS IN J. S. BACH'S AND G. F. HANDEL'S VOCAL WORKS

Although it would be very fruitful to trace the appoggiaturas in the two great baroque masters' instrumental works, lack of space forbids. Their accompanied instrumental works belong in the category of chamber music and are outside the scope of this book. But their vocal compositions give ample opportunity to discuss the appoggiaturas. Johann Sebastian Bach, in his book of instructions for Wilhelm Friedemann (Fig. 136) shows the appoggiatura from above and from below. Both start on the beat and both take half the value of the main note.

Johann Sebastian Bach gives no other hint of how to execute appoggiaturas, so we must consult Quantz in order to compare theory with probable practice. We

Figure 136. **J. S. Bach's embellishments**
A facsimile of page 8 of his *Klavierbüchlein für Wilhelm Friedemann Bach*

First measure, trill (shake); second, mordent; third, trill plus mordent; fourth, turn; fifth, double turn from below; sixth, double turn from above; seventh, double turn from below plus mordent; eighth, double turn plus mordent; ninth, appoggiatura from below; tenth, appoggiatura from above; eleventh, appoggiatura plus mordent; twelfth, appoggiatura plus trill; thirteenth, appoggiatura plus trill from above.

find that appoggiaturas before dotted notes or in triple time receive two thirds of the value of the main note. In most cases this rule will prove right, but there are exceptions, usually when the execution according to rule would change the intended harmony or the rhythmical pattern of a phrase. Bruno Walter cites the violin solo (Fig. 137) in the alto aria "Erbarme dich" of Bach's Matthew Passion as an example of how ambiguous the original notation is. It seems to me that the appoggiatura cannot be executed according to rule — receiving two thirds of value of main note (execution A, Fig. 138)

Figure 137. Bach, Matthew Passion, violin solo in alto aria, "Erbarme dich," as written

Figure 138. Three ways of playing the preceding passage

— because the rhythmical pattern of a dotted eighth, a sixteenth, and an eighth would be destroyed. In order to keep the pattern unchanged one would have to change the long appoggiatura into a short one (execution C, Fig. 138). This was certainly not Bach's intention. Short appoggiaturas in Bach's time take place only in fast passages or in passing. I think, therefore, that execution B must have been the right one. It preserves the rhythmical pattern. The accent, of course, must fall on the heavy beat, i.e., on the appoggiatura. Another exception which does not appear until one looks not only at the woodwinds' part (Fig. 139) but also at the vocal part (Fig. 140) in the full score is the duet with chorus "So ist

Figure 139. Bach, Matthew Passion, "So ist mein Jesus nun gefangen," woodwinds

Figure 140. Bach, Matthew Passion, "So ist mein Jesus nun gefangen," voice

mein Jesus nun gefangen" from the same Passion. The woodwinds have the appoggiaturas written in, which, according to the rule, ought to receive two thirds of the

value of the dotted note. The vocal part has no appoggiaturas at all. For this reason and unless one dares to put the appoggiaturas also in the voice line, they should be executed like eighth notes (one third of the value of the main note). This will not distort the melodic pattern.

Albert Schweitzer says: "The more one studies the inner meaning of Bach's appoggiatura the more one understands that the real value of the note itself makes no difference and that the importance lies only in the loudness of the appoggiatura and the accent on it." This sounds to me like the best definition of Bach's appoggiaturas. One word only about Bach's passing appoggiaturas. They are always comparatively short and, though not played on the beat, accentuated (Fig. 141).

Figure 141. Example of Bach's passing appoggiatura

It seems certain that Handel's appoggiaturas in concerted numbers should be executed in approximately the same way as Bach's. Since Handel's operas and oratorios are written in a richer baroque style and contain more Italianisms, one need not be quite so strict with his appoggiaturas as with Bach's more linear and northern works. A sentimental, sweet style has, however, wormed its way into Handel's church oratorios, especially in the Anglo-Saxon churches, by way of playing and singing appoggiaturas in every possible place. I cannot warn enough against this ugly distortion.

Christoph Willibald Gluck's appoggiaturas belong more to the classic than to the baroque. He uses all kinds, though he notates them rather sloppily. A. Beyschlag, in his *Die Ornamentik in der Musik*, advises us to treat most of Gluck's appoggiaturas in concertante pieces in a short manner. I do not see the necessity for it. You will have to decide for yourself which is the right one for a given phrase. Let us take a few examples from Gluck's operas.

In No. 7 of *Orfeo* the beginning is sung as shown in Figure 142 while the violins have the passage notated as shown in Figure 143. There can be no doubt about

Chia - mo il mio ben co - si.   Quan - do si mo-stra il dí.

Figure 142. Gluck, *Orfeo*, passage as sung

Figure 143. Gluck, *Orfeo*, same passage for violins

the execution. "Che farò senza Euridice" has the one-third-value appoggiatura on "dove andrò senza il mio ben." We find here a favorite of Gluck's, the appoggiatura from below. The two-thirds-value traditional appoggiatura appears, for instance, in the passage from *Alceste* shown in Figure 144. In the orchestra, the same passage reads as in Figure 145. Short appoggiaturas are frequently employed (see Fig. 146).

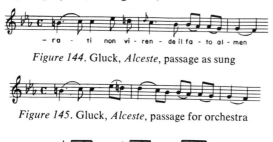

Figure 144. Gluck, *Alceste*, passage as sung

Figure 145. Gluck, *Alceste*, passage for orchestra

Figure 146. A. Short appoggiatura. B. Usual execution. C. Incorrect execution

Before discussing in detail the appoggiaturas of our masters of the classic and romantic period, I must mention here the great surprise — yes, even shock — that I got from studying what the theoreticians had to say about appoggiaturas before dotted notes. Quantz, Philipp Emanuel Bach, Leopold Mozart, D. G. Türk — all without exception give the appoggiatura *two thirds* of the dotted note, one third only where the wrong harmony would otherwise result. Even Johann Nepomuk Hummel, who wrote his *Anweisung* about forty years after Türk's book, still gives the two-thirds theory. While studying Mozart's and the other classical composers' appoggiaturas in the light of the two-thirds theory, I was about to revise my whole concept of the classical appoggiaturas and to abjure what I had learned from my teachers and the whole performance style of my formative years, when I read the remarks of J. A. Hiller about the appoggiaturas before dotted notes. Hiller was a composer, music teacher, and writer, a contemporary of Haydn and Mozart. In his *Anweisung zum musikalisch richtigen Gesang*, published in 1774 and 1780, he says that the appoggiatura before a dotted note "nowadays" *frequently* receives the value of one third of the main note instead of the two thirds of the earlier period. Here, finally, was proof of the correctness of my musical education in this respect. All the questionable pieces now fell into place. Hiller, who wrote some early German Singspiel-type operas that pleased no less a man than

Goethe, was more modern in his theory than the whole array of famous theoreticians who in all probability copied from one another. Likewise, Muzio Clementi, in his *Introduction to the Art of Playing the Pianoforte*, published in 1801, gives the versions shown in Figure 147.

Figure 147. Clementi's two versions (B, C) of appoggiatura before a dotted note (A)

Figure 148. Mozart, *Die Zauberflöte*, passage for violins

Figure 149. Mozart, *Die Zauberflöte*, same passage for voice

Now, suddenly, one direct proof for the one-third-value theory did not appear as an illogical exception but fitted into the over-all picture. I am speaking about the spot in the first-act Finale of Mozart's *Die Zauberflöte*, where the violins have the notes written out (Fig. 148), while the voice line has the appoggiatura (Fig. 149). This dots the *i* on the question of appoggiaturas before dotted notes and definitely establishes the one-third-value theory for our classicist masters.

APPOGGIATURAS IN CONCERTANTE PIECES OF HAYDN, MOZART, BEETHOVEN, AND WEBER

Outside of those in recitatives, appoggiaturas in our classicist composers' works are not common. Haydn had already begun to abolish the notation of long appoggiaturas as embellishments. In a very interesting letter to his publisher Artaria, Haydn explains how a certain appoggiatura (Fig. 150A) should be executed (Fig.

Figure 150. Haydn's explanation (B) of the playing of a certain appoggiatura (A)

150B). And this is the way that many of Schubert's appoggiaturas are to be played. The other masters of of the classicist school also made use of this kind of appoggiatura. In general, Haydn's appoggiaturas are not different from Mozart's. We may assume that in his youth Mozart's execution of appoggiaturas followed the directions his father gave in the *Thorough School for the Violin.* Later on, Mozart's appoggiaturas assumed different meanings. Let's take his *Nozze di Figaro*, for instance. In the concerted numbers there are very few appoggiaturas in the orchestral parts, mostly of the kinds shown in Figure 151. They are to be played as

Figure 151. Mozart, *Le Nozze di Figaro*, appoggiaturas from concerted numbers

four even sixteenth or eighth notes. Sometimes Mozart uses short appoggiaturas in the orchestral parts, as, for instance, in No. 17, measure 17 and following, or in No. 18 (Sextet), measure 25 and following, both times in the violins. A very piquant combination of short and long appoggiaturas appears in the Fandango (Fig. 152).

Figure 152. Mozart, *Le Nozze di Figaro*

I have heard these measures executed with short appoggiaturas only, which sounded very strange, to say the least, and is, of course, not in accord with Mozart's intention; he uses the formula of four even sixteenth notes over and over again.

Appoggiaturas in vocal arioso lines appear very seldom. Mozart writes them out sometimes, as in Susanna's aria No. 27 on the words "notturna face." In the same aria, there are two genuine long appoggiaturas (Fig. 153), which must be executed as two sixteenth notes, and at the very end (Fig. 154), a passage where the

Figure 153. Mozart, *Le Nozze di Figaro*

Figure 154. Mozart, *Le Nozze di Figaro*

appoggiatura gets a third of the value of the main note and has to be sung *on* the fourth beat. Appoggiaturas in concerted numbers in *Don Giovanni* should be handled in the same fashion. In the duet No. 2, the "te" of Ottavio's "Che vive sol per te" (Fig. 155A) must be sung as shown in Figure 155B. In the No. 7 duet, the appoggiatura (Fig. 156A) in "mi trema un poco il cor" must be sung as shown in Figure 156B. But later, Don Giovanni's "andiam" (Fig. 157) must be sung as two

Figure 155. Mozart, *Don Giovanni.* A. Appoggiatura as written. B. Appoggiatura as it should be sung

Figure 156. Mozart, *Don Giovanni.* A. Appoggiatura as written. B. Appoggiatura as it must be sung

Figure 157. Mozart, *Don Giovanni*

eighth notes. In No. 13, Zerlina's aria, all appoggiaturas before dotted notes receive the one-third value. Similarly in No. 24, Elvira's aria.

The situation becomes somewhat more involved in *Die Zauberflöte.* Since there are no secco recitatives, appoggiaturas, with the exception of the great accompagnato recitative of Tamino and the Priest, appear only in concerted numbers. This is because *Die Zauberflöte* is a genuine German opera as compared with Mozart's earlier Italian-style operas. Let us take Pamina's aria as an example. The very beginning "Ach, ich fühl's" creates a real problem. If the passage shown in Figure 158 were sung according to the rule, as two straight

Figure 158. Mozart, *Die Zauberflöte*

sixteenth notes, the effect would be very dry and unemotional. If, on the other hand, "fühl's" is treated as two eighth notes, which would match the following phrase ending, the eighth rest would become unnecessary and Mozart undoubtedly would have written out the appoggiatura. In my performances, I have this appoggiatura executed by a slight portamento, which lengthens the small note to a point just short of an eighth note and shortens the main note to a point just a little shorter than a sixteenth note. Similarly with the words "hin" and "allein." In Tamino's aria (No. 3), the appoggiaturas before the dotted notes assume one third the value of the main notes, as do those in No. 4 (aria of the Queen of the Night). The same in Sarastro's aria (No. 15) except that eighth notes take the place of sixteenths. The appoggiatura (Fig. 159) in Pamina's solo line in

Figure 159. Mozart, *Die Zauberflöte*

No. 21 is, of course, sung as two quarter notes. The pattern stays the same for the rest of the opera.

Of Mozart's songs let me mention only "Das Veilchen" (Fig. 160) as another example of the one-third-value theory. Mozart's short appoggiaturas are mostly executed as if they were long.

Figure 160. Mozart, "Das Veilchen"

Beethoven used all kinds of appoggiatura. In his song "An Die Hoffnung" we find additional support for the one-third-value theory before dotted notes. Though the vocal line reads as shown in Figure 161, the accompaniment is as shown in Figure 162. In his song "Feuerfarb," the appoggiatura (Fig. 163A) must be executed as shown in Figure 163B, to parallel the accompaniment. His song "Neue Liebe, neues Leben" (Fig. 164) con-

Figure 161. Beethoven, "An die Hoffnung," vocal line

Figure 162. Beethoven, "An die Hoffnung," accompaniment

Figure 163. Beethoven, "Feuerfarb," appoggiatura as written (A) and as sung (B)

Figure 164. Beethoven, "Neue Liebe, neues Leben," "classical" appoggiatura as written (A) and as sung (B)

tains the classical appoggiatura — two-thirds value before dotted notes; this is also clear in the accompaniment. In *Fidelio* there is another one-third appoggiatura in the Trio No. 5 at the words "Ich gab die Hand" and at corresponding places later in the same number; the orchestral part has the notes written out. In Florestan's aria No. 11, at the words "Wahrheit wagt ich kühn zu sagen," the appoggiatura is written and played as shown in Figure 165, as in the majority of Schubert's songs (see p. 151). The finale (No. 16) of *Fidelio* contains the appoggiatura shown in Figure 166, which must be exe-

Figure 165. Beethoven, *Fidelio*, appoggiatura as written (A) and played (B)

Figure 166. Beethoven, *Fidelio*, appoggiatura as written

Figure 167. Beethoven, *Fidelio*, appoggiatura as it should be played

cuted short but accented, approximately as shown in Figure 167.

A few of Weber's appoggiaturas must be played in the style of Schubert. This means that the appoggiatura assumes the full value of the main note, which is actually eliminated. Proof of this may be found in Kaspar's Song in *Der Freischütz*. At the words "die Rache gelingt" the orchestra plays as shown in Figure 168A, while the voice line reads as shown in Figure 168B.

Figure 168. Weber, *Der Freischütz*. A. Orchestral part. B. Appoggiatura in voice line

Weber also makes good use of the short appoggiaturas. The famous Horn Quartet in the Hunting Chorus (No. 15) of *Der Freischütz* has short appoggiaturas. The horns imitate hunting sounds. It must have been difficult to play these appoggiaturas short on the technically limited horns of Weber's times. Therefore, the appoggiaturas were, and sometimes still are, done long. In the old chorus parts of the Berlin Royal Opera House that were used in Weber's time these appoggiaturas are notated long. But short appoggiaturas much better depict the intended idea. The traditionally long appoggiaturas may

Figure 169. Weber, *Euryanthe*, passing appoggiaturas as written (A) and executed (B)

still be found in Agathe's aria on the words "auf zum Sternenkreise" and "Himmelshalde." In *Euryanthe*, passing appoggiaturas, in spite of their notation (Fig. 169A) should be executed as if they were sixteenth notes (Fig. 169B).

Weber is the last of the great composers to write long appoggiaturas consistently. Starting with Mendelssohn and Berlioz they gradually vanish from musical script, although even Verdi uses them on rare occasions — for instance, in *Aïda*. Franz Schubert's appoggiaturas are so varied that they deserve a special chapter. His songs, which are among the basic requirements for any accompanist and coach, can tolerate no misunderstanding with respect to the execution of his appoggiaturas.

APPOGGIATURAS IN RECITATIVES

Appoggiaturas in recitatives are the most difficult problem in all ornamentation. In the beginning of Italian operatic music, they were never indicated. It was assumed that singers would execute them at their own discretion, and they were sung from above, from below — at all kinds of intervals. Even in Mozart's time and later in Donizetti's and Rossini's operas, they were made in almost all possible and impossible places. Telemann left us a set of very good formulas for recitative appoggiaturas in his *Harmonischer Gottesdienst*, published in 1725. Some of his tables kept their validity for more than a century; some became archaic rather quickly. With the exception of Johann Christian Bach's recitatives, Telemann's tables are a good mirror of the performance style of the times. Gluck took great care to mark appoggiaturas in his works; we will not go wrong if we avoid appoggiaturas in his recitatives unless they are strongly demanded by reasons of expression, or occasionally in phrase endings, when intervals of a third are involved.

When I now propose my own way of handling the recitative appoggiaturas, it will be good to consider what I said about the innate style, original performance style, and present performance style. The problem is easiest to solve in the case of Johann Sebastian Bach's recitatives. He usually wrote out the appoggiaturas where he wanted them; therefore, do not change any of Bach's recitatives by putting in appoggiaturas. I have already discussed the exaggerated, over-sentimental manner in which Handel's recitatives are generally performed in American churches and concert halls. Take for instance the recitative from the *Messiah* shown in Figure 170. In order to stress the word "people," I would advocate doing the appoggiatura only at the end, taking out the other one, marked with an x. Again, I want to say that the performance style of yesteryear certainly favored all appoggiaturas. But our musical taste at the moment

Figure 170. Handel, *The Messiah*

holds the middle ground between romanticism and purism. During the nineteenth century the taste in performance oscillated between romanticization and complete purism. Southern Europe, including Vienna, stuck to its old way of singing appoggiaturas whenever possible. The North, with Berlin as center, went overboard to abolish them. In my youth the battle in favor of appoggiaturas was led by Franz Schalk and Bruno Walter (who had inherited the performance style from Gustav Mahler), the fight against by Otto Klemperer and Fritz Busch. Erich Kleiber, Fritz Reiner, and George Széll stood between the two camps. This is also my position. I have learned from experience in some of the best opera houses of the world that *expression* is the main justification for or against appoggiaturas. Their use is and will always be a matter of musical taste and culture.

Here is what I think is right; it may be useful for accompanists and coaches.

1. Never make an appoggiatura in secco recitative when the meaning of the phrase or word is heroic, harsh, hard, unbending.

2. Make an appoggiatura in secco recitative when it serves to soften, smooth, or relax the expression, and also in cases of dramatic distress, especially on intervals of a third.

3. Do not execute an appoggiatura in a secco recitative too many times in a row. Save the effect for the end.

4. Make it at the end of a definite cadence or at the end of a secco recitative.

5. Be very careful about making an appoggiatura from a note below. This should be done only in very rare cases when a strong stress or an expression as noted under 2 is indicated.

6. Appoggiaturas in accompagnato recitatives ought to be made only in the rarest cases. Think it over for a long time before you decide to do it — and then, at the last moment, shrink from it. The spots in Mozart's, Beethoven's, and Weber's accompagnato recitatives where an appoggiatura should be made will be noted below.

Beethoven writes out his appoggiaturas in recitatives.

In the few cases where he does not do so, as in the recitative in the last movement of his Ninth Symphony, the meaning becomes clear by comparison with the parallel place in the part of the cellos and double-basses (Fig. 171). This phrase is repeated later by the solo voice, with the last measure as in Figure 172. There is no doubt that Beethoven intended an appoggiatura from above. In *Fidelio* Beethoven uses the accompagnato recitative only in Leonore's great aria. Appoggiaturas there should be avoided, although they undoubtedly were executed in earlier times.

Figure 171. Beethoven, Ninth Symphony

Figure 172. Beethoven, Ninth Symphony

Weber's *Der Freischütz* contains a few recitatives that puzzle us today. Should appoggiaturas be made in places like "O wie hell die goldnen Sterne" or "Dort tönts wie Schritte" in Agathe's aria (No. 11)? I am against it because Weber, as a purely German composer of the northern school, hardly had them in mind. But I know that many musicians will insist on the appoggiaturas.

One word about appoggiaturas in recitatives of Italian opera from Bellini to Verdi. Here the rules are much less strict. I would suggest that appoggiaturas in fast parlando secco recitatives of Rossini's buffo operas should be executed freely. The same holds true for Donizetti's buffo operas. In Bellini's, Donizetti's, and Rossini's serious operas, the appoggiaturas in the recitatives should be done only in cases where artistic taste and musical culture warrant it. No appoggiaturas at all must be executed in Verdi's operas. Wherever he wanted them he indicated them. The old habit, however, was still so strong among singers and conductors that Verdi, in *Rigoletto*, had to state expressly that he did not want any voluntary appoggiaturas. In the recitative after the famous quartet he says: "This recitative must be sung without the usual appoggiaturas." With Verdi the old custom of neglecting to notate appoggiaturas where they were expected to be sung comes to an end.

I shall now give examples of appoggiaturas in accompagnato recitatives in Mozart's operas.

Le Nozze di Figaro

No. 6, Cherubino's aria. Appoggiatura should be done on the *o* of m'oda in "e se non ho chi m'oda."

No. 19, Countess's recitative and aria. Appoggiaturas should be done on the *i* of ardito in "Alquanta ardito il progetto me par," on the *e* of cielo in "O cielo," and on the second *a* of amata in "Prima amata."

No. 22, finale, Count's recitative. Appoggiatura should be done on the *o* of pompa in "Colla più ricca pompa."

No. 26, Figaro's recitative and aria. Appoggiaturas should be done on the *i* of vicina in "l'ora dovrebbe esse vicina," and on the *i* of marito in "a fare il scimunito mestiero di marito."

No. 27, Susanna's recitative and aria. Appoggiaturas should be done on the *i* of mio in "in braccio all' idol mio!" and on the *e* of terra and the *o* of seconda in "l'amenità del loco, la terra e il ciel risponda, come la notte i furti miei seconda!"

Così fan tutte

No. 11, Dorabella's aria. Appoggiatura should be done on the *i* of spiro in "Odio l'aria, che spiro."

No. 27, Ferrando's recitative and aria. Appoggiatura should be done on the first *o* of ritrovo in "io mi ritrovo?"

Don Giovanni

No. 2, Don Ottavio's recitative and duet. Appoggiaturas should be done on the first *o* of tesoro in "Ah! soccorete amici, il mio tesoro," on the second *a* of tardate and the first *a* of Anna in "Ah, non tardate! Donn' Anna," on the *i* of amica in "Sposa! Amica," on the *i* of uccide in "la meschinella uccide," and on the *o* of core in "Fa core." All these appoggiaturas should be made in accordance with the soft aspect of Don Ottavio's character. But when he swears to avenge Donna Anna's father's death ("Lo giuro!"), appoggiaturas should not be made.

No. 11, Donna Anna's recitative and aria. Appoggiaturas should be made on the *a* of coraggio on Don Ottavio's "Mio bene, fate coraggio!" and on the *o* of sciolsi in Donna Anna's "Da lui mi sciolsi."

No. 23, Donna Elvira's recitative and aria. Appoggiatura should be made on the *a* of nasce in "che contrasto d'affetti in sen mi nasce!"

No. 25, Donna Anna's recitative and aria. Appoggiatura should be made on the first *e* of "Crudele?"

Die Zauberflöte

No. 8, recitative of Tamino and the High Priest. Appoggiaturas should be done on the *a* of Knaben in "Die

Weisheitslehre dieser Knaben," the *ä* of näher in "Erklär dich näher mir," and the *e* of bewiesen in "Durch ein unglücklich Weib bewiesen."

SCHUBERT'S APPOGGIATURAS

Schubert notated appoggiaturas when he wanted them; no appoggiatura ought to be made in his works when it is not expressly written. Confusion sets in only when the question arises of how his appoggiaturas ought to be sung. They follow the tradition of the eighteenth century, meaning that they are usually long, even when Schubert notates them as sixteenth notes. Mozart used to write them as shown in Figure 173A, which was exe-

Figure 173. Mozart's and Schubert's appoggiaturas

cuted as shown in Figure 173B. Schubert's copyists changed his "B" appoggiatura back to "A," the sign in use before Schubert's time, a custom that has given rise to problems in our time. How should a given appoggiatura be performed? "A" or "B" forms in Schubert's printed songs are almost always long. An exception is made when a "B" form stands before a triplet: then the "B" turns into a "C" (short appoggiatura). In his song "Morgengruss," for instance, the appoggiatura written as shown at the left in Figure 174 must be executed as

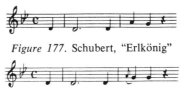

Figure 174. Schubert, "Morgengruss," appoggiatura as written (left) and as executed (right)

shown at the right. There are other exceptions which become evident through comparison with repeats of the same phrases in the vocal or accompaniment line. The list of songs with appoggiaturas of different kinds given a little further along will deal with these exceptions. But it is the long appoggiatura that interests us most here. The same notation is executed in several different ways. For each of the four kinds of appoggiatura discussed below, I shall give examples taken from Max Friedländer's edition of the first volume of Schubert's songs. The rules may be applied to the appoggiaturas in the other volumes as well.

The first kind of appoggiatura. If the appoggiatura stands above or below two notes of the same pitch, the second of which is unaccented, it takes the place of the first note, assuming its full value. This is an old rule

that had already appeared in Philipp Emanuel Bach's standard work of the eighteenth century. We may be absolutely sure about this interpretation of the appoggiatura in Schubert's songs. Franz Lachner, composer, conductor, and close friend of Schubert, died as late as 1890 and was able to give us a lot of information about the performance style of Schubert's works. Among his observations the one important to us here is that Schubert himself sang the appoggiaturas in his songs almost always as I have described them here. But beyond the testimony of Lachner, Schubert himself has given us uncontestable proof. In his piano introduction to "Frühlingstraum" he writes the passage shown in Figure 175, and a little later, in the voice line, the passage in Figure 176. There is no other reason for his substituting the appoggiatura than that singers and accompanists knew exactly what was meant and were able to execute it correctly.

Figure 175. Schubert, "Frühlingstraum," piano introduction

Figure 176. Schubert, "Frühlingstraum," vocal line

Another striking example of the execution of Schubert's appoggiatura may be found in his different versions of the "Erlkönig." In this song, which he set to music several times until it suited his artistic conscience, he wrote out the appoggiatura in one version (Fig. 177) while the same measure in another version is notated as shown in Figure 178.

Figure 177. Schubert, "Erlkönig"

Figure 178. Schubert, "Erlkönig," another version

This first kind of appoggiatura may also stand in front of two notes of which the first is a long dotted note. Then the appoggiatura assumes the full value of the dotted note. In some isolated cases where expression may warrant it, this kind of appoggiatura may be sung by connecting the appoggiatura with the following note by slight portamento, the following note assuming a short dotted value. Take, for example, the appoggiatura in Schubert's song "Die Krähe." It may be done in the usual

Figure 179. Schubert, "Die Krähe"

Figure 180. Schubert, "Frühlingstraum"

Figure 181. Schubert, "Frühlingstraum"

way, eliminating the first note after it, but it also may be justifiable to sing it with a slight portamento (Fig. 179).

The song "Frühlingstraum" serves as another example of how an exception to the rule may be made if likeness to a phrase before or after the one which contains the appoggiatura warrants it. The first appoggiatura, by analogy with the melody two measures before, should be of type 1, while four measures later the same appoggiatura should be executed as two sixteenth notes, conforming with the slight change of the melodic line two measures before (Fig. 180). Another interesting exception appears in the "Erlkönig." The line "er hat den *Kna*ben wohl in dem Arm" should be sung as shown in Figure 181 because of the pattern of the melody throughout the first part. The heavy beat always falls on a long note.

Examples of the First Kind of Appoggiatura

"Die Wetterfahne." Er hätt' es *eher* bemerken *sollen*.

"Gefrorne Tränen." Ei *Tränen*, meine *Tränen*.

"Erstarrung." Ich will den Boden *küssen* / Wo find ich eine *Blüte*.

"Auf dem Fluss." Ob's unter seiner *Rinde*.

"Irrlicht." Wie ich einen Ausgang *finde*. Jeder Strom wirds Meer gewinnen.

"Rast." Es war zu kalt zum *Stehen*.

"Frühlingstraum." Ich träumte von bunten *Blumen* / Da war es kalt und *finster*. / Ich träumte von Lieb um

Liebe. / Nun sitz ich hier al*eine* / Noch *schlägt das* Herz so warm (first time).

"Einsamkeit." Ach, dass die Luft so *ruhig*.

"Der greise Kopf." Und hab mich sehr ge*freuet*. / Wie weit noch bis zur *Bahre*!

"Die Krähe." *Krähe*, wunderliches Tier, willst mich nicht ver*lassen*? / *Meinst wohl* bald als Beute hier meinen Leib zu *fassen*.

"Letzte Hoffnung." Spielt der Wind mit meinem *Blatte*.

"Im Dorfe." Tun sich im Guten und Argen er*laben*; / Und morgen früh ist alles zer*flossen* / Wiederzufinden auf ihren *Kissen*. / Ihr wachen *Hunde*, / Mit allen *Träumen* (by analogy).

"Erlkönig." Er fasst ihn *sicher*. / Dem Vater *grauset's* / Er hält in *Armen*.

"Lob der Tränen." Was die Sinnen nur ge*winnen* / Wie vom Regen Blumen *pflegen* (the same in the following stanzas).

"Sei mir gegrüsst." Mit meiner Seele glühendstem Er*gusse* / In dieses Arms Um*schlusse*.

"Ave Maria." Sieh der Jungfrau *Sorgen* / O *Mutter*, hör ein bittend Kind! Der Jungfrau wolle hold dich *neigen*.

"Lied der Mignon." Es brennt mein Einge*weide*.

"Rastlose Liebe." So viel Freuden des Lebens er*tragen*. / Alles, alles ver*gebens*!

"Schäfers Klagelied." Ich breche sie ohne zu *wissen*, / Die Türe dort bleibt ver*schlossen*.

"An die Musik." Zu warmer Lieb ent*zunden* / Den Himmel bessrer Zeiten mir ent*schlossen*.

"Ganymed." Deiner ewigen *Wärme*.

"An die Nachtigall." Er liegt und schläft an meinem *Herzen*.

"Das Rosenband." Da band ich sie mit Rosen*bändern*!

The second kind of appoggiatura. Some appoggiaturas, above or below a repeated or an unrepeated note, do not take the place of the first note, but are connected with it, always starting *on* the beat. It is not easy to decide when this should be done. Melodic patterns and vocal phrasing will always be the deciding factors.

In "Des Baches Wiegenlied," the phrase "bis das Meer will trinken die Bächlein aus," is first written with appoggiatura, and right afterwards without it (Fig. 182), changing the sixteenth appoggiatura quarter note and the following note into two even eighths. In "Der Neugierige," the words "ein Wörtchen um und um" are

Figure 182. Schubert, "Des Baches Wiegenlied," phrase with appoggiatura (above) and without (below)

Figure 183. Schubert, "Der Neugierige," phrase with appoggiatura

Figure 184. Schubert, "Der Neugierige," appoggiatura as it should be sung

repeated, first with appoggiatura (Fig. 183), then without it. This second phrase should be sung as four even sixteenth notes. The reason for this way of notating lies in the fact that the F sharp which Schubert wanted on the heavy beat does not belong to the harmonic structure of the chord and is for this reason less objectionable if notated as an appoggiatura. It should therefore be sung as shown in Figure 184.

Examples of the Second Kind of Appoggiatura

"Wohin." Und immer heller der *Bach.*

"Danksagung an den Bach." Dein *Sing*en, dein Kling-en / Für die *Hän*de, fürs Herze.

"Der Neugierige." Ein *Wört*chen um und um.

"Mein." Unverstanden in der weiten Schöpfung *sein.*

"Pause." Da wird mir so *bang*e.

"Des Baches Wiegenlied." Bis das Meer will *trin*ken die Bächlein aus.

"Gefrorne Tränen." Aus der Quelle der *Brust* so glühend heiss.

"Erstarrung." Ich such im *Schnee* vergebens nach ihrer *Tri*tte Spur, / Wo find ich grünes *Gras*? / Soll denn kein *A*ngedenken ich nehmen *mit* von hier? / Wenn meine *Schmerz*en schweigen, / Ihr *Bild* dahin (end of song).

"Auf dem Flusse." Mit einem spitzen *Stein* / Den Tag, an dem ich *ging.*

"Frühlingstraum." Wer *mal*te die Blätter da? (second time) / Noch *schlägt* das Herz so warm (second time).

"Einsamkeit." Ach, dass die Welt so *licht!*

"Täuschung." Dass es verlockt den *Wand*ersmann. / Nur Täuschung ist für *mich* Gewinn!

"Das Wirtshaus." Nur weiter, mein treuer *Wander*-stab!

"Der Wanderer." Ich komme vom Gebirge *her.*

"Lob der Tränen." Reihentanz und Spiel und *Scherz* / Löscht es jede wilde *Glut!* (the same in following stanzas).

"Frühlingsglaube." Nun, armes *Herz,* vergiss der Qual!

"Jägers Abendlied." Da schwebt so licht dein liebes *Bild.*

"An die Musik." Hast mich in eine bessre Welt ent-*rückt,* / Du holde Kunst, ich danke dir da*für.*

"Litanei." Die vollbracht ein banges *Quäl*en.

The third kind of appoggiatura. If the appoggiatura stands in front of an unrepeated dotted note, it is usually treated as a long note assuming either a third or two thirds of the dotted note. "An die Musik" illustrates this

Figure 185. Schubert, "An die Musik"

kind of execution of the appoggiatura (Fig. 185). In this case the appoggiatura should take a third of the value of the note following.

Examples of the Third Kind of Appoggiatura

"An die Musik." In *wie*viel grauen Stunden, / Oft hat ein Seufzer, *dei*ner Harf' entflossen.

The fourth kind of appoggiatura. There are times when Schubert wanted an appoggiatura to be short; this depends upon the tempo, the passage in question, and

Figure 186. Schubert, "Wohin"

the mood of the phrase. In Schubert's "Wohin," the appoggiatura "ich musste auch *hin*unter" is short, in keeping with the fast tempo and the sixteenth notes before which it stands (Fig. 186).

Examples of the Fourth Kind of Appoggiatura

"Wohin." Ich musste auch *hin*unter / Es singen wohl *die* Nixen / Mir *ganz* berauscht den Sinn.

"Halt!" Wilkommen, süsser *Mühl*engesang!

"Ungeduld." Accompaniment, third measure.

"Morgengruss." Als wär dir *was* geschehen!

"Tränenregen." Wir sassen so *trau*lich beisammen.

"Die Post." Mein *Herz*, mein Herz.

"Das Wirtshaus." Allhier will ich *ein*kehren.

"Der Leiermann." First two measures of the accompaniment.

"Lob der Tränen." Reihentanz und *Spiel* und Scherz / Löscht es jede *wil*de Glut (the same in following stanzas).

"An die Nachtigall." Mein *gu*ter Schutzgeist.

"Liebe schwärmt auf allen Wegen." Aufgesucht *will* Treu*e* sein (by analogy with the triplet of the same word appearing earlier).

I have already mentioned that an appoggiatura before a triplet is always short. An unusual appoggiatura appears in "Frühlingsglaube." The best way of singing it seems to be to execute it as the first note of a quintole, starting on the beat (on the words "alles wenden") (Fig. 187). Although the execution of appoggiaturas in

Figure 187. Schubert, "Frühlingsglaube"

Schubert's compositions is not so complex as in Mozart's works it will be well to close this part of the current chapter with the words of Max Friedländer, the foremost authority on Schubert's songs, from the foreword to his edition of them: "The instances in which complete clarity reigns as to how the appoggiaturas should be executed do not constitute a majority. Rather one must resign oneself to leaving the execution to the musical taste of singers and pianists." It is interesting to note that the "Schwanengesang" does not contain a single appoggiatura. This, Schubert's last work, was written at a time when the appoggiatura had already become a thing of the past. From then on, the composers' intentions were much clearer, owing to the abolishment of the old-fashioned appoggiatura.

THE TRILL

The other ornaments can be treated only insofar as they concern us today, and at that only perfunctorily; otherwise this book could not continue beyond the chapter about ornamentation. When in doubt, the accompanist and coach will have to consult special works about ornaments, some of which are mentioned in the

bibliography. The most frequently encountered ornament is the trill or shake. Notated in Johann Sebastian Bach's manuscript (see Fig. 136, p. 144) as shown in A, B, C, and D of Figure 188, it usually started with the upper note, a half or a whole step above the main note. "B" or "D" meant that no Nachschlag (termination) was intended; "E," on the other hand, made one necessary, as shown, for example, in Figure 189. The

Figure 188. Notations for the trill or shake

Figure 189. Trill with Nachschlag

notation shown in Figure 188A was ambiguous, and left the question of the Nachschlag open: the musician had to decide from the context what was right. The trill in Bach's time was played less rapidly than today: the single notes were hardly faster than thirty-seconds — often slower. The best definition, indeed a very modern one, of the speed at which trills ought to be performed is given by Quantz: "All the shakes must not be made with the same speed. One must consider not only the place where one practises, but where the performance will take place. The echo of a large hall will confuse the movement of the shake and it may become blurred. If, on the contrary, one plays in a small, stuffy room, where the auditors are very near, a rapid shake will be better than a slow one. Besides one must make a difference according to the piece played and not confuse everything as so many people do. In a sad piece, the shake should be slow: but more rapid in a merry one."

Quantz also says that the speed of a shake depends on the ability of the musical instrument to execute it: a soprano voice or a violin will trill faster than a bass voice or a violoncello; organ trills in the lower register will always have to be done slower than shakes on the pianoforte. Furthermore, trills before ascending notes should be made with a Nachschlag; trills before descending notes do not warrant one. A. Beyschlag finds that Handel's shakes started on the main note because of the Italian influence on his writing. Gluck's trill always started with the main note unless he notated it as shown in Figure 190. Frequently his trills had no Nachschlag.

Figure 190. Gluck's trill not beginning on the main note

Around 1800, the trill beginning with the main note became the universal rule if not notated as above. Hummel in 1820 and Spohr in 1832 were very outspoken about this rule. Haydn's shake started with the main note, otherwise he wrote the upper note separately as shown in Figure 191. In such a case as Gabriel's solo in "Die Schöpfung" (Fig. 192), where the trill serves as an illustration of the cooing of the doves, the tempo will not allow for more than a short shake (Pralltriller). Mozart's trill followed Haydn's example closely. He usually notated the Nachschlag when he wanted it executed.

Figure 191. Haydn's trill not beginning on the main note

girrt   das   zar - te   Tau - ben-paar

Figure 192. Haydn, "Die Schöpfung"

Figure 193. Beethoven, Violin Concerto

Beethoven wanted his trills to start with the upper note, but in his works we can find many spots where he contradicted himself. In the third movement of his Violin Concerto, for instance, the trill must definitely start on the main note and is to be executed with Nachschlag (Fig. 193). Beethoven's famous chains of trills are usually played without Nachschlag unless he marked them otherwise. Weber's and Schubert's trills and other ornaments are not perceptibly different from Beethoven's shakes.

THE SHORT SHAKE (PRALLTRILLER OR SCHNELLER) AND THE MORDENT

The Pralltriller as well as the Schneller has as symbol ◆. Although Bach uses this sign for both a trill and a short shake downwards, beginning with the upper neighboring note, composers after him have restricted it to a half shake with the upper whole or half step (Fig. 194). When this embellishment is supposed to be done with the lower neighboring note the sign is as shown in Figure 195; it is called a *mordent*. It becomes clear from the above that the two signs still meant the same in Philipp Emanuel Bach's time. The difference was that the Pralltriller could be used only on descending seconds (Fig. 196), the mordent on ascending seconds (Fig. 197).

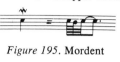

Figure 194. Half shake with upper whole or half step

Figure 195. Mordent

Figure 196. Pralltriller

Figure 197. Mordent

The differentiation shown in Figure 198 was made later. The difference between Pralltriller and Schneller lies in the fact that the Pralltriller starts on the note over which it is written. The execution of the Schneller, on the other hand, starts before the note over which it is written.

Figure 198. Later differentiation between Pralltriller and mordent

The tempo of these Pralltrillers and mordents in the baroque age was always fast, since not too much agility of the fingers was required to execute them. The accent always fell on the first note of the embellishment, not on the termination. Later on, however, they became means of expression, and the context in which they stood was decisive for their execution. Mozart does not use the signs; he always writes out the music. While these embellishments were usually played or sung before the beat, there are cases when their execution seems to warrant slower speed and beginning on the beat. For instance, the expression of Elsa's serene thankfulness, as she tells her happiness to the night air (in *Lohengrin*) will gain from execution of the Pralltrillers, written out in this case, on the words "ihr lächeltet der Fahrt" and "hab' ich euch oft gemüht," in a relaxed tempo. These expressive embellishments should also be started *on the* beat.

THE TURN

In Bach's times the turn was executed starting on the upper neighboring note. Its tempo was directly dependent on the speed of the music. In an adagio it would

Figure 199. Adagio turn, starting on upper neighboring note, in Bach's time

be executed as shown in Figure 199. In a vivace it would sound like four equal sixteenth notes. If a composer wanted to start the turn with the principal note he would have to notate as shown in Figure 200. A turn which was to start with the lower neighboring note had to be notated with the sign inverted (Fig. 201). The turn sign was also sometimes used in a vertical position.

Figure 200. Turn of Bach's time, starting on the principal note

Figure 201. Turn of Bach's time, starting on lower neighboring note

Haydn was very much concerned about the notation of his turns. In a letter to his publishers he demands that they be set correctly: as in Figure 202 (left) if he intended it to start with the upper neighboring note, and as in Figure 202 (right), after the note, when the main note was to be sounded first. In phrases with dotted

Figure 202. Haydn's turns, beginning with upper neighboring note (left) and with main note (right)

Figure 203. Haydn turn on dotted note, as written (left) and as executed (right)

Figure 204. Mozart, Don Giovanni, turn as written (above) and as sung (below)

notes (Fig. 203, left), the turn assumes triplet character (Fig. 203, right), as for instance in Mozart's Don Giovanni No. 25 (Donna Anna). The turns are to be sung as triplets on the words "Tu conosci la mia fè" (Fig. 204). Usually, however, Mozart wrote out his turns, except in some of his early piano solos.

In Beethoven's "Adelaide" the turn should actually **stand over the E natural** (Fig. 205, above). The only

Figure 205. Beethoven, "Adelaide," passage as written (above) and two possible executions (below)

possible executions are shown in the lower part of Figure 205.

In recent times the kind of turn starting with the lower neighboring note was asked for by Richard Wagner in his *Rienzi* overture, but *not* in his *Tannhäuser* (entrance of the guests), which, according to contemporaries such as Franz Liszt, began with the upper neighboring note. The turns in the orchestra before the words "So stehet auf" and "Nie darf ich hier euch sehen," according to Anton Rubinstein's vocal score, which was made under Wagner's eye, were notated from below. This assertion, however, may easily be contradicted by the known fact that Wagner went through various periods of personal taste, favoring at times one, at times another execution of his embellishments. In the end the decision must be left to the accompanist and coach, or, more likely, to the conductor. In later years Wagner wrote out all embellishments. He kept his predilection for the turn from below, as we find it for instance in *Götterdämmerung* (Fig. 206).

Figure 206. Wagner, *Götterdämmerung*

The turn has run through all stages from pure ornament to innermost means of expression. A very late use of the turn appears in Gustav Mahler's *Das Lied von der Erde* (last movement) (Fig. 207). It is some-

Figure 207. Mahler, *Das Lied von der Erde*

times doubtful at what point between two notes of a melody the turn should be executed. In such a case I advise playing the melody without the turn first and then fitting the turn in where it comes most logically. Figure 208, from Beethoven's Romance in G major for Violin and Orchestra, Opus 40, will provide us with **an example.**

Figure 208. Beethoven, Romance in G major, as written (above) and as it should be played (below)

THE SLIDE (SCHLEIFER)

The slide was notated as shown at the left in Figure 209 in the old musical script of Johann Sebastian Bach, but was always written out later. Its execution starts always *before* the beat (at the right in Fig. 209). Bach gives us his execution of the slide by writing the passage shown in Figure 210 in the solo violin part of the alto aria "Erbarme dich" in his Matthew Passion, while the voice reads as shown in Figure 211. The slide must be sung on the first syllable of Zähren.

Figure 209. The slide as indicated in Bach's time (left), as written out later (center), and as executed (right)

Figure 210. Bach, St. Matthew Passion, violin passage

mei   ner   Zäh - ren

Figure 211. Bach, St. Matthew Passion, part of same passage for voice

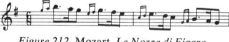

Figure 212. Mozart, *Le Nozze di Figaro*

Figure 213. Beethoven, *The Ruins of Athens*

Handel's and Gluck's slides follow the same rule. The masters of the classical period use the slide quite frequently, always beginning before the beat. Two examples may suffice: the bridal girls' little chorus (No. 21) in *Le Nozze di Figaro* (Fig. 212) and Beethoven's March from *The Ruins of Athens*, which is still frequently used for ballet (Fig. 213).

GERMAN LIED STYLE

Every musical art form springs from humble beginnings and rises to a period of great culture and beauty,

whence it slowly glides back into a more or less moderate existence. In the meantime, another musical art form has found its way to the top. At times several of these art forms may coexist in a high state of perfection. Such a time would be a truly golden age of music, and the classic and romantic period was just such an age. The classicists had perfected the sonata form to an unheard-of degree; their symphonies were the high point of their time. Mozart's Italian and German operas could not be surpassed. The romantic composers brought the German lied to perfection. Their operatic masters invested their work with fairy-tale qualities, mysticism, love of nature, the search for the "blue flower," the folk-like quality. Their symphonies, though not able to fill Beethoven's gigantic footprints, found new ways of expression and grew new branches on the tree of musical creation, culminating in the symphonic works of Brahms, Bruckner, and Mahler.

It must have been sheer delight for the progressive Viennese musiclover of the early nineteenth century to look back to the season of 1814–1815. Haydn's and Mozart's symphonies, Gluck's and Mozart's operas, had become the common property of the general musical public; Beethoven's *Fidelio*, eight of his nine symphonies, all but his last four piano sonatas, all his violin and violoncello sonatas, and all but his last five string quartets had appeared in print or had been performed.

An eighteen-year-old former Viennese choirboy, Franz Schubert, had finished two masses; if the enthusiast wanted to hear them, he had to go on a pilgrimage to a small church in the suburbs. We may assume he liked them and became interested in knowing what else this Franz Schubert had composed: there were songs — as a matter of fact about a hundred fifty of them. Our Viennese musiclover took pains to hear most of them, and Schubert and his friends were only too eager to sing and play them. After hearing Schubert's "Gretchen am Spinnrad" and "Erlkönig" the cultured musiclover could be certain that a new age had dawned. Only a few years later he could even name this age: the age of the "Deutsches Lied."

Up to the season of 1814–1815, musiclovers and amateur and professional singers had not been spoiled by a rich production of songs. True, Haydn, Mozart, and Beethoven had written a number of songs, and the poetry of the great German classicist poets, with Goethe in the lead, had been popularized by Zelter, Zumsteeg, and Reichardt (see also p. 15). But the last three were very careful with their vocal line and their piano accompaniment lest the music overpower the words and rob the lyrics of their beauty. The same was true of Haydn and, up to a point, Mozart. Beethoven, when he put his personality into his music, would reach towering heights; but most of his songs were more or less conventional, written for some wealthy or lovable members of the nobility or the well-to-do bourgeoisie.

I have earlier, however, excepted a few of Mozart's and Beethoven's songs (p. 15). These songs are true predecessors of the German lied and may even be counted among the first representative examples of it. Mozart in "Das Veilchen" is not content to follow the verse pattern of the poem — a cute but not very significant poem, at that, from Goethe's Anacreontic period — but makes a little drama out of it. The music assumes much more than the usual importance, effected by Mozart's avoiding strophic repetition. A little recitative is written into the song, and although the end is reminiscent of the beginning, one cannot speak about a da capo form. The song is clearly "durchkomponiert" (through-composed). We have here another hardly translatable term of great importance to the accompanist and coach who want to understand German lied style. The term may be best got at in the following definition: the continuous musical setting of a song, without the use of strophic, variation, or da capo composition, constantly employing new musical material.

Beethoven's long and very expressive song "Adelaide," composed in 1795, follows no easily recognizable pattern of his time. Mattheson, who wrote the poem, called it a lyrical fantasy. He said that Beethoven's music put his lyrics in a more insignificant position than other, more conventional settings. This could hardly have been meant as a compliment, and shows the point of view of the time, represented principally by Goethe, who did not appreciate Schubert's settings for his poems because they did not merely underline the words but strove to match their quality. I have already mentioned the importance of Beethoven's song cycles to lyrics by Gellert and his "An die ferne Geliebte" (p. 15).

In Franz Schubert we find the amazing phenomenon of a single artist developing a completely new style all by himself, bringing it to a height never since surpassed. It usually takes generations to bring a style to a climax. Schubert, in his six hundred songs, did it all in about fifteen years. Nor did he favor one special pattern of lied style: he mastered them all and used them as he saw

fit. It is generally agreed that Schubert modeled his first songs after songs by Reichardt and ballads by Zumsteeg (see p. 15). This is undoubtedly so. But among his first songs is "Gretchen am Spinnrad," a masterful conception of Gretchen's mind and her growing love for Faust. The minor key presages an unhappy outcome of the adventure. The accompaniment consists of groups of six notes to a half-measure, imitating the motion of the spinning wheel. The bass notes are very definite. The syncopated knocks in the accompaniment between bass and treble may be likened to the recoil of the spinning wheel's axle as well as to Gretchen's irregular heartbeat in her anxiety and her dreams. At the point where the remembrance of Faust's kiss overwhelms her, the constant motion is stopped and a sequence of two diminished seventh chords injects a dissonance into her sensuous dreaming. Slowly, the spinning wheel is put into action again. It purrs on under Gretchen's plaintive words, to end in an almost unconsciously uttered repetition of the beginning. This early lied already shows all of Schubert's mastery in composing the vocal line and the right accompaniment. It shows even more: the complete grasp of the words' meaning, of their underlying, half-hidden psychological background, and of the dramatic situation.

Thus we have established not only Schubert's personal lied style, but also some of the main qualities of the German lied style.

I shall continue to discuss Schubert's and the other lied composers' personal style and, at the end of this chapter, try to find a common denominator for the German lied style. "Gretchen am Spinnrad" is not a strophic song. It is a combination of a varied strophic form with new elements and a coda. We might even call this song *durchkomponiert*. It is clear that such a through-composition leads us away from the classical-objective pattern of strophic composition and right into a romantic-subjective way of subduing the form to the emotion.

At seventeen, Schubert found and founded the romantic lied as one of his principal means of artistic expression. It is true that he returned to the classical manner of composing strophic songs in all stages of his short life; he even changed lyrics to fit the strophic meter when he deemed it proper to do so; but essentially we must regard him as the originator of the romantic song and through him we may call the entire German lied style after him a romantic style.

This does not contradict, by any means, what I said

about Schubert's being a classicist composer as well as a romantic. Schumann's lieder, for instance, would fit only into the romantic category. Schubert's gift of feeling the most subtle nuances of the meaning of the lyrics and his ability to make the meaning clear in his own way make him the first real romantic lied composer. He tells us all that is contained in the lyrics — and even more. He puts into his lieder, his accompaniments, his preludes and his postludes everything hidden behind the words or between the lines. Moreover, he is not obtrusive in putting such inner meaning into music. He chooses the shortest, most modest, most tasteful way. He lifts his accompaniments up to share the vocal lines' importance equally. But he does not give preponderance to the piano part as, for example, Schumann did after him. In this respect — in the moderation and the balance with which he uses his vocal and piano material — he proves himself the classicist he also was. Here we have again his dual position: a romantic in his feelings, a classicist in his application of the golden rule of moderation. Perhaps the best example of his concise style may be found in one of his last songs, "Der Doppelgänger," set to Heine's lyrics. Fitted into some somber chords of a passacaglia or a basso ostinato pattern we find a nostalgic, pessimistic, hopeless outlook on life, on love, on faithfulness, freely recited but in a monotonous, psalmodizing tone which later rises up to a violent accusation. Brahms, the great pessimist, could not have composed a song which would better express the complete futility of human hopes and dreams. This song, written only a few months before Schubert's death, belongs to another lied style pattern: the free, declamatory type.

Schubert created, developed, or used the following lied-style patterns or lied forms for his songs:

1. *The strophic song.* He used this pattern whenever he was able to create a melody whose expression would fit all stanzas of a poem, divergent in mood as they might be. Some of these songs are "Das Wandern," "Ungeduld," "Der Jäger," "Heidenröslein," "Litanei," "Ave Maria." Knowing that some stanzas might be cut by singers or accompanists, he wrote out the whole song without repeats, as for instance in "An die Musik" or "Frühlingsglaube," whenever he wanted to avoid such cuts.

2. *The varied strophic song.* The variation may be recognizable by way of different harmonies, changed piano accompaniment, modulations, added codas, and so on. Schubert used this pattern when strict strophic composition could not express the meaning of the song. Some examples are: "Gute Nacht," "Die Wetterfahne," "Der Lindenbaum," "Im Frühling," "Die Sterne."

3. *Strophic songs with altered last stanza (Abgesang).* When the poetic idea of one stanza is different from that of preceding stanzas and would not fit into a strict strophic form, Schubert composed a new last stanza in the style of what Wagner's Hans Sachs calls an Abgesang. Among such are "Du bist die Ruh," "Die Forelle," "Der Leiermann."

4. *The modified or free strophic song.* This loosely defined term contains all patterns between categories 1 to 3 and the through-composed songs. Usually there is one strophic stanza, after which the song, depending upon its meaning, changes melody, leads somewhere else, but later returns to the strophic stanza. This group includes songs written in two parts, some of which repeat the two parts (ABAB) so that a semblance of strophic pattern is still preserved, as in "Frühlingstraum." It also includes songs written in more than two parts, such as "Wohin," "Der Neugierige," "Gefrorne Tränen," and many many more.

5. *The da capo song.* This pattern is closely related to the arioso type. It has its origin in the old operatic forms, such as Handel's da capo arias. Schubert used this type not for formal reasons but only if the inner content of the lyrics asked for it. Examples are "Der Kreuzzug," "Ihr Bild," "Die Stadt," "Die Liebe hat gelogen."

6. *The through-composed song.* No resemblance to the strophic song is recognizable here. Some of these songs, such as "Die Allmacht," are rather long; some remind us of operatic arioso pieces without da capo pattern such as "Dem Unendlichen," where an aria follows the recitative. Some are written in the form of ballads, the best known of which is the "Erlkönig." Some could be best classified as dramatic scenes, such as "Die junge Nonne," "Nachtstück," or the freely declaimed "Prometheus."

Another way of grouping different kinds of lied styles takes as a basis the relationship between voice line and accompaniment.

1. The vocal line — the melody — dominates the song. The accompaniment gives only the harmonic background. Most strophic songs are constructed in this way.

2. The accompaniment assumes the leading role, and the balance is shifted heavily in the direction of the piano. The accompaniment paints, explains, and illuminates the overt and hidden meaning of the song. The vocal line is

still written in a melodious manner, but it moves freely without formal enchainment. This kind lends itself to being through-composed.

3. The vocal line is more declamatory than musical, giving greater importance to the meaning of the song than to the formal structure of the lyrics, and the accompaniment goes hand in hand with this principle. The over-all impression is one of freedom of form. Schubert was and still is the greatest master of this type. After his death, it was not much favored by other composers until Hugo Wolf revived it, building on the foundation that Schubert had laid.

Altogether, Schubert freed accompaniment from its former limitations; the pianistic requirements grew tremendously as the accompanist assumed full partnership with the singer. In a letter to his brother Ferdinand, Schubert wrote: "The way Vogl sings and I accompany him, we seem to be *one*; such a moment is something quite new, unheard of to the audience."

Voice and accompaniment express the whole gamut of human feelings. Frequently, Schubert used the same thematic or rhythmic elements to paint and to express the same feelings. A very interesting research into these elements of Schubert's personal style was undertaken by Felicitas von Kraus in her *Beiträge zur Erforschung des malenden und poetisierenden Wesens in der Begleitung von Franz Schuberts Liedern*. A few of these elements — horses' hoofbeats, a woodpecker, a cuckoo, and a quail — are shown in Figure 214. Schubert's nightingales sing in a minor key, expressing plaintive longing. Birds' voices are usually represented by repetitions of a motif, most often in the framework of a triad.

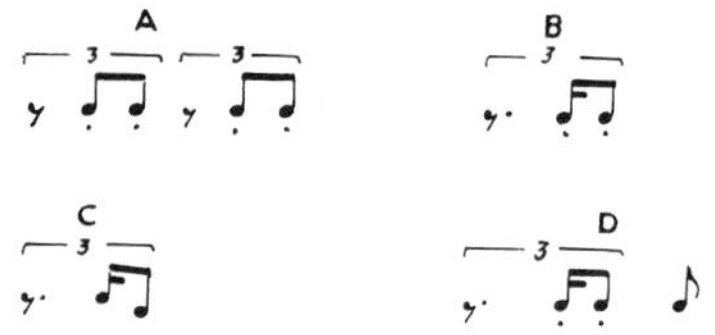

Figure 214. Schubert's representations of horses' hoofbeats (A), woodpecker (B), cuckoo (C), quail (D)

Hunting songs are usually written in 6-8 time ("Jagdlied," "Der Alpenjäger"). Hunting horns or post horns are mostly written in E♭ major ("Ellens Gesang," "Die Post"). Imitations of harps or lyres are usually done by chords in triplets ("An Laura," "Der Liedler") or arpeggios ("Abschied von der Harfe," "Nachtstück," "Liebesend"). Lute imitations are plucked bass and plucked accompaniment in right hand ("Ständchen," "Sprache der Liebe").

In "Dem Unendlichen," Schubert puts the arpeggios of the harp into the right hand, the trombone chords into the left. Bells are imitated in accordance with their imagined size ("Die junge Nonne," "Abendbilder," "Das Heimweh"). Deep bells are sounded in "Romanze."

Gladness is often expressed by chords of the seventh in long note values ("Dem Unendlichen," "Stimme der Liebe"). Sadness, sorrow, depression, and tears are frequently put into music by a downward chromatic movement ("Hagars Klage," "Tränenregen"). Sorrow and nostalgia are many times represented by Schubert's "own" chord, the Neapolitan sixth ("An Mignon," "Des Mädchens Klage," "Wonne der Wehmut," "Die Stadt"). Sadness may also be expressed by altered chords. Heartbeats may be notated as shown in Figure 215, or suggested by syncopation or dotted rhythms. Syncopation is usually the sign of disturbed physical movement or of an inner imbalance. The accompanist and coach will find in Schubert's songs many more musical patterns expressing different thoughts and emotions.

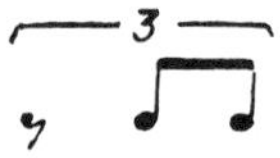

Figure 215. Schubert's notation of heartbeats

The ballad form did not belong exclusively to Schubert. Karl Loewe, whose songs were extremely popular until thirty or forty years ago, is generally considered the master of the form. His "Tom der Reimer," "Archibald Douglas," "Harald," and many other ballads belonged to the permanent repertoire of concert stages, and his "Erlkönig" was considered superior to Schubert's by many critics and writers. Today we do not cherish the ballad form so much as we used to. We search instead for inner qualities in the German lied and we rarely find these in Loewe's ballads. One of them, however, the "Prinz Eugen," strikes us as very forceful; it keeps our interest alive by its use of a genuine 5-4 rhythm.

"He has sounds for the most subtle feelings, thoughts, even happenings, and as human imagination and striving shows itself in a thousand facets, so does his music." These words about Franz Schubert's songs were written by Robert Schumann. Schumann came to appreciate the lied form rather late. At twenty-nine he wrote, "All my life I have put song compositions beneath instrumental music. Never did I think that they were great art." But only a few months later he said in a letter: "I am working exclusively on vocal pieces, big and small ones, even on male vocal quartets. I hardly can tell you what joy it is to write for the voice compared with instrumental compositions and how it rumbles and grumbles in me when I sit at my writing desk."

He did not continue where Schubert left off, but approached the lied from a different direction. He started his composing career with piano pieces, and the sung word did not mean much to him until he fell in love with Clara Wieck. Then his feeling for lyricism bloomed and he created songs that must be counted among the best of the German lieder.

Schumann's style is much more romantic than Schubert's — rooted more in the over-all impression that a poem makes on him than in the inner meanings of the lyrics. He is at his best when he dreams ("Der Nussbaum," "Im wunderschönen Monat Mai"); often losing sight of the metric form, he improvises without knowing where his musical invention will lead him. Always sensitive to pianistic effects, he elevates the accompaniments to a leading position, leaving the vocal part, which interests him less, subservient. On the other hand, he can be hymnically inspired by the mood of a poem ("Widmung"), he falls in love with simple folk tunes ("Volksliedchen"), he feels with the pure mind of a child ("Marienwürmchen"). His sense of humor can sometimes be quite earthy ("Die Soldatenbraut"), sometimes rather unrefined and very typically German ("Wohlauf noch getrunken").

Schumann was lucky to live in the time of Heine's lyrical outpouring. Even if he could not always follow Heine's biting sarcasm and cynicism he completely amalgamated his music with Heine's deeply felt melancholy. Schumann's selection of lyrics, *Dichterliebe*, from Heine's *Buch der Lieder*, has left us with virtually the greatest songs that the height of the romantic period was able to produce. Each song is small, and they are connected by very elaborate piano preludes and postludes that shift the main task of performing to the accompanist. The cyclic lied form is, of course, not Schumann's invention: Beethoven's "An die ferne Geliebte" and Schubert's "Müllerlieder" and "Winterreise" had already paved the way for a synthesis of songs in an ideologically connected unit. Schumann uses related keys to bind the songs to each other. The postlude of the last song of his cycle "Frauenliebe and -leben" is reminiscent of the first song; thus is the chain of romantic emotion linked into one circle.

Of the few ballad types among his compositions, Heine's "Die zwei Grenadiere" impresses us with its somber, through-composed grandeur and the use of the "Marseillaise" to symbolize the dying soldiers' vision of returning French glory.

There can be no doubt that Schumann's contribution to the German lied is most important, largely because he developed the highly romantic, dreamy, improvisatory style and because of his pianistic freedom, expressed mainly in his preludes and postludes. Apart from all differences of form and content, Schubert was an Austrian musician, breathing in every measure of his songs the light and lovely air of the Austrian landscape, whereas Schumann was a Rhenish-Saxon composer, which gave his songs a definite German tinge.

Many lesser stars shine in the sky of German lied composition. Some of them, like Robert Franz, sparkle increasingly with age, and accompanists and coaches would be well advised to familiarize themselves with Franz's songs. Born in the immediate neighborhood of Wagner's birthplace (Halle in central Germany), he lived from 1815 to 1892, survived Wagner, but never fell under his spell. This is in itself quite an achievement and required strong artistic conviction. He also remained independent of Brahms's more introspective, darker colors.

Felix Mendelssohn's lyric star, on the contrary, is on the wane as far as his songs are concerned, and his influence on the development of the German lied style is negligible. Looking backward rather than forward, his songs are beautifully built and contain all the loveliness of his orchestral and instrumental works; but for our hard-bitten age they are too soft, too shallow, and often too sentimental.

Johannes Brahms's pronouncement that the strict strophic song represents the highest form of the lied stamps him as the great conservative who reaches back to Schubert to bring simplicity, even austerity, to his songs. But Brahms was also a tremendous innovator in sensitivity and emotion. One of the greatest objective masters in his musical form, he is also one of the most subjective, individualistic, creative musicians of all ages. This combination has given us some of the most profound songs of the German lied style. A very short song of his (opus 95/5) — only twenty measures long — contains the key to all his musical production. The words are by Halm: "No home, no country, no wife, and no child. I whirl like a feather through storms and through winds! I'm carried by waves, now there and now here. World, if you don't miss me, why should I miss you?" * No biographer could more concisely describe Brahms's psychological makeup. His greatest songs are saturated with resignation, bitterness, pessimism. Even in rare moments of happiness his bliss is hardly ever outgoing: rather it is an almost bashful happiness, a more inward contentedness, a quiet relaxation that can be found in some of his songs, such as "Feldeinsamkeit" or "Geheimnis." Although Brahms was capable of expressing passionate love, as in the "Magelone" romances or in "Wie bist du meine Königin," one does not feel that his passion had an outlet with a resulting happy end. The only example of a really passionately happy song is "Meine Liebe ist grün" to lyrics by Felix Schumann, Robert's youngest son. It may be that the memory of happy hours in Schumann's home, especially with the adored Clara, inspired the song. Brahms's humor follows the same pattern as his seriousness: it can be rough and earthbound, as in "Der Schmied," or tenderly joking as in "Vergebliches Ständchen" or "Therese."

His first important song, "Liebestreu" (opus 3), sets the pattern for his theme of complaint and resignation. His late songs are still variations on the same theme; resignation and foreboding of death have the upper hand. His last songs, the "Vier ernste Gesänge" (opus 121), close the circle. The strange combination of Brahms's northern depth and introspectiveness and the more southern lively outgoing atmosphere of his adopted home, Vienna, give his personality a sharp profile. Not one of his two hundred-odd solo songs fails to mirror his dual personality, not one measure falls short of being unmistakably genuine and honest. Brahms further enriched the German lied by introducing Slavic and Hungarian influences, by his artful arrangements of folk songs, and by his numerous duets and quartet songs.

Musically, Brahms is the most erudite and conscientious composer of songs. One of his principal musical contributions to the German lied style is the thematic and organic connection he established between voice line and accompaniment. Never before had there been so much melodic unity; never before had there been such a mastery of compository technique. One feels, because his style is the most concise of all the great song composers', that Brahms operates with an absolute minimum of musical matter. With his technique of widely spread

out, broken chords in the bass accompaniment (see p. 140) and his hard, stubborn rhythms, he elicits from the modern piano a maximum of sound and variety. Contemporary listeners tell us that Brahms accompanied his songs with strong, sometimes even rough, dynamics. His music, like Beethoven's, reminds one of a continuous fight against the strong resistance of an unseen wall of air, a wall that has to be broken through. Transfer this feeling to your accompaniments, apply inner relaxation for playing his contemplative songs, imbue his lighter songs with his caressing tenderness toward children, and you will have mastered the right style for Brahms's lieder.

With Franz Liszt and Peter Cornelius, the German lied style turns toward Wagner's principles. Wagner himself wrote a few songs — the "Wesendonk Lieder," which are beautiful monuments to his love of Mathilde Wesendonk, and form studies for his operas, especially for *Tristan und Isolde*. Wagner demands complete unity of accents in the spoken and in the sung words; melodic phrases must not continue when the language stops for a caesura or when the declamation asks for interruption. In making these laws, which both his contemporary adherents and later musicians followed, Wagner influenced not only operatic production but also the German lied style for a long time to come. How far this went we shall see in the following section, particularly in the correspondence of Richard Strauss and Romain Rolland on pages 168–169.

Liszt followed Wagner's laws, but he was too internationally inclined to give up writing beautiful melodies even if he did imbue them with a sentimentality that sounds somewhat antiquated to our ears. Such sentimental songs as the "Lorelei," "Es muss ein Wunderbares sein," "Oh, quand je dors," and many others were idolized by the generation at the turn of the century. It is more important to the development of the German lied style that Liszt was influenced to some extent also by Berlioz, thus forming a link between the newly awakening French national style and the German lied.

Cornelius was inspired to his songs by his love for his faraway fiancée. His song cycle *Brautlieder* grew out of this love. In sending the songs to his fiancée, he said: "The poet in me was born in labor pains, the musician has always been a child of sorrow. But now arrived the child of fortune that took the best from the two others and smiled at the world in a free and artistic manner. The result was the poet-musician." Cornelius, though he sat at Wagner's feet, did not lose the simplicity of honest

---

* Kein Haus, keine Heimat, / Kein Weib und kein Kind, / So wirbl' ich, ein Strohhalm, / In Wetter und Wind! / Well' auf und Well' nieder, / Bald dort und bald hier, / Welt, fragst du nach mir nicht, / Was frag' ich nach dir?

emotion. It would pay the accompanist and coach to get acquainted with his songs, especially the *Brautlieder*.

Hugo Wolf is usually described as an outright follower of Wagner's theories of declamation; this is a blatant oversimplification. True, Wolf adored Wagner and Wagner's principles and he hated Brahms and all the conservatism that he detected in Brahms. It is also true that Wolf did not write one line of vocal music that neglects correct declamation in favor of a sweeping melody. But Wolf was much more than a simple imitator of Wagner. He searched for and found new means of expression, audacious new harmonies, new colors for the palette of the German lied style. In the sixty-odd years that lie between Wolf's last songs, the *Michelangelo Sonnets*, and today, his position as a master of the German lied has not been weakened a bit. On the contrary, his stature has grown and he has not been surpassed since then, notwithstanding some great songs by Richard Strauss, Gustav Mahler, and Hans Pfitzner.

Hugo Wolf composed his songs in a few eruptions of productivity interrupted by years of barrenness. He did not choose his lyricists aimlessly. He would take one author at a time — Mörike, Goethe, Eichendorf, Keller, Heyse, or Michelangelo — and dig so deeply into every little nook of his author's style that he was finally able to identify himself completely with the poet's finest inflections of language, meaning, and form. He would then go to work on each song in detail, establishing the rhythm of declamation, the proper accents, and the cadence of speech. During this detailed work, the nucleus of the song was usually created. What remained was for Wolf to find for the whole song the common denominator of a melodic, harmonic, or rhythmic theme or pattern. Finally, he wrote down the song, hardly ever changing it afterwards. The amazing thing in Wolf's creative method is that he was able to completely amalgamate himself with each poet's personal style without losing his own. The *Mörikelieder* and the Spanish and Italian song books are quite different in their musical language and still they all bear Hugo Wolf's personal stamp. Only a most sensitive composer, whose nerve ends remind one of tiny antennae, receiving the written and even the unwritten messages of his poets, could succeed in creating such masterpieces. Wolf's musical diction is above reproach. His articulation marks are less stilted than Wagner's more epic interruptions, his themes or motives usually short. They are repeated many times by the voice, by the accompaniment, in variation, and in

transposition. Thus, he is able to create a kaleidoscopic variety without really possessing the faculty of writing "infinite melodies" such as Wagner introduced in his works.

Wolf is not much concerned with the laws of form and harmony. His forms are dictated to him by the lyrics, his harmonic changes and combinations are rich and unfettered. *Tristan und Isolde* served as an example for Wolf's many chromatic harmonies. During his lifetime and after, his modulations and harmonic shifts created real difficulties for his hearers. His rhythms — there is usually one dominant rhythm for the whole song — appear principally in the accompaniment. The rhythm shown in Figure 216A, for instance, is the sole basis for his song "Das verlassene Mägdlein," and the rhythm shown in Figure 216B returns throughout his song "Der Gärtner." The hymnic "Weyla's Gesang" rises on the simple rhythm shown in Figure 216C, supported, however, by rich, broad, harp-like arpeggios. Wolf's sense of humor is one of his loveliest qualities: it is so fine and tasteful that it will never evoke a loud laugh, but always the smile of an appreciative connoisseur. The end of "Nimmersatte Liebe," the "Storchenbotschaft," "Elfenlied," "Der Musikant," and many others are delightful examples.

Figure 216. Wolf's rhythms. A. In "Das verlassene Mägdlein." B. In "Der Gärtner." C. In "Weyla's Gesang"

One of the most important style elements of the German lied, the reaching into the depth, is fully realized by Wolf in songs that are among the most beautiful ever written by a German composer, such as "Und willst du deinen Liebsten sterben sehen" (one of the greatest love songs), "Nun lass uns Frieden schliessen," "Kein Schlaf noch kühlt das Auge mir," "Herr, was trägt der Boden hier," and the ever popular "Verborgenheit." Hugo Wolf's accompaniments are difficult but highly interesting and rewarding to an accompanist and coach of culture.

Richard Strauss's place in the story of the German lied style is slowly changing. Celebrated as a national genius during his lifetime, he is judged by today's critical musical public with more detachment. One fact comes immediately to mind: with the exception of an irreproachable declamation — and the question arises whether "correct" declamation really is so overwhelmingly important — Strauss is not very typically German. In his long life, he was subject to so many cultural influences that he could not but show them in his songs. Most of his lieder lack the typical German "depth manner," as Debussy has called it (p. 165). Some are simply shallow, written mostly with an eye to public success, as for instance the popular "Cäcilie." Some are truly great — the Schumann-style song "Morgen" or the almost mystical "Traum durch die Dämmerung." Some songs breathe Brahmsian roughness — "Schlechtes Wetter" or "Lied des Steinklopfers." His "Four Last Songs" shed new light on Strauss's equally divided gifts: on his immense craftsmanship and on the resignation of his old age, as mild as some precious old vintage wine; but also on his loss of firm control of form, on his toying with endless harmonic modulations.

Because Gustav Mahler died in 1911, our age is at a greater remove from his songs, and at this esthetic distance his contribution can be evaluated more safely. The controversy that has raged over his symphonies and still rages today does not include his songs: he is generally accepted as a song composer of the highest rank. Indeed, quite a few of his symphonic movements grew out of simple songs. His great contribution to the German lied consists in his having invented folk melodies and embroidered them with piano accompaniment that he conceived with orchestral effects in mind. His affinity for folk music found its richest source in an anthology of anonymous Southern German folk poetry, *Des Knaben Wunderhorn*, collected by the German romantic poets Achim von Arnim and Clemens Brentano. Mahler not only injects into his songs all kinds of animal voices (nightingale, finch, cuckoo, goose, oxen, donkey), trumpet and horn signals, bells, drums, yodeling, and the whole array of music of the angels, he also recreates the romantic atmosphere of the German forest and the beauty of the German fields and meadows glittering with morning dew.

He is equally free in ranging over the scale of emotions, starting at one end with wild desperation ("Das irdische Leben," "Ich hab' ein glühend Messer") and reaching the other end with angelic bliss ("Wir geniessen die himmlischen Freuden"). His facility for identifying his music with the German folk character would in itself secure him a place in the hierarchy of German lied composers; and he also reaches into the other main component of German lied style, the depth of feeling, of creating. In his "Seven Last Songs," set to lyrics by Rückert, he leads us as near as is humanly possible to the secret source of an artist's creative power: loneliness ("Ich bin der Welt abhanden gekommen"). This song, as much Mahler's personal credo as Brahms's is his "Kein Haus, keine Heimat," plumbs the unconscious. His song cycle *Kindertotenlieder* is a profoundly moving expression of grief and fits my description of grief's emotional impact on someone who has grown up in the atmosphere of German culture (see p. 167).

Stylistically, Mahler turns back to Brahms and Schubert, and most of all to the old German folk song. His musical language is of course his own and encompasses the bizarre ("Die Fischpredigt des heiligen Antonius") as well as the nostalgic, which is expressed in his childhood reminiscences of Austrian military band music ("Wo die schönen Trompeten blasen," "Revelge," "Der Tamburgesell.")

At my choice of Hans Pfitzner to close the circle of German lied composers, I can see quite a few raised eyebrows. Pfitzner is very little known among American musicians and music students. Yet he embodies the best that German lied style has to offer: romanticism, folklore, simplicity, introspection or inner fulfillment (it is hard to find a good translation for the German "Innerlichkeit"), genuine feeling, soul (here again I am groping without success to find an equivalent for the German "Gemüt"), depth, honesty, idealism, sentimentalism (as opposed to naivety), and the philosophical search for the primary cause of all matter.

Pfitzner is by no means a modernist. He is a conservative whose work is based on tradition, especially upon Schumann's songs. Suffering from competition with the more commercial, more extroverted Richard Strauss, Pfitzner spun himself into his dreams and his lyric emotions. We not only have him to thank for one of the mightiest, most profound German operas (*Palestrina*), but we are grateful for his sincere struggle to avoid anything that did not spring genuinely from his inner self. I recommend the study of his songs to all accompanists and coaches who would like to vary their vocalists' programs and who are intent on their students' mastering the German lied style.

I have enumerated above a few of the most basic, positive traits of German lied. Let me continue with some others, gained by the insight into the creative work of German composers from Mozart to Pfitzner: mysticism, nearness to nature, humor from idyllic to sarcastic, uninhibited passion. There are, of course, some German traits expressed in German lied style that could be evaluated by putting a minus sign in front of them, such as the strong nationalism ("Deutschland, Deutschland über alles"), a homespun pedantry, an excessive Weltschmerz expressing itself in an overemphasized sentimentality, a cruelty which may be an overcompensation of sentimentality, and a perverted sense of humor. But in the scales of art appreciation the weight of the positive traits will easily overbalance the negative and will forever establish the German lied style as one of the most important of musical styles.

FRENCH MUSICAL STYLE

What we today call French musical style is the product of centuries of national and musical evolution. Nationally, the age of the Bourbons, the French Revolution, the Napoleonic era, and the frequent alternations between Empire and Republic have contributed toward shaping the French character as it appears to us in the French music of the nineteenth and twentieth century. Musically, France — as we saw in the chapter about the historical background of accompanying and coaching — was at times the world's leader and at times the follower and imitator of other nations. During the seventeenth century and most of the eighteenth, with the exception of a few outstanding musical personalities such as Grétry, Rameau, and Couperin, the French musical ship sailed in the wake of Italian melody. With the appearance of the great German classicists and romanticists — Haydn, Mozart, Beethoven, Schubert, and Schumann — France turned the rudder sharply toward the neighbor to the east. In Halévy and Meyerbeer, France found musicians who were creating grand opera by integrating the operatic styles of Italy with the deeper ideas of German operatic style — an integration which Gluck had initiated and Weber had continued. The musical genius Berlioz, although he was a fanatic admirer of Beethoven, was one of the first to realize the need for a national French musical style, and he was a great enough master to create works that were definitely French. The appearance of Wagner on the musical scene in general and in the French musical arena in particular brought French music nearer to the Rhine than ever before, but Berlioz held his position steadfastly and even influenced such German masters as Liszt. From Berlioz's time on, the development of a French musical style progressed steadily. The fight between Wagner's and Brahms's followers in Germany had its repercussions in France, but still, with all the noise going on, French music was able to

put down roots into the national soil. The greatest French poets of their time, Baudelaire, Mallarmé, and Verlaine, were faithful apostles of Wagner. It is not without some twist of irony that these self-same poets became the main lyricists for the most famous composers of the newly awakened French musical spirit.

By and by, the French love for German music turned into a hate-love. Political relations worsened; Napoleon the Third did not possess the diplomatic or military genius of his uncle, and the culmination of France's national misery came with its defeat in the 1870–71 war against Prussia. But, as so often happens in times of distress, the national spirit soared higher and higher. In 1871, the Société Nationale de Musique was founded. Its main purpose was the furthering of the ars gallica, French national music. French composers searched for and found new ways of expression. The long-neglected art form of the song was the best vehicle to carry and to express the newly found French soul. The great composers of songs — Duparc, Chausson, Debussy, Fauré, Ravel, and many others — are the products of this renaissance of the French spirit. Debussy, who had a more international cultural background than his colleagues — he had traveled widely in Italy and Russia — became the epitome of French musical style. His opera *Pelléas et Mélisande* is rightly looked upon as the climax of this national movement. Its music was conceived and written as a direct counterpoise to Wagner's Musikdrama. It is a masterwork of underplay, of utmost thriftiness of musical means, of creating mood with the help of impressionistic elements that became known to French music through the works of the avant-garde painters of the day.

What did Debussy himself say about the new style? Where did he locate its roots? We find some very characteristic lines in his short essay about Jean Philippe Rameau:

"We had . . . a pure French tradition in the work of Rameau. It consisted of a delicate and charming tenderness, of right accents, of a strict declamation in the recitatives, without that affectation in the German depth manner. There is no need to stress it (the music) with a swinging fist and to explore it until the breath gives out. All this seems to say: You are a collection of idiots; you do not understand anything unless one forces you beforehand to believe that the moon is made of green cheese. One may regret that French music had during too long a period of time been following roads that, in a perfidious way, led us astray from that clarity of expression, from that preciseness and that concentration of form which are particular and significant qualities of the French genius."

It is rare to find a Frenchman defining French musical style. Debussy is one of the very few who have analyzed it. We are much more likely to find definitions and explanations in foreign writings, by German, English, American, or Italian authors. Their opinion, however, will always be based on their own musical culture, on their musical mother's milk. How much more valuable it is, then, to find great Frenchmen who have occupied their minds with the problem of French musical style and the differences between it and other styles. More than a century before Debussy, Jean Jacques Rousseau, whose ideas and works were to give France its direction for years to come, was also deeply interested in music, both as a composer and as a writer. He and Rameau were among the first Frenchmen to raise the issue of a French musical style. Though Rousseau was mostly critical of contemporary French music, including Rameau's operas, his writings imply very clearly the trend he foresaw for French music. Criticizing an opera buffa by Rameau he wrote: "I am not raising the question whether the buffo genre in French music exists in reality. What I do know very well is that it necessarily should be different from the buffo genre of Italian music: a fat goose does not fly like a swallow."

In his famous "Lettre sur la musique française," Rousseau criticized almost everything in contemporary French music: the melody, the harmony, and the French language itself, which he characterizes as being unfit for music. This letter, no doubt highly unfair and exaggerated, brought a flood of polemic answers; but it served to stimulate interest in creating a genuinely French musical style.

No one was better qualified to write about the problem of French musical style than Romain Rolland, the great modern author, musicologist, and all-round genius. I shall have to quote him frequently. His musicological background makes him one of the foremost authorities on French musical style. In his *Musicians of Today*, Rolland names Berlioz as the first pure representative of French national music. He juxtaposes Berlioz with the great German composers of Berlioz's day and finds that he has emancipated himself from foreign influences, especially from the German ones that were predominant in France during the middle of the nineteenth century.

The outstanding qualities of French music — including lyrics and diction — that Rolland mentions are clarity, elegance, simplicity, naturalness, grace, plastic beauty. I shall later devote an entire paragraph to Rolland's explanation of French musical accents. One of the first to recognize Debussy's greatness and his importance to French music, he says: "The aesthetic sensualism of the French race seeks pleasure in art and does not willingly admit ugliness even when it seems to be justified by the need of the drama and of truth. Like the impressionistic painters of today, Debussy paints with primary colors but with a delicate moderation that rejects anything harsh as if it were something unseemly. Anyone who lives in foreign parts and is curious to know what France is like and understand her genius should study 'Pelléas et Mélisande.'" And in another place: "Not that Debussy's art entirely represents French genius; for there is quite another side to it which is not represented there; and that side is heroic action, the intoxication of reason and laughter, the passion for light, the France of Rabelais, Molière, Diderot, and in music, we will say — for want of better names — the France of Berlioz and Bizet. It is the balance between these two Frances that makes French genius. In our contemporary music, 'Pelléas et Mélisande' is at one end of the pole of our art and 'Carmen' is at the other. The latter is all on the surface, all life, with no shadows and no underneath. The former is below the surface, bathed in twilight and enveloped in silence. And this double ideal is the alternation between the gentle sunlight and the faint mist that veils the soft, luminous sky of the Ile de France."

Rolland explains Debussy's feelings as expressed in *Pelléas et Mélisande*: "During the last 10 or 20 years scarcely one French musician has escaped Wagner's influence. One understands too well the revolt of the French mind, in the name of naturalness and good taste against exaggerations and extremes of passion whether sincere or not. 'Pelléas et Mélisande' came as a manifestation of this revolt. It is an uncompromising reaction against over-emphasis and excess, and against anything that oversteps the limits of imagination. The distaste of exaggerated words and sentiments results in what is like a fear of showing the feelings at all even when they are most deeply stirred. With Debussy, the passions almost whisper; and it is by the imperceptible vibrations of the melodic line that the love in the hearts of the unhappy couple is shown by the timid 'Oh — où allez vous?!' at the end of the first scene, and the quiet 'Je t'aime aussi' in scene four of the last act. Think of the wild lamentations of the dying Isolde and then the death of Mélisande, without cries and without words."

How influential Rousseau's opinion was on Debussy's style may be seen by quoting again from Rousseau's "Lettre sur la musique française": "The kind of recitative that would best suit us should fluctuate between little intervals and neither raise the voice very much nor lower it beyond a certain interval. It should have a minimum of sustained sound, no noise and no outcries of any kind — in fact, nothing that resembles [arioso] singing. Furthermore, there should be but little inequality in the duration or the value of the notes or in their intervals." This sounds very much like Debussy's own interpretation of what a recitative should be like.

Some of the characteristic qualities of the French musical style are mentioned in the quotations above. Here are some more: logical sense, tenderness, sense of balance, and restraint in emotions. Listening to French vocal music of the second half of the nineteenth century and the beginning of the twentieth, a period that has rightly been called the Golden Age of French music, one finds that the French are almost afraid to show too much emotion. They prefer what we today call underplaying a feeling to stressing it. It is as if there were an invisible watchman standing at the door of the emotions and allowing past only those that have first been purified. This watchman is the leveling spirit of self-criticism, of order and balance in the most subtle stirrings of heart and soul. He is like a brain center that rules over different parts of the body and sees to it that no everlasting harm should be done anybody — performing artist or listener.

Underplaying does not mean, however, that French music lacks depth. Depth is not a Germanic or Slavic attribute alone. Great German or Russian music not only stresses the notes but searches also for what lies behind the notes — for the music's psychological, ethical, and moral quality — but French music is not so much concerned with this search. It maintains a happy medium among Italian sensuality, German philosophy, and Russian exhibitionism.

Let us take a simple example. Grief is one of the simplest but at the same time deepest emotions of man. It can be expressed in many ways. A German — as perhaps best exemplified by the Funeral March of Beethoven's Eroica — will sit in his room, alone, numb, staring into space, not able to say a word. His grief fluctuates between the absolute end of everything material and the heroic apotheosis of immortality. The Russian, in a similar situation, as exemplified by the first movement of Tchaikovsky's Sixth Symphony, will run out into the street, rend his clothes, and yell out his grief to all the world. The Italian's grief, though just as profound, will never lose sight of sensuous beauty in his melodic phrases. Take, for instance, Verdi's *Requiem.* It is a work of greatest ethical and moral depth and sincerity; yet not without justification has it been called an opera. The Italian, moreover, will always find solace in his religion. This also holds true for the Frenchman. His musical expression of grief may best be traced in a simple art song, such as Fauré's "La Chanson d'un Pêcheur." Deep emotion is there, all right; but it is hidden behind a mask of objectivism — of cool, self-critical observation. The grieving fisherman is afraid to show his emotions: he does not want to bother the listener by presenting grief in a crude way. This refinement — our age, trained to affix technical terms even to mysterious inner stirrings, would call it sophistication — is the great secret of French musical style. There is no doubt that such refinement can be understood only by a person of culture, and culture, therefore, is what the composer of the ars gallica era expects to find in his listener. The accompanist and coach must implant this refinement in the artist; this, in turn, means that the accompanist and coach must first have acquired musical culture. Thorough study of French musical style is one of the many steps that will lead the student toward the desired goal of over-all musical culture.

THE ACCENTS IN FRENCH VOCAL MUSIC

Before I turn to dealing further with the musical part of French musical style I must discuss problems of accents in French vocal music. The accompanist and coach will notice that French accents are fluid: the same word may be accented on any syllable. At first, one might interpret this to mean that the French are careless in their musical diction. In particular, musicians schooled in the German and, above all, the Wagnerian tradition will find fault with this seemingly sloppy way of composing and declaiming. One very prominent representative of this group of objectors is the young Richard Strauss who studied French accents when he translated Oscar Wilde's *Salome* — which had been written in French by its English author — into German. He compared Bizet's and Gounod's accents with the meticulously correct accents of Wagner's music dramas and found the French composers wanting in care. In his doubt he turned to Romain Rolland, asking the great Frenchman to explain why the same word could have different accents in French. Richard Strauss to Romain Rolland (July 15, 1905): "I ordered and received the Debussy *Pelléas et Mélisande* [which Rolland had recommended for study]. But there again I find the same nonchalance in declamation that has always surprised me so much in all of French music. Why does the Frenchman sing differently from the way he speaks? In speaking, do you pronounce: le ter′ rain or le ter rain′? Why then does Debussy declaim [Fig. 217]? Why [Fig. 218]? Does one say pe′ tite or peti′ te? In this country, Wagner has regenerated the feeling for the meaning of the language. France seems to me to be still stuck in the mire of deceit of the cothurn tragedy of the 18th century! Teach me, please, if you can, how to get rid of these old bad customs."

Figure 217. Debussy, *Pelléas et Mélisande*

Figure 218. Debussy, *Pelléas et Mélisande*

Romain Rolland to Richard Strauss (July 16, 1905): "I do not know of too much to answer you and I am afraid I might have to be a little severe. Would you allow me to tell it to you in a friendly way? You are amazing, all you Germans, you understand nothing about our poetry, absolutely nothing; and you judge it with imperturbable certainty. You will answer that we in France are doing the same? — No. We do not judge your poets, we do not know them. But it is better not to know them at all, than to believe one knows them when it is not true."

After discussing differences among regional accents, Rolland continues in his proud defense of the French musical accents:

"The French language is our most beautiful work of art and you desire that we ourselves should smash it to pieces? We in France possess too many qualities that only artists possess. Our language will not die but with us. . . . What you are calling 'nonchalance of declamation' is flexibility and psychological truth. We do not have just one single way of accenting a word, once and forever: it is accented differently in accordance with the meaning of the phrase and above all in accordance with

the psychological makeup of the person who utters it. Je ne peux pas le dire may be accented either:

"1) Je′ ne peux pas le dire (if obstinacy is involved) or 2) Je ne peux′ pas le dire (if it is really an impossibility) or 3) Je ne peux pas′ le dire (if the person is tired of answering that he can not say, if it involves lassitude).

"Why, you ask, does Debussy stress: 'Selon′ le ter′-rain et le vent?' because this is the rhythm of the phrase and of the person who says it. Does not everybody have his rhythm, defined by his breath? Here the breath is short and a little panting. . . . You are too proud at this moment, in Germany. You all think you understand everything and you do not spend any effort to try. Too bad for you if you do not understand us. We will exist no less and we will go on existing for a long time still, I hope."

Rolland's answer is very characteristic of the defensive position in which the adherents of French musical style found themselves against the Wagnerian dictate of definite accents. Rolland turns the defense into a friendly but outspoken attack on the German "know-it-alls."

In another letter, he explains to Strauss that the fluidity of accents in French vocal music has its origin in the old French music, the Gregorian chant still preserved by the Benedictine order of Solesmes: "I do believe, in summing up, that the present movement to free the rhythm from the inflexible regularity of the bar conforms to an old French tradition before the conquest of our music in the seventeenth century by Italianism."

We have seen that accents in French vocal music may have many different shadings, in accordance with the inner rhythm of the phrase and the emotion it expresses. How beautiful is the explanation of the different accents on the che-veux′ or che′-veux, as Rolland gives it!

Richard Strauss to Romain Rolland (August 2, 1905): "Yesterday I re-read 'Pelléas et Mélisande' by Debussy and again I am very uncertain about the principle of French vocal declamation. Thus, I have found on page 113 [Fig. 219] and on page 115 [Fig. 220]. I ask you, for the love of God, of these three versions there can be but only *one* right one."

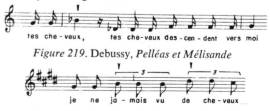
Figure 219. Debussy, *Pelléas et Mélisande*

Figure 220. Debussy, *Pelléas et Mélisande*

Romain Rolland to Richard Strauss (August 9, 1905): "Les cheveux. I take the liberty of reminding you of an observation which I made to you earlier about the change of stress on certain syllables, in accordance with the rhythm and the emotional aspect of the phrase in which the word is encased. The natural stress on cheveux is 'tes che-veux'.' But someone in love will put a particular stress on it: 'tes che'veux.' We have here some sort of slight, imperceptible trembling of voice and lips (the stress is very slight, anyway). It is as if one would say: 'tes *chers* cheveux.' You see: the great difficulty with our language is that the stress is variable for a great number of words, never arbitrarily but following logical and psychological reasons. When you say: 'Of these 3 versions only one can be right' this is no doubt true for a German but not for a Frenchman. In French, there is a certain number of words with an absolutely fixed stress: they are part of the ossification of the language. The others are fluid and proteiform; they obey logical and psychological circumstances etc. and lend themselves to be bent in accordance with these circumstances."

Thus the correspondence of two great artists of their representative countries. The moral for accompanists and coaches: look at French lyrics with the eyes of a Frenchman, understand the flexible accents, the meanings of inflections, the fine differences of moods, the variety of pastel colors in French vocal diction. What the accompanist and coach has learned from the study of lyrics and their accents he can readily transfer to the musical side of songs, arias, and recitatives of French vocal composition.

THE MUSICAL QUALITIES

Returning now to the musical qualities of French musical style, I shall try to group the French art song into a few different categories, highly characteristic of the genre. I know, of course, that this can only be a rough and approximate grouping.

Expanding French colonialism brought new exotic countries and peoples to la patrie. Oriental influences are clearly present in such operas as Bizet's *Les Pêcheurs des perles*, Delibes' *Lakmé*, Massenet's *Thaïs*, *Hérodiade*, and many others. A great number of poems tried to catch this exotic and erotic atmosphere of sweetly scented perfume, and French composers avidly set them to music—Debussy's "Chansons de Bilitis," Duparc's "Phidilé," Fauré's "Les Roses d'Ispahan" and many songs of lesser quality, such as Xavier Leroux's "Le Nil,"

Paladilhe's "Psyché" and others. The voluptuous environment and mood of these songs are subject to the Frenchman's control of emotions: the clarté, tendresse — mere suggestion of erotic feelings that never become plainly sexual.

No other poems are more suitable to French musical style than the calm verses that deal with moonlight, with the cool sound of a flute, such as Reynaldo Hahn's "L'heure exquise" or Saint-Saëns's "Le Lever de la lune." It is no accident that almost every French composer of the golden age has set Verlaine's "Claire de lune" to music. The cool — but not cold — light of the moon corresponds so well to French clarté, sobriety, underplay, and cool charm.

Another group of French songs is dedicated to painting the sea on the coasts of Brittany and Normandy, and on the Mediterranean. Fauré has composed some of his most beautiful songs to words describing this element — "Les Matelots," "Les Berceaux," "Chanson du Pêcheur." Another geographical region fascinating to French composers is the Basque country and neighboring Spain. Not only *Carmen*, the greatest masterwork of French operatic music, but many other works make use of Spanish rhythms and guitar-like accompaniments: Delibes' *Les Filles de Cadix* and Ravel's *Don Quichotte* song cycle, for example. Most French art songs indicate their inner contents by their titles: Chanson Triste, Soupir, Lamento, Elégie, En Sourdine. One is able to recognize in them all the above-mentioned watchfully controlled emotions.

Perhaps the purest composer of the French golden age of song is Gabriel Fauré. Nadja Boulanger, an expert on French music, says this about him: "His smiling suavity disdains all violence of mood or gesture and shuns the solemn effects of oratory and eloquence. He is never aggressive, but conceals his strength beneath the quiet force of the unemphatic voice and the untroubled serenity of a soul that has found inner peace and certitude." Contemporaries of Fauré called him the French Schumann. This is, of course, an oversimplification. Fauré has Schumann's simplicity but a much more highly developed sense of finesse, a great imagination, and a variety of colors on his palette. In his late years, Fauré devised a very advanced harmonic language, an audacious freedom from the rules of harmony that even our time has not yet conclusively analyzed.

From all that has been said above, it becomes clear that the word with all its nuances is the most important element of the French art song. The whole song, musically, has to be built on the word. Never must the voice become so dominant as to drown out or to muddy the word. Only when the lyrics can be recited with the proper inflection may music be added. The *raffinement* ("sophistication" is a rough translation) of the word is supported and brought out by the *raffinement* of the vocal phrase and by the accompaniment. The accompanist must study the printed dynamics and must invent scores of new dynamic variations, new shades, and new color mixtures on his sound palette. The pianistic touch must be subtle and flexible, and must follow the slightest inflections of the voice. The clarity of the accompaniment's figurations must be stressed; the genuine, but at the same time somewhat detached and controlled, emotions must be discreetly underlined. The apparent simplicity of, for instance, a Fauré song which actually is saturated with *raffinement* in the best and highest sense of the word must be made understandable to the audience. The tenderness, the charm of a French song must not be disturbed; the elegiac melancholy of many songs must not turn into sentimentality or heavy-handed sadness. The accompanist should make a special study of pedaling: the sustaining pedal should be used whenever impressionistic treatment of the song is indicated, and the soft pedal is

an absolute necessity. New shades can be created thus, new effects brought into play. The construction of French pianofortes is a help in playing French music. A Pleyel or an Erard concert grand has softer colors and more subdued sound, offers possibilities for finer shadings than the more powerful pianofortes of other countries. Contemporaries of Debussy said of his touch in playing the piano: "His manner was quite inimitable. So exquisite was the delicacy, the richness of his sonorities, and so masterly were the effects of color which he conjured forth from his pedals that one forgot the piano was an instrument with hammers." (Nadja Boulanger.)

I do not want to close this chapter without mentioning that recently a new French school of vocal music has followed different trends. The supersophistication of Poulenc and the contrasting archaizing catholicism of Messiaen, for instance, created another type of French vocal music. Everything today is becoming less subtle and is moving away from the style of the golden age of French vocal music. Today's trend toward the global unification of taste and custom has not stopped short of musical performance. It is to be hoped that it will not destroy the performance style of what many feel is the finest and noblest period in the history of French music, the real golden age of French vocal art.

✗ 10

Program-Building

THE building of a recital program is one of the most difficult and responsible tasks of an accompanist or a coach. The right program can make an artist; the wrong one — even wrong only in part or in a single number — can break him for a long time, if not forever.

Into successful programing goes an immense sum of experience in the psychology of audiences, a feeling for the weak points of the artist, and a knowledge of the artist's best instrumental or vocal features. Every artist, even the greatest, has some technical or interpretative deficiencies. There are passages, stops, harmonics, trills, vocal tessituras, that do not "lie well" for him. It is the job of the accompanist or coach to avoid numbers that come dangerously close to these technical or interpretative pitfalls. Again, in a choral ensemble, one group of voices may be stronger than another. It is the coach's art to select a program which will do justice to the choral group as a whole and will cover some weak spots.

But a recital or concert is not only a showcase for the artist, designed just to show off the best features of a particular virtuoso and cover his bad ones. It must also — most importantly — give the public enjoyment through the particular selection of compositions, the balancing of all numbers, and the contrasts formed by their juxtaposition.

A great amount of time and a great number of hit-and-miss tryouts of repertoire go into the making of a program. Let there be no mistake about it: an artist who comes to an accompanist or coach announcing that he has rented a hall for a date in the near future, and wants help in arranging a program, will never make the grade. Artistic humility, conscientiousness, and sensitivity are the most necessary preliminary ingredients for a successful recital. The absence of nerves, so important for the

overwhelming success of the American athlete, will not help to create a like success for the American artist.

The building of a recital program starts with considering and weighing different points of view.

First of all, the artist himself will have his preferences, pieces he thinks he does extremely well, pieces he has tried on different occasions. It may be important for practical and time-saving reasons to accept some of his preferences and to choose some numbers that he already has in his repertoire, although it may be even harder to correct old mistakes than to start studying an entirely new piece.

Secondly, there are the very important influences of the teacher, instrumental or vocal. Of course, nobody knows the artist's technical weaknesses and strong points better than his teacher. But, on the other hand, the teacher is likely to overstress technical problems in order to show off his pupil — or his method — and the most precious unity of a program, its harmony and contrast blended into an organic balance, may get lost. Unbiased advice requires a certain aesthetic distance which a teacher cannot always maintain.

Thirdly, there is the very strong influence of the whole array of interested persons — managers, agents, personal and press representatives. True, their experience with audiences should not be underestimated: sizing up audiences is a most important element in programing, especially if recitals are to be given outside the cultural centers of the United States. But here lies the root of a fundamental problem of music in our country. Should the artist play down to an arbitrarily assumed audience level in smaller towns, or try to lift the public up to the level of the main cities of musical culture — to a level which may be way over their heads? Both alternatives are fraught with danger. The managers' advice is no doubt well meant, if even founded on commercial considerations. They tend, however, to bend too far in the direction of popular appeal, thus perpetuating an audience taste that was artificially created in the first place. I believe in the existence of a good sound audience taste which, though not sophisticated, is not so low as some public relations firms want us to believe.

On a recent trip to Mexico, in a provincial town in the far South, I watched an audience composed largely of pure Indians, descendants of the ancient Mayas, listen in rapturous silence to an excellent band of musicians of the same origin. The band played the overture to Mozart's *The Magic Flute* and other good music. After each piece the audience burst into spontaneous applause. Nobody can convince me that the artistic taste of a Texas farmer or an Oregon lumberjack is not at least on a level comparable with that of these Indians.

The success of concerts in small towns does not depend solely on the familiarity of the music, either. To include some familiar numbers in a program is one thing, but to build a whole concert of hackneyed, often-played music is to insult the intelligence of the listener.

It is the task of the accompanist or coach to scrutinize closely all of the opinions and influences, weed out numbers that do not belong, balance climaxes with pieces that allow artists and audiences to relax, and obtain over-all harmony of creative and re-creative effort.

Many artists, especially the young ones, love to pile difficult numbers upon difficult numbers. In their enthusiasm they forget that with such a program they would be exhausted by intermission time. Here again, the experience of the accompanist or coach will have to put a damper on the artist's youthful exuberance. It is extremely important to space a program so that easier numbers follow difficult ones, not only for technical reasons but also so as not to overburden and tire the audience's attention. Another point to be considered is the choice of numbers in relation to the keys in which they are written. It is not good to have, for instance, a piece in D major followed by another one in the same key. Good taste and the principle of contrasting musical keys will guide the accompanist and coach in their selections.

As I have said before, the majority of programs which an accompanist or coach helps to build will be recital programs of instrumentalists (with the exception of pianists) and vocalists. Occasionally, a choral concert may be programed by an accompanist or coach, although usually the choral leader himself will do the programing.

Instrumentalists, for all practical purposes, will be confined to violinists and 'cellists. Viola virtuosos, such as William Primrose or Lyonel Tertis, do from time to time give full recitals, but as a rule the limitations of their instrument and their literature make it unlikely that they can hold the interest of an audience for a whole evening. The same is true for double bass and wind players.

It is also theoretically possible that dancers may ask for help in building a recital program. Most of the time, however, dancers will choose the music themselves. They either visualize their dances by listening to music, or create the idea for the dance first and try to find appropriate music afterwards. Some, especially modern dancers, will want to have original music composed. Then the accompanist may become the composer, and the composer the accompanist, like Louis Horst (for Martha Graham) or Friedrich Wilckens (for Harald Kreutzberg). At other times, the accompanist may be asked to arrange or cut music for a dance recital, which is not an enviable task. But we can dispense here with a discussion of the building of dancers' programs.

There are several kinds of recital, each requiring a different sort of program: the debut recital, the recital or recitals on tour, the regularly recurring recital, the refresher recital, the one-language recital, the one-composer recital, the topical recital, the critic's recital. If these names sound like a variation of the different modes about which David sings in *Die Meistersinger von Nürnberg*, the blame should not be put on me. The complications of the American musical scene are the reason for the manifold types of recital I have found it necessary to describe.

THE DEBUT RECITAL

The debut recital is the program that will most often require the help of an accompanist or coach. Typically, a young artist wants to show himself for the first time in a complete program and wants to collect reviews which he will be able to use to further his career. The money invested in such a recital has more often than not been scraped together by the young performer during months of saving, because few are lucky enough to be sponsored by private persons or by organizations. The program must show the artist at his best in technique and interpretation, handling of styles and languages, stage appearance, poise, and every other trait that makes an artist. It must be built to satisfy the professional critic as well as the public at large.

Here, a special problem arises in the big cities, especially in New York, where the number of recitals during a season is well up in the hundreds. Critics rush from one concert to the other to catch at least one group of each before they hurry to the nearest telephone to dictate their reviews before the deadline. News must be fresh in the big American cities. The reviews must appear the next morning. It is different in the capitals of Europe, where a critic can write his review at leisure and where it appears in print on the second day after the recital or even later. Besides, the New York, Chicago, or Boston critic — to name only some of the most hectic cities — has heard the same pieces so many times during recent seasons that he is hungry for something new and unusual.

The program must take into account this peculiarity of our musical scene. Not only should there be some unknown or rarely performed pieces, or a whole cycle or group of such numbers, but it would be advisable to dig up a "first performance" or possibly a "first performance anywhere" for inclusion in the program.

This is still not enough. The most interesting part of the recital must be programed so that the critic can catch it on his nightly tour of the concert halls. Usually, the best spot is just before or just after the intermission. In the immediate neighborhood of this group should be put some more familiar music that will give the critic a chance to compare the artist's work with established standards. It may happen, of course, that the critic spends precisely this time at another concert and arrives too late to hear these two groups. The artist, in this case, is out of luck and his efforts and his money have been spent in vain. A conscientious critic, however, will time his presence at a recital in such a way that he is sure to listen to the most interesting part of the program.

How then should a debut recital program be built? I have said before that variety is essential to show the different facets of the young artist. Every performer will be — or ought to be — nervous at the start of a concert. This is only natural. A lack of nervousness would show lack of artistic sensitivity. But nervousness may develop into loss of self-control. It is up to the accompanist or coach to suggest a first number or first group that will put the artist at ease and help him overcome his stage-fright. For instrumentalists this will mean avoiding a starting piece that asks for long-spun phrases which only a very steady bowing arm can execute. Vocalists have the same problem: they should shy away from songs or arias that require perfect breath control. Artists' varying temperaments have to be taken into consideration at this point. Like race horses which may be fast starters but fade out in the stretch, some artists warm up very fast, but have little staying power as far as intensity is concerned. Other performers, especially vocalists of the lower voice ranges or possessors of heavy voices, need more time to warm up, and should, therefore, be given longer opening pieces with more dramatic impact in order that they may be at the height of their performing capacities sooner. For coloratura sopranos or light tenors, whose voices must be very flexible, light legato numbers without overlong phrases are recommended. Instrumentalists have an easier way out of the difficulty of starting a program. They should begin with a sonata, classical or contemporary, which puts half the burden on the accompanist, who thus becomes a full partner. A sonata, furthermore, gives the artist time to warm up and contains in itself enough contrast of mood and expression. Its dimensions are large enough to make the audience overlook any momentary insecurity of bowing technique or pitch.

What each young artist, instrumental as well as vocal, must face is the absolute necessity of starting out on the highest possible level of mental and spiritual intensity. He must be keyed to it from the very first measure of the first number. No warming up here!

The accompanist should try to keep outward disturbances away from the artist before the start of the recital. Last-minute hitches in costuming, arrangement, transportation, and the like should be avoided. The first number of a recital is like a *carte de visite* which an artist leaves with his audience. The first impression, as psychologists will tell you, is a lasting one.

It is traditional for instrumentalists to start with a classical or preclassical sonata — let us say with a Beethoven sonata (easier as a starter than a Mozart sonata) or a Tartini or Handel sonata, if they are violinists, or one of the earlier Beethoven or Brahms sonatas or a Boccherini concerto or like piece, if they are 'cellists. There is nothing against such a beginning, but I should like to make it clear that the opening piece of a recital need not be prompted by historical considerations, with the concert then continuing chronologically all the way down to contemporary music. A recital may start with a piece from any period, as long as the inner relation between the different groups is logical and harmonious. A recital may as well start with Stravinsky or Hindemith as with Bach. But the rest of the program will still have to be in harmony with the principles of programing outlined earlier. There are recitalists who give their audiences the shock treatment. Aggressive musical numbers follow one after the other. Rhythmic and dynamic attacks repeatedly arouse audiences from their lethargy — until they are so exhausted that the effect is nil. Such a procedure is not recommended for debut recitalists.

One more question of principle: should recitals include concerti played with piano accompaniment instead of orchestral support? The answer, generally, is No. Even the best accompanist, one who is able to embellish the piano part with all the orchestral coloring, and who can recreate each instrument on the piano, cannot approach the richness and the grandeur of an orchestra. Today the smallest communities have ample occasion to acquaint themselves with all concerti through recordings by first-rate orchestras, conductors, and soloists. For these reasons of comparison it is dangerous to include a concerto with piano accompaniment. There is, however, one exception: concertos of preclassical times were scored for small string orchestra accompaniment with the addition of maybe a few wind or brass instruments, supported by the percussive effects of a harpsichord; these orchestrations are not so colorful as to preclude their successful substitution by a good piano accompaniment.

The traditional start for vocalists is a group of old Italian, old English, old French, or just "old" pieces, pieces which they usually have learned in voice studios. Though this is an easy beginning, interpretatively speaking — these songs do not require great personality — it is far from safe. These period compositions, more than compositions of a later era, are likely to tax the technical capacities of a singer to the utmost right from the start. For example, a Monteverdi aria or a Purcell song offers more difficulties than any selection of the classic or modern repertoire. It can be sung, of course, but only if the artist is very sure of himself and can trust his breath control.

I would prefer a longer first number, some piece into which the singer can sink his teeth emotionally while he has time to warm up vocally. As I have said before, the choice of a first group depends largely on the voice category. A Mozart concert aria, for instance, would be a good choice for coloratura sopranos or basses (just so it is not one of the devilishly difficult ones). Something like "Ah Perfido" by Beethoven may be right for a dramatic soprano. Altos, tenors, and baritones have ample choice among works by Handel, Grétry, and Haydn, to name just a few, unless they choose to start with something more modern.

Operatic and oratorio arias, while not to be avoided entirely, should be programed sparingly. I should say that not more than two or three should be sung in a debut recital — just enough to show the aptitude of the young artist for an operatic or oratorio career.

Now that the hurdle of a starting number or group has been got over, I can go on to discuss the build-up of a debut recital.

A debut recital should not be overlong. Impressions are not improved by a quantity of musical interpretations but by their quality. Although many deviations from the standard are possible, depending on the length of the various numbers, a four-part concert with one long intermission seems the reasonable form for instrumentalists. Vocalists need more breathing space between groups. For this reason it may be safer for them to sing three groups in the first half of the concert — the initial warming-up number being a group in itself — and two groups in the second half. In any case, the first half of a concert should be longer than the second. Encores should bring the concert to its full length. The net duration of music (without the encores) should not exceed an hour and a quarter. If we add to this an intermission of fifteen minutes, and shorter pauses between groups, amounting to about ten minutes, and allow furthermore for the conventional delay of ten minutes at the beginning, for applause after each number, and for bows at the end of groups, the entire concert, including encores, should not be longer than two hours.

Let me point out a danger which always faces the not-so-experienced accompanist or coach when he is timing a program. His timing will invariably be too fast, even if done with a stop watch while the artist is playing or singing. In performance, all tempi will be slightly slower. This phenomenon can be explained by the facts that the artist puts more expression into his concertizing, and that the accompanist — and the artist — will start the pieces somewhat slower than in rehearsal for reasons of safety. So choose less music rather than too much if you want to avoid stretching the recital to tedious length. A total of between sixteen and twenty-one numbers, depending on their length, seems to be right for vocalists.

Fewer numbers are needed for instrumentalists, since their selections are always longer.

The choice of a second group for a debut recital will be dictated by the availability of "interesting" material. This is the spot that the critics are likely to catch. Instrumentalists should not play another sonata, because this would give the recital too much of a chamber-music aspect. If the recitalist is very strong, musically and technically, one of the great solo works by Bach may be programed here, especially in a 'cello recital. Otherwise, there are enough compositions available from the classics and romantics to Bartók and the modern composers of the American, Russian, German schools. The last number of this group should have a brilliant ending, since it will be played just before intermission. This group would also offer the best spot for a novelty or a first performance of a serious new work.

For vocalists, the problem is to program the second group in one of the languages in which the debut recitalist is expected to show his versatility of style and his mastery of foreign tongues. The group may be sung in a different language, or it may continue in the same language as the first group. It is better, however, to change both the cultural milieu and the style of the compositions. The vocalist has a wide choice of musical material here. I recommend using either a cycle of songs by one composer, or, if the artist can afford it, a song or a group of songs with an obbligato instrument. This will add more color to the recital and show the versatility of the young singer in his ability to combine soloistic effects with chamber-music style.

Sometimes a combination of both suggestions (unusual music and obbligato instruments) can be found in one composition, such as Ravel's *Chanson Madégasses,* scored for voice with flute and violoncello. Another possibility: the two Brahms songs with viola obbligato (Bratschenlieder), best performed by an alto voice. Other songs with obbligato instruments: Mozart's aria from *Il Re Pastore* with violin solo (which could be used also for a starting number of a light coloratura or lyric soprano), Schubert's "Der Hirt auf dem Felsen" with clarinet obbligato (done rather frequently, and best for coloratura soprano), Schubert's "Auf dem Flusse" for tenor voice and French horn. Spohr has written beautiful songs for voice and clarinet. Brilliant coloratura voices will, at some dominant point in the program, use arias with flute obbligato, especially in cadenzas, as, for instance, in the Mad Scene from *Lucia,* or the "Shadow Song" from *Dinorah.*

For even more ambitious singers, there is a whole literature of voice and trio or quartet combinations, as, for instance, in the Scottish Songs by Beethoven or in many contemporary song cycles with the accompaniment of string quartet. Here, again, it is up to the accompanist or coach to know the available literature and to choose wisely and always to the advantage of the singer. In the accompanying list are a few of the song cycles that would fit well into the second group. The great Schubert song cycles, the Schumann cycles, and some other difficult cycles, such as Fauré's *La bonne chanson,* should not be attempted by debut recitalists in their entireties, but should be reserved for one-language and one-composer recitals. The reason for the inclusion in the accompanying list of English translations of Slav songs will be discussed later.

German

Beethoven: *An die ferne Geliebte* (for tenor or baritone); *Geistliche Lieder* (best for low voice); *Klärchen Lieder,* from Goethe's *Egmont* (for soprano)

Brahms: *Vier ernste Gesänge* (for low voice); *Folk Songs*

Cornelius: *Brautlieder* (for female voice — beautiful and seldom done)

Wagner: *Wesendonk Songs* (for heavier soprano voice)

Wolf: *Michelangelo Songs* (for low male voice)

Richard Strauss: *Vier letzte Lieder*

Alban Berg: *Sieben frühe Lieder* (it is possible to omit one or two songs)

French

Debussy: *Chansons de Bilitis* (for female voice); *Fêtes Galantes* (for female voice)

Ravel: *Don Quichotte* songs (for male voice); *Five Greek Songs*

Canteloube: *Chants d'Auvergne*

Italian

Pizzetti: *Sonnets of Petrarch*; *Greek Songs*

Spanish

De Falla: *Canciones Nacionales* (for female voice)

English

Mussorgsky: *Songs and Dances of Death* (for male voice); *In the Nursery* (for female voice)

Dvořák: *Biblical Songs*; *Gypsy Songs*
Benjamin Britten: *Les Illusions*; *Sonnets of Michelangelo* (for tenor); *Songs from the British Isles*
Samuel Barber: *Cinque Melodies passagères*

Of course, a one-language group consisting of songs by different composers can also be programed as the second group. I want to warn, however, against the mixing of too many composers. If the group consists of 4 songs, the division should be $2 + 2$ (for instance, 2 Fauré and 2 Poulenc songs). If the group consists of 5 or 6 songs, the relation should be $2 + 2 + 1$, or $3 + 2$, or $2 + 2 + 2$.

The second group may also, as I have said before, be the spot where a possible first performance of a group of songs may be scheduled. These songs would in most cases be by American composers. But they should be programed in this group only if they have enough musical and textual value. Such a group could also be programed right after the intermission while critics still have a chance to hear and write about it.

A solid operatic aria in a language different from that of the second group could constitute the third group, and end the first part of the program. Such an aria must show the young singer at the zenith of his art in every respect.

After the intermission the reins of seriousness may be loosened somewhat. This creates no problem for the instrumentalist, who has at his disposal a vast number of shorter pieces — all made to order to show his technical achievements. These pieces may be classical or modern, by composers of any nationality. But they must not become shallow or downright cheap. The accompanist or coach must choose them with great taste and care. This third group too must have substance. Novelties and first performances may still be programed here.

From the third to the fourth group the pieces can gradually become lighter and more virtuoso. They should offer contrasts of tempo — a slow one should be followed by a fast — and melodic lines should be alternated with strong rhythms. Each should contain a different tonal or technical problem to display the artist's versatility. The violinist, furthermore, has a chance to use some of the more serious transcriptions, according to his taste and his audience's presumed taste. For the 'cellist, there are the inevitable compositions by Popper and the many Spanish transcriptions in which the 'cello imitates the guitar.

The only problems in the after-intermission program of an instrumental debut recitalist are to contrast the numbers, to hide the artist's weaknesses by leaving out specifically dangerous pieces, and to choose the right brilliant closing number. There are lots of *perpetuum mobiles*, Rumanian dances, and other entertaining and dazzling numbers, known to every instrumentalist, to bring the concert to a successful close.

The vocalist, after intermission, should again change the language. The songs should become lighter without becoming trite. Tradition has it that the last group must be in English, but there is no reason at all why this must be so. If the young singer is of a certain national background, the last group might well be sung in his native tongue and style. Not only will he have a special feeling for these songs and do them extremely well, but the audience will probably be partly recruited from his co-nationals and will receive the group with special appreciation. This holds true equally for the Armenian, Swedish, or Negro artist. But it should in no wise be construed to mean that the Negro singer should confine himself to spirituals. He should, on the contrary, strive to attain mastery in all fields of the vocal art. But it is also true that the Negro singer of spirituals cannot be matched by any other artist.

The last group may also possibly be tailored to the regional provenance of a singer. Southern United States folk songs, ballads, mountain songs, all in tasteful transcriptions, contain much beautiful material.

A special discussion is necessary to pinpoint the character of the closing number of the program, especially if the last group is to be made up by songs of American composers. It must be said that in the past the choice of this particular number was very much cliché and routine, largely because there are comparatively few American songs of quality that have spirited, brilliant endings. The overabundance of seashells, exhortations addressed to the wind, loves going a-riding, and hearts full of song becomes nauseating, and the Lord's Prayer at the very end will not help much, since by that time the critic has already filed his review. I have, in many instances, taken refuge in the magnificent songs from Gershwin's *Porgy and Bess*, even if they are serious ones; or some of Menotti's effective arias; or even songs from some of the outstanding American musicals — Rodgers and Hammerstein's *Carousel*, or Kurt Weill's *Street Scene*; and many others which meet the highest artistic standards of vocal recitals.

The accompanist and coach must spend a great

amount of time in music stores looking through the amazing quantity of new American songs. He is sure to find some beautiful, sincere, and effective compositions. It only needs some special effort. One of the most important duties of the accompanist and coach is to keep abreast of contemporary music, American and European. A doctor must continuously study the latest medical journals — why shouldn't the pianist study the scores of the latest songs and arias?

If a singer is especially talented for opera, his closing number may well be an aria that embodies all his technical and musical faculties and his understanding of contemporary music.

In a way, the last number is not the end of the program but only the appetizer to another dish — the encores. These ought to be short light pieces which bear some relation to the recital proper. The first should be a more or less quiet one since after it the applause will not die down anyway. Then there should be very gay and possibly familiar pieces. If the applause should continue and the artist feels too tired to go on much longer, a quiet song will probably do the trick and kill the applause.

The accompanist and coach must see to it — even to the extent of spending time rehearsing the names — that the artist announces his encores clearly and audibly. Nothing is more annoying than listening to music without knowing what it is. And even if the encore is familiar to the audience, its announcement will invariably produce applause.

One word about repeating songs: this should be avoided in debut recitals. Time is short and the young artist seldom has the faculty of topping his first rendition. This is the prerogative of mature artists who have at their command so many colors and shades that a repetition will always be different and delightful.

The accompanist or coach must also insist that the young artist is properly coached in walking onto the stage and bowing. Many appearances have been spoiled by lack of self-assurance in these technical details, resulting in tenseness.

Another job for the accompanist or coach, at least supervisory, if not actually participating, is the preparation of program notes. They should be short, to the point, and not too flowery. Foreign poetry cannot be successfully put into English prose: it will sound clumsy. The meaning of the song should be clear without transcribing the song word for word. No story should be given for songs in English. If the artist's diction cannot be understood, the cause is lost anyway.

After having so thoroughly discussed the building of a program for a debut recital, it will be easy to adjust the same principles for application to the other kinds of recitals.

THE RECITAL ON TOUR

Concerts on tour should be constructed very similarly to debut recitals. There are two differences.

Firstly, if the tour is of considerable length and a large number of concerts is to be given, the physical stamina of the artist becomes a problem. Programs should be shorter, and technical difficulties should not be heaped on each other. If possible, slight variations of program should be scheduled; otherwise the artist's renditions may become stale.

Secondly, the program should be somewhat lighter than a New York recital. This does not mean that it should become out and out popular: I cannot warn enough against underestimating the musical intelligence and appreciation of out-of-town audiences. The last few years have made them grow up considerably in culture. However, since there will always be some people in the audience who have never heard a live recital, more old favorites may be programed, even to the extent of including some semiclassical numbers here and there. It would also be advisable to lengthen the intermission. People should have a chance to talk up the program, exchange views, and read the program notes — which should be more elaborate than for a New York recital.

A special kind of out-of-town recital is the university or college recital. Here the program may be very discriminating at times. The accompanist or coach should inform himself well about the musical standards in each of these educational centers and plan the program accordingly. For some of these institutions of learning even the heaviest fare will be too light. But this will be the exception rather than the rule.

THE REGULARLY RECURRING RECITAL

After an artist establishes himself on the concert stage, he must give recitals regularly, yearly or even more often. Such recitals may even turn out to be profitable.

The artist has now grown into a mature, regularly concertizing performer. Needless to say, his program has to be changed year by year, although some of the best numbers may be repeated either at the request of the audience or by his own wish. The accompanist or coach must impress on the artist that he must not fall into a routine, but must always include some new, interesting elements in his programs. A financially successful artist should spend part of his earnings to commission new works by our own American composers. This happens too seldom.

The accompanist usually also serves the artist as coach; sometimes he is even hired by the year. His influence on the artist is substantial. He becomes a partner not only in the music, but also takes part in the artist's daily life, his travels, his ups and downs, and his unavoidable psychological tensions and releases.

THE REFRESHER RECITAL

From time to time it becomes necessary for an artist to get himself back into the public eye. This is especially true for an artist who has been out of town or out of the country for a considerable time. It may also happen that an artist has given a successful debut recital, found a manager, and been booked well for a few seasons, when suddenly the public's interest in him diminishes — people hardly remember him any more. The United States, in this respect, is especially cruel. The tempo of life is so fast and hectic that memory cannot be faithful to an artist for long. His management may require him to give another concert for publicity's sake, or because he needs new reviews to fill his press book. Or perhaps an artist has given a debut recital that was not very well received, but he has been helped through constructive criticism to remove his shortcomings and to deepen his musical conception. He feels ready now to give his best and wants to try again.

There are many other reasons for wanting to give another recital. The responsibility of the accompanist or coach in such cases is great. He had to find some "best" numbers for the first recital; now he must look for some other pieces, just as good, if not better. More unusual compositions and more first performances have to be planned. The artist's progress has to be made evident to critics and audiences. The whole nervous excitement of preparing a debut recital is felt again, only more intensely and more desperately. This recital must not only be as good as the first one, it must top it in every respect. This can be done, but it takes nerves of iron, lots of patience, good will, and, especially, knowledge and experience on the part of the accompanist or coach to bring such a program to a successful conclusion.

THE ONE-LANGUAGE RECITAL

Naturally, the one-language recital is only for vocalists, usually of French or German origin, and of secure reputation. The German lied or the French art song is so much a style in itself and the literature is so valuable and abundant that a whole evening of it can be satisfying and entertaining. The ideal interpreters for these are to be found mainly among the German and French singers — to mention only a few: Lotte Lehmann, Elisabeth Schumann, and Richard Tauber in bygone days, and Dietrich Fischer-Dieskau, Elisabeth Schwartzkopf, Irmgard Seefried, and Hans Hotter today; on the French side of the roster are artists like Martial Singher, Pierre Bernac, Roger Bourdin, and others who have reached the stage of consummate artistry. Italian singers are somewhat handicapped by the lack of a wide literature of songs. But since they themselves are mostly operatic artists, they build their one-language programs around operatic arias, with a starting group and some fill-ins of old and new songs. Outstanding in our time is Renata Tebaldi. In earlier days we had singers like Beniamino Gigli and the incomparable Tito Schipa who liked to program recitals of mainly Italian compositions.

But it is not absolutely necessary to have been born in the country of one's musical choice. Quite a few Anglo-Saxon singers have given the most exquisite programs in German or French, among them Maggie Teyte and Mack Harrell.

The accompanist's or coach's task in this kind of program is of a merely advisory nature. The above-mentioned artists and their kind know very well what they want to do. I would not recommend that a young American artist plan a one-language recital unless he is unusually talented for it.

One word about programs in English: There is no doubt that a recital of songs by English and American composers can be genuinely interesting and valuable. Artists have done such concerts in the past and if they had enough personality to hold the attention of the audience, the results were excellent. It is also advisable that Russian, Czech, Polish, Yugoslav, Finnish, and Scandinavian songs be done in English translations, unless performed by singers of these nationalities. A good translation is always preferable even to phonetical spellings of these foreign lyrics — lyrics which are hardly ever pronounced correctly by American singers. Only artists who are proficient in these languages and can, in addition, feel an inner relation to the most minute details of mood of these songs should attempt to study them in the original. I would go even further and contend that this also holds true for the languages in which the American artist by tradition is expected to perform.

Sometimes the reason that an artist wants to give a whole program in English can be found in his conviction that *all* vocal music performed in an English-speaking country should be performed in English. If this is a genuine conviction, and not just the result of the artist's inability to master a foreign tongue, a discussion about the pros and cons of song recitals in English is entirely possible. Though the case for opera in English is very strong, the issue seems different in the concert field. An opera can be compared with a drama or a comedy, whereas a song is a lyrical, or possibly an epical piece. The bases for songs are poems. In songs, the finest shadings, the most subtle nuances of diction, become important and the music is built entirely on the musical content of the spoken word. This interplay of word and music constitutes the art form of the song. Although it is a possibility, theoretically, and could surprise us one day in the future, no translation, even by the greatest poet, has yet constantly conveyed the esthetic pleasure of a song in its original language. French, Italian, Spanish, and German — languages which have given us some of the most wonderful songs — ought to be preserved in recitals. Every singer ought to be thoroughly familiar with some of these languages and be able to sing in them without difficulty. The accompanist or coach ought to impress on his artists that they sing French, Italian, Spanish, and German songs in the original languages and should work untiringly to perfect them.

THE ONE-COMPOSER RECITAL

This is a rather rare kind of program and is mainly employed by mature artists who specialize in one language and further narrow the choice of songs in it down to one composer. Usually, it will be a program of lieder, since there are enough song cycles available to fill at least the major part of a program. Thus, most frequently encountered on programs of this sort are Schubert's *Müllerlieder*, his *Winterreise*, and the collection of his songs known as "Schwanengesang," which is not actually a cycle. Few other composers have written songs with so much unity of conception and variety of expression. One-composer recitals can also be programed by putting together various separate songs. For such a recital the accompanist or coach has great latitude in advising the artist which songs to choose and how to put them together so that the requirements mentioned before — unity and variety (or contrast) — are met. There are hundreds of little-known lieder by Schubert, Schumann, Brahms, and Wolf, some of them extremely beautiful and worthy of performance. They should be mixed with some of the better-known songs.

It happens from time to time that composers feature their own songs in recitals, playing their own accompaniments. Notable in this category was Richard Strauss, who toured Europe and the Americas widely with various singers, of whom the best known was Elisabeth Schumann, a perfect interpreter of his lieder. More recently, Benjamin Britten came here to play recitals of his own songs with Peter Pears as his soloist. This kind of program profits immensely by the perfect harmony between singer and accompanist and by the air of authenticity that hovers over it. But it need not be the composer himself who performs the songs. One of the last great conductors of our time, Bruno Walter, an accomplished pianist, found relaxation and at the same time gave his audiences sheer joy by playing the accompaniments in lieder recitals with such artists as Lotte Lehmann and more recently Irmgard Seefried. Especially enjoyable were his Gustav Mahler lieder recitals, in which he recreated the vocal art of his old master. Other composers performed in one-composer recitals are Brahms (by Lotte Lehmann) and Wolf (by Dietrich Fischer-Dieskau).

A well-established subtype of these recitals is the two-composer recital, a Schubert and Schumann concert, or a Debussy and Ravel concert, for example.

It is possible that instrumentalists of wide renown may play a whole program consisting of works by one composer. These programs, however, will almost always come under the heading of chamber music or sonata concerts.

THE TOPICAL RECITAL

From time to time we encounter programs which are built around a certain topic, as, for instance, a recital of Shakespearean poems set to music by various composers, or a concert of lyrical poetry by Goethe or ballads by Robert Burns. These topical programs allow the accompanist or coach to run the gamut of musical material. It is a pleasure to roam through stacks of songs by many composers; the only difficulty is to find the best possible blend of styles and tunes. It is always harder to limit oneself to certain selections than to let the imagination run wild.

Another popular topic for concerts is music for children. Children's song recitals offer a wonderful choice of musical material from classical to modern times. They open very valuable possibilities for educating our children in an entertaining way, so that they may enjoy serious vocal art as well as folk songs.

Topics can be found for almost any occasion. Some may not be important enough to sustain a whole recital but may come in handy for radio programs and the like. Here are a few topics: seasons (especially spring), love, religion, humor, the sea, ballads.

THE "CRITIC'S RECITAL"

This kind of recital is an absurdity, and arises from some artists' hope of arousing the interest and gaining the good will (and, incidentally, good reviews) of some important critic. They heap the Pelion on the Ossa, dig out the most unknown or forgotten (most rightly so) compositions, and schedule a lot of "firsts." These programs serve no constructive purpose. It must further be said that they usually backfire and fail to achieve the desired results. Accompanists and coaches should not be parties to such calculating purposes.

The particular likes and dislikes of some music critics used to be a professional hazard for young artists. Some critics wrote well only about modern music, and one critic never hid the fact that he hated Mozart, to cite only two instances. Luckily, these temporarily bizarre conditions have been eliminated by the newspapers themselves. Fearing these critics, some artists were induced to put on recitals especially designed to catch their attention and their good will.

It must be said that critics in general know how important their reviews are for the career of a debut recitalist. They treat the young artist very fairly and, if they see a special talent in one of them, try to give him encouragement and constructive criticism.

The accompanying samples of actual recital programs will serve as examples for accompanists and coaches in building programs along the lines that I have developed in this chapter.

VIOLINIST'S DEBUT RECITAL
(Paul Zukovsky)

I

Sonata in D major . . . . Corelli

II

Partita No. 1 in B minor . . . . Bach

III

Concerto in A minor . . . . . Glazounov

Intermission

IV

Suite Italienne . . . . Stravinsky
Polonaise Brillante in D major . . Wieniawski

VOCALIST'S DEBUT RECITAL (Angelica Lozada)

I

El jilguerito con pico de oro . . . Blas de Laserna
Minué cantado . . . . José Bassa
Las majas de Paris . . . . . . Blas de Laserna
El amor es como un niño . . . . Anonymous
La maja y el ruiseñor (*Goyescas*) . . Granados

II

September . . . . Richard Strauss
Schlagende Herzen . . . . . Richard Strauss
Freundliche Vision . . . . . Richard Strauss
Amor . . . . Richard Strauss

Intermission

III

Green . . . . Claude Debussy
L'Ombre des Arbres . . . . . Claude Debussy
Fleur des Blés . . . . Claude Debussy
Extase . . . . Henri Duparc
Non, monsieur mon mari (*Les
Mamelles de Tirésias*) . . . . . Francis Poulenc

IV

O Cool Is The Valley . . . . . Arnold Freed
Sister Awake . . . . Arnold Freed
The Bird . . . . John Duke

V

Jicarita . . . . Blas Galindo
Paloma Blanca . . . . Blas Galindo
Canción Epigramática . . . . . Amadeo Vives

REGULARLY RECURRING RECITAL
(Joseph Schuster — violoncello)

I

Chorale-Prelude . . . . . . Johann Sebastian Bach
Concerto in C minor . . . . . Johann Christian Bach

II

Sonata, Opus 69 . . . . . . Ludwig van Beethoven
Fantasie Pieces, Opus 73 . . . . Robert Schumann

Intermission

III

Sonata, Opus 119 (1949) . . . . Serge Prokofieff
Introduction and Polonaise
Brilliante, Opus 3 . . . . . . Frederic Chopin

FIRST OF THREE ONE-LANGUAGE RECITALS
(Lotte Lehmann)

I

Ganymed . . . . Franz Schubert
Lied der Mignon (So lasst
mich scheinen) . . . . Franz Schubert
Fischerweise . . . . Franz Schubert

Der Jüngling an der Quelle . . . Franz Schubert
Sei mir gegrüsst . . . . Franz Schubert

II

Am Meer . . . . Franz Schubert
Schlummerlied . . . . Franz Schubert
Litanei . . . . Franz Schubert
Suleika II . . . . Franz Schubert
Die Post . . . . Franz Schubert

III

Schöne Wiege meiner Leiden . . . Robert Schumann
Der Himmel hat eine Träne geweint . Robert Schumann
Er ist's! . . . . Robert Schumann
O ihr Herren . . . . Robert Schumann
Belsazar . . . . Robert Schumann

IV

Provençalisches Lied . . . . . . Robert Schumann
Im Westen . . . . Robert Schumann
Jemand . . . . Robert Schumann
Allnächtlich im Traume . . . . Robert Schumann
Aus alten Märchen winkt es . . . Robert Schumann

SECOND ONE-LANGUAGE RECITAL
(Lotte Lehmann)
I

Minnelied . . . . Johannes Brahms
Geheimnis . . . . Johannes Brahms
Spanisches Lied . . . . Johannes Brahms
Sandmännchen . . . . Johannes Brahms
Auf der Heide weht der Wind . . Johannes Brahms

II

An eine Aeolsharfe . . . . . Johannes Brahms
Hier, wo sich die Strassen scheiden Johannes Brahms
Wir wandelten . . . . Johannes Brahms
Der Kuss . . . . Johannes Brahms
Frühlingstrost . . . . Johannes Brahms

III

Der Tod das ist die kühle Nacht . . Johannes Brahms
Wenn du mir zuweilen lächelst . . Johannes Brahms

Nachtigallen schwingen . . . . . Johannes Brahms
Serenade . . . . Johannes Brahms
Der Jäger . . . . Johannes Brahms

IV

An die Nachtigall . . . . . . Johannes Brahms
O wüsst' ich doch den Weg
zurück . . . . Johannes Brahms
Es liebt sich so lieblich im
Lenze . . . . Johannes Brahms
Salamander . . . . Johannes Brahms
Vergebliches Ständchen . . . . . Johannes Brahms

THIRD ONE-LANGUAGE RECITAL
(Lotte Lehmann)
I

Auf einer Wanderung . . . . . Hugo Wolf
Nun lass uns Frieden schliessen . . Hugo Wolf
Dass doch gemalt all' deine
Reize wären . . . . Hugo Wolf
Geh', Geliebter, geh' jetzt . . . . Hugo Wolf
In dem Schatten meiner Locken . . Hugo Wolf

II

Schlafendes Jesuskind . . . . . Hugo Wolf
Peregrina . . . . Hugo Wolf
Nein, junger Herr . . . . . . Hugo Wolf
An eine Aeolsharfe . . . . . . Hugo Wolf
Waldmädchen . . . . Hugo Wolf

III

Erinnerung . . . . Gustav Mahler
Liebst du um Schönheit . . . . . Gustav Mahler
Das irdische Leben . . . . . . Gustav Mahler
Serenade . . . . Gustav Mahler
Lob des hohen Verstandes . . . . Gustav Mahler

IV

Im Spätboot . . . . Richard Strauss
Geduld . . . . Richard Strauss
Mit deinen blauen Augen . . . . Richard Strauss
Ruhe, meine Seele . . . . . . Richard Strauss
Zueignung . . . . Richard Strauss

The Art of
Accompanying and Coaching

WHAT I have said thus far should have shown how much knowledge is necessary to form the basis on which the art of the accompanist and coach will grow. Those who read the introduction will recall my attempt to have them realize how elusive the meaning of the word "art" is, and how difficult it is to describe artistry adequately. The specific art of accompanying and coaching lies in the ability to deeply feel the soloist's intentions and his artistry; to attune oneself to his artistic style; to recognize his artistic shortcomings and to make up for them by extending a helping hand to lead him, giving him a sense of artistic mastery and matching it by following him. In short, the art of accompanying and coaching is a continuous give and take, a molding of two personalities into one. It consists in serving the music humbly, but with a secure conviction that one is performing it properly. Nobody can describe the elation and the deep happiness that come when this oneness is achieved.

Of course, if your soloist gets *his* satisfaction from *his* work alone, there is not much you can do to share it with him, except to derive satisfaction from accompanying him well. Many instrumentalists and singers insist on putting themselves into the foreground. Yet though they may be strong personalities or have complete mastery of their medium, still I would not call them real artists. A real artist must be humble. Vanity has been the core of many virtuoso careers but it also has been the end of genuine artistic growth. Psychologically, an accompanist and coach must try to search for and understand where the roots of his soloist's artistry lie. These roots are as varied as the individual artists. Faith — religious, metaphysical, or materialistic — is one of the strongest roots; faith in oneself is part of it. Some great artists —

Richard Wagner, for instance — were extremely self-centered, compensating for this fault by preaching altruism in their works. This brings us to another root of artistry: compensation for shortcomings in one's make-up — atonement for real or imagined sins and errors. A third very important root is rebellion against family, upbringing, or an adverse fate. Among those who rebel are some of our greatest artists, who have become what they are by surmounting seemingly overwhelming odds. Complacency is not a good stimulus to artistry.

All these things would not be sufficient to produce an artist if he had not at the same time a good deal of sensitivity. Without sensitivity — the ability to feel influences from without and within and to sublimate them into art — there can be no artistry. The understanding of what makes a particular artist tick may be very valuable to the process through which the accompanist and coach must go if he wants to become one with the artist. But rarely can an artist be read like an open book.

Up to now I have been speaking only of the best artists. But an accompanist and coach will have ample opportunity to work with less favored artists and even with amateurs, on concert stages as well as in homes, churches, and studios. With such performers it is of great importance that the accompanist and coach not use his powers to the fullest and thereby overpower the artist. The real accompanist and coach must be able to place himself not on the level of the soloist but on a somewhat higher level; he will thus bring out the best in his soloist without capturing for himself the whole success of the performance. That he is not in conformity with the soloist is about the worst that could be said about an accompanist. If you feel you are born to dominate, do not try to become an accompanist. Neither choose this vocation if you are prone to subdue yourself to the extent of losing your personality completely. These two extremes of personality will make you unhappy as an accompanist — and I do not refer to the kind of happiness the pursuit of which is guaranteed by our Constitution, nor to the feeling of having fun, but to a deeply rooted content, a quietly glowing happiness, a deep satisfaction, a fulfillment of one's dreams and aspirations.

THE ART OF COACHING

After having struggled step by step through the dense thicket of technical knowledge, the accompanist and coach is now ready for the artistic problems he will have to cope with. When we discuss and explain art, we must necessarily leave the grounds of exact description. Art can be analyzed to a great extent, but there will always remain an unknown, elusive quality that cannot be caught on paper or in speech. Like anything else beyond the realm of intellect, the description of art must make use of imagery, comparison, circumscription, and other non-exact means of explanation. Herein lies the difference between science and art, and between artisanship and artistry. No matter where the spark of artistry really comes from — be it God-given or simply a particular combination of chromosomes, genes, or cells — without it, nobody can become an artist.

The gift of artistry is not rare. Most of mankind has it in early youth. Environment, parental care, and teaching must combine to fan this spark, develop this talent. Otherwise it may lie dormant for years and break through suddenly, sometimes too late to be realized as a vocation. It may, on the other hand, spurt out all at once in a gigantic flame. And it can be extinguished by bad teaching.

But the purpose of this book is not to speculate philosophically about the phenomenon of artistry. In these last pages I mean to guide the accompanist and coach as close to the source of his art as is humanly possible, and the best way I know how is to draw on my own forty years of experience.

This is the point where the roads for accompanists and coaches turn in different directions. As I said before, specialization has to come eventually. Should you become a coach or an accompanist? Of course, the musician's struggle for a living makes it imperative that he follow both roads and take any job that offers itself. But professional heights in both vocations can be reached only by very few. I do not know a single artist who, even if equally great as both accompanist and coach (which happens very rarely) can pursue both specialties with the same opportunity and success. With the exception of this small handful of combination coaches and accompanists, there are some top accompanists, vocal as well as instrumental, not so proficient in coaching as some others who, on the other hand, just have not got the pianistic armament to make the playing of concert accompaniments their life's vocation. Coach and conductor — that is a very good combination. Accompanist and conductor is rare; in our time, I know of only a few: Richard Strauss for one (in his own lieder), Bruno Walter, and George Széll.

What then are the respective criteria for the professionals of accompanying and of coaching? When should the talented student concentrate on one, when on the other? I would say simply this: If he is mostly interested in performing, if he has outstanding pianistic ability, and if he is able to share the give and take of musical emotions equally with his soloist, the student should try to become an accompanist. If, on the other hand, his urge to teach is greater than his desire to perform in public, if asserting his leadership is more important to him than the submersion in somebody else's feeling, he should become a coach. I repeat once more: a very few lucky ones have the good fortune to choose for themselves. More often a quirk of fate, opportunity, or chance determines the direction in which one will be thrown. But in any case, it is important to *know* where one's strength lies. And knowledge paired with energy and, no doubt, some good luck will frequently get one where he wants to be.

In this chapter I shall try to explain the art of coaching. As I have suggested, the main ingredients that go into the making of a good coach are: the ability to teach, an inner conviction that will establish authority and is based on knowledge, the assertion of leadership, and the love of imparting artistic guidance. Add to these the complete mastery of all the technical and stylistic problems discussed in this book; a feeling for, if not a thorough knowledge of, psychology; a sound pianistic background; excellent sightreading and transposing faculties; and — last but not least — an even temper, patience, and perseverance.

I know of no better way to start this chapter than to tell what happens when a singer calls me with the intention of coaching with me. I use the specific term singer purposely, because more than ninety per cent of coaches will have to coach singers. The number of instrumentalists who seek a coach is negligible; they get their coaching from their specialist teachers, just as dancers follow the advice of choreographers or ballet masters.

I always ask the prospective pupil for references; as you would not want to invite just anybody off the street into your house, so you must have some kind of reference for somebody who may become your pupil. This point cleared up satisfactorily, I ask the student to come for an audition so that we may get acquainted with each other. This is another necessary step because of the many crackpots among singers. Singing, in my opinion, is a primitive urge in mankind, and near and dear to the healthy mind as well as to the not so healthy one. This audition must not be confused, however, with one given with the purpose of having me utter an opinion about the student's artistic future — an audition that amounts to a consultation.

Well, the appointment has been made and the first approach to employ is psychology. A coach must develop a faculty for sizing up the prospective pupil and for questioning him in such a way as to find out his makeup, his artistic possibilities, his problems, his attitude. The main point is to determine whether the pupil is really interested in a career to the point of being obsessed by it. I call this being bitten by the bug.

The pupil's individuality will show itself the moment he enters the room: the timid one, the one who compensates for his inner insecurity by trying to appear dead sure of himself, the nervous one, the one without any nerves, the one with the businesslike approach. I try to put the newcomer at ease by asking him to sit down and rélax and by making small talk for a minute or so. Then I ask him to tell me his musical background. His answers are always revealing. One can deduce from them not only his actual musical training but his family problems and his financial state. Knowing all this beforehand is very important. Complicated family problems or the necessity of having a full-time or part-time job will influence my judgment of whether the coaching will lead to a more or less fast success or to no success at all, even before he opens his mouth to sing.

After these introductory probings, I fire one of my strongest shots. I give him to understand that with the tremendous number of beautiful voices in this country only the singers who are really *possessed* by the thought of a career have a chance to survive the tough competition. Again, his reaction will be very revealing. As a rule, he assures me that he would undergo any privation in order to achieve his goal — which, most often, is nothing less than the Metropolitan Opera. But a few fall by the wayside right there by confessing that they are interested in a career as a means of making a living. These people, though honest and realistic, do not stand much chance. Economic freedom, of course, is a wonderful if rare prerequisite for a career in our society. On the other hand, it may create a too easygoing attitude.

After this preparatory conversation I ask the prospective pupil to sing for me something in which he thinks he can show his best side. Hardly ever does he sing a selection his voice can do justice to. Usually, it is an aria or a song much too heavy and dramatic for his budding voice. After deducting about fifty per cent for nervousness, I can already form a preliminary first impression. I then ask the prospective pupil to name the selections he knows, and I choose one in a different language and mood. By and by, he finds his heart, his voice, his nerve. By the time he is singing the third selection he is usually at his best possible. Sometimes I even ask for a semiclassical song or a show tune if a career as an opera or lieder singer seems doubtful to me. I also try to put to him some artistic suggestions and watch his response closely to see how quickly he understands me and whether he is sufficiently responsive to criticism.

By now, the vocal state, the musicality, the facility of diction, the talent for foreign languages, the personality, the artistic nucleus, the ability for opera, lied, or oratorio — in short, the potentialities of the singer — have become pretty clear to me, as have his psychological problems. This is not to say that I have not made terrible errors in judgment. But on the whole my batting average has been good.

The first thing after the actual audition is to calm down the pupil. In any critique I always tell him the good things first — and there is nobody who hasn't at least something good to be talked about. Then comes the real criticism, which I may make a little harsher than necessary if I think the pupil can take it, to see how he responds. I also venture my ideas about the long-range planning of his career. I close the interview by accepting the pupil, first for a period when both of us will be on trial, or by turning him back to his voice teacher if he is not yet ready vocally to be coached, or by suggesting to him that he should first catch up with elementary musical background such as sightreading and ear training.

I never criticize any of his teachers. A teacher, especially a voice teacher, occupies a very sensitive spot in any pupil's affections and this kind of criticism should be left until much later, when the pupil will trust me more fully. Even if a new pupil is not happy with his voice teacher and asks me to recommend another, I would not do so right away. Recommending a voice teacher is like recommending a surgeon: the responsibility is overwhelming. Besides, each singer has particular problems and not every voice teacher is suited to tackling every problem. There are, for instance, some voice teachers, not necessarily the most famous, who are good for relaxing the voice, others who are good for demanding more intensity. Some teachers concentrate on building up breath support; others specialize in repair work on damaged voices, and so on. If, at a later date, I feel I ought to accede to the pupil's wish to have me name a new voice teacher, I usually give him three names, all selected with a view to helping his particular problem; I tell him to choose the one that appeals to him most after taking at least a few lessons from each.

All this brings me to a very important element in the work of a coach: his relation to the voice teacher. It is of the utmost importance that they get in touch with each other, that they discuss the problems of the pupil, and that they handle him in a very similar way. It is, for instance, harmful to the pupil if his voice teacher tells him to use the "smiling" or horizontal mouth position, and his coach insists upon the pupil's "lowering his jaw," thus opening the mouth vertically. If the coach must have the last say in musical and stylistic questions, the voice teacher certainly ought to decide on the voice technique. Voice teacher and coach must not have a tug of war with the poor pupil.

They must try to get together on imagery for the pupil. The technical terms teachers and coaches use are usually very flowery — and indefinite. One must find the right language for each pupil. Some singers' imaginations need to be stimulated, others have their heads too high in the clouds of imagery and should be brought down to a more sober terminology. Sometimes teacher and coach use diametrically opposed images to explain the same thing. For instance, the coach may say, "Sing more forward, the voice does not carry, and the diction becomes mushy." The teacher, trying to remedy the same shortcomings, may say, "Think of producing the tone further back," meaning that resonance should be added. Teacher and

coach must agree which terms to use; otherwise utter confusion will follow.

Coach and teacher must also let one another know whenever one of them spots possible danger signals, vocal or musical, in the pupil. Another important part of the cooperation between teacher and coach is the choice of music for the pupil. Here the coach should be aware that teachers tend not to hear their pupils as they actually sound at the moment of their lesson, but as they want them to sound in the future. This is why arias and songs given pupils by their teachers are usually too heavy. A serious telephone conversation may bring about agreement on the right musical literature. Unfortunately, cooperation in this respect is not always easily achieved.

There are many other points where the interests of teacher and coach intersect — too many, in fact, to be enumerated here. The main thing for the coach to remember is: always do things by agreement, and insist on being allowed to aid in the choice of literature. Do not shrink from summit meetings!

Teacher and coach should also discuss the psychological and pedagogical approach to be used with their different pupils. I have found out through bitter experience that no method, no one way of treating the singer, can be adopted. The coach's psychology and his pedagogical approach must be flexible. Overly nervous pupils must be calmed down; phlegmatic ones must be whipped up into a frenzy of studying. Too-diligent ones must be braked, lazy ones ought to be given a daily assignment. Self-conscious pupils must be encouraged, conceited ones should be hit unmercifully (if the conceit is genuine and not an overcompensation for insecurity). I have seen hysteria so severe that not one tone would come out of a singer's throat. In such cases, the artificial creation of a minor breakdown with tears has proved very helpful. After the breakdown, the singer relaxes and his voice becomes better. In such extreme cases, family or other personal difficulties usually can be blamed.

In general, I have had very good success with changing the approach every few lessons. If, for instance, a pupil comes to a lesson unprepared, I listen to his explanations, try to be understanding, and wait for the next lesson. If this laxity continues, I crack down on him hard.

Never let a pupil become stale. Work on every sixteenth note; but when you see that his performance is becoming too mechanical, change the part, aria, or song, and read through something the pupil has never done.

Keep his interest awake, increase it, make him hunger for more, broaden his musical horizon.

If a pupil comes to a lesson complaining about a sore throat, headache, or other symptoms of oncoming sickness, and you are sure he is not malingering or finding excuses for being unprepared, send him home and make up the lesson later. You will lose more money if you make him sing in such a state, and force him to cancel a number of succeeding lessons.

After a while, you will notice that you have lost your ability to evaluate your pupil's progress and also lost the distance from him that enables you to see his shortcomings. You have grown so familiar with his voice and his habits that you are not able to improve him any more. This is the moment for you to suggest that he look for another coach, who will have a fresh ear and a fresh approach to his problem. Don't worry! A new pupil usually will already be ringing your bell. Remember: singing is a primitive urge!

Whenever I feel uncertain about my pupil's progress or my own usefulness to him, I like to get the opinion of a colleague. And when I feel sure that I cannot improve a pupil any more I tell him so and suggest that he find another coach. This is true for hopeless pupils as well as for pupils with prolonged artistic or vocal stagnation.

Coaching has two main purposes: building repertoire and preparation for specific performances — concerts, auditions, or contests. In such preparation, the coach must be very persistent, even to the most minute details, so that a piece is completely ready to be performed. He must put the singer on a special training schedule, like an oarsman training for a race. It will not do for the pupil to know only two or three audition pieces and nothing else. If one wants to open a business one must have goods to sell; these goods encompass not only voice, personality, and the like — in short, quality — but also quantity, a repertoire. The right psychology to be used for divining the particulars of coming auditions is usually more than half of the success. One could write a book about the psychology of audition judges. Keep in mind that they want variety in order to learn the auditionist's potentialities. But, above all, know that judges do not want to listen to long selections. Any coloratura soprano, for instance, auditioning the Bell Song or the entire Mad Scene has already one strike against her. Judges have only a limited time to listen to a singer. Do not have him strain their patience too much! If you can, find out what the audition is supposed to accomplish, what

vacancies there are, what the forthcoming repertoire of an opera company will be, what kinds of selection the judges may lend a benevolent ear to. If you are able to determine this, your auditionist is already a step ahead of the others. Coach your student in appearance, projection, and poise at auditions. Give him self-assurance. A coach's main success in placing a pupil lies in knowing the right selection for the right opening at the right moment.

Group or class coaching requires a different approach from individual coaching. Some coaches teach in music schools, others may form a class in their studios. In both situations they have to cope with groups that are usually very unevenly assembled in regard to voice categories: there may be five lyric sopranos, two mezzo-sopranos, no tenor, a baritone, and three basses. What to do with them? The first job of a coach working with a group is to keep everybody's interest aroused. In coaching songs, the coach should make the whole class listen while he demonstrates problems of interpretation, style, and so on with one of his pupils. He should make the others repeat particular vocal phrases and have them become conscious of violations of taste, rhythm, phrasing, and pitch. A fair distribution of the opportunity to sing is essential for group coaching.

Constructive criticism and the absence of favoritism will be appreciated by the pupils. If one of them has an important performance or audition coming, the coach should tailor the selections to this particular singer. Otherwise, a repertoire should be chosen that includes parts for the voice combinations present in the class. To keep a healthy sense of competition alive and to keep everybody happy are the first laws for group coaching.

A decided advantage in group coaching lies in the possibility of acquainting the singers with operatic concertati — larger ensembles. Too often these operatic ensembles are neglected in favor of arias, duets, and trios; morever, at a later stage in his career the singer will have very little time to study them. Here is a chance for the coach to save the singers future difficulty by preparing them in time.

If a singer is weak or timid, group coaching may give him an opportunity to overcome this shortcoming. Let him sing along in unison with another, more self-assured pupil. All in all, it can be said that group coaching, like group psychotherapy, though not so valuable as individual "treatment," has its merits.

But enough of psychological and pedagogical approaches. I must now discuss the musical ingredients necessary to the art of coaching.

First of all, the coach must be a good sightreader. This is even more important than his being a good pianist. As we shall shortly see, the coach's pianistic style is very different from the accompanist's. You will hardly have time to practice new musical material brought to you by the pupil; instead you must be able to scan it very quickly and to play it, if not perfectly, well enough at least to stress all the essentials. Not all good coaches have been good sightreaders originally. But just as Demosthenes trained himself to overcome his stuttering and became a great orator, a coach can train himself to become a good sightreader. If, however, after years of trying (and nothing less than years will do) you find that you still cannot simultaneously read the piano part and the vocal line or lines of a score, play the essentials of the accompaniment, be in absolute control of the vocal line, and give cues in addition, you had better give up and become something else. A certain presence of mind and a certain ability to omit less essential figurations in difficult accompaniments may be helpful.

I remember that, during my first year of professional coaching, at the Berlin State Opera, my boss, the late Hermann Weigert, one of the greatest Wagnerian and Straussian coaches of our time, gave me an important assignment: to coach in the composer's presence the main role of one of Franz Schreker's very difficult, bombastically inflated opera scores, entirely unknown to me at that time. To my frantic protests that I did not know the score, Weigert answered, "None of the other coaches knows it either, but you at least will be able to fake your way through." Which I did.

Another important ingredient of the art of coaching is the ability to transpose. Most transpositions will be made a half step or a whole step up or down. There are shortcuts and several technical ways of making this task easier. Good books exist, as do books about sightreading. Transposing usually involves mentally changing sharps to naturals, naturals to flats, flats to double flats, or vice versa. No pupil will fly into a rage if you are not able to transpose a harmonically complicated Hugo Wolf or Debussy song at first sight. But simple transpositions, such as playing Rosina's aria from *The Barber of Seville* half a tone up from the original E major, as is always done if a soprano sings the part, must be performed without mistakes. A Schubert or Schumann song

also is not difficult to transpose if a talent for it and perseverance in training oneself are present.

Every young coach's bugaboo is the problem of how much of the piano accompaniment transcribed from an original orchestral piece he should play. The first rule here is: do not play everything; it only confuses the singer. Leave the pianistic fireworks to the accompanist. Know what is important for the singer. In operatic literature you will have to know the orchestration and the harmonic and rhythmic structure. Then decide how much or how little to play. As I shall discuss in more detail later on, this will be different at different phases of the singer's preparation. Generally, however, it is safe to say that the most important part of the music for the singer to hear in opera is the *harmonic and rhythmic skeleton.* And in this skeleton the backbone is created by the bass notes — sounds of the bass instruments that stand out in every musical composition. They are the most prominent sounds a singer will hear in an orchestration and the sturdiest pillars for him to lean on. It has been said that a good coach can do his work with one finger of each hand. Though this is a gross exaggeration there is an element of truth in it: the finger on the left hand plays the bass and the right hand helps with a primitive harmony. I am not advocating this except for occasional checkups by the coach to see with how little playing he is still able to give the essentials of a piece.

It is most desirable that coaches be able to play from full scores (partituras), but this is not absolutely essential. The coach must, however, know how to condense vocal ensembles — trios, quartets, sextets, and large choral settings — into compact harmonic structures. Vocal ensembles like the canon from Beethoven's *Fidelio,* the quartet from Mozart's *Don Giovanni,* the sextet from the same opera or from Donizetti's *Lucia* must be played without a part missing. The ability to condense orchestral or vocal lines can only be acquired by an intense study first of full-score reading and then of full-score playing.

Here are some examples of harmonic and rhythmic skeletons, marked by the heavier notes: Figure 221 shows harmonic skeleton (lied); Figure 222, harmonic skeleton (opera); Figure 223, rhythmic skeleton (opera); Figure 224, not clearly recognizable harmonic structure changed temporarily into pure harmony for coaching purposes; Figure 225, twelve-tone patterns; Figure 226, a cappella music. After imparting to the student coach the realization that there are these different patterns, I

Figure 221. Schubert, "Mein," harmonic skeleton

Figure 222. Wagner, *Die Walküre*, harmonic skeleton

Figure 223. Wagner, *Das Rheingold*, rhythmic skeleton

Figure 224. Strauss, *Salome*, unclear harmony changed temporarily to pure harmony for coaching purposes

Figure 224 continued

can now proceed to show how each pattern should be coached.

After all's said and done, the harmonic and rhythmic skeleton is the basis for coaching. Even in modern music where the harmonic structure is not evident, harmony should be created temporarily until it is safe for the singer to discard it. Our ear since the sixteenth century has been trained to hear harmonically; our scales, triads, and other chords are based on harmony. In old polyphonic music, as well as in modern linear or atonal compositions, the linear (horizontal) line is more important. Though the coach should make this weave of counterpoint or twelve-tone combinations clear to the pupil, our ears will still be searching for some latent harmony. In some compositions, rhythmical patterns predominate over melodic and harmonic structures, and these patterns must be stressed by the coach. Likewise, harmonic accompaniment should be used temporarily in a cappella passages to be discarded as soon as the student knows his music.

In addition to the harmonic skeleton, the coach must play the melody (if any) with the singer, must mark the pauses in the voice line, must decide whether the singer should rely on counting the pauses or should listen

for a musical cue, must give (sing) these cues, must put breath marks and phrasing divisions into the singer's part, and must make him conscious of the proper dynamics. This done, the coach must then proceed to explain to the singer the meaning of the part; help translate foreign lyrics into English; and not only explain the words, but the ideas, inflections, moods behind the words. At the same time he must fill in the accompaniment with fuller harmonies, more and more rhythmical figurations and contrapuntal voices, playing less and less of the melody, urging the pupil on to start memorizing the music.

The last stage of preparation is reached with the coach working out details and shadings, insisting on full intensity of expression and projection, ironing out mistakes in diction, marking the time with one hand, and, if possible, acquainting the singer with the peculiarities of a conductor's beat, encouraging, criticizing, helping, giving, giving, giving. Quite a bill to fill!

Let's tackle each of these points separately and distinguish between operatic or oratorio coaching and song coaching.

OPERATIC AND ORATORIO COACHING

In the very beginning when coach, voice teacher, and singer have decided on a part, the coach should give the pupil a short synopsis of the story and the character's particular place in it. He should insist that the pupil underline his part in the score and mark the pages where the part continues. This done, the coach should mark the beat of the lesson's portion of the part. This can be done in two ways: either by marking the beat of the more complicated spots by vertical strokes (Fig. 227a) or by writing in the units of time pertaining to the pauses (Fig. 227b). There are two possible methods of marking the units of time, as shown in Figure 228. One may either mark the rests in progression (a), or one may mark each measure with progressive numbers, filling in the rest of each measure with its time unit (b). I prefer the second method although some singers are good mathematicians and get faster results from method (a).

Pauses are music. The coach will notice that every pupil is reluctant to count pauses. In difficult places or in long periods of rest, make the pupil count the rests *aloud* in the beginning, so he'll be conscious that they belong to his part. Insist on that, notwithstanding the resistance the pupil is sure to offer.

Now the coach should play the singer's part, sup-

Figure 225. Berg, *Wozzeck*, twelve-tone patterns

Figure 226. Wagner, *Lohengrin*, a cappella music

Figure 226 continued

Figure 227. Verdi, *Requiem*, sample of coach's marking
of the beat

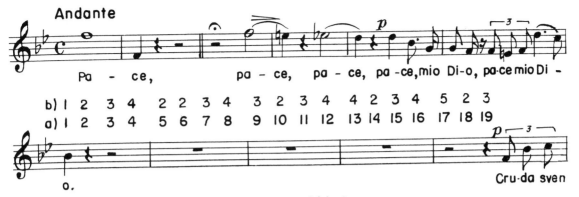

Figure 228. Verdi, *La Forza del destino*, two ways
of marking pauses

Figure 229. Verdi, *Il Trovatore*

Figure 230. Tchaikovsky, *Eugene Onegin*, part of an aria as written
(upper staves) and as played by the coach (lower staves)

ported by a simplified harmony in the left hand, encouraging the pupil to sing with him. If the harmony is sustained by simple figuration, as for instance in Count di Luna's aria "Il Balen" from Verdi's *Il Trovatore*, this kind of figuration will not confuse the singer and should therefore be played from the very beginning (Fig. 229). The psychological insight and the experience of the coach will determine whether he should concentrate on a thorough treatment of a small section of the role, stopping to correct all mistakes in diction, dynamics, and so on, or handle only one problem at a time and cover more ground. There can be no set rule, but the realization of what is right for a particular student marks the difference among good, bad, and indifferent coaches. At this stage, part of an aria printed in the score as shown in the upper staves of Figure 230 will be played by the coach as shown in the lower. If a pupil is weak musically, one must not grow impatient with playing the melody over and over again. Insistence on elementary musical training (solfeggio, ear training) with the proper teachers may help the coach. One must decide whether a singer learns by the visual method (seeing the music and impressing this picture in his mind), or by the acoustical method (hearing the sound and keeping the image in mind). There is still another way, the motoric way of memorizing, which means that the pupil beats time with feet or body, conducting with hands or other parts of the body. This should be stopped at all cost by the coach. Bad habits like these have a way of hanging on. Nothing is more disturbing than to see a singer on stage beating time while he is singing, or indicating syncopations or grace notes by jerks of his head.

At later stages, the same arias may be played with increasingly rich harmonies and rhythmical figurations.

All in all, the various phases of pianistic accompaniment for an average musical student's operatic coaching may be summed up in this way:

1st phase. Play voice line in upper voice, simplified harmony in left hand, and, if possible, with fingers of right hand not busy with playing melody. Do not play any harmony above melody.

2nd phase. The same, except repeating in left hand harmony in chords in accordance with the beat unit.

3rd phase. The same, but play bass in original rhythm; if indicated, start playing harmony also above melody.

4th phase. Same as 3rd, but start playing contrapuntal patterns wherever indicated. In ensembles play other singing voices.

5th phase. Same as 4th, but start leaving out voice line gradually. Be sure, though, to play first note of voice line if student is not yet secure in pitch.

6th phase. Final stage of preparation. Play score as pupil will hear it in orchestral sound, leaving out voice line entirely. If students show more talent, one or the other phase may be eliminated. If the pupil is extremely slow, more time must be given to each phase.

Rhythmically difficult voice parts should first be *spoken* in the rhythm and tempo of their music. Only after rhythm and diction have been established firmly should the singing voice be added to the words. If the singer is not coached to master the rhythm right in the beginning, later will be too late. This rhythmical recitation is also very necessary in choral passages where clarity of rhythm is of prime importance. And, of course, in the few melodramas in musical literature, the whole effect of this particular art is based on exact rhythmical recitation. A good example may be the clipped speech in Schoenberg's *Gurrelieder* (Fig. 231). Modern works

Figure 231. Schoenberg, *Gurrelieder*

sometimes make use of the half-spoken, half-sung word. This Sprechgesang has no relation to Wagnerian recitative. It is a recitation on pitch. The heads of notes are usually marked by crosses. The example from Alban Berg's *Wozzeck* (Fig. 232) will make this clear. The

Figure 232. Berg, *Wozzeck*

coach must insist that the words first be spoken in the proper rhythm. Then the student should try to add a little voice, *not* a real singing voice, on the desired pitch. If this sounds too much like singing it is better later to alter the pitch slightly, bringing it back to natural recitation, than to have the composer's intentions ruined by arioso singing. Of course, some phrases in operas or oratorios are just spoken or shouted. Take as an example Marcello's outcry in *La Bohème*, as shown in Figure 233. In opera, a singer will not know when and on what pitch to come in unless he is thoroughly conditioned to it by his coach. In fact, most of a singer's musical mistakes stem from either counting wrongly, or from not counting the rests at all. Singing or playing cues is therefore basic to good coaching. Two kinds of cues—vocal cues and orchestral ones—teach a singer the right entrances.

Figure 233. Puccini, *La Bohème*

The vocal cue contains another operatic character's last sung line, or, if the vocal lines overlap, the last word before our student's entrance. A vocal cue may be either sung by the coach, if he has something that faintly approaches a singing voice, or played on the piano and at the same time spoken on pitch. I should like to use for this technique of half-singing the term "marking."

"Marking" should be taught pupils by their voice teachers. Germans call this process *markieren*. There is no one word in English to express the same meaning, but the use of the verb "mark" may be excused for this purpose. Normally, marking means something different, but in the singer's vernacular it means singing in half voice. Half-voice singing is recommended in learning a new part before it sinks in. "Marking" at that stage conserves the voice and gives the pupil a chance to study without tiring the vocal cords. Which brings me back to the matter of cues. Vocal cues should be "marked" by the coach. It is a sign of a good coach that he knows exactly how much of a cue the singer ought to be given. Too short a cue, especially in fast tempo, might not bring him in on time; too long a cue may make him lose

his concentration. The logical way of giving the right cue is always the most musical way. In general, the last complete vocal phrase should be given and the pauses before the singer's entrance must be counted (Fig. 234). Where the tempo changes at an entrance, a cue should be chosen that starts in the old tempo. Thus the singer will grow accustomed to the change of tempo at this particular point and it will not come as a surprise (Fig. 235).

In ensembles, the best cue is the one that the singer will hear on stage either because he will be standing near the artist who sings it (something that a coach can not always foresee since ways of staging vary) or because it predominates by reason of its melodic or dynamic value. If there is no real melody contained in a vocal line, the last sequence of words or a logical part of such a sequence should be given (Fig. 236). Sometimes, especially in complicated ensembles, the vocal cue may confuse a singer. When this happens, an orchestral cue should be found that can easily be heard by the singer. From then on, it's count the rests until the entrance. Take for instance Herodias's entrance in *Salome* after the very complicated ensemble of the Jews who sing the same music for a long stretch. The only sure way is to find an outstanding spot in the predominating trombones' part and to count the pauses and the patterns until the entrance comes (Fig. 237). In some ensembles, however, the harmonic and rhythmic patterns appear in the voice lines, the orchestra just playing less important figurations. When this happens the coach must play all vocal lines, reading them at a glance and finding a way to distribute them between his two hands. A good example is the famous quintet from *Carmen* (Fig. 238).

Sometimes, after a cue is given the singer must continue his part, but it will be interrupted by a number of rests. It is the job of the coach to help the singer memorize this pattern of rests, usually by "magical" numbers. The beginning of the part of Uncle Bonzo in Puccini's *Madama Butterfly* has to be established backstage by the coach's giving the entrance to the singer. From there on the solution is strict counting, the magical numbers being 1, 1, 1, 3, 2, 2, 3 (Fig. 239). In the absence of any nearby vocal cue, the orchestral cue takes over entirely (Fig. 240). In general, I prefer giving the singer musical cues whenever possible. When conditioned to vocal cues, he depends entirely on the musicality of his fellow singer. How often does it befall a singer to come in too late because he knows nothing but his partner's

Figure 234. Mozart, *Le Nozze di Figaro*

Figure 235. Leoncavallo, *Pagliacci*

Moderato

Octavian: Das ist ein Kerl!— dem möcht' ich wo be-geg-nen mit mei-nem

Faninal: als wär' sie ihm schon an - ge-traut. Und

De - gen da,— wo ihn kein Wäch-ter schrei — en hört.— Ja das ist

da steht ein Ro-fra - no, grad' als müsst's so sein____

Sophie:

al - les was ich möcht! Ei lass er doch. Wir sind nicht so ver-traut!

ein Graf Ro - fra - - no, son-sten nix,

Figure 236. Strauss, *Der Rosenkavalier*

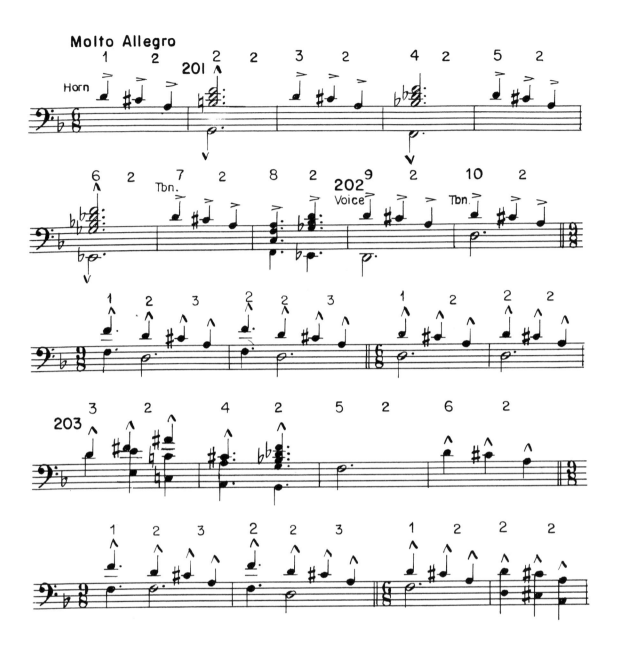

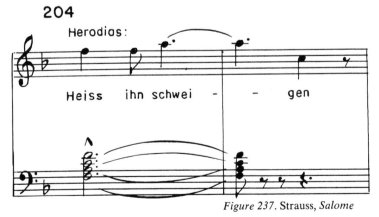

Figure 237. Strauss, *Salome*

Et   sans   el – les   Mes tou-tes belles, on   ne   fait   ja – mais   rien   De bien.   Quoi!   sans nous

Figure 238. Bizet, *Carmen*

Cio-cio - san! ___   Cio-cio - san! ___

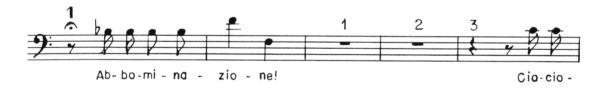

Ab- bo-mi - na - zio - ne!   Cio-cio -

san! ___   Cio-cio - san! ___   Cio-cio -

san! ___   Cio-cio- san! ___

Figure 239. Puccini, *Madama Butterfly*

Figure 240. Wagner, *Die Walküre*

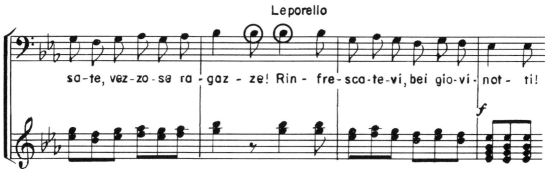

Figure 241. Mozart, *Don Giovanni*

Figure 242. Verdi, *La Traviata*

Figure 243. Wagner, *Lohengrin*

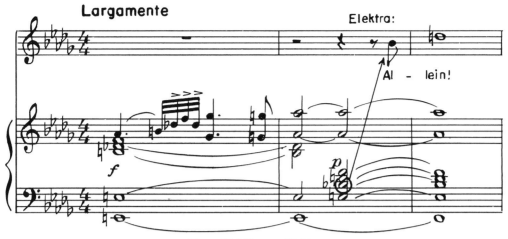

Figure 244. Strauss, *Elektra*

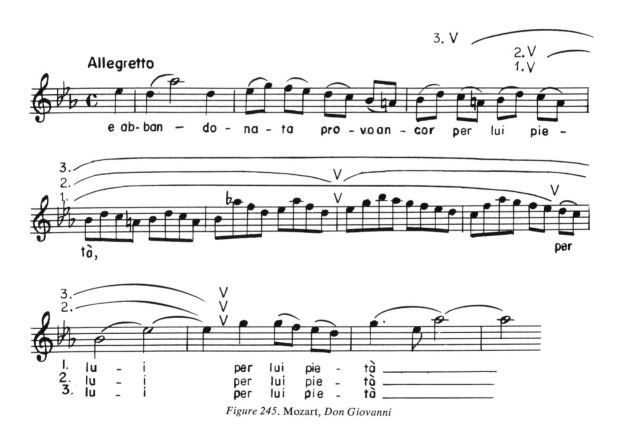

Figure 245. Mozart, *Don Giovanni*

line and his partner just happened to be late himself? One could imagine that in such a circumstance the curtain, too, would start falling too late. The conductor or prompter will usually be able to straighten things out.

How does a singer find the tone on which he has to come in? In the majority of older operatic and oratorio scores the tone will belong to the harmony of the orchestral accompaniment. Assuming normal musicality in a student, the coach must point out to him which tone in a chord is the one to come in on. The pitch can be established either from the vocal line of one of the other characters (Fig. 241) or from the orchestral accompaniment (Fig. 242).

Finding the right pitch becomes difficult if the orchestral accompaniment is very soft, or if the cue tone lies in a much higher or lower part of the musical scale, or if it comes after a long pause. Then the coach must accustom the singer to hearing these faint tones and mentally transferring them into the octave in which he must start his phrase (Fig. 243). Sometimes applause after a set number may interrupt the flow of music for a time. If this happens, the coach must urge the singer to think or even to hum the tone during the applause.

In harmonically more complicated operas or oratorios, no direct connection between cue and first tone may be found. Up to the operas of Richard Strauss, however, there is always present a latent harmony which will divulge the desired pitch. Otherwise, a related tone in an interval to be easily associated by the singer must be used as pitch cue. Sometimes it will be a tone in the orchestral bass, sometimes even in an orchestral middle voice. The coach must condition the singer to hear this

tone and to take his pitch from it. If there is no harmony at all, as in very old or very new music, some relationship between tones must be constructed temporarily by the coach and kept up until the singer is able to hit his tone without hesitation. Then the temporary bridge may be abandoned (Fig. 244).

An efficient coach always chooses the right cue tone. Musical and logical thought and experience will be of greatest advantage in this. If the tempo is fast and there is the danger that the singer may be surprised by a quick entrance and therefore miss it, it is more than advisable for the coach to insist that the singer learn the vocal cue line as if it belonged to his part — humming it or singing it along soundlessly (Fig. 245).

Although phrasing is mainly a question of style, and breath should be taken whenever a musical phrase ends or whenever proper diction and recitation warrant it, exceptions exist. I have discussed phrasing and breathing in other chapters of this book; here, it is timely to remind coaches that breath marks can and should be changed according to the singer's individual needs. The main purpose of a coach's art is not only to make his student proficient in singing but also to make him feel at ease while performing. Some students have less breath support than others. Even while making the student work just a bit harder, trying to train and improve his breath support, the coach nevertheless should feel free, even obliged, to put in more breath marks, change existing ones, and increase the intensity of expression by doing so. This can be done on a temporary basis. Considerable time will elapse before a singer feels a phrase "in his voice." Until then, the phrase should be made

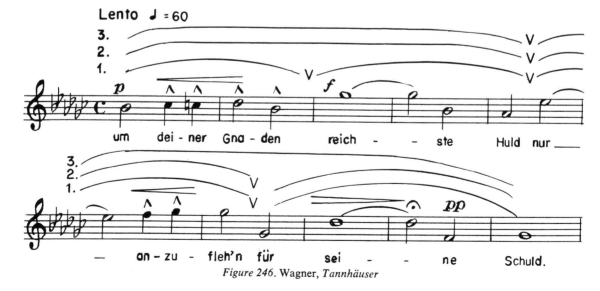

Figure 246. Wagner, *Tannhäuser*

easier by the addition of more breath marks. Once the student is thoroughly familiar with the phrase, some of these auxiliary breath marks can be taken away.

Here is an example of phrases famous for being difficult to sing in one breath. It is given in three sets of breath marks, the last version being the most desirable (Fig. 246). The breath marks of the earlier stage should be left in the scores for emergencies. It may well happen that a singer will sometimes not feel very well during a performance. When that happens he can fall back on these additional emergency breaths.

It takes time to breathe. However short a phrase between breaths is, it will shorten the notes adjoining to the breath mark. The coach must see to it that the note *before* the breath mark is shortened somewhat. Otherwise the phrase after the breath mark would start too late. The beginning of a phrase must never be shortened. If shortening has to be done it must be the end of a phrase that is shortchanged.

The coach in extreme cases is even justified in changing the lyrics — repeating one word, or putting in another fitting one if beauty of sound and intensity of feeling can thus be saved (Fig. 247). One of the greatest sopranos of the last forty years, Lotte Lehmann, needed a lot of breath to make her phrases expressive. At present, Renata Tebaldi uses the same kind of breathing. Both take a breath wherever it helps to make the meaning of music and lyrics clearer to their audiences. One word of caution: the coach must not overstep the boundaries of good taste by plucking phrases apart.

Figure 247. Beethoven, *Fidelio*

Changes are also permissible in cadenzas. A cadenza is meant to show a singer's vocal brilliance, his flexibility in rapid passage work, his range, and his ability to sing with proper expression. In bass cadenzas the profoundness of voice is stressed; in coloratura cadenzas the extreme top notes, the agility of a soprano's voice, her ability to sustain a long-spun trill, and so on. Each singer has some strong points and some weak ones. Composers used to fit their cadenzas to their star singers, and these are the cadenzas that got into the printed vocal score. It is quite possible that a student has other strong points that should be stressed and weak points

that should be covered up. If this is true, the coach is justified in altering a cadenza and giving the student a different one. Needless to say, the coach must be extremely careful not to give the student a cadenza which could not possibly be identified with a composer's style. The coach must also have it in mind that a cadenza is not just a means of showing vocal technique: it must also express emotion. Knowledge of style and artistic taste will help him find the golden middle road.

If the coach has been able to teach the student all the different elements of role study contained in the last paragraphs, the singer should now be able to *read* through a part with ease. At this point the second plateau of coaching should start. By this I mean that the student is now ready to be taught expression, the meaning of words and music and their interplay, symbolism, realism or verism, the psychology of a role, the reaction of an operatic character to the other persons in the same opera — in short, he is ready to develop his personality and artistry. A good coach knows that a role has been perceived by the composer in one way, but that there are as many individual approaches to it as there are artists. The coach will have to modify the composer's "right" way by bringing out the singer's particular personality and fitting it to the part.

There have, for instance, been great Boris Godunovs past and present. Of the ones known to me, I shall mention only Chaliapin, Pinza, Siepi, London, Hines, Christoff, and Rossi-Lemmeni. Each of them was or is great but each of them perceived the part differently. Chaliapin, of course, was the most perfect Boris. But each of them fitted the part to his own personality, adding to it something of his own that the others did not have. It is the task of an operatic coach to recognize the artist's individuality, to bring it out of hiding, make it grow, and implant it into the parts.

This also holds true for oratorio singers. An Evangelist in Bach's St. Matthew Passion, for instance, can sing his music in many different ways. The greatest Evangelist to my taste was the German tenor Karl Erb, who brought to this part an absolute lack of personality in his voice that made him ideal for the impersonal words of the chronicler. His reading impressed me in the same way as did the printed lines in the Passion — factually and unemotionally. He left emotion to the ariosos of the other characters.

Many great artists owe their early successes to their coaches, who imbued them with the spirit of their roles, among them Kirsten Flagstad (coach Hermann Weigert), Helen Traubel (coach Ernst Knoch), Rosa Ponselle (coach Romano Romani), Lily Pons (coach Pietro Cimara).

The question arises, at what point in their coaching should the artists be initiated into the fine points of characterization of operatic roles? I think that the singer should first be able to read through a part without mistakes. He should then start again from the beginning, but this time on a higher level. This does not mean that extraordinarily gifted singers cannot be given pointers at an earlier stage. It is extremely hard to systematize rules. The coach's common sense must determine when to start working on expression in each individual case.

This work begins with complete analysis of the written word. No librettist, no composer uses words for words' sake. Though some lyrics may sound corny and cliché to us, at the time they were written they really were right for the emotion they were supposed to convey, even if they were a simple "O Dio!" or "Que vois-je!" And all these corny expressions are founded in a particular national temperament.

Composers are very meticulous about the lyrics that their writers deliver to them. No coach should fail to read the very revealing correspondence between Verdi and his librettists, or Richard Strauss's correspondence with Hugo von Hofmannsthal and Stefan Zweig. He will see how much thought, how much detailed work goes into a good libretto, and this knowledge will help him to treat the lyrics the way they deserve to be treated.

Lyrics in a foreign language must be translated word for word even if the construction of a sentence becomes weird or downright impossible. The singer must at all times know the meaning of *every word* he sings. There are no shortcuts to easy understanding. A coach ought to have two or three dictionaries on his piano for quick reference. Once the meaning of every word is clear, each sentence should be translated as a whole. I have always found it best to translate it into the vernacular whenever possible, to bring the meaning closest to the singer. The accompanying lines from Cherubino's aria ("Le Nozze di Figaro") show literal and idiomatic translations.

The coach will frequently encounter repetitions of sentences. Though such repetitions were characteristic in the old days of *da capo* pieces or any set numbers, repeating words still means something: it always means stressing an important thought or feeling, a buildup — which may be expressed by use of stronger dynamics as

Original	Literal Translation	Idiomatic Translation
Non più andrai, far-fallone amoroso.	No more will you go, big amorous butterfly.	No longer will you gad about, you lovesick butterfly.
Notte e giorno d'intorno girando.	Night and day in a circle turning.	Fluttering and circling night and day.
Delle belle turban-do il riposo.	Of the beautiful ones disturbing the repose.	Disturbing our beauties' peace of mind.
Narcisetto, Adon-cino d'amor.	Little Narcissus, little Adonis of love.	You little self-enchanted lover-boy.

well as by softer ones. A repetition of words in solo lines should never be sung exactly the same as the original sequence. The great Czechoslovak composer Leoš Janáček loved to repeat sentences, sometimes as many as three or four times. They always were logically and psychologically justifiable repeats. His translator, Max Brod, himself a writer of renown, once asked him, "Master, why do you repeat your sentences so often?" No answer came from Janáček. Brod had to make his question more urgent: "Master, *why* do you repeat your sentences so often?" "But, you see, you yourself repeated your sentence!" Janáček finally answered.

All lyrics have two meanings, an immediate one, springing from the momentary situation, and another, inner one which shows the psychological and the human development of an operatic character. Both meanings must be explained to the singer by the coach. All parts, even the smallest, should be portrayed in such a way that a definite personality becomes evident. Where the score does not offer any background for the personality, as for instance in the many different servant or confidante parts of the older lyric theater — Alisa in *Lucia*, Inez in *Il Trovatore*, Gastone in *La Traviata*, Curra in *La Forza del Destino* — it will repay the coach to do a little research into the literary source of the libretto. Invariably he will find there more information about a character's psychology. The greatness of some singers of character parts — the wonderful Alessio de Paolis and George Cehanovsky, for example — stems from their deep immersion in the psychology and history of their parts, however small. When they portray a servant, they convey the very idea of being the best, the most conscientious servant in the world. Their spies and their courtiers are so sharply defined, so deeply analyzed and synthesized, that one forgets the smallness of the parts.

Of course, unusual artistry and intelligence are the source of such portrayals. But these and many other artists reached perfection because coaches and conductors showed them the way to complete understanding of lyrics and dramatic situations. I have said that each genuine operatic character goes through an unbroken ascent — or descent — of development. Though it is very difficult to generalize in this respect, I want to give a few examples of such development of operatic heroines.

Leonora (*Trovatore*): love, resignation, self-sacrifice.

Violetta (*Traviata*): joie de vivre, coupled with incurable sickness, genuine love, resignation, euphoric death in ultimate happiness.

Eva (*Meistersinger*): young girl's first love maturing to a woman's deep feeling.

Carmen (*Carmen*): flirtatious, showing a thousand different facets of femininity, a believer in fate, courageous, true to her passion, unflinching when death is the consequence.

Susanna (*Marriage of Figaro*): coquetry, practical sense, jealousy, genuine love for Figaro.

This list could be prolonged indefinitely. The coach must point out to the singer the line of development that each role takes, and the singer must never lose his sight of this line. Each part takes on new meaning through such understanding.

In Wagner's music, the task is made somewhat easier by his use of the leitmotiv to explain, musically, inner development and conscious as well as unconscious thoughts. All the coach need do is translate literally, explain the often twisted language, and point out the meaning of the leitmotiv. A very characteristic element of Wagnerian and post-Wagnerian style is the treatment of syncopations in the vocal line and of the pauses preceding these syncopations. A syncopation in the voice part is almost always the sign of an inhibition or hesitation, however slight. The operatic character hesitates for a split second before proceeding with his thoughts — the result, musically, is a syncopated note and a slight pause before it. A pause may be motivated by this hesitation, by sudden tension, by preparation for a new mood or a new emotion, by punctuation, stress, or by quite a few other causes. Insistence on strict observance of these pauses, coupled with explanation of motivation, will considerably help the singer in understanding a part. In Verdi's music, accents on weak beats sometimes take the place of syncopations.

Things become more difficult when we look at Mozart or pre-Mozart operas. Here the formality of classical and baroque music does not allow for obvious psychological characterization. The coach must know Mozart's, Gluck's, and Bach's styles and the meaning of their musical language. This music expresses the same emotions we find in romantic, impressionistic, and modern music, but they are woven into the canvas of musical form. Key, tempo, rhythm, certain patterns of melody, certain modulations and cadences — all are indicative of certain emotions. The coach must understand this and also make it understandable to the singer.

Here again I can only give hints. Take, for instance, the very problematic part of Donna Elvira in *Don Giovanni*. Her path crosses Don Giovanni's repeatedly, each meeting unexpected by him — and by the audience. She constantly complains of her fate, even to the point of sometimes being ridiculous. I have heard audiences chuckle at some of Elvira's unexpected interferences. This means that something is wrong: Mozart certainly did not intend his character to be funny or maudlin or stupid. As a matter of fact, Donna Elvira is a passionate noblewoman driven by two strong impulses: morality resulting from religious fanaticism, and infatuation with Don Giovanni. These impulses clash violently, and the result of the clash is twofold: Elvira tries to save Don Giovanni from himself — and for herself, threatening him with heaven's wrath otherwise. Scorned, her love turns to hate, and henceforth her character has no other driving force. The coach must explain this force to the singer, pointing out constant repetitions of such words as "il giusto ciel," "scellerato," "traditor." The choice of E flat for her two main numbers is a sure sign that Mozart intended her to be a hurt but noble woman, by no means hysterical. Compare it with the Countess's "Porgi amor" in *Nozze di Figaro* and other arias in the same key. The rhythm and style of Elvira's D major aria (in the manner of Handel) adds greatness and restraint to her character. The coach must lay the fundamentals for the right expression of Elvira's part, a foundation on which conductor, stage director, and the singer herself can continue to build.

I hope this very abbreviated analysis may give the coach an idea of how to go about teaching expression.

An ideal clue to a composer's intention in regard to his characters' make-up may be found in the recitatives. Recitatives push the action ahead; in all operatic and oratorio literature, they are the dramatic elements, the arias and ensembles being epic or lyric interludes. There are two kinds of recitative: the secco (dry), sustained only by chords of a harpsichord or pianoforte, and the accompagnato, supported by chords and figurations of the orchestra. The accompagnato recitative is usually very carefully marked by the composer; dynamic and tempo signs leave the coach in very little doubt as to how these recitatives should be performed. Pauses must be strictly observed. The only question of interpretation left to the coach is the degree of dramatic intensity.

In Mozart's most famous accompagnato recitative, Donna Anna, bereaved by the assassination of her father, unveils to her fiancé, Don Ottavio, how she came to recognize Don Giovanni as her attacker and the murderer of her father. The chords and figurations in the orchestra depict her wrestling with the intruder as well as her being torn between doubt and certainty about his identity. Her pent-up emotions finally find release in the grandiose aria of vengeance.

The accompagnato recitative may be called the musical form for elevated, dramatic speech; the secco recitative, on the other hand, is simply everyday speech or dialogue put into a musical language which does not alter the informality and naturalness of the spoken word. It is the old masters' way of presenting what later on was called Sprechgesang. The secco recitative moves along on a natural speaking pitch, leaving it only when the natural up and down cadence of speech would require it. The secco recitative is indigenous to Italian opera and its imitations. French and German operas used the spoken word instead. The greatest masters of the secco recitative are Mozart and Rossini. The time signature (4-4 or 3-4) is more or less conventional; a stiff rhythmical recitative would kill the natural flow of musical speech. The tempo, which is hardly ever indicated by the composer, can be deduced from the meaning of the words and from the relation of the written note values to each other. This relationship of note values must be kept intact. If, for instance, there is a great number of sixteenth notes, followed by some eighth notes, the latter must be sung slower, although not necessarily exactly half as slow. In a secco recitative all is relative — the tempo, the length of notes, even the length of pauses and the right places for them. I should like to compare a secco recitative to an elastic rubber band that can be stretched and released at will — not, of course, at just any will but at a will founded on thorough understanding of the spoken word, of the situation in which it is used, and of the mental and emotional condition the operatic character finds himself in at the particular moment. In a dialogue between two persons it is fair to say that one of

them will always be more excited than the other. The more excited should sing his recitative lines faster. This may change, however, just as dialogue may change in everyday life. The choleric type may suddenly calm down, the phlegmatic one may even more suddenly blow up. There must be a constant interplay of variety, change, and elasticity.

In teaching the student to sing secco recitatives, the coach must first of all translate the lines into the vernacular; literary translation is not important here, since everyday language is usually spoken in the recitatives. In analyzing the spoken lines the coach will find the spots where the natural breaks for breath lie — always in accordance with the natural recitation of the lines. It is permissible to change the rests when they do not fit the natural accents of speech. A pause, moreover, does not always mean a breath, but most of the time an almost imperceptible break, a hold, a division between thoughts. In the example given in Figure 248, it would not be nat-

Figure 248. Mozart, *La Nozze di Figaro*

ural for the count to say "Susanna, tu mi sembri (break) agitata e confusa." The natural way would be to say "Susanna, (break) tu mi sembri agitata e confusa."

Figure 249, from Rossini's *Barber of Seville*, shows the different tempi at which a secco recitative must be sung. Bartolo is slow in his speech; Figaro is quick-witted and therefore usually speaks rapidly.

After teaching the student how to speak secco lines naturally — a difficult undertaking because of singers' clumsiness in *speaking* lines, the coach must proceed to the next phase. The singing of seccos must be done by slightly adding voice to the spoken word but with full vocal intensity in order to reach the parlando singing style. Recitatives are not arias. There must be a distinct difference in the vocal approach. The coach must stop any attempt by the student to give real voice in secco recitatives. He must find a way to show the student how to do it. The best way is to use his own untrained voice to demonstrate how, through inflections and elasticity, a secco recitative should be sung. One principle, however, must never be abandoned: pitch and intervals must never

Figure 249. Rossini, *Il Barbiere di Siviglia*

Figure 249 continued

be changed. Whatever voice is added must come on pitch.

The secco recitative is usually followed by an aria or a set number. Sometimes the last words of a secco recitative lead directly into the arioso, confirmed and underlined by the final cadence, sometimes in the accompanying instruments, sometimes in the voice line alone. In such a case the last notes of the recitative should be sung in arioso style so that no break is noticeable (Fig. 250).

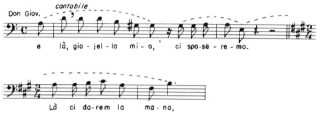

Figure 250. Mozart, *Don Giovanni*

I repeat what I have said so many times before: a whole book could be written about this most important operatic element. But I must be content to confine myself here to giving in full a secco recitative showing my treatment of it with directions and notes (Fig. 251). This treatment of operatic secco recitatives with necessary adjustments for the different styles is also valid for oratorio recitatives. Some modern operas, such as Richard Strauss's *Ariadne auf Naxos* or Stravinsky's *The Rake's Progress*, recreate the old secco recitatives. But these composers did not write them in conventional, approximate style. They wanted them to be executed exactly as they wrote them. The coach has nothing to do but to follow the printed vocal lines.

Nineteenth-century Italian opera developed a recitative style which combines elements of the accompagnato and the secco recitative. The best examples for it may be found in the earlier Verdi and the Donizetti operas. This kind of recitative is accompanied in the orchestra by a few chords, but these chords actually do nothing more than remind the singer and audience of the harmonic background. They are of no importance as means of expression. The recitative line fluctuates between more or less rapidly excited speech and weightier phrases. Verdi usually marks such passages with directions such as "quasi recitativo," "prestissimo." The feverishly spoken passage before Azucena's dramatic narrative may serve as a good example (Fig. 252). It is the coach's job to instruct the student to sing most of these recitatives in a modified secco way; a little more tone

Figure 252. Verdi, *Il Trovatore*

should be given, but still not so much as in arioso singing. The endings of these recitativo passages, however, are cadences and must be sung in arioso style. The tempo variations should be done as in the secco recitative. Elasticity and freedom to produce the necessary inflections and accents are indispensable.

Related to the recitative style is operetta singing style. In this art form, slight inflections and unnoticeable changes from arioso singing to parlando are essential. Constant arioso singing would be boring. The gaiety of an operetta's action warrants a definite lightening of vocal power. The voice must be extremely flexible; dozens of nuances between singing and speaking must be found. This will prove easier for light, pert voices, such as lyric-coloratura sopranos. "Soubrette" has been applied to this kind of voice. The best way of pronouncing in operettas may be to search for a key word in each sentence, project this word thoroughly, go easy on the rest, and let the audience guess the sentence as a whole. The words used in operettas are as a rule not very elaborate, not very poetic, but taken from everyday life. The rhymes likewise are simple. The operatic coach who does not often come to grips with these problems ought to speak the lyrics with his student and practice all kinds of parlando inflections until the right ones are achieved.

The student is now ready for the third and last stage of preparation. This will consist mainly in picking up loose ends and tying them together — in other words, in cleaning up and synthesizing all the elements I have discussed. At this stage great importance should be given to the proper dynamics. Full voice should be used at all occasions in this last cleaning-up process. The singer's endurance, or lack of it, will now become apparent. The right level of dynamics may have to be modified by the coach so that the student's voice will not give out before the end of a phrase, a scene, an act, or the whole part. Playing the full piano score as the student will hear it

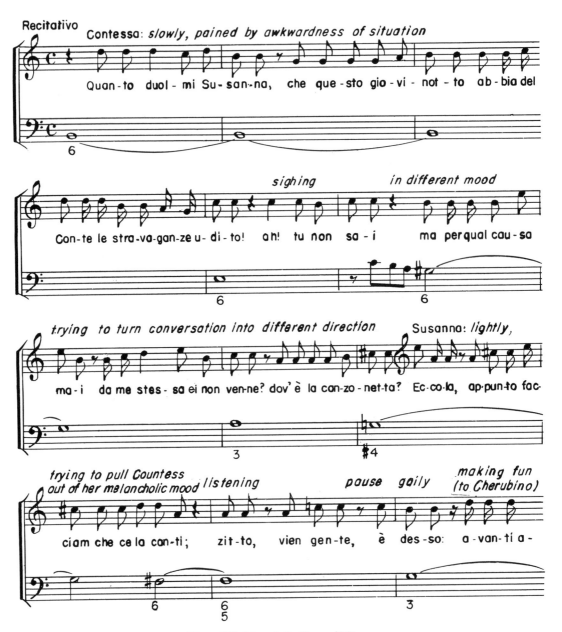

Figure 251. Mozart, *Le Nozze di Figaro*

Figure 251 continued

Figure 251 continued

later in the orchestra will also contribute to a sensible spacing of dynamic buildups and climaxes. The coach has to show the students where accents are meant to be harsh, where cutting, and where just a cantabile stressing of a certain expression. This will usually become clear from the meaning of the words and from the particular situations.

A special word has to be said about sforzatos (accents not marked by > or ʌ but with sf, or sfz). Sforzatos are always meant to be relative, their strength determined by the level of dynamics of the whole phrase. If, for instance, a sforzato stands in a piano passage, the voice must not overstep mf. Sfp accents are eo ipso less harsh. A sforzato may also be purely espressivo; then the accent should be softened and be actually made *after* the note under which it stands has been attacked.

Full-voice singing will allow the coach to check the smoothness of the vocal line, the faculty of making music and diction perfectly understandable to everybody in a theater, concert hall, or studio. Projection can be achieved only by full intensity, full concentration, full dedication, always supervised by the controlling intellect. It is only natural that piano singing requires *more* projection than loud singing. It also stands to reason that projection will be different in different surroundings. In big halls, great care must be taken to spit out the consonants, especially the final ones. Any student or coach who has ever had a chance to stand in the wings of a big opera house and see first-rate singers project will understand what hard work, what concentration are required. Intimate concert halls require just as much projection but in softer shades. Sometimes voice and diction should sound as if a damper was being used. A special kind of projection was formerly used for the microphone technique of radio and television, especially in singing popular music: the main rule was not to stress final consonants. But the development of modern microphones has put an end to this old technique. Modern recordings need the same projection that one would employ in a concert hall or on stage. In more popular, lighter radio and television work, as for instance in performing light opera and operetta, the use of the key-word technique may be advantageous.

A good coach must now acquaint the singer with the conductor's beat by beating the rhythm with his hand. The coach must know how to beat time and how to beat the different kinds — nonexpressive, expressive, legato, staccato, and so on. I need not waste another word about this. Max Rudolf's excellent and most comprehensive book, *The Grammar of Conducting*, contains all possible kinds of beat, and is a must for every coach. If they know who the conductor will be, it is up to the coach to inform the singer about this particular conductor's style, his requirements, his method of rehearsing, his idiosyncrasies.

Now the work is almost done. One last checkup, one last smoothing out of mistakes, one last touching up of expression, and then only one thing is missing, albeit the most important one: the coach must deeply impress upon the singer the fact that every artist has a sacred duty to the work as it is written, a duty to perform it true to the composer's intentions, without changing its inner values. I have written in another chapter (pp. 112–113) about the different styles of a musical work. Style of performance is in constant flux. What was accepted yesterday may not be fashionable tomorrow. The most valuable send-off present a coach can give his student is the deep conviction that fidelity to the written music is the greatest achievement, the greatest victory for an artist. Our time has not known a greater conductor than Arturo Toscanini, a greater musician than Pablo Casals. To both of them, fanatical adherence to the composer's wishes has always been the holiest creed. It should be the same with every coach and accompanist.

SONG COACHING

A song may be a drama, an epic, a comedy, or just an expression of a mood, an impression set to music — all in capsule form. In this capsule form lies the difference of this art form from opera, oratorio, or operetta. The song may have one or all elements of the larger form, but they are compressed into a very few minutes.

This different form requires a different approach by the coach. Whereas details in a long operatic part may pass unnoticed, may get lost in the huge canvas of orchestral and vocal colors, the same kind of detail, like the detail in a miniature, will invariably engrave itself on the mind of the listener to a song recital. Detail, then, is the element of the song, and the sum of the details synthesized to create its mood is the song. Despite opinions to the contrary, the song is nothing else than a poem set to music, a poem inspiring a musical thought which is then expressed in the song. The poem, therefore, assumes great importance. A good song coach must not only understand the poem but should know a goodly number of other poems by the same author, giving him better insight into the poet's style. To know one poem by Verlaine, for instance, is only confusing. But if you read his cycle of poems, a new poetic world will open up for you and you will suddenly understand the poem of the song which you are coaching. The same holds true for the music of a song. If you knew but one song by Brahms its meaning might remain a mystery. Only by knowing Brahms's other songs and a good deal of his orchestral and chamber music will you be able to understand fully the meaning of a particular song.

This leads me back to what I said at the beginning about the cultural background of coach and accompanist. The deeper and better founded it is, the better will his work turn out to be. Many singers regard studying songs as something easy, something that can be done between "more serious" studies of roles, something that can be improvised in no time. Such singers should quickly be convinced of the absurdity of their opinion. The study of songs is just as time-consuming as the study of opera, if not more so. Quality is all-important, not quantity. There is not one song that could be taught in less than one lesson, and very few that could be learned in one. Patience and love of detail are necessary qualities for successful lieder singers. Add to this a rich and deep inner life, a firm belief (see p. 182), and the ability to mold diction and voice into a thousand shapes.

Still more important is a singer's idealism. Very rarely can a career be made on song recitals alone, and the artist will have to suffer economic privations unless he has made enough of a name in opera or in other musical performances to draw audiences to his concerts. The coach will do well to make all these difficulties clear to the singer lest there be sad disappointments later on.

But there are also compensations. A well-delivered song is one of the singer's greatest inner satisfactions. The song is such an entity in itself that the artist really feels happy after he has finished singing a beautiful one. Moreover, though many voices do not have the power, the vocal expansion for an operatic career, nature has endowed them with a variety of color and with feeling for finest shadings. All this can be put to work in reproducing a song. Finally, how many thousands of people who never will make singing their career bring joy to their families and their friends by being able to sing songs, starting with simple folk tunes? The field for the song coach, therefore, is not so narrow as it would seem. As a matter of fact, there are more American song coaches than any other kind of musical coaches.

Songs as generally sung today can be classified into religious, folk, and art songs. For all practical purposes English song literature starts with the Elizabethan composers; the German lieder with Schütz, Mozart, and some of his contemporaries; the French art song with the chansons and other forms of the seventeenth century (see pp. 13–14).

A song coaching session must begin with a study of the lyrics. Unlike the procedure at an operatic coaching session, no music should be played until the student is able to comprehend and pronounce the words, and until he thoroughly understands the meaning of the whole song. As a matter of fact, the inflection and the emotional connotation, the fine shadings, the idiomatic undertones of every word, phrase, sentence are of the utmost importance. Problems of diction must be settled at the beginning. The coach must give the student a word-by-word translation if the song is in a foreign language. Printed translations are never right, because they are usually tailored to fit the meter, the rhyme, and the general thought. Meanings of songs are not always clear. Sometimes a song is only an impression, a mood, an image. It takes considerable thought, plus the ability to put oneself in the poet's place, to understand the meaning of the poem. Naturally, several ways of interpreting a poem are possible. This becomes very obvious when you realize that many composers have set the same poem to music, with entirely different results. Goethe's poem "Mignon," for example, has been set to music by Schubert, Brahms, Wolf, even by Ambroise Thomas in his famous opera. Each time a different aspect is accentuated.

Most songs were conceived by the composer in a certain key and for a certain kind of voice. Schubert himself, for instance, had a tenor voice, and it is natural that most of his songs lie in that range. Many composers wrote songs for certain men and women of the nobility, for friends, and for famous singers. These songs were conceived in a key to suit the particular interpreter. But even if no such interpreter was particularly in the composer's mind when he wrote a song, he always had in his thoughts a definite tonality, the color of which would best express the mood of the song.

It is not always possible to sing a song in the original key. Almost all classical song collections have been edited in three, or at least in two different ranges, high, medium, and low. Though I prefer singing in the original key, I fully understand that this would sharply curtail the song literature for a particular singer. The coach must choose the right key for his singers. This should not be done mechanically by just choosing the "high" edition for sopranos or tenors, the medium one for mezzo-sopranos or baritones, and the low key for contraltos or basses. I believe in carefully trying out any key in the singer's voice range and choosing the definite key only after a trial-and-error period. The vocal criterion for the choice of key is the singer's "passaggio," the change from one voice register to another one. Songs in which the voice line moves dangerously near this transition point should be transposed into an easier, less exposed key. But here again good taste must prevail. In general, it is better to transpose songs a whole tone up or down which affects the color of tonality less than a change of a half tone. When songs are transposed down, furthermore, the bass notes of the accompaniment may come to lie in an impossibly low position, where the tones do not sound any more, but simply drone on an indefinable pitch (Fig. 253). It is better not to sing such a song than to transpose it down too far. I must also strongly deplore the bad practice of men's singing song cycles or even single songs that because of their lyrics and typical feminine emotions should be sung by women, and vice versa. But quite a few songs express feelings common to both men and women. After scrutinizing the lyrics, the coach may be able to put things right by changing a "he" to a "she" or a "Liebster" to "Liebste." Our greatest interpreters may be excused for singing any song, but for the voice student enough literature is available to fit his or her sex.

At this point I shall show practical ways to coach songs. The earliest kind of song to be encountered in today's repertoire is the strophic song. The happenings and the various emotions are expressed in this kind of song by a musical pattern which is repeated as many times as there are stanzas. Naturally, the projection of different emotions will necessitate different dynamics, sometimes even almost imperceptible modifications of tempo from stanza to stanza. The coach is justified in making these changes if they support the modifications of expression.

This may be the moment to talk about possible cuts in these strophic songs. Take, for instance, Schubert's "Das Wandern," which has five stanzas, the mood remaining the same throughout. It will not only not damage the song but actually help it if one or two stanzas are cut. These cuts must be made with taste and understanding to keep the line of thought unbroken.

Unlike operatic scores which have the piano part condensed from orchestrations, song accompaniments must be played as written. I shall elaborate upon this later. Here let it suffice to say that the coach must play for the student the exact accompaniment from the very start of the coaching session, because this is what the student will hear in performance. The voice line, too, ought to be played in the beginning. This may necessitate omitting some of the right-hand accompaniment in the first phases of coaching. But otherwise, no attempt to condense or to "orchestrate" the piano part should be made. The only exception to this occurs with a song that was composed for accompaniment by an orchestra in the first place. Mahler, for instance, and to a degree Strauss, are mainly symphonic composers. Their songs are conceived with the thought of orchestral background, even if they are written with piano accompaniment. In these songs, the coach may color the piano part to imitate the orchestral instruments, which will help the singer to recognize the orchestral support later on. In some folk songs and in almost all Spanish songs, the piano accompaniment is actually a substitute for guitar-playing. The coach should accustom the student right away to these broken chords and plucked figurations.

The coach must make clear to a student that preludes and postludes are integral parts of a song, serving to create the mood of a song before the vocal line starts and complete it after the vocal line is ended. The musical setting of the poem begins with the first note of the introduction and does not end before the very last chord of the postlude. The singer must regard the prelude as the beginning of his immersion into the mood of the song, and he must keep his concentration alive throughout the postlude, until the very end of the music. The artist must, so to speak, start "singing" with the first note of the prelude and must not finish "singing" before the pianist lifts his hands from the keyboard.

I have always found it very useful to construct a person as the hero or the antagonist of a song, fitting out this imaginary person with every nuance of feeling that the song expresses. Give this idea to the student and let him identify himself with this person in the song he is studying; he will then have a much more vivid conception of the song. If he has enough imagination he may create such a person in his mind himself. I always try to animate the student's imagination by saying, "Who, in your opinion, is singing this song? How does he look? Is he young? Is he old? Try to form an exact picture of

Figure 253. Schubert, "Der Atlas," in original key (above) and
transposed too far down (below)

his personality and keep it alive during the song." The results have been amazingly good. Even if no such person can be determined from the song itself, there is always one inherent in it.

In outlining such an imaginary person the coach will have to correct possible errors of style on the student's part. Just as it is not appropriate, for instance, to construct an imaginary fiery Italian as the hero of a German song, you cannot "create" a Midwestern college girl as the heroine of a French art song. In other words, century and nationality have to be considered. No generalization is possible. I am not attempting to set rules: I only want to show the coach a way of kindling the student's imagination and his faculty of characterization. Here are some of the best-known patterns:

Early English songs (not ballads): somewhat distant, depersonalized, sophisticated — as if an Elizabethan fop were musing about love and nature.

Eighteenth-century French songs (bergerettes): naive, but with tongue in cheek.

Nineteenth- and twentieth-century French songs: see pages 165–170.

German lieder of the classic and romantic era: see pages 157–165.

Russian songs: passionate, brooding, heavy-hearted.

In all other means of projecting expression song coaching follows the technique of opera or oratorio coaching.

One word about the performance of songs in concert. The artist has no costumes, no scenery, and no other outside help to project the feeling of a song to his audience. He is all by himself, guarded only by the accompanist. The coach must see to it that the artist does not dramatize his songs by operatic or other gestures. On the other hand, a stiff posture will destroy any illusion of lyricism. Very slight gestures, discreetly underlining important points, are permissible, but should be rehearsed — not left to improvisation. A relaxed stance is recommended, with no frantic wringing of handkerchiefs or emoting with the help of any part of the body. The artist should give the impression of self-assured poise, of naturalness, of quiet concentration. Too much showmanship is harmful.

I shall not delve into the specialty of coaching authentic folk songs. An over-all coach, even a very good one, will not be able to communicate to his artists the regional traditions and inflections of a folk song. This is a specialist's work, just as coaching popular songs is a specialty which lies outside the scope of this book.

COACH AND CONDUCTOR

In operatic, oratorio, and operetta coaching for a definite performance the shadow of the conductor looms large. If the coach knows who the conductor is going to be and if it is technically possible, he should get in touch with him beforehand and find out as much as possible about the conductor's interpretation, his tempi, his way of beating time, his idiosyncrasies. The coach will thus possibly save his student some unpleasant surprises, and the conductor, on the other hand, will appreciate the singer's familiarity with his intentions. If the conductor is not available for a conference before the coach's work starts, the coach will have to deduce a plan of action from his knowledge of the conductor's style.

The coach may be one of the lucky few with jobs in the nation's opera companies, or he may hope to get one. As such he may be called upon to perform the following duties: (a) rehearse artists individually (solo rehearsals); (b) rehearse ensembles; (c) play musical rehearsals with the conductor beating time; (d) play stage rehearsals with the stage director in charge, with or without the conductor present; (e) fulfill backstage duties.

For (a) and (b) no additional information is necessary; leadership and authority are absolutely essential. The opposite holds true for (c) and (d). In playing rehearsals with the conductor present the coach must not have a musical opinion of his own at all; he must understand and follow the beat of the conductor at all times, and subordinate himself to the conductor's wishes. The utmost flexibility is necessary. At the same time, the coach must be relaxed, in order quickly to find the suggested place in the score as he resumes playing after an interruption. This is not at all easy. It requires an excellent knowledge of the score and, in addition, alertness. This strange combination of authority and submission to the will of the conductor is also necessary for the various backstage duties of a coach.

The coach may be called upon to relay the conductor's beat to the singer. This is best done by direct eye connection. Through a hole in the scenery, the coach watches the conductor and synchronizes the beating of time with him, always allowing, however, for the distance. Sound travels much more slowly than light. Anticipation of the beat — sometimes by a remarkably long interval — is necessary. Where direct communication with the conductor in the pit is not possible, such instruments as time-beaters must be used. The coach has to learn how much time elapses between the depressing of the time-beater's key (like a Morse code key) and the start of the backstage music (singing or stage band). The right anticipation will help bring the backstage music together exactly with the conductor's beat. In most European opera houses and in our opera theaters of the future, television monitors, stationary and portable, will undoubtedly take the place of the hole in the scenery. The coach will then see the conductor's beat clearly, but he will still have to anticipate in conducting the backstage music.

Other backstage duties include the cueing in of a singer and sending the singer out on stage when his entrance is due. Scores should be marked clearly. Nothing must be left to improvisation. If a singer misses his entrance, the whole performance may be jeopardized.

Further backstage duties: The playing of organ and harmonium (see pp. 5, 34–37), the beating of bells or anvils (always check to see whether your mallets are all right and whether the bells are hung in the right order). Coaches must know how much strength to employ in pounding the backstage floor with a more or less heavy wooden stick (to imitate knocking on a door), when to turn a key in a metal keyhole, how to shake sleighbells (signifying approaching carriages). Sometimes they are even required to don a costume and appear on stage to play an instrument. The operatic coach must have an idea of how to prompt from the wings when an artist is too far from the prompter's box. There is hardly an end to the coach's backstage duties. The question arises at the end of this chapter: how can a coach possibly learn all his different functions? The answer is simple: through talent and experience. If you are interested in becoming a coach you should start by playing the piano for voice teachers. As you grow more proficient, try to improve your coaching by playing the piano for first-class voice teachers, stage director's classes, and small operatic groups. Keep eyes and ears open, learn through your mistakes, watch your more advanced colleagues, and coach with singers as much as you can. One can never learn more than by teaching others. Thus, the time will come when you, with a clear conscience, can call yourself a coach.

SELF-ACCOMPANYING

On the amateur level, in homes, self-accompanying has its very definite place. The performer will find it extremely difficult, however, to find the right balance between singing and accompanying; usually, one will dominate at the expense of the other. Balancing pianistic ability against vocal gifts will take a great deal of judgment. Still, a great deal of pleasure may be derived from accompanying oneself on piano or harmonium or small home organ.

On the professional level, self-accompaniment is useful in entertainment. Your facial expression is very important for this purpose; your profile will not do the trick. In order to have your personality reach the audience, you will have to use a spinet piano. If you try to use a concert grand, and turn away from it to face the audience, your accompaniment will suffer. At this level, I have only known two or three self-accompanying singers. In these words—self-accompanying singers—lies one of the reasons for the shortcomings of self-accompaniment. In all these cases the singing was much superior to the accompanying; the balance was shifted toward the vocal part. Self-accompanying in a concert hall may have some value as a curiosity, but I think art will always be the loser.

PIANO-PLAYING AND ACCOMPANYING

It is an open secret that piano virtuosos are very rarely good accompanists. Even chamber music may suffer from the domination of one musician over the others. The reason is clear: a virtuoso pianist wants to express himself, and his instrument is his medium of expression. He has not learned to attune or to subordinate himself to a partner. He is a lone wolf, not a member of the pack. The first requirement for a good accompanist is, therefore, a psychological one. He must be willing to do teamwork. As in all teamwork, he will have to lead at times, follow at other times, and be one with his soloist most of the time.

But this is a big order, even if the willingness is there. It requires first of all the technical and mechanical mastery of piano playing. Since we except chamber music, including sonatas, the technical requirements should not be an insurmountable obstacle. The passage work in a song, an aria, or an accompanied instrumental work is hardly ever forbidding. The few pieces in the literature that present special problems are known and will have to be prepared especially.

Before an accompanist takes the first step into professionalism, he must have in his repertoire the technically and rhythmically difficult pieces. The problems are different for song and instrumental accompaniment. In only one branch of the accompanist's duties is virtuoso technique important: the dance accompanist frequently will have to play difficult compositions — Chopin, Debussy, De Falla, or Prokofiev. Dance accompanists, therefore, are usually recruited from the ranks of concert pianists who, besides having a satisfactory technique, possess the other requirements necessary to lead or to follow a dancer.

If technique is not the main pianistic hurdle to be taken by a first-class accompanist, then, you say, there must be other obstacles in his path. Indeed there are. They can be summed up in one word: musicianship. Only a good musician can become a good accompanist. This differentiates him from a vocal soloist. Many singers are excellent musicians, but lack the necessary beauty of their organ; many more possess an exceptionally beautiful voice, but are weak musically. Although these latter cannot count on a career as song recitalists or choral singers, they may become outstanding opera singers, to the delight of the audience and the desperation of conductors and accompanists. An instrumentalist must be at least a competent musician if he wants to qualify for a solo career. Sometimes, he can get by with a dazzling technique, but even then his lack of musicianship will be felt by the audience. We have seen that it is up to the coach to try to improve his charges' musicianship. An accompanist may have to do the same, but in a much shorter length of time, usually in the course of a few rehearsals. If he is not a first-rate musician himself, he will never succeed.

In addition to sightreading and transposing, the pianistic elements for good musicianship are mainly tonal beauty and variety of touch. The accompanist must make sure that his tone lives, sings, mourns and jubilates, caresses and beguiles. A good piano can produce a great variety of tonal shadings if the pianist feels what he wants to express and has the means to translate it into touch. A large collection of tools is at his command: fingertips, fingers, wrist, arm, body weight, and the mechanical aid of pedalization which, used wisely, will help the accompanist to spin out phrases, to bridge otherwise impassable gorges.

Furthermore, the right fingering for passage work and for connection and separation of chords must be established. It is not always the traditional way of fingering that the accompanist will employ: each will have some weak fingers, usually the fourth and fifth. The piano virtuoso cannot afford such a weakness. Unless he overcomes it, he will never reach the top. But the accompanist can still be outstanding in his métier, even if he does not do exercises for eight hours a day to strengthen his weak fingers. A piano virtuoso would be able to play the octave triplets of "Erlkönig" as written and come out of it fresh as a daisy. The accompanist may use unorthodox fingerings, but that still will not mean cheating.

In much legato playing, the accompanist should use organ fingering. Especially when excessive pedalization is foreign to a composer's or to an era's style, as in all music up to the time of Chopin, the legato fingering must be perfect. Here, accompanist and organist walk the same road. A principal legato and tonal problem for the accompanist lies in the necessity for the even distribution of the fingers' strength in quiet piano or pianissimo figurations. Depressing one key with a different amount of weight can ruin the mood of a whole song or a stringed instrument's beautiful cantilena melody.

The accompanist, however, must also be concerned with all kinds of leaps and jumps, and with a great variety of staccato nuances. A virtuoso who plays from memory can keep his eyes on the keyboard and see ahead of time how far his hands will have to jump to reach certain keys. The accompanist, however, must play from the music, and his eyes must follow the soloist's musical line so that if the soloist suffers a mishap, he will know in a flash what to do. He must, therefore, be infallible in leaping; he also must know where the most dangerous leaps are, and his eyes must, for a split second, leave the music to glance quickly at the key or the keys on which the hands are to fall. The eye, reading the music and especially the solo line, must always be a few beats or measures ahead of the hands. Otherwise, the accompanist may be surprised by a sudden change in harmony, accidentals, or key. The mental anticipation of the measures following may also help him to detect mistakes and compensate for them quickly.

Page-turning is another real problem for any accompanist. Printed editions hardly ever take into consideration difficult page turns and seldom try to avoid them. If you do not have a page turner — and I suggest you don't, because even such help may be futile if the page turner is nervous or inexperienced — what can you do?

Well, there are several possibilities open to you. If you can, have two copies of the same song on the piano with two succeeding pages open. If the song is only four pages long, affix a cardboard to each of these four pages. If there are more than four pages, do not use cardboard but mark the pages, toward the bottoms, for turns at easy spots. Copy the rest of such a page and paste the copied music to the top of the following page. If only a few measures are involved, memorize them. Also memorize difficult interludes and postludes. You will then be able to concentrate on the keyboard. I do not like the "accordion" system of folding together many pages, like pleats. Something is likely to go wrong when you turn them. It is never good to have more than four pages open on the rack. If you have to mend pages, especially in the fold, do not use Scotch tape. The pages will stick together just when you need to turn them, or they will suddenly close. Lately, other kinds of tape have become available that do not stick together. I am waiting for the invention of a music prompter similar to the tele-prompter in television — some device by which the music, clearly legible, would keep rolling by on the rack at the tempo of your playing. That will be the day!

Let us hope that the page-turning problem is no more. Now we come to piano dynamics. Here, the accompanist must observe two rules: firstly, he must not only know all dynamic shades from ppp's to fff's with special attention to such in-between shades as mezzopiano and mezzoforte, but he must also be able to employ them in the right degree. There are, for instance, many different kinds of simple forte; the mood of the song will determine which to use. This leads to the second rule: all dynamics are relative. They depend on acoustical circumstances — room, instrument, soloist's volume, and breath or bowing-arm control. The accompanist must study all these and then decide which basic dynamics to use for a particular musical piece in order to be of most help to a particular soloist. If the concert hall is big enough for an open or at least a half-open grand piano, use it by all means, change your basic dynamics, and play the entire program somewhat less loud. The richness of sound resulting from the open piano lid will more than compensate for the softer dynamics. It may be advisable to play the accompaniment of a concerto or a dramatic operatic aria with open lid and play the next, more intimate group with the lid only half open. In small halls, of course, the lid should be down.

Should the accompanist "orchestrate" as he accompanies? This will depend on the works he plays. Concerti should be "orchestrated," and so should operatic arias and some songs that were composed with orchestral sound in mind (Mahler, Strauss, and some Hugo Wolf). In all other accompaniments, variety and sensitivity of pianistic touch should take the place of the imitation of orchestral colors. In a Bach composition, for instance, the use of articulation is absolutely essential: the melody should be played as Bach indicated, cantabile or staccato, while the bass accompaniment should be played portato. In a polyphonic piece, the leading voice should be brought out, whether it is an outer or inner voice. (For hints as to how to achieve this independence of touch and articulation, see p. 132).

Do not use pedal in Bach's works unless you want to sustain organ points with the help of the sustaining pedal. Use the pedal most sparingly in Haydn's and Mozart's music; rely instead on phrasing, articulation, dynamics, and impeccable rhythm. Favor harsher accents and dynamic contrasts in playing Beethoven. The romantic composers can stand more pedal but be *very* careful with the sustaining pedal when you play works of the French impressionists, especially Fauré. This music requires a constant use of all three pedals in combination, with the soft pedal predominant.

The foregoing is a generalization, of course. In special cases, for special effects, and for solving special problems in connecting tones, the sustaining pedal will prove of greatest help. But treat it as something *very* special. Nothing is worse than sound constantly blurred because the pedal is being overused.

I have said that pianistic technique is not the main obstacle on the way to professional accompanying. But, after discussing the main obstacles, we now must return to technique and its applications to accompanying. Schubert himself was not able to play the difficult triplets of his "Erlkönig." A singer, Josef Barth, once asked him: "Why don't you play the triplets you composed, instead of changing them into figurations of eighth notes?" Schubert answered: "You see, I don't need to. It is enough that I composed the song with triplets. Let the others play them." Schubert's answer sounds like a good excuse for all accompanists who must play the "Erlkönig." Still, there are other ways out of the dilemma of lack of technique. For years I played my own version of "Erlkönig," which does not miss a single note, but is based on special fingering and distribution into both hands of some of the octave triplets. And then, in 1954, in Gerald Moore's excellent *Singer and Accompanist*, I found confirmation of my version. He also advocates dividing the octave triplets and playing them with both hands. As a matter of fact, he begins the accompaniment as shown in Figure 254; three measures later he plays the passage in Figure 255. I start the accompaniment as written, with

Figure 254. Schubert, "Erlkönig," Gerald Moore's beginning of the accompaniment

Figure 255. Schubert, "Erlkönig," Moore's accompaniment three measures after

Figure 256. Schubert, "Erlkönig," my accompaniment

Figure 257. Schubert, "Erlkönig," Moore's accompaniment

Figure 258. Schubert, "Erlkönig," my accompaniment

the octave triplets in the right hand, to give the impression of the thunderous figuration from the very beginning. Before my right hand grows too tired, though, I change to the two-handed distribution in measure 3 and continue as shown in Figure 256. I shift occasionally to the use of both hands, as the need arises to relax the right hand. I also change fingerings to rest the fourth and fifth fingers now and then.

In a later part of the song, Moore advocates leaving out notes from time to time (Fig. 257). I do not find this necessary, and use instead the way shown in Figure 258. I do not mean to imply that my arrangement is better than Moore's: I simply want to point out that there are several ways of solving a difficult technical problem. The accompanist must search for the best solution compatible with his technical limitations.

Fingering, of course, is very important. I suggest that each song should be thoroughly fingered by the accompanist, with the fingering written into the music. Chances are that under fire the accompanist will take different fingerings; but it is always reassuring, and gives you a feeling of security, to have your fingerings looking at you.

Some songs that present no problems in the original key become very difficult as soon as they are transposed. The reason is that in transposing, black keys sometimes become white and vice versa, thereby changing the hand position radically. The same fingers fall on different keys. Strauss's "Cäcilie" is a good example. Not a technically easy song even in its original E major, it presents many difficulties if the soprano must avoid the high B at the end and does not want to sing below B flat, which means transposition a half tone down. The fingering must be different: fingers accustomed to striking the white keys do not want suddenly to strike black keys. And if an alto sings the same song, the accompanist probably will have to play it in C major, which creates another problem, because there will be fewer black keys used in this accompaniment than in the other two. Usually, anything in C major is much harder to play than a piece in another key. The only remedy for these difficulties in adjusting fingering is practice. The accompanist must know technically difficult songs and should have them ready for concert performance in one high, one medium, and one low key.

The following is Coenraad V. Bos's list of technically difficult songs, given in his *The Well-Tempered Accompanist*, which he suggests that accompanists have ready:

SCHUBERT "Erlkönig"

BRAHMS "Blinde Kuh," "Vier Ernste Gesänge," "Sommernacht"

WOLF "Ganymed," "An eine Aeolsharfe," "Lied vom Winde," "Der Rattenfänger," "Waldmädchen," "Prometheus," "Abschied"

RICHARD STRAUSS "Cäcilie," "Schlechtes Wetter," "Frühlingsfeier," "Lied des Steinklopfers," "Des Dichters Abendgang," "Der Arbeitsmann"

I should like to add to this list the following:

SCHUBERT "Nacht und Träume," "Litanei," "Du bist die Ruh" (all because of the required even pianissimo sixteenth notes)

SCHUMANN "Frühlingsnacht"

BRAHMS "Meine Liebe ist grün"

WOLF "Er ists," "Ich hab in Penna einen Liebsten wohnen," "Auf ein altes Bild" (evenness of touch), "Fussreise," "Der Feuerreiter"

STRAUSS "Ständchen," "Wiegenlied" (both for lightness and dexterity)

RACHMANINOFF Most of his songs

DUPARC "L'Invitation au voyage"

TRANSPOSING

I spoke earlier about transposing (pp. 220–221). Here I shall add only a few observations connected with the application of transposing to the art of accompanying. We have just seen that some songs become more difficult when transposed because of changed accidentals and hand and finger positions. Yet fingering is not the only change that transposition will cause. The tonal quality of a song or an aria also changes with transposition. As I have said, composers wrote their vocal music with a certain key in mind, a key that would best fit the mood to be expressed. Transposing destroys this ideal marriage of tonality and mood. Imagine a transposition from C major, a key that expresses classic simplicity (as in Mozart's Sonata Facile) or hymnic jubilation (the finale of Beethoven's Fifth Symphony) to C sharp major or B major. An element of artificiality will invade the composition, the mood will change. A transposition of more than a half step might do even more harm to the tonal quality of the original. Take, for instance, the noble and yet simple lines of Beethoven's "Ich liebe dich" in the G major of the original. Transpose it up to A major and it will assume a much lighter tonal quality. Transpose it down to, let's say, F major and it will become much richer, something that Beethoven wanted to avoid.

Or take Brahms's "Liebestreu" in a low key: the bass notes will lose their clarity and sound louder because of the greater thickness of the lower bass strings.

Yet transposing is necessary. The singer must feel at ease, his best tones must be used and his worst avoided. The accompanist can do very much toward achieving the original mood of a song or an aria, even in transposition. He can change his touch according to the desired expression. If a low song has to be transposed up, the resulting lighter sound must be counteracted by playing the bass notes in a darker hue, with more weight, and the right-hand accompaniment must be sounded with more sonority. Brahms's "Von ewiger Liebe," for instance, is a passionate, dark song if played and sung in the original key of B minor. A soprano with great expressional force but weak extreme low notes has every right to sing this song in a higher key, which will give the brooding bass tones a somewhat lighter texture. This may be counteracted in the accompaniment by more stress on the bass, even by playing some particularly high-sounding note an octave lower. In the opposite case, in the downward transposition of a song, the brilliancy should be preserved by employing a lighter touch than the original key would require. Schubert's "Die Post" is composed in the traditional post horn key of E♭ major. A contralto or a bass would probably sing it in C major, depriving the accompaniment of the gay sound of the post horn. But the accompanist may save much of the original flavor by brightening the tonal quality and by strongly stressing the rhythm of the song. The tempo, of course, must remain the same: it must be so chosen that the gay major and the sad minor mood of the song will sound right without any tempo differentiation. We see, therefore, that although transposition should be avoided, in principle, whenever possible, it may be changed from a great to a lesser evil by the accompanist's intelligent control of his touch.

THE INSTRUMENTAL ACCOMPANIST

An instrumental accompanist's work will be confined almost entirely to stringed instruments, principally the violin and the violoncello. The problems of accompanying strings differ from the problems of accompanying vocalists. Strings and piano do not blend as well as voice and piano; only in staccato or pizzicato passages will there be an amalgamation of the sound of both instruments. The accompanist must be careful never to cover the instrumentalist's cantilena in either concerti or in solo pieces, always to make his melody sing exactly as a stringed instrument does — even to the point of phrasing and articulating alike. He must, furthermore, imitate the different kinds of bowing. In simple harmonic background accompaniments, he must be discreet and must never drive the soloist to force the tone.

We shall examine three main kinds of instrumental accompaniment: (1) the orchestral sound in concerti; (2) the background accompaniments in cantilenas, dance forms, and virtuoso pieces; (3) the newer kinds of violin-piano or violoncello-piano pieces that try to do justice to both instruments' technical and tonal possibilities, making the job of the accompanist more satisfying.

When accompanying concerti, the pianist will have to scrutinize very closely the piano reduction of the score. Arrangers of all times have been guilty of aberrations in style that may be explained by the performance style of their own times. Instrumental music of the baroque and the preclassical periods has been doctored by unscrupulous, or, at best, untalented arrangers. I have already emphasized that accompanists and coaches must study the original full scores of such compositions. The full score should be compared with the piano reduction and the unnecessary doodads cut out; or the accompanist can add harmony or lower bass octaves, if the arrangement is too skimpy.

Especially in figured-bass compositions such re-editing may be very useful. Romanticizing editors have weakened the straight lines of figured-bass accompaniment with musical matter foreign to the age in which the piece was conceived and foreign also to our modern performance style, which favors simple objectivity.

The simplest and best manner which I could recommend for performing the accompaniments of early concerti is to play the harmony of the figured bass in chords, sometimes connecting them by counterpoint melodies in outer or inner voices consisting preferably of movement contrasting with the solo. In the tutti parts, the accompaniment may be full, but never richer than the composer's orchestration would sound. In the solo parts, the accompaniment must be discreet, and should be set in a range that contrasts with the solo instrument's momentary field of action. This means that the accompaniment should be in a moderately low range if the violin has figuration on the higher strings, or if the 'cello is playing on the A string. If the violin has extended passages on the G string or the 'cello has some low-lying melodies or figurations, it is advisable to put the piano accom-

Figure 259. Tchaikovsky, Violin Concerto

Figure 260. Mendelssohn, Violin Concerto

paniment above the solo instrument's tessitura. Otherwise, muffled sound or covering of the soloist might result.

With the concerti of Haydn and Mozart, and with Beethoven's violin concerto, the situation becomes simpler: their orchestral parts are much easier to reduce to piano accompaniments. But some piano accompaniments to these concerti resemble piano partituras because they were put together to give the accompanist a complete picture of the orchestration, short of a full score. Such an arrangement may not be pianistic and the accompanist, if he cannot find a better one, should feel free to reduce the piano part to playable dimensions. Such piano partituras exist, for instance, for the Beethoven, Mendelssohn, Brahms, Tchaikovsky, Glazunov, and many other concerti. Musicians of high stature, such as Carl Flesch, have done piano scores of these concerti, scores which are easier to read than to play. If the accompanist is either a first-class pianist, able to play such a score without endangering the plasticity of the accompaniment, or if he is well-versed enough to do his own reduction from these scores, he may use them. Otherwise, he should look for a more pianistic reduction.

In playing accompaniments to concerti, the accompanist will encounter a problem that is present in accompanying all swift passages of the violin literature, namely catching the exact moment when a chord should be played during or after fast virtuoso figurations. The same difficulty, even more intricate to master, confronts the conductor. Violin virtuosos have a way of smearing such passages so that the rhythm is no longer recognizable. When this happens it is catch as catch can, a very bad practice to which a conscientious accompanist will never assent. In rehearsals, the accompanist should try very hard to make the soloist play such passages rhythmically, insisting on ever so slight accents on the heavy beats, especially with irregular passages such as groups of five, seven, nine, and more notes to a beat. If this method does not lead to success, the accompanist must train himself to virtually subdivide such passages into manageable groups, listening to and looking for landmarks such as the shift of the bow from one string to the other. In any case, the accompanist must rehearse the difficult spots as many times as necessary. Figures 259–261 give examples of such fast spots. Of course, the accompanist himself must play his chords with the most precise rhythm, offering the soloist a valuable chance to get a toehold on the sheer cliffs of technical difficulty.

Figure 261. Saint-Saëns, "Introduction and Rondo Capriccioso"

The violin has much more agility than the swiftest-moving human coloratura voice. Not only in rapid passage work, but in any fast piece for the violin, the accompanist will encounter the problem of staying with the soloist. The problem becomes even more acute when the accompaniment must be played in a dainty staccato style, in imitation of the soloist's articulation. The third movement of Mendelssohn's violin concerto is a dainty elfin-like piece that soloists sometimes play at breakneck speed. Although I do not myself approve of a tempo faster than rhythmic precision and airy elegance will allow, I must caution the accompanist to be prepared for such a race. His hands must never be lifted high. The staccato must be short, weightless; after striking one chord, the hands must skip to the next position immediately, waiting just above the keys to strike again. The eye will have to cooperate by always being at least two measures ahead of the hands (Fig. 262).

The problem is the same for all fast violin music and, to some extent, also for accompanied violoncello pieces. Modern composers, from Fritz Kreisler on, have complicated matters by writing graceful but harmonically difficult piano accompaniments (Fig. 263). Accompanists who play a lot for instrumentalists must know these tricky pieces and practice them beforehand.

Simple background accompaniments present no difficulties. Neither are they overly interesting. Still, the accompanist must find some details to make his work more agreeable to himself and the audience. He can always derive pleasure from discriminate shadings, dynamics, finesse of touch, balance, holding the soloist to a steady rhythm. Depending on the soloist's bowing, the accompaniment must try to imitate — but not to cover — the violin's staccato, spiccato, martellato, détaché.

There exists a very large number of excellent violin solo pieces with interesting piano accompaniments. Fritz Kreisler was the first to add spice to the piano part by means of exotic harmonies, imitations of the melody,

Figure 262. Mendelssohn, Violin Concerto

Figure 263. Kreisler, "Tambourin Chinois"

complicated rhythms. Some of his little pieces are exceedingly difficult to read and to accompany; the accidentals are colorful, but not always logical. The accompanist must prepare himself well and never give the impression of being stunned by such piano parts. From Sarasate to transcriptions by Casals, Cassadò, and others, Spanish music is a favorite for the last group in violin and 'cello recitals. Here, the pianist's touch must be seemingly unemotional, rather dry, but driven by a nervous sensitivity, and must imitate guitar sounds much as the soloist does. Sometimes, the articulation is extremely elaborate, as for instance, in De Falla's "Jota," originally written for voice and piano. Staccatos, semistaccatos, tenutos, accents in various degrees of shading—all these are called for and must be executed (Fig. 264).

The most gratifying pieces, except for sonatas, are those that distribute musical matter evenly between instrumentalist and pianist. Here real music can be made. The purely technical aspects will recede into the background and the joy of teamwork will compensate the accompanist for many hours of musical dearth. More about this real fulfillment later on.

As we near the end of this chapter, I should like to give a few practical hints about the details of presentation. A soloist must be given ample time to tune his instrument. This should be done straightforwardly, unobtrusively. A few middle A's with the D minor chord below should be quietly struck by the accompanist, followed by the other unstopped string sounds in fifths. Before starting, wait for the nod from the soloist. Do not get nervous if the 'cellist does not immediately find the right spot to anchor his instrument on; wait for the adjustment of bow and chin holder by the violinist. In difficult simultaneous beginnings, make sure you discuss with your artist which of you should give the upbeat and how it should be done. Either a movement of the head or a lifting of the bowing arm in the right tempo should be the sign to start. If a piece ends on a long-held chord, look at the bow and lift your hands from the keyboard the instant you see your soloist take his bow off the strings. Thus, start and finish will impress the audience with your perfect teamwork.

THE DANCE ACCOMPANIST

Dance accompanying is a very special form of accompanying. The main thing that it has in common with the other branches of accompanying is its goal: oneness in style; the unification of expression between soloist and accompanist; the amalgamation of two different personalities, both devoted to the service of art.

The basic difference between all other forms of accompanying and dance accompanying is the substitution by the soloist of the visual expression of the body for the acoustical means of expression used by other soloists. The elements of expression remain the same. Melody, rhythm, dynamics, phrasing, counterpoint, form — all can be expressed by the human body moving in space. This music of the body can only be seen, not heard. The acoustical part of the dance must be carried entirely by the accompanist. For this reason, the dance accompanist must be much more a piano soloist than the vocal, choral, or instrumental accompanist. The musical material that he will play is much more varied, ranging from any pianistic piece of the baroque and the classic age to the most modern compositions, some of them written especially for the dance. The dance may be one of several kinds: classical or modern ballet, character dancing, modern dancing, ethnic (oriental, American Indian) dancing, to say nothing of ballroom, tap, jazz, or acrobatic dancing. The dancer may want to follow the accompanist's playing or may ask to be followed by the pianist. The musical terms used by the dancer are very different from any musician's because the terminology has to do with the movement of the body in space. At first, this language sounds like a secret code, and the accompanist must learn to translate it into musical terms. The dancer's counting bears very little relation to musical counting in regular periods. Furthermore, the accompanist must not only be able to play all the above-mentioned kinds of music, he may also be asked to cut it to pieces to fit the dancer's creative ideas. This is about the toughest thing that can be asked of a musical and conscientious pianist. He should try to convince the dancer to accept logical, musical cuts, or he should suggest that special music be written for the particular dance. Finally, the accompanist must be able to improvise, usually for dancing classes and rehearsals.

THE DANCE STUDIO ACCOMPANIST

The first thing a dancer does in class is warm up. Legs and entire body would be harmed if intense training were started without this warming up. The warm-up of all types of dancers is done first at the bar at the sides of the studio, then in the center, and conforms to the classic ballet bar exercises. The accompanist must play

Allegro ma non troppo e pesante

Figure 264. De Falla-Kochansky, Ritual Dance from
El Amor Brujo

appropriate music. Some exercises in class recur every day. I have chosen the bar exercises of one of the purest classic ballet masters, Enrico Cecchetti, who not only laid the scientific and artistic foundation for Italian ballet, but also strongly influenced Russian ballet by his work in St. Petersburg and his travels with Anna Pavlova as her ballet master. Cecchetti's definition of the dance is as follows: "The dance expresses the most perfect equilibrium. At the same time, it lifts spirit and gestures and links together poses and movements, not by chance but following the rules of unspoken poetry and musical rhythm."

The singer's breathing and the string player's change of bow are analogous to the dancer's flexing of the leg muscles, to the bending and stretching of the knees as preparation for any dance figure. This is called the *plié*, one of the many ballet terms, all French, which the accompanist must know. The plié is the first exercise to be done at the bar.

All bar-exercise music is played in several periods of four or eight measures, the number of periods for a particular exercise to be determined by the ballet master. The accompanist should never interpret music for these exercises by adding expression. He should just play it at a steady rhythm. Beginners and intermediate pupils do the bending and stretching in even time, two beats for going down and two beats for coming up. The music played for this should be an even, flowing 4-4 beat, such as Chopin's C minor prelude. Advanced pupils and professional dancers do the plié in three beats — two down and one up. A slow waltz, like Weber's "Invitation to the Dance," is the appropriate music. Each measure should be done in three beats. Occasionally, male dancers will use only one beat to go down, two beats to come up. In general, the dancer has at his disposal four directions in space: up and down, in and out. The music must be chosen to take these directions into consideration.

The next bar exercise in Cecchetti's routine is the *grand battement*. Beginners do this exercise in four stages. The music should have a light 4-4 rhythm. For advanced and professional dancers, the music should be a grand march (such as the Triumphal March from *Aïda*), but not too fast — a quarter note = about 86. The heavy beat comes when the dancer's leg is down.

The *battement tendu* gets its musical accent from the movement of the leg. The music should be faster or slower, as needed. A good piece for this exercise is Mozart's *alla turca* music from his A major piano sonata.

The music for *battement dégagé* should be played fast and lightly, in a 2-4 or 6-8 rhythm. Accents should be light and on the third count.

For the *ronde des jambes à terre*, the accompanist is usually asked to play two chords as preparation. He should start playing his music when the dancer's leg is passing through the first position. The music should be a smooth, slow waltz, counted in one. *Battement frappé* requires a 2-4 or 6-8 fast music, preferably some staccato piece in dotted rhythm. It should start with a musical upbeat and should have a sharp accent on one, when the dancer's leg moves *out*. *Petit battement* has the accent on the leg movement *in*. Advanced dancers do this exercise in a continuous movement. The best musical rhythm for this is a polka. Musically, the accent falls on the second beat.

Ronde des jambes en l'air has the musical accent on the stretching out of the legs. A slow, sustained, sweeping waltz, like the one from Delibes' *Coppélia*, will fit this exercise perfectly.

These are Cecchetti's basic bar exercises. One more is occasionally done, the *retiré*, to music that is the same as for the grand battement. All other exercises are combinations of the basic patterns. The accompanist will have to learn to understand and to translate into music the French terms for the sometimes very complicated combinations. One simple example may suffice: the *jetté petit battement* with the accent at the end.

All elevation steps are up, with the heavy musical beat when the dancer comes down. The *temps à terre* is a balletic down with the musical accent on the down. You will have noticed that I distinguish between musical and terpsichoreal language. For instance, upbeat, musically, means the beat before the heavy beat, usually before the first beat of a measure. In the dancer's language, upbeat means simply the beat in which the leg or body movement goes upward. This may very well happen on a musical downbeat. Accordingly, the dancer's downbeat means simply that the movement is directed downward. Ambiguities like these make communication between musician and dancer extremely difficult and contribute to the necessity of specialization for the dance pianist.

The dancer, of course, also knows the musical upbeat. He usually expresses it by the word "and." The accompanist will do well always to listen to the ballet master's or the dancer's "and." The command is usually given in the desired tempo and makes it easier for the pianist to divine the following tempo.

A dancer's accents are the same as a musician's, except that they are made by body movement. When a dancer's accent is to be up, the accompanist will have to take it from the "and." In performance, when no "and" can be uttered, the accompanist will have to start on his own. When a dancer's accent is down, the accompanist takes it from the dancer.

On jumps, the musician must always start before the jump takes place. The plié before will give him his exact cue, corresponding to the singer's inhaling before starting a phrase. On lifts, especially sustained ones, supported by a partner, the accompanist must lead the dancer to come down after staying in the air. The length of the stay depends on the elevation. It should be timed beforehand; otherwise, the pianist may wear out dancer and partner or make the dancer come down too soon.

A very beautiful ballet figure is the *pirouette*, which may be sustained (the best music for this is a slow waltz) or rapid, especially in chains of several pirouettes, as, for instance, in the *fouettés*. The best kind of music for this is a *galop* (as in the last part of the *La Gioconda* ballet music).

Generally, accompanists playing for exercises should use minor keys but sparingly because they contribute a certain deadness of movement. Modern music with dissonances should not be avoided entirely in class, so that the dancer will be at least familiar with it, but neither should it be overdone. If a dancer wants a slower or faster tempo, he probably means only a hairbreadth's difference. Also, ritardando and accelerando in a dancer's vocabulary mean very slight decrease and increase of tempo. But slower may also mean heavier, musically speaking, and faster may mean lighter. Heavy in a dancer's terminology means more volume, marcato, but not heavier musically. Quicker, on the other hand, does not mean faster but lighter, almost pizzicato. Stronger does not mean louder, but more fluent, more supported. These hints must suffice. The rest of the accompanist's task is adjustment to the dancer's terms, good instincts, and a feeling for movement.

I have said that dancers do not count in measures but in phrases, some of which differ greatly from musical phrases. A dancer, for example, may start counting a phrase from a musical upbeat. He also may include in his count the preparation and the ending of his movements. He needs time for both — time that he may find only in the last measure of the preceding, or the first measure of the succeeding phrase. Thus he may create many irregular musical phrases, but they should not stump the accompanist.

THE DANCE RECITAL ACCOMPANIST

The principal question for the dance recital accompanist is: should he lead the dancer or should he be led by him? The answer will depend on the individual dancer. It is, of course, not only very desirable but more musical that the dancer execute his choreography to the music as it is being played, and as it has been rehearsed. In character dancing (Spanish, Russian, Hungarian, and so on) this must be the dancer's general approach. In ballet, the dancer should follow the music, with the exception of some especially intricate technical steps, where the music may have to adjust itself to help the dancer. In modern dancing, we will find dancers who are trying to bend the music to fit their often esoteric ideas. It would be better to have special music composed for such purposes, and indeed, our leading modern dancers discuss their choreographic ideas with composers who may also act as accompanists. The composers then know what the dancers have in mind and can write original music accordingly. One of the best known composer-accompanists was Louis Horst, dean of dance accompanists, who had traveled with Martha Graham for many years. Another is Friedrich Wilckens who was Harold Kreutzberg's composer-pianist. Improvised accompaniments in rehearsals may often form the nucleus for a finished composition. If the accompanist is a good improviser, he might very well become a dance composer.

In accompanying all kinds of dancing, the accompanist must watch the dancers' legs and be ready for the "and" which, we now know, is the preparation for the dance step. It is advisable to have the piano put backstage right, or on whichever side the curtain is being drawn from, because the accompanist may often be called upon to give curtain and light cues. The keyboard should face downstage so that the accompanist has as much view of the stage as the wings or the scenery of the concert hall will permit. This position of the piano is preferable even if the space backstage is small and part of the piano may be visible to the audience. If there is absolutely no space in the wings, the piano should go at the front of the stage, to the right. Wherever the piano is, the dancer should be visible to the pianist as much as possible. The dancer may begin a dance standing on stage or he may enter from backstage. In the latter case, the accompanist, before he starts his music, should watch for the dancer's nod. If the dancer starts onstage, watch for his preparation.

Pianistic sonorities ought to take into consideration the size of the auditorium and the support which a full sound will give to the dancer. The piano lid should always be open.

The potential musical literature for a dance recital is so vast that the pianist cannot be expected to know all music likely to be used by the dancer. A good sight-reader, therefore, will have a much better chance of success as dance accompanist than a slow reader. But after the accompanist has gone through the first rehearsals, he must thoroughly familiarize himself with the music, mastering difficulties of technique and touch, imitating an orchestra on the piano wherever necessary.

I have always found Spanish music the most difficult to play, especially the intricate compositions of Joaquin Niñ, De Falla, Granados, and Turina. Rhythmically, however, a good Spanish dancer will lead you with the language of the castanets, and they can be sounded with so much expression and variety that they may tell a whole story or express any feeling. Once the accompanist grasps the particular rhythmic pattern, he will know exactly what rhythm to follow. In oriental dancing, ankle bells and finger bells will have the same usefulness. In more primitive ethnic dancing, as well as in some modern dancing, a whole array of drums, beaten by a percussionist, will give the pianist the basic rhythm. The dynamics of the piano will depend on the dynamics of castanets, bells, drums, or heel beats. The dancer will hardly hear the piano while the percussion instruments play, so the piano sound must therefore be rather loud.

At the highest level of dance accompanying, the problems are the same as in all other branches: the accompanist, through his playing, must create the right mood and be one with the dancer in conveying this mood to the audience — at the same time giving him all support, and in the last analysis leading him so discreetly that the dancer will not even notice that he is being led.

TEAMWORK

With that last sentence I almost gave away the secret that I intend to unveil in this last section. The highest achievement of soloist and accompanist is teamwork — the molding of both personalities into a firm unity of purpose and execution. Only such a unity can serve the work and bring out the music's highest values, its inner meanings, its deepest stirrings. We have seen how many preparatory steps are necessary to give the accompanist the tools with which to attain this crowning achievement. Now the scientific, the technical, the stylistic, the psychological, and the artistic elements must be put to work, be synthesized into the work of creative art that a recital of quality represents. Such a synthesis will be effected by a very simple process: by both artists' transmitting and receiving feelings, based on complete agreement about the poetic, musical, and spiritual content of a musical piece.

The first steppingstone to teamwork, therefore, will be complete understanding of each piece to be performed. I have shown (p. 184) how the accompanist ought to employ psychology to reach an understanding of his soloist's artistic make-up. Suppose he has been successful. He knows where the artist's roots spring from. Armed with this knowledge, he must now discuss with his soloist each song and each aria, or each instrumental piece. He must try to uncover the meaning of each phrase, each stanza, and each movement, be it evident or hidden. There may be many explanations for one and the same musical detail. Take, for instance, the knocking bass rhythm in Schubert's "Gretchen am Spinnrad," which I explain as the recoil of the spinning wheel axle (overt meaning) or the irregular heartbeat caused by Gretchen's anxiety (inner meaning) in addition to its purely rhythmic and harmonic function (see p. 158).

It is up to the accompanist to explain each detail to his soloist in a manner that the latter will best understand. The approach may be factual or sentimental, materialistic or poetic. I do not mean, of course, to advocate long sessions of debate. On the contrary. First of all, accompanist and soloist, when they meet for the first time, should make music right away. Both may be so sensitive that many words are unnecessary; the transmitting and receiving of invisible rays may take place instantly. But it may also be that the first singing and playing will disclose two entirely different outlooks. If that is true, discussion may be beneficial to both.

The initiative may also come from the soloist, especially if he is a more experienced or — to put it bluntly — a greater artist than the accompanist. If he is, listen to his arguments, and agree with him if he convinces you. Many times I have had to radically change my artistic opinion of years' standing about a certain song, a certain phrase, a certain meaning; my soloist's explanation of it was an eye-opener, and I was not at all ashamed to accept his conception. In fact, such alterations are necessary for your artistic development. Otherwise, you will grow fossilized and autocratic, revolving in circles.

In time, you will learn to look at problems of interpretation from many different points of view and be ready to change your interpretation according to your soloist's temperament and personality. A good accompanist may play the same song three times in a week for three different soloists. He will have to vary his interpretation three times — seeing to it, however, that his artistic integrity is preserved at all times. Listen, for instance, to recordings of Schubert's "Die Post," sung by some great artists of the immediate past: Leo Slezak, Richard Tauber, Lotte Lehmann, Aksel Schiøtz. They are all wonderful and all different. Now imagine that you had played for all of them. Naturally, if you are a good accompanist, you would have played the same song differently each time, bringing out different details, employing different shadings. It does not matter, as long as the total of two artists adds up to the figure one, as long as there is artistic union.

Not only different artistic conceptions, but also different vocal temperaments may make pianistic adjustment imperative. The immolation scene from Wagner's *Götterdämmerung*, for example, may be sung with the greatest beauty. Flagstad's exceptional voice, soaring into space, made an immense impact on her audience, as her personality expressed itself in the purity and majesty of her tones. The same scene, sung by a more emotional artist, with a less gorgeous voice but with more understanding of the climactic situation that brings the tetralogy to the end which was its beginning — the fateful gold is again a harmless plaything of the Rhine daughters — this same scene may also be performed without the sensuous beauty of Flagstad's voice, but with profound comprehension and overwhelming personality. The accompanist, called upon to play this very difficult scene, must assimilate the singer's conception by either stressing the purely musical side of it or giving more weight to the thematic material and the ethical and moral values of the music.

The team of soloist and accompanist is now attuned to the same wave-length of purpose and execution. What else is there to be done? For one thing, the music to be performed must be so securely rehearsed that rigidity of execution can be broken in performance by a continuous give and take, an improvisatory creativeness that will spell success. Such improvisation within clearly defined bounds will express itself in details of blending and balance, and in imitation of each other's tonal quality, phrasing, articulation, tempo, dynamics. An accompanist must go along with the soloist, must be with him at all points — this is the first maxim that an accompanist learns. But the reverse is also true: the soloist must be with the accompanist. Both artists have to allow for sudden physical or psychological indispositions that may change a concert's planned course. And I am not talking only of the soloist's lapses of memory that may happen anytime and never fail to happen at some time during a performance. Such mishaps must be immediately corrected by the accompanist, who has the music in front of him, and who must know in a split second whether to jump with the soloist, to repeat measures (in the event of a late entrance), to prompt a vocalist, or to play the soloist's part on the piano to help him find his place again. As a matter of fact, the accompanist will know after rehearsals where the main danger spots lie; he must foresee them. He must always show presence of mind and react very fast. No accompanist is worthy of the name who lacks the above qualities.

The tempo of a composition should be agreed upon during rehearsal. If a team has been together for some time, both will know that nervousness in performance may cause tempo changes, usually making fast music slower and slow music faster. The accompanist should, under normal circumstances, try to initiate the right tempo and maintain it if the soloist begins to change it during the performance. But he also must sense a singer's sudden vocal indisposition and help him by changing the tempo on his own, or by following him. The same goes for dynamics and phrasing. The accompanist must go with the sudden accelerandos necessitated by the soloist's physical weakness; physical incapacities may force the singer to give less voice or breathe more often, or an instrumentalist to use less pressure and to change bowing oftener. The accompanist must, on the spur of the moment, change his dynamic range by playing softer. He must listen to the singer's phrasing and watch his mouth for unexpected changes of breath; he must watch the string-player's bow at all times for the same reason. He must then phrase his own music accordingly. But the accompanist must also sense when his soloist has the jitters simply because of nervous tension. When this happens, the accompanist should keep to the prearranged tempo and other details of performance, shepherding his soloist back to the fold. A singer or instrumentalist may get off pitch because of nervousness or sudden indisposition, and the accompanist can make his soloist aware that not all is well in the pitch department by intensifying the melodic line of the accompaniment. There will be some — very few — soloists who will help nervous accompanists to calm down. But accompanists, do not rely on your soloists; do not give in to your own nerves. Be as much above the situation as you are in it.

Any soloist, even the greatest artist, expects to be given support by his accompanist. Pianistic support is like feeling solid ground under his feet: he needs this support. In musical language, support will mean playing the bass with distinct, if not overly loud, dynamics; preparing for the entrance of the soloist by some such device as a slight ritardando, a slight diminuendo, or whatever is indicated in a particular case; leading the soloist on to more intense singing or playing by an increase in the intensity of the accompaniment; encouraging the soloist during the entire performance. The accompanist may immediately convey a sense of his reliability and support by playing the prelude before the soloist's first entrance with great competence, conviction, and immersion in the meaning of the piece. The accompanist will also give support to the very end by playing the postludes at the same high pitch of intensity as the rest of the composition. The soloist will feel this intensity after finishing his own part, and it will prevent him from slackening his concentration before the last echo of the last chord has disappeared.

By teamwork, complete unity and understanding of the performed work's meaning has now been achieved. Both soloist and accompanist feel sure of one another, and are at ease during the performance. The invisible rays or waves emanate and are received in an ever-alive interchange of emotions, and, at the same time, are being transmitted to the listeners. The groundwork for a very good performance has been laid. What will make such a performance stand out as truly great? What will elevate it from the competent and routine into an unforgettable experience for soloist, accompanist, and audience alike? One single word is the answer: *creativeness*. Not very often during an artist's career does the spark of understanding develop into a surging flame that — far beyond merely recreating a musical work — brings into being new depths of emotion, new ethical and moral values; shows an entirely new side of the work; presents it not only as the author conceived it but imbued also with new life, new feelings that spring forth from the fusion of two personalities into one. This flame of creativeness will make the accompanist feel servant and master at the same time: humble servant of the composer and faithful guardian of the work, but also master of the free interplay of personality; recreator and creator of music. In such a moment, the accompanist will stand on the highest rung of the ladder that leads into the elysium of Art.

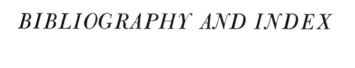

BIBLIOGRAPHY AND INDEX

Bibliography

Abert, Hermann. *Illustriertes Musik Lexikon*. Stuttgart: J. Engelhorns Nachfolger, 1927.

Ademollo, Alessandro. *La bell'Adriana a Milano*. Milan: R. stabilimento musicale Ricordi, 1885.

Ademollo, Alessandro. *La bell'Adriana ed altre virtuose*. Città di Castello: S. Lapi, 1888.

Adler, Guido. *Handbuch der Musikgeschichte*. Berlin: H. Keller, 1930.

Alton, Robert. *Violin and 'Cello Building and Repairing*. London and Toronto: Cassell and Co., 1946.

Apel, Willy. *Harvard Dictionary of Music*. Cambridge: Harvard University Press, 1945.

Arnold, F. T. *The Art of Accompaniment from a Thorough Bass*. London: Oxford University Press, 1931.

Bach, Carl Philipp Emanuel. *Versuch über die wahre Art das Klavier zu spielen* (edited by Walter Niemann). Leipzig: C. F. Kahnt Nachfolger, 1917.

Bartholomew, Wilmer T. *Acoustics of Music*. New York: Prentice-Hall, Inc., 1942.

Bauer, Moritz. *Die Lieder Franz Schuberts*. Leipzig: Breitkopf and Härtel, 1915.

Beethoven, Ludwig van. *Sämtliche Briefe* (edited by Emerich Kastner and Julius Kapp). Leipzig: Hesse and Becker, 1923.

Beetz, Wilhelm. *Das Wiener Opernhaus 1869–1945*. Zürich: The Central European Times Verlag A.G., 1949.

Berlioz, Hector. *Memoirs* (annotated and the translation revised by Ernest Newman). New York: A. A. Knopf, 1932.

Beyschlag, Adolf. *Die Ornamentik der Musik*. Leipzig: Breitkopf and Härtel, 1908.

Bie, Oskar. *Das deutsche Lied*. Berlin: S. Fischer Verlag, 1926.

Bischoff, Hermann. *Das deutsche Lied*. Berlin: Bard, Marquard & Co., 1905.

Blüthner, Julius, and Heinrich Gretschel. *Der Pianofortebau*. Leipzig: B. F. Voigt, 1909.

Blume, Friedrich. *Die Musik in Geschichte und Gegenwart*. Kassel and Basel: Bärenreiter Verlag, 1949–1960.

Bodmer, Frederick. *The Loom of Language*. New York: W. W. Norton & Co., 1944.

Böttcher, Hans. *Beethoven als Liederkomponist*. Augsburg: Dr. Benno Filser Verlag, 1928.

Bos, Coenraad V. *The Well-Tempered Accompanist*. Bryn Mawr, Pa.: Theodore Presser Co., 1949.

Boulanger, Nadja. *Lectures on Modern Music*. Houston: Rice Institute, 1926.

Brelet, Gisèle. *Temps Musical et Tempo*. Paris: Polyphonie, 1948.

Brodnitz, Friedrich S. *Keep Your Voice Healthy*. New York: Harper and Brothers, 1953.

Bücken, Ernst. "Die Musik des Rokokos und der Klassik," *Handbuch der Musikwissenschaft*. Vol. 5. Potsdam: Akademische Verlagsgesellschaft Athenaion, 1928.

Bücken, Ernst, and Paul Mies. "Grundlagen, Methoden und Aufgaben der musikalischen Stilkunde," *Zeitschrift für Musikwissenschaft*. Vol. 5. Leipzig: Breitkopf and Härtel, 1923. Pp. 219–225.

Busnelli, M. D., and U. Pittola. *Guida per l'insegnamento pratico della Fonetica Italiana*. Perugia: Regia Università Italiana per stranieri, 1940.

Camilli, Amerindo. *Pronunzia e grafia dell'Italiano*. Florence: Sansoni, 1947.

Capell, Richard. *Schubert's Songs*. New York: Macmillan Co., 1957.

Castiglione, Pierina Borrani. *Italian Phonetics, Diction, and Intonation*. New York: S. F. Vanni, 1957.

Cauvet, Alfred. *La prononciation Française et la diction*. Paris: Albin Michel, n.d.

Chrysander, Friedrich. *Georg Friedrich Händel*. Leipzig: Breitkopf and Härtel, 1858–1867.

Clementi, Muzio. *Introduction to the Art of Playing the Pianoforte*. London: Clementi, Collard, Davis, & Collard, 1821.

Colorni, Evelina. *Lessons in Italian Lyric Diction*. New York: published by the author, 1956.

Cooper, Martin. *French Music from the Death of Berlioz to the Death of Fauré*. New York: Oxford University Press, 1957.

Crankshaw, Geoffrey. "The Study of Musical Style," *Musical Opinion* (December, 1949), pp. 137–139.

Darrell, Robert Donaldson. *Schirmer's Guide to Books on Music and Musicians*. New York: G. Schirmer, Inc., 1951.

David, Lucien. *La prononciation Romaine et le chant Grégorien*. Grenoble: Librairie Saint-Grégoire, 1929.

De Angelis, Father Michael. *The Correct Pronunciation of Latin, According to Roman Usage*. Philadelphia: St. Gregory Guild, Inc., 1937.

Debussy, Claude. *Monsieur Croche, antidilettante*. Paris: Dorbon-aîné, 1921.

Decsey, Ernst. *Die Spieldose*. Stuttgart: J. Engelhorns Nachfolger, 1928.

Deutsch, Otto Erich. *The Schubert Reader*. New York: W. W. Norton & Co., 1947.

Dickinson, Clarence. *The Technique and Art of Organ Playing*. New York: H. W. Gray Co., 1922.

Dolmetsch, Arnold. *The Interpretation of the Music of the XVII and XVIII Centuries*. London: Novello & Co., Oxford University Press, 1946.

Dorian, Frederick. *The History of Music in Performance*. New York: W. W. Norton & Co., 1942.

Drinker, Henry S. *Bach's Use of Slurs in Recitativo Secco*. Merion, Pa.: published by the author, n.d.

Duncan, Edmondstoune. *The Story of Minstrelsy*. New York: Charles Scribner's Sons, 1907.

Edgren, Hjalmar. *An Italian and English Dictionary*. New York: Henry Holt & Co., 1944.

Einstein, Alfred. *Mozart, His Character, His Work*. New York: Oxford University Press, 1945.

Einstein, Alfred. *Music in the Romantic Era*. New York: W. W. Norton & Co., 1947.

Ellis, Alexander J. *Pronunciation for Singers*. London: J. Curwen & Sons, 1877.

Emery, Walter. *Bach's Ornaments*. London: Novello & Co., 1953.

Emil Naumanns Illustrierte Musikgeschichte (edited by E. Schmitz). Stuttgart: Union Deutsche Verlagsgesellschaft, 1918.

Enria, Umberto. *Lèssico Ortofònico*. Milan: Il Maglio, 1953.

Fletcher, Harvey. *Speech and Hearing in Communication*. New York: D. Van Nostrand Company, Inc., 1953.

Freer, Dawson. *The Teaching of Interpretation in Song*. London: Evans Brothers Ltd., 1924.

Friedländer, Max. *Das deutsche Lied im 18. Jahrhundert*. Stuttgart: J. G. Cotta'sche Buchhandlung, 1903.

Friedländer, Max. Supplement to Schubert's Songs, *Schubert Song Collection IIa*. Leipzig: C. F. Peters, n.d.

Friedländer, Max. "Über die Vorschläge in Schuberts Liedern," introduction to Franz Schubert, *Die schöne Müllerin*. Leipzig: C. F. Peters, 1922.

Fuller-Maitland, John Alexander. *Schumann*. London: S. Low, Marston, Searle, & Rivingston, 1884.

Gasc, Ferdinand E. A. *Dictionary of French and English Languages*. New York: Henry Holt & Co., 1938.

Giltay, J. W. *Bow Instruments, Their Form and Construction*. London: William Reeves, 1923.

Gosling, Henry F. *The Violinist's Manual*. New York: Charles Scribner's Sons, 1935.

Greene, Harry P. *Interpretation in Song*. London: Macmillan Co., 1924.

Greilsamer, Lucien. *L'Anatomie et la Physiologie du Violon, de l'Alto et du Violoncelle*. Paris: Librairie Delagrave, 1924.

Grove's Dictionary of Music and Musicians (5th edition, edited by Eric Bloom). New York: St. Martin's Press, 1955.

Haas, Robert. "Aufführungspraxis der Musik," *Handbuch der Musikwissenschaft*. Vol. 6. Potsdam: Akademische Verlagsgesellschaft Athenaion, 1931–1932.

Haas, Robert. "Die Musik des Barocks," *Handbuch der Musikwissenschaft*. Vol. 7. Potsdam: Akademische Verlagsgesellschaft Athenaion, 1928.

Hahn, Reynaldo. *Du Chant*. Paris: Editions Pierre Lafitte, 1920.

Hall, James Husset. *The Art Song*. Norman: University of Oklahoma Press, 1953.

Hartmann, Rudolf. *Handbuch des Korrepetierens*. Berlin: Max Hesses Verlag, 1926.

Heuberger, Richard. *Franz Schubert*. Berlin: "Harmonie" Verlagsgesellschaft für Literatur und Kunst, 1902.

Hiebner, Armand. *Französische Musik*. Olten: Verlag Otto Walter, 1952.

Hiller, Johann Adam. *Anweisung zum musikalisch richtigen Gesange*. Leipzig: J. F. Junius, 1774.

Hopkins, Edward J. *The Organ, its History and Construction*. London: R. Cocks & Co., 1870.

Hugo Riemanns Musik-Lexikon (edited by Alfred Einstein). Berlin: Max Hesses Verlag, 1919.

Hummel, Johann Nepomuk. *Anweisung zum Pianofortespiel*. Vienna: T. Haslinger, 1828.

International Phonetic Association. *The Principles of the International Phonetic Association*. London: University College of London, Department of Phonetics, 1957.

Jahn, Otto, and Hermann Abert. *W. A. Mozart*. Leipzig: Breitkopf and Härtel, 1919–1921.

Keller, Hermann. *Die musikalische Artikulation, insbesondere bei J. S. Bach*. Stuttgart: C. L. Schultheiss, 1925.

Keller, Hermann. *Phrasierung und Artikulation*. Kassel and Basel: Bärenreiter Verlag, 1955.

Keller, Hermann. *Schule des Generalbassspiels*. Kassel: Bärenreiter Verlag, 1931.

Klotz, Hans. *Das Buch von der Orgel*. Kassel and Basel: Bärenreiter Verlag, 1955.

Kohn, Arthur. *Was soll der Klavierspieler vom Bau des Klavieres wissen?*. Vienna: published by the author, 1925.

Kolisch, Rudolf. "Tempo and Character in Beethoven's Music," *Musical Quarterly*, XXXIX, 2 and 3 (1943), pp. 169–187, 291–312.

Kraus, Felicitas von. *Beiträge zur Erforschung des malenden und poetisierenden Wesens in der Begleitung von Franz Schuberts Liedern*. Mainz: Zeberndruck, 1927.

Krehbiel, Henry E. *The Pianoforte and its Music*. New York: Charles Scribner's Sons, 1911.

Kwasnik, Walter. *Die Orgel der Neuzeit*. Cologne: Staufen-Verlag, 1938.

Laird-Brown, May. *Singers' French*. New York: E. P. Dutton and Co., 1926.

Leet, Leslie. *An Introduction to the Organ*. Cranford, N.Y.: Allen Publishing Co., 1940.

Lehmann, Lotte. *More than Singing*. New York: Boosey & Hawkes, 1945.

Lindo, Algernon H. *The Art of Accompanying*. New York: G. Schirmer, Inc., 1916.

Locher, Carl. *Dictionary of the Organ*. New York: E. P. Dutton and Co., 1914.

Malagoli, Giuseppe. *L'accentazione Italiana*. Florence: Sansoni, 1946.

Marafioti, P. Marion. *Caruso's Method of Voice Production*. New York: D. Appleton-Century Co., 1937.

Marcello, Benedetto. *Il teatro alla moda*. Venice: Tip. dell'Ancora, 1887.

Marshall, Madeleine. *The Singer's Manual of English Diction*. New York: G. Schirmer, Inc., 1953.

Martinon, Philippe. *Comment on prononce le Français*. Paris: Librairie Larousse, 1913.

Mattheson, Johann. *Der vollkommene Capellmeister* (facsimile reprint of 1739 edition). Kassel and Basel: Bärenreiter Verlag, 1954.

Meyer, Kathy. "Zum Stilproblem in der Musik," *Zeitschrift für Musikwissenschaft*. Vol. 5. Leipzig: Breitkopf and Härtel, 1923. Pp. 316–332.

Meyer, Leonard B. *Emotion and Meaning in Music*. Chicago: University of Chicago Press, 1956.

Mies, Paul. *Schubert, der Meister des Liedes*. Berlin: Max Hesses Verlag, 1928.

Mies, Paul. *Stilmomente und Ausdrucksstilformen im Brahmsschen Lied*. Leipzig: Breitkopf and Härtel, 1923.

Migliorini, Bruno. *Pronunzia Fiorentina o pronunzia Romana*. Florence: Sansoni, 1945.

Moore, Gerald. *Singer and Accompanist*. New York: Macmillan Co., 1954.

Moore, Gerald. *The Unashamed Accompanist*. New York: Macmillan Co., 1956.

Mosel, Ignaz Franz von. *Versuch einer Ästhetik des dramatischen Tonsatzes*. Vienna: A. Strauss, 1813.

Moser, Hans Joachim. *Das deutsche Lied seit Mozart*. Berlin: Atlantis Verlag, 1937.

Mozart, Leopold. *A Treatise on the Fundamental Principles of Violin Playing*. London: Oxford University Press, 1948.

Mozart, Wolfgang Amadeus. *Briefe* (edited by Ludwig Schiedermair). Munich: Georg Müller, 1914.

Mozart, Wolfgang Amadeus. *The Letters of Mozart and his*

Family (translated and edited by C. B. Oldman). London: Macmillan Co., 1938.

Nalder, Lawrence M. "The Modern Piano," *Musical Opinion.* (March–May, 1927), p. 34.

Nohl, Hermann. *Stil und Weltanschauung.* Jena: Eugen Diederichs, 1920.

Ochs, Siegfried. *Der deutsche Gesangsverein.* Berlin: Max Hesses Verlag, 1926.

Peyrollaz, Marguerite, and M. L. Bara de Tovar. *Manuel de phonétique et de diction Française à l'usage des étrangers.* Paris: Librairie Larousse, 1954.

Pfordten, Hermann von der. "Franz Schubert und das deutsche Lied," *Wissenschaft und Bildung.* Leipzig: Quelle-Meyer, 1916.

Pius X. *The Motu Proprio of Church Music.* Toledo, Ohio: Gregorian Institute of America, 1950.

Pougin, Arthur. *Jean-Jacques Rousseau Musicien.* Paris: Librairie Fischbacher, 1901.

Quantz, Johann. *Versuch einer Anweisung die Flöte traversière zu spielen* (edited by Arnold Schering). Leipzig: C. F. Kahnt Nachfolger, 1906.

Reissman, August. *The Life and Works of Robert Schumann* (translated by A. L. Alger). London: G. Bell and Sons, 1908.

Ricci, Luigi. *Puccini interprete da se stesso.* Milan: G. Ricordi & Co., 1954.

Riemann, Hugo. *Katechismus der Orgel.* Leipzig: Max Hesses Verlag, 1911.

Riemann Musik Lexikon (edited by Willibald Gurlitt). Mainz: B. Schotts Söhne, 1959.

Rogers, Clement F. "The Pronunciation of Latin," *Musical Opinion* (December, 1942), pp. 79–80.

Rolland, Romain. *Musiciens d'aujourd'hui.* Paris: Librairie Hachette, 1947.

Rolland, Romain. *Musiciens d'autrefois.* Paris: Librairie Hachette, 1908.

Rostand, Claude. *French Music Today.* New York: Merlin Press, 1957.

Rothschild, Fritz. *The Lost Tradition in Music.* New York: Oxford University Press, 1953.

Rothschild, Fritz. *Musical Performance in the Times of Mozart and Beethoven.* New York: Oxford University Press, 1961.

Rudolf, Max. *The Grammar of Conducting.* New York: G. Schirmer, 1950.

Russell, G. Oscar. *Speech and Voice.* New York: Macmillan Co., 1931.

Sachs, Curt. *Commonwealth of Art.* New York: W. W. Norton & Co., 1946.

Sachs, Curt. *Handbuch der Musikinstrumentenkunde.* Leipzig: Breitkopf and Härtel, 1920.

Sachs, Curt. *Real-Lexikon der Musikinstrumente.* Berlin: Julius Bard, 1913.

Sachs, Curt. *Rhythm and Tempo.* New York: W. W. Norton & Co., 1953.

Schering, Arnold. "Zur Geschichte des begleiteten Sologesangs im 16. Jahrhundert," *Zeitschrift der Internationalen Musikge-sellschaft.* Vol. 13. Leipzig: Breitkopf and Härtel, 1911. Pp. 190–196.

Schneider, Max. "Die Begleitung des Secco Rezitativs um 1750," *Gluck Jahrbuch.* Vol. III. Leipzig: Breitkopf and Härtel, 1917. Pp. 88–107.

Schneider, Max. *Zur Geschichte des begleiteten Sologesangs.* Leipzig: Breitkopf and Härtel, 1918.

Schweitzer, Albert. *J. S. Bach.* Leipzig: Breitkopf and Härtel, 1929.

Siebs, Theodor. *Deutsche Bühnenaussprache-Hochsprache.* New York: Frederick Ungar Publishing Co., 1944.

Smith, Fanny Morris. *A Noble Art: Lectures on the Evolution and Construction of the Piano.* New York: Charles F. Tretbar, 1892.

Steglich, Rudolf. "Über Mozarts Adagio Takt," *Mozarteum Jahrbuch* (1951), pp. 90–111.

Stilz, Ernst. "Über harmonische Ausfüllung in der Klaviermusik des Rokoko," *Zeitschrift für Musikwissenschaft.* Vol. 13. Leipzig: Breitkopf and Härtel, 1930–1931. Pp. 11–20.

Strauss, Richard. *Betrachtungen und Erinnerungen* (edited by Willy Schuh). Zürich: Atlantis Verlag, 1949.

Strauss, Richard, and Hugo von Hofmannsthal. *Briefwechsel* (edited by Franz and Alice Strauss and Willy Schuh). Zürich: Atlantis Verlag, 1952.

Strauss, Richard, and Romain Rolland. *Correspondance* (foreword by G. Samazeuilh). Paris: Albin Michel, 1951.

Strauss, Richard, and Stefan Zweig. *Briefwechsel* (edited by Willy Schuh). Frankfurt on the Main: S. Fischer Verlag, 1957.

Thayer, Alexander Wheelock. *Ludwig van Beethovens Leben* (edited by Deiters-Riemann). Leipzig: Breitkopf and Härtel, 1917.

Thurwanger, Camille. *French Musical Diction.* Boston: published by the author, 1910.

Torchi, Luigi. "L'accompagnamento degli instrumenti nei melodrami Italiani nella prima metà del seicento," *Rivista Musicale Italiana.* Vol. I. Turin: Fratelli Bocca Editori, 1894. Pp. 7–38.

Türk, Daniel Gottlob. *Klavierschule.* Halle: Hemmerde und Schwetsche, 1802.

Varney-Pleasants, Jeanne. *Pronunciation of French.* Ann Arbor, Michigan: University of Michigan Press, 1949.

Vennard, William. *Singing: The Mechanism and the Technic.* Los Angeles: published by the author, 1950.

Verdi, Giuseppe. *Copialettere* (edited by Gaetano Cesare and Alessandro Luzio). Milan, 1913.

Wagner, Richard. "Über das Dirigieren Beethovenscher Tonwerke," in *Sämtliche Schriften und Dichtungen.* Leipzig: Breitkopf and Härtel, 1911.

Walker, Ernest. "Some Questions of Tempo," in *Free Thought and the Musician, and Other Essays.* New York: Oxford University Press, 1946.

Weingartner, Felix. *Über das Dirigieren.* Leipzig: Breitkopf and Härtel, 1905.

Zuckerkandl, Viktor. *Musikalische Gestaltung der grossen Opernpartien.* Berlin: Max Hesses Verlag, 1932.

Index

a: 45, 46; Italian, 48, 50, 51, 52, 54, 56, 58, 59, 65; French, 65–66, 71, 72, 74, 81, 85; Spanish, 89, 90; German, 92–93, 95, 97, 98, 107
a cappella music, 187, 192, 193, 194
a punta d'arco, 23
abdominal breathing, 37
Abgesang, 159
abgeschliffen, 138
abgezogen, 138
About Conducting (Wagner), 126
absolute music, 122
Abzug, 137–138, 140
accelerando, 119, 122, 125, 126, 133, 237, 239
accents: grave, 48, 49, 50, 66; circumflex, 66, 70, 71, 74; acute, 67
accents, dancer's, 237
accents, musical: 52, 65, 120, 121, 125, 126, 129, 130, 134, 137, 140, 145, 155, 165, 168, 211, 215, 226, 234, 236; heavy, 111, 127; weak, 111, 127, 129; strong, 126, 130; even, 130; expression, 134; melodic, 134; positive, 134; relative, 134; sudden, 134; minute, 137, 232; French, 166, 167–169; fluid, 167, 169; definite, 168, 169; light, 236
accents, speech, 163, 212
accidentals: 187, 225, 229, 234
accompagnato recitative, 14, 15, 147, 149, 150–151, 212, 215
accompanied music, Greek, 8
accompaniment: art of, 5, 6, 7; craft of, 6; self-, 7, 10, 19, 224; choral, 8; for dance, 8, 230; vocal, 15, 16, 148, 224; instrumental, 16, 17, 215, 224; on organ, 37; on piano, 114, 159, 160, 161, 162, 163, 164, 170, 187, 192, 221, 232; guitar-like, 169; orchestral, 174, 215; for concerti, 174, 226, 230; for string quartet, 175; of own compositions, 179; difficult on piano, 187, 232, 234; harmonic on piano, 192; orchestral on piano, 208, 221; for cantilena, 230; for modern pieces, 230; for virtuoso pieces, 230; background, 230, 232
accompanist: dance, 4, 10, 16, 125, 225, 234–238; professional, 4, 12, 183, 224, 226; instrumental, 4, 16, 183, 224, 230–234; vocal, 4, 63, 183, 223, 224, 234;

choral, 4, 63, 234; defined, 5; rehearsal, 5; semiclassical repertoire, 5; and teacher, 40, 41; and coach, 183; and conductor, 183; recital, 237–238
accordion system of folding pages of music, 226
acoustical conditions, 34, 114, 118, 226
acoustical expression, dancer's, 234
acoustical method of learning, 184, 192, 197
Acoustics of Music (Wilmer T. Bartholomew), 39
action, piano: 27, 29; Viennese, 25; English, 26
acute accent, 67
adagietto, 117
adagio, 116, 117, 118, 119, 120, 121, 123, 124, 125, 126, 155, 156
adagio, French and Italian, 117
adagio assai: 115, 119, 120; cantabile, 115, 119, 124; ma non poco, 124; sostenuto, 124; un poco mosso, 124
Adam's apple, 38
ä, 93. *See also* è
Affektenlehre, 117, 118, 119, 120
agents, artist's, 171, 172
agraffes, 27
"Ah Perfido" (Beethoven), 174
Aïda (Verdi), 20, 51, 54, 57, 58, 59, 60, 97, 149, 236
aigu, 67
air chamber, of harmonium, 34
air pressure, 38
Alberti bass figures, 14
Alcaeus, 8
Alceste (Gluck), 146
alla breve, 114, 115, 116, 117, 118, 120–121, 124, 125, 128
allegretto: 115, 117, 118, 119, 120, 121, 124; scherzando, 118; agitato, 124; ma non troppo, 124; vivace, 124
allegro: 116, 117, 118, 119, 123, 125, 126; assai, 115, 117, 118, 119, 123; moderato, 115, 117, 118, 124; commodo, 117; non troppo, 117; maestoso, 118; ma non troppo (tanto), 118, 119, 124; con brio, 118, 123; molto, 118, 123; vivace, 123
alliteration, 107, 110
altered chords, 160

altered rhythm, 127, 128, 129
alto voice, 114, 174, 175, 229
alveolars, 46, 53, 54, 56, 57, 58, 59, 79
Amati, violin builders, 22
American music, 17, 140, 176
American organ, 35
El Amor Brujo (de Falla), 89, 235
amphibrach, 126
Amphion, 8
"An die Musik" (Schubert), 159
Anacreon, 8
anapest, 126
"and" (dancer's upbeat), 236, 237
andante: 117, 118, 119, 120, 121, 123, 124, 126; flebile, 117; amoroso, 118; mesto, 118; grazioso, 120; con moto, 120, 124; sostenuto, 120, 124; moderato, 121; cantabile, 124; espressivo, 124; ma non troppo, 124; piuttosto allegretto, 124; quasi allegretto, 124; scherzoso, 124
andantino: 117, 124; Italian, 119; Viennese, 119; poco agitato, 124
Anderson, Marian, 20
Andrea Chenier (Giordano), 54
animal voices in songs, 160, 164
ankle bells, 238
anterior sound, 65
anvils, 224
Anweisung zum musikalisch richtigen Gesang (Hiller), 146
anxiety, 238
Apel, Willi, 5, 111
apostrophes, poetical, 103
appearance at auditions, 186
applause, 172, 174, 177, 208
appoggiato, 136, 137
appoggiaturas: 143–154; J. S. Bach's, 143, 144–145; Handel's, 143, 144–145; long, 143, 144, 145, 146, 147, 148, 149, 151; Mozart's, 143, 146–148, 150–151; Schubert's, 143, 146, 151–154; Beethoven's, 143, 148, 150; before main beats, 144; short, 144, 145, 146, 147, 148, 151, 153, 154; on main beats, 144, 145, 147, 152; passing, 144, 145, 148; in concerted numbers, 144, 146, 147; in accompagnato recitatives, 144, 146, 147, 148–154; in secco recitatives, 144, 146, 147, 149, 150; from below, 144, 146,

149, 151, 152; from above, 144, 149, 150, 151, 152; before dotted notes, 145, 146, 147, 148, 152; one-third theory, 145, 146, 147, 148, 152; two-thirds theory, 145, 146, 148, 150; Gluck's, 145–146, 149; Haydn's, 146; Weber's, 148–149, 150; Berlioz's, 149; Mendelssohn's, 149; Donizetti's, 149, 150; Rossini's, 149, 150; Verdi's, 149, 150; Bellini's, 150

approach, vocal, 212
Archilochos, 8
architectural dynamics, 131, 132, 133
archlute, 12
Argentinian pronunciation of Spanish, 89, 91
argot, 65
Ariadne auf Naxos (R. Strauss), 29, 97, 106, 215
arie antiche, 12
Arion, 8
arioso, 115, 147, 159, 198, 209, 215
Arne, Thomas, 16
Arnim, Achim von, 164
arpeggio, 14, 23, 118, 125, 140, 160, 163
arpeggione, 16
arrangers: 112, 139, 173, 230, 232; for dance music, 172
ars nova, 10–11
art of accompanying, 5, 6, 7, 224–240
"The Art of the Fugue" (J. S. Bach), 132
art song, French, 16, 17, 165–170, 178, 179, 220, 223
Artaria and Company, music publishers, 146
articulation, musical: 127, 135–142, 163, 230, 232, 234, 239; of vowels, 92; marks, 135, 136, 137, 138, 139, 140, 141, 142, 163; baroque, 138–139; Handel's, 138–139; J. S. Bach's, 138–139, 226; Beethoven's, 139–140; classicist, 139–140; Mozart's, 139–140, 226; Chopin's, 140; irregular, 140; Mendelssohn's, 140; neoclassicist, 140; Schumann's, 140; Brahms's, 140–141; romantic, 140–141; Wagner's, 140–141; Verdi's, 141; contemporary, 141–142; Bartók's, 142; Berg's, 142; French Impressionist, 142; Mahler's, 142; Schoenberg's, 142; R. Strauss's, 142; Stravinsky's, 142
artist, 209, 221, 234, 238, 239, 240
artistic growth, 171, 176, 182, 183, 184, 236, 238, 239
artistry, defined, 6, 182–183, 209, 210
arytenoid cartilage, 38
aspiration of consonants, 56, 57, 58, 65, 68, 76, 77, 84, 98, 99, 102, 103, 105, 106, 108
assai vivace, 123
assistant conductor, 5, 19, 20
atonal music, 4, 192
Attaignant, Pierre, 11
audience, 171, 172, 173, 176, 177, 178, 179, 211, 215, 224, 225, 232, 234, 237, 238, 239, 240
audition, 184, 186
auditorium size, 238
Aufführungspraxis für "Tannhäuser" (Wagner), 123

aulos, 8, 9
Ausführliche Anweisung zum Pianoforte-spiel (Hummel), 143, 146
"Ave Maria" (Schubert), 159

b: 46; Italian, 55, 57; French, 71, 77, 78, 80, 86; German, 99, 102; English, 102
b, weak: Spanish, 89–90; American, 90
Bach, Johann Christian, 15, 16, 149, 180
Bach, Johann Sebastian: 5, 13, 14, 34, 35, 111, 112, 113, 114, 115, 116, 118, 125, 127, 128, 131, 132, 133, 136, 137, 138, 139, 143, 144, 145, 149, 154, 155, 156, 157, 174, 175, 180, 209, 211, 226; Lieder, 98, 101; passions, 112, 118, 132, 139, 145, 157, 209; suites, 115; partitas, 115, 180; cantatas, 118, 132, 139; concerto for flute, violin, and harpsichord, 128; French suites, 129; chorales, 132; "A Musical Offering," 132; sonatas, 132; Brandenburg concerti, 132, 139; B minor mass, 139; Christmas Oratorio, 139; solo works, 175; chorale-prelude, 180
Bach, Philipp Emanuel, 15, 118, 127, 133, 143, 146, 151, 155
Bach, Wilhelm Friedemann, 143, 144
Bachelet, Alfred, 67, 76, 79, 87
back check, 27
backfalls, 143
background: musical, 6, 12, 110, 112; harmonic, 159, 215; national, 176; orchestral, 221
backstage, 34, 198, 237; duties, 20, 223, 224
backward pronunciation or production, 54, 65, 70, 96, 185
bagpipe, 10
balance rail, 26
Baldwin piano, 26
ballad, 9, 10, 11, 16, 98, 158, 159, 160, 161, 176, 179, 180, 223
ballet: 11, 13, 157, 237; master, 5, 184, 236; class, 125, 237; classic, 234; Italian, 236; music for exercises, 236; Russian, 236; terms, 236; figure, 237
Un Ballo in Maschera (Verdi), 50, 54, 58, 59
bar, dance studios, 234
Barber, Samuel, 17, 176
Der Barbier von Bagdad (Cornelius), 95
Il Barbiere di Siviglia (Rossini), 49, 50, 53, 55, 56, 59, 61, 187, 212, 213, 214
Bardi, Count, 19
barform, 10
Bariera y Calleja, 90
baritone, 174, 175, 186, 221
baroque era, 11, 12, 13, 14, 25, 29, 112, 118, 119, 125, 127, 128, 131, 132, 139, 142, 143, 145, 155, 211, 230, 234
baroque organ, 118
The Bartered Bride (Smetana), 98
Barth, Josef, 226
Bartholomew, Wilmer T., 39, 41
Bartók, Béla, 17, 130, 142, 175
barytone, 16
bass, 12, 18, 127, 131, 140, 158, 187, 197, 221, 229, 238
bass, orchestral, 208
bass accompaniment, 162, 197

bass instruments, 187, 226
bass strings (piano), 27
bass tones, 230
bass voice, 114, 154, 174, 186, 221, 230
Bassa, José, 180
bassbar, 25
basso ostinato, 159
bassoon, 11, 137
battement: dégagé, frappé, grand, petit, petit jetté, tendu, 236
Baudelaire, Charles, 165
Bay, Emanuel, 20
Bayreuth tradition, 100
beat, 232, 236; steady, 125, 127; strong (heavy), 128, 143, 145, 152, 153, 211, 232, 236; weak, 128, 211; expressive, 219; legato, 219; nonexpressive, 219; staccato, 219; anticipating conductor's, 223
beating time, 197, 219, 223
Bechstein piano, 26
Beethoven, Ludwig van: 3, 13, 15, 16, 17, 26, 111, 114, 116, 121, 122, 123, 124, 125, 129, 133, 134, 135, 139, 140, 148, 149, 150, 155, 156, 157, 158, 161, 162, 165, 167, 173, 174, 175, 180, 187, 209, 229, 232; chamber music, 3, 121, 124, 157; symphonies, 15, 97, 121, 122, 124, 133, 134, 150, 157, 167; song cycles, 15, 124, 156, 158, 161; folk songs, 15, 124, 175; variations, 16; songs, 100, 121, 124, 148, 157, 158, 175, 229; Leonore Overture No. 3, 113; letters, 121, 122, 123, 124, 140; piano works, 121, 124, 157; choral works, 124; Violin Concerto in D major, 124, 139, 140, 155, 232; Romances for Violin and Orchestra, 124, 156, 157; conducting, 134; piano playing, 134; conversations, 139, 140; sonatas, 173
beginners, 236
beginning, simultaneous, 234
Beiträge zur Erforschung des malenden und poetisierenden Wesens in der Begleitung von Franz Schuberts Liedern, (von Kraus), 160
bel canto singing, 92, 99, 109, 141
bel canto, style, 48, 52, 65, 71, 97
Bellini, Vincenzo, 17, 141, 150
bellows: organ, 29; harmonium, 34, 35
bells: 5, 9, 20, 160, 164, 238; beating, 238; dynamics of, 238
belly, violin, 24, 25
Bemberg, Henri, 67, 71, 79
Benedict XV, Pope, 64
Benedictine order of Solesmes, 168
Berg, Alban, 4, 17, 142, 175, 193, 197
bergerettes, 14, 223
Bériot, Charles, 16
Berlin, 119, 149
Berlin Royal (State) Opera House, 148, 187
Berlioz, Hector, 16, 17, 67, 77, 79, 80, 82, 84, 87, 88, 130, 135, 143, 149, 162, 165, 166
Bernac, Pierre, 178
Bernstein, Leonard, 17
Beyschlag, Adolf, 145, 154
Bible, 7
bilabials, 46, 52, 55, 57

biomechanics, 22
birds' voices, 160
Bizet, Georges, 17, 66, 67, 68, 69, 71, 73, 74, 75, 76, 78, 79, 80, 81, 84, 85, 86, 88, 166, 167, 169, 198, 203, 211
blending: 48, 49, 50, 92, 239; piano and instrument, 230; piano and voice, 230
blocks, violin, 24, 25
Blondel de Nesle, 10
blowers, organ, 29
Blüthner piano, 26
Boccherini, Luigi, 14, 133, 173
body: feeling, 41; weight, 225; visual expression, 234; music of the, 234; movement, 236, 237
Bösendorfer piano, 26
La Bohème (Puccini), 48, 49, 50, 51, 53, 54, 55, 56, 57, 58, 59, 60, 61, 63, 198
Boito, Arrigo, 60
bolero, 129
Bologna, center of monodic Renaissance music, 19
La bonne chanson (Fauré), 175
Boris Godunov (Mussorgsky), 130
Borodin, Alexander, 17, 130
Bos, Coenraad V., 229
Boulanger, Nadja, 169, 170
Bourdin, Roger, 178
bourée, 116
bow, violin: 22, 23, 25, 118, 119, 234; back of, 23; point of, 23; curved, 118, 131; changes of, 137, 140, 236, 239; shifting of, 232
bowing: 22, 26, 173, 226, 234; marks, 139; technique, 173
bowing (acknowledging applause), 174, 177
bowings: 232; articulation, 136, 137, 139, 141, 230; phrasing, 136, 139, 230
Brahms, Johannes: 16, 17, 41, 125, 130, 135, 137, 140, 157, 159, 161–162, 163, 164, 165, 173, 175, 179, 181, 220, 229, 230, 232; songs, 94, 95, 96, 99, 100, 101, 102, 103, 104, 105, 106, 107, 108, 109, 140, 159, 161–162, 175, 179, 181, 220, 229, 230; Ein deutsches Requiem, 95, 98, 102; symphonies, 137, 220; Waltz in A flat major for piano, 140; duets, 162; quartets, 162; sonatas for violoncello, 173; chamber music, 220; Violin Concerto in D major, 232
brass instrument, 118, 119, 174
bratsche, 22
Brautlieder (Cornelius), 162–163
breaks, natural, 212
breath: 37, 141, 168, 208, 209, 212, 226; control, 22, 139, 141, 173, 174; support, 34, 37, 141, 185, 208; abdominal, clavicular, rib, 37; fresh or stale, 38; audible, 76; flow of, 108; of wind players, 137; auxiliary, 141; emergency, 209; more frequent, 239
breath marks: 135, 136, 139, 192, 208, 209; auxiliary, 139, 209; changing, 208
Brentano, Clemens, 164
breve, 114, 116
bridge: violin, 22, 23, 24, 25, 27, 28; piano, 24, 27
bridge pin, 27
brightening tone quality, 230

Britten, Benjamin, 17, 176, 179
Brod, Max, 210
Brodnitz, Dr. Friedrich, 37
bronchi, 37, 39
Bruckner, Anton, 157
Buch der Lieder (Heine), 161
Bücken, E., 113
Bülow, Hans von, 134
buildup, 210
Bull, John, 12
Burney, Charles, 133
Burns, Robert, 179
Busch, Fritz, 149
busine, 11
Busoni, Ferruccio, 17
button, violin, 24
Byrd, William, 12

c: Italian, 58, 105; French, 76, 77, 78–79, 81, 82, 83, 86, 87, 88, 90, 105; Spanish, 89, 90, 91; voiceless dental fricative, 90; English, 104, 105; German, 105
caccia, 11
Caccini, Giulio, 12, 53, 128, 131, 132
cadence: 126, 149, 211, 212, 215; declamatory, 132, 163; of speech, 212
cadenzas, 10, 175, 209
caesura, 135, 142, 162
Caldara, Antonio, 53
Callas, Maria, 18
Canciones Nacionales (de Falla), 175
Cannabich, Christian, 133
cantabile, 219, 226
Canteloube, Joseph, 175
cantilena, 132, 225, 230
capo d'astro bar, 27
Capriccio (R. Strauss), 43
"Capriccio on the Departure of a Beloved Brother" (Bach), 119
capstan screw, 26
career: artistic, 172, 180, 182, 184, 225, 240; oratorio, 174; operatic, 174, 184, 220; as lieder singer, 184, 220; solo, 225
Carmen (Bizet), 66, 67, 68, 69, 71, 73, 75, 76, 78, 79, 81, 84, 85, 86, 88, 166, 169, 198, 203, 211
"Carnaval" (Schumann), 129
Carpenter, John Alden, 17
cartilages: arytenoid, cricoid, epiglottis, thyroid, 38
Casals, Pablo, 219, 234
Cassadò, Gaspar, 234
castanets, 238
Castilian pronunciation, 89, 90
castrati voices, 18, 119
Catalani, Alfredo, 58
Cavalleria Rusticana (Mascagni), 54
Cecchetti, Enrico, 236
Cehanovsky, George, 210
celesta, 5, 21, 29
'cello. See violoncello
center exercises (ballet), 234
Cesti, Marc Antonio, 19
ch sound, 58, 90, 106; Italian, 58; French, 79, 82; German, 83, 90, 93, 94, 95, 96, 103, 106, 107, 108; Spanish, 90; English, 104, 106, 107
Chabrier, Alexis Emanuel, 86, 87

chaconne, 116, 127
Chaliapin, Feodor, 209
chamber music, 5, 12, 16, 144, 175, 179, 224. See also individual composers
Chaminade, Cécile, 66, 73, 74, 75, 79
chanson, 9, 10, 220
"Chansons madécasses" (Ravel), 67, 70, 75, 78, 79, 175
Chants d'Auvergne (Canteloube), 175
character parts, 210
charm, 169, 170
Charpentier, Gustave, 29, 68, 69, 71, 72, 74, 75, 78, 80, 86, 87, 88
Chausson, Erneste, 66, 71, 73, 74, 75, 77, 78, 79, 80, 84, 86, 88, 165
cheng, 7
Cherubini, Luigi, 17
chest: cavity, 37, 38; quality, 39; resonance, 39; voice, 41
chewing muscles, 40
children's songs, 180
Chilean pronunciation, 89, 91
chin holder, 234
choir expression pedal, 33
Chopin, Frédéric: 125, 129, 130, 140, 180, 225, 236; songs, 125; works for 'cello and piano, 125; piano works, 125, 129, 225; Bolero, 129; Funeral March, 129; "Introduction and Polonaise Brilliante," Op. 3, 180; piano prelude in C minor, 236
choral composition, 142
choral groups: 5, 8, 20, 135, 171, 225; music, 10, 12, 109, 110, 197; masses, 18, 132; technique, 110; voices, 114; leader, 172; settings, 187; singers, 225
chorale, 13, 132, 136
chords: 12, 14, 22, 23, 111, 118, 121, 126, 134, 136, 140, 153, 158, 159, 160, 192, 197, 208, 211, 212, 215, 221, 225, 230, 234, 236, 240; altered, 160; broken, 162, 221; connections, 225; separation, 225
choreography, 18, 184, 237
chorus master, 5, 20
Christoff, Boris, 209
chromatic harmonics, 163
chromatic movement, 160
chronometer, 121
churches and church music, 9, 10, 13, 34, 63, 115, 118, 131, 145, 149, 182
Le Cid (Massenet), 75
Cilea, Francesco, 17
Cimara, Pietro, 210
Cimarosa, Domenico, 14
Cinque Melodies passagères (Barber), 176
circumflex accent, 66, 70, 71, 74
citole, 9
clarinet, 13, 31, 32, 137, 141, 175
clarity, 166, 170, 197, 230
clarté, 142, 169
class exercises, 236
classes, vocal, 186
classical period, 13, 14, 16, 118, 125, 133, 139, 140, 143, 145, 146, 157, 175, 180, 211, 223, 234
classicism, 113, 118, 158, 159, 165
clavecin, 25
clavichord, 11, 13, 25, 116, 118, 131, 142

clavicular breathing, 37
clavicymbalum, 25
clavier, 19
clavis, 25
Clementi, Muzio, 119, 143, 146
closing number, 176
coach: vocal, 4, 5, 20, 63, 183–225; instrumental, 4, 183; defined, 5; ballet and dance, 5, 20, 125; choral, 5, 37, 63; and conductor, 5, 183, 223–224; and voice teacher, 6, 40, 41, 185; craft and art of, 6, 183–224; pedagogical work, 183–186; psychological work, 183–186; purpose of, 186; musical, 187–224, 225; operatic, 192–219; oratorio, 192–219; operetta, 215, 219, 223; of folk songs, 221
Coci, Johann, 20
coda, 158, 159
col legno, 23
colloquial language, 68
coloratura soprano, 10, 40, 119, 139, 173, 174, 175, 186, 209, 215, 232
combination exercises, 236
combination of consonants. *See* consonant combinations
combination piston (organ), 30, 33
comedy, 179, 219
comma: complete, 135; suspended, 135; elevated, 135, 141
common time, 115–117
composer-accompanists, 237
composers, American, 176
concentration: 198, 219, 221, 223, 240; slackening of, 240
concert, 6, 172, 173, 174, 175, 176, 177, 178, 179, 180, 186, 220, 239
concert grand, 118, 224, 226
concert hall: stage in, 12, 34, 57, 99, 109, 112, 135, 139, 149, 160, 171, 173, 182, 219, 224, 226, 237; big, 219, 226; intimate, 219, 226
concertati, operatic, 186
concerted numbers, 147
concerto: with orchestra, 174; with piano, 174, 226, 230, 232
conducting (while singing), 197
conductor: 6, 12, 18, 19, 61, 113, 114, 120, 122, 124, 126, 130, 133, 134, 142, 143, 150, 151, 156, 174, 179, 192, 208, 211, 219, 223, 225, 232; assistant (associate), 5, 19, 20; auxiliary, 20; mode of rehearsing, 219, 223, 224
confidante parts, 210
connection of German consonants, 108–109
consonance, 111
consonant combinations: 47, 59, 60, 83, 105, 106, 108
consonants: 43, 44, 45, 46, 219; labials, 46; linguals, 46; classification of, 46–47; nasals, 46, 52, 53, 65, 71, 90; bilabials, 46, 52, 55, 57; alveolars, 46, 53, 54, 56, 57, 58, 59, 79; velars, 46, 53, 56, 58, 65, 90; gutturals, 46, 53, 98, 107; labiodentals, 46, 54; fricatives, 46, 54, 57, 59, 89, 90, 101, 106, 107; glottal fricatives, 46, 76; plosives, 46, 109; liquids, 53; palatals, 53, 54, 56, 58, 59, 79, 90, 101, 106, 107; dentals, 54,

55, 57, 58, 90; uvular, 107; homorganic, 108–109; non-homorganic, 109
consonants, double: Italian, 48, 49, 50, 52, 59–60, 91, 99; voiceless Italian, 59; German, 59, 99, 107–108; voiced Italian, 59, 107; French, 76, 77, 78, 80, 81, 83, 107; Spanish, 91; voiced German, 107–108, 109; voiceless German, 108
consonants, final, 53, 56, 60, 67, 68, 69, 70, 71, 72, 76, 77, 78, 79, 80, 81, 82, 84, 85, 86, 87, 88, 90, 91, 99, 100, 102, 103, 104, 105, 106, 108, 109, 219
consonants, initial, 52, 53, 54, 55, 56, 57, 58, 60, 69, 72, 73, 76, 77, 78, 79, 80, 81, 82, 89, 91, 98, 99, 100, 101, 102, 103, 104, 105, 106, 107, 108, 109
consonants, medial, 54, 55, 56, 57, 58, 76, 77, 78, 79, 80, 81, 82, 89, 91, 98, 99, 100, 102, 103, 104, 105, 106
consonants, mute: French, 66, 67, 68, 71, 72, 73, 76, 77, 78, 79, 80, 81, 82, 83, 84, 85, 86, 88; German, 99; English, 104
consonants, single: Italian, 44, 48, 52–60, 76, 89; French, 44, 67, 68, 69, 70, 71, 72, 73, 74, 75, 76–84; Spanish, 44, 89–91; German, 44, 92, 93, 94, 95, 96, 97, 98–107, 108; Czech, 98
consonants, voiced: Italian, 46, 52–56, 57, 58; French, 66, 78, 87; Spanish, 89, 90, 91; German, 99–104, 105, 106, 108, 109
consonants, voiceless: Italian, 46, 52, 54, 56–59; French, 68, 78; Spanish, 90, 91; German, 100, 102, 103, 104–107, 109
Les Contes d'Hoffmann (Offenbach), 66, 70, 72, 73, 74, 80, 81, 84, 85
contests, 186
contractions, 49
contradance, 130
contralto, 221, 230
Copland, Aaron, 17
Coppélia (Delibes), 236
Corelli, Arcangelo, 12, 14, 180
Cornelius, Peter, 16, 17, 95, 162–163, 175
cornet: biblical, 7; curved, 11; straight, 11
corona, 61, 127, 135, 136, 142
Der Corregidor (Wolf), 100
Così fan tutte (Mozart), 59, 119, 120, 121, 150
costuming, 173, 223
counterpoint: 12, 131, 197, 230, 234; technique, 11; vertical, 12; linear, 12, 192; study of, 111
counting rests, 192, 198
country dances, 16
Couperin, François, 14, 127, 135, 165
coupler, 30, 31, 33, 35
courante, 115
court dances, 115, 116, 120, 129
Covent Garden, 20
covering (vocal), 34, 92, 232
Cramer, Jean Baptiste, 143
The Creation (Haydn), 120, 155
creativeness, 161, 164, 239, 240
Cremona school of violin-building, 12, 22, 25
crescendo, 23, 30, 31, 126, 132, 133, 134
cricoid cartilage, 38
Cristofori, Bartolomeo, 25

critic: 173, 175, 176, 178, 180; recital aimed at, 172, 180
criticism of pupil, 178, 180, 184, 185, 186, 192
cromorne, 11
crosses (heads of notes), 197
crwth, 10
cue: 187, 198, 208, 237; musical, 192, 198; orchestral, 198; vocal, 198, 208, 224; curtain, 237; light, 237
curtain, 208, 237
curved bow, 118, 131
cuts, 159, 172, 221, 234
Cuzzoni, Francesca, 19
cymbals, 7, 9
Czerny, Josef, 126

d: 46, 56; Italian, 55, 56, 57, 58; French, 71, 77, 78, 80–81, 86; Spanish, 90; German, 102–103, 106; English, 103, 106
da capo: form, 158; song, 158, 159, 210; aria, 159
dactyl, 126
Dafne (Peri), 12, 18
La Damoiselle élue (Debussy), 82
damper, 27, 29, 219
damper pedal, 27, 28, 35
dance: 8, 234; accompanying, 4, 10, 16, 125, 225, 234–238; music, 11, 12, 16, 234; tempo, 115, 130; forms, 127, 230
Dancla, Jean Charles, 16
David, King, 7
death, of Carmen and Violetta, 211
Debussy, Claude, 17, 65, 66, 67, 68, 69, 70, 71, 72, 73, 75, 76, 77, 78, 80, 81, 82, 83, 85, 86, 87, 88, 164, 165–169, 170, 175, 179, 180, 187, 225
debut recital, 172–177, 178
declamation, musical, 131, 142, 162, 163, 165, 167, 168
decrescendo, 30, 31, 131, 132, 134
dégagé, 236
Delibes, Léo, 17, 66, 82, 85, 169, 186; songs, 70, 73, 169, 236
Delius, Frederick, 17
denasalized sounds, 87
dentals, 54, 55, 57, 58, 90
détaché, 23, 232
detail, 219, 232, 234, 238, 239
detail dynamics, 131, 132
details of performance, 239
Deutsches lied, 15, 97, 109, 158, 178, 179, 220, 223
Ein deutsches Requiem (Brahms), 95, 98, 102
Deutsches Singspiel, 15, 146
development of an operatic character, 210, 211
dialect, 55, 57, 65, 104, 105, 168
dialogue, 212
diaphragm, 37
diction: 5, 43–47, 53, 97, 166, 177, 179, 185, 197, 208, 219, 220; Italian, 45, 48–63, 64; English, 45, 63, 64; French, 45, 63, 65–88, 167, 169; German, 45, 63, 65–88, 167, 169; German, 45, 63, 95–110; Spanish, 45, 89–91; clarity of, 53, 110; Latin, 63–64, 82; modern, 77; in theaters, concert halls, studios, 92, 219; Russian, 101

Diderot, Denis, 166
digamma, 51
diminuendo, 61, 126, 131, 132, 133, 137, 138, 144, 240
Dinorah (Meyerbeer), 175
diphthongization, 43, 45, 47
diphthongs: 43, 45, 47; Italian, 51, 52, 60, 89, 97; Latin, 64; French, 66, 69; Spanish, 89; German, 89, 97–98; English, 94, 96, 98
directions to dancers, 236, 237
discharge pallet, 34
dissonance, 111, 158, 237
distribution: of music between both hands, 198, 226, 229; of music between instrumentalist and soloist, 234
Ditters von Dittersdorf, Karl, 133
Doctor Faustus (Mann), 3, 4
Doktor Faust (Busoni), 17
Dolmetsch, Arnold, 128, 132
Don Carlo (Verdi), 53, 57, 59
Don Giovanni (Mozart), 15, 19, 52, 53, 54, 56, 57, 58, 59, 62, 120, 128, 129, 138, 139, 147, 150, 156, 187, 205, 207, 211, 212, 215
Don Pasquale (Donizetti), 49, 50
Don Quichotte songs (Ravel), 169, 175
Donizetti, Gaetano, 17, 49, 50, 53, 57, 58, 61, 81, 149, 150, 175, 186, 187, 210, 215
Donna Anna (*Don Giovanni*), 212
Donna Elvira (*Don Giovanni*), 139, 211
Dorian, Frederick, 126, 131
dots: single, 127, 129, 136, 137; double, 128, 129
dots (articulation marks), 23, 139, 140, 141, 142
dotted notes, 115, 127, 128, 129, 145, 146, 147, 151, 153, 156, 160, 236
double bass, 150, 172
double escapement, 27
double flats, 187
double stops, 24
Dougherty, Celius, 17
Dowland, John, 12
downbeat: musical, 127, 236; dancer's, 236
dramatic effects, 98, 100, 107, 108, 109, 110, 158, 159, 173, 211, 212, 223
draw knob, 30
Dresden, 119
drop screw, 27
Druckluftharmonium, 35
drums, 5, 9, 164, 238
"Du bist die Ruh" (Schubert), 159
Du Bois, Louis, Cardinal, 63, 64
duets, 186
Dufay, Guillaume, 11
Duke, John, 180
Duparc, Henri, 17, 66, 69, 70, 73, 78, 80, 81, 165, 169, 180, 229
Durante, Francesco, 14
durchkomponiert (through-composed), 158, 159, 160, 161
Dussaut, Robert, 123
duties of an operatic coach, 223
Duvernoy, Victor Alphonse, 87
Dvořák, Antonin, 17, 130, 176
dynamic markings: 132, 212; attacks, **174**; value, 198; range, 239

dynamics: 25, 26, 40, 41, 131–135, 140, 142, 162, 169, 192, 197, 215, 221, 234, 240; fortissimo, 22, 23, 41, 131, 133, 134; pianissimo, 22, 40, 41, 61, 131, 133, 134, 225; piano, 23, 30, 52, 131, 132, 133, 134, 219, 225; forte, 30, 40, 131, 132, 133, 134, 226; forte subito (sudden), 30, 134; piano subito (sudden), 30, 134; organ, 31, 131; mezzoforte, 52, 131, 133, 134, 219, 226; clavichord, 131; declamatory, 131; harpsichord, 131; detail, 131, 132; stringed instruments, 131, 132; terrace, 131, 132; architectural, 131, 132, 133; emotional, 131, 132, 133; hairpin, 131, 132, 133; J. S. Bach's, 131–133; baroque, 131–133; contrasting, 131, 133; Handel's, 131–133, 139; vitalizing, 132; light and shade, 132, 133; Jomelli's, 133; Stamitz's, 133; pppp, 133; ppppp, 133; preclassical, 133; fff, 133, 134, 226; mezzo-piano, 133, 134, 226; classical, 133–135; ppp, 133, 226; Beethoven's, 134–135, 226; changes of, 134, 136, 239; Haydn's, 134, 226; Mozart's, 134, 226; suppressed, 135; Brahms's, 162; stronger, 210; softer, 210, 226; level of, 215, 219; buildups, 219; basic, 226; contrast of, 226; piano, 226, 238

e: 46; Italian, 46, 49, 51, 52, 54, 56, 58, 59, 60, 66, 67, 89; Latin, 64; English, 66, 67; French, 66–69, 71, 74, 75, 76, 79, 81, 82, 93; German, 67, 93, 97, 98, 106; Spanish, 89, 90, 91
e, mute: French, 66, 67, 68–69, 70, 74, 76, 79, 84, 94; English, 68, 93, 94; German, 94, 99, 101, 102
e, nasal, 67, 70, 71, 72–73, 75, 76, 77
ear training, 184, 192, 197
echo, 114, 118, 131, 154, 240
edition of songs (high, medium, low), 221
editions, original vs. later, 112, 139, 151, 154, 221, 225
Eichendorf, Joseph von, 163
Einstein, Alfred, 133
elasticity, 135, 212, 215
elegance (quality of French music), 166, 232
Elektra (R. Strauss), 207
elevated comma, 135, 141
elision of sounds, 68, 69, 72, 78, 79, 81, 84, 93, 103
Elisir d'amore (Donizetti), 61
Elizabethan lutenists, 12, 115, 220
embellishments, 7, 14, 24, 62, 142, 143, 155, 156
emotion, 15, 16, 56, 76, 90, 98, 99, 104, 108, 113, 115, 117, 118, 119, 131, 132, 133, 158, 160, 161, 163, 164, 167, 168, 183, 209, 210, 211, 212, 221, 239, 240
Emotion and Meaning in Music (Meyer), 111
empty measures. *See* rests
encores, 174, 177
endurance, 215
energizer: 21; violin, 22–23; piano, 26–27; organ, 29–31; voice, 37–38, 41; harmonium, **43**
L'Enfance du Christ (Berlioz), 82, 87

L'Enfant prodigue (Debussy), 78
ensembles, operatic, 186, 187, 197, 198, 211
Die Entführung aus dem Serail (Mozart), 15, 94, 103, 108
entrances: 198, 224, 240; late, 198, 239; quick, 208; anticipating, 224
entrée (court dance), 116
enunciation, 43
epic quality, 179, 219
epigastrium, 37
epiglottis, 38
equilibrium, 236
Erard piano, 26, 170
Erb, Karl, 209
"Erlkönig" (Schubert), 16, 159, 225, 226, 227, 228
Ernani (Verdi), 54, 58
erotic feelings, French songs, 169
escapement, 26, 34
esophagus, 38
espressivo, 24, 219
Estey, builder of harmoniums, 35
esthetic sense, 111, 126, 179
ethical sense, 3, 4, 6, 13, 15, 113, 167, 239, 240
eu sound: German, 67, 69, 95, 98, 106; French, 69, 71, 73, 75, 76, 82
Eugene Onegin (Tchaikovsky), 196
euphony, 69, 82, 85, 86, 88, 103, 109
Euridice (Caccini), 12
Euridice (Peri), 12
Euryanthe (Weber), 123, 128
evaluation of a pupil's progress, 186
Evangelist (St. Matthew Passion), 209
exercises, 225, 236
explosion of sounds, 57, 58, 59, 76, 80, 81, 90, 99, 100, 102, 103, 104, 105, 106, 108, 109, 134
expression, musical, 15, 16, 61, 113, 122, 124, 125, 126, 128, 131, 132, 133, 134, 135, 136, 139, 144, 149, 151, 155, 156, 157, 158, 159, 163, 165, 166, 173, 174, 179, 192, 209, 210, 211, 215, 219, 221, 223, 224, 230, 234, 236, 238
eye connection, 223

f: 46, 53; Italian, 57; French, 67, 69, 78, 80, 86; German, 99, 104–105; English, 105
f holes, 24
faith, 182
de Falla, Manuel, 17, 89, 90, 91, 175, 225, 234, 235, 238
falsetto voice, 41
Falstaff (Verdi), 57, 58
fandango, 129, 147
Fauré, Gabriel, 17, 66, 67, 69, 70, 72, 73, 74, 76, 77, 78, 80, 82, 84, 87, 88, 165, 167, 169, 170, 175, 176, 226
Faust (Gounod), 66, 67, 69, 70, 71, 72, 73, 74, 76, 77, 78, 79, 81, 82, 83, 84, 86, 87, 88
fermata, 61, 127, 135, 136, 142
Fidelio (Beethoven), 94, 103, 106, 107, 108, 124, 129, 134, 139, 148, 150, 157, 187, 209
figurations, 187, 197, 198, 212, 221, 225, 226, 229
figured bass, 3, 5, 12, 13, 14, 16, 230

La Fille du régiment (Donizetti), 81
final consonants, 53, 56, 60, 67, 68, 69, 70, 71, 72, 76, 77, 78, 79, 80, 81, 82, 84, 85, 86, 87, 88, 90, 91, 99, 100, 102, 103, 104, 105, 106, 108, 109, 219
finger bells, 238
fingerboard, 22, 23, 24
fingering: 226, 229; on piano, 35, 36, 119, 225; on organ, 35, 36, 138, 225; on harpsichord, 138; unorthodox, 225; change of, 226
fingers: substitution, 35, 36; pressure, 131, 132; lifting, 137; strength of, 225; positions of, 229
first performance, 173, 175, 176, 178, 180
Fischer-Dieskau, Dietrich, 98, 178, 179
Five Greek Songs (Ravel), 175
Flagstad, Kirsten, 210, 239
flamenco guitarists, 11
flange, 26
Die Fledermaus (J. Strauss), 85
Flesch, Karl, 232
Der Fliegende Holländer (Wagner), 96
Florence, 10, 12, 19
Florilegium (Muffat), 128
Flotow, Friedrich von, 101
flute, 31, 169, 175
folk music: 14, 15, 17, 89, 90, 107, 124, 161, 162, 164, 175, 176, 180, 220, 221; Hungarian, 129; Scottish, 129; Slovak, 129; Finnish, 130; German, 164
following: a conductor, 192, 223; a dancer, 237; a soloist, 239
forcing the tone, 230
forefalls, 143
foreign origin, words of, 49, 51, 54, 55, 58, 72, 76, 79, 80, 81, 82, 83, 96, 100, 101, 104, 106, 107
"Die Forelle" (Schubert), 159
form, musical, 111, 113, 124, 136, 140, 158, 160, 161, 163, 164, 211, 219, 234
forte. *See* dynamic scale
forte piano, 134
fortissimo. *See* dynamic scale
forward position (singing), 185
forward production, 54, 68, 90, 96, 100
La Forza del Destino (Verdi), 48, 50, 54, 56, 57, 58, 59, 195, 210
forzato, 134
fouetté, 237
frame (piano), 27, 28
Franck, César, 17
Franz, Robert, 16, 161
frappé, 236
Die Frau ohne Schatten (R. Strauss), 29
Frederick II of Prussia, 115
Freed, Arnold, 180
Der Freischütz (Weber), 98, 100, 105, 107, 108, 110, 129, 148, 150
French, language, 47, 65, 83
French horn, 13, 148, 175
French music, 165–170
frequencies of high and low tones, 39
fricatives: 46, 54, 57, 59, 89, 90, 101, 106, 107; glottal, 46, 76
Friedländer, Max, 112, 151, 154
frog (of a bow), 25
frottola, 11
"Frühlingstraum" (Schubert), 159
fugue, fugato, 138

full score: 131, 145, 187, 230, 232; reading and playing, 187; studying, 230
full voice, 215, 219
funeral music: 34; funérailles (Liszt), 129
Furtwängler, Wilhelm, 113, 114, 125

g: 46, 64; Italian, 53, 55, 56, 58, 90, 106; French, 69, 71, 72, 77, 78, 79, 81–82, 86, 106; Spanish, 89, 90; interior Spanish, 90; German, 99, 103–104; English, 104, 106
da Gagliano, Marco, 18
gagliarda, 127
Galindo, Blas, 180
galop, 237
Gasparri, Cardinal Pietro, 63
gauklers, 9, 12
gavotte, 116
"Gefrorne Tränen" (Schubert), 159
geige, 22
Gellert, Christian Fürchtegott, 158
Geminiani, Francesco, 12, 132, 133
Gemüt, 164
German dances, 16, 116, 127, 129
German Singspiel, 15, 146
Gershwin, George, 17, 176
gestures, 223, 236
Gigli, Beniamino, 178
gigue (dance form), 116
gigue (giga), predecessor of violin, 22
La Gioconda (Ponchielli), 49, 50, 53, 56, 58, 59, 237
Giordani, Tommaso: 14; arietta, 53, 58
Giordano, Umberto, 17, 54
Glazunov, Alexander, 17, 180, 232
gleemen, 8, 10
Glinka, Michail, 17, 130
glissando: 24; organ, 35, 36
glottal fricatives, 46, 47
glottal stroke, 72, 109, 110
glottis, 38
Gluck, Christoph Willibald von, 14, 15, 17, 51, 61, 121, 128, 129, 145–146, 149, 154, 157, 165, 211
gn sound: English, 53; Portuguese, 53; French, 53, 69, 77, 82, 90, 101; Spanish, 53, 90, 101; Italian, 53, 101; German, 101
Godunov, Boris, 209
Goethe, Johann Wolfgang von: 8, 15, 146, 157, 158, 163, 179, 220; "Mignon" (from Wilhelm Meister), 220
Die Götterdämmerung (Wagner), 94, 98, 101, 102, 108, 156, 239
golden age of music, 15, 135, 157, 167, 169
golden mean, 43, 108, 159, 209
Gonzaga, Vincent, Duke of Mantua, 18
Gounod, Charles, 17, 66, 67, 69, 70, 71, 72, 73, 74, 75, 76, 77, 78, 79, 81, 82, 83, 84, 85, 86, 87, 88
Goyescas (Granados), 89, 90, 180
graduation (violin), 24
Graham, Martha, 172, 237
The Grammar of Conducting (Max Rudolf), 219
Granados, Enrique, 17, 89, 90, 180, 238
grand battement, 236
grand détaché, 23
grave accent, 48, 49, 50, 66

grazioso, 137
Greek music, 8
Greek origin, words of, 49, 51, 54, 55, 58, 64, 72, 76, 79, 80, 81, 82, 83, 96, 100, 101, 104, 106, 107
Greek Songs (Pizzetti), 175
Gregorian chant, 9, 10, 63, 168
Grétry, André Erneste, 165, 174
grief, ways of expressing, 164, 167
Grieg, Edvard, 17
Griffes, Charles, 17
group coaching, 186
"Grundlagen, Methoden und Aufgaben der musikalischen Stilkunde" (Bücken and Mies), 113
gu sound: Italian, 51; French, 82; Spanish, 90
Guarnerius, violin builders, 22
gü sound, Spanish, 90
guilds, musical, 12, 13
guitar, 9, 10, 11, 169, 176, 221, 234
gum ridge, 46, 54, 58, 59, 105, 107
Gurrelieder (Schoenberg), 197
"Gute Nacht" (Schubert), 159
gutturals, 46, 53, 98, 107
gz sound: Latin, 64; French, 83

h: 46; Italian, 56, 58, 59, 76; Latin, 64; French aspirated, 65, 68, 76–77, 84; French mute, 65, 76–77, 83, 84; Spanish, 91; German, 96, 98–99; German aspirated, 98, 99, 104; German mute, 99; English, 106
Hageman, Richard, 17
Hagen, Oskar, 139
Hahn, Reynaldo, 17, 71, 72, 83, 85, 88, 169
hairpin dynamics, 131, 132, 133
Halévy, Jacques Fromental, 17, 76, 80, 83, 165
half falls, 143
half-spoken words, 197
half-stopped pipes, 32
half-sung words, 197
half-voice, 198
Halm, Friedrich, 161
hammer: piano, 26, 27, 170; harmonium, 35
hammerhead, 26, 27, 28
hammershank, 26, 27
Hammerstein, Oscar III, 176
Handel, George Frederick: 13, 14, 16, 19, 35, 114, 115, 116, 118, 125, 127, 128, 129, 131, 132, 133, 136, 138, 139, 143, 149, 154, 157, 159, 173, 174, 211; concertos, 132; operas, 132, 143; sonatas, 132, 173; oratorios, 143; arias, 159
hands: substitution, 35; transposing, 229; in accompanying, 232; skipping, 232; lifting, 234
Hänsel und Gretel (Humperdinck), 105, 106
harmonics: 24, 27, 31, 32, 33, 171; pattern, 113, 163, 198; structure, 143, 153; background, 159, 230; skeleton, 187, 188, 192; function, 238
Harmonischer Gottesdienst (Telemann), 149
harmonium, 5, 21, 34–35, 224
harmonium technique, 34–37

harmony: 11, 22, 29, 140, 143, 145, 146, 159, 163, 166, 169, 187, 191, 192, 197, 208, 225, 230; latent, 11, 13, 192, 208; study of, 111; full, 192, 197; simplified, 197; sustained, 197; complicated, 208; exotic, 232
harps, 7, 9, 10, 160
harpsichord, 11, 12, 13, 14, 25, 116, 118, 128, 131, 133, 142, 174, 211
Harrell, Mack, 178
Harris, Roy, 17
Harvard Dictionary of Music (Apel), 5, 111
Hasse, Johann Adolf, 14
Haydn, Joseph, 14, 15, 16, 114, 118, 119, 120, 121, 123, 124, 126, 129, 133, 134, 139, 143, 146, 155, 156, 157, 158, 165, 174, 226, 232
head (of a bow), 25
head voice, 41
hearing, 14
heartbeats (imitating), 160, 238
heavy, musician's vs. dancer's terminology, 237
heel beats, 238
"Heidenröslein" (Schubert), 159
Heifetz, Jascha, 20
Heine, Heinrich, 159, 161
Henneberg, Johann Baptist, 19
Hérodiade (Massenet), 76, 83, 169
heroines, operatic, 211
hesitation, 127, 208, 211
Hesse, Hermann, 3, 4
Heyse, Paul von, 163
hiatus: 51, 61; marks, 135, 136, 138, 141. *See also* separation
Hilfskapellmeister, 20
Hiller, Johann Adam, 15, 143, 146
Hindemith, Paul, 3, 174
Hines, Jerome, 209
The History of Music in Performance (Frederick Dorian), 126, 131
Hofmannsthal, Hugo von, 210
holds, 135, 136, 142, 212
hole in scenery, 223, 224
homophonic style, 10, 112, 132
homorganic consonants, 108, 109
Honegger, Arthur, 17
horns: biblical, 7; Greek, 9; of classical times, 148; signals, 164
Horst, Louis, 172, 237
Hotter, Hans, 98, 178
Hubay, Jenö, 17
Hüe, Georges, 74, 78, 87
human development, 210, 211, 234
humility, artistic, 171, 182
Hummel, Johann Nepomuk, 143, 146, 155
humming, 52, 53, 122, 208
humor, 161, 162, 163, 164, 165
Humperdinck, Engelbert, 105, 106
Hungarian influences, 129, 162
hunting horn, 14, 160
hurdy-gurdy, 9, 10
hyoid bone, 38
hysteria, 185, 211

i: 46; Italian, 49, 50, 51, 54, 56, 58, 59, 60, 69, 94; French, 69–70, 71, 73, 74, 75, 77, 79, 82; English, 69, 94; Spanish,
89, 90, 91; German, 94, 97, 98, 106, 107
iambus, 126
idealism, 164, 220
idiom: in translations, 210; idiomatic undertones of lyrics, 220
Les Illusions (Britten), 176
"Im Frühling" (Schubert), 159
imagery, 41, 183, 185, 197, 220
imaginary hero of song, 221
imagination, 166, 169, 179, 185, 221, 223
imitating: of orchestral instruments on piano, 221, 226, 230, 238; of soloist's articulation, 232; of soloist's nuances, 239
immolation scene (*Götterdämmerung*), 239
impetus: dramatic, 59, 61, 107, 108; rhythmic, 61
impressionism, 26, 142, 165, 166, 170, 211, 219, 226
improvisation: 9, 10, 12, 161, 223, 224, 239; for dancers, 234, 237
"in" (dancer's direction in space), 236
In the Nursery (Mussorgsky), 175
indisposition, 239, 240
individual coaching, 186
individual needs (of a singer), 208
individuality, 161, 184
d'Indy, Vincent, 67, 83
infinite melody, 141, 163
inflection, 142, 163, 169, 170, 192, 212, 215, 220
innate style, 84, 112, 113, 136, 149
Innerlichkeit, 164
instrumental accompaniment, 16, 17, 215, 224
instrumental style, 112
instrumentation, 111
integrity, artistic, 239
intellect, 183, 210, 219
intensifying melodic line, 240
intensity: 41, 173, 185, 212, 219, 240; vocal, 22, 41, 42, 185, 212; of diction, 59, 76, 103, 104, 105, 107, 219; dynamic, 131, 135; of expression, 192, 208, 209
intention: composer's, 211; conductor's, 223
interludes, 211, 226
intermezzi, 14
Intermezzo (R. Strauss), 122
intermission, 172, 173, 174, 175, 176, 177, 180
International Phonetic Alphabet, 43, 50
interpretation, 5, 6, 107, 134, 135, 139, 174, 183, 186, 212, 220, 223, 236, 239
The Interpretation of the Music of the XVII and XVIII Centuries (Dolmetsch), 115, 128, 132
interpreters, 178, 179, 220, 221
interruptions, 127, 135, 162, 208, 223
intervals: 111, 167, 208, 212; quarter tones, 24; half tones, 24, 28; wide, 138
intonation, 24
introduction, 221
"Introduction and Rondo Capriccioso" (Saint-Saëns), 232
Introduction to the Art of Playing the Pianoforte (Clementi), 146

"Invitation to the Dance" (Weber), 129, 236
IPA (International Phonetic Alphabet), 43, 50
Isaac, Heinrich, 11
Ives, Charles, 17

j: Italian, 56; Latin, 64; French, 78, 79; Spanish, 89, 90; German, 99, 101; English, 106
j semivowel: Italian, 51; French, 73, 74, 75, 76, 77; Spanish, 89, 90, 91; German, 104
jack, piano, 26
jack fly, 26
"Der Jäger" (Schubert), 159
Janáček, Leoš, 17, 210
janissary music, 129
jaw, 40, 46, 49, 50, 66, 67, 69, 71, 185
jazz, 127, 130, 140
jetté petit battement, 236
Jews, musical instruments of, 7, 9
Joachim, Joseph, 17, 23
Jomelli, Niccolò, 19, 133
Jones, Robert, 19
jongleurs, 9
Joseph and His Brothers (Mann), 8
Jubal, 7
La Juive (Halévy), 76, 80, 83
jumps: musical, 140, 225; dancer's, 237; with soloist, 239
"Die junge Nonne" (Schubert), 159

k: 46, 64; Italian, 53, 57, 58; French, 79, 80, 82–83, 87, 88; Spanish, 90; German, 99, 100, 103, 104, 107; English, 104
Kaulich, Josef, 20
Keep Your Voice Healthy (Brodnitz), 37
Keller, Gottfried, 163
Keller, Hermann, 137
keras, 9
key: 211, 220, 221, 222, 225, 230; related, 161; contrasting, 172; original, 220, 222, 229, 230; definite, 221; right, 221; medium, 229; high, 229, 230; low, 229, 230; minor, 237
key: piano, 26, 27, 225, 229, 232; organ, 30, 31, 136; harmonium, 34; harpsichord, 128; time-beater, 224
keyboard: piano, 27, 28, 137, 221, 225, 226, 234, 237; organ, 30, 34, 35, 36; harmonium, 35
keyboard instruments, 11, 12, 13, 19, 21, 24, 29, 118, 119, 127, 132, 136
keyboard wind instruments, 5, 31, 34
key-word technique, 215, 219
Kilpinen, Yrjö, 17
kithara, 8
klavier, 25
Klavierbüchlein für Wilhelm Friedemann Bach (J. S. Bach), 144
Kleiber, Erich, 149
Klemperer, Otto, 113, 149
Des Knaben Wunderhorn (von Arnim and Brentano), 164
knee attachments, harmonium, 35
knees (dancer's), 236
Knoch, Ernst, 210
knocking, imitating, 224, 238
knuckle, 26, 27

Kochanski, 235
Kodaly, Zoltán, 17
Kolisch, Rudolf, 122, 124
Korngold, Erich Wolfgang, 104
Korrepetitor, 5
Kraus, Felicitas von, 160
Kreisler, Fritz, 17, 232, 233
Křenek, Ernst, 4
Kreutzberg, Harald, 172, 237
Kreutzer, Rodolphe, 16
"Der Kreuzzug" (Schubert), 159
krummhorn, 11
ks sound: Italian, 58; Latin, 64; French, 82, 83; Spanish, 91; German, 104, 105, 107
Ktesibios, 7, 9
Kucharz, Johann Baptist, 19
kw sound: Italian, 58, 104; French, 83; Spanish, 90; English, 104; German, 104

l: 46; English, 54; Italian, 54, 55, 56, 58, 60, 100; Italian gl, 54, 75, 90, 101; Spanish ll, 54, 90–91, 101; French, 69, 71, 75, 77, 80, 82, 87, 100; German, 99, 100, 102, 103, 105, 106; German ll, 101
l mouillé: French, 75, 77, 78, 87, 90; Spanish (Central American), 91
La Favorita (Donizetti), 50
labials, 46
labiodentals, 46, 54
Lachner, Franz, 151
lacquer, 21
Ländler, 129, 130
Laird-Brown, May (*Singers' French*), 76
Lakmé (Delibes), 66, 82, 85, 169, 186
Lalo, Edouard, 76, 87
Landino, Francesco, 10
languid, 31
Lanner, Joseph, 130
lapses of memory, 239
larghetto, 117, 119, 120, 121, 124
largo, 117, 119, 120, 124
largo assai, 124
larynx, 21, 37, 38, 41, 45, 56
de Laserna, Blas, 180
latent harmony, 11, 13, 192, 208
Latin origin, words of, 49, 51, 54, 55, 58, 72, 76, 79, 80, 81, 82, 83, 96, 100, 101, 104, 106, 107
leaps: musical, 140, 225; dancer's, 237
learning, methods, 197
Leclair, Jean Marie, 14
leg (dancer's), 234, 236, 237
legato, 52, 86, 135, 137, 138, 139, 140, 142, 173, 219, 225; on organ, 5, 30, 35, 36, 136; on piano, 15, 26, 225; bowing, 22, 139; on celesta, 29; singing, 109, 110, 142; slurs, 136, 137; fingering, 225
Legrenzi, Giovanni, 57
Lehmann, Lotte, 98, 178, 179, 180, 181, 209, 239
Leich, 10
"Der Leiermann" (Schubert), 10, 159
leitmotiv, 211
lengthening of notes, 136
lento, 117, 119, 124
Leoncavallo, Ruggiero, 53, 54, 59, 200
Leopold I, Emperor, 19
Leroux, Xavier, 74, 169
Lesbos, school of, 8

letoff regulating button, 26
"Lettre sur la musique française," essay by J. J. Rousseau, 166, 167
levers, piano, 26, 27
Liadoff, Anatol, 81
liaison, French consonant and vowel: 65, 67, 68, 69, 76, 78, 79, 81, 84–88; forbidden, 84–85; required, 84, 85–86; optional, 84, 86
liaison, German consonant and vowel, 109–110
liaison, Italian vowels, 60–62
liaison, Spanish vowels, 9
librettist, 210
lied: 15, 97; J. S. Bach's, 98, 101, 109, 158, 178, 179, 220, 223
Das Lied von der Erde (Mahler), 156
lieder singer, 184
lift, dancer's, 237
ligatura, 135, 137, 140
light cues, 237
light opera, 5, 219
lighter (musical terminology), 237
"Der Lindenbaum" (Schubert), 159
linear music, 192
linguals, 46
lip (of an organ pipe), 31
lip technique (brass and wind instruments), 13, 21, 118, 119
lips: 21, 40, 45, 46, 52, 54, 55, 57, 59, 66, 67, 69, 90, 97, 98, 101, 105, 108, 109; rounded, 46, 49, 50, 59, 68, 69, 71, 73, 75, 95, 96, 98; protruded, 50, 68, 69, 73, 75, 95, 96
liquid l sound: French, 75, 77, 78, 87, 90; Spanish (Central American), 91
liquids, 53
listeners, 240
listening to singer's phrasing, 239
Liszt, Franz: 16, 129, 130, 156, 162, 165; songs, 84, 87, 162; funérailles, 129
"Litanei" (Schubert), 159
literal translation, 177, 210, 211, 212, 220
Locatelli, Pietro, 12
Loewe, Karl, 16, 160
Lohengrin (Wagner), 94, 95, 99, 101, 104, 106, 110, 155, 193, 194, 206
Lombardian manner, 129
London, George, 209
Lorenzo il Magnifico, 11
Lortzing, Albert, 17
Louise (Charpentier), 29, 68, 69, 74, 75, 78, 80
loure, 116
Lozada, Angelica, 180
Lucia di Lammermoor (Donizetti), 53, 57, 58, 175, 186, 187, 210
Lully, Jean Baptiste, 13, 19, 128
lungs, 37
Die lustigen Weiber von Windsor (Nicolai), 102
lute, 10, 11, 12, 13, 14, 116, 118, 142, 160
lutenists, 12, 115, 220
lyra, 9, 16, 160
lyric poetry, 179
lyric soprano, 175, 186, 215
lyric tenor, 173
lyrical, 100, 179
lyricism, 161, 164, 223
lyricist, 163, 165

lyrics: 210, 215; meaning, 131, 159, 161, 209, 210; of songs, 158, 159, 160, 161, 163, 166, 169, 170, 178, 220, 221; foreign, 192; changing, 209, 221; understanding, 211

m: 46; Italian, 52–53, 55, 60, 99; French, 66, 67, 70, 72, 73, 77, 80, 82, 87; Spanish, 90; German, 99, 100, 102, 105
Machaut, Guillaume de, 10, 11
Madama Butterfly (Puccini), 49, 50, 51, 52, 53, 56, 57, 58, 61, 198, 203
Madame l'Archiduc (Offenbach), 68
madrigal, 11, 12
"Madrigal Amarilli" (Caccini), 53
Mälzel, Johann Nepomuk, 121, 122
maestoso, 120
maestro al cembalo, 12, 18
maestro sostituto, 5
"magical numbers," 198
Magister Ludi (Das Glasperlenspiel) (Hesse), 3, 4
Mahler, Gustav, 17, 95, 98, 112, 113, 123, 142, 149, 156, 157, 163, 164, 179, 181, 221, 226
Mallarmé, Stéphane, 165
mallet, 224
Les Mamelles de Tirésias (Poulenc), 180
manager, artist's, 171, 172, 178
mandora, 9
manichord, 9
Mann, Thomas, 3, 4, 7
Mannheim style, 125, 133, 134
Manon (Massenet), 56, 59, 70, 72, 73, 74, 75, 76, 77, 78, 83, 84, 85
Manon Lescaut (Puccini), 59, 61, 62
Mantua, 19
manuals: organ, 29, 30, 31, 33, 34, 35, 36, 131, 136, 138; harmonium, 35
marcato, 35, 36, 237
Marcello, Benedetto, 14
Marcellus, Pope, 131
march alla breve, 116
marches, 129, 236
markieren, 198
marking: time units, 192; the beat, 192, 194; rests, 192, 195; pages, 192, 225; scores, 224
Marschner, Heinrich, 17
"La Marseillaise," 70, 161
Marshall, Madeleine, 45
martellé (martellato), 23, 26, 137, 232
Marty, Georges Eugène, 87
Mascagni, Pietro, 17, 54
Massenet, Jules, 17, 66, 68, 69, 70, 71, 72, 73, 74, 75, 76, 77, 78, 79, 80, 82, 83, 84, 85, 86, 88, 169
master (setter) piston, 30
Il matrimonio segreto (Cimarosa), 14
Mattheson, Johann, 126, 135, 158
Mavra (Stravinsky), 130
Mazas, Jacques, 16
mazurka, 129, 130
Mazzocchi, Domenico, 131
meaning: of a song or part, 159, 160, 163, 177, 192, 211, 220, 238, 240; covert, 159, 238; overt, 159, 238; of a phrase, 168, 238; of music, 209; of lyrics, 209, 210; inner, 238; of a stanza, 238
mechanical aids: organ, 33; piano, 225

mechanical reproduction, 141
mechanics of musical instruments: 21–41, 42; stringed instruments, 22–25; piano, 25–28; celesta, 29; organ, 29–37; voice, 37–42; harmonium, 43–47
Medici, the, 11, 18
Mefistofele (Boito), 60
Méhul, Etienne Nicolas, 17
Meistersinger, 10
Die Meistersinger von Nürnberg (Wagner), 10, 96, 99, 100, 102, 103, 104, 105, 106, 107, 108, 172, 211
melisma, 62, 139
melodic accents, 134
melodic pattern: 113, 152, 163; line, 135, 136, 137, 142, 143, 166, 176, 240; value, 198
melodrama, 15, 124, 197
melos, 126
memorizing, 192, 197, 225, 226, 239
men singing women's songs, 221
Mendelssohn-Bartholdy, Felix: 16, 112, 123, 125, 129, 140, 144, 149, 161, 231, 233; songs, 109, 161; Wedding March, 129; Violin Concerto, 231, 233
mending pages, 226
ménestrier, 10
Menotti, Gian Carlo, 17, 176
mensural notation, 11, 113, 114
Mersenne, Father Marin, 131
messa di voce, 22, 131, 133
Messiaen, Olivier, 170
The Messiah (Handel), 143, 149
meter: 126, 140, 220; amphibrach, 126; anapaest, 126; dactyl, 126; iambus, 126; trochee, 126; strophic, 158; metric form, 161
methods of learning, 197
metronome marks: 114, 116–117, 121–123, 125, 126; Beethoven's, 121–123, 124; Schubert's, 122; Weber's, 122–123; Bartók's, 123; Brahms's, 123; Mahler's, 123; Mendelssohn's, 123; Poulenc's, 123; Puccini's, 123; Sibelius's, 123; Strauss's, 123; Stravinsky's, 123; Verdi's, 123; Schumann's, 123, 125; Wagner's, 123, 126
Metropolitan Opera, 84, 113, 184
Mexican folk songs, 89, 90, 91
Meyer, Käthe, 112
Meyer, Leonard B., 111
Meyerbeer, Giacomo, 17, 70, 74, 79, 165, 175
mezza voce, 137
mezzo forte, 52, 131, 133, 134, 219, 226
mezzo piano, 133, 134, 226
mezzo soprano, 186, 221
mezzo staccato, 137
"Mi tradì" (Mozart), 139
Michelangelo Buonarotti, 3, 163
microphone technique, 219
Mignon (Thomas), 74, 75, 81, 82, 220
Milhaud, Darius, 17, 69, 72, 75, 77
military bands, 12, 164
mimes, 9
Minnesänger, 9, 10
minstrels, 9, 10
minuet: classical, 16, 116, 124; Haydn's, 116, 120; Mozart's, 116, 120, 124; Bee-

thoven's, 116, 124; pre-classical, 116, 127
minute accents, 132, 232
Mireille (Gounod), 85, 86
Missa da Requiem (Verdi), 167, 194
Missa Solemnis (Beethoven), 120, 124
mistakes: correcting, 171, 197, 218; musical, 198, 210; learning through, 224
moderato, 117, 119, 120, 121, 125
modern compositions, 234
modified secco recitative, 215
modulation, 159, 163, 164, 211
Mörike, Eduard, 163
Mörikelieder (Wolf), 163
molding of personalities, 182, 238
Molière, Jean Baptiste, 166
molto allegro, 117, 119
molto vivace, 119
Monn, Georg Mathias, 15
monody, 12, 13, 18, 19
monosyllables, 49, 50, 51, 53, 66, 67, 73
Monsigny, Pierre Alexandre, 82
Montalto, Cardinal, 18
Monteclair, Michel Pignolet de, 14
Monteux, Pierre, 84
Monteverdi, Claudio, 12, 14, 19, 174; aria, 174
mood of a piece or phrase, 118, 120, 124, 130, 135, 153, 165, 169, 173, 179, 184, 192, 211, 219, 220, 221, 225, 226, 229, 230, 238
mood, major and minor, 230
Moore, Gerald, 226, 227, 228, 229
mordents, 143, 155
morendo, 133
Morley, Thomas, 12
Mosel, Ignaz von, 123
motets, sacred, 13
motoric method of learning, 197
mountain songs, 176
mouth: 38, 40, 45, 46, 49, 50, 53, 71, 90, 184, 239; shape of, 22, 40, 69; positions, 40, 53, 71, 72, 95, 96, 97, 185
movement of voices (outer and inner), 230
Mozart, Leopold, 114, 117, 119, 129, 143, 146, 147
Mozart, Wolfgang Amadeus: 12, 14, 15, 16, 17, 19, 36, 41, 62, 111, 112, 114, 118, 119, 120, 123, 125, 126, 129, 133, 134, 136, 137, 138, 139, 140, 143, 146, 147, 149, 150, 151, 154, 155, 156, 157, 158, 164, 165, 173, 174, 175, 180, 187, 199, 205, 207, 211, 212, 215, 216, 217, 218, 220, 226, 232, 236; songs, 15, 100, 104, 107, 148, 157, 158, 220; symphonies, 138; Rondo in A minor for piano, 139; Gigue for piano, 140; sonatas, 173, 229, 236; concert arias, 174; concerti, 232
Muffat, George, 128
Mugnone, Leopoldo, conductor of Puccini operas, 20
murky bass figures, 14
musette, 116
music: 219, 220, 237, 239; classical, 5, 65, 68, 86, 211; semiclassical, 5, 177; vocal, 8, 10, 11, 16, 28, 97, 115, 131, 135, 136, 160, 163, 167, 179; secular, 9, 10, 12,

13, 127; sacred, 9, 10, 13, 115, 131, 145; popular, 9, 45, 68, 219; instrumental, 10, 14, 115, 136, 137, 160, 230, 238; choral, 10, 45, 136; dance, 11, 12, 16, 115; symphonic, 28, 127; contemporary, 68, 86, 130, 173, 175, 177, 180, 192, 208, 211, 237; operatic, 109, 127, 169, 197; classicist, 119; romantic, 124, 125, 211; mechanized, 126; a cappella, 187, 192, 193, 194; baroque, 211; impressionistic, 211; primitive, 211; ballet, 237
musical accents, 52, 65, 120, 121, 125, 126, 130, 134, 137, 140, 145, 155, 165, 168, 211, 215, 219, 226, 234, 236
musical comedy, 176
musical phrase, 23, 85, 88, 101, 110, 126, 128, 134, 135, 137, 138, 139, 140, 141, 142, 143, 145, 149, 150, 152, 153, 168, 169, 198, 203, 219, 220, 225, 237, 238
musical scene, American, 171, 172, 173
Musicians of Today (Romain Rolland), 166
musicologist, 136, 143, 166
Die Musikalische Artikulation, insbesondere bei Johann Sebastian Bach (Keller), 137
Musikdrama (Wagner), 165
Mussorgsky, Modest Petrovich, 3, 17, 130, 175
mutation stops, 32
mute, violin, 24

n: 46; Italian, 53, 55, 60, 99; Spanish, 53, 90, 91; French, 67, 69, 70, 72, 73, 77, 80, 82, 87; German, 99, 102, 104, 105, 106
n mouillé: English, 53; Portuguese, 53; French, 53, 69, 77, 82, 90, 101; Spanish, 53, 90, 101; Italian, 53, 101; German, 101
Nachschlag, 154, 155
Nalder, Lawrence M., 27
Naples, 14, 19, 119
Narváez, Luiz de, 11
nasal vowels, 71, 73, 76, 77, 81, 82
nasals, 46, 52, 53, 65, 71, 90
national music: 17, 84, 162, 165–170; Russian, 17, 112, 130, 167, 175; French, 17, 129, 130, 165–170, 178; Spanish, 17, 129, 234, 238; Czech, 17, 130; Finnish, 17, 130; Slovak, 129; African, 130; Latin American, 130; German, 157–165, 167, 175; Italian, 166; American, 175; Rumanian, 176
national spirit, 165, 210, 223
naturalness, 166, 212, 223
Neapolitan sixth, 160
neck, violin, 23, 24, 25
negative accents, 134
Negro artist, 176
nervousness, 171, 173, 184, 185, 225, 234, 239, 240
"Der Neugierige" (Schubert), 159
ng sound: 46, 53; Spanish, 90; German, 90, 99–100; English, 90, 100, 103. *See also* gn sound
Nicolai, Otto, 17
Nietzsche, Friedrich, 3
Niñ, Joaquín, 89, 90, 91, 238
nodes on vocal cords, 109

nomoi (Greek melodies), 8
non espressivo, 24, 219
non legato, 137
Norma (Bellini), 141
nose: physical structure, 30, 40, 41, 65, 71; sounds produced by, 40, 46, 53, 65, 66, 68, 70, 71–73, 77, 85, 87, 100
nostrils, 37, 40
notes: 145, 212; sustained, 22, 35; short, 23, 52, 127, 128, 151; long, 52, 126, 151, 153, 160; semibreve, 114, 116, 134; breve, 114, 116; half, 115, 116, 117, 119, 121, 134; eighth, 115, 116, 117, 120, 127, 128, 134, 145, 147, 152, 212, 226; quarter, 115, 116, 117, 134, 148, 152, 236; dotted, 115, 127, 128, 129, 145, 151, 153, 156; triplets, 115, 127, 151, 154, 156, 160, 225, 226; smallest, 116, 117, 118; sixteenth, 116, 117, 127, 128, 138, 147, 148, 152, 153, 155, 185, 212; whole, 114, 116, 134; thirty-second, 117, 154; small, 125, 127, 143, 147; syncopated, 128, 129, 134, 141, 158; capital, 128, 143, 145, 152, 153, 211, 232, 236; main, 143, 144, 145, 147, 148, 154, 155, 156; quintoles, 154
novelty, 175, 176
Le Nozze di Figaro (Mozart), 15, 19, 48, 49, 50, 51, 53, 55, 56, 57, 58, 59, 61, 119, 120, 129, 133, 138, 147, 150, 157, 199, 210, 211, 212, 216, 217, 218
nuances: 179, 215, 225; of feeling, 221
Nuove Musiche, 12, 13, 128, 131

o: 46, 69; Italian, 50, 51, 54, 56, 58, 59, 60, 70; French, 69, 70, 71, 72, 73, 74, 81, 82; German, 70, 94, 97, 107; Spanish, 89, 90. *See also* eu sound
o, open: Italian, 49–50, 51, 54, 56, 58, 59, 60, 70, 89, 106; French, 69, 70; German, 70, 94–95, 98, 107; Spanish, 89; English, 95
obbligato instrument, 175
oboe, 11, 31, 138
Obradors, Fernando, 89, 90, 91
occlusion, 55, 56, 57, 58, 59, 89, 90
octave: division of, 28; interval, 208; triplets, 225, 226, 229
ö: German, 68, 95
Oedipus Rex (Stravinsky), 64
Offenbach, Jacques, 66, 68, 70, 72, 73, 74, 76, 80, 81, 82, 84, 85
Olympos, 8
omission of part of accompaniment, 221
omission of vowels, 62
one-composer recital, 172, 175, 179
one-language recital, 172, 175, 178–179, 180
onomatopoeia, 57, 92, 97, 98, 99
opening number, 173
opera: 12, 18, 45, 53, 64, 84, 107, 142, 184, 187, 198, 208, 215, 219, 220, 223; buffa, 14, 15, 150, 166; seria, 14, 150; theaters, 20, 49, 62, 75, 135, 149, 219, 224; in English, 179; modern, 215; light, 219
operatic style: 112; Italian, 147, 149, 150, 165, 167, 212, 215; German, 147, 165, 212; French, 212

operetta, 5, 68, 215, 219, 223
oratorio, 13, 53, 64, 143, 145, 184, 208, 209, 211, 215, 219, 223
orchestra: 12, 114, 119, 133, 174, 198, 212, 219; accompaniment by, 9, 174, 215; score, 131, 145, 187, 230, 232; effects, 164; middle voice, 208; instruments, 221; parts, 232
orchestrating piano part, 174, 221, 226, 238
orchestration, 114, 135, 187, 221, 230, 232
Orfeo ed Euridice (Gluck), 61, 145–146
Orff, Carl, 17, 64, 126
organ: 5, 12, 13, 21, 29–51, 116, 118, 119, 131, 136, 224; first mentioned, 7; hydraulic, 7, 9; portative, 11; electrical, 29, 35; pipe, 29–37; baroque, 118
organ bench, 36
organ pipes, 22, 29, 30, 31, 32, 33, 34
organ point, 28, 226
organ stops, 32–33
organ technique, 11, 29, 35–37
organist, 5, 13, 225
organistrum, 10
oriental influences, 129, 130, 169
ornamentation: 116, 126, 142–157; baroque, 142, 143, 144–145, 149, 154, 155, 156, 157; classical, 143, 145–148, 149–151, 155, 156, 157; preclassical, 143, 149, 155; romantic, 148–149, 151–154; modern, 156
Die Ornamentik in der Musik (Beyschlag), 145
orthography, 67, 69, 75, 99, 102, 103, 104, 105, 107
Otello (Verdi), 49, 50, 51, 52, 53, 55, 56, 57, 58, 59, 60, 141
ou sound, French, 70, 73, 74, 81, 82
"out" (dancer's direction), 236
overplaying, 98, 99, 166, 187
overtones, 38, 39

p: 46; Italian, 57; German, 57, 99, 102, 104, 105, 106; French, 69, 71, 77, 80, 87; English, 104
Paesiello, Giovanni, 14
Paganini, Nicolò, 17, 23
page turner, 225, 226
Pagliacci (Leoncavallo), 53, 54, 59, 200
Paladilhe, Emile, 80, 87, 169
palatals, 53, 54, 56, 58, 59, 79, 90, 101, 106, 107
palate: 40, 50, 83; soft, 39, 40, 46, 53, 56, 58, 65, 71, 72, 73, 90, 107; hard, 46, 47, 53, 54, 55, 56, 59, 101, 105
Palestrina (Pfitzner), 164
Pallavicino, Carlo, 19
Palmgren, Selim, 17
panpipe, 9
de Paolis, Alessio, 210
Papageno, 20
parlando, 150, 212, 215
Parsifal (Wagner), 4, 96, 103, 137, 141
partials, upper, 34
partitura, 131, 145, 187, 230, 232
passacaglia, 159
passage work, 224, 225, 226, 232
passaggio, 221
Passavant's cushion, 40

passecaille, 116
passepied, 116
passions: Schütz, 13; Bach, 112, 118, 132, 139, 145, 157, 209
pauses: 108, 109, 114, 126, 127, 128, 135, 136, 137, 141, 142, 192, 198, 208, 211, 212; counting, 192, 198; patterns, 198; length, 212; slight, 212
Pavlova, Anna, 236
Pears, Peter, 179
Les Pêcheurs des perles (Bizet), 169
pedagogy, 6, 186
pedal, celesta, 29
pedal, harmonium, 35
pedal, harpsichord, 133
pedal, organ, 29, 30, 31, 33, 36
pedal, piano: 28, 140, 226; damper, 27, 28, 35, 170; sustaining, 27, 28, 170, 226; middle, 28, 35
pedalboard, organ, 30, 31
pedaling technique, 30
pegs: violin, 23, 25; piano, 24
Pelléas et Mélisande (Debussy), 76, 81, 165, 166–169
percussion instruments, 7, 25, 26, 27, 238
performance: 185, 186, 209, 220, 221, 223, 229, 237, 239, 240; style, 84, 112, 113, 119, 126, 136, 146, 149, 151, 170, 219; live, 114, 122, 223, 224; preparation for, 186; details of, 239
Pergolesi, Giovanni Battista, 14, 53
Peri, Jacopo, 12, 18
La Périchole (Offenbach), 82
perpetuum mobile, 122, 176
personality, 6, 174, 178, 182, 183, 184, 186, 209, 210, 223, 224, 234, 239, 240
petit battement, 236
petit jetté, 236
Petrucci, Ottavigno dei, 11
pf sound, German, 105
Pfitzner, Hans, 17, 163, 164
Phantasie Stücke für 'cello (Schumann), 180
pharynx, 39, 40, 46
phonation, 38
phonetic chart, 44
phonetic symbols, 44
phonetics: 43–47; Italian, 48–63; Latin, 63–64; French, 65–88; Spanish, 89–91; German, 92–110
phrase, legato, 136
phrase, melodic, 162, 167
phrase, musical, 23, 85, 88, 101, 110, 126, 128, 134, 135, 137, 138, 139, 140, 141, 142, 143, 145, 149, 150, 152, 153, 168, 169, 198, 208, 219, 220, 225, 237, 238
phrase, vocal, 37, 38, 92, 97, 141, 152, 170, 186, 198, 208, 209, 215
phrases, dancer's, 237
phrases, long-spun, 173, 225
phrasing: 61, 88, 92, 120, 127, 134, 135–142, 152, 186, 208, 226, 230, 234, 239; defined, 135; marks, 135, 139, 192; of various composers, 136–142; in various periods, 138–142; irregular, 139, 140, 237
physical condition of performers, 239
pianissimo, 22, 40, 41, 61, 131, 133, 134, 225
pianists, 4, 13, 179, 234

piano (dynamics), 23, 30, 52, 131, 132, 133, 134, 219, 225, 226
piano arrangement, 232
piano e forte, 25
piano part, 187, 221, 232, 234
piano partitura, 215, 232
piano playing and accompanying, 224–229
piano score: 215, 230, 232; reduction of, 230, 232
pianoforte, 5, 14, 25–28, 29, 30, 119, 132, 134, 162, 170, 210, 211, 237, 238
pianos: 5, 114, 225; Baldwin, 26; Bechstein, 26; Blüthner, 26; Bösendorfer, 26; Steinway, 26; Erard, 26, 170; Pleyel, 26, 170; concert grand, 224, 226
Picasso, Pablo, 3
Piccini, Nicola, 14, 50
"Pictures at an Exhibition" (Mussorgsky), 130
Pierné, Gabriel, 67, 69, 87
Pinza, Ezio, 209
pipes, organ. *See* organ pipes
pitch: 7, 22, 24, 32, 33, 34, 38, 136, 151, 173, 186, 197, 198, 208, 212, 215, 221, 240; cue, 208; changes, 215; indefinable, 221
più allegretto, 124
più moderato, 121
Pius X, Pope, 63, 64, 82
Pius XI, Pope, 64
Pizzetti, Ildebrando, 17, 175
pizzicato: 23, 230, 237; left hand, 23; right hand, 23
plaque (of a bow), 25
Plato's definition of rhythm, 126, 127
playing: on stage, 224; from music, 225; soloist's part, 239
plectron, 9, 11
Pleyel piano, 26
plié, 236, 237
plosives, 46, 109
plucking (imitating guitar), 221
poco allegretto, 124
poco allegro, 115
poise, 173, 186, 223
polka, 236
polonaise, 129
polyphony, 7, 10, 29, 112, 131, 132, 138, 192, 226
polyrhythmics, 127, 129, 130
polysyllables, 48, 49, 50, 51
Ponce, Manuel, 89
Ponchielli, Amilcare, 17, 49, 50, 53, 56, 58, 59, 237
Pons, Lily, 210
Ponselle, Rosa, 210
Popper, David, 176
Porgy and Bess (Gershwin), 176
Porpora, Nicola, 14
port de voix, 143
portamento, 141, 147, 151, 152
portato, 35, 36, 136, 137, 138, 140, 141, 142, 226
post horn, 160, 230
posterior sound (phonetics), 65
postludes, 159, 161, 221, 226, 240
Poulenc, Francis, 17, 68, 81, 82, 123, 170, 176, 180
Praetorius, Michael, 13

pralltriller, 155
preclassical period, 14–15, 16, 118, 133, 139, 143, 174, 230
preludes, 15, 16, 159, 161, 221, 240
preparation, dancer's, 236, 237, 238
preparation for performance, 186, 192, 197, 234
press, 171, 172, 178
prestissimo, 117, 119, 123, 215
presto: 115, 117, 118, 119, 123, 124, 125; assai, 117; agitato, 123; con fuoco, 123
Primrose, William, 172
production of sounds, 41, 43, 66, 67, 68, 69, 70, 71, 72, 73, 76, 77, 78, 79, 80, 81, 82, 83, 90, 93, 94, 95, 96, 97, 99, 100, 101, 102, 103, 104, 105, 106, 107
program music, 16, 119, 122
program notes, 177
programing, 171, 172, 173, 174, 175, 176, 177, 178, 179
progress, artist's, 178, 186
projection, 41, 57, 58, 99, 104, 186, 192, 215, 219, 221, 223
Prokofiev, Sergei, 17, 180, 225
prompting, 208, 224, 239
Le Prophète (Meyerbeer), 70, 74, 79
proportion, mathematical, 21, 24
Proses lyriques (Debussy), 82
psaltery, 7, 10
psychological development of a character, 209–210, 211, 238
psychology, in coaching, 6, 183, 184, 186, 197, 210
public, 171, 172, 173, 176, 177, 178, 179, 211, 215, 224, 225, 232, 234, 237, 238, 239, 240
Puccini, Giacomo, 17, 20, 61, 62, 123, 126, 141, 198, 203
Pugnani, Gaetano, 14
punctuation, 61, 85, 88, 135, 211
pupils, 185, 186, 192, 197, 236
Purcell, Henry, 12, 16, 114–115, 174
purfling, 25
pushing the voice, 69
Pythagoras, 4

q sound (French), 83, 87
qu sound: Italian, 58, 104; French, 83; Spanish, 90; English, 104; German, 104
Quantz, Johann Joachim, 113, 114, 115–116, 120, 127, 128, 132, 143, 144, 146, 154
quartets: vocal, 161, 187; string, 175
quasi recitativo, 215
Quilter, Roger, 17

The Rake's Progress (Stravinsky), 123, 215
Il Re Pastore (Mozart), 50, 175
recital: dance, 5, 125, 172; types of, 172–179; programs for, 180–181; accompanying, 237–238
recitation: 208, 212; rhythmical, 197; on pitch, 197, 198
recitative: 12, 146, 149–151, 158, 159, 167, 169, 211, 212, 215; accompagnato, 14, 15, 147, 149, 150–151, 212, 215; secco, 14, 15, 147, 149, 150, 211, 212, 215; J. S. Bach's, 149; Gluck's, 149; Handel's, 149; rules for, 149; Donizet-

ti's, 149, 150; Mozart's, 149, 150–151, 158, 212; Rossini's, 149, 150, 212, 213, 214; Beethoven's, 150; Bellini's, 150; Weber's, 150; Debussy's, 167; Wagner's, 197; rhythmical, 212; oratorio, 215
recordings, 114, 122, 123, 126, 174, 219, 239
reduction of orchestral parts and scores, 232
references, pupils', 184
refresher recital, 172, 178
regional variations in pronunciation, 55, 57, 65, 101, 104, 105, 168
register, voice, 41, 221
regularly recurring recital, 172, 177–178, 180
rehearsal, 174, 177, 223, 225, 232, 237, 238, 239
Reichardt, Johann Friedrich, 15, 157, 158
Reiner, Fritz, 149
relative accents, 134, 219
relative dynamics, 133, 226
relative tempo, 117, 119, 125–126
relaxation of tension, 38, 185, 223
relaying conductor's beat, 223
Renaissance, 11, 18, 19, 29, 112
repeats, 130, 132, 151, 159
repertoire, 171, 174, 186, 221, 224
répétiteur, 5
repetition: of words, 139, 209, 210, 211; of motifs, 160, 163; of musical numbers, 177; of sentences, 210; of measures, 239
representative, artist's, 171, 172
reputation, artist's, 178
Requiem (Verdi), 167, 194
resonance: 22, 23, 25, 38, 39, 40, 52, 185; cavities for, 34, 39, 40, 41, 65; nasal, 40, 41; head, 41
resonator: 21, 22, 29, 38, 41, 42; of stringed instruments, 24; of piano, 28; of organ, 31, 32, 34; of human voice, 38–39
Respighi, Ottorino, 17
respiratory system, 21, 37
rests: 85, 127, 128, 139, 147, 192, 212; counting, 192, 198; changing, 212
retiré, 236
Reuenthal, Neidhart von, 10
reviews, 172, 173, 180
Revueltas, Silvestre, 89
Das Rheingold (Wagner), 96, 98, 101, 102, 104, 105, 107, 190
rhythm: 100, 126–131, 142, 143, 160, 163, 168, 169, 174, 186, 197, 198, 211, 219, 230, 232, 234, 236, 238; primitive, 7, 130; pattern of, 54, 111, 113, 126, 140, 145, 163, 192, 198, 238; emphasis in, 109; definite, 126; weak, 126; defined, 126, 127; occidental, 126, 127; strong, 126, 127, 128, 176; combinations of, 127; J. S. Bach's, 127–128; Handel's, 127–128; altered, 127, 128, 129; dance, 127, 129; syncopated, 127, 129; Gluck's, 128; Haydn's, 129; innovations in, 129; Mozart's, 129; shifts in, 129; oriental, 129, 130; Stravinsky's, 129, 130; Beethoven's, 129, 134; irregular, 130; accents for, 134; elements of, 160; dotted, 160, 236; Brahms's, 162;

structure of, 187; skeleton of, 187, 192; figurations of, 192, 197; of recitation, 197; of recitatives, 212; precision in, 232; steady, 232, 236; complicated, 234; light, 236; functions of, 238

Richter, Hans, 20

Riemann, Hugo, 136, 138, 139

Rienzi (Wagner), 156

rigaudon, 116

Rigoletto (Verdi), 18, 48, 49, 50, 51, 55, 56, 57, 58, 59, 150

Rimsky-Korsakov, Nikolai, 17, 130

rinforzando, 134

Ring cycle (Wagner), 20

ritardando, 119, 122, 125, 126, 237, 240

robbed tempo, 125–126

rococo, 14, 15, 118, 119, 139, 142, 143

Rode, Jacques, 16

Rodgers, Richard, 176

Le Roi et le fermier (Monsigny), 82

Rolland, Romain: 162, 166–167, 168–169; correspondence with R. Strauss, 162, 168–169

Roman music, 8, 9

Romani, Romano, 210

Romantic era, 13, 16, 125, 126, 140, 143, 146, 157, 161, 211, 223

romanticism, 113, 118, 125, 132, 143, 149, 158, 159, 161, 164, 165, 175, 226

Rome, 19

Roméo et Juliette (Gounod), 66, 67, 69, 75, 78, 85

ronde des jambes: à terre, 236; en l'air, 236

rondeau, 9, 10, 116

Der Rosenkavalier (R. Strauss), 29, 94, 95, 99, 100, 104, 106, 130

Rossi-Lemmeni, Nicola, 209

Rossini, Gioacchino, 17, 49, 50, 53, 55, 56, 59, 61, 149, 150, 187, 212, 213, 214

rota, 10

Rothschild, Fritz, 116

Rousseau, Jean Jacques, 166, 167

rubato, 125–126

rubebe, 10

Rubinstein, Anton, 156

Rudolf, Max, 210, 219

Rückert, Friedrich, 164

The Ruins of Athens (Beethoven), 129, 157

Rumanian dances, 176

Rupp, Franz, 20

Russell, G. Oscar, 46

s: 46, 64; Italian, 55, 57, 58; English, 57; German, 57, 99, 100, 104, 105, 106, 108; French, 60, 77, 78–79, 81, 83, 84, 87, 88; Spanish, 90, 91

s, voiced: 46; Italian, 54–55, 57; French, 70, 71, 78, 83, 87; Spanish, 91; German, 100–101, 108

Sachs, Curt, 113, 114

Sachs, Hans, 10

"Le Sacre du Printemps" (Stravinsky), 130

Sadko (Rimsky-Korsakov), 130

St. Thomas (J. S. Bach's church in Leipzig), 118

Saint-Saëns, Camille: 169, 232; songs, 73, 78, 82, 84, 169

Salieri, Antonio, 14, 121

Salome (R. Strauss), 29, 97, 103, 191, 192, 198, 202

Salonwalzer, 129, 130

salpinx, 9

saltato (sautillé), 23

Samson et Dalila (Saint-Saëns), 72, 73, 74, 75, 78, 79, 84, 88

Sappho, 8

sarabande, 116, 127

Sarasate, Pablo de, 17, 23, 234

Sartorio, Antonio, 19

Satie, Eric, 130

Sauglufetharmonium, 35

scale, musical: 36, 192, 208; Chinese, 129

scaling system: piano, 27; organ, 31, 32

scanning music, 187

Scarlatti, Alessandro, 14, 19

scenery, 223, 224, 237

sch sound (German), 105, 106

Schalk, Franz, 149

Schenker, Heinrich, 136

scherzando, 120

scherzo, 116, 124, 127

Schikaneder, Emanuel, Jr., 20

Schiller, Friedrich von, 15

Schindler, Anton, 134

Schiøtz, Aksel, 239

Schipa, Tito, 178

Schleifer, 157

Schlick, Arnolt, 11

Schneller, 155

Schobert, Johann, 16

Schoenberg, Arnold, 3, 4, 142, 197

School for the Pianoforte (D. G. Türk), 143

Schott und Söhne, 121, 122

Schreker, Franz, 187

Schubart, Christian Friedrich Daniel, 119

Schubert, Ferdinand, 160

Schubert, Franz: 10, 14, 16, 112, 114, 122, 125, 129, 140, 143, 146, 149, 151–154, 155, 157–160, 164, 165, 175, 179, 180, 181, 187, 188, 220, 221, 222, 226, 227, 228, 229, 230, 238, 239; songs, 10, 15, 16, 85, 97, 98, 99, 100, 101, 102, 103, 104, 105, 106, 107, 108, 109, 110, 112, 122, 125, 148, 149, 151–154, 157–160, 161, 175, 180, 181, 187, 188, 220, 221, 222, 225, 226, 227, 228, 229, 230, 238, 239; Sonata for arpeggione, 16; works for violin and pianoforte, 16; chamber music, 112; orchestral, 112, 125; Masses, 112, 157; Impromptu, G flat major, 125; military marches, 129; song cycles, 161, 175, 179

Schütz, Heinrich, 13, 220

Schumann, Elisabeth, 98, 178, 179

Schumann, Felix (son of Robert), 162

Schumann, Robert: 3, 15, 16, 123, 125, 129, 130, 140, 159, 160–161, 162, 164, 165, 169, 175, 179, 180, 181, 186, 229; songs, 95, 97, 99, 100, 101, 102, 103, 106, 109, 125, 159, 160–161, 179, 181, 186, 229; song cycles, 102, 109, 161, 175; piano sonata in G minor, 125

Schuster, Joseph, 180

Schwartzkopf, Elisabeth, 98, 178

Schweitzer, Albert, 131, 138, 145

scores: 136, 177, 187; original, 112, 139; operatic, 187, 197, 208, 209, 221, 223, 224; oratorio, 208; vocal, 209; reduced, 230, 232

scoring, 118

Scotch snap, 128, 129

Scott, Cyril, 17

scroll box, 23

The Seasons (Vivaldi), 129

sec, 23

secco recitative, 14, 15, 147, 149, 150, 211, 212, 215

Seefried, Irmgard, 178, 179

Segovia, Andrés, 11

Seidl, Anton, 20

Seiffert, Max, 139

self-accompanying, 7, 10, 19, 224

self-assurance, 173, 177, 185, 186, 223

Semet, Théophile, 82

semibreve, 114

semiclassical music, 5, 177

semiconsonants, 49, 73, 101

semilegato, 35, 36

semioccusive sounds, 55, 56, 58, 59, 79

semistaccato, 234

semivowels: 43, 45, 47; Spanish, 44; Italian, 44, 49, 51–52, 56, 60; French, 44, 65, 73–76, 84; German, 44, 101

sensitivity, artistic, 161, 163, 171, 173, 182, 226, 234, 238

sentimentality, 161, 162, 164, 165, 170, 238

separation (hiatus): 51, 61; of sounds, 51, 60–63, 74, 76, 85, 86, 91, 108, 109, 110, 142; of phrases, 135, 136, 138, 141

separation marks, 135, 136, 138, 141

septum, 40

servant parts, 210

set numbers, 208, 210, 215

sextets, 187

sforzando, 134, 219

sforzato, 134, 219

sforzato piano, 219

sh sound: 46; Italian, 59; French, 79–80; English, 105; German, 105, 106

shadings, 26, 98, 109, 132, 135, 140, 168, 170, 177, 179, 192, 219, 220, 232, 234, 239

shake, 24, 126, 142, 154–155, 171

Shakespeare, William, 12, 179

shallot, 32

shawm, 11

shofar, 7

shortening: pauses, 136; notes, 136, 209

Shostakovich, Dimitri, 17

Sibelius, Jean, 17, 123, 130

siciliana, 115

Sieben frühe Lieder (Berg), 175

Siebs, Theodor, 92, 107, 108

Siegfried (Wagner), 97, 98, 103, 104, 107

Siepi, Cesare, 209

sightreading, 19, 183, 184, 187, 225, 238

Silbermann, Gottfried, 25, 132

simplicity, 161, 166, 169, 170

Singer and Accompanist (Moore), 226

The Singer's Manual of English Diction (Marshall), 45

Singher, Martial, 178

Singing, The Mechanism and the Technique (Vennard), 37
singing diction, 5, 43–47, 97, 166, 179
Singspiel, 15, 146
sinuses, 22, 41
Sistine choir, 131
sk sound (Italian), 59
skolion, 8
Slavic influences, 162
Slezak, Leo, 239
slide (embellishment), 157
slide (glissando), 24
sliding technique, on organ, 36
slur: 135, 138, 139, 140; articulation, 135, 136, 138, 140, 141, 142; phrasing, 135, 136, 140, 141; legato, 136, 137; technical, 136, 137
Smetana, Bedřich, 17, 98, 130
smiling position, 40, 49, 185
smorzando, 134
Société Nationale de Musique, 165
solfeggio, 184, 192, 197
song coaching sessions, 220, 221
song collections, classical, 220
song cycles, 15, 98, 102, 109, 124, 156, 158, 161, 164, 169, 175, 179, 221
song recital, 219, 220
songs: 11, 12, 45, 53, 83, 142, 162, 173, 177, 179, 184, 185, 219–223, 224, 225, 226, 229, 230, 238, 239; part, 11; German, 12, 15, 157–165, 175, 179, 220, 223; English, 12, 16, 99, 107, 220, 223; shepherd's, 14, 98; hunting, 14, 160; folk, 14, 162, 220, 221; French, 16, 17, 165–170, 175, 178, 179, 220, 223; Italian, 53, 175, 179; Hebrew, 98; art, 165, 167, 169–170, 178, 179, 220; of the sea, 169, 180; Slavic, 175; Spanish, 175, 179, 221; American, 176, 177; Czech, 178; Finnish, 178; Polish, 178; Scandinavian, 178; Yugoslav, 178; children's, 180; humorous, 180; love, 180; seasonal, 180; religious, 180, 220; semi-classical, 184; Russian, 223
Songs and Dances of Death (Mussorgsky), 175
Songs from the British Isles (Britten), 176
La Sonnambula (Bellini), 55
Sonnets of Michelangelo (Britten), 176
Sonnets of Petrarch (Pizzetti), 175
sonority, 21, 170, 230, 238
soprano: 114, 141, 154, 175, 187, 209, 221, 229, 230; coloratura, 119, 173, 174, 175, 186, 209, 215, 232; dramatic, 174; spinto, 175; lyric, 175, 186, 215
soundboard: 21; piano, 22, 26, 27, 28
soundbox, 24, 25
soundpost, 24, 25
sp sound (German), 105, 106
Spanish rhythms, 238
Spanish singing diction: 89–91; Castilian pronunciation, 89, 90; Central American (Mexican) pronunciation, 89, 90, 91; South American pronunciation, 89, 91
Speech and Voice (G. Oscar Russell), 46
speech apparatus, 45, 46, 52, 59, 106
spiccato, 23, 232
spinet, 11, 118, 224
spirituals, Negro, 176

Spohr, Louis, 134, 155, 175
sprechgesang, 98, 197, 212
st sound (German), 105, 106
staccato: 135, 137, 138, 139, 140, 219, 226, 230, 232, 234, 236; bowing, 23; on piano, 26, 225; on celesta, 29; on organ, 30, 35, 36; singing, 109
stage: 198, 219, 224; stage director, 211, 223; stage band, 224
stage presence, 5, 173
Stamitz, Johann, 15, 133
starting: a number, 173, 174, 175, 234; a dance, 237, 238
Stein, Johann Andreas, piano builder, 119
Steinway and Sons, 26
stentato, 137
"Die Sterne" (Schubert), 159
Stilmomente, 113
Stokowski, Leopold, 112, 125
Stradivarius, Antonio, 22
Strauss, Johann, the elder, 130
Strauss, Johann, the younger, 130
Strauss, Richard: 17, 29, 43, 119, 122, 123, 130, 142, 162, 163–164, 167–169, 175, 179, 180, 181, 183, 187, 191, 202, 207, 208, 215, 221, 226, 229; songs, 99, 100, 106, 108, 163–164, 175, 179, 180, 181, 183, 226, 229; correspondence with Romain Rolland, 162, 168–169; correspondence with Hofmannsthal and Stefan Zweig, 210
Stravinsky, Igor, 3, 17, 64, 112, 123, 129, 130, 142, 172, 180, 215
Street Scene (Weill), 176
string orchestra, 174
stringed instruments, 8, 11, 21, 24, 34, 38, 118, 119, 128, 131, 132, 133, 136, 137, 140, 225, 230
strings: violoncello, 22, 230; violin, 23, 24, 25, 230, 232, 234; piano, 27, 28, 230
strophic song, 15, 16, 158, 159, 221
Strozzi, Gian Battista, 19
structure: beats, 116; rhythmic, 187; harmonic, 187, 191, 192; melodic, 192
sts sound (German), 108
studio: dance, 3, 234–237; instrumental or vocal, 174, 182, 186, 219
style, cycles of, 112–113
style (musical): 135, 136, 139, 165, 173, 183, 186, 208, 219; French, 17, 84, 162, 165–170; performance, 84, 112, 113, 119, 126, 136, 146, 149, 151, 170, 219; contemporary performance, 84, 112, 113, 136, 143, 149, 230; innate, 84, 112, 113, 136, 149; of a composition, 84, 112, 175; defined, 111–112; of a period, 111, 112, 113, 225, 230; of a composer, 111, 112, 209, 211, 225; of a medium, 112; additions to, 113; classical phase of, 113; counter movements, 113; decline of, 113; deviations from, 113; phases of, 113; romantic phase, 113, 125, 158, 161; conventional, 115; classical lied, 125; German lied, 157–165; operatic, 165; chamber music, 175; post-Wagnerian, 211; Wagnerian, 211; parlando, 212; arioso, 215; of recitatives, 215; operetta, 215; of a particular conductor, 219

subdivision: of passages, 120; of beats, 138, 232
subjectivity, 113, 118, 131, 132, 158, 161
sublimation into art, 182
Suite Italienne (Stravinsky), 180
Suk, Josef, 17
sul ponticello, 23
sul tasto, 23
Sulzer, Johann Georg, 137
support, breath, 34, 37, 141, 185, 208
sussurrando, 133
Swedish artist, 176
syllables: accented, 48, 49, 50, 71, 169; unaccented, 48, 49, 95; final, 66, 73, 77, 92, 94, 98, 101, 102; initial, 68, 94; medial, 94
symphonies. *See individual composers*
syncopation, 128, 129, 134, 140, 141, 158, 160, 197, 211
syrinx, 9
Széll, George, 149, 183
Szymanowsky, Karol, 17

t: 46; Latin, 55; Italian, 57–58; German, 57, 99, 102, 103, 104, 105, 106; French, 70, 71, 77, 80, 81, 86, 88; English, 104
t, voiceless alveolar palatal semiocclusive: Italian, 58, 90, 106; Spanish, 90; English, 106; German, 106
tailgut, 24
tailpiece, 23, 24
talent, 6, 180, 183, 187, 197, 224
"Tales from the Vienna Woods" (J. Strauss), 130
tambourin, 116
"Tambourin Chinois" (Kreisler), 233
Tannhäuser (Wagner), 10, 96, 103, 104, 105, 107, 109, 129, 156, 208
tape recorder, 65, 73, 95
Tartini, Giuseppe, 14, 173
taste, artistic, 86, 92, 108, 110, 149, 150, 166, 172, 176, 186, 209, 221
Tauber, Richard, 98, 178, 239
Taylor, Deems, 17
Tchaikovsky, Peter Ilich: 17, 130, 167, 196, 231; 6th Symphony, 130, 167; violin concerto, 231
teacher: 146, 183, 185, 197; vocal, 5, 18, 40, 41, 61, 171, 184, 185, 192, 198, 224; instrumental, 5, 40, 171, 184; dance, 5, 184
teamwork, 224, 234, 238–240
Tebaldi, Renata, 18, 178, 209
technical problems, 107, 171, 174, 176, 177, 183, 224, 229, 230, 232, 234, 237, 238
technique: 172; organ, 11, 29, 35–37; vocal, 22, 41, 109, 185, 209; piano, 29, 35, 170, 224, 225, 226; pedal (organ), 30; harmonium, 35–37; composing, 162; microphone, 219; pedal (piano), 225; lack of, 226
teeth: 40; upper, 46, 53, 54, 55, 57, 105; lower, 49, 50, 53, 54, 56, 83, 101
Telemann, Georg Philipp, 15, 149
teleprompter, 226
television, 219, 224, 226
temperament, artist's, 173, 239
tempered pitch, 24, 28
tempered scale, 34

tempo: 113–126, 135, 142, 153, 174, 197, 198, 211, 212, 223, 230, 232, 239; improvised, 113; today's performance, 113, 114; pre-Bach, 113, 114–116; giusto, 113, 114, 116, 118, 121, 123, 124, 126, 135, 234, 239; performance, 113, 116, 122; innate, 113, 122; Mozart's, 114, 116, 118–121; Beethoven's, 114, 116, 122, 123–124; Purcell's, 115; relations, 115, 116; dance, 115, 130; indications, 116, 117–118, 119, 120, 121, 122, 123, 124, 125, 126, 212; J. S. Bach's, 116–118; Handel's, 116–118; Haydn's, 116, 118–121; modifications of, 117, 118, 119, 126, 215; relative, 117, 119, 125–126; scale of classicist masters, 119, 123; absolute, 119, 126; Weber's, 122–123; ordinario, 122, 123; changes in, 122, 126, 198, 239; initial, 123; Schubert's, 124–125; Mendelssohn's, 125; Schumann's, 125; rubato (robbed), 125–126; contrasts of, 176; fast, 208; differentiation of, 230; desired, 236; following, 236; faster, 237; slower, 237
tempo of life, 114, 178
temporary bridge, 208
temps à terre, 236
tempus imperfectum, perfectum, 114
tendresse, 165, 167, 169, 170
tenor: 114, 174, 175, 176, 186, 220, 221; lyric, 173
tenuto, 234
terminology: vocalist's, 185; dancer's, 234, 237
Terpander of Lesbos, 8
terrace dynamics, 131, 132
Tertis, Lyonel, 172
tessitura, 171, 232
Teyte, Maggie, 178
Thaïs (Massenet), 68, 169
theater auditorium, 34, 99, 219
themes, 160, 162, 163, 239
Thomas, Ambroise, 74, 75, 81, 82, 220
Thomson, Scottish music publisher, 124
thorough bass, 3, 5, 12, 13, 14, 16, 230
Thorough School for the Violin (Leopold Mozart), 114, 117, 143, 146–147
throat, 37, 40, 45, 50, 53, 67, 69, 96, 107, 185
through-composed, 158, 159, 160, 161
ti sound, French, 81
timbre, 21, 22, 33, 34, 39
timbrels, biblical, 7
time, unit of, 113, 114, 192, 194, 195
time signatures: 114, 115, 116, 120, 123, 124, 125, 126, 212; Haydn's, 114, 123; Mozart's, 114, 123; Beethoven's, 114, 123, 124; Schubert's, 114, 125; Purcell's, 115; J. S. Bach's, 116–117
time-beater, 223, 224
timidity, 186
timing, 174, 237
Titus (Mozart), 19
tone quality, 25, 34, 39, 41, 221, 225, 229, 230
tongue, 39, 40, 45, 46, 47, 49, 50, 53, 54, 55, 56, 57, 58, 59, 66, 67, 68, 69, 71, 83, 90, 94, 97, 99, 100, 101, 105, 107, 108, 137

topical recital, 172, 179–180
Tosca (Puccini), 20, 29, 49, 51, 53, 54–62
Toscanini, Arturo, 20, 113, 114, 123, 124, 219
Die tote Stadt (Korngold), 104
touch: 26, 42, 170, 226, 230, 232, 234, 236; shadings of, 6, 26, 170; flexible, 170; subtlety in, 170; variety of, 225; control of, 230; finesse in, 232; dry, 234; difficulties in, 238
Tourte, François, 25
trachea, 39, 41
Traité de l'harmonie (Rameau), 13
transcriptions, musical, 11, 12, 13, 176, 187, 234
transcriptions, phonetic: from Italian, 63; from Latin, 64; from French, 88; from Spanish, 89, 91; from German, 110
translations: of songs, 175, 178, 179; literal, 177, 210, 211, 212; into English, 192; into idiomatic language, 210; into the vernacular, 210, 212; word-by-word, 210, 220
transposition: 163, 187, 221, 229, 230; downward, 187, 221, 222, 229, 230; upward, 187, 221, 229, 230
Traubel, Helen, 210
La Traviata (Verdi), 48, 49, 50, 51, 52, 59, 63, 142, 206, 210, 211
treadles, 34, 35
tremolo, 23, 24, 34, 35, 40
triad, 160, 182
trigonon, 9
trill (shake): 24, 126, 142, 154–155, 171; rapid, 154; slow, 154; starting with main note, 154, 155; starting with upper note, 154, 155; for various voices, 154, 209; short, 155; starting with lower note, 155; long, 209
trios, 186, 187
triphthong: 43, 45, 47; Italian, 52, 60; English, 98
triplets, 115, 127, 151, 154, 156, 160, 225, 226
Tristan und Isolde (Wagner), 95, 96, 100, 103, 104, 130, 140, 141, 162, 163
trochee, 126
trombone, 11, 21, 160, 198
trouvères, 9, 10
Il Trovatore (Verdi), 10, 48, 50, 51, 53, 54, 56, 59, 141, 142, 197, 210, 211, 215
trumpet: 9, 11, 21; biblical, 7; curved, 9; signal, 164
trumscheit, 11
ts sound: Italian, 55, 58; German, 105, 108
Türk, Daniel Gottlob, 143, 146
tuning, 28, 32, 38, 234
Turandot (Puccini), 56
Turandot (Weber), 129
turbinates, 40, 41
del Turco, Giovanni, 19
Turina, Joaquín, 17, 89, 90, 91, 238
turn, 62, 143, 155–157
twelve-tone music, 4, 135, 187, 192, 193
tympanum, 9

u sound: 46, 50; Italian, 50, 51, 54, 56, 58, 59, 71, 96; French, 70, 73, 74, 75, 81, 82; English, 71, 96; Spanish, 89; German, 95–96, 97, 98, 107
umlaut: ä, 93, 106; ö, 94, 95, 98, 106; ü, 95, 96, 97, 106
underlining, 158, 170, 192, 215
underplaying, 98, 165, 167, 169
understanding a part, 211, 212, 238, 239, 240
"Ungeduld" (Schubert), 159
unification: of phrases, 135, 136, 138, 139; of taste, 170; of expression, 234
unit of time, 113, 114, 192, 194, 195
unity: of spoken and sung words, 162; of program, 171, 179
"up" (dancer's direction in space), 236, 237
upbeat, 121, 127, 130, 136, 138, 234, 236, 237
uvula: 53, 90; uvular consonants, 107

v sound: 53; Italian, 53, 55, 100; French, 66, 69, 70, 71, 78, 86, 100; in American Southern English, 90; German, 99, 100; English, 100
Valderrabano, Enriquez de, 11
values: artistic, 3; spiritual, 3, 4, 6, 12, 13, 15; ethical, 3, 4, 6, 13, 15, 167, 239, 240; musical, 12, 238; inner, 219, 238; moral, 239, 240
Valverde, Joaquín, 89
valves: on wind instruments, 13, 118; organ, 29, 30, 32; harmonium, 34
varied strophic song, 158, 159
variety: 238; in program, 179, 186; of expression, 212; of color, 220; of tonal shadings, 225; of touch, 225, 226
Vaughan Williams, Ralph, 17
velars, 46, 53, 56, 58, 65, 90
velum, 39, 40, 46, 53, 56, 58, 65, 71, 72, 73, 90, 107
Venice, 19
Vennard, William, 37, 40, 46
Veracini, Francesco, 12
"Verborgenheit" (Wolf), 163
Verdi, Giuseppe: 16, 17, 123, 133, 141, 142, 149, 150, 167, 194, 195, 197, 206, 210, 211, 215; correspondence with librettists, 210
verism, 209
Verlaine, Paul, 165, 169, 220
vernacular: 198; in translations, 210, 212
vertical stroke, 135, 137, 192, 194
Viadana, Lodovico, 12
vibrations: of strings, 23, 24, 27, 28; of piano case, 28; of vocal cords, 38, 41
vibrato, 24, 40
vibrator: 21, 29, 42; of violin, 23–24; of piano, 26, 27–28; of organ, 31–34; of harmonium, 34; of voice, 38, 41
vielle, 10
Vienna, 14, 15, 119, 130, 137, 138, 149, 162
Viennese waltz, 129, 130
"Village Swallows from Austria" (J. Strauss), 130
Villon, François, 75
viol, 10, 11
viola, 12, 22, 172
viola da braccio, 22
viola da gamba, 16

violin: 10, 12, 16, 19, 22–25, 141, 145, 146, 147, 154, 157, 172, 175, 230, 232, 234; literature, 232; virtuosos, 232

violoncello, 12, 14, 16, 22, 110, 150, 154, 172, 175, 180, 230, 232, 234

Viotti, Giovanni, 14, 16

virelai, 9, 10

virginal, 11, 12, 25

virtuoso: 171, 182; pieces, 176, 230; pianist, 224, 225; technique, 225; figurations, 232

visual method of learning, 197

vivace: 115, 117, 119, 123, 124, 156; ma non troppo, 123

vivacissamente, 123

Vivaldi, Antonio, 12, 13, 14, 50, 119

Vives, Amadeo, 180; song, 180

vocal cords, 21, 38, 39, 41, 109, 198

vocal line, 49, 52, 53, 59, 60, 65, 83, 85, 97, 99, 101, 109, 134, 141, 142, 145, 146, 147, 148, 151, 158, 159, 160, 162, 187, 192, 197, 198, 208, 211, 215, 221

vocal literature, 43, 75, 221

vocal music, 8, 10, 11, 16, 28, 43, 75, 97, 115, 131, 135, 136, 160, 161, 163, 167, 179, 187, 221

vocal part, 145, 161, 197, 211, 219

vocal qualities: defects in, 40; color, 65, 219; style, 112; agility, 209; brilliance, 209; approach to, 212; intensity, 212; power, 215, 220; expansion, 220; gifts, 224

vocal score, 11, 19, 97, 156, 209

vocal teacher, 5, 18, 40, 41, 61, 171, 184, 185, 192, 198, 224

vocalise, 45

Vogelweide, Walther von der, 10

Vogl, Johann Michael, 160

voice: 11, 22, 28, 34, 37–42, 99, 127, 131, 132, 133, 137, 150, 157, 160, 161, 163, 167, 169, 170, 173, 175, 184, 185, 186, 197, 198, 209, 212, 219, 220, 225, 239; register, 41, 221; range, 114, 209, 220, 221; categories, 174, 186

voice part, 145, 161, 197, 211, 219

voice teacher, 5, 18, 40, 41, 61, 171, 184, 185, 192, 198, 224

voicebox, 21, 37, 38

voices: 131, 132, 138; main (leading), 131, 132, 226; contrapuntal, 131, 192; secondary, 132; even movement of, 139; uneven movement of, 139; upper, 197; inner, 226, 230; outer, 226, 230

"Voices of Spring" (J. Strauss), 130

Der vollkommene Capellmeister (Mattheson), 126

Vorhalt, 143

Vorschlag, 143

vowels. See specific vowels

w consonant, German, 99, 100

w semivowel: Italian, 51; French, 73–74, 75; Spanish, 89, 91

Wagenseil, Johann Christoph, 15

Wagner, Richard: 15, 16, 17, 100, 119, 123, 124, 125, 126, 127, 130, 135, 137, 140, 155, 156, 159, 161, 162, 163, 165, 166, 168, 182, 187, 189, 190, 193, 194, 197, 204, 206, 208, 211, 239; school of diction and singing, 92, 109, 167

Wagnerian Sprechgesang, 98, 197, 212

walking on stage, 177

Die Walküre (Wagner), 94, 95, 101, 102, 104, 106, 189, 204

La Wally (Catalani), 58

Walter, Bruno, 4, 124, 145, 149, 179, 183

waltz, 116, 120, 127, 129–130, 236, 237

"Das Wandern" (Schubert), 159

warm-up: singer's, 173, 174; dancer's, 234

Weber, Carl Maria von, 15, 17, 20, 122, 148, 149, 150, 155, 165, 236

Webern, Anton von, 4, 135

wedge-shaped staccato signs, 137, 140

Weigert, Hermann, 187, 210

Weigl, Joseph, 19

Weill, Kurt, 176

Wekerlin, Jean Baptiste, 67, 78

"Wellington's Victory" (Beethoven), 122

The Well-Tempered Clavichord (J. S. Bach), 116, 129

The Well-Tempered Accompanist (Coenraad V. Bos), 229

weltschmerz, 165

werktreue, 113, 219

Wesendonk, Mathilde, 162

"Wesendonk Lieder" (Wagner), 162, 175

"Die Wetterfahne" (Schubert), 159

Widor, Charles-Marie, 85

Wieck, Clara (Schumann), 161, 162

Wieniawski, Henri, 17, 180

Wilckens, Friedrich, 172, 237

Wilde, Oscar, 167

Williams, Ralph Vaughan, 17

wind chest, 29, 30, 32, 34

wind instrument, 21, 39, 118, 119, 128, 133, 136, 137, 145, 172, 174

windpipe, 34, 37, 38, 39

wings: in opera house, 219; in concert hall, 237

wippen, 26

wire, piano, 27

"Wohin" (Schubert), 159

Wolf, Hugo: 3, 17, 160, 163, 175, 179, 181, 187, 220, 226, 229; songs, 94, 97, 99, 100, 101, 102, 103, 104, 106, 108, 109, 163, 175, 179, 181, 187, 220, 226, 229

women singing men's songs, 221

wood for musical instruments, 21, 28

word: sung, 43, 73, 132, 138, 141, 142, 149, 154, 158, 161, 162, 169, 170, 198, 215; spoken, 43, 142, 162, 166, 167, 169, 170, 177, 179, 197, 198, 212, 220, 238; and music, 43, 179; meaning of, 158, 159, 192, 209, 210, 212, 219; half-spoken, 197; half-sung, 197, 198; written, 210

word-by-word translation, 177, 210, 211, 220

Wozzeck (Berg), 142, 193, 197

wrest plank, 27

wrestling, Don Giovanni and Donna Anna, as expressed in music, 212

wrist, 225

x: Italian, 58; Latin, 64; French, 71, 83, 88; Spanish, 89, 91; German, 104, 105. See also ks

x sound: German, 90; Scottish, 90; Spanish, 90, 91

y: 49; Italian, 49; Latin, 64; French, 69–70, 73, 75, 76, 81, 82; German, 71, 96–97, 98; English, 74, 90, 101; Spanish, 89, 90

yod, 74

yodeling, 164

Ysaye, Eugène, 17

z: 64; Italian, 58, 105; French, 66, 78, 79, 88, 105; Spanish, 89, 91; English, 105; German, 105

Zacconi, Ludovico, 113

Zar und Zimmermann (Lortzing), 105

Die Zauberflöte (Mozart), 9, 19, 94, 97, 100, 105, 109, 121, 146, 147, 148, 150–151, 172

Zelter, Karl Friedrich, 15, 157

Ziani, Marc Antonio, 19

zither, 7, 8, 9

zh sound: 46, 56; French, 69, 70, 71, 79; English, 106; German, 106

Zukovsky, Paul, 180

Zum Stilproblem in der Musik (Käthe Meyer), 112

Zumsteeg, Johann Rudolf, 15, 157, 158

Zweig, Stefan, 210